archithese reader

Critical Positions in Search of Postmodernity, 1971–1976

Gabrielle Schaad and Torsten Lange (Eds.)

Triest

Contents

5
Critical Positions in
Search of Postmodernity
    by Gabrielle Schaad
    and Torsten Lange

I   HISTORICITY
    AND MEANING

23
Expanding Notions
of the Past:
Approaches and Forms
    by Marie Theres Stauffer

38
Architecture Today
and the Zeitgeist:
A Critical Retrospective
    by Charles Jencks

62
The Reconstruction of the
Kornhaus in Freiburg im
Breisgau and Several
Observations on Architecture
and Historical Understanding
    by Jürgen Paul

77
History as a Part of Architectural
Theory: Notes on New Projects
for Zurich, Bellinzona, Modena,
and Muggiò
    by Bruno Reichlin
    and Fabio Reinhart

93
Phase Shifts
    by Stanislaus von Moos

111
Shrunken Metropolis
    by Rosemarie Bletter

II   REALISM
    AND AUTONOMY

123
From Idealism
to Disenchantment:
Realism in and
beyond *archithese*
    by Irina Davidovici

142
To Laugh in Order Not to Cry:
Interview with Robert Venturi
and Denise Scott Brown
    by Stanislaus von Moos

167
Rules, Realism, and History
    by Alan Colquhoun

177
Problems of Architecture
and Realism
    by Giorgio Grassi

188
A Realist Education
    by Aldo Rossi

194
On The Problem of
Inner Architectonic Reality
    by Bruno Reichlin
    and Martin Steinmann

III   URBANISM
    AND CONSUMPTION

213
Between Crisis and Myth:
The City at the
End of Modernity
    by Torsten Lange

232
Questions for Henri Lefèbvre
    by Jean-Claude Widmer

242
Three Warnings against
a Mystical Rebirth of Urbanism
    by Superstudio

252
Collective Housing:
Theories and Experiments
of the Utopian Socialists Robert
Owen (1771–1858) and
Charles Fourier (1772–1837)
    by Franziska Bollerey
    and Kristiana Hartmann

273
"New Babylon": The New
York of the 1920s and
the Search for Americanism
    by Manfredo Tafuri

296
Roxy, Noah, and
Radio City Music Hall
    by Rem Koolhaas

481
A Conversation
with Stanislaus von Moos

IV USE
   AND AGENCY

311
Whose Agency?
Impact of User, Appropriation,
and Consumerism in the
Built Environment
   by Gabrielle Schaad

329
Project-Based Learning
at the ETH: Critical Rather
Than Technocratic
   by Seminar Janssen [AA.VV]

339
Citizens' Action Groups:
How, Where, Why?
   by Marianne Günter
   and Roland Günter

350
Group Portraits and
Self Portraits: Some Remarks
on Recent Approaches
to Town-Planning
   by David P. Handlin

364
Atelier 5, 1955–1975:
Experiments in
Communal Living
   by Jacques Blumer

378
Signs of Life: Symbols
in the American City
   by Denise Scott Brown

V TERRITORY
   AND SHELTER

389
The Colonial Order
of Things
   by Samia Henni

405
Immigrant Worker
Housing in Switzerland
   by Eliane Perrin

420
Military Theories and
Collective Housing
   by Teresa Zarebska

431
Remarks on an Ill-Defined
Problem: The Architecture
of Nonarchitects
   by André Corboz

450
Squatters: The Seven
Housing Systems of Nairobi
   by Praful C. Patel,
   Jeff Racki, and Reena Racki

468
An Architecture of Resistance:
Slums in Asia
   by Jin-Bak Pyun

V APPENDIX

521
Name index

524
Contributors

526
Acknowledgments
Imprint

527
Register of *archithese*
1971–1976

Critical Positions in Search of Postmodernity

Gabrielle Schaad
and Torsten Lange

The journal *archithese* may have started as the modest mouthpiece of a professional association with headquarters in central Switzerland. But already with its first issues it was able to attract an impressive range of international contributors. Moreover, it quickly achieved critical acclaim beyond national borders. Running from 1971 to 1976 under its founding editor, Stanislaus von Moos, the periodical drew, on the one hand, from the tradition of little magazines of the 1920s and 1930s avant-garde. On the other hand, it departed from the speculative outlook of late 1960s radical architecture magazines.[1] In doing so, it prepared the ground for a more substantial shift of focus in architectural discourse: from criticizing technocratic visions (e.g., of modernist urban planning) to revisiting and mining modern concepts with an astute sensibility for the historicity of form and meaning. In this vein, the magazine featured articles that tackled topics from the seventeenth to the twentieth centuries and covered politically relevant topics from architectural pedagogy to the impact of grassroots movements on urban planning. In its visual aesthetic, the magazine's layout differed from the provocative, comic, and pop aesthetic of its radical precursors in Italy and the United Kingdom, like *Casabella* and *Architectural Design*. Still, the collisions between different sets of typographies and the deployment of images as argumentative evidence rather than glossy project illustrations gave *archithese* a fresh and playful appeal.

Well before postmodernism crystallized into a set of clearly distinguishable architectural gestures in the 1980s, the positions laid out on the magazine's pages responded to the (post-)1968 condition. They each wrestled with the consequences of postwar socioeconomic and political upheaval: urbanization and environmental crisis, social diversification, and the questioning of welfare state interventionism, as well as Cold War politics and decolonization, to name but a few. Rather than drawing on a common theoretical basis, most featured authors shared an interest in the polysemy of architectural form. Their readings of buildings and cities as layered cultural expressions drew from established and novel interpretive frameworks, ranging from history to aesthetics, phenomenology, literary theory, politics, and sociology. The new sociological approach, in particular, was applied not only to "high" architecture but also to the less spectacular everyday phenomena that make up the built environment.

Postmodernism vs. Postmodernity
In this publication, we deliberately use the term *postmodernity* instead of *postmodernism*. In recent years, historians, curators, and architects have begun to critically interrogate and historicize postmodernism both as style and concept. In their far-ranging review exhibition cutting across the arts, design, and popular culture, *Postmodernism: Style and Subversion, 1970–1990* (Victoria and Albert Museum, September 2011– January 2012), curators Glenn Adamson and Jane Pavitt abridge postmodernism as a set of "gestures [that] marked a moment in the long trajectory of dissatisfaction, beginning in the early 1960s, with the commercial and institutional mainstreaming of the Modern Movement."[2] Answering Hal Foster's question from 1985, whether postmodernism was "a matter of local style or a whole new period or economic phase," they argue that it is best understood as a contested territory, hybrid style, and peripheral practice.[3] While they present interiors and furniture of late-1970s Italian radical design as one of postmodernism's multiple points of origin, they also see its rapid global spread beyond such regional manifestations in the ability to forge new

relations between "late capitalist, post-Fordist service culture" and "localized, specialist and traditional forms of production," establishing the "subversive entrepreneur" as a type of (un)disciplined practitioner.[4] Moreover, the dissatisfaction with a (techno-)utopian spirit that underpinned many modernist —and even some of the radical—projects further propelled the "unthinking of utopia" that Reinhold Martin deems one of the characteristics of postmodernism.[5]

Especially on this last point, *archithese* takes a slightly different angle. While its thematic plurality and semiological approach place it squarely within postmodernism's interest in difference and meaning, the periodical's take on modernity and modernism appears far less clear. Of course, such generalizations are inherently tricky, given the distributed nature of the magazine's production and, thus, the lack of a unified editorial line. Nevertheless, instead of simply denouncing twentieth-century modernist utopias, many of the contributors turned to their (pre)history to unearth overlooked potentials in all too easily dismissed projects. At the same time, they also addressed problematic aspects such as these projects' universal claims, their polemic (at times bombastic) tone, technocratic gestures, political opportunism, and links to colonial violence.

In its early years, the editors and authors of *archithese* were thus less intent on setting a specific formal agenda or promoting a postmodern style out of discontent with modernism. Rather than focus solely on present-day architectural production, they sought to establish a forum that would allow them to reflect critically on the historical and theoretical dimensions of recent sociospatial developments. This differed from viewing history as a precedent for creative practice (e.g., by establishing historical, formal, programmatic, or typological references). Instead, architectural history and iconography were often mobilized in *archithese* to comment on the architectural output of the time. As a result, difference and repetition came into play not only when authors turned to questions of historic preservation and reconstruction but also in the transfer and translation of North American discourse—for example, regarding the aesthetics of the everyday, pop culture, or suburban sprawl—to the context of Switzerland, with its diverging geographic scale and cultural traditions. Because of this critical-inquisitive rather than polemical-assertive character, we have chosen the term *postmodernity* instead of *postmodernism* as a header for this reader.

Thinkers like Jean-François Lyotard, Fredric Jameson, and Zygmunt Bauman view the postmodern as a discursive formation and an economic and geopolitical condition that collapses familiar notions of historical time and geographically distinct locations. Egyptian literary theorist Ihab Hassan further defines *postmodernity* "as a world process, by no means identical everywhere yet global nonetheless." "The term," he continues, acts "as a vast umbrella under which stand various phenomena: postmodernism in the arts, poststructuralism in philosophy, feminism in social discourse, postcolonial and cultural studies in academe, but also multinational capitalism, cybertechnologies, international terrorism, assorted separatist, ethnic, nationalist, and religious movements."[6] This world process follows a "cultural logic," as Jameson would say, and leads to a situation where the logic of capital pervades all aspects of life and thought.[7] However, while Jameson's totalizing critique of postmodernism emphasizes the dystopia of presentness, with its hollowing out of the past and total commodification of historical traces, Hassan's use of the term *postmodernity* strikes a less pessimistic chord by embracing difference. When we adopt Hassan's notion here, we deem it more inclusive by shifting the frame from the cultural sphere—postmodernism's connection to technologically advanced and media-driven consumer societies—to the realm of geopolitics, where conflict-laden processes of globalization and localization play out simultaneously. The contemporary world in flux, with its crisis of cultural and personal identities mirrored in its infancy on the pages of *archithese*, contributes to historical introspection and epistemic self-reflexivity. Hence, postmodernity is connected to the ethicopolitical challenge of working with and from difference, even at the risk of conflict, of recognizing distinctions, and "cultivat[ing] a keener, livelier, more dialogical sense of ourselves in relation to diverse cultures, diverse natures, the whole universe itself."[8]

Critical Positions

archithese was founded in 1971 as a more discourse-oriented version of the already existing bulletin of the Fédération Suisse des architectes indépendants (Association of Independent Swiss Architects, FSAI) on the initiative of the association's president, Hans Reinhard. His motivation was to cultivate current architectural and planning debate instead of primarily reflecting professional politics and concerns. In contrast to the more academically oriented Bund Schweizer Architekten (Union of Swiss Architects), the FSAI represented the interests of smaller architectural practices without an explicit cultural agenda. The founding editorial team of the bilingual German-French journal consisted of the art historian von Moos, who had been a casual friend of Reinhard's; von Moos's wife, Irène von Moos, as a translator; and the French-Swiss architecture journalist Jean-Claude Widmer. The association provided a modest budget; hence, hiring the professional designer Paul Diethelm and working with a large printing press (Imprimeries Réunies Lausanne) quickly broke the cost ceiling. The *archithese* experiment thus almost failed within a year due to a lack of funding.

In its first year of publication, *archithese* with its four thematically open issues met with a certain skepticism, if not resistance—the political thrust of contributions challenged the sensibilities of many architects in "neutral" Switzerland. Thanks to Reinhard's mediation and persuasion efforts, however, a "relaunch" succeeded in 1972 under changed auspices. The journal redefined itself as a "publication series," with each issue highlighting a specific topic from multiple angles. In the second issue of the original run, Reinhard, the president of the FSAI, had defined the journal's mission as pluralistic. The "neutrality" of the association was thus transferred to *archithese* by Reinhard as a mission of openness to diversity of opinion, an approach persistently followed in the journal's subsequent years by the editor-in-chief von Moos. This was also the moment when Niggli Verlag, Teufen, known for its architecture and typography books, entered the stage. To redefine the journal as a publication series had been Arthur Niggli's idea. Through 1976, the Niggli/

von Moos team produced twenty issues in the handy brochure format that would become the trademark of the journal's formative years under Diethelm's initial graphic lowercase "archithese." Von Moos, in dialogue with Niggli, more or less single-handedly managed the magazine for five years, overseeing not only the editorial work but also the graphic design. In 1977, the merger with the long-established magazine *werk*, whose editor-in-chief, Lucius Burckhardt, had left, offered the opportunity to enlarge *archithese*'s readership and overcome its financial hardships. *werk.archithese* was coedited with Diego Peverelli from 1977 to 1979. Since 1980, the journal has existed under its original name with changing editors.[9]

In its founding phase, *archithese* held a unique position in the European landscape of architectural publications due to its focus on an often sociologically informed architectural criticism that drew from historical and theoretical scholarship—as opposed to dry professional debate, architects' self-promotion, or pure scholarly writing. From today's perspective, the field of architectural criticism of the time appears more heterogeneous. The magazine presented a plurality of voices, all of whom were, in different ways, "in search of postmodernity." Among these were architects Gian Piero Frassinelli of Superstudio, Rem Koolhaas, Bruno Reichlin, and Denise Scott Brown; sociologists such as Henri Lefebvre and Eliane Perrin; and architectural historians and critics including Rosemarie Bletter, Franziska Bollerey, André Corboz, Charles Jencks, and Manfredo Tafuri.

Establishing a Transatlantic Dialogue

Architectural historian Léa-Cathrine Szacka writes that by 1980 the "distant realities" that European and American traditions still represented in the 1970s had "converged into a global architectural culture."[10] We deem *archithese* one of the means and media producing this transatlantic dialogue; it was a "medium on the move." Among its "material conditions" of production, we may count, for example, increased mobility through transatlantic flight, job opportunities in the United

States, and emerging friendships and professional networks between scholars and architects—notably, the connection between von Moos and Venturi, Scott Brown. Articles that testify to this were written, for example, by Swiss architects and historians who either worked or held teaching positions in North America, including von Moos himself, as well as Corboz, Kurt W. Forster, and Niklaus Morgenthaler. Furthermore, the global spread of American pop and consumer culture, as well as petro-modernity, across all scales of the built environment meant that familiar models of the "old" and "new" world were becoming increasingly obsolete. Thus, recent spatial phenomena and their architectural manifestations—suburbanization, urban sprawl, shopping malls, etc.—visible on both sides of the big pond could be brought into productive dialogue. The cross-fertilizing effects of personal mobility surface in similar lines of thought and features when comparing *archithese* to the later-founded *Oppositions* (1973–1984). If *archithese* was not imbedded in an institutional context, *Oppositions* famously emerged from the discursive constellations at Peter Eisenman's Institute for Architecture and Urban Studies in New York. Both periodicals shared a "provenance being neither academic nor professional."[11] *Oppositions*' orientation could be termed "strongly European" because it covered "several major currents of contemporary European discourse, mainly the ideological, Marxist oriented Frankfurt school and the more linguistically oriented French structuralist school."[12] *archithese* had ventured into similar terrain a few years earlier. Thus, we might call it the European "cousin" thanks to its orientation toward U.S. architecture culture.

Another context was that of Italy. During his research stays at the Istituto Svizzero di Roma, von Moos was exposed to publications produced and distributed between Venice, Florence, and Rome and established contacts with colleagues—among them Tafuri. From the mid-1970s, the outspoken Marxist architectural historian contributed several articles to *archithese*. Before that, Tafuri was strongly associated with the short-lived Italian *Contropiano: Materiali Marxisti* (1968–1971), which had escaped von Moos's attention. It was founded by Alberto Asor Rosa, Massimo Cacciari, and Antonio Negri. The journal's editors treated architecture and the city as a field of political *operaist* analysis, among other theoretical (or perhaps better, dialectical) dissections of literature and film. The journal was an important outlet for members of the newly formed Institute of History at the Istituto Universitario di Architettura di Venezia, Venice's architecture school. Its decidedly political stance stands in sharp contrast to the pluralist approach of *archithese*. Yet, this did not stop authors like Tafuri, Giusi Rapisarda, and Francesco Dal Co from presenting their views on its pages.

Apart from *Contropiano*, there were other periodicals whose thematic focus resonates with that of *archithese* but with whom direct exchange cannot be tracked. Briefly looking at these examples strengthens the argument that the discursive affinities were transatlantic, while the vicinity of the European publishing context yielded surprisingly fewer intersections.

In Germany, assistants and students at Stuttgart University's Institute for the Foundations of Modern Architecture and Design (Institut für Grundlagen der modernen Architektur und Entwerfen), founded in 1967 by Jürgen Joedicke, kickstarted the journal *ARCH+*. Its initial objective was to ground architecture in scientific criteria. In the 1970s, the agendas of *ARCH+* and *archithese* grew close, as *ARCH+* based its systems thinking approach on the cybernetically underpinned semiotics of Max Bense, Horst Rittel, and Christopher Alexander. The attention to social movements in architecture and urbanism pops up in several monographic issues of *archithese*. However, for *ARCH+*, its sociopolitical agenda, bolstered by Marxist theory, became an increasingly defining characteristic that eventually differentiated it once again from *archithese*'s pluralist stance.

Because *archithese* appeared throughout its run in a bilingual format (French and German), its lack of reception in the French architectural discourse of the time—prominently featured in the journal *utopie*—is equally surprising. Other than Henri Lefebvre's early contribution in conversation with *archithese*'s Lausanne-based founding coeditor Widmer, we search in vain for overlaps among the two journal's contributors. In terms of topics, the historical approach to utopia as a "no-place" (*ou-topos*) rather than a "good place" (*eu-topos*), which Craig

Buckley describes as characteristic of the "cautionary tales" presented in the French periodical's first issue (1968), could be considered a point of intersection.[13] Examples from *archithese* that resonate with this reading are Martin Fröhlich and Martin Steinmann's article dealing with Karl Moser's 1930s plan for a modernist rebuilding of Zurich's old town or Franziska Bollerey and Kristiana Hartmann's discussion of socialist utopias (e.g., by Charles Fourier).[14]

When we consider *archithese* against its immediate backdrop of the discursive landscape within Switzerland, a similar tendency for dissociation can be observed. This is most noticeable in the (non)relationship between *archithese* and the Institute for the History and Theory of Architecture (gta) within the architecture school of the Swiss Federal Institute of Technology, ETH Zurich, founded four years before the journal in 1967.[15] While some of its members contributed and later even became coeditors of the journal, *archithese* always remained independent of, and coexisting with, the gta Institute. The latter distinguished itself through its "rainbow series" of publications issued by Birkhäuser Verlag. In 1970, von Moos criticized the institute's series of publications as a medium whose contemporary graphic design surpassed the modernity of the methods and academic style it represented.[16] *archithese* can be understood as an unconscious commentary on these gta publications. With its iconographic and monographic features, it complemented and occasionally countered the more formalist approaches to architectural theory and the historical topics championed by scholars from the architecture department.[17] Perhaps it was precisely this original attitude that turned *archithese* into a compass for interested architecture students at ETH, as Ruth Hanish has noted.[18]

At times, *archithese* also consciously held up a mirror to Switzerland's leading architecture school. For example, it published an issue dedicated to the politics of higher education. Moreover, in 1971, it offered a platform to the collective formed around the infamously expelled guest lecturer Jörn Janssen to present the sociological and anti-capitalist thrust of their bottom-up seminar analyzing the operations of Swiss general contractor Goehner.

Thematic Axes

The articles chosen for translation and republication in *archithese reader: Critical Positions in Search of Postmodernity* were selected from the four issues of the first series in 1971 and from issues one to twenty of the "magazine in the form of a publication series" published by Niggli from 1972 to 1976. Several among these miniature monographs were curated by guest editors who drew on their scholarly and professional networks. The monographs form a series of relatively hermetically themed issues. However, specific topics such as history and preservation, housing, American architecture and planning, urbanism, realism, and the metropolis feature across multiple issues. Recontextualizing the articles by combining them under a series of contemporary keywords opens the arguments in the source material to readings in the present, allowing us not only to assemble a digest of the periodical and point to thematic strands but also to acknowledge the farsightedness of the selected contributions, highlighting their continued relevance without overlooking their areas of weakness.

From today's perspective, the difference in vocabulary and tone—the audacity of the arguments—in the translated sources assembled here is immediately apparent. In a few instances, the originals presented challenges to the translator, but overcoming them granted additional insight into their historicity. Our argument that *archithese* had, in many ways, a visionary character is supported by the fact that several featured articles or early versions of them grew into volumes that became milestones in architectural historiography and criticism. Examples include Koolhaas's article "Roxy, Noah, and Radio City Music Hall," published in issue 18 (1976) and later turned into a chapter in *Delirious New York* (1978), or Tafuri's contribution to issue 20 (1976) titled "New Babylon," which was later revised and extended for his *La sfera e il labirinto* (1980; translated into English as *The Sphere and the Labyrinth* in 1987). Where (partial) translations existed, we carefully integrated them with the earlier versions' not-yet-translated parts. The book highlights these textual hybrids by referencing the sources.

To highlight texts whose approach to crucial questions in postmodernist discourse is relevant to present-day analysis, we introduced new thematic axes. They are reflected in the section titles, offering a lens onto discursive arenas, as suggested by the specific case studies in this section. Five critical historiographic essays contextualize the reprinted articles, considering and reflecting on their continued relevance.

The first section, "Historicity and Meaning," dissects the multiple ways *archithese* engaged the past and the practice of history. As Marie Theres Stauffer points out, during the second half of the twentieth century, history gained significance within international architectural debates. Yet, despite forming a common reference point, no consensus was achieved around this new appreciation of historicity. In fact, how the past was mobilized depended on an author's disciplinary and cultural background. Debates about the relationship between old and new stood side-by-side with the embrace of heritage protection and calls for preserving historic buildings, neighborhoods, and old towns. These were paralleled by criticism of the modern movement's alleged ahistoricism and break with history—even if those critiques followed a similar logic of historical cycles to argue for a postmodern rupture. The articles presented in this section share the architectural interest, especially among those following Rossi, in the permanence of autonomous form.

This thread is taken up in section two, "Realism and Autonomy." Just as *archithese*'s authors shared no single definition of history, the much-discussed notion of realism also eluded stable meaning. As Irina Davidovici stresses in her introductory essay, any appeal to a universal notion of "reality" has been eclipsed by the recognition of (epistemic) difference and the embrace of multiple perspectives, an approach that germinated in the 1970s with thinkers like Lyotard. Post- and decolonial scholars in the humanities, such as Dipesh Chakrabarty and Walter Mignolo, have since expanded this position. These pluriversal realities can no longer be contained within the synthetic notion of "realism" championed by the editors of *archithese* in issues dedicated to the theme. The divergent realities and, hence, competing notions of realism upheld on either side of the Atlantic —represented in the journal through figures such as Scott Brown and Venturi versus Rossi—were a harbinger of this fractured perspective. Moreover, revisiting this discourse exposes a paradox: a shared and constitutive aspect of the various appeals to realism in architecture is its idealism, the very thing realism claims to counter.[19]

The third section, "Urbanism and Consumption," charts and unpacks the intense, multidisciplinary debates concerning the city and urban planning from the early to mid-1970s. The array of positions assembled in *archithese* testifies to the palpable sense of crisis that large-scale modernist planning had encountered since the mid-1960s and to which these new perspectives—ranging from sociology to critical theory, history, economics, psychology, and literature/fiction—sought to respond. Using various means, from critical historical analysis to design speculation, the new perspectives confronted a perception that utopian ideals had been exhausted and that the underlying myths of modernity needed to be deconstructed. In hindsight, the articles furthermore reveal the late capitalist shift from the modern industrial metropolis to the postmodern global city and its role in novel forms of flexible accumulation, linked foremost to cities' increasing culturalization during the past fifty years, a process having two dimensions: first, a transition to new forms of production, with culture and immaterial labor at their heart; second, the city as a cultural object —visible, for instance, in the revitalization of historical inner cities or the blending of past and present in urban image making and place marketing.

The commentary on the texts assembled in "Use and Agency" assesses the various ways authors evaluated a transition from the imagined, normed, and relatively passive figure of the unmarked user of buildings and urban infrastructures to active "citizen participation" in architecture—at a time when large-scale social housing projects were, despite their social agenda, being criticized primarily for their reductive molding of everyday routines. Recall Jencks's preface to *The Language of Postmodern Architecture* (1977), conflating the "death of modern architecture" with the destruction of the social housing complex Pruitt Igoe in St. Louis, Missouri, in 1972.[20] The section illuminates the potentials and pitfalls of emancipatory initiatives, open-process planning, participation, and citizen activism. It showsß that the *archithese* authors not only destabilized the position of architects as prescient planners but even questioned their ability to shape the use and adaptation of buildings. The social criticism of the time covered a wide range of differing, if not dissonant positions, from open criticism of the capitalist (building) economy on the one hand to the celebration of the everyday that the work of Venturi and Scott Brown represented on the other. Acknowledging the expansion of architectural discourse today—that is, architecture becoming an increasingly transdisciplinary, diverse, and inclusive field—this section critically renders the question of "agency" in architecture against the backdrop of larger emancipatory struggles and initiatives around and after 1968.

"Territory and Shelter" testifies to geopolitical aspects in the debates around housing in various cultural and climatic settings and characterizes the spatial discrimination and violence ingrained in modern architecture. Critically situating the early 1970s texts and their contents, Samia Henni argues that coloniality went hand in hand with modernity as a project of spatial expansion and domination. She goes on to question whether *postmodernity* amounted to *postcoloniality*, especially when looking, for example, at the establishment of the United Nations Human Settlements Program (UN-Habitat). In her commentary, Henni draws connections among the disparate phenomena explored by the sources in this final section, from "informal settlements" over immigrant worker housing to the architecture of military fortifications. She shows how architecture, buildings, and other constructed environments could be weaponized against people who were otherwise praised for their nonspecialized constructions or worked as subaltern minorities in the building industry during the explosion of urban renewal projects in the 1970s across many countries globally.

This book is the work of many minds and hands. After picking up the threads laid out in journal articles historicizing *archithese*, we began to consider the seminal role of *archithese* as a critical medium within the Swiss architectural landscape, particularly within the frame of the "Critical Issues" seminar we cotaught at the gta Institute, ETH Zurich in 2018.[21] Our thanks go to the students who contributed to this course and whose ideas helped shape the inquiries that led to this publication. From the outset, we were lucky enough to have the journal's founding editor, von Moos, at reach for questions and advice on the project. From this close collaboration sprang an extensive conversation about the early years of the journal, which is also included in this volume. The content and selection of source material took shape in a joint workshop with contributing authors Davidovici, Henni, and Stauffer in the summer of 2019. We thank them for their invaluable work. The workshop itself was conducted with the support of Blanka Major, Lisa Maillard, and Ina Stammberger. Later, Erich Schäli helped research and prepare the original texts for translation. Tracing and reconstructing the publication histories of the twenty-five original articles would have been impossible without their help. We also thank Sara Finzi-Longo and Michael Gnehm for their assistance. The final manuscript was reviewed by Ákos Moravánszky, whom we thank for his generous feedback and suggestions. Nina Paim and Eliot Gisel were key partners in the making of the book, thanks to their sensitive graphic concept. Finally, our thanks go to Andrea Wiegelmann of Triest Verlag, our publisher, who has supported and guided the project from day one.

1   See *CLIP/STAMP/FOLD: The Radical Architecture of Little Magazines, 196X to 197X* (New York: Actar; Princeton, NJ: Media and Modernity Program, Princeton University, 2010).

2   See *Postmodernism: Style and Subversion, 1970–1990*, exh. cat., ed. by Glenn Adamson and Jane Pavitt (London: V & A Publishing, 2011), 15.

3   Ibid., 13.

4   Ibid., 14.

5   Reinhold Martin, *Utopia's Ghost: Architecture and Postmodernism, Again* (Minneapolis: University of Minnesota Press, 2010).

6   Ihab Habib Hassan, "From Postmodernism to Postmodernity: The Local/Global Context," *Philosophy and Literature* 25, 1 (2001): 1–13, here 3.

7   Fredric Jameson, *Postmodernism, or, the Cultural Logic of Late Capitalism* (London: Verso, 1991).

8   Hassan, "From Postmodernism to Postmodernity" (see note 6), 13.

9   Hubertus Adam, "40 JAHRE ARCHITHESE," *archithese* 4 (2011): 38–43.

10 Léa-Catherine Szacka, *Exhibiting the Postmodern: The 1980 Venice Architecture Biennale* (Venice: Marsilio, 2016), 83.

11 Joan Ockman, "Resurrecting the Avant-Garde: The History and Program of Oppositions," in *EAV—Enseignement architecture ville 10* (Versailles: École d'architecture Versailles, 2004/2005), 31–44.

12 Ibid.

13 See Craig Buckley, "Introduction: The Echo of Utopia," in *utopie: Texts and Projects 1967–1978*, ed. Craig Buckley, Jean-Louis Violeau, and Jean-Marie Clark, 9–21 (New York: Semiotext(e); Random House, 2011), 16.

14 Martin Fröhlich and Martin Steinmann, "Zürich, das nicht gebaut wurde," *archithese* 3 (1972): 25–33; Franziska Bollerey and Kristiana Hartmann, "Collective Housing: Theories and Experiments of the Utopian Socialist Robert Owen (1771–1851) and Charles Fourier (1772–1837)," 252–71 in this publication, first published *archithese* 8 (1973): 15–26.

15 According to Sylvia Claus, the founding of the gta Institute is emblematic of a more significant trend to establish research centers for history and theory within schools of architecture in Italy, Germany, and the United States circa 1967–1968. See Sylvia Claus, "Phantom Theory: The gta Institute in Postmodernist Architectural Discourse," *gta papers* 3 (2019): 121–35, here 121.

16 Stanislaus von Moos, "Schriftenreihe des Instituts für Geschichte und Theorie der Architektur an der ETH Zürich," *Zeitschrift für Schweizerische Archäologie und Kunstgeschichte* 27, 4 (1970): 236–43, here 236.

17 See Adolf Max Vogt, "Die französische Revolutionsarchitektur und der Newtonismus," *SD, aus: Stil und Ueberlieferung in der Kunst des Abendlandes* I (1967): 229–32; Colin Rowe and Robert Slutzky, *Transparenz*, trans. Bernhard Hoesli (Basel: Birkhäuser, 1968).

18 Ruth Hanisch and Steven Spier, "'History Is Not the Past but Another Mightier Presence': The Founding of the Institute for the History and Theory of Architecture (gta) at the Eidgenössische Technische Hochschule (ETH) Zurich and Its effects on Swiss Architecture," *The Journal of Architecture* 14, 6 (2009): 655–686, here 669.

19 In 1977, von Moos had already made forays into this topic in *werk.archithese*. Stanislaus von Moos, "Zweierlei Realismus," *werk.archithese* 7–8 (1977): 58–62.

20 Charles Jencks, *The Language of Postmodern Architecture* (New York: Rizzoli, 1977).

21 See Marie Theres Stauffer, "Geschichte der Archithese: Kontexte der neueren Schweizer Architektur," *Kunst + Architektur in der Schweiz*, 55, 4 (2004): 6–14; Stanislaus von Moos interviewed by Hubertus Adam and Hannes Mayer, "Architektur und Architekturkritik," *archithese* 4 (2011): 48–51.

I HISTORICITY AND MEANING

23
Expanding Notions
of the Past:
Approaches and Forms
    by Marie Theres Stauffer

38
Architecture Today
and the Zeitgeist:
A Critical Retrospective
    by Charles Jencks

62
The Reconstruction of the
Kornhaus in Freiburg im
Breisgau and Several
Observations on Architecture
and Historical Understanding
    by Jürgen Paul

77
History as a Part of Architectural
Theory: Notes on New Projects
for Zurich, Bellinzona, Modena,
and Muggiò
    by Bruno Reichlin
    and Fabio Reinhart

93
Phase Shifts
    by Stanislaus von Moos

111
Shrunken Metropolis
    by Rosemarie Bletter

Expanding Notions of the Past

Approaches and Forms

Marie Theres Stauffer

When an art historian in the early 1970s proposed creating a series of texts on architecture, it is hardly surprising that the historical dimension of building played a role. That aspect probably also benefited from the fact that Stanislaus von Moos founded *archithese* while living in Rome. The presence and significance of the history in that environment need not be especially emphasized. In the Rome of that time, however, other significant factors were also present. Von Moos's choice to live in the Eternal City was connected with a research project on Italian Renaissance architecture.[1] In the context of that project, von Moos was part of a scholarly community whose members maintained a lively exchange while conducting research at various countries' Italy-based study centers.[2] A not insignificant number of scholars from that network later wrote articles for *archithese*. Furthermore, Italian debates on architecture, long conscious of history, had since the 1960s only increased their reflections on the debates' historical dimensions.

Beyond Italy, the significance of the history had increased in international discourses on building as well. Von Moos was thus positioning his series in a broader context and establishing particular emphases by doing so. Accordingly, *archithese* quickly stood out from other specialist journals as both independent-minded and original for its emphasis on text and its broad horizon of cultural history, as well as for the topics it addressed and its formal design. This approach especially differed from the way architecture was reported on in Swiss circles, to which von Moos attributed a lack of exacting criticism.[3] His view was shared by the architect Hans Reinhard, who, while president of the Fédération Suisse des architectes indépendants / Verband freierwerbender Schweizer Architekten (Swiss Federation of Independent Architects, FSAI), was also involved in the founding of *archithese*.[4] The avowedly pragmatic FSAI was prepared to finance a decidedly theoretical debate in order to "once again focus on architecture as a design problem and as a conveyor of cultural meaning."[5]

The comments that follow engage with the five essays from various issues of *archithese* that precede this text. Special attention is paid to historicity, which is treated from the viewpoints of "Historicity and the Present," "Rise and Reversal," "Cycles," and "Constants (and Rifts)." In restricting the present discussion to selected aspects, the intent was to better confront the arguments of various authors against a backdrop of separate themes and in their historical cultural context.

History and the Present; or, Old and New
Various contributions to *archithese* emphasize the question of historicity by relating antithetical concepts to one another—"old" and "new" or "historical" and "contemporary." These antitheses are made even more trenchant by pitting "modern architecture" against "traditional construction" or "inherited building fabric."

In the essay "Phase Shift," von Moos presents his own reflections on the relatedness, interdependence, and relativity of "old" and "new." He uses examples of architectural objects and urban planning phenomena that have enjoyed a certain boom and appeared in various places and times. His title refers to the fact that that which has only just emerged reaches a next stage through enduring presence and lasting use. In such cases, that which broke with conventions at the time it originated will transition over the years into its own convention and eventually into the phase of "being old(-fashioned)." That does not have to be the case, however. From von Moos's discussions one could also conclude that the new preserves some of its unconventional aspect if it collides with conservative attitudes and is therefore unable to establish itself. This outcome is revealed, for example, in the disapproving attitude in the "New World" toward architectural innovations: "In the meantime, the sentiments of the 'common man' continue to cling to bourgeois ideas of sensual gratification."[6] By contrast, modernism is "affiliated with the world of business, bureaucracy, and schools—as well as, more recently, with 'urban renewal'"; under those circumstances, architectural modernism "remains a concern of the intellectual elite; it appears to be unattractive to the majority of people."[7]

Whether the original difference between the new and the traditional is preserved, one must also consider the fact that, over the years, architectural innovations "grow old" in the sense that they become historical. An additional element comes into play, too, as inadequate maintenance can cause innovative buildings to look disproportionally "outdated," as von Moos observes of American cities of the 1970s, with their "skyscrapers, freeways, and billboards."[8] At the time they were built, these constructions were symbols of a (seemingly) unlimited progress based on an extremely liberal economic system that benefited from far-reaching deregulation. In the United States, construction projects are understood primarily as short-term investments—and in that sense also as episodic signs of the efficiency of the market economy. As much as possible, American architects take advantage of the great design freedoms offered by the task of creating a "monument to uniqueness," but hardly consider questions of durability. Once the "monument" has become a "kind of gigantic scrap," it has passed its moment of relevance and is at risk of losing even its use value. Two decades into the twenty-first century, this situation has only grown worse, as demonstrated, for example, by the many scaffolds placed over sidewalks in Manhattan to protect passersby from falling facade elements!

Von Moos observes a somewhat inverted correspondence in Switzerland, a country of the "old continent."[9] There, a discreet but continual progression of architectural modernism is taking place that affects even the worlds of the middle class: the "new" is spreading in parallel, as it were, with the preserved traditions.

As a result of this "sidling" openness to "modern architecture," broader strata are open to accepting inspiration from the land of unlimited opportunities, only to immediately clothe them in a high "mediocrity" and implement them with "propriety." But that is not yet enough. In "Phase Shifts," von Moos also observes that the "highly industrialized" countries of the "old continent" have the ability to make the new even newer: architectural forms and construction methods developed in the New World are assimilated in old Europe after a time—that is, they are "phase shifted."[10] Once borrowed, however, high-rises, highways, and urban infrastructure become (technologically) more "solid, modern, tasteful, and 'clean.' In a word: new."[11]

Rise and Reversal

Certain preconditions must be met for building types and methods of construction to be adopted in places that are at considerable geographical distance. In the 1960s and 1970s, these preconditions were essentially based on the fact that in the twentieth century the United States had risen to become a world power. This position of political supremacy was also tied to advanced positions in many other sectors, including construction technology. At the latest from the 1950s onward, the latter was a point of reference for building construction in Switzerland and communicated the mythos of the skyscrapers of Chicago and, especially, New York. A broad swath of the Swiss public at the time was impressed, both positively and negatively, by American metropolises and their architectonic monuments. Against the backdrop of this general attitude, which could acquire the features of an idealization, von Moos's reading is fresh—and deconstructive in the literal sense. It attests both his fundamental critical distance and his personal, on-site exploration, which permitted him a look at and behind the scenes. In the 1970s, when transatlantic flights were expensive, such experiences were available to only a few Europeans, which is why many knew the Manhattan skyline or the multilane viaducts of the U.S. Interstate Highway System only from films and photographs. As Rosemarie Bletter explains in her article "Shrunken Metropolis," such media put the looming residential and office towers of urban America in a particularly advantageous light.[12]

In the United States, too, skyscrapers were avowedly objects of self-glorification, as Bletter notes.[13] She addresses the most outstanding examples built during the construction boom of the 1920s in Manhattan with an eye toward a special kind of decor. It consisted of these buildings being made accessible to urban people a second time in the form of models or photographs: "Often these skyscrapers feature lavishly decorated portals" or special decorative elements in the halls on which the building in question is shown in miniature form.[14]

Bletter hypothesizes that the miniature is supposed to offer a more tangible picture of the high-rise, whose overall form is difficult to take in because of its height, the tapering required by the building code, and the building density of the local context. She also notes among those architects who built skyscrapers a certain discomfort resulting from the economic pressure that demanded the optimization of profits and consequently enormous building heights. In Bletter's view, reproducing the building as a model restored it to a human scale. One may also assume that the architects wanted to illustrate their work fully to passersby and users of the building to ensure that their creative achievement was appreciated. Likewise, the decoration of portals and lobbies must have served the client's interest in creating a status symbol. The additional financial investment in "miniatures" was surely intended to firmly establish the particular form of a building—whether the Empire State Building or the Chrysler Building—in the visual memory of New Yorkers and thereby give wing to the mythos that had grown up around the tall towers with respect to one's own building.

If the mythical high-rises of Manhattan were about excessive heights (initially) passed off as futuristic, the later Swiss reception of this building type reveals a combination of excessive height and reversal—though this combination was not perceived as such. In postwar Europe, skyscrapers were considered the building forms of the future.[15]

Another kind of reversal in combination with a certain excessive height concerns the value of historical architecture.

Von Moos opens up both old and new to debate, whereas Bletter, Jürgen Paul, and Bruno Reichlin and Fabio Reinhart express in their texts their appreciation for historical forms of architecture and settlements. Recall that until the nineteenth century the new was preferred. The only exceptions were buildings of high symbolic capital and special meaning for society. Everything else that had existed for a long time and no longer conformed to current taste or was worn out and defective was replaced whenever possible. The existence at the beginning of the twenty-first century of a broad consensus on the cultural meaning and material value of historical buildings is a "modern" approach and the result of a multistage process. What follows is a synthesis of several important aspects of this development that were significant with respect to the situation in the 1970s and hence at the time the *archithese* contributions discussed here were being written.

The first significant factor is the increasing centrality in the second half of the twentieth century of historical architecture and building traditions in debates among specialists but also among a broader public with an interest in culture. This centrality was connected to the loss of historical buildings in the context of the postwar economic miracle and the associated building boom. Interventions in the existing urban fabric that were careless and of dubious quality occurred in many places in industrially advanced Europe, peaking in the period around 1970 especially, as von Moos and Jürgen Paul note in their articles.[16] Criticism of this "destruction" also grew in parallel with its spread.

The increased interest in the historical and the need to protect it led to the founding of institutions such as the International Council on Monuments and Sites (1965), which followed the signing of the Venice Charter (1964). This and other initiatives urged a differentiated approach to architectural heritage, encouraged it to be understood as a witness of its time, and established the foundations for protecting cultural sites and individual structures. One other important factor was that the buildings of architectural modernism were becoming historical artifacts themselves. This was particularly true of the buildings and projects of the 1920s and 1930s but also for those from the period immediately after the war. The emerging historical distance took on an additional, concrete reality from 1965 to 1976 as the "great masters" of "modern architecture"—Le Corbusier, Walter Gropius, Ludwig Mies van der Rohe, and Alvar Aalto—passed away.

In some European countries of the 1970s, especially in West Germany, the two decades of reconstruction following the Second World War also had a major influence. In many places, the approach had been to replace historical districts that had been heavily or even just slightly damaged with superficially "modern" buildings. Design and sociocultural dimensions were neglected in favor of purely functional and economic considerations. The result was formal impoverishment and monotony on a large scale and for those reasons rightly met with various sorts of resistance.

In his essay on the Kornhaus in Freiburg im Breisgau, which had been built at the end of the fifteenth century, Paul discusses one aspect of the postwar approach to the historical building fabric; namely, the reconstruction of historical buildings that were destroyed in the war.[17] As Paul shows in his text, the historical dimension of lost (monumental) buildings was closely intertwined with their symbolic value, so that approaches to reconstruction also appealed to ethical standards. These crystallized especially in the question of whether to reconstruct the lost monument faithfully or "in the form of a free recreation" based on "specific values of formal structure."[18]

The practicality of faithful reconstruction depends on adequate documentation of the historical building and whether it can be adapted to the functional, technical, and legal requirements of a later era. All of this led to a construction process that was as complicated as it was expensive and nevertheless resulted in practice in a new building in terms of materials. For that reason, faithful reconstructions are rare. By contrast, the freely recreated landmark building can be built at lower cost using current technologies. One significant disadvantage of this approach, however, is that the reduction to "specific values of formal structure" results in the loss of the very decoration that was an indispensable source of meaning in the original historical context. For those reasons, the middle road that is often taken is to cloak a "new" core in an "old" shell. This creates a commercially optimized interior that remains hidden beneath the old garb.

Projects from the early twenty-first century such as the Berliner Schloss (Berlin Palace) make clear that the subject has lost nothing of its currency. As in Freiburg, in the German capital a historicizing shell was literally "glued" to a concrete core, but there it does not even extend across all of the facades. Superficial recreation thus results in an incoherent picture. One of the problems posed by—more or less faithful—reconstruction, combined with contemporary facades on the other sides, is that the outcome lacks both architectural and conceptual qualities. The juxtaposition of contrasting architectural forms should ideally generate a tension that has aesthetic qualities. With both the Kornhaus in Freiburg and the Berliner Schloss, however, the resulting side-by-side architectural forms are unconvincing for two reasons. First, the contrast does not succeed on formal grounds; second, the old and new differ in quality. The Berlin newspaper *taz* remarked on historical value: "this architectural hybrid simulates for us a history that we never had."[19] The author was writing with the Berliner Schloss in mind, but the words also apply to the example in Freiburg. The (naive) will and (understandable) desire to repair "a history that cannot be repaired" quickly become evident in such projects.[20] To find a persuasive solution is incomparably more difficult.

Cycles
Charles Jencks's essay "Architecture Today and the Zeitgeist" also addresses the theme of reversal, in the sense of a new orientation around a historical approach; specifically, the cyclical emergence of architectural forms in the language of classicism.[21] Jencks associates this periodic phenomenon with repressive power structures, which deserve to be questioned critically.[22] The intent of this essay, however, is to emphasize the historical and its significance, which is why it is more relevant here that the

classical approach, in its reference to the architecture of antiquity, represents a paradigm that has the concerted influence of a centuries-old tradition.[23] The cyclical emergence of classicism is thus manifested on a powerful foundation. Modern architecture, which was not only oriented toward the future in its ideas but also broke with the past by introducing new forms and construction methods, had an incomparably shorter tradition. The relationship between (neo)classical and modern architecture also must be differentiated in another way: modern architecture's approaches to construction and design were above all opposed to nineteenth-century historicism—and to the question of style. Yet admiration for the outstanding monuments of earlier eras was widespread among the great modernist architects. One need think only of Mies van der Rohe's interest in the work of Karl Friedrich Schinkel or Le Corbusier's grappling with the Athenian Parthenon or Rome's monumental historical buildings.[24] The formal idiom of modernism, which countered classical models with abstract forms, asymmetrical dispositions, and refusal of historical decorative elements, can nevertheless echo the earlier models on a structural or typological level. These echoes are, however, downplayed in the look of the buildings and are overshadowed on the discursive level by a rhetoric that presents itself as vehemently futuristic.

Constants (and Rifts)
In his contribution to *archithese*, however, Jencks did not so much address the architectural works of the modern era as the ethical and moral stance of their authors. According to him, it is typical that architects appeal to the zeitgeist and very much bend to it; accordingly, one could speak of a "constant." As examples, Jencks mentions several of the great figures of the modern movement who tried to come to arrangements with the fascist dictators of the twentieth century or received architectural commissions from them.[25] That these attempts often failed should be seen as a blessing of history; that such efforts should be condemned is beyond question.

Jencks's reproaches, however, are intended to discredit modernism and its architects. The historian was not alone in that effort but rather was joining in a debate that became widespread in the 1970s. First and foremost, it condemned a specific architectural practice of the postwar period that must be characterized as a vulgarized form of the International Style and placed itself at the service of speculative architecture without spatial quality. One of the prominent voices in the debate was Robert Venturi, who, as early as 1966 in his *Complexity and Contradiction in Architecture*, turned against "orthodox Modern architecture," by which he meant a superficial and simplified version that was widespread in the United States—although not just there.[26] This condition is often blamed on the first generation of modern architects, and in North America the focus was on those influential representatives who from the late 1930s onward had taught at American universities. Another factor, however, is that numerous large building projects of the New Deal era and, especially, many examples of American public housing were planned without trained architects; that is, they were designed solely by investors and construction companies.[27] Apart from the flat roof and unframed windows of the modern movement, the resulting buildings have no connection to it whatsoever. That does not mean that modern architecture should not be criticized, however, as it was in various ways in the 1970s. Among the more reflective voices were those who criticized the abstract formal language of modern architecture as inaccessible and elitist or found fault with its distance from architectural traditions. Even proponents of the modern movement understood that it could no longer be a universal reference system on which a transformed world could rely.

If the growing esteem for the long history of architecture, in both its outstanding and modest manifestations, corresponds to the zeitgeist of the 1970s, another of Jencks's contributions in "Architecture Today and the Zeitgeist" was to historicize the use of the zeitgeist as an argument. Jencks related themes from the zeitgeist to "powers" of a specific era: those difficult to recognize factors that emerge only indirectly, of which it is often said that they inevitably determine events and the course of history.[28]

Also characteristic of the 1970s is Jencks's categorical distancing of himself from the concept of a singular "force" that can be historically determined, such as "the Marxist appeal to inevitable laws of history" or Sigmund Freud's concept of a drive that underlies everything and is said to feed on the libido. Jencks thus abandons the idea of one external force or of one internal necessity to which human beings are completely subjected and operates instead with the concept of the "system." By doing so, he switches from one constant powerful concept to another. The idea of the system spread during the second half of the twentieth century through the reception of publications by Karl Ludwig von Bertalanffy such as *An Outline of General Systems Theory* (1950) and *General System Theory: Foundations, Development, Applications* (1969), as well as Claude Lévi-Strauss's *Anthropologie structurale* (1958), Arthur Koestler's *The Ghost in the Machine* (1967), and Fred E. Emery's *Systems Thinking* (1969).[29]

The concept of the system made it possible to introduce not only complexity but heterogeneity. "The system" was accordingly conceived as a structured set of (extremely) different elements with certain relationships between them. For that reason, Jencks's concept also includes the idea of the "dissectibility" of the system, a notion of particular interest to the broader idea of historical development. According to this understanding, a given zeitgeist is not simply "replaced" by another zeitgeist, with the human being remaining its unconscious victim. The idea of the system permits instead an analytical confrontation with structure, which can be disassembled so that its individual aspects may be critically assessed. That means, in turn, qualifying the entities thus reflected on, and on that basis "putting the system back together" without its dysfunctional parts.[30]

Jencks's discussions also contain aspects of the discourses that emerged in the context of the revolts of the 1960s, such as the calls for change and participation. Jencks takes the side here of those demanding participation and intervention in the existing structures. He thus finds himself at odds with his period's more radical positions, which viewed any constructive intervention in the system as an improvement of a capitalist world order and hence as a task requiring critical distance. The call for active intervention and participation also has an architectonic dimension; it focuses especially on integrating users in order to break up the architect-investor power relationship. Another point of agreement between Jencks's essay and the radical movements of the 1960s lies in its combative, sometimes polemical tone and preference for commentary and argument over balanced and detailed discussion. At one point, however, Jencks trails far behind issues that would have been current around 1970. He counsels going "along with" and understanding an "inexorable" fate and to that end makes an analogy to rape: when it is "inevitable," he writes, "lie back and enjoy it." Such chauvinistic making light of a serious crime, one that not only feminists of the period but theorists such as Michel Foucault branded as a form of torture, is not just reactionary but discrediting.[31]

Constancy and Permanency
The *archithese* article by Bruno Reichlin and Fabio Reinhart shares with the other texts examined here the great weight placed on the historical dimension. The title already points to this: "History as a Part of Architectural Theory: Notes on New Projects for Zurich, Bellinzona, Modena, and Muggiò."[32] However the distinctive quality of the discourse of these two architects from Ticino is the theme of constancy. This factor concerns the staying power of architectural traditions and their historical-social meanings, which are constitutive not only of approaches to historical preservation but also of new projects. Within this framework, Italian *razionalismo* and, in a broader sense, the modern movement represent a phase of history that the two architects recognize as a specific tradition.

This attitude is expressed when Reichlin and Reinhart explain their project for the Kratz district of Zurich, between Paradeplatz and Bürkliplatz. In their plan for the district, they focus on the historical context, specifically on traditions that are local but linked to significant aspects of a more universal history of architecture. Thus, they refer on the one hand to Gottfried Semper's nineteenth-century plans for the Kratz district, plans that convey a classicistic approach both on the formal level and in the construction type of the block perimeter. On the other hand, they refer to the modernism of German-speaking Switzerland, which in their eyes also has classicistic aspects.[33] The broader horizon—"contesto in assenza"—of the project in Zurich is ultimately formed by typologically or functionally comparable realizations that are part of the cultural memory of the history of architecture and are mobilized by every architect in a personal way.

The attention the architects from Ticino pay to the context of an architectural brief can be traced back to debates in Italy; for example, over Vittorio Gregotti's book *Il territorio dell' architettura* (*The Territory of Architecture*; 1962), which discusses the relationship between the architectural intervention and its urban surroundings, as well as that between architecture and history.[34] With reference to Giulio Carlo Argan, Gregotti also took up the theme of typology; that is, of a kind of constant structural basis underlying certain architectural traditions and permanently shaping their disposition.[35]

An even stronger basis for Reichlin's and Reinhart's approach were the ideas of Aldo Rossi, with whom they collaborated at the ETH Zurich and beyond. Rossi had pointed out as early as 1966 in his book *L'architettura della città* (*The Architecture of the City*) that "established building types [play a role] in determining the morphological structure of urban form as it develops in time."[36] Accordingly, Rossi based his projects on historical architectural elements that are "abstracted from the vernacular, in the broadest possible sense."[37] This implies that the design also integrates an inventory of the surrounding buildings with the idea of inscribing an aspect of memory in the completed building that is formally analogous to its context. In this way, the old lives on in the new; temporary interventions nevertheless guarantee the permanence of that which is established locally. With projects such as the Gallaratese apartment block (1968–1976) or the San Cataldo Cemetery in Modena (1971–1984), Rossi demonstrated this mediation between historical traditions and the elementary geometric forms of architectonic rationalism.

Historicity is for Reichlin and Reinhart thus a true point of departure for both their theoretical reflections and their design practice.[38] To some extent, historicity is also the objective of their work, since, following a dictum of the German philosopher Hans Heinz Holz that they cite in their text, their projects are appropriate to the present "to the extent [they] have absorbed the past," yet they can also be recognized as being of the present because they both "absorb what we have not experienced ourselves in existing forms ... and expand it."[39]

Relations

The wealth of topics discussed here reflects the heterogeneity of the discourses of the 1970s. These diverse debates must be viewed not least as signs of the extent to which architecture and its historiography were undergoing a process of upheaval in those years. With regard to the central question of that era concerning future approaches and architectural forms, which was swallowed by the multifariousness and contradictoriness of various proposals, awareness of the historical seems to have been a kind of leitmotif.

The *archithese* of the 1970s presented an extremely informative selection of contemporaneous themes with an astonishing density. The fact that articles from these years can still be read, discussed, and reflected on in ever-new ways shows that the ideas and hypotheses presented in them have not exhausted their importance for the historical and theoretical discourse today. The "strange seventies" are, however, both a point of contact and a point of repulsion for the important architects of our time, in which the connection to history, too, is present and significant in ever-new ways.

1   See Stanislaus von Moos, *Turm und Bollwerk: Beiträge zu einer politischen Ikonographie der italienischen Renaissancearchitektur* (Zurich: Atlantis, 1974), in which he takes up again the subject of his dissertation at the Universität Zürich.

2   Many nations have research institutes in Italy's capital that focus on art, archaeology, history, and art history, including the American Academy in Rome, the British School at Rome, the German Bibliotheca Hertziana—Max-Planck Institut für Kunstgeschichte, the Académie de France à Rome, and the Istituto Svizzero. The discussions have been referred to by Kurt W. Forster.

3   Stanislaus von Moos in conversation with the author, November 24, 1997, and October 27, 2007.

4   Before the first issue of the journal appeared, von Moos had already published, at Reinhard's invitation, contributions to the quarterly journal of the FSAI. On the circumstances of the founding of *archithese*, see Hubertus Adam, "40 Jahre *archithese*," *archithese* 4 (2011): 38–42; "Fokus: *archithese*: Stanislaus von Moos im Gespräch mit Beatriz Colomina und Marie Theres Stauffer," *Arch+*, 186–187 (2008): 68–75; Marie Theres Stauffer, "Geschichte der Archithese: Kontexte der neueren Schweizer Architektur," *Kunst und Architektur in der Schweiz*, 4 (2004): 6–14.

5   Stanislaus von Moos in Hubertus Adam and Hannes Meyer, "Architektur und Architekturkritik: Ein Gespräch mit Stanislaus von Moos," *archithese* 4 (2011): 48–51; Stanislaus von Moos in conversation with the author, Zurich, November 24, 1997.

6   Stanislaus von Moos, "Phase Shifts," 92–108 in this publication, esp. 93. First published in *archithese* 16 (1975), 26–36, esp. 26.

7   Ibid.

8   Ibid.

9   The focus on a comparison between the United States, a country in the "New World," and Switzerland in the "Old World" is made against the backdrop of the issue's theme, but one could also think of Scandinavian countries where similar phase shifts are manifested.

10   Von Moos, "Phase Shifts" (see note 6), 92. The "phase shift" of the title refers to a physical phenomenon: the difference in the phases of two waves or vibrations of the same frequency.

11   Ibid.

12   Rosemarie Bletter, "Shrunken Metropolis," 110–19 in this publication, esp. 117. First published in *archithese* 18 (1974), 22–27.

13   Ibid., 110–19.

14   German summary of Rosemarie Bletter, "Metropolios réduite," in *archithese* 18, 1974, S. 22 ; see also Bletter, "Shrunken Metropolis" (see note 12), 113 and figs. 1-5.

15   The skyscraper remained a central theme in architecture in the United States as well. The competition to have the tallest building encouraged the development of both construction and formal design.

16   Von Moos, "Phase Shifts" (see note 6); Jürgen Paul, "The Reconstruction of the Kornhaus in Freiburg im Breisgau, and Several Observations on Architecture and Historical Understanding," 62–75 in this publication. First published in *archithese* 11 (1976), 10–19.

17   Ibid.

18   Ibid., 66 (16 in original).

19   Esther Slevogt, "Wiederaufbau Berliner Stadtschloss: Neurose aus Beton," in *taz*, September 3, 2016, https://taz.de/Wiederaufbau-Berliner-Stadtschloss/!5332988/ (accessed February 16, 2020).

20   Ibid.

21   Charles Jencks, "Architecture Today and the Zeitgeist: A Critical Retrospective," 38–61 in this publication. First published in *archithese* 2 (1971), 25–41.

22   Ibid., 44–52 (33–35 in original).

23   The reading of the writings of Vitruvius, which became available to a broader readership from the fifteenth century onward, established ancient architecture as a reference system— and hence revived discussion of its arguments over and explanations of the construction, structure, and decoration of diverse types of buildings. That happened again and again in ever-new forms over the course of centuries.

24   The ABC group, to which architects from Switzerland, the Netherlands, and the Soviet Union belonged, did the most to distinguish itself from historical architecture in the 1920s and 1930s. On this, see, for example, *ABC: Beiträge zum Bauen, 1924–1928*, ed. Mart Stam et al. (Baden: Lars Müller, 1993); Sima Ingberman, *ABC: Internationale konstruktivistische Architektur, 1922–1933*, Bauwelt-Fundamente 105 (Wiesbaden: Vieweg, 1995).

25   Jencks, "Architecture Today and the Zeitgeist" (see note 21), 44–52 (26–28 in original).

26   By contrast, Robert Venturi greatly admired the modern architects of the first generation, such as Le Corbusier and Aalto. See Robert Venturi, *Complexity and Contradiction in Architecture*, Museum of Modern Art Papers on Architecture 1 (New York: Museum of Modern Art; Garden City, NY: Doubleday, 1966).

27   On this, see also Von Moos, "Phase Shifts" (see note 6), 26.

28   Jencks, "Architecture Today and the Zeitgeist" (see note 21), 25.

29   Karl Ludwig von Bertalanffy, "An Outline of General Systems Theory," *British Journal for the Philosophy of Science* 1–2 (1950): 134–65; Karl Ludwig von Bertalanffy, *General System Theory: Foundations, Development, Applications* (New York: George Braziller, 1969); Claude Lévi-Strauss, *Anthropologie structurale* (Paris: Plon, 1958); Arthur Koestler, *The Ghost in the Machine* (London: Hutchinson, 1967); Fred. E. Emery, ed., *Systems Thinking* (London: Penguin, 1969).

30   Jencks, "Architecture Today and the Zeitgeist" (see note 21), 38–43, 52–59 (25–26 in original).

31   Ibid., 44–52 (26–28 in original).

32   Bruno Reichlin and Fabio Reinhart, "History as a Part of Architectural Theory: Notes on New Projects for Zurich, Bellinzona, Modena, and Muggiò," 76–91 in this publication. First published in *archithese* 11 (1976), 20–29.

33   Ibid., 77–84 (20–24 in original).

34   Vittorio Gregotti, *Il territorio dell'architettura* (Milan: Feltrinelli, 1962).

35   Giulio Carlo Argan, "Sul concetto di tipologia architettonica," in G.C. Argan, *Progetto e destino* (Milan: Casa Editrice il Saggiatore, 1965).

36   Kenneth Frampton, *Modern Architecture: A Critical History*, rev. ed. (London: Thames and Hudson, 1980), 294. See also Aldo Rossi, *L'architettura della città* (Padua: Marsilio, 1966), translated by Diane Ghirardo and Joan Ockman as *The Architecture of the City* (Cambridge, MA: MIT Press, 1984).

37   Frampton, *Modern Architecture* (see note 36), 294.

38   On this, see especially the introductory section of Reichlin and Reinhart, "History as a Part of Architectural Theory" (see note 32), 76 (20 in original).

39   Ibid.

Architecture Today and the Zeitgeist

A Critical Retrospective

Author:
Charles Jencks

Sources:
archithese, 2 (1971): 25–41
Charles Jencks, *Architecture 2000: Predictions and Methods* (London: Studio Vista, 1971), 20–32 (EN)

Translated by:
Steven Lindberg

La trahison perpétuelle des clercs[1]

The idea that man is an unconscious victim of external forces, or internal necessities, is one of the greatest intellectual orthodoxies of our time. Ever since the waning of traditional religions, men have been convincing themselves of one inevitable necessity after another, until the point has been reached where some of them have actually started to become operative in detail. Whether or not this desire to discover some omnipotent, external force signifies an intellectual rage for order and understanding or rather a deep psychological drive to identify with a superhuman force and avoid responsibility is open to question: but its existence is beyond dispute.

It can be seen in the Marxist appeal to inevitable laws of history, in the Freudian appeal to basic drives of the libido and most recently in the appeal to underlying forces of technology by Galbraith and McLuhan. It might seem at first, with such a superabundance of prime movers, that each one would largely serve to undermine the idea that any one was primary and therefore, perhaps, the whole idea of inevitable fate itself.

But quite the reverse has happened. What we have received is one fundamentalist explanation after another, with each supersession giving added hope to the belief that something really ultimate lies beneath the series of external appearances. Thus history could be seen as the gradual peeling back of layer after layer of partially true explanations which promised an absolute truth as their end. Recently, however, this search for an ultimate prime mover has reversed its direction and it now appears that if there is any such thing as an overwhelming fate it has to be considered as the concatenation of many forces together into a system, but it is even doubtful that this implies necessity.[2] For even within a rigidly deterministic system there always exists the *possibility* of transcendence and this transcendence often has an indeterminate element of chance. In any case, we have continually made the mistake of substituting a single force for the general system and having given up beliefs in a transcendental existence have located it behind and external to us. Thus Karl Marx:

"When a society has discovered the natural law that determines its own movement, even then it can neither overleap the natural phases of

Heutige Architektur und 'Zeitgeist'

Kritische Rückschau

Rétrospective critique

Charles Jencks, London   La trahison perpétuelle des clercs[1]

Die Idee, der Mensch sei ein unbewusstes Opfer äusserer Kräfte oder innerer Notwendigkeiten, ist eine der beliebtesten intellektuellen Maximen unserer Zeit. Seit dem Verblassen der traditionellen Religionen suchte sich die Menschheit ständig von der Existenz dieser oder jener unausweichlicher Notwendigkeit zu überzeugen, bis der Punkt erreicht wurde, wo eine davon tatsächlich begann, bis in Einzelheiten hinein wirksam zu werden. Ob dieser Wunsch, irgendeinen allmächtigen äusseren Kraftfaktor zu entdecken, gleichbedeutend sei mit intellektueller Sehnsucht nach Ordnung und Einsicht, oder vielmehr einem tiefliegenden psychologischen Bedürfnis entspreche, sich mit einer übermenschlichen Kraft zu identifizieren und Verantwortung zu vermeiden, ist eine offene Frage: Seine Existenz ist jedenfalls ausser Diskussion.

Er kann herausgelesen werden aus der marxistischen Beschwörung unausweichlicher geschichtlicher Gesetze, aus der Lehre Freuds von den fundamentalen Antriebskräften der Libido und neuerdings auch aus der Evozierung der unterschwelligen Kraft der Technologie etwa bei Galbraith und McLuhan. Angesichts einer solchen Überfülle an Erstbewegern könnte man in der Tat annehmen, dass jeder einzelne von ihnen genügen würde, um die Vorstellung, wonach überhaupt eine dieser Antriebskräfte am Anfang stand ins Wanken zu bringen — und so möglicherweise die ganze Idee vom unausweichlichen Schicksal überhaupt.

Aber genau das Gegenteil geschah. Was uns beschert wurde, ist eine fundamentalistische Erklärung nach der andern, und jede Ablösung erhöhte die Hoffnung im Glauben, dass unter einer Reihe von äusseren Erscheinungen etwas wirklich Letztgültiges verborgen liegt. So konnte die Geschichte als schichtweises Herausschälen von partiell wahren Erklärungen verstanden werden, das — im Endeffekt — eine absolute Wahrheit zu enthüllen versprach. In jüngerer Zeit änderte jedoch diese Suche nach einem letzten Erstbeweger ihre Richtung, und es scheint jetzt, dass, wenn es

L'idée selon laquelle l'homme est la victime inconsciente de forces extérieures et de nécessités intérieures est aujourd'hui une des maximes intellectuelles les plus répandues. On en trouve les éléments chez Marx et chez Freud, aussi bien que plus récemment chez Galbraith ou McLuhan. Cependant, depuis un certain temps on tend plutôt à admettre que ce ne sont pas des forces isolées, sociales, psychologiques ou inhérentes à la technologie

qui déterminent le cours de l'histoire, mais plutôt leur enchaînement dans des systèmes (structuralisme).

Dans cette situation beaucoup d'hommes — et en particulier beaucoup d'architectes — tendent vers un « déterminisme passif ». Incapables de changer le « destin » de l'histoire, ils essayent de s'y adapter.

Les conséquences de cette attitude pour l'avenir sont souvent fatales. Il existe toujours dans l'architecture

moderne une tradition qui aime à se référer au « Zeitgeist »; c'est en effet une tactique très répandue parmi les architectes d'infliger au public leurs idées en les présentant comme la suite logique de leurs inéluctables.

Le Corbusier a parlé de « l'industrie envahissante comme un fleuve qui roule à sa destinée ». On trouve des formules analogues chez Mies van der Rohe, Philip Johnson et d'autres architectes qui, en effet, non seule-

überhaupt sowas wie ein überwältigendes Schicksal gibt, dieses als die Verkettung verschiedenster Kräfte zu einem System betrachtet werden muss [2]. Aber selbst für ein starr deterministisches System gibt es immer die *Möglichkeit* der Transzendenz, und diese Transzendenz hat oft ein unbestimmtes Zufallselement. Jedenfalls haben wir beständig den Fehler begangen, das allgemeine System durch eine einzelne Kraft zu ersetzen; auch wenn wir den Glauben an eine transzendente Existenz verloren haben, so blieben wir doch dabei, diese Kraft hinter uns und ausserhalb von uns zu plazieren. So Karl Marx:

« Auch wenn eine Gesellschaft dem Naturgesetz ihrer Bewegung auf die Spur gekommen ist (...), kann sie naturgemässe Entwicklungsphasen weder überspringen noch wegdekretieren. Aber sie kann die Geburtswehen abkürzen und mildern » [3].

Oder wie es später McLuhan formulierte: « Es gibt solange keine Unausweichlichkeit als die Bereitschaft vorhanden ist, das, was laufend geschieht, nüchtern zu verfolgen. » [4]

Mit anderen Worten: Das Schicksal ist solange nicht gänzlich schicksalshaft, als wir bereit sind, uns dreinzuschicken und es zu verstehen. Ein tschechisches Sprichwort drückt diese Fügsamkeit noch besser aus: « Wenn du der Vergewaltigung nicht ausweichen

ment par leur vocabulaire rhétorique mais aussi par leurs positions politiques, tendaient fatalement à s'intégrer dans les courants fascistes et répressifs des années 30. Ils étaient d'autant plus enclins à faire un compromis avec le statu quo politique qu'ils proclamaient être complètement apolitiques.

Le « déterminisme passif » de beaucoup d'architectes et leur penchant vers de naïfs pronostics technocratiques (comme ceux d'un Buckminster-Fuller) néglige le fait que les tendances historiques ont bien un caractère inexorable mais ne sont point inévitables. Elles se développent uniquement jusqu'au point où l'équilibre du système est gravement troublé et où des contre-mouvements sont engagés. C'est pourquoi les pronostics scientifiques conçoivent l'avenir non pas sous forme de tendance univectorielle mais de courbe en S.

Il est cependant important de concevoir les systèmes comme démontables, en dépit de leur prédisposition à s'enchaîner dans des unités compactes. Ceci permet d'identifier des tendances positives et de les disséquer de tendances négatives: ceci pour dépasser le caractère fatal d'événements inexorables. Au lieu du déterminisme fataliste courant, l'auteur propose le principe d'une « évolution critique » dans laquelle des valeurs sociales et culturelles contrôlent à chaque moment le progrès technologique.

† fig. 1 Vehicle Assembly Building, Cape Kennedy, view of exterior. An example of "technological determinism." The fact that these objects transcend individual determinants and appear to be determined by many precise parameters gives them a certain moral, not to say religious, authority, especially among architects.

↓ fig. 2 Vehicle Assembly Building, Cape Kennedy, view of interior. The VAB, "the largest building in the world," is so large that it creates its own weather conditions in its interior.

kannst, so lehne dich zurück und geniesse sie!» Aber dieser Fatalismus — Beispiele dazu werden wir kurz anhand einiger moderner Architekten anführen — ist lediglich ein kraftloser Determinismus. Er steht nicht einmal auf dem Niveau des strengen Determinismus wie zum Beispiel des Islams, der lehrt, dass das Unausweichliche nur deshalb unausweichlich ist, weil wir es nicht kennen können. Dieser kraftlose Determinismus behauptet, dass wir in Wirklichkeit machtlos seien, die Naturgesetze und die unausweichlichen Kraftströme zu ändern, obwohl wir sie erkennen können. Folglich trägt er dazu bei, unseren Willen zu schwächen, uns zu versöhnen, mit dem, wovon wir *denken*, dass es über unsern Kräften steht, und endlich, im Fall der Vergewaltigung, uns in die Stimmung zu versetzen, die es uns erlaubt, diese zu geniessen.

Die Auswirkungen dieser Haltung auf die Zukunft sind oft dermassen unglücklich, dass «sie verdient, in der brutalsten Weise zerschmettert zu werden», wie es Bertrand de Jouvenel einmal formulierte [5]. Was tatsächlich geschieht ist folgendes: Wir leugnen, dass das Wissen um eine Kraft uns in die Lage versetzt, irgendwas gegen sie zu unternehmen; wir verwechseln einen *unerbittlichen* Trend mit einem *unausweichlichen* Trend und folglich ein «ist» mit einem «sollte.» Um es in der Sprache der Zukunftprognosen zu sagen: Wir akzeptieren die Vorzüge irgendeines evolutionären Trends selbst dann, wenn eine der Begleiterscheinungen darin besteht, dass die «Reichen immer reicher und die Armen relativ ärmer werden». [6]

Welches war nun die Haltung von Intellektuellen und führenden Architekten gegenüber diesen äusseren Kräften oder Einflüssen? Sie war offensichtlich höchst verschieden: Zugleich kritisch und passiv, moralisierend und ergeben. Noch immer gibt es eine sehr lebendige Tradition in der modernen Architektur (und man kann ihr Fortdauern in die Zukunft prophezeien), die sich auf den Zeitgeist beruft. Man könnte sogar sagen, dass es immer wieder den Versuch gegeben habe, die Gesellschaft zu verängstigen und sie zu zwingen, gewisse vom Architekten geförderte Strömungen zu akzeptieren, indem diese als unausweichlich hingestellt werden. Das ist eine allgemein übliche Taktik. Um jedoch klarzustellen, dass sich mein Angriff keineswegs gegen bestimmte Architekten oder gar gegen die ganze moderne Bewegung richtet, sondern vielmehr bloss gegen *die Haltung eines kraftlosen Determinismus*, so werde ich hier eine Reihe von Architekten zitieren, mit denen ich in anderen Zusammenhängen übereinstimme.

In den frühen Zwanzigerjahren sagte Le Corbusier: «L'industrie, *envahissante comme un fleuve qui roule à sa destinée*, nous apporte les outils neufs adaptés à cette époque nouvelle animée d'esprit nouveau. La loi d'économie gère impérativement nos actes et nos conceptions». Ihm folgte kurz darauf Mies van der Rohe: «Das Individuum verliert an Bedeutung; sein Schicksal ist nicht länger von Interesse für uns. Die entscheidenden Leistungen in allen Bereichen sind unpersönlich und ihre Urheber sind zumeist unbekannt. Sie nehmen *teil am Strom* unserer Zeit zur Anonymität.» Beide Auffassungen werden zusammengefasst von Nikolaus Pevsner in seiner 1936 verfassten Rechtfertigung des modernen Stils: «Wie dem auch sei, der grosse schöpferische Geist wird seinen eigenen Weg auch in Zeiten von *übermächtiger kollektiver Energie*

its evolution, nor shuffle them out of the world by a stroke of the pen. But this much it can do: it can shorten and lessen the birth pangs."[3]

Or as McLuhan later put it:"There is absolutely no inevitability as long as there is a willingness to contemplate what is happening."[4]

In other words, fate is not altogether fatal as long as we are willing to go along with and understand it. A Czech proverb puts the acquiescence even better: "When rape is inevitable, lie back and enjoy it." In fact, this fatalism, and the examples of it that will be quoted shortly from modern architects, is merely weak determinism. It doesn't even have the virtue of strong determinism such as is found in the religion of Islam which argues that the inevitable is only inevitable because we cannot know it. Rather, weak determinism asserts that although we can be aware of natural laws and inevitable trends we are actually powerless to change them. Thus it tends to undermine our will and reconcile us to that which we *think* is beyond our power.

The effects of this attitude on the future are often so unfortunate that, as Bertrand De Jouvenel says, "it deserves to be battered in the most brutal manner."[5] What effectively happens is that we deny that knowledge of a force allows us to do anything about it; we mistake an *inexorable* trend for an *inevitable* trend and thus implicitly mistake an "is" for an "ought." Or in terms of a former example, we assume the positive virtues of some evolutionary trend even when its correlation is that the "rich get richer and the poor relatively poorer."[6]

What has been the attitude of intellectuals and leading architects toward these external forces or pressures? Obviously it has been varied: both critical and passive, moral and acquiescent. Yet there is a very strong tradition in modern architecture, and one can predict its continuance into the future, of appeals to the Zeitgeist, or the underlying spirit of history. One might even say there has been an attempt to coerce or stampede society into accepting certain trends which the architect favors, under the guise of making them appear inevitable. I would like to substantiate this statement, but in order to avoid the misunderstanding that I am attacking particular architects or the whole modern movement, rather than an *attitude of weak determinism*, I will cross quote from a number of architects, all of whom I agree with in other contexts.

In the early twenties Le Corbusier said: "Industry, *overwhelming us like a flood which rolls on toward its destined ends*, has furnished us with new tools adapted to this new epoch, animated by the new spirit. Economic law unavoidably governs our acts and thoughts." He was followed shortly by Mies van der Rohe's *"The individual is losing significance; his destiny is no longer* what interests us. The decisive achievements in all fields are impersonal and their authors are for the most part unknown. *They are part of the trend* of our time toward anonymity." Both attitudes were summarized by Nikolaus Pevsner in his justification of the modern style in 1936: "However, the great creative brain will find its own way even in times of *overpowering collective energy*, even with the medium of this new style of the twentieth century, which, because it is a genuine style as opposed to a passing fashion, is *totalitarian*." Although the last word was perhaps a slip of the pen and was later changed to "universal," it is a significant slip, underlining the attitude of "overpowering energy" or "overwhelming flood" which is often connected with a particular style or technological determinism. Indeed we find a continuation of this tradition today in many places. Because of what he terms "an unhaltable trend to constantly accelerating change," Reyner Banham suggests to the architect that he "run with technology and discard his whole cultural load including the professional garments by which he is recognized as an architect" or else the "technological culture" will "go on without him"[7] or Buckminster Fuller uses the example of the rigorously designed space technology, to chide architects for not keeping up with the Zeitgeist and lessening the birth pangs of history. Common to all these prophecies is the appeal to a mixture of both moral choice and amoral inevitability: the conflation of an "ought" with an "is," or "will be." This position then leads to a form of pragmatism that says whatever exists, or works, is alright, or successful.

This step to pragmatism is a natural consequence of weak determinism, and its pitfalls have long been pointed out—particularly with respect to intellectuals in Julien Benda's *La Trahison des Clercs* [The betrayal of the

clerics] (1927) and Noam Chomsky's *American Power and the New Mandarins* (1969). In fact the pitfalls are so well known (*Time Magazine* formulated them explicitly)[8] that only one example among many will suffice to illustrate the problem. It concerns the way in which "the new intellectual elite," the pragmatists of the coming "Post-Industrial Society," discuss the bombing of North Vietnam. Instead of concerning themselves with whether it is moral in principle to intervene in a foreign country and bomb, or whether these principles apply in this particular case, they are concerned with whether or not it can be successful:

"I believe we can fairly say that unless it is severely provoked or unless the war succeeds fast, a democracy cannot choose war as an instrument of policy."

Chomsky comments:

"This is spoken in the tone of a true scientist correcting a few of the variables that entered into his computations—and, to be sure, Professor Pool is scornful of these 'anti-intellectuals,' such as Senator Fulbright, who do not comprehend 'the vital importance of applied social science for making the actions of our government in foreign areas more rational and humane than they have been.' In contrast to the anti-intellectuals, the applied social scientist understands that it is perfectly proper to 'rain death from the skies upon an area where there was no war,' so long as we 'succeed fast.'"[9]

The social scientists whom Chomsky is referring to are the "New Mandarins," or the new class of intellectuals who tend to accept the assumptions and ideology of the *status quo* and then apply themselves to ameliorating its conditions. Their weak determinism consists in accepting the overall system, whatever it might be, and then applying their very real expertise to technological problems, to making the system more efficient, or humane, or smooth-running. Thus they are ready to make their peace with whatever system happens to be extant—whether it be a dictatorship, capitalism or Socialism—claiming, in Daniel Bell's famous terms, "the end of ideology" and the fact that social problems are physical and technical rather than ideological.

The most extreme statement of this view and its consequences for the future comes from Buckminster Fuller:

"It seems perfectly clear that when there is enough to go around man will not fight anymore than he now fights for air. When man is successful in doing so much more with so much less that he can take care of everybody at a higher standard, then there will be no fundamental cause for war …

Within ten years it will be normal for man to be successful—just as through all history it has been the norm for more than 99 per cent to be economic and physical failures. Politics will become obsolete."[10]

Aside from the naivety in assuming that most, if not all, wars are caused by a scarcity of material wealth, the most dubious part of Fuller's prediction consists in assuming that if man gave up his political power and turned the whole world over to administrators then all would be well. At best we would have well-fed sycophants; at worst we would live under the most successful form of Totalitarianism ever known, where no one was responsible for anything, where all tensions could be blamed on the system and where political action, or shaping collective destiny, had been perverted into occasional outbursts of violence. For, as shown in the study of past government and revolutions, when men hand over their political powers to a party or government which is not directly responsive to their will, they give up their fundamental right to shape their destiny and alternate between passive submission and violent aggression.[11] In politics, as in an individual's way of life, there is no such thing as efficiency or specialization. To say there is would be as absurd as saying that an individual is a specialist at living.

Nonetheless, weak determinists and pragmatists assume this when they accept the present situations of politics. They assume that whoever holds political power at a given time is fated to hold it and that, in any case, the political problems will "wither away" as the increases in production make plenty for everyone. It is therefore not surprising that the advocates of this view, let us call them "service intellectuals," will sell their services to whoever is in power.

For instance, when the Nazis came to power in Germany in 1933, many modern architects such as Gropius, Wassili Luckhardt and Mies van der Rohe made many pragmatic attempts to achieve conciliation.[12] Gropius justified

finden, sogar mit dem Mittel dieses neuen Stils des 20. Jahrhunderts, der, weil es sich um einen ursprünglichen Stil und nicht bloss um eine modische Laune handelt, *totalitär* ist.» Obgleich das letzte Wort vielleicht ein Ausrutscher war und denn auch später durch «universal» ersetzt wurde, ist es doch ein bedeutsamer Ausrutscher, weil es jene «übermächtige Energie» oder jenen «überflutenden Strom» unterstreicht, die so oft im Zusammenhang mit einem besonderen Stil oder technologischem Determinismus zum Zeugen aufgerufen werden. Tatsächlich finden wir heute bei vielen Autoren eine Fortsetzung dieser Tradition. Wegen des «unaufhaltbaren Trends zu immer schnellerem Wechsel», empfiehlt Reyner Banham dem Architekten, «den Anschluss an die Technologie zu finden... und sich seines ganzen kulturellen Ballastes zu entledigen, alle Kleidungsstücke, die ihn als Architekten kennzeichnen, miteinbegriffen», sonst werde «eine technologische Kultur ohne ihn weitergehen»[7]. Buckminster Fuller gebraucht das Beispiel der bis ins letzte Detail geplanten Weltraumtechnologie, um die Architekten dafür zu tadeln, dass sie mit dem Zeitgeist nicht Schritt halten und so die Geburtswehen der Geschichte nicht lindern helfen.

All diesen Prophezeiungen gemeinsam ist der Appell an eine Mischung von moralischer Entscheidung und amoralischer Unausweichlichkeit: das Ineinanderfliessen von «sollte» und «ist» oder «wird sein». Diese Einstellung führt leicht zu einer Form von Pragmatismus, die besagt, dass alles, was existiert oder arbeitet, in Ordnung oder erfolgreich sei. Dieser Schritt hin zum Pragmatismus ist eine natürliche Konsequenz des kraftlosen Determinismus, und seine Fallgruben sind schon lange aufgezeigt worden — im Hinblick auf die Intellektuellen etwa in Julian Bendas *La trahison des clercs* (1927) und Noam Chomskys *American Power and the new Mandarins* (1969). Die Fallgruben sind in der Tat so gut bekannt (sogar das *Time Magazin* hat sie aufgezählt[8]), dass ein einziges Beispiel unter vielen genügen soll, um das Problem zu illustrieren. Es betrifft die Art und Weise, wie etwa die «neue intellektuelle Elite», die Pragmatiker der kommenden «nachindustriellen Gesellschaft» die Bombardierung Nordvietnams diskutieren. Statt sich damit zu befassen, ob es grundsätzlich moralisch sei, in einem fremden Land zu intervenieren und Bomben abzuwerfen, oder ob diese Grundsätze im konkreten Fall Anwendung finden, fragen sie sich, ob dies erfolgreich sein könne oder nicht:

«Ich glaube, wir können gerechterweise sagen, dass eine Demokratie, sofern sie nicht ernsthaft provoziert wird oder sofern der Krieg nicht zu sofortigem Erfolg führt, den Krieg nicht als politisches Instrument benutzen darf.»

Chomsky kommentiert:

«Dies wird gesagt im Tonfall des aufrechten Wissenschaftlers, der einige wenige Variabeln korrigiert, die in seine Berechnungen eingedrungen sind — und, um sicher zu sein, blickt Professor Pool voller Verachtung auf diese 'Antiintellektuellen', wie etwa Senator Fulbright, welche 'die vitale Bedeutung angewandter Sozialwissenschaft im Hinblick darauf, die Handlungen unserer Regierung in fremden Gebieten vernünftiger und menschlicher zu gestalten als es früher der Fall gewesen', nicht begreifen. Im Gegensatz zu diesen Antiintellektuellen versteht der angewandte Sozialwissenschaftler, dass es vollkommen in Ordnung ist, 'vom Himmel herab auf ein

Gebiet, wo kein Krieg herrschte, den Tod regnen zu lassen', sofern dies 'zu sofortigem Erfolg führt'. » [9]

Die Sozialwissenschaftler, auf die sich Chomsky bezieht, sind die « New Mandarins », oder die neue Klasse von Intellektuellen, welche geneigt sind, die Ideologie des status quo zu akzeptieren und sich der Verbesserung seiner Voraussetzungen widmen. Ihr *kraftloser Determinismus* besteht darin, dass sie das Gesamtsystem akzeptieren, worin es auch immer besteht, und ihre sehr reale Erfahrung mit technologischen Problemen dafür verwenden, das System wirkungsvoller oder humaner oder reibungsloser zu gestalten. Folglich sind sie bereit, Frieden zu schliessen mit jedwelchem System, das zufälligerweise vorkommt — sei es eine Diktatur, sei es Kapitalismus oder Sozialismus —, indem sie mit den berühmten Worten von Daniel Bell « das Ende der Ideologie » sowie die Tatsache proklamieren, dass soziale Probleme eher physisch und technisch bedingt sind als ideologisch.

Die extremste Ausformung dieses Standpunktes und seiner Konsequenzen für die Zukunft stammt von Fuller:

« Es scheint vollkommen klar zu sein, dass der Mensch, sobald er genügend Platz zum spazieren hat, dafür nicht mehr kämpfen wird als er jetzt für die Luft kämpft. Wenn die Menschen mit so viel weniger so viel mehr erreichen, dass sie sich auf einem höheren Niveau um jedermann kümmern können, dann wird es keine grundlegende Ursache mehr geben für den Krieg...

In zehn Jahren wird es für die Menschen normal sein, Erfolg zu haben — genauso wie es durch die ganze Geschichte hindurch für mehr als 99 % aller Menschen normal war, wirtschaftliche und physische Fehlschläge zu sein. Politik wird sich erübrigen. » [10]

Abgesehen von der naiven Annahme, dass die meisten, wenn nicht alle Kriege durch den Mangel an materieller Wohlfahrt entstanden seien, liegt die zweifelhafteste Stelle von Fullers Voraussage in der Vermutung, dass es zum allgemeinen Glück und Frieden genügen würde, dass die Menschen auf die politische Gewalt verzichten und die ganze Welt einigen Verwaltern anvertrauen. Im besten Fall wären wir wohlgenährte Hydrophanten, im schlimmsten Fall lebten wir unter der erfolgreichsten Form von Totalitarismus, die es je gegeben hat, in der niemand für nichts verantwortlich ist, wo alle Spannungen dem System zur Last gelegt werden können und wo politische Aktion — oder die Gestaltung des kollektiven Schicksals — pervertiert werden in gelegentliche Gewaltausbrüche. In der Tat zeigt das Studium vergangener Herrschaftsformen und Revolutionen, dass die Menschen ihr Grundrecht auf Gestaltung ihres eigenen Schicksals aufgeben und zwischen passiver Unterwerfung und heftiger Aggression abwechseln, sobald sie ihre politische Gewalt einer Partei anvertrauen, die ihrem Willen nicht unmittelbar entspricht. [11] In der Politik gibt es ebensowenig wie im privaten Leben des Individuums « Efficiency » oder Spezialisierung. Die Behauptung, dies sei der Fall, wäre ebenso absurd wie zu sagen, dass ein Individuum ein Spezialist in der Kunst des Lebens sei.

Trotzdem behaupten dies *kraftlose Deterministen* und Pragmatiker, wenn sie die gegenwärtige Lage der Politik akzeptieren. Sie behaupten, dass, wer immer zu einer bestimmten Zeit zufälligerweise die politische Gewalt innehabe, schicksalshaft dazu

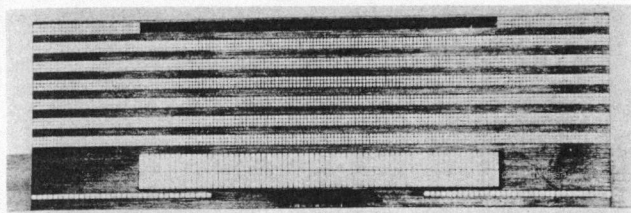

↓ fig. 3   Ludwig Mies van der Rohe, Reichsbank, Berlin (elevation), 1933.
The combination of "modern" and classical architecture in connection with the building of a national bank anticipates the analogous trends of many modern architects in the 1950s.

bestimmt sei und dass, so oder so, alle politischen Probleme in dem Masse dahinschwinden werden, als der Produktionszuwachs Überfluss für jedermann schaffen wird. Es kann folglich nicht überraschen, dass die Befürworter dieses Standpunktes, die wir « Dienstintellektuelle » nennen wollen, ihre Dienste jedem verkaufen, der gerade an der Macht ist.

So konnten etwa, als 1933 die Nazis in Deutschland an die Macht gelangten, manche moderne Architekten wie Gropius, Wassili Luckhardt oder Mies van der Rohe verzweifelte pragmatische Versuche anstellen, um eine Versöhnung zuwegezubringen.[12] Gropius begann, moderne Architektur in nationalistischer Terminologie zu rechtfertigen, d.h. in der Terminologie des « Deutschtums ». Mies van der Rohe ging so weit, einen rassistischen Appell des Architekten Schultze-Naumburg zu unterzeichnen, der genug Faschist war, um während seiner Vorlesungen über rassistische Kunst opponierende Künstler durch SA-Leute niederknüppeln zu lassen. Wie Sibyl Moholy-Nagy schreibt: « Als er (Mies) im Juli 1933, nach der Machtübernahme Hitlers, den Auftrag für die Reichsbank annahm, war er ein Verräter an uns allen und ein Verräter an allem, wofür wir gekämpft hatten. Er unterzeichnete zu dieser Zeit einen patriotischen Aufruf Schultze-Namburgs, den dieser als Kulturkommissar erlassen hatte, worin alle Künstler, Schriftsteller und Architekten Deutschlands aufgefordert wurden, ihre Kräfte vereint hinter den Nationalsozialismus zu stellen. Ich würde sagen, dass Mies als einziger unter den leitenden Bauhausleuten unterschrieb. Und er akzeptierte den Auftrag. Das war für uns ein schrecklicher Dolchstoss in den Rücken. »[13]

Aber Mies war wohl schwerlich der einzige « Pionier der modernen Bewegung », der mit der vorherrschenden Machtstruktur seinen Privatfrieden schloss. Le Corbusier verbrachte einen Teil des Jahres 1941 in Vichy damit, die Marionettenregierung zu überreden, ihm Arbeit zu geben.[14] Frank Lloyd Wright bereiste auf Einladung der Sowjetregierung Russland zu einem Zeitpunkt, als eineinhalb Millionen Bolschewiken den Säuberungswellen zum Opfer fielen. Philip Johnson, der eine demagogische Gruppe nach der andern unterstützte, stattete in Danzig Hitler einen Besuch ab, kurze Zeit nachdem dieser in Polen eingefallen war und so den Zweiten Weltkrieg ausgelöst hatte.[15] Der Fall der modernen Architekten im faschistischen Italien war sogar noch zwiespältiger, teilweise weil Futuristen wie Marinetti von der Ästhetik der Macht fasziniert waren (er schrieb sogar ein futuristisches Pamphlet voller Lob für die « Ästhetik des Krieges », nachdem 1934 Äthiopien bombardiert worden war), und weil Mussolinis Faschismus ein ausgesprochen rationalistisches und technizistisches Element barg (« er

31

↓ fig. 5 Kremlin Palace of Congresses, Moscow, 1961.

fig. 4 →
Guerrini,
Lapadula,
Romano,
Palazzo
della Civiltà
Romana, EUR,
Rome, 1942.

↑ fig. 7   Minoru Yamasaki, Northwestern National Life Insurance, Minneapolis, 1965.

fig. 6   Oscar Niemeyer, Palace of the Highland (seat of the president), Brasilia, 1961.

sorgt dafür, dass die Züge pünktlich abfahren»). Pier Luigi Nervi erbaute Flughangars und praktisch jeder «moderne» Architekt von Rang, von Ponti bis Pagano und Terragni arbeitete in dieser oder jener Weise für das Regime.[16] Wie so oft in der Geschichte schien es, dass der Architekt, gleich wie der Bankier und ganz im Gegensatz zum Künstler, für die herrschende Ordnung arbeiten *muss*, wenn er seinen Beruf ausüben will.

Die im faschistischen Auftrag erstellte Architektur (Abb. 4; 8) weist offensichtlich formale Parallelen mit dem späteren halbklassischen Modernismus auf, wie er unter ähnlichen, wenn auch etwas liberaleren, sozialen Bedingungen geschaffen wurde. Man könnte sogar von einem klassischen Repressionsstil sprechen, der in Brasilia (Abb. 6), Moskau (Abb. 5) Minneapolis (Abb. 7) und New York (Abb. 10; 12) anzutreffen ist, und der so gleichartig ist, dass er einem den Gedanken nahelegen könnte, es bestehe ein natürlicher Zusammenhang zwischen Form und Inhalt, Ausdruck und sozialer Ordnung — auch wenn man weiss, dass solch deterministische Zusammenhänge theoretisch falsch sind.[17] Die Tendenz des Klassizismus, sich mit Repression zu verbünden, und umgekehrt, erscheint beinah als ein unabänderliches Gesetz, oder doch zumindest als eine Sache hoher Wahrscheinlichkeit. Jedenfalls

haben sich in der Vierzigerjahren manche Architekten mit einer Sozialordnung eingelassen, gegen die sie in den Zwanzigerjahren mehr oder weniger vereint gekämpft hatten.

Die Gründe, weshalb so viele derartige Zwischenfälle mit Architekten vorkommen konnten, deren Verhalten sonst eher kompromisslos ist, bleiben solange unklar, als wir uns nicht daran erinnern, wie ausdrücklich « unpolitisch » sie angeblich sind. Ihre Verachtung oder ihr Abscheu gegenüber der Politik macht sie nur allzu willig für die Annahme des politischen status quo — wenn auch nur um zu behaupten, dass er in Wirklichkeit gar nicht existiere und verschwunden sei. Sobald wir einmal diesen Fatalismus und seine natürliche Verwandtschaft mit dem Pragmatismus realisiert haben, werden verschiedene andere wahrscheinliche strukturelle Zusammenhänge klar. Wir sehen die Parallelen zwischen dem Ausspruch von Mies: « Das Individuum verliert an Bedeutung; sein Schicksal ist nicht länger von Interesse für uns » und Goebbels Satz: « Das wesentlichste Prinzip unserer siegreichen erobernden Bewegung heisst: Entthronung des Individuums ». Oder wir merken, wie Philip Johnsons Verteidigung der « neuen Sehnsucht

fig. 9 →
The architects of Lincoln Center for the Performing Arts in New York.
Left to right:
Wallace Harrison, Philip Johnson, Pietro Belluschi, Eero Saarinen, Max Abramovitz, and Gordon Bunshaft.

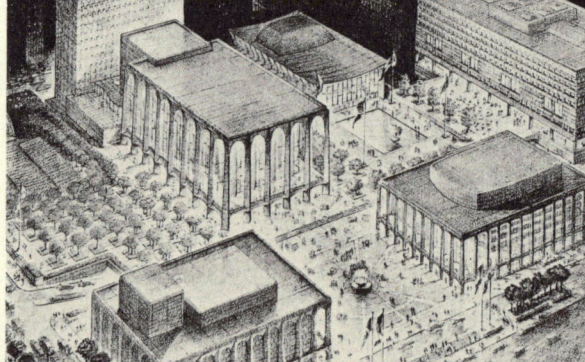

↑ fig. 8 Albert Speer, Zeppelinfeld, entrance side, 1934.

↑ fig. 10 Plan drawing for Lincoln Center, New York, 1961. The fact that neoclassicism recurs in twenty- to thirty-year cycles is common to public buildings. The fact that it is normally the result of teamwork makes prediction relatively easy. Unfortunately, it must be said that each of the architects on the team would have been able to produce a better complex as a whole than the one that resulted from collaboration.

modern architecture in nationalistic terms, that is in terms of its "Germanness." Mies van der Rohe went so far as to sign a racist appeal from Schultze-Naumburg, an architect who was fascist enough to have dissenting artists "bludgeoned" by stormtroopers when he gave lectures on racist art. In fact as Sibyl Moholy-Nagy has written:

"When he (Mies) accepted in July 1933, after the coming to power of Hitler, the commission for the Reichsbank he was a traitor to all of us and a traitor to everything we had fought for. He signed at that time a patriotic appeal which Schultze-Naumburg had made as Commissar to the artists, writers and architects of Germany to put their forces behind National Socialism. I would say that, of the leading group of the Bauhaus people, Mies was the only one who signed. And he accepted this commission. This was a terrible stab in the back for us."[13]

But Mies was hardly the only "pioneer of modern design" who made his private peace with the dominant power structure. Le Corbusier spent part of the year 1941 in Vichy trying to persuade the puppet regime to give him work.[14] Frank Lloyd Wright toured Russia at the invitation of the Soviet government at a time when one and a half million Bolsheviks were falling victim to the waves of purges. Philip Johnson, who supported one demagogical group after another, paid a visit to Hitler in Danzig just after the latter had invaded Poland to start the Second World War.[15] The case of the modern architects in Fascist Italy was even more conflicted, in part because Futurists such as Marinetti were fascinated by the aesthetic of power (he even wrote a Futurist pamphlet full of praise for the "aesthetic of war" after Ethiopia had been bombarded in 1934), and because Mussolini's Fascism concealed a decidedly rationalist and technicistic element ("he saw to it that the trains run on time"). Pier Luigi Nervi built plane hangars, and practically every "modern" architect of significance, from Ponti to Pagano and Terragni, worked for the regime in one way or another.[16] As so often in history, it seems that the architect—just like the banker and very much in contrast to the artist—*must* work for the ruling order if he wants to practice his profession.

The architecture commissioned by the Fascists (figs. 4, 8) has obvious formal parallels to the later semiclassical modernism created under similar albeit somewhat more liberal social conditions. One could even speak of a classical style of repression, which can be found in Brasilia (fig. 6), Moscow (fig. 5), Minneapolis (fig. 7), and New York (figs. 10, 12), and which is so similar that it could suggest a natural connection between form and content, expression and social order—even if one knows that such deterministic connections are wrong in theory.[17] The trend of classicism to ally with repression, and vice versa, almost seems to be an unalterable law or at least a matter of high probability. In any case, some architects got involved in a social order in the forties against which they had fought, more or less united, in the twenties.

The reasons why such incidents can occur among architects, who are otherwise rather uncompromising, remains obscure until we remember how explicitly "apolitical" they say they are. Their disdain or hatred for politics makes them all too willing to accept the political status quo—if only to pretend that it really doesn't exist and has withered away. Once we have realized this fatalism as well as its connection to pragmatism, several other structural connections become clear.

We see how Mies's statement "the individual is losing significance; his destiny is no longer what interests us," has parallels with Goebbels' "It is the most essential principle of our victoriously conquering movement that the individual has been dethroned." Or how Philip Johnson's defense of the "new craving for monumentality" under the Nazis is parallel to the "new craving for monumentality" in the United States thirty years later (figs. 7, 10, 12).[18] These parallels can be drawn on social, psychological and formal levels. In fact they allow us to identify structural tendencies and thus in broad outline to predict the future. Thus one could point to the tendency for neo-classicism to recur, in America for instance, every twenty-five years, and its association with public building and communal design, and then predict that the next large revival will occur, significantly enough, around 1984 or so (see the self-conscious tradition). But here we come to the core of determinism and pragmatism, or the difference between an inexorable and inevitable trend.

In fact, it is a characteristic of all open or biological systems to become unbalanced. This is another way of saying that in all life there is always a trend toward something or other. The systematic pessimist about the future, for example, can collect all the negative trends, which he will have little trouble finding: the population explosion, the pollution explosion and the explosive growth of deadly weapons to take a few instances. Indeed, if things keep growing at their present rate, he can say that sometime in the twenty-first century there will not be any room to move in, everyone will be living in one, dense city, everyone will be wearing gas-masks when they leave their fallout shelters and all those people between the ages of twenty-five and thirty-four who are not bureaucrats will be scientific hippies on a jag of LSD doing Research and Development for one large corporation, General, United Dynamics Inc. All the present trends show this to be inevitable; they are all growing at exponential rates. Thus the pragmatic thing to do would be to jump on all combined bandwagons at once—a recommendation that we actually hear from some architects such as Doxiadis.[19] But, in fact, all trends do not continue indefinitely; they always reach a point of equilibrium either because counter-action is taken, because the environment is saturated or because of a counter-trend.

Counter-action depends on our knowing that a trend is inexorable, that if we do not decide to do something rather emphatic about it, it will continue into the future. Thus we may say, contrary to Marx and in accord with Islam, that the only social trends which are inevitable are those which we don't know about, and that the rest are inexorable and subject to our changing them. Fortunately, not all negative trends depend on our knowledge and desire for counter-action to disappear, but rather reach equilibrium because of an equal and opposite trend. For instance, the exponential growth of population, cities and pollution might be countered by a similar growth in contraceptive devices, decentralization, and exhaust converters. Any sophisticated accounting of trends will show how simple-minded it is to generate hysteria over any single trend such as the population explosion.[20] There are always enough balancing forces to make any particular long-term imbalance improbable. Hence the characteristic S-curve of growth common to so many social and natural phenomena.

The importance for prediction of the S-curve, or Verhulst curve, cannot be overrated, as it represents the most typical and basic kind of force the forecaster tries to deal with. Essentially it is concerned with the growth of a force across time, or an imbalance or pressure within an open system. Often, as in the case of population growth, it is made up of many smaller growth forces which are usually misunderstood or neglected by initial assumptions. Thus many demographers predicted a population limit at too low a point because they did not assume large break-throughs in medicine, food cultivation and transport. Hence it is often safer to avoid specifying exact breakthroughs in advance and draw an hypothetical "envelope curve" over a series of superimposed S-curves and project this into the future. This method is used in predicting future transport speeds without predicting exact methods of vehicles to attain them.

However, the concept of the S-curve is introduced here not just to explain its general validity for prediction, but to emphasize the point that at any time there are always some imbalances in a system, which are felt as pressures. This overpowering feeling is probably as constant as the imbalances are perpetual. Since all open systems will remain inherently dynamic and unstable, it is quite likely that certain pragmatists and *weak determinists* will remain ready to exploit these changes without regard for their moral consequences. Thus one may postulate a perpetual *"trahison des clercs"* as long as their ideology persists.

Put in an entirely different way, we could say that there will always be "reasonable intellectuals" who regard systems as closed and deterministic, who say that given a trend X, certain consequences Y *must* follow. For instance, given our values of "liberty and equality" in housing, it must follow that we cannot achieve "fraternity." The anthropologist Edmund Leach has argued that the architect's desire to create "communities" based on kinship (or fraternity) naturally conflicts with the social values of democracy, liberty and equality.[21] Thus it is eminently "reasonable" to argue as he did, that one may have either alternative but

↓ fig. 11   Luigi Moretti, Project for the Piazza Imperiale, EUR, Rome, 1941 (First prize *ex aequo*).

nach Monumentalismus» bei den Nazis in den Vereinigten Staaten dreissig Jahre später seine Entsprechung gefunden hat (Abb. 7; 10; 12). Diese Parallelen können auf der sozialen, psychologischen und formalen Ebene gezogen werden. Sie erlauben uns in der Tat, strukturelle Tendenzen zu identifizieren und folglich in breiten Umrissen die Zukunft vorauszusagen [19]. So könnte beispielsweise jemand die Tendenz des Neoklassizismus zu periodischer Wiederkehr, in Amerika etwa alle 25 Jahre, zum Anlass nehmen, die nächste neoklassizistische Welle für das Jahr 1984 — bezeichnenderweise — vorauszusagen. Aber damit stossen wir auf den Kern von Determinismus und Pragmatismus, oder auf den Unterschied zwischen einer unerbittlichen und einer unausweichlichen Tendenz.

Es ist in der Tat ein Merkmal aller offenen oder biologischen Systeme, unausgeglichen zu werden. Das ist lediglich eine andere Formulierung der Tatsache, *dass in jedem Leben ein Trend zu irgendetwas zu finden ist*. Wenn jemand ein systematischer Zukunftspessimist ist, kann er alle negativen Tendenzen sammeln, die er mit wenig Aufwand finden wird: Bevölkerungsexplosion, Umweltverschmutzung, explosive Zunahme tödlicher Waffen, usw... Wenn

↑ fig. 12   Lincoln Center for the Performing Arts, New York.

sich die Dinge im heutigen Tempo weiterentwickeln, so können wir tatsächlich voraussagen, dass irgendwann im 21. Jahrhundert kein Bewegungsraum mehr übrig bleibt, dass jedermann in einer einzigen, dichtbesiedelten Stadt leben wird, dass jedermann Gasmasken tragen wird, um seinen Bunker zu verlassen, und dass alle Leute zwischen 25 und 34, die nicht zufällig der Bürokratie angehören, wissenschaftliche Hippies sein werden, die mit einem LSD-Schwips Forschung und Entwicklung für eine einzige grosse Gesellschaft mit Namen General United Dynamics Inc. (mit Hauptsitz überall) betreiben werden. Alle gegenwärtigen Tendenzen zeigen, dass dies unausweichlich ist; sie schreiten in der Tat mit schwindelerregendem Tempo voran. Folglich wäre das einzig Vernünftige, sich allen siegreichen Lagern gleichzeitig anzuschliessen — eine Empfehlung, die wir gegenwärtig von gewissen Architekten wie etwa Doxiadis zu hören bekommen.[20] Leider entwickeln sich aber nicht alle Zeittendenzen ins Unendliche hinein; sie erreichen immer ein Gleichgewicht: Entweder weil eine Gegenaktion unternommen wurde, oder weil die Umgebung gesättigt ist oder eine Gegentendenz entstanden ist.

Was die erste Alternative anbetrifft, so hängt sie haargenau von unserem Wissen davon ab, dass eine Tendenz unerbittlich ist und dass sie, wenn wir nicht etwas Entschlossenes dagegen unternehmen, in die Zukunft hinein fortdauern wird. Wir könnten also sagen, im Gegensatz zu Marx und in Übereinstimmung mit dem Islam, dass nur diejenigen sozialen Tendenzen unausweichlich sind, die wir nicht kennen, und dass alle übrigen lediglich unerbittlich und unserer Bereitschaft, sie zu ändern, unterworfen sind. Glücklicherweise sind nicht alle negativen Tendenzen von unserem Wissen darüber abhängig, wie eine Gegenaktion erfolgreich durchzuführen sei, sondern erreichen sozusagen automatisch ein Gleichgewicht; ganz einfach, weil ein gleichstarker und entgegengesetzter Trend wirksam ist. So *könnte* zum Beispiel die Bevölkerungsexplosion, die Verstädterung und Luftverschmutzung durch einen ebenso explosiven Zuwachs an empfängnisverhütenden Mitteln, durch Dezentralisation und Abgasumwandler neutralisiert werden. Jede vernünftige Zusammenstellung von Tendenzen kann zeigen, wie einfältig es ist, wegen eines einzelnen Trends wie etwa der Bevölkerungsexplosion[21] Hysterie zu erzeugen. Es gibt immer genügend ausgleichende Kräfte, um jede langfristige Unausgeglichenheit unwahrscheinlich zu machen. Von daher stammt die charakteristische S-Kurve des Wachstums, die so vielen sozialen und natürlichen Phänomenen eigen ist.

Die Bedeutung der S-Kurve (oder Verhulst-Kurve) für die Zukunftsvoraussage kann gar nicht überschätzt werden, da sie die typischste und grundlegendste Art von Kraft darstellt, mit welcher der Prognostiker arbeitet. Sie befasst sich wesentlich mit dem Wachstum einer Kraft im Ablauf der Zeit, oder mit dem Ungleichgewicht oder dem Druck in einem offenen System. Wie gerade der Fall des Bevölkerungswachstums zeigt, wird sie oftmals aus vielen kleinen Wachstumskräften zusammengesetzt, die gewöhnlich wegen anfänglicher Vermutungen missverstanden oder vernachlässigt werden. So sagten viele Demographen eine Bevölkerungsgrenze voraus, die viel zu tief lag, weil sie die grossen Durchbrüche in Medizin, Ernährung und Transport nicht voraussahen. Darum ist

↓ fig. 13 This S-curve (Verhulst curve) shows the growing speed of means of transportation over time. Frequently, exponential growth results from the sum of many individual growth trends that cannot be predicted. As a result, it often happens that the summarizing S-curve is placed too low.

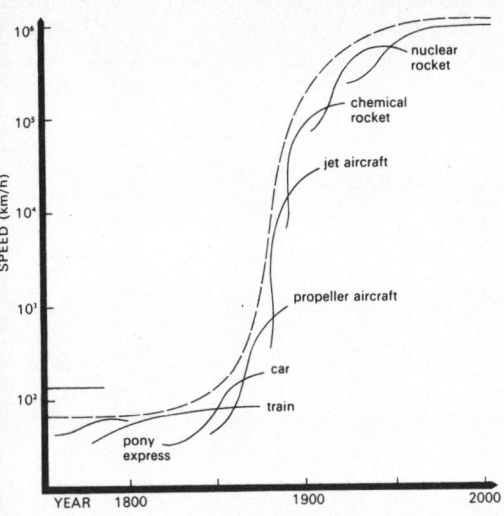

es oft sicherer, exakte Fortschrittsprognosen zu vermeiden und eine hypothetische, die Einzeltendenzen zusammenfassende Kurve über eine Reihe von übereinandergelegten S-Kurven zu zeichnen und diese in die Zukunft zu projizieren. Diese Methode wird denn auch tatsächlich gebraucht, um zukünftige Transportgeschwindigkeiten vorauszusagen, ohne dass man sich genau auf die Art des Vehikels festlegt.

Trotzdem wird die S-Kurve hier nicht vorgestellt, um lediglich ihre allgemeine Gültigkeit für Voraussagen zu erläutern, sondern vielmehr um hervorzuheben, dass jederzeit irgendwo in einem System Ungleichgewichte vorhanden sind, die als Druck empfunden werden. Dieses übermächtige Gefühl ist wahrscheinlich ebenso beständig wie die Ungleichgewichte selbst. Solange alle offenen Systeme von Natur aus dynamisch und unstabil sind, wird es sehr wahrscheinlich immer eine gewisse Zahl Pragmatiker und *kraftloser Deterministen* geben, die bereit sind, diesen beständigen Wechsel ohne Rücksicht auf moralische Konsequenzen auszubeuten. Folglich kann man eine beständige «trahison des clercs» postulieren, solange deren Ideologie fortdauert.

Von einem völlig anderen Standpunkt aus könnten wir sagen, dass es immer «vernünftige Intellektuelle» geben wird, die die Systeme als geschlossen und determiniert betrachten, die behaupten, dass bei einem gegebenen Trend X gewisse Konsequenzen Y folgen *müssen*. So müsste man z.B. folgern, dass in Anbetracht der gegebenen Werte wie «Freiheit und Gleichheit» im Wohnungsbau konsequenterweise die «Brüderlichkeit» nicht realisiert werden kann. Der Anthropologe Edmund Leach hat aufgezeigt, dass der Wunsch des Architekten, gemeinschaftliche, auf Verwandtschaft (oder Brüderlichkeit) aufbauende Lebensräume zu schaffen, natürlicherweise mit den sozialen Werten der Demokratie (eben Freiheit und Gleichheit) in Konflikt gerät.[22] Deshalb ist es in hervorragender Weise «vernünftig», mit Leach zu argumentieren, dass

↓ fig. 14   The Flying Bedstead developed by Rolls Royce Inc.

man eine, aber nicht beide Möglichkeiten einer Alternative haben könne. Das Problem liegt bei solchen Gedankengängen darin, dass sie den Fall nicht berücksichtigen, dass alle Systeme zerlegbar und zusammensetzbar, oder mit einem Wort: transzendierbar sind. Der Fatalismus besteht in diesem Fall darin, dass alle System für ganzheitlich statt für zerlegbar gehalten werden.

Zerlegbarkeit

Alle Systeme haben die Tendenz, dichtverwobene Einheiten zu bilden. So können wir sagen, dass in den meisten Gesellschaftsordnungen eine dichte Verbindung besteht zwischen Ehe, sexuellem Vergnügen und Zeugung von Nachkommenschaft. In der weiten Mehrheit der Fälle konnte niemand nur einen Teil ohne das Ganze haben. Heute hingegen ist es aufgrund der veränderten Werthierarchien und sicherer Kontrolle möglich, Sex ohne Zeugung, Ehe ohne Zeugung und Zeugung ohne Ehe oder gar ohne Sex zu haben. Soviele Mittel stehen uns heute zur Verfügung (eingeschlossen Ehescheidung, Empfängnisverhütung, Pille und bevorstehende Techniken wie etwa künstliche Gebärmütter, Samenbanken, Hormonkontrolle usw.) [23], dass wir das System in seine Einzelteile zerlegen und die Teile in irgendeiner gewünschten

↓ fig. 15 Rocket Belt developed by Bell Aerosystems.

Kombination haben können — frei von jeder Notwendigkeit, sie als Gesamtheit nehmen zu müssen. Dieses einzelne Beispiel für die Zerlegbarkeit steht wenigstens grundsätzlich stellvertretend für alle ganzheitlichen Systeme. Seine Auswirkungen auf die Zukunft unterscheiden sich ziemlich von denjenigen, die von den meisten Prognostikern vorgelegt werden. Denn es geht davon aus, dass es immer möglich ist, die Systeme in ihre positiven und negativen Konsequenzen zu zerlegen und mit genügender Anstrengung die negativen zu unterdrücken, solange es für die meisten Systeme die Tendenz *gibt*, sich unerbittlich als untereinander verbundene Einheiten in gewisse Richtungen zu bewegen. Um auf ein vorangegangenes Beispiel zurückzukommen: Theoretisch war es beim Aufkommen des Automobils möglich, gewisse seiner negativen Konsequenzen wie Lärm, Verkehrsstauung und Luftverschmutzung vorauszusehen. Wenn diese Konsequenzen vorausgesagt worden wären, und wenn die Gesellschaft willens gewesen wäre, einen gewissen Preis zu zahlen, dann wären wir heute nicht mit kostspieligeren Alternativen konfrontiert.

Die gleiche Ambivalenz der Kräfte begegnet uns heute jeden Tag. So wurde zum Beispiel während der vergangenen zehn Jahre an der Entwicklung verschiedener Formen von Fahrzeugen gear-

←fig. 16
Hovercraft
assault vehic
developed
by Bell
Aerosystems

beitet, die unabhängig von jeder Oberfläche sich bewegen können (Abb. 14; 15). Diese Fahrzeuge werden, wie Galbraith voraussagen würde, von den wirklich grössten Gesellschaften mit der nötigen Investitionskraft für Spezialistenwissen und Produktionskosten entwickelt. Überdies unterstützt das militärische Establishment das Projekt, da solche Fahrzeuge von offenbarem Interesse für den Guerillakrieg sind (Abb. 16). Wenn wir hierauf die übliche Faustregel anwenden, derzufolge das, « was heute wenige besitzen, morgen Allgemeingut ist », dann kann man unter Einberechnung einer genügenden zeitlichen Verzögerung zwischen Erfindung und

↑ fig. 17 Surface-free vehicles have the obvious consequence that men can move anywhere independent of streets. This will entail legislation to control traffic and protect the private sphere.

not both. The problem with such thinking is that it does not allow for the fact that all systems can be dissected and restructured—or, in a word, transcended. The fatalism in this case consists in regarding all systems as wholistic rather than dissectible.

Dissectibility

Consider the tendency for all systems to form tightly interrelated wholes: in most societies, for instance, there has been a tight relationship between marriage, sexual pleasure and reproduction. In the large majority of cases, one could not have any part of the system without the whole. Now, however, because of changing values and increased technological control, it is possible to have sex without reproduction, marriage without reproduction and reproduction without sex or marriage. There are so many means at our disposal (including divorce and contraceptive devices),[22] that we can dissect the related parts of the system and have those parts we desire in any new combination we want— freed of the necessity of having them as a whole. This single example of dissectibility holds true for all wholistic systems, at least in principle; and its implications for the future are radically different from those put forward by most predictors. For it assumes that while there *is* a tendency for most systems to move inexorably in certain directions as interrelated wholes, it is always possible to dissect their positive from their negative consequences and, given sufficient effort, suppress the negative ones. To return to a former example, it was theoretically possible when the automobile came into use to foresee some of its negative consequences such as noise, congestion, and pollution. If these consequences had been predicted and if society had been willing to pay a certain price, we would not now be confronted with more costly alternatives.

The same ambivalence of forces confronts us at every moment. For instance, there have been under development for the last ten years various forms of vehicle which move independently of any surface, route, or road (figs. 14, 15). These vehicles are being developed, as Galbraith would predict, by the very largest corporations which can invest the necessary capital in specialist knowledge and production costs. Furthermore, they are being supported by the military establishment as they have very obvious consequences for use in limited guerilla warfare (fig. 16). If we apply the normal rule of thumb that "what the few have today, the many will have tomorrow" plus a sufficient time-lag between invention and mass-production of thirty years—then we can see that by about 1990 we could have on a large scale the consequences that plague our airports even today (fig. 17). We have to dissect very consciously the obvious positive and negative consequences which these surface-free vehicles imply. On the positive side, they imply that men will be able to move over any surface they wish including ice, water and land and thus be able to cross all boundaries, which have hitherto divided vehicles into specialized types. This will have the effect of cutting some transit times in half, removing interchange points such as ports and stations and lessening such geographic obstacles as have previously constrained location. In short the trade routes will shift, along with political boundaries which are certified by natural obstacles. For instance, the political problems arising from the Suez or Panama Canal will have to move on to other constraints when hovercraft shipping becomes feasible. Cities will become more decentralized and location, due to economic factors, will take on a more even spread. As for the obvious negative consequences, they include the loss of visual and acoustic privacy, the invasion of secluded areas and the various forms of pollution with which we are already too well acquainted.

It is clear from this and other examples that to a large extent we are implicated with, and dependent on, very questionable forces and ideas. A large part of the hardware which we shall use in the future was used first in Vietnam, was developed for warfare by the largest monopolies in the world. Many of the ideas adopted here, such as the postindustrial society, come from those fatalists we have just criticized. The object of dissectibility is to take those consequences and ideas which we favor, cut away those we dislike and project forward the new combinations. This method avoids the either/or fatalism of accepting or rejecting wholistic systems the way they are presented to us. As a method, it is close to that natural evolution on which it depends; but as it demands the presence of human value and intervention, it should be distinguished from the former concept as the idea of "critical evolution."

Critical evolution accepts—as the dualistic terminology already suggests—the tendency of inexorable trends to form a baseline for social coexistence; at the same time, however, it denies the fatality of these trends and confronts them with the desires of society. It proceeds according to the usual scientific analytical method of dissecting an unmanipulable whole into manipulable components but then exceeds the purely scientific foundation in order to establish new combinations based on subjective and cultural values.

ENDNOTES

1 See Julien Benda, *La trahison des clercs* (1927), an attack on those intellectuals who, leaving their traditional role of criticizing temporal power, have succumbed to various forms of nationalism and fanaticism because of their pragmatic philosophy.

2 For example, in structuralist terms the idea of the langue and in systems theory the idea of the "closed system." See *Systems Thinking*, ed. F. E. Emery (London: Penguin Books, 1969); Arthur Koestler, *The Ghost in the Machine* (London: Hutchinson, 1967), 197–221. Claude Lévi-Strauss, *Structural Anthropology* (New York: Basic Books, 1962), argues for "historical determinism" (240), but denies "mechanical causality" (233).

3 Preface to *Capital*, quoted from Karl Popper, *The Poverty of Historicism* (London: Routledge and Kegan Paul, 1957), 51.

4 Marshall McLuhan, *The Medium Is the Massage* (London: Penguin Books, 1967).

5 Bertrand de Jouvenel, *Forecasting and the Social Sciences*, ed. Michael Young (London: Heinemann, 1968), 121; and Bertrand de Jouvenel, *The Art of Conjecture* (New York: Basic Books, 1967)—an excellent albeit somewhat conservative exposition of the philosophical problems underlying scientific prognoses.

6 For instance, by the year 2000 Herman Kahn predicts that per capita income in the USA will be about $15,000 and in India $200, compared to about $4,000 and $100 today (in 1965 US dollars).

7 The quotations are from Le Corbusier, *Vers une architecture* (Paris: Éditions Crès, 1923); Ludwig Mies van der Rohe, *Der Querschnitt* (1924); Nikolaus Pevsner, *Pioneers of Modern Design* (1936); and Reyner Banham, *Theory and Design in the First Machine Age* (1960). Italics added by the author.

8 "The Tortured Role of the Intellectual in America," *Time Magazine*, May 9, 1969.

9 See *The New York Review of Books*, January 2 and 16, 1969. Chomsky's text was also published in his book *American Power and the New Mandarins* (London: Penguin, 1969).

10 See "2000 +," *Architectural Design*, February 1967, 63.

11 Hannah Arendt discusses the fact that when men hand over or lose political power they will resort to two species of violence: covert bureaucratic violence and overt coercion. In *Reflections on Violence*; see also *New York Review of Books*, February 27, 1969.

12 See B. M. Lane, *Architecture and Politics in Germany, 1918–45* (Cambridge, MA: Harvard University Press, 1968), 181.

13 Sibyl Moholy-Nagy, *Journal of the Society of Architectural Historians*, March 1965, 84.

14 See Stanislaus von Moos, *Le Corbusier: Elemente einer Synthese* (Frauenfeld-Stuttgart: Huber, 1968), 220, 236, 265–71. Le Corbusier's faith in authority cannot be discussed here; there are countless incriminating and extenuating arguments.

15 See William Shirer, *Berlin Diary* (New York, 1941), 213 (revealingly, this episode is not mentioned in the version of the book published in England).

16 See Giulia Veronesi, *Difficolta politiche dell'architettura in Italia* (Milan, 1958).

17 At least since Ferdinand de Saussure's first contributions to semiology (*Cours de linguistique générale*, 1915), the "random" or "unmotivated" nature of signs is generally known.

18 Philip Johnson, "Architecture in the Third Reich," *Hound and Horn*, 1934.

19 Indeed, Doxiadis uses the metaphor of jumping on a moving train of trends—a metaphor which is fatalistic and uncritical with respect to the "dissectibility" of forces.

20 The following list of inexorable trends is divided crudely into those we might regard as positive and negative; some of them are mutually balancing:

Positive (?): exponential growth in scientists, intellectuals, universities, computers, education, students; information, knowledge, technology, Research and Development (3% of GNP), mass research, health, recreation, leisure; affluence, tertiary and quarternary services; discoveries, micro-miniaturizations, aerospace, speed, etc.

Negative (?): population, pollution, weaponry; bureaucrats, alienated, dispossessed, relatively poor; overcrowding, urbanization, suburbanization; fashion, pragmatists, middle class; centralization, loss of privacy, spying, waste, ugliness; small wars, change.

21 In a lecture at the Architectural Association, London, May 1, 1969. See *New Society*, May 9, 1969.

22 See G. R. Taylor, *The Biological Time Bomb* (London: Thames and Hudson, 1968). Whenever we do "dissect" holistic systems, we have to pay a very heavy price to make new combinations satisfactorily; another biological analogy of this "dissectibility" is transplant surgery in medicine (where the heavy price is immunosuppressive drugs).

Massenproduktion von etwa 30 Jahren unschwer vorausahnen, dass wir etwa um 1990 herum in grossem Ausmasse diejenigen Konsequenzen zu spüren bekommen werden, die heute schon unsere Flughäfen heimsuchen (Abb. 17). Wir müssen sehr sorgfältig die offensichtlichen positiven und negativen Folgen auseinanderhalten, die solche oberflächenunabhängige Fahrzeuge mit sich bringen. Auf der positiven Seite steht, dass die Menschen in der Lage sein werden, sich über jeder Oberfläche, sei es Eis, Wasser oder Land, zu bewegen, und dass demnach alle Grenzen überschritten werden, die bisher eine Spezialisierung der Fahrzeuge nötig machten. Das wird zur Folge haben, dass gewisse Fahrzeiten halbiert, dass die traditionellen Orte für Fahrzeugtypenwechsel wie etwa Hafen oder Bahnhof verschwinden und dass schliesslich geographische Hindernisse, die bis anhin eine Besiedlung gehemmt haben, sich vermindern werden. Kurz: Die Handelsstrassen werden ebenso verschwinden wie jene politischen Grenzen, die durch natürliche Hindernisse bestimmt wurden. So werden sich zum Beispiel die politischen Probleme, die heute mit dem Suez- oder Panamakanal zusammenhängen, andere kritische Punkte suchen müssen, sobald Luftkissenschiffahrt möglich sein wird. Die Städte werden dezentralisierter und die von wirtschaftlichen Faktoren bestimmte Besiedlung wird eine weitere Streuung erfahren. Was die offensichtlichen negativen Konsequenzen anbetrifft, so handelt es sich dabei vor allem um den Verlust an optischer und akustischer Ruhe, um die Invasion abgeschlossener Gebiete und die verschiedenen Formen von Umweltverschmutzung, mit denen wir mittlerweile nur allzu vertraut geworden sind.

Dieses Beispiel kann zeigen, dass wir in sehr hohem Ausmasse miteinbezogen und abhängig sind von Kräften und Ideen, die fragwürdig sind. Ein grosser Teil der «hardware» die wir in Zukunft gebrauchen werden, wurde zuerst in Vietnam ausprobiert, wurde also von den weltgrössten Monopolgesellschaften entwickelt. Viele der Ideen, die ich hier für die Voraussage benutzt habe, stammen von jenen Fatalisten, die ich soeben kritisiert habe. Der Sinn der Zerlegbarkeit besteht darin, die von uns bevorzugten Idee und Folgen zu fördern, die missliebigen Folgen zu unterdrücken und neue Kombinationen zu entwerfen. Diese Methode umgeht den Entweder/Oder-Fatalismus, der immer ein System als Ganzes akzeptiert oder verwirft — so wie sie uns vor Augen geführt werden. Als Methode steht sie jener natürlichen Evolution nahe, von welcher sie zugleich abhängig ist. Doch da sie die Anwesenheit menschlicher Werte und menschlichen Willens verlangt, sollte sie unterschieden werden von der früheren deterministischen Vorstellung als die Idee der «kritischen Evolution».

Die kritische Evolution akzeptiert — wie bereits die dualistische Terminologie andeutet — die Neigung unerbittlicher Tendenzen, eine Basislinie für das gesellschaftliche Zusammenleben zu bilden; gleichzeitig aber leugnet sie die Fatalität dieser Tendenzen und konfrontiert sie mit den gesellschaftlichen Wünschen. Sie geht nach der üblichen wissenschaftlichen analytischen Methode vor, indem sie ein unmanipulierbares Ganzes in manipulierbare Einzelteile zerlegt, aber sie überschreitet anschliessend die rein wissenschaftliche Grundlage, um neue Kombinationen zu errichten, und zwar aufgrund subjektiver und kultureller Werte.

Eine frühere Fassung dieses Aufsatzes erschien in Charles Jencks' *Architecture 2000, Predictions and Methods*, London 1971. Der Abdruck grosser Partien erfolgt mit der freundlichen Genehmigung des Verlages Studio Vista Ltd., London. Übersetzung: Albert Gnägi und S.v.M.

Abbildungsnachweis:

USIS: 1, 2, 7, 10, 12
The Arts Council, London: 5
Brasilianische Botschaft, London: 6
La Casa, 6, Roma, o.J.: 11
Jencks, Architecture 2000, London, 1971: 8, 9, 13
Rolls Royce Ltd.: 14
Bell Aerosystems Company: 15, 16

An earlier version of this essay was published in Charles Jencks's *Architecture 2000: Predictions and Methods* (London, 1971). Studio Vista Ltd., London, has kindly granted permission to reprint large sections.

The Reconstruction of the Kornhaus in Freiburg im Breisgau

and Several Observations on Architecture and Historical Understanding

Author:
Jürgen Paul

Source:
archithese, 11 (1974): 11–19

Translated by:
Steven Lindberg

In Freiburg im Breisgau, on the north side of the Münsterplatz, which had been completely destroyed during the war, the last remaining gap was closed with the reconstruction of the Altes Kornhaus [Old Granary] (fig. 1) in 1970–71. The building that had stood there until its utter destruction in 1944 had been built in 1497 as a municipal dance hall and granary. Despite several conversions of the interior, most recently into a concert hall, that had also caused changes to the exterior—on the ground floor and the sides—it had preserved its late Gothic form with a stepped gable and elaborate cross windows and was one of the outstanding historical architectural landmarks of old Freiburg (fig. 2).

After its complete destruction, its reconstruction was heatedly debated for years, for reasons of architectural principle and economics. A series of new uses of diverse cultural character were discussed until finally a private group of companies took the problem of its use and funding out of the hands of the city, the building's owner.

An architectural competition was announced to design a historically faithful reconstruction of the two gabled facades. The design, which was carried out with subsidies from the preservation authorities, fulfills this task but has nothing else in common with the historical building's technique and interior subdivision.

Behind the gabled facades stands a six-story skeleton construction whose two main floors under the gable of the facade contain three interior floors and extends to three-fourths of the roof height. The roof slope up to that height is a concrete shell above which lies a small, doubled remnant of a roof truss that has been flattened on top and contains the ducts. The gabled facades, which were previously made of undressed stone with frames of hewn stone, were constructed from bricks, entirely independently of the structure of the skeleton. The stonemasonry is colored cast stone; the former corner ashlar was simulated with thin slabs. The form of the lower floors was slightly altered to accommodate three floors: the center arch on the ground floor was tripled in front and back. The side facades are modern in design with exposed concrete and washed-concrete infill.

The building, which receives natural light through elongated triangular openings that follow the vanishing lines from the cellars to the ceiling, is used commercially by restaurants, cafés, night bars, smaller shops and boutiques, and a few offices.

Jürgen Paul

Der Wiederaufbau des Kornhauses in Freiburg i. B.

und einige Betrachtungen über Architektur und Geschichtsverständnis

↑ fig. 1   Freiburg im Breisgau: the Altes Kornhaus

↑ fig. 2   The Altes Kornhaus (1497) before its

In den Jahren 1970—71 wurde an der im Kriege völlig zerstörten Nordseite des Münsterplatzes in Freiburg im Breisgau die letzte Lücke durch den Wiederaufbau des «alten Kornhauses» geschlossen (Abb. 1). Der Bau, der bis zu seiner völligen Vernichtung 1944 an der Stelle gestanden hatte, war 1497 als städtisches Tanzhaus und Kornspeicher errichtet worden. Trotz mehrmaliger innerer Umbauten, zuletzt als Konzertsaal, die auch im Aeusseren — im Erdgeschoss und an den Seiten — gewisse Veränderungen mit sich brachten, hatte es mit den steilen Treppengiebeln und reich profilierten Fensterkreuzen seine spätgotische Form bewahrt und gehörte zu den herausragenden historischen Baudenkmälern des alten Freiburg (Abb. 2).

Sein Wiederaufbau war angesichts der totalen Zerstörung eine über die Jahre heftig umstrittene Frage, aus prinzipiell architektonischen Gründen und wirtschaftlichen Erwägungen. Immer neue Nutzungen verschiedenen kulturellen Charakters wurden diskutiert, bis schliesslich eine private Firmengruppe dem Besitzer, der Stadt, das Problem der Nutzung und Finanzierung abnahm.

Mit der Auflage der historisch getreuen Wiederherstellung der beiden Giebelfassaden wurde ein Architektenwettbewerb ausgeschrieben. Der mit Zuschüssen der Denkmalpflege ausgeführte Entwurf erfüllt diese Auflage, hat aber sonst in Technik und Innenaufteilung mit dem historischen Bau nichts mehr gemeinsam.

Hinter den Giebelfronten steht eine sechsgeschossige Betonskelettkonstruktion, die in den beiden Hauptgeschossen unter dem Giebelsatz der Fassade drei innere Stockwerke unterbringt und bis in drei Viertel der Dachhöhe reicht. Die Dachschräge besteht bis zu dieser Höhe aus einer Betonschale, über der ein kleiner doppelter und oben abgeplatteter Restdachstuhl liegt, der die Versorgungsleitungen enthält. Die Giebelfronten, früher aus Bruchstein mit Hausteinrahmungen, wurden von dem Betonskelett konstruktiv ganz unabhängig aus Ziegel erstellt. Die Steinmetzarbeiten sind in gefärbtem Steinguss ausgeführt, die einstigen Eckquader durch dünne Platten nur vorgetäuscht. Die Masse der Untergeschosse wurden zur Unterbringung dreier Stockwerke leicht verändert, der mittlere Erdgeschossbogen vorn und hinten verdreifacht. Die Seitenfronten sind modern gestaltet in Sichtbeton mit Waschbetonausfachung.

Das Haus ist von den über die Fluchtlinien ausgedehnten Kellern bis ins Dach hinein, dieses durch langgezogene dreiecksförmig ausgeschnittene Oeffnungen belichtet, kommerziell genutzt von Restaurants, Cafés, Nachtbars, kleineren Geschäften und Boutiquen, sowie einigen Büros.

Obwohl der Wiederaufbau des Freiburger Kornhauses also ein wirtschaftliches Unternehmen ist, bei dem jeder Quadratzentimeter renditebringend gefüllt wurde, ist seine eigentliche Aufgabe nicht dies, sondern es ist die, der Stadt ein historisches Bauwerk wiederzugeben. Ist dieses neue «alte Kornhaus» noch oder wieder ein historisches Bauwerk? Ueber den baugeschichtlichen Authentizitätswert zu streiten ist müssig. Als Aufgabe ist das Kornhaus ein historisches Bauwerk, als Erfüllung der Aufgabe aber gleichzeitig ein Bau des 20. Jahrhunderts. Es gehört in das unübersehbare Heer von historischen Baudenkmälern, die nach den Zerstörungen des letzten Krieges wiederaufgebaut wurden. Nach den mitunter heftigen Debatten der ersten Nachkriegsjahre über ihre Wiederherstellung haben wir uns inzwischen an sie gewöhnt und aufgehört, viel über sie und die Motivationen, die sie hat wiedererstehen lassen,

La reconstruction du «Kornhaus» à Fribourg-en-Brisgau

Le grenier à blé de Fribourg-en-Brisgau, qui datait de 1497, fut complètement démoli en 1944. Il fut reconstruit en 1970/71, après de longues controverses. Le nouvel édifice restitue presque textuellement les deux façades principales, derrière lesquelles un squelette en béton armé permet une exploitation commerciale maximum de l'espace. Cette opération marque un tournant dans la théorie de la rénovation urbaine en Allemagne Fédérale. Jusque là toute reconstruction avait visé non à une restitution «archéologique» de l'état d'avant-guerre, mais à la recréation dans son ensemble de l'image de la ville, tout en traitant les détails de manière «moderne» (cf. par exemple Thomas Mann et son idée de «roman historique»). L'auteur discute les différents modèles culturels et principes de style qui déterminèrent la conception de la reconstruction urbaine en République Fédérale depuis la deuxième guerre mondiale. Ces méthodes de reconstruction ne reflètent pas seulement différents points de vue envers le problème de la conservation des monuments; il s'agit d'un important aspect de l'histoire de l'architecture depuis 1945.

Although the reconstruction of the Kornhaus in Freiburg is a business venture in which every square centimeter has been filled to bring in profit, its purpose is to return to the city a historical building. But is this new "Altes Kornhaus" still, or once again, a historical building? It is futile to quarrel over the value of authenticity regarding building history. The Kornhaus is a historical building in its brief; to fulfill that brief, however, it is also a twentieth-century building. It belongs to that immense army of historical architectural landmarks that were rebuilt after the destruction of the last war. After the at times vehement debates of the early postwar years about whether to reconstruct them, we have in the meantime grown used to them and stopped thinking much about them and the motivations that led to their reconstruction. We always view them—both the single building and the restored historical image of the city, with its reconstructed cathedral and reused baroque facade, the Renaissance portal inserted into a new building, or the relocated half-timbered building—with very different eyes, sometimes as authentic documents of history, sometimes as a reflection of something lost, in isolation or as part of an urban-planning context, but always primarily as a historical object. They all have in common that they have not been removed as a worthless ruin but rather restored. As a result, even when their form has regained so very precisely the old image, as sociological products they are twentieth-century architecture. Even when we can scarcely see them as our era's legitimate contribution to the history of architecture, these reconstructed images of history are just as important as an expression of our time—of its self-image and its relationship to the present and to history—as is modern architecture.

The new Kornhaus is the late consequence of the general historical concept of the reconstruction of Freiburg's center. There are, however, fundamental differences between the one and the other in the concern with and criteria for historical architecture that reflect a crucial change in the relationship to history and the historical object in now nearly thirty years of postwar history. This example was chosen in order to make several observations on that subject.

The reconstruction of Freiburg's old town is based on then-municipal director of building Schlippe's development plan of 1946, which countered the optimistic programs motivated by the impetus in the early days for a radical new order and total rebuilding of the cities on the basis of tabula rasa and principles of modern urban planning and modern architecture oriented around economics and technology with a compromise solution seeking to restore the old order.[1] Schlippe's plan for Freiburg represents with rare consistency (plans for nearly all blocks of the destroyed old town had, by that time, been carefully laid out) the attitude and objectives of the conservative side in the embittered conflict then being fought over the question of the reconstruction of historical cities in which both sides postulated their programs as an ethical mission: on the one hand, the requirement of the present and the necessity of vital self-confidence and historical honesty; on the other hand, the obligation to the everlasting, timelessly valid values of the past as a cultural mission.

Schlippe's plan for Freiburg set itself the task of restoring the character of the medieval look of the city by preserving the elements that were perceived as essential: preserving the planned layout of this Zähringer town, which was recognized as an urban-planning work of art, with its lines of streets and facades; preserving a limited and uniform overall height subordinated to the dominance of the cathedral; restoring the small-scale structure of individual homes of burghers; retaining the local housing type on the eave side: steep roof, executed with appropriate masonry technique, coherent surface form, and large windows; restoration of the partially destroyed important architectural landmarks; and reuse of historical architectural parts that had been preserved (figs. 3, 4).

Our concern here is not an architectural or urban-planning assessment of this program, or of that which was offered as an alternative at the time, but rather the question of which principle of the theory of history and art it reveals. A reconstruction like that of Freiburg rejects the reproduction of the city that was destroyed. It was instead intended as a revival of a familiar architectural structure in which one saw not only an artistic value but the expression of a way of life; namely, that of the historical city as the visible and experienceable form of an unbroken historical and national continuity.

The reconstruction was thus justified as the fulfillment of an ethical requirement not to undo the destruction of historicity caused by the catastrophe of the war—as had been done in Warsaw—but to repair the torn historical thread. It was supposed to restore the unity of historicity and contemporaneity in the ideal image of a historical city that can also function as a modern city, as an architectonic image of a compressed historicity, as a historical novel, so to speak, built in a language that freely connects to the past—comparable to, say, Thomas Mann's *Doktor Faustus*; and the spirit of the educated bourgeoisie à la Mann is in fact what was expressed here.

Reading the apologies for this and similar reconstruction programs, one encounters a wealth of biological and musical analogies in which the destroyed city is compared to a multicellular creature whose injuries are healed not by rebuilding the individual destroyed part as a dead backdrop, not by aping faded melodies, but by taking up the old rhythm again, so that the old harmony will resound again, by growing new tissue over the old bone. This vitalist metaphor reveals the antirational philosophy of life with romantic features that runs through the entire nineteenth century as an antithesis to positivism, materialism, and faith in progress and lives on unbroken in twentieth-century architecture alongside and opposed to functionalism and the aesthetic of technology. And the image of lebensraum that is recreated in this reconstruction—a medieval city of artisans and the bourgeoisie centered around the church—corresponds to this movement's ideal image of a middle-class society opposed to the metropolis, industrialization, and technology (fig. 5).

Artistically, after all, this image of the city is a reformation of certain aesthetic categories of experience of a modern reception of historical urban planning and architectural history: scale, restricting dimensions and compartmentalization, irregular lines, limited individuality within a larger order, a self-contained structure of open spaces, and an organic ethics of materials. What is revealed here is the urban planning ideal of the aesthetic of empathy of Camillo Sitte and his followers and the principles of the traditionalist architecture movement in the manner of Theodor Fischer and Schultze-Naumburg, with their fierce rejection of functionalist urban planning, the technological aesthetic, and the high-rise. With an awareness of an unbroken artistic tradition based on timeless values, this urban-planning synthesis of old and new is the model of a social utopia of the identity of history and present, that counters the relentless demands of the modern metropolis of capitalism. That this model could not get far, because it contradicts the social and economic preconditions and was therefore soon overrun by architectural developments, is demonstrated by what the city of Freiburg ultimately became with the increasing alteration of Schlippe's plan and is only too clear just as in all the other reconstructed cities.

The artistic program of Freiburg's reconstruction plan distinguishes, in sternly moral terms, between recreating and copying, between the repeatable and unrepeatable aspects of historical form. The artistic object is thereby divided into two formal spheres: an overall form and an individual form. This corresponds to a specific level of the theory of historical preservation as found, for example, in the statements of Paul Clemens. Very much in contrast to Dehio's positivist stance, Clemens postulates a symbolic value of the historical object that goes beyond its physical existence as an individual document of history. Clemens, who, as we know, lived to experience the destruction of the Second World War, also belongs to the theoretical advocates of a historical reconstruction in the form of a free recreation of specific values of formal structure.

The crucial problem with this concept, from the viewpoint of historical preservation, is defining the hypothetical line between the universal form of the symbolic value that is elevated over the decline of history and the individual form tied to a time. Famously, this line was drawn anew and differently over and over in debates of often moral and ideological vehemence, from the Prinzipalmarkt in Münster to the cathedral in Würzburg, from the Goethehaus in Frankfurt to the Marktplatz in Hildesheim. Several factors play a role in this, having to do with the understanding of style—that is, the aesthetic closeness to or distance from specific historical styles—with the problems of the theory of materials, and with the individual emotional value of the historical object. The most essential criterion was the distinction between architectonic form and decorative form. Despite its claim

nachzudenken. Wir betrachten sie, das einzelne Bauwerk wie das wiederhergestellte historische Stadtbild, den wiederaufgebauten Dom und die wiederverwendete Barockfassade, das in einen Neubau einbezogene Renaissanceportal wie das versetzte Fachwerkhaus mit ganz verschiedenen Augen, teils als authentische Dokumente der Geschichte, teils als Reflex von etwas Verlorenem, als Einzelnes oder als Teil eines städtebaulichen Zusammenhanges, doch immer primär als historisches Objekt. Gemeinsam haben sie aber alle, dass sie nicht als wertlose Ruinen beseitigt, sondern wiederhergestellt worden sind. Und dadurch sind sie, auch wenn sie in ihrer Form das alte Bild noch so genau zurückerhalten haben, als soziologische Produkte Architektur des 20. Jahrhunderts; auch wenn wir sie kaum als legitimen Beitrag unserer Epoche zur Geschichte der Baukunst betrachten, sind diese wiederhergestellten Bilder der Geschichte als Ausdruck unserer Zeit, ihres Selbstverständnisses, ihres Verhältnisses zur Gegenwart und zur Geschichte ebenso wichtig wie die moderne Architektur.

Das neue Kornhaus ist die späte Konsequenz des historischen Gesamtkonzeptes des Wiederaufbaus der Freiburger Innenstadt. Im Anliegen und in den Kriterien der Wiederherstellung historischer Architektur, bestehen zwischen diesem und jenem der grundlegende Unterschiede, die einen wesentlichen Wandel des Verhältnisses zur Geschichte und dem historischen Objekt in den fast 30 Jahren der Nachkriegszeit widerspiegeln. Für einige Beobachtungen darüber wurde dieses Beispiel gewählt.

Dem Wiederaufbau der Freiburger Altstadt liegt der Bebauungsplan des damaligen Oberbaudirektors Schlippe von 1946 zugrunde, der den vom Impetus der ersten Stunde getragenen optimistischen Programmen, die auf der Basis der tabula rasa eine radikale Neuordnung und einen totalen Neubau der Städte nach den an wirtschaftlicher und technischer Funktion orientierten Prinzipien des modernen Städtebaus und der modernen Architektur forderten, eine restaurative Kompromisslösung entgegenstellte.[1] Der Schlippesche Plan für Freiburg repräsentiert in seltener Konsequenz (vorsorglich wurden damals schon die Entwürfe für fast alle Baublöcke der zerstörten Altstadt festgelegt) die Haltung und Ziele der konservativen Seite in dem erbitterten Streit, der um die Frage des Wiederaufbaus der historischen Städte ausgefochten wurde und in dem beide Seiten ihre Programme als ethische Aufgabe postulierten: hier die Forderung der Gegenwart, das Gebot von vitalem Selbstbewusstsein und geschichtlicher Ehrlichkeit, dort die Verpflichtung an die unvergänglichen und zeitlos gültigen Werte der Vergangenheit als kulturelle Aufgabe.

Der Schlippesche Plan für Freiburg setzte sich die Aufgabe der Wiederherstellung des mittelalterlichen Stadtbildcharakters durch Wahrung seiner als wesentlich empfundenen Elemente: also Wahrung des als städtebauliches Kunstwerk erkannten planmässigen Grundrisses der Zähringer Stadt mit seinen Strassenlinien und Baufluchten, Wahrung einer sich der Dominanz des Münsters unterordnenden beschränkten und einheitlichen Gesamthöhe, Wiederherstellung der kleinteiligen Struktur individueller Bürgerhäuser, Beibehaltung des lokalen traufseitigen Haustypus mit Steildach, Ausführung in werkgerechter Mauertechnik und hochformatigen Fenstern, Wiederherstellung der teilzerstörten bedeutenden Baudenkmäler und Wiederverwendung erhaltener historischer Bauteile (Abb. 3, 4).

Es soll hier nicht auf eine architektonische oder städtebauliche Bewertung dieses Programmes oder dessen, was als Alternative dazu damals angeboten war, ankommen, sondern auf die Frage nach dem geschichtstheoretischen und künstlerischen Leitbild, das sich hier zeigt. Ein Wiederaufbau wie der Freiburgs lehnte die Reproduktion der zerstörten Stadt ab. Er war vielmehr als Wiederbelebung einer vertrauten architektonischen Struktur gemeint, in der man nicht nur einen künstlerischen Wert, sondern darüberhinaus den Ausdruck einer Lebensform sah, nämlich die der historischen Stadt als sichtbare und erlebbare Form einer bruchlosen historisch-nationalen Kontinuität. Der Wiederaufbau rechtfertigt sich somit als Erfüllung einer ethischen Forderung, nicht die Zerstörung der tatsächlichen historischen Substanz, wie man es in Warschau tat, sondern die Zerstörung der Geschichtlichkeit durch die Katastrophe des Krieges rückgängig zu machen, den abgerissenen historischen Faden wieder zu knüpfen. Er soll die Einheit von Geschichtlichkeit und Gegenwärtigkeit wiederherstellen im Idealbild ei-

↓ fig. 3 Joseph Schlippe, development plan for Freiburg im Breisgau (1946).

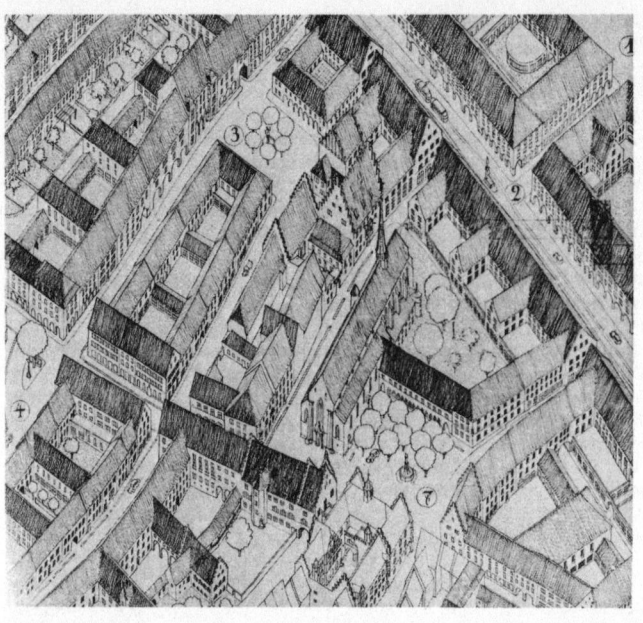

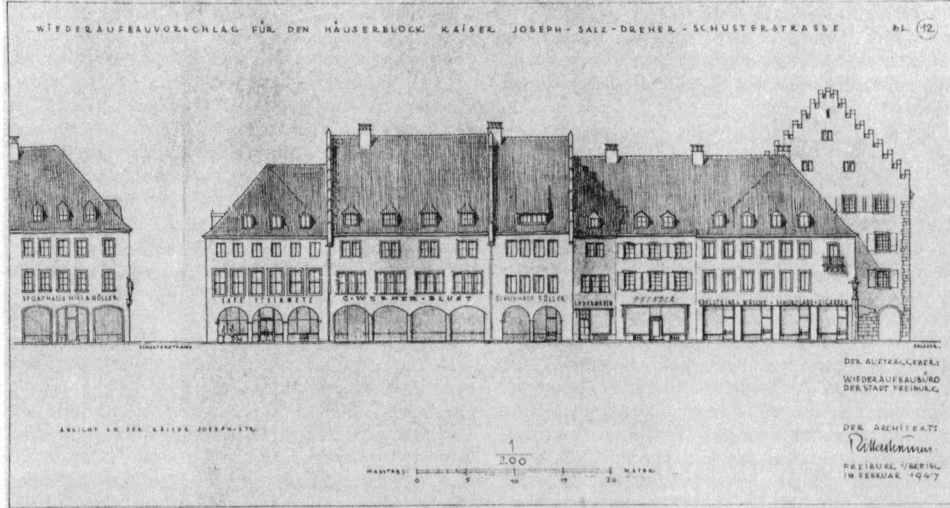

14

↑ fig. 4 Typical street facade based on Schlippe's plan.

ner historischen Stadt, die auch als moderne Stadt funktionieren kann, als architektonisches Bild einer kondensierten Geschichtlichkeit, sozusagen als gebauter historischer Roman, in einer an die Vergangenheit frei anknüpfenden Sprache, vergleichbar etwa dem «Doktor Faustus» von Thomas Mann; und der Geist des Bildungsbürgertums Thomas-Mannscher Prägung ist es in der Tat, was hier seinen Ausdruck fand.

Liest man die Apologien dieser und ähnlicher Wiederaufbauprogramme nach, so stösst man auf eine Fülle biologischer und musikalischer Analogien, in denen die zerstörte Stadt mit einem vielzelligen Lebewesen verglichen wird, dessen verwundeter Organismus geheilt werde, nicht indem der einzelne vernichtete Teil als tote Kulisse wiederaufgerichtet wird, nicht indem verklungene Melodien nachgeäfft werden, sondern indem der alte Rhythmus wiederaufgenommen werden soll, die alte Harmonie wieder aufklingen soll, indem man das alte Bein mit neuem Gewebe verwachsen lässt. Diese vitalistische Metaphorik zeigt die antirationalistische Lebensphilosophie mit romantischen Zügen, wie sie als Antithese zu Positivismus, Materialismus und Fortschrittsglauben das ganze 19. Jahrhundert durchzieht und im 20. Jahrhundert auch in der Architektur neben und gegen Funktionalismus und technischer Aesthetik bruchlos weiterlebt. Und das in diesem Wiederaufbau nachgeformte Lebensraumbild einer mittelalterlichen, um die Kirche zentrierten Handwerker- und Bürgerstadt entspricht dem mittelständischen, gegen Grosstadt, Industrialisierung und Technik gerichteten sozialen Idealbild dieser Strömung (Abb. 5).

Künstlerisch schliesslich ist dieses Stadtbild eine Nachformung bestimmter ästhetischer Erlebniskategorien einer modernen Rezeption des historischen Städtebaus und der Architekturgeschichte: Masstäblichkeit, Beschränkung der Dimensionen und Kleinteiligkeit, unregelmässige Linien, begrenzte Individualtität innerhalb einer grösseren Ordnung, geschlossene Freiraumstruktur und organische Materialethik. Was sich hier zeigt, ist das städtebauliche Ideal

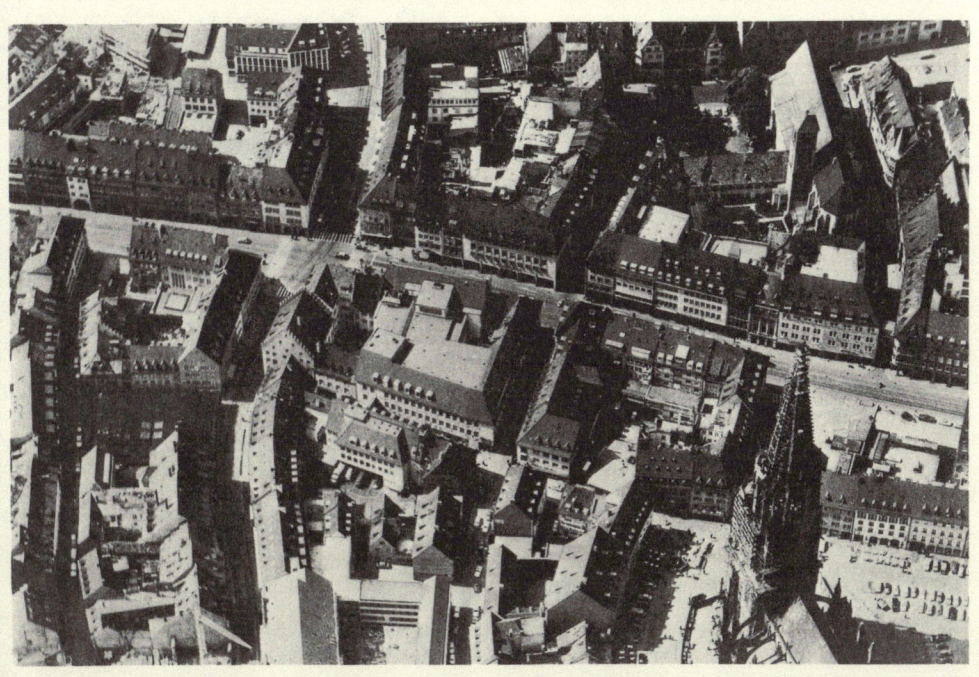

↑ fig. 5 Freiburg im Breisgau: the center of town after reconstruction. Lower right: cathedral.

fig. 6   Munich, Heiliggeistkirche, after being damaged in the war.

der Einfühlungsästhetik Camillo Sittes und seiner Nachfolger und die Prinzipien der traditionalistischen Architekturströmung in der Richtung Theodor Fischer und Schulze-Naumburgs mit ihrer scharfen Absage an den funktionalistischen Städtebau, die technische Aesthetik und das Hochhaus. Im Bewusstsein einer ungebrochenen künstlerischen Tradition auf der Grundlage zeitloser Werte ist diese städtebauliche Synthese von Alt und Neu das Modell einer gesellschaftlichen Utopie der Identität von Geschichte und Gegenwart, die sich gegen die unerbittlichen Forderungen der modernen Grossstadt des Kapitalismus stellt. Dass dieses Modell nicht weit kommen konnte, weil es den gesellschaftlichen und wirtschaftlichen Voraussetzungen widersprach, und daher von der baulichen Entwicklung bald überrannt wurde, zeigt das heutige Stadtbild von Freiburg, wie es schliesslich in zunehmender Veränderung des Schlippe-Planes wurde, so wie das aller übrigen wiederaufgebauten Städte überdeutlich.

Das künstlerische Programm des Freiburger Wiederaufbauplanes trifft eine streng moralisch formulierte Unterscheidung zwischen Nachschaffen und Kopieren, zwischen dem Wiederholbaren und Unwiederholbaren in der historischen Form. Das künstlerische Objekt wird dabei in zwei formale Bereiche geteilt: in eine Gesamtform und eine Individualform. Dies entspricht einer bestimmten Stufe der Denkmalpflegetheorie, wie sie z. B. in den Aeusserungen Paul Clemens zu finden ist. Ganz im Gegensatz zur positivistischen Haltung Dehios postulierte Clemen einen Symbolwert des historischen Objekts, der über seine physische Existenz als individuelles Dokument der Geschichte hinausgeht. Clemen, der bekanntlich die Zerstörungen des zweiten Weltkrieges noch miterlebt hat, gehört auch zu den theoretischen Anwälten eines historischen Wiederaufbaus in der Form eines freien Nachschaffens spezifischer formaler Strukturwerte.

Das entscheidende Problem dieses Konzepts vom Gesichtspunkt der Denkmalpflege ist die Definition der hypothetischen Grenze zwischen der Allgemeinform des über den Verfall der Geschichte erhobenen Symbolwertes und der an die Zeit gebundenen Individualform. Diese Grenze wurde bekanntlich in heftigen Auseinandersetzungen von oft moralischer und weltanschaulicher Wucht von Fall zu Fall, vom Prinzipalmarkt in Münster zum Würzburger Dom, vom Goethehaus in Frankfurt zum Hildesheimer Marktplatz immer wieder neu und anders gezogen. Eine Fülle von Faktoren spielen dabei eine Rolle, die mit dem Stilverständnis, also der ästhetischen Nähe oder Ferne zu den einzelnen historischen Stilen, mit den Problemen der Materialtheorie wie mit dem individuellen emotionalen Wert des historischen Objekts zusammenhängen. Das wesentlichste Kriterium war die Unterscheidung zwischen architektonischer Form und dekorativer Form. Es ist deutlich, dass auch diese ästhetische Zerlegung des historischen Objekts, trotz ihres historischen Absolutätsanspruches, eine rezeptive Interpretation ist. Die ästhetischen Erfahrungsqualitäten, die den vereinfachten Wiederherstellungen von Stadtbildern ebenso wie dem kahl re-romanisierten Dom von Hildesheim, oder dem Betonmuster des neuen Gewölbes von St. Michael in München zugrunde liegen, sind eine Reduktion

fig. 7 Munich, Heiliggeistkirche after its "restoration" of 1952.

auf die abstrakten Grundstrukturen von Körper und Raum, Linie und Umriss, Fläche und Proportionen, wie sie die moderne Kunst verwendet. Am deutlichsten wird dies im dekorativ vereinfachten oder völlig dekorationslosen Wiederaufbau von barocken Innenräumen, wie der scharfkantig-umrisshaften Neugestaltung der Münchner Heiliggeistkirche von 1952, die damals als beispielhafte Wiederaufbaulösung galt (Abb. 6, 7).

Wie verhält sich nun das neue Freiburger Kornhaus zu dem historischen Wiederaufbauprogramm der Freiburger Altstadt? Dass überhaupt ein Baudenkmal, von dem nichts an alter Substanz, an die man hätte anknüpfen können, mehr erhalten war, wiedererrichtet wurde, verstösst entscheidend gegen den lebensphilosophischen Gedanken einer organischen Heilung der historischen Stadt als lebendigem Wesen. So hatte man schweren Herzens in der ersten Nachkriegsphase zum Beispiel auf einen Wiederaufbau des Knochenhaueramtshauses in Hildesheim verzichtet, weil weder seine Bausubstanz noch sein Zusammenhang mehr vorhanden war, und die Rekonstruktion des Frankfurter Goethehauses von 1949, von Denkmalpflegern und Architekten heftig befehdet, musste sich schuldbewusst mit der ausgelagerten Ausstattung und vorhandenen Erdgeschossresten rechtfertigen.

Weiterhin verzichtet das wiederaufgebaute Freiburger Kornhaus nicht nur in der Konstruktion auf eine organische Verbindung von «Alt» und «Neu», der formale und materielle Gegensatz der unvermittelt aufeinanderprallenden Gegensätze der historischen Giebelkopien und der modernen Seitenfassaden, der Durchblick durch die ungeteilten grossen Scheiben in das moderne Innere werden sogar als gestalterische Qualitäten forciert.

Im Sinne des ursprünglichen Wiederaufbaukonzeptes wäre dieses neue Kornhaus eine unehrliche, ausgestopfte historische Attrappe, das genaue Gegenteil von dem, was man wollte. Doch offensichtlich trifft der damals an die Wiederherstellung historischer Bauten gestellte Anspruch hier überhaupt nicht mehr zu. Die nur vorgetäuschte Eckquaderung, das falsche Material der Zierteile zeigen, dass diese historischen Fassaden gar nichts anderes sein wollen als eine Kulisse, eine mit ökonomischen Mitteln erzielte Reproduktion, die einem konstruktiv und gestalterisch modernen Bau, der möglichst offen gezeigt wird, vorgeheftet ist (dasselbe hat man in den letzten Jahren auch mit vorhandenen Fassaden praktiziert).

Ein besonders aufschlussreiches Motiv sind die aufgefalteten langen Dreiecke der Dachöffnungen. Sie wirken im Zusammenhang mit den Giebeln und dem Steildach als spielerisch verfremdete Paraphrase von historischen Dachgauben. Verfremdende Umsetzung historischer Formen, wörtliche Kopie, auch in modernem Material, und forcierter Gegensatz von Alt und Neu, das sind Erscheinungen, die heute in den verschiedensten künstlerischen Zusammenhängen begegnen: in der Pop Art wie im Wohnstil (gotische Madonna vor der weissen Wand), in der Werbung wie in der Mode, in der Musik (Kagels *Beethoven '70)* wie auf dem Theater *(Der nackte Hamlet).*

In der Architektur hat sich die programmatische Einheit von Alt und Neu aufgelöst. Aus

17

der Kompromissarchitektur der ersten Nachkriegsjahre hat sich einerseits eine abstrakte historisierende Anpassungs- und Anspielungsarchitektur entwickelt, die sich besonders im Zusammenhang von Altstadtsanierungen ausbreitet. Mehr und mehr wird hier neuerdings die Giebelhausabstraktion in Beton oder mit vorgehängter Rasterfassade, eine Form, bei der von den früheren komplexen Ansprüchen nur noch die formalen Kriterien von Masstäblichkeit und Umriss übriggeblieben sind (Abb. 8), verdrängt von geistreicheren, spielerischen Verfremdungen und Umsetzungen historischer Formen (Abb. 9).

Die andererseits vorhandene Bereitschaft zu detailgetreuer Kopie oder Reproduktion zeigt sich ebenso in der plötzlich allgemeinen enthusiastischen Bewertung des früher zumindest im Westen heftig kritisierten Wiederaufbaus in Polen oder in dem hohen Lob, das der ebenso heftig abgelehnte Wiederaufbau des Frankfurter Goethehauses nun von Seiten der Denkmalpflege erhält, wie in neueren Wiederherstellungen zerstörter historischer Bauten und Räume. Die Münchner Heiliggeistkirche, obwohl in ihrer kargen Form von 1952 als endgültig gedacht, hat in jüngster Zeit in genauer Detailrekonstruktion ihre Stuck- und Freskendekoration doch wiedererhalten.

Bekanntlich ist dies kein Einzelfall. Erbdrostenhof und Clemenskirche in Münster, Würzburger und Münchner Residenz, die Klosterkirche in Kreuzlingen in der Schweiz sind nur herausgegriffene Beispiele, die Pläne, das Leibnizhaus in Hannover an anderer Stelle zu rekonstruieren und das Knochenhaueramtshaus, obwohl sein Platz längst besetzt ist, nun doch wiederaufzubauen, sind besonders prononcierte.[2]

Es geht in diesen Betrachtungen nicht um eine Bewertung dieser Dinge aus denkmalpflegerischer Sicht oder als künstlerische Produkte. Es soll vielmehr versucht werden, einiges zu sagen über die Motive, die sie hervorbringen, die Bedürfnisse, die sie befriedigen. Von dieser Frage her betrachtet gehören Verfremdung und Kopie historischer Formen zusammen, als Dokumente nicht der Geschichte, sondern unseres Verhältnisses zur Geschichte. Die unbegrenzte Freiheit, mit der man sich heute des historischen Objektes bedient, es reproduziert, versetzt, seine Formen als ästhetische Assoziation und Verfremdung benutzt, ist zwar eine konsequente Weiterführung des langen Autonomisierungsprozesses der Kunst und der schliesslich inflationären Ausweitung der künstlerischen Erfahrung, die nun auch das freie Spiel mit der historischen Form im universalgeschichtlichen Musée Imaginaire als eine neue, zusätzliche ästhetische Dimension entdeckt hat. Doch sie ist nicht nur eine neue künstlerische oder modische Geschmacksform, sondern es handelt sich hier um ein verändertes Verhältnis zum historischen Objekt, das diesem eine neue Funktion gibt, ein Wandel, der sich in einem langsamen Uebergang aus der ersten Nachkriegszeit entwickelt hat.

Die Verwendung des Historischen, wie wir sie heute finden, ist alles andere als ein totaler Historismus, sondern gehört bestimmten, abgegrenzten Sphären des Lebens an: dem Kulturbetrieb, der Freizeit- und Privatwelt, jedenfalls nicht der alltäglichen, der Wirtschafts- und der Arbeitswelt. Dass man im Freiburger Kornhaus Boutiquen und schicke Lokale angesiedelt hat und für eines davon auf dem hier völlig unsinnigen neuen Namen «Ratskeller» bestanden hat, ist dafür ebenso bezeichnend wie der jetzt modische Innenausstattungsstil von Gaststätten mit viel Holzverkleidung, Schmiedeeisen und gedrechselten Stuhlbeinen, wie die Formen exklusiver Ferienquartiere an der Côte d'Azur oder der Wiederaufbau der Münchner Oper mit seinem um mehrere Meter versetzten, doch getreuer als jemals zuvor rekonstruierten Zuschauerraum.

Der historische Wiederaufbau der ersten Nachkriegszeit stellte den hohen Anspruch, eine totale Einheit von Geschichte und Gegenwart zu schaffen als allgemeingültige Lebensform, die Kultur und Arbeitswelt in sich vereint. Diese romantische Utopie, getragen vom Geist des Bildungsbürgertums, hat sich auch dort, wo sie Fuss fassen konnte, aufgelöst in den ökonomischen und technischen Forderungen der Entwicklung, die das Wirtschaftswunder hervorbracht, ihren sozialen und wirtschaftlichen Veränderungen, ihrem Optimismus und Fortschrittsglauben — und der daraus resultierenden Architektur der Stadt.

Die heutige Nostalgiewelle und die emotionale Rückkehr zu historischen Formen ist eine Fluchtbewegung vor deren totalen Konsequenzen, das Bedürfnis, der in dieser zweiten Phase der Nachkriegszeit geschaffenen technischen Arbeitswelt eine ganz andere, schönere Reservatswelt entgegenzustellen; doch nicht als

to historical absoluteness, this aesthetic dissection of the historical object is clearly a passive interpretation. The qualities of historical experience that underlie the simplified reconstructions of cityscapes and the sparsely re-Romanesqued cathedral of Hildesheim or the concrete patterns of the new vault of St. Michael in Munich amount to a reduction to the abstract basic structures of volume and space, line and outline, plane and proportions as modern art employs them. This becomes most clear in the decoratively simplified or completely undecorated reconstruction of baroque interiors, such as the sharp-edged, contour-like redesign in 1952 of the Heiliggeistkirche [Church of the Holy Spirit] in Munich, which at the time was considered an exemplary reconstruction solution (figs. 6, 7).

How does the new Kornhaus in Freiburg relate to the historical reconstruction program for Freiburg's old town? The very fact that an architectural monument of which none of its original fabric remained to which it could be connected was nevertheless reconstructed decidedly violates the philosophy of life that the historical city should be organically healed like a living creature. In the first postwar phase, for example, the idea of reconstructing the Knochenhaueramtshaus [Butchers' Guild Hall] in Hildesheim was abandoned with heavy heart because neither its fabric nor its context existed any longer, and the reconstruction of the Goethehaus of 1949, which was vehemently attacked by preservationists and architects, was guiltily justified with decorations taken from storage and existing remnants on the ground floor.

Moreover, the reconstructed Kornhaus in Freiburg dispensed not only with an organic connection of "old" and "new" in its construction; the formal and material contrast of the directly clashing antitheses of copies of historical gables and modern side facades and the view through the undivided large panes into the modern interior were compelled as qualities of the design.

In the spirit of the original reconstruction concept, this new Kornhaus would have been seen as a dishonest, filled-in, historical mock-up — the exact opposite of what was wanted. Yet clearly the former ambition for the reconstruction of historical buildings was no longer relevant. The merely faked corner ashlar and the faux material of the decorative parts show that these historical facades are not intended to be anything other than a stage set, a production achieved by economic means, attached to the front of a building of modern design that is displayed as openly as possible (the same thing has been practiced in recent years with existing facades).

One especially revealing motif is the long, unfolded triangles of the roof openings. In connection with the gables and the steep roof, they seem like a playfully defamiliarized paraphrase of historical dormer windows. Defamiliarized implementation of historical forms, literal copy, even using modern materials, and a recherché antithesis of old and new — these are the phenomena encountered today in a wide range of artistic contexts: in pop art as well as home decorating (Gothic Madonna in front of a white wall), in advertising, in fashion, in music (Kagel's *Beethoven '70*), and in the theater (*The "Naked" Hamlet*).

In architecture, the programmatic unity of old and new has broken down. The compromise architecture of the early postwar years has evolved, on the one hand, into an abstract, historicizing architecture of adaptation and allusion that is spreading especially in the context of renovating old towns. More and more, gabled house abstraction in concrete or grid curtain facades — a form in which all that remains of the former complex ambitions are the formal criteria of scale and outline (fig. 8) — are superseded by more imaginative, playful defamiliarizations and realizations of historical forms (fig. 9).

The willingness, on the other hand, to faithfully copy or reproduce details is also revealed in the suddenly universal, enthusiastic assessment of the reconstructions in Poland that were previously vehemently criticized, at least in the West, as well as in the high praise that the once equally vehemently rejected reconstruction of the Goethehaus in Frankfurt now gets from preservationists, and in the newer reconstructions of destroyed historical buildings and spaces. The Heiliggeistkirche, whose sparse form of 1951 was considered to be final, has recently been given a precise reconstruction of the details of its stucco and fresco decoration.

Famously, this is not an isolated case: the Erbdrostenhof [High Steward's Court] and the Clemenskirche [St. Clement's Church] in

Münster, the Würzburg and Munich Residences, and the Klosterkirche [Monastic Church] in Kreuzlingen, Switzerland, are just some examples chosen at random. The plans to reconstruct the Leibnizhaus in Hanover in another location and now to rebuild the Knochenhaueramtshaus, even though its place has long since been occupied, are particularly pronounced examples.[2]

The point of these observations is not to evaluate these things from the perspective of historical preservation or as artistic products. Rather, it is intended as an effort to say something about the motifs they produce and the needs they satisfy. Seen from that perspective, the defamiliarization and copying of historical forms go together as documents not of history but of our relationship to history. The unlimited freedom with which the historical object is used today is a logical continuation of the long process of art becoming autonomous and the ultimately excessive expansion of the artistic experience, which has now also discovered free play with historical form in the *musée imaginaire* of universal history as a new, additional aesthetic dimension. It is not, however, merely a new form of artistic or fashionable taste but rather a changed relationship to the historical object that lends it a new function, a transformation that has evolved in a slow transition from the early postwar period.

The use of the historical that we find today is anything but a total historicism and rather belongs to certain, demarcated spheres of life: the cultural scene, the worlds of leisure and privacy, but not to the everyday, the world of the economy and work. The fact that boutiques and chic stores were located in the Kornhaus in Freiburg and that one of them insisted on the name "Ratskeller" [Town Hall Cellar], which makes no sense at all there, is just as characteristic as the now fashionable style of decorating the interiors of restaurants with lots of wood paneling, wrought iron, and turned chair legs, as well as the forms of the exclusive vacation spots on the Côte d'Azur or the reconstruction of the Munich opera house, whose auditorium has been shifted several meters but reconstructed more faithfully than ever before.

The historical reconstruction of the early postwar period set itself the ambitious goal of creating a total unity of history and present as a universally valid way of living that unites culture and the work world. This romantic utopia, borne by the spirit of the educated bourgeoisie, has, where it could gain a foothold, been assimilated into the economic and technical requirements of the development that resulted from the postwar economic miracle, its social and economic changes, its optimism and faith in progress—and the architecture of the city that resulted from it.

Today's wave of nostalgia and emotional return to historical forms is a flight from its ultimate consequences, reflecting the need for a completely different, more beautiful reserve world to counter the technological work world created in this second phase of the postwar period—not as a total ideological antithesis but merely as a supplement.

The new emotional popularity of preserving old towns results not from a new interest in history that has suddenly seized all social strata. People today prefer to live in modern housing, but they prefer to see old buildings; people satisfy their practical needs with modern architecture, but they spend their leisure time and prefer to see themselves represented by historical architecture. Old towns and historical buildings derive their significance above all from their connection to this reserve world. The Kornhaus in Freiburg would not have been rebuilt so late if it had not been located on the tourist center Münsterplatz. Other historical buildings in remote locations of the same old town were being demolished at the very same time.

Nevertheless, we have begun to develop this sociologically constantly growing reserve world by, among other ways, the now popular use of historical forms for aesthetic appeals. Because the historical object is no longer identified as a document of history (being adopted free of content) and because formal affinities to specific historical styles have also become less significant as a result of aesthetic pluralism, the entire store of history is available for arbitrary use.

ENDNOTES

1   Joseph Schlippe, "Der Wiederaufbauplan für Freiburg," *Die neue Stadt* 1 (1947): 115–22; Joseph Schlippe, *Freiburger Almanach* 1 (1950): 13–47; *Freiburger Almanach* 10 (1959): 73–101; and *Badische Heimat* 39 (1959): 214–71.

2   See *Deutsche Kunst und Denkmalpflege*, 1965–68.

typical street facade of the early years of reconstruction. typical street facade of the 1960s.

totale weltanschauliche Antithese, sondern nur als Ergänzung.

Die neue emotionale Popularität der Altstadterhaltung entspringt ja nicht einem plötzlich alle Schichten ergreifenden neuen Interesse an der Geschichte. Die heutigen Menschen wohnen lieber in modernen Wohnungen, aber sie sehen lieber alte Bauten, sie befriedigen ihre praktischen Bedürfnisse in moderner Architektur, doch sie verbringen ihre Freizeit und sehen sich repräsentiert lieber in historischer Architektur. Ihre Bedeutung erhalten Altstädte und historische Bauten vor allem durch ihren Zusammenhang mit dieser Reservatswelt. Das Freiburger Kornhaus wäre kaum so spät noch wiederaufgebaut worden, wenn es nicht am Touristenzentrum des Münsterplatzes stünde. An entlegener Stelle werden gleichzeitig in derselben Innenstadt vorhandene historische Bauten abgebrochen.

Doch wir haben begonnen, diese soziologisch sich stetig vergrössernde Reservatswelt auszubauen, unter anderem durch die beliebig gewordene Verwendung historischer Formen als ästhetische Reizwerte. Da eine Identifizierung mit dem historischen Objekt als Dokument der Geschichte nicht mehr stattfindet, es als inhaltliches Vakuum übernommen wird, und da zudem auf der Grundlage eines ästhetischen Pluralismus auch formale Affinitäten zu bestimmten historischen Stilen an Bedeutung verlieren, steht der ganze Fundus der Geschichte zur beliebigen Verwendung zur Verfügung.

Bruno Reichlin und Fabio Reinhart

DIE HISTORIE

als Teil der Architekturtheorie

Anmerkungen zu
neuen Projekten
für
Zürich, Bellinzona, Modena und
Muggiò

Dieser Beitrag beabsichtigt, in groben Zügen eine Betrachtungsweise der Architektur darzulegen und zu illustrieren, der die folgenden Ueberzeugungen und Einsichten zugrunde liegen:
— die Ueberzeugung, dass sich die grundsätzlichen Probleme des Restaurierens und des Bauens im historischen Kontext diejenigen der Architektur im Ganzen sind.
— die Einsicht in die Notwendigkeit einer «operativen Kritik», die Denken und Handeln zu vereinen sucht, indem sie der historischen Analyse, der Architekturkritik und dem Entwerfen dieselben Kriterien zugrundelegt (ein Vorgang, der allerdings mit der naiven «imperialistischen» Vorstellung einer Verschmelzung der historischen und architektonischen Disziplin nichts zu tun hat). Diese Einsichten oder Hypothesen beruhen ihrerseits auf Ueberzeugungen: Ueberzeugungen einerseits hinsichtlich der Frage, was als spezifische Bedeutung der Architektur anzunehmen sei, und andererseits hinsichtlich der Konsequenzen, die sich aus der Annahme ergeben, wonach sich der Bedeutungsgehalt der Architektur jeweils nur im Bezugsfeld der eigenen architektonischen Tradition definiert. Unter Tradition verstehen wir dabei zugleich die Werke und das Verständnis, das wir von ihnen haben. Wir beziehen uns auf die umfassendere Definition, die

H. H. Holz in «Tradition und Traditionsbruch» gibt: «Tradition ist . . . eine ebenso anthropologische wie erkenntnistheoretische Kategorie: denn wir sind nur gegenwärtig, insofern wir Vergangenheit in uns aufgenommen haben, und wir erkennen nur, insofern wir in vorgegebenen Denkformen Unerfahrenes aufnehmen und um dieses erweitern.»

Diese nur andeutungsweise ausgeführten grundsätzlichen Ueberlegungen zum Problem der «Bedeutung» von Architektur, die weit davon entfernt sind, eine kohärente Theorie zu bilden, stehen am Beginn der Untersuchungen und Bemühungen, die sich bei Aldo Rossi (*L'architettura della città*) und in seinem

History as a Part of Architectural Theory

Notes on New Projects for Zurich, Bellinzona, Modena, and Muggiò

Authors:
Bruno Reichlin
Fabio Reinhart

Source:
archithese, 11 (1974): 20–29

Translated by:
Steven Lindberg

The intent of this article is to roughly outline an approach to architecture based on the following convictions and insights:
— the conviction that the fundamental problems of restoring and building in the historical context are those of architecture as a whole.
— the insight into the need for an "operative critique" that tries to unite thought and action by basing historical analysis, architectural criticism, and design on the same criteria (an approach that has nothing to do, however, with the naive "imperialist" idea of fusing the historical and the architectural disciplines). These insights or hypotheses are based in turn on convictions: convictions, on the one hand, about the issue that is to be assumed as the specific significance of architecture and, on the other hand, about the consequences that result from the assumption that the semantic content of architecture is defined in each case only within the field of reference of architecture's own tradition. We understand *tradition* to mean both the works and the understanding we have of them. We refer to the more comprehensive definition that H. H. Holz offers in "Tradition und Traditionsbruch" [Tradition and Breaking with Tradition]: "Tradition is ... an anthropological category as much as an epistemological one, since we are only present to the extent we have absorbed the past into us, and we know only insofar as we absorb what we have not experienced ourselves in existing forms of thought and expand it."

These merely suggestively elaborated fundamental reflections on the problem of "significance" in architecture, which are far from forming a coherent theory, stand at the beginning of the studies and efforts that can be discovered in the work of Aldo Rossi (*L'architettura della citta* [*The Architecture of the City*]) and his circle, above all in the fields of semiological studies (especially those that appeal to Russian formalism or should be ascribed to structuralism of French influence), and finally in certain orientations of more recent American architecture.

These reflections will be briefly summarized in what follows. Subsequently, we will attempt at least to explain their operative scope for criticism and design in the discussion of designs and buildings.

The study of the architecture of the city, the analysis of modern buildings, and design activity itself represent structurally interrelated attempts to understand architecture as a sign. Dealing with architecture in this way tends toward an operative discourse on the relationship—and on the nature of this relationship—that ties an empirical object (architecture) to the cognitive experience that belongs to it and that is developed from it. That means, in other words: this empirical object becomes the signifier of a sign that, on the one hand, finds its signified in the most general context of the social life and of the institutions of society in which it occurs. On the other hand, architecture creates its signified itself insofar as every example of architecture essentially reflects its own "nature" (the *autoriflessività* of the work of art). In this view, the significance (signified) of a work of architecture is providing an object with "meaning": a meaning that is inherent in social use in the broadest framework. In the process, the activities of design and of historical-critical analysis are assigned a categorically preferred role in that they try to capture the meaning of the history of the creation of architecture and the gene-specific significance of their object; that is, its particular quality as an architectural work of art. This significance refers to, on the one hand, a typological, morphological, technological-constructional, functional, iconographic, and finally ideological knowledge and, on the other hand, to the epistemology of architecture as a specific product according to the concepts and categories of the theory of architecture. The task of an architectural semantics would be to develop a terminology that would permit one to describe, study, and classify architectural significances abstractly defined in this way.

For us architects—and this will subsequently represent a necessary restriction—the activity of design stands in the foreground. We try to explain in the process that along with the architectural work its significance is created as well. The synthetic aspect of our study is thus the work, the design; this procedure, however, makes use of diverse, eclectic approaches that are continually modified and perfected as work progresses. This procedure is justified by the conviction (already expressed above) that the fundamental dimension of architectural significance lies in the reference of architectural language to itself (*autoriflessività*). That is, to the same extent that architecture develops on its own foundation, it signifies its own logical construction. Aldo Rossi elaborates on this, commenting that historical works of architecture such as "Roman monuments, Renaissance Palazzi, Gothic cathedrals, constitute architecture and are part of its construction. As such they will not only come back as history and memory, but as elements of design." In this view, then, the history of architecture is not an enormous field of stored experiences, design results, and attempted possibilities but the site where the significance of architecture is defined according to our interpretation. Every work refers conversely to the history of its own type, to the relevant reference to technology, to nature, to related figurative phenomena, and so on. Understanding the significance of an architecture work thus means situating it in a dense network of relationships, assigning it a place in a value system. Under such conditions, the concept of context takes on a new, more comprehensive dimension. We can speak of a context *in presenza* (the architecture of the place, the usual "historical" context); we can also supplement this by the context *in assenza* and by that mean, roughly, the architectural imagination that produced a project by way of manifold associations, the formative energies that emerge from grappling with the history of architecture, and so on. Building is thus always a building in context, even if the latter is not physically tangible.

Architectural significance is understood in a way similar to that of a language: it is a system—albeit one that is constantly evolving— a coherent whole of parts whose generative rules have to be learned arduously in practice. We speak this language and are spoken by it. A study that attempts to inventory the typological, morphological, technological-functional norms that are defined by a historically datable collective use obtains an exact meaning in this way. For the design, these insights make possible the articulation of an exact and intelligible discourse insofar as the various codes are updated in an *acte de parole*. This updating is unique and unrepeatable because it is also tied to a specific site and to the architect's will to express. Given the self-referential, "self-reflexive" language of architecture, it is necessary to explore how this "self-reflexivity"

Umkreis, überhaupt in Bereichen semiologischer Studien (insbesondere denjenigen, die sich auf den russischen Formalismus berufen oder dem Strukturalismus französischer Prägung zugerechnet werden müssen) und schliesslich in bestimmten Ausrichtungen der neueren amerikanischen Architektur feststellen lassen.

Diese Ueberlegungen sollen im folgenden kurz zusammengefasst werden. Anschliessend werden wir bei der Diskussion von Entwürfen und Bauten versuchen, ihre operative Tragweite für Kritik und Entwurf zumindest zu erläutern.

Die Untersuchung der Architektur der Stadt, der Analyse der Bauten der Moderne und die Entwurfstätigkeit selbst bilden strukturell aufeinander bezogene Versuche, Architektur als Zeichen zu verstehen. Eine solche Beschäftigung mit der Architektur tendiert auf einem operativen Diskurs über die Beziehung – und über die Natur dieser Beziehung –, welche einen empirischen Gegenstand (die Architektur) mit der ihm zugehörigen und von ihm aus entwickelten kognitiven Erfahrung verbindet. Das heisst mit anderen Worten: dieser empirische Gegenstand wird als Signifikant eines Zeichens verstanden, das sein Signifikat einerseits im allgemeinsten Kontext des sozialen Lebens und der Institutionen der Gesellschaft findet, in der es auftritt. Andererseits schafft sich die Architektur ihr Signifikat selbst, insofern jede einzelne Architektur im wesentlichen ihre eigene «Natur» reflektiert («autoreflessività» des Kunstwerks). Die Bedeutung (Signifikat) einer Architektur ist demnach die Ausstattung eines Gegenstandes mit «Sinn»: einem Sinn, der also dem sozialen Gebrauch im weitesten Rahmen inhärent ist. Dabei kommt nun der Entwurfstätigkeit wie der historisch-kritischen Analyse insofern eine kategoriell bevorzugte Rolle zu, als sie den Sinn der architektonischen Entstehungsgeschichte und die spezifische Bedeutung ihres Gegenstandes, d. h. die besondere Eigenart als architektonisches Kunstwerk zu erfassen sucht. Diese Bedeutung bezieht sich auf ein typologisches, morphologisches, technologisch-konstruktives, funktionales, ikonographisches und schliesslich ideologisches Wissen, andererseits auf die Epistemologie der Architektur als einem spezifischen Produkt gemäss den Begriffen und Katego-

La tendance qui s'est formée autour des études théoriques et des projets d'Aldo Rossi en Italie, les écrits et projets de Robert Venturi et des «Five Architects» (Eisenman, Graves, Gwathmy, Hejduk, Meier) etc. . . . , ainsi que les plus prudentes approches sémiotiques de l'architecture, proposent une compréhension de l'architecture qui tend toujours plus à rapprocher la manière de faire un projet à celle de la critiquer.

En face d'une historiographie sociologique et idéologico-critique aguérie, qui a souvent préfiguré en termes apocalyptiques la fin de l'objet même de son analyse, une nouvelle tendance se dessine. Celle-ci propose l'étude des liens internes à la construction, à la genèse de l'architecture, et revendique des tâches assez semblables à celles que le formalisme russe avaient remplies, dans les deux premières décennies du siècle, en s'occupant de la «littérarité» de la littérature.

Pour ce mouvement l'histoire de l'architecture est non seulement un immense dépôt d'expériences, d'indications et de projets, mais aussi le lieu où se définit la signification de l'architecture. Dans cette perspective, la recherche est dirigée vers l'étude des structures rhétoriques et poétiques du discours architectural.

L'histoire de l'architecture est le contexte nécessaire et indispensable des projets. Ainsi il n'y a plus de séparation en catégories entre les problèmes de restauration et de construction dans les «centres historiques» d'une part, et tout le reste de l'architecture d'autre part. On pourra le cas échéant parler d'un contexte «en présence» ou bien «en absence».

Finalement, la restauration et la construction dans les centres historiques sont des révélateurs de la rationalité et de la valeur cognitive de l'architecture contemporaine. Les projets préfigurent une «critique opérative», qui récupère la recherche historique et défend le droit à un «plaisir de l'architecture» contre l'impassibilité scientifique de l'histoire de l'art traditionnelle, le puritanisme de l'analyse idéologique et le vieux mythe réactionnaire du «cœur de la ville».

rien der Architekturtheorie. Es wäre Aufgabe einer architektonischen Semantik, das begriffliche Instrumentarium zu entwickeln, das es erlaubte, die so abstrakt definierten architektonischen Bedeutungen zu beschreiben, zu untersuchen und zu klassifizieren.

Als Architekten – und dies bildet in der Folge eine notwendige Einschränkung – steht vor uns die Entwurfstätigkeit im Vordergrund. Wir suchen dabei zu erklären, dass zusammen mit dem architektonischen Werk auch dessen Bedeutung geschaffen wird. Synthetisches Moment unserer Untersuchung ist somit das Werk, der Entwurf; das Vorgehen jedoch bedient sich eklektisch verschiedenster Annäherungsweisen, die im Fortgang der Arbeit ständig modifiziert und vervollkommnet werden. Dieses Vorgehen rechtfertigt sich durch die (schon ober geäusserte) Ueberzeugung, wonach die grundlegende Dimension der architektonischen Bedeutung in der Bezogenheit der architektonischen Sprache, auf sich selbst liegt («autoreflessività»). Oder anders ausgedrückt: In demselben Ausmasse, in dem sich die Architektur auf ihrer eigenen Grundlage weiterentwickelt, bedeutet sie ihre eigene logische Konstruktion. Aldo Rossi führt dazu aus: «Die Werke der Architekturgeschichte . . . die römischen Monumente, die Paläste der Renaissance, die Schlösser, die gotischen Kathedralen bilden die Architektur: als solche werden sie nicht sosehr und nicht nur als Geschichte und Erinnerung auftauchen, sondern auch als Elemente des Entwerfens wiederkehren.» Danach wäre also die Architekturgeschichte nicht ein gewaltiges Feld abgelagerter Erfahrungen, Entwurfsergebnissen und erprobten Möglichkeiten, sondern vielmehr der Ort, wo sich gemäss unserer Darlegung die Bedeutung der Architektur definiert. Jedes Werk verweist umgekehrt auf die Geschichte seines eigenen Typs, auf den jeweiligen Bezug zur Technologie, zur Natur, zu verwandten figurativen Erscheinungen, usw. Die Bedeutung eines architektonischen Werkes verstehen heisst somit, es in einem dichten Netz von Beziehungen zu situieren, ihm einen Platz in einem Wertsystem zuzuweisen. Unter solchen Umständen gewinnt der Begriff des Kontextes eine neue, umfassendere Dimension. Wir können von einem Kontext «in presenza» sprechen (die Architektur des Ortes, der übliche «historische» Kontext); wir können diesen aber zudem ergänzen durch den Kontext «in assenza» und meinen damit etwa die architektonische Imagination, die ein Projekt über mannigfache Assoziationen hervorgerufen hat, die formenden Kräfte, die aus der Auseinandersetzung mit der Architekturgeschichte hervorgegangen sind, usw. Bauen ist also immer ein Bauen im Kontext, auch wenn dieser nicht physisch greifbar ist.

Die architektonische Bedeutung wird ähnlich derjenigen einer Sprache aufgefasst: sie ist ein — wenn auch in stetiger Entwicklung begriffenes — System, ein zusammenhängendes Ganzes aus Teilen, dessen generative Regeln wir erst im Gebrauche mühsam erlernen. Wir sprechen diese Sprache und werden von ihr gesprochen. Eine Untersuchung, die sich vornimmt, den Bestand an typologischen, morphologischen, technologisch-funktionalen Normen aufzunehmen, die von einem historisch datierbaren kollektiven Gebrauch definiert worden sind, gewinnt damit einen exakten Sinn. Für den Entwurf gestatten diese Erkenntnisse die Artikulierung eines exakten und intelligiblen Diskurses, insofern die verschiedenen Codes in einem «acte de parole» aktualisiert werden. Diese Aktualisierung ist einmalig und nicht wiederholbar, weil sie stets an eine bestimmte Situation und an den Ausdruckswillen des Architekten gebunden ist. Aufgrund der auf sich selbst bezogenen «autoreflexiven» Sprache der Architektur muss die Art und Weise erforscht werden, in der sich diese «Autoflexivität» zeigt. Dies kommt dem Postulat einer architektonischen Poetik, d. h. einer architekturimmanenten Theorie gleich, die sich der Erarbeitung von Kategorien vornimmt, die geeignet sind, gleichzeitig Einheit und Verschiedenheit aller architektonischen Werke und also die dort vorfindbaren poetischen Verfahrensweisen zu erfassen.

Die systematische Analyse der Architekturwerke müsste zur Feststellung der poetischen Strukturen führen und zugleich verifizieren, ob Begriffe wie Homologie zwischen verschiedenen Systemen (dem typologischen, distributiven, statischen, konstruktiven usw.), Vergleich, Norm und Normbruch, Verfremdung usw., geeignet seien, die Natur des architektonischen Diskurses zu beschreiben.

Zürich

Der erste Entwurf, den wir vorstellen, ist eigens für eine Ausstellung von Entwurfsuntersuchungen der internationalen Abteilung für Architektur an der 15. Triennale di Milano ausgearbeitet worden. In ihm wurden die hier vorgebrachten Hypothesen als operatives Modell verwendet: von der Wahl des Standortes, der typologischen Form bis hin zu den morphologischen — und Detailentscheidungen beabsichtigt das Projekt einen Diskurs über die Architektur, über das Bild der Stadt Zürich, über ihre gebauten und gedachten Architekturen im besonderen. Wir werden den Entwurf von diesem Gesichtspunkt her beschreiben.

Wenn in Zürich, wie jemand scharfsinnig bemerkt hat, Kultur und geschäftiger Bürgersinn der Stadt mit der Bahnhofstrasse und dem Seequais ein ideologisches Antlitz gegeben haben, so prägen anderseits diese beiden Elemente auch in entscheidendem Masse die Individualität der Stadt. In einem Punkte aber erbrachte der beharrliche Wille zur Eigenzelebration keine architektonische Lösung. Trotz wiederholter Versuche bleibt die Nahtstelle zwischen Bahnhofstrasse und Seequais ein ungelöster Punkt im Stadtsystem des 19. Jahrhunderts.

Die Schwierigkeiten hinterlassen ihre Spuren in der Widersprüchlichkeit der städtebaulichen Pläne, der aufeinanderfolgenden Gestaltungsideen und auch in den topographischen Eigenarten des Ortes.

In der Tat hat diese Zone, die zum grössten Teil durch Seeaufschüttungen (zwischen 1834 und 1885) entstanden ist, ganze Architektengenerationen angeregt, eine Idee Gottfried Sempers zu interpretieren und weiterzuentwickeln. Dieser hatte 1858 in einem Wettbewerb vorgeschlagen, die Stadt zum See hin zu öffnen und sie aus ihrer überlieferten Ausrichtung auf den Fluss hin zu lösen. Wenn das heutige Quartier in den grossen Linien Sempers Schema bewahrt, so nimmt ihm die Schaffung des Quais durch die gleichwertige Ausrichtung aller Gebäude auf den See die Bedeutung, die ihm Semper verleihen wollte. Die heutige bescheidene Panoramaterrasse ist nur ein bescheidener Notbehelf, die die Verlegenheit angesichts dieses unbewältigten Konflikts verrät.

Die späteren Vorschläge erklären die Natur des architektonischen Problems. Beim Wettbewerb von 1924 schlagen einige Entwerfer auf der anderen Seite des Quais eine szenographische Verdoppelung der Semperschen Anlage im See vor, allerdings unter Berücksichtigung der axialen Struktur der Quartieranlage. Andere hingegen zeigen einen bereits grösseren Abstand, wenn nicht schon Unverständnis, gegenüber dem bisherigen Stadtbild, und suchen ihren kompositorischen Ausgangspunkt allein in der topographischen Begebenheit, wie etwa jenes Projekt, das eine Nahtstelle (Zäsur) zwischen Fluss und See konstruiert und mit einer «romantisch» autonomen Volumenkomposition das gesamte Quartier umkrempelt.

Die öffentlichen Räume, die sich gegen den See hin aneinanderreihen, finden ihren Ansatzpunkt in der Typologie des Kappeler- und Zentralhofes. Der städtische und halböffentliche Charakter dieser Hofbebauungen (die Zeit spricht von «Squares») wird radikalisiert und mit dem Bild einer rationalistischen Siedlung verschmolzen, deren Basis in ambivalenter Weise die Stelle zwischen Natur und Architektur zugewiesen ist. Dieses Bild hat entfernte, jedoch nicht zufällige Bezugspunkte in der Idealkonstruktion des Templum Salomonis von Fischer von Erlach, aber auch in Hilbersimers Konzept der Vertikalstadt. Wenn von der Stadt her das Projekt immer noch als grosser, der Architektur des Quartiers wesensverwandter Palast erscheint, präfiguriert die Innengestalt jedoch ein autonomes Stück Stadt, mit Wohnungen, öffentlichen Gebäuden und Plätzen. Eine Stadt, typologisch sosehr von Zürich unterschieden, dass aus der Gegenüberstellung ein gültiger paradigmatischer Bezug resultiert. Die Wirksamkeit dieser synoptischen Stadtdarstellung wird in einem typologischen und ikonographisch-emblematischen Bezug gesucht: die rationalistische Siedlung für Wohnungsbau, die Architektur der Aufklärung — temperiert durch den einem Neoklassizismus zustrebenden Schweizer Rationalismus — steht für öffentliche Gebäude.

Die Gegenüberstellung Architektur vs. Natur findet ihre Fortsetzung in den Abwandlungen des «Basaments», die die «naturalistischen»

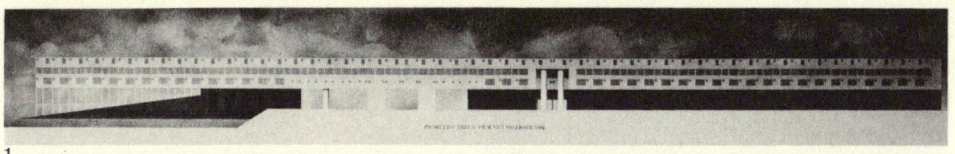

fig. 1 Reichlin / Reinhart: Project for developing the Kratz neighborhood in Zurich. View from Fraumünsterstrasse (1973).

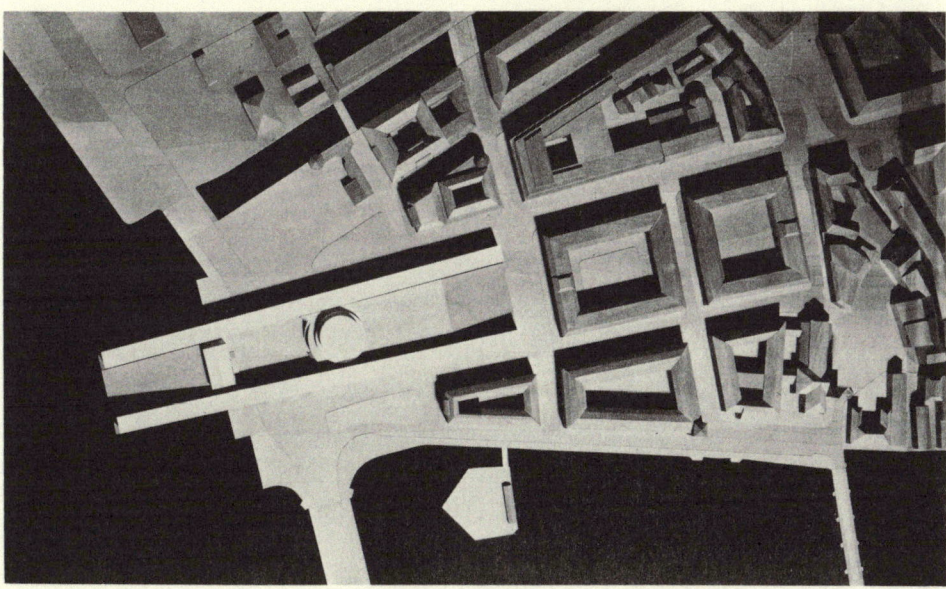

← fig. 2
Model seen from above. Left: the lake; below: Limmat River with the Bauschänzli [artificial island].

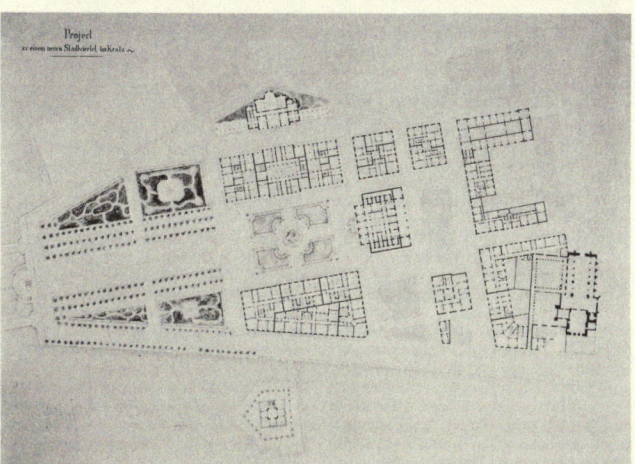

← fig. 3
Gottfried Semper, Project for a new neighborhood in Kratz (1858).

↓ fig. 4   Reichlin / Reinhart: View of the complex of new buildings seen from the lake.

→ fig. 5   Project for a design of the lakeshore in Zurich, 1926.

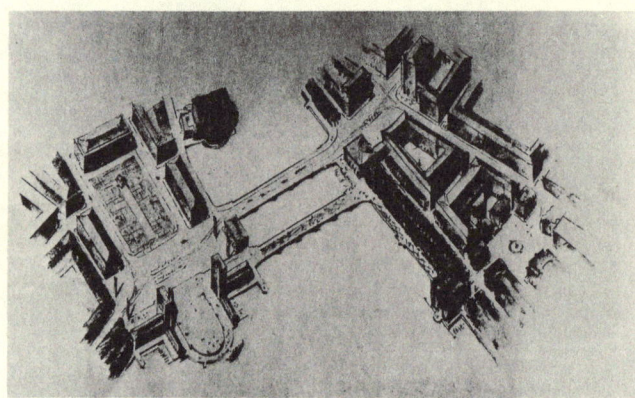

Konnotationen dieses Elementes entfalten. Bereits auf den Frontseiten der Strassen wir der «Rustico»-Charakter des Basamentes stärker betont als bei den Gebäuden im Quartier.

Wo das Gebäude auf den See hinausgeht, erlangt dieses Element immer deutlicher topographische Konnotationen und endet bei der schiefen Terrasse zum Wasser hin.

Die Reihenhäuser der Siedlung sind auf drei Geschossen organisiert. Die Zeichnung der Prospekte macht die analytische Natur von Methode und Resultaten des Rationalismus sichtbar, auf den sie Bezug nehmen. Die Form soll sich der Spur des Sinnes angleichen — als Paraphrase von Pope's Ratschlag an die Dichter: «der Ton soll das Echo des Sinnes aufnehmen.»

Im Entwurf finden wir zwei geneigte Ebenen: die erste verbindet Siedlung und Stadt, indem sie die Höhe des Sockels überwindet, die andere öffnet die Siedlung zum See hin. Die Zeichnung dieser letzteren — ein vergrössertes Fragment des Platzes, an den Canovas Tempel von Possagno grenzt — betont den gerichteten Charakter des Platzes.

Dieses Projekt gewann seine Form aus der Diskussion der vorausgegangenen Entwürfe. Und indem es sich diesen Entwürfen anschliesst, liefert es schliesslich deren Bewertung. Die Sempersche Idee eines Architekturparkes, als Keil in den See projiziert, ist in der geneigten Ebene erreicht, die, so wie sie ausserhalb des Quais situiert ist, zum Angelpunkt zwischen See und Fluss wird; wie in Sempers Entwurf steht auf der Hauptachse der Panoramaterrasse ein öffentliches Gebäude.

Der Entwurf umfasst zwei Elemente, die die leicht konvergierenden Linien der Bahnhof- und Fraumünsterstrasse bis in den See hinaus verlängern und grenzt mit den Schmalseiten, an denen sich die öffentlichen Gebäude finden (der gedeckte Platz und der Pavillon über dem See) einen inneren offenen Hof ab. Die langen zeilenförmigen Baukörper sind in der Höhe in zwei Zonen gegliedert: die untere, von der Ebene der Stadt aus zugänglich, sieht im Erdgeschoss und Mezzanin Ladengeschäfte vor. Die obere Zone, durch einen Laubengang sechs Meter über dem Strassenniveau erschlossen, umfasst in erster Linie dreigeschossige Reihenwohnungen und im Abschnitt über der Strasse Büro- und Geschäftsräume, sowie auf einen kleinen Hof, im obersten Stock Kleinwohnungen.

Der Hypothese, die die Bezogenheit der architektonischen Sprache auf sich selber zugrundelegt, entspricht der Wille, den Gegenstand und die Art und Weise der eigenen entwerferischen Auseinandersetzung exakt zu bestimmen. Der Entwurf umfasst, zumindest als «objet trouvé», den Bezugskontext, den er sich gegeben hat und den er statuiert: Kontext «in presenza»: die Architektur des Ortes — Kontext «in assenza»: die Entwürfe und Bauten, die durch Assoziation (in einer ikonographischen Montage) evoziert sind.

reveals itself. It is like the postulate of an architectural poetics; that is, like a theory immanent to architecture that works out categories that are suitable to grasping simultaneously the unity and difference of all architectural works and hence the poetic procedures that can be found there.

The systematic analysis of works of architecture must lead to the determination of poetic structures and at the same time verify whether concepts such as homology between different systems (typological, distributive, static, constructional, and so on), comparison, norm and the violation of norm, alienation, and so on, are suited to describing the nature of architectural discourse.

Zurich

The first design we introduce was worked out especially for an exhibition of design studies for the international architecture section of the fifteenth Triennale di Milano. The hypotheses put forward with it were used as an operative model: from the choice of site to the typological form to the morphological and detailed decisions, the project intends to spark a discourse on architecture, on the image of the city of Zurich and, in particular, its built and conceived architectures. We will describe the design from this viewpoint.

If in Zurich, as someone once incisively remarked, culture and bustling public spirit have lent the city, with its Bahnhofstrasse and lakeside quays, an ideological visage, these two elements have also decisively shaped the individuality of the city. In one instance, however, the stubborn will to self-celebration did not provide an architectural solution. Despite repeated attempts, the seam between Bahnhofstrasse and the lakeside quays has remained an unresolved point in the nineteenth-century system for the city.

The difficulties have left their traces in the contradictions of urban planning, in a series of design ideas, and in the unique topographic features of the place.

Indeed, this zone, created largely by a series of land reclamations (from 1834 to 1885) has inspired entire generations of architects to interpret and develop an idea from Gottfried Semper. In a competition in 1858, he had proposed opening up the city to the lake and freeing it of its traditional orientation toward the river. Although the neighborhood today has preserved Semper's schema in broad outlines, the creation of the quay—by orienting all of the buildings equally toward the lake—deprived it of the significance Semper wanted to give it. Today's modest panorama terrace is merely a stopgap that betrays the embarrassment over this unresolved conflict.

The later proposals explain the nature of the architectural problem. In the competition of 1924, several designers proposed a scenographic doubling of Semper's structure in the lake on the other side of the quay, albeit taking into account the axial structure of the arrangement of the neighborhood. Other designers, in contrast, revealed a greater distance from— if not already a misunderstanding of—the cityscape until that point, seeking the point of departure for their composition solely in the topographical feature—for example, one project would have constructed a seam (caesura) between the river and the lake and completely altered the entire neighborhood with a "romantically" autonomous composition of volumes.

The public spaces facing the lake find their point of reference in the typology of the Kappelerhof and the Zentralhof. The urban and semi-public character of these courtyard structures (in their day, they were called "squares") is radicalized and fused with the image of a rationalist development whose basis is ambivalently assigned a place between nature and architecture. This image has remote but not coincidental points of reference in the ideal construction of the Temple of Solomon by Fischer von Erlach but also in Hilberseimer's concept of the vertical city. Although from the city the project still looks like a large palace closely related to the architecture of the neighborhood, the interior design prefigures an autonomous section of city, with apartments, public buildings, and squares—a city typologically so very different from Zurich that the juxtaposition results in a valid paradigmatic reference. The effectiveness of this synoptic account of the city is sought in a typological and iconographic-emblematic reference: the rationalist development stands for residential architecture; the architecture of the Enlightenment, tempered by a Swiss rationalism that strives for a neoclassicism, stands for public buildings.

The juxtaposition of architecture versus nature finds its continuation in the transformations of the *basamento* [base] that develop the "naturalist" connotations of this element. Already on the street facades, the *rustico* character of the *basamento* is emphasized more than on the buildings in the neighborhood.

Where the building extends to the lake, this element takes on increasingly clear topographical connotations and ends at a steep terrace sloping down toward the water.

The rowhouses of the development are organized on three floors. The drawing of the prospects reveals the analytical nature of the rationalist methods and results to which they refer. The form is supposed to adapt to the trace of the sense—as a paraphrase of Pope's advice to the poet: "The sound must seem an echo to the sense."

In the design, we find two inclined levels: the first connects the development and the city by overcoming the height of the base; the other opens the development to the lake. The drawing of the latter—an enlarged fragment of the piazza adjacent to Canova's temple in Possagno—emphasizes the oriented character of the square.

This project derives its form from the discussion of the previous designs. And by taking up these designs, it ultimately provides an assessment of them. Semper's idea of an architectural park projecting like a wedge into the lake is achieved by the inclined level, just as it is situated outside the quay, at the fulcrum between the lake and the river; as in Semper's design, a public building is standing on the main axis of the panoramic terrace.

The design comprises two elements that extend the slightly converging lines of Bahnhofstrasse and Fraumünsterstrasse out to the lake and demarcate, with the short sides where the public buildings are located (the covered square and the pavilion above the lake), an inner, open courtyard. The long, ribbon-like building volumes are divided vertically into two zones: the lower one, accessible from the level of the city, has retail stores on the ground floor and mezzanine. The upper zone, accessed via a loggia six meters above street level, comprises primarily three-story row apartments and, in the section above the street, office and commercial spaces, as well as, in a small courtyard on the top floor, small apartments.

Corresponding to the hypothesis based on architectural language relating to itself is the will to determine exactly the object and the way of addressing it in one's own design. The design includes, at least as an objet trouvé, the context of reference that it established for itself and that it sets as an example: context *in presenza*—the architecture of the place—and context *in assenza*—the designs and buildings evoked by association (in an iconographic montage). We will go into somewhat more detail about that.

The vertical division of the design into two parts has its precise correspondence in the architecture of the nineteenth-century neighborhood: the Zentralhof and the Kappelerhof with their upscale businesses on the ground floor and mezzanine and prestige apartments on the upper stories propose as models the design of a conflict that emerged along with the capitalist city: the separation of the place of work and that of living. This distributive separation into two relates analogously to the stylistic differentiation of the exterior. Iconographically, the rustic wall assigns the role of the base to the ground floor and mezzanine. The column orders, which are often reduced to ciphers even on main facades, are, as a rule, limited to the upper stories. A revealing juxtaposition in the distribution systems: apartments versus commercial spaces. And iconographic juxtaposition in the system of styles: naturalistic versus nonnaturalistic architectural elements correspond to one another in a "unity of two."

Few requirements of the nineteenth century could be expressed in as unmistakable a building type as the gallery, a creation of private speculation in the retail trade. That a place of honor is granted to this building type in the unbuilt parts of Zurich is no coincidence. One is almost tempted to attribute the later designs of a gallery in the form of an autonomous building on the quay, between cultural institutions, more to a sense of incompleteness than to a real need. A gallery—significantly at the opposite end of Bahnhofstrasse from the train station—completes as an equal element the iconographic

↓ fig. 6 Reichlin / Reinhart: View of the complex of new buildings seen from the city.

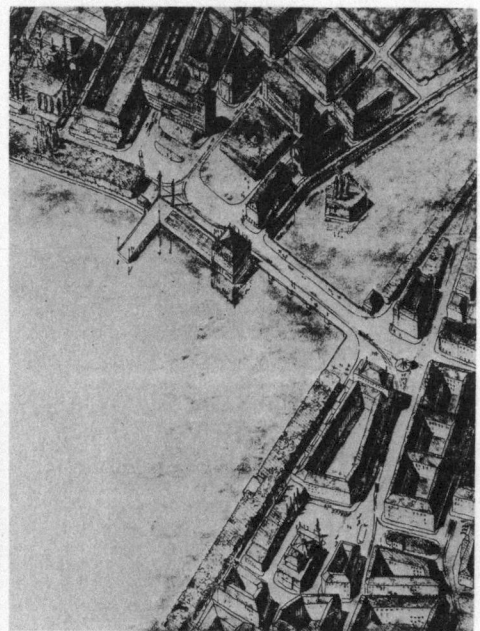

Darauf gehen wir im Folgenden etwas näher ein.
Die vertikale Zweiteilung des Entwurfs hat ihre genaue Entsprechung in der Architektur der Quartieranlage aus dem 19. Jahrhundert: Zentral- und Kappelerhof mit den anspruchsvollen Geschäften im Erdgeschoss und Mezzanin und den herrschaftlichen Wohnungen an den oberen Geschossen schlagen modellhaft die Gestaltung eines Konfliktes vor, der zusammen mit der kapitalistischen Stadt entstanden ist: die Trennung von Arbeits- und Wohnort. Diese distributive Zweiteilung verhält sich analog zu der stilistischen Differenzierung im Aeusseren. Ikonographisch teilt die Rustikamauer dem Erdgeschoss und Mezzanin die Rolle des Sockels zu. Die Säulenordnungen, häufig sogar bei den Hauptfassaden auf Chiffren reduziert, bleiben in der Regel auf die oberen Geschosse beschränkt. Bezeichnende Gegenüberstellung im Distributionssystem: Wohnungen vs. Geschäftsräume. Und ikonographische Gegenüberstellung im stilistischen System: naturalistisches vs. nichtnaturalistisches Architekturelement entsprechen sich «zweieindeutig».
Wenige Erforderungen des 19. Jahrhunderts vermochten sich in einem ähnlich unverwechselbaren Bautyp auszudrücken wie Privatspekulation im Detailhandel in der Schöpfung der Galerie. Es ist nicht Zufall, dass diesem Bautypus im nichtgebauten Zürich ein Ehrenplatz zusteht. Fast ist man versucht, die späteren Entwürfe einer Galerie in der Form eines autonomen Gebäudes am Quai,

25

↑ fig. 7 Project for a design of the lakeshore in Zurich, 1926.

figs. 8–10 M. Campi, F. Pessina, and N. Piazzoli, Restoration of the Castello di Montebello in Bellinzona. Details (1974).

zwischen kulturellen Institutionen, eher einer empfundenen Unvollständigkeit als einem realen Bedürfnis zuzuschreiben. Eine Galerie, bedeutungsvoll und dem Bahnhof am anderen Ende der Bahnhofstrasse gegenübergestellt, vervollständigt als ebenbürtiges Element die ikonographische Ausstattung der Stadt des 19. Jahrhunderts, die dem Flaneur auch heute noch das trügerische Bild der Metropole, der weltbürgerlichen Grosszügigkeit und Liberalität zukehrt. In Uebereinstimmung mit der kanonischen Beschreibung des Typs verbindet sie zwei Strassen, die auf dem Plan, jedoch nicht im aktuellen Gebrauch gleichwertig erscheinen: Bahnhof- und Fraumünsterstrasse. Diese letztere ist — verglichen mit den Plänen, die sie parallel zur ersten durch das ganze historische Zentrum ziehen wollten — Torso geblieben.

Die Einfügung eines rundförmigen Elementes zwischen zwei leicht konvergierende tangenziale Körper, die der zufälligen geometrischen Form des Grundstückes folgt, bereichern den Plan um Kompositionsprobleme, die uns viele Bravourstücke aus der Architektur des 19. Jahrhunderts eingebracht haben.

Bellinzona

Im zweiten hier vorgestellten Beispiel, der Restaurierung des Castello di Montebello in Bellinzona, scheinen der alte viscontinische Befestigungsbau und die neuen Strukturen im Verhältnis morphologischer, technologischer, statischer Ungleichheit zu sein. Bei genauerem Hinsehen lassen sich diese Gegensätze auf gezielt berechnete Analogien in Form von Antithesen zurückführen. Die erste betrifft zwei verschiedene statische Prinzipien (Zug und Druck): eine Metallstruktur ist oben an den dicken Mauern des Turmes aufgehängt. Die zweite betrifft verschiedene technologische Auffassungen: Minimum an Differenzierung (funktionale Morphologie der rauhen Steinkonstruktion des Schlosses); grösster Differenziertheitsgrad der neuen Konstruktion in Metall und Holz (Gelenke, Verzahnungen, Platten, Bolzen, Doppel-T-Profile usw.), die jedoch auch als bewusste thematische Wahl aufzufassen sind, die die Gesamtausstattung miteinbe-

↓ fig. 11   Aldo Rossi, Cemetery project for Modena (1971).

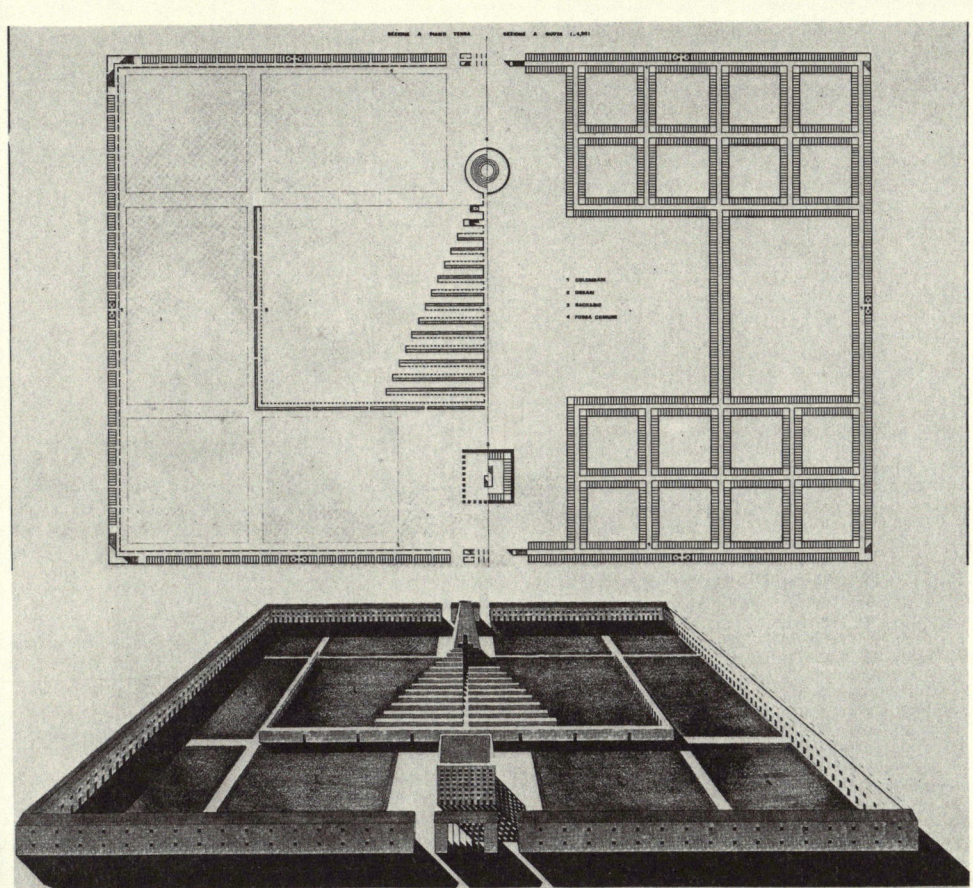

zieht. Die Gleichförmigkeit der Detailbehandlung in Gelenkstellen wie Profilen steht zusätzlich im Kontrast zu diesem Diskontinuum einer Assemblage. Die dritte Antithese betrifft die verschiedenen Morphologien: geometrische Indifferenz im unregelmässigen alten Gebäude; vollendete Geometrie mit dem Quadrat als Grundform in der neuen Konstruktion.

In Anbetracht einer an Sinngebungen reichbefrachteten Architektur, wie sie eben ein mittelalterliches Schloss mit all seinen Fabelhintergründen darstellt, will die Restaurierung des Castello di Montebello auf dem Prinzip der Antithese («figure de style par rapprochement») die Distanz zwischen Alt und Neu überbrücken und versucht gleichzeitig, die Grenzen einer historisieren-

den, anpassenden Restaurierung zu überwinden, die weder der Imagination freien Raum lässt, noch an die Möglichkeiten einer echten Integration glaubt. Alte und neue Struktur entsprechen sich aufs beste in der Definition des gemeinsamen Ortes als einer vertikal-bestimmten, dynamischen Einheit. Das ganze Museum wird dementsprechend zu einer kontinuierlichen Abfolge rhythmisch von

↓ fig. 12 Aldo Rossi, Project for the town hall in Muggiò, Milan, 1971.

Podest zu Podest sich folgender Raumzellen und vermeidet die brutale Unterteilung in langweilig übereinandergeschichtete Geschosse.

Modena

Wenige Werke der Architektur spiegeln so unmittelbar und mit so grosser Intensität den historischen Sinn architektonischer Formen wie das Projekt Aldo Rossis für den Friedhof San Cataldo in Modena. Das hervorgerufene Bild ist aufs engste mit der typologischen Tradition des Friedhofes verknüpft: der Stadt der Toten als der Entsprechung zur Stadt der Lebenden. Folgen wir der Beschreibung des Architekten: «Die Gesamtheit dieser Bauten formiert sich zu einer Stadt; in dieser Stadt wird die private Beziehung zum Tod zur bürgerlichen Beziehung zur Institution. Der Friedhof ist somit noch ein öffentliches Gebäude mit der notwendigen Klarheit und Logik seiner Strukturen und mit einer vernünftigen Ausnützung des Raumes; nach aussen abgeschlossen von einer Mauer mit Fenstern. Das düstere Thema lässt ihn nicht allzusehr von den übrigen öffentlichen Gebäuden unterscheiden. Seine Ordnung und Stellung lassen sich auch den bürokratischen Aspekt des Todes mitbeinhalten. Der Friedhof ist ein definierter Ort: dieser Friedhof weicht nicht von der Idee eines Friedhofes ab, die ein jeder besitzt. Die Architektur braucht ja lediglich die eigenen Elemente sinnvoll, im richtigen Zusammenhang zu verwenden, indem sie alle Möglichkeiten von sich weist, die nicht dem eigenen Entstehungsprozess entstammen: demzufolge definiert sich der Bezugsrahmen des Friedhofes in der Architektur des Friedhofes, des Hauses, der Stadt. Die Monumente entsprechen hier dem Verhältnis von Leben und Behausung in der modernen Stadt. So stellt der Würfel ein verödetes oder unvollendetes Haus dar, mit leeren Fenstern, ohne Dach, und der Kegelbau ist ein Kamin einer verlassenen Fabrik. Die Analogie mit dem Tod erfasst der Verstand lediglich in den ausgeführten Dingen, am Ende der Dinge: jeder andere Bezug bleibt unsagbar. . . . . Der Tod drückte einen Zustand des Ueberganges zweier Bereiche aus, deren Grenzen nicht festgelegt waren. Aber die etruskischen Aschenurnen in Form von Häusern und das Grab des Bäckers Eurysaces in Rom bezeugen den historischen Zusammenhang zwischen verlassenem Haus und verlassener Arbeit.»

Muggiò

Aldo Rossis Entwurf für das Rathaus in Muggiò in der Provinz Mailand zeigt, wie die Architektur ihre Bezugspunkte auch in anderen Kunstgattungen, im Bereiche des Figurativen finden kann. Dadurch, dass ein Bild in seinem selektiv-synthetisierenden Charakter eine bewusste kulturelle Wahl darstellt, vermag es beim Aufbau des Sinnes als ausgesprochener Bezugspunkt und Paradigma zu funktionieren.

In einem individualisierenden architektonischen und städtebaulichen Elementen armen Kontext wie in demjenigen einer kleinen Stadt an der Mailänder Peripherie kann der Bezug zu den vom Maler De Chirico porträtierten italienischen Plätzen einer städtebaulich anonymen Situation Individualität verleihen.

Seitenblick

auf Ernst May und die Siedlung «Römerstadt»

Unser letztes Beispiel zeigt auf eindrückliche Weise, wie auch die Werke des Neuen Bauens — also einer sich als ausgesprochen antihistorisch gebärdenden Tendenz — ihre Bedeutung durch die mittelbare und unmittelbare Auseinandersetzung mit der Tradition gewinnen.

Ernst May's «Römerstadt» beruht in ihrer rationalen Lösung der Erschliessungs- und der übrigen funktionellen Probleme, die sich von keinen pseudo-psychologischen Scheinargumenten irreführen lässt, auf derselben Siedlungs- und Bautypologie, die wir aus unzähligen Siedlungen der Geschichte kennen.

Die knappe, präzise Morphologie des Neuen Bauens beschreibt den Typ und verleiht ihm die Einprägsamkeit eines Exempels. Wo aber die Siedlung durch das beabsichtigte organische Anschmiegen an die Topographie sich aufzulösen drohte, setzte Ernst May ein klassisches städtebauliches Element ein: die

outfitting of the nineteenth-century city, which even today offers the flaneur the deceptive image of the metropolis, of cosmopolitan generosity and liberalism. In correspondence with the canonic description of the type, it is connected by two streets, which seem equals on the map but not in actual use: Bahnhofstrasse and Fraumünsterstrasse. The latter remains a torso despite plans proposing to continue it through the entire historical center in parallel with the former.

The insertion of a round element between two slightly converging, tangential volumes, following the arbitrary geometric form of the property, enriches the plan with the compositional complications that yielded many bravura works of nineteenth-century architecture.

Bellinzona

In the second example presented here—the restoration of the Castello di Montebello in Bellinzona—the old Visconti fortification and the new structures seem to be in a relationship of morphological, technological, and static inequality. On closer inspection, these contradictions can be traced back to deliberately calculated analogies in the form of antitheses. The first concerns two static principles (tension and compression): a metal structure is suspended on the thick walls of the tower. The second concerns different technological conceptions: a minimum of differentiation (functional morphology of the rough stone construction of the castle); highest degree of differentiation of the new construction in metal and wood (joints, gears, plates, bolts, double-T profiles, and so on), which are, however, also to be understood as a conscious thematic choice that integrates the overall design. The uniformity of the treatment of the details in the joint areas and the profiles also contrasts with this discontinuous assemblage. The third antithesis concerns the different morphologies: geometric indifference in the irregular old building; perfected geometry with the square as a basic form in the new construction.

In view of an architecture richly laden with meanings, as represented precisely by a medieval castle with all its fabulous backgrounds, the restoration of the Castello di Montebello seeks to bridge the distance between old and new based on the principle of the antithesis (*figure de style par rapprochement*) and at the same time tries to overcome the limits of a historicizing, adapting restoration that neither leaves free play for the imagination nor believes in the possibilities of a genuine integration. The old and the new structure correspond perfectly in the definition of the common place as a vertically determined, dynamic unity. Accordingly, the entire museum becomes a continuous sequence of spatial cells that follows rhythmically from half-landing to half-landing and avoids the brutal subdivision into one floor boringly stacked above another.

Modena

Few works of architecture mirror so directly and with such great intensity the historical meaning of architectural forms as does Aldo Rossi's project for the San Cataldo Cemetery in Modena. The image evoked is very closely tied to the typological tradition of the cemetery: the city of the dead as the correspondence to the city of the living. Let us follow the architect's description: "Together, all of the buildings read as a city in which the private relationship with death happens to be the civil relationship with the institution. Thus the cemetery is also a public building with an inherent clarity in its circulation and its land use. Externally, it is closed by a fenestrated wall.

The elegiac theme does not separate it much from other public buildings. Its order and its location also contain the bureaucratic aspect of death. The project attempts to solve the most important technical issues in the same manner as they are solved when designing a house, a school, or a hotel. As opposed to a house, a school, or a hotel, where life itself modifies the work and its growth in time, the cemetery foresees all modifications; in the cemetery, time possesses a different dimension. Faced with this relationship, architecture can only use its given elements, refusing any suggestion not born out of its own making; therefore, the references to the cemetery are also found in the architecture of the cemetery, the house, and the city. Here, the monument is analogous to the relationship between life and buildings in the modern city. The cube is an abandoned or unfinished house; the cone is the chimney of a deserted factory. The analogy with death is possible only when dealing with the finished object, with the end of all things: any relationship, other than that of the deserted house and the abandoned work, is consequently untransmittable. ... Death expressed a state of transition between two conditions, the borders of which were not clearly defined. The urns, shaped like Etruscan houses, and the Roman Baker's tomb express the everlasting relationship between the deserted house and the abandoned work."

Muggiò

Aldo Rossi's design for the town hall in Muggiò in the province of Milan shows how architecture can find its points of reference in other artistic genres as well, in the realm of the figurative. Because an image in its selective-synthesizing character represents a conscious cultural choice, it can function as a decided point of reference and paradigm in the construction of meaning.

In a context lacking in individualizing architectural and urban planning elements, such as that of a small town on the periphery of Milan, the reference to the Italian squares portrayed by the painter de Chirico can lend individuality to an anonymous urban planning site.

A Side-Glance at Ernst May and the "Römerstadt" Housing Development

Our final example demonstrates impressively how even the works of modern architecture—that is, a trend with a decidedly antihistorical gesture—obtain their significance through direct and indirect engagement with tradition.

Ernst May's "Römerstadt" is based—in terms of its rational solution to access and other functional problems, which cannot be misled by any specious, pseudopsychological arguments—on the same typology of the development and the building that we know from countless historical developments.

The concise, precise morphology of modern architecture describes the type and lends it the impressiveness of an example. But where the housing development was at risk of being broken up by the intended organic embrace of the topography, Ernst May employed a classic urban planning element: a quay promenade extending toward the Nidda Valley. By doing so, he gave Römerstadt its unmistakable individuality and distinguished its urban character—something that could never succeed in our much more densely built developments. In Römerstadt, the housing development and the quay promenade follow the topography and trace it, but a classical architectural element in the sense of an *embellissement de la ville* draws a precise line between the development and nature, between inside and outside.

These few examples, which are, however, representative of many, should have demonstrated how every example of architecture—the author's conscious intention is not decisive here—and every design expresses a judgment about the architectural tradition, a historical knowledge or ignorance.

Accordingly, restoration and building in the historical context are merely striking aspects of a broader problem: no work can be seen and understood separate from the tradition of architecture.

Restoring and building in the historical context become rather the genuine touchstone of the rational and cognitive value of contemporary architecture.

[Editor's note: For the non-referenced citations, see Aldo Rossi, "Architecture for Museums," in *Aldo Rossi: Selected Writings and Projects*, ed. John O'Regan (London: Architectural Design; Dublin: Gandon, 1983), 21; and Aldo Rossi, "The Blue of the Sky," in ibid., 47.]

↓ fig. 13 Giorgio de Chirico, "Semantic reference point" for the design of the center of Muggiò.

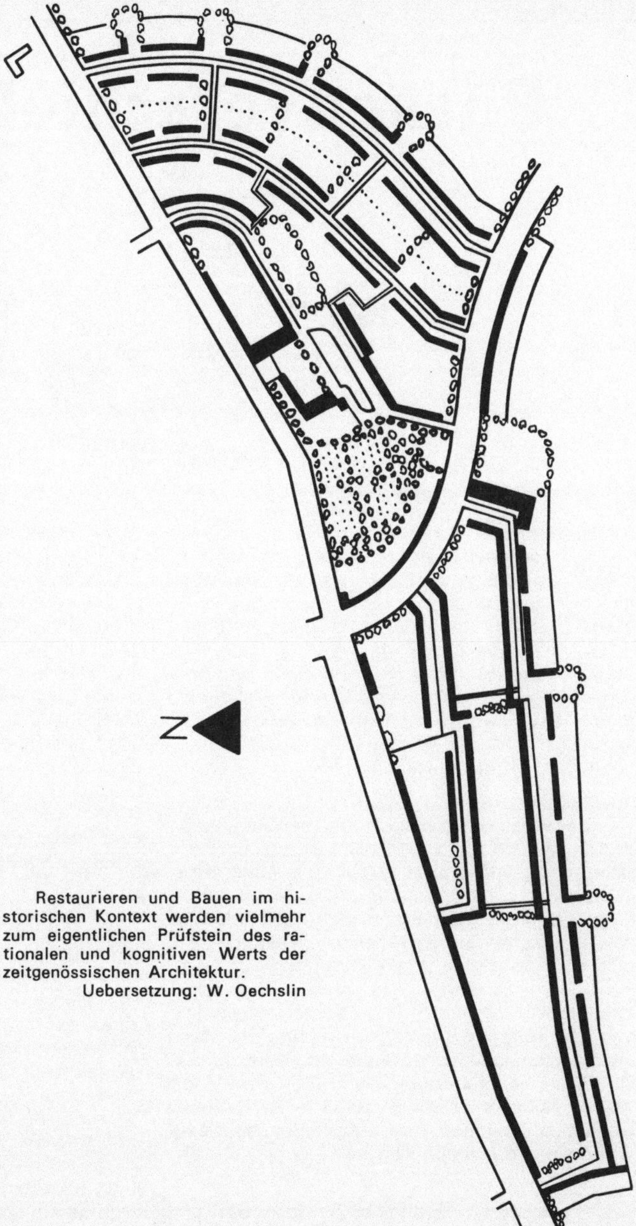

← fig. 14
Ernst May,
Site plan for
the Römerst
housing
developmen
Frankfurt
(after 1926).

Quaipromenade gegen das Niddatal hin. Dadurch verleiht er der Römerstadt ihre unverkennbare Individualität und unterscheidet ihren städtischen Charakter: etwas, das in unseren viel dichter bebauten Siedlungen nie gelingen konnte. In der Römerstadt folgen Siedlung und Quaipromenade der Topographie und zeichnen diese nach; aber ein klassisches architektonisches Element im Sinne eines «Embellissement de la ville» zieht eine präzise Grenze zwischen Siedlung und Natur, zwischen Innen und Aussen.

Diese wenigen Beispiele, die jedoch repräsentativ für viele sind, sollten gezeigt haben, wie in jeder Architektur – die bewusste Absicht des Autors ist hier nicht entscheidend – wie in jedem Entwurf ein Urteil über die architektonische Tradition, ein geschichtliches Wissen, beziehungsweise Nichtwissen zum Ausdruck kommt.

Demnach sind also Restaurieren und Bauen im historischen Kontext nur augenfällige Aspekte eines umfassenderen Problems: kein Werk kann losgelöst von der Tradition der Architektur betrachtet und verstanden werden.

Restaurieren und Bauen im historischen Kontext werden vielmehr zum eigentlichen Prüfstein des rationalen und kognitiven Werts der zeitgenössischen Architektur.

Uebersetzung: W. Oechslin

S. von Moos

Phasenverschiebungen

Als Hintergrund
Der vorliegende Aufsatz nimmt den Umweg über Amerika unter die Füsse, um über das Naheliegende, die Situation daheim, in der Schweiz, etwas unverblümter reden zu können. Er handelt — der Mode zum Trotz — vornehmlich von Aeusserlichkeiten: von Erscheinungen und persönlichen Eindrücken. Diese können vielleicht in drei lose zusammenhängenden Thesen subsummiert werden — Thesen, die für das Folgende als Hintergrund dienen sollen:

1.
Die Vorstellung von Amerika als der «neuen Welt» will sich nicht mehr decken mit der Erfahrung; sie ist veraltet. Wohl ist drüben alles grösser und mächtiger, aber nicht neuer. Von dem Zerfall der Städte nicht zu reden: auch die amerikanischen Strassenkreuzer, Wolkenkratzer, Autobahnen, Plakatwände stehen heute Teils herum als eine Art gigantischen Schrotts. Es gibt dieselben Dinge inzwischen auch bei uns, oft (zumindest technisch) solider, moderner, geschmackvoller, «sauberer». Kurz: neuer. Der Boom hat später eingesetzt; ihm stand, so will es scheinen, mehr Know-How zu Gebote. Ist Europa (zumindest der hochindustrialisierte Teil davon) die «neue Welt»?

2.
Die moderne Architektur hat in Amerika Fuss gefasst vor allem im Zeichen des New Deal (nach dem «reinigenden» Schock der Krise von 1929) und im Bereich des tertiären Sektors (Bürobauten). Dazu kommt — v. a. seit 1948 — der soziale Wohnbau, der die modernen Prinzipien gründlich in Verruf gebracht hat. Die Wohnkultur, das Sentiment des kleinen Mannes, klammert sich nach wie vor an die traditionellen Zeichen bürgerlicher Sinnenfreude. (Man beachte das Möbelassortiment irgendeines populären Warenhauses.) Die Moderne, einerseits mit dem Hochschul- und Verwaltungssektor, anderseits mit der Welt des «urban renewal» assoziiert, blieb weitgehend eine Sache von Big Business und intellektueller Elite; sie scheint für die Mehrheit nicht attraktiv zu sein.
Anders das industrialisierte Nachkriegseuropa, vorab die Schweiz: hier vermochte die Moderne (d. h. die Reformbewegung, die etwa vom Bauhaus ausging und von den Werkbünden getragen wurde) bis in den Mittelstand hinein Fuss zu fassen. So scheint sich z. B. der Schweizer Kleinbürger (im Gegensatz zum amerikanischen) wohlzufühlen angesichts von guter, zumindest «sachlicher» Grafik. (Man vergleiche MIGROS-Werbung mit derjenigen von A—P oder FINAST.) «Moderne Gestaltung» trifft sich da mit einer puritanisch-bürokratischen Vorliebe für «saubere Lösungen» und mit dem Wohlgefallen an einer Ordnung, wo der Durchschnitt hoch, das Hervorragende aber selten ist.

Phase Shifts

Author:
Stanislaus von Moos

First published in:
archithese, 16 (1975): 26–36

Translated by:
Steven Lindberg

Background

The present essay takes America as an excuse to speak somewhat more frankly about the obvious; that is, the situation at home, in Switzerland. Albeit going against the trend, it focuses on outward appearance and personal impressions. They can perhaps be subsumed in three loosely connected propositions, which may serve as a background to what then follows.

1.

The notion of America as the "New World" no longer concurs with our experience; it has become outdated. Everything may be bigger and mightier across the Atlantic, but not newer. Not to mention the urban degradation: Today, America's big cars, skyscrapers, freeways, and billboards are scattered around like colossal pieces of junk. We have those things in our country, too, by now—though in general they come in an impeccably crafted form, solid, modern, tasteful, and "clean." In a word: new. The boom started later and appears to have benefited from greater know-how. Is Europe (or at least its highly industrialized parts) now the "New World"?

2.

"Modern architecture" in America mainly established itself as part of the New Deal (triggered by the "purgative" shock of the 1929 crash) and primarily so in the tertiary sector (office buildings). The big housing projects followed later—particularly so after 1948—and they did much to seriously damage modernism's popular reputation. In the meantime, the sentiments of the "common man" continue to cling to bourgeois ideas of sensual gratification (see the furniture ranges in any big department store). Modernism, affiliated with the world of business, bureaucracy, and schools—as well as, more recently, with "urban renewal"—largely remains a concern of the intellectual elite; it appears to be unattractive to the majority of people.

The situation is different in industrialized postwar Europe, and particularly in Switzerland, where modernism (i.e., the reform movement that emerged roughly during the Bauhaus period and was supported by the Werkbund) has managed to gain a foothold in the middle class. As a result, and rather unlike his American counterpart, the Swiss petit bourgeois appears to feel at home with "functional" graphics (compare MIGROS or CO-OP advertising with campaigns by A+P and FINAST). "Modern design" thus appears as an equivalent to a puritanical preference for "tidy solutions" as well as to an equally visceral delight in the orderly; in short: a rationalized everyday where the average standard is high but outstanding achievement is rare.

3.
The American city gives architecture a leeway that was lost long ago in Europe—if it ever existed in the first place. Office buildings are part of the corporate identity of leading interest groups and trusts. Thus, the nonconformity (with respect to the historical and topographical context), overwhelming scale, and design originality are perceived as desirable, since they contribute to the "visibility" of the respective corporation or patron. Unlike Europe, with its restrictive roof lines, and so on, American zoning regulations encourage the staging of particular achievements.

Thus, architects have "more say" in the USA. They have a greater chance of slipping into positions with *plein pouvoirs* [complete authority]. Although only a few manage to do so, once that status has been reached fewer design boards tend to "meddle" with their work, and the architects are not continually called upon by a grumbling environment of professional jealousy and parochial politics to scale down their dreams. That explains the enthusiasm of many European architects for what they primarily perceive as genuine openness toward imagination and creative endeavor.[1] From a sociological perspective, such generosity, after all, indicates nothing so much as a surviving distribution of roles in society that respects the "master" in the architect. In that sense, too, the New World appears to be functioning as a hothouse for upholding the "old" social order.

Be that, as it may: time and again, the American experience forces one to recognize that the "old" in America—that is, the jungle of laissez-faire—produces a vibrancy and a freshness that makes the "newness" in our much more controlled Swiss reality look stale. Such "oldness" enables adventure, while our "newness" merely ensures decency and mediocrity.

"Environmental Destruction"

What I mean by "phase shifts" can be illustrated by two books. The first of the two is Peter Blake's *God's Own Junkyard* (1964). Blake was editor of *Architectural Forum* at the time. The title is a mocking allusion to the notion of the United States as "God's Own Country." Architects will be familiar with some of the book's imagery, though most likely via Venturi, who used them in some of his own works— albeit in miniature format—the best known being the picture of a duck restaurant (figs. 1, 2, 3).[2] The text is worth recalling, both for its content and its rhetoric. The book's subtitle castigates "The planned deterioration of America's landscape." Blake compares the campus of the University of Virginia (which was built by President Thomas Jefferson around 1820) to Canal Street in New Orleans as follows:

> "Jefferson's serene, urban space has been called 'almost an ideal city'—unique in America, if not in the world. Canal Street, one fervently hopes, has not been called anything in particular in recent times. It is difficult to believe that these two examples of what a city might be were suggested by the same species of mammal, let alone by the same nation. Jefferson called his campus 'an expression of the American mind'; New Orleans' Canal Street, and all the other dreary Canal Streets that defile America today, have not been called 'expressions of the America mind' by any but this nation's mortal enemies."

Other outbursts of rage spice up the text. Blake's indignation reaches biblical heights when he speaks of the "Moloch" of vehicle traffic:

> "Most of them [Blake is referring to 'highways'] are hideous scars on the face of this nation—scars that cut across mountains and plains, across cities and suburbs, poisoning the landscape and townscape with festering sores along their edges."

Filtering out some of the tirade's undisputed journalistic verve and pepping up its apocalyptic fervor with a shot of parochial stubbornness, one finds oneself at about the level of Rolf Keller's successful *Bauen als Umweltzerstörung* [Building as environmental destruction] of 1973, which, revealingly, was published in Switzerland nearly a decade after Blake's book. The same themes, the same tacitly accepted concept that the environmental disaster is basically a "moral" issue, and the same angry urge for a change from within, always dangerously close to the involuntary humor of a penitentiary sermon to Boy Scouts, yet this time dressed up in a

↓ figs. 1–3   Illustrations from Peter Blake, *God's Own Junkyard*: Charlottesville (1), New Orleans (2).

3.
Die amerikanische Stadt gewährt der Architektur einen Spielraum, den sie in Europa längst eingebüsst hat — oder eigentlich gar nie besass. Bürobauten sind Teil der «corporate identity» der führenden Interessengruppen und Trusts. Nonkonformität (gegenüber dem historischen wie auch gegenüber dem topografischen Kontext), «Grosszügigkeit» und Originalität des Entwurfs gelten daher als erstrebenswert: sie tragen zur «Sichtbarkeit» des betreffenden Auftraggebers bei. Im Gegensatz zu Europa mit seinen restriktiven Baulinien usw. dienen amerikanische Zonenordnungen dazu, die Inszenierung partikularer Leistungen zu fördern.

So hat auch der Architekt in den USA «mehr zu sagen». Er hat grössere Chancen, als Entwerfer in Positionen mit «pleins pouvoirs» hineinzurutschen. Obgleich das nur wenigen gelingt: wenn es einmal soweit ist, gibt es weniger nörgelnde Kommissionen, die ihm «am Zeug herumflicken». Man verlangt von ihm nicht ständig den Kompromiss. Daher die Begeisterung vieler europäischer Architekten in Anbetracht dessen, was ihnen primär als Grosszügigkeit, als Offenheit in schöpferischen Belangen erscheint.[1] Soziologisch ist diese Grosszügigkeit zunächst nichts anderes als das Ueberleben einer gesellschaftlichen Rollenverteilung, die den «Maestro» im Architekten respektiert. Auch diesbezüglich will einem die neue Welt bisweilen erscheinen als Treibhaus einer «alten» Ordnung.

Freilich: zur Amerikaerfahrung gehört, dass das «Alte» an Amerika, der Dschungel, in mancher Hinsicht vitaler und frischer ist als das «Neue» unserer helvetischen Realität. Jenes «Alte» ermöglicht das Abenteuer; dieses «Neue» garantiert Anstand und ordentliches Mittelmass.

«Umweltzerstörung»
Was ich mit «Phasenverschiebungen» meine, sei anhand von zwei Büchern illustriert. Zunächst, von Peter Blake: *God's Own Junkyard* (1964). Peter Blake war damals Redaktor des *Architektural Forum* und der Titel («Gottes eigener Müllhaufen») ist eine recht scharfmacherische Anspielung an die amerikanische Nationalhymne, «God's Own Country». Einige der Abbildungen aus diesem Buch — zumal das Bild eines Enten-Restaurants — dürften vielen Architekten vertraut sein; wenn auch, paradoxerweise, auf dem Umweg über Venturi, der sie in seinen Büchern zitiert hat (**1, 2, 3**).[2] Aber es lohnt sich, Text und Tonart in einigen Stichproben zu vergegenwärtigen. Der Untertitel des Buches geisselt «die geplante Zerstörung der amerikanischen Landschaft». Zu dem Vergleich des (vom Präsidenten Thomas Jefferson um 1820 erbauten) Campus der University of Virginia mit der Canal Street in New Orleans heisst es:

> Man hat Jeffersons heiter abgeklärten Platzraum als beinahe eine ideale Stadt bezeichnet, als einmalig in Amerika, wenn nicht in der Welt. Was die Canal Street

↓ figs. 4–6   Illustrations from Rolf Keller, *Bauen als Umweltzerstörung*: Dübendorf yesterday / here (4) and today (5).

anbelangt, so kann man nur inständig hoffen, dass diese Strasse in der jüngsten Vergangenheit nicht irgendeine Bezeichnung erhalten hat. Es ist schwer zu glauben, dass diese beiden Beispiele dafür, wie eine Stadt aussehen könnte, von der gleichen Spezies von Säugetieren, ja sogar von derselben Nation vorgeschlagen worden ist. Jefferson nannte seinen Campus einen «Ausdruck des amerikanischen Geistes». Die Canal Street in New Orleans und alle anderen Canal Streets, welche Amerika verwüsten, werden von niemandem Ausdruck des amerikanischen Geistes genannt, ausser von den Todfeinden dieser Nation.

Weitere Zornesausbrüche würzen den Text — und natürlich nimmt die Empörung geradezu biblische Töne an, wo vom «Moloch Verkehr» die Rede ist:

Die meisten von ihnen (es ist von Autobahnen die Rede) sind entsetzliche Wunden auf dem Gesicht dieser Nation, Wunden, die Berge und Ebenen, Städte und Vorstädte zerschneiden, die Länder und Städte verseuchen mit dem stinkenden Unrat, der ihre Ränder säumt.

— Wenn man etwas von dem unbestreitbaren journalistischen Schmiss dieser apokalyptischen Vision substrahiert und durch einen Schuss provinzieller Borniertheit ersetzt, befindet man sich ungefähr auf dem Niveau des erfolgreichen Buches von Rolf Keller, *Bauen als Umweltzerstörung* (1973), das bezeichnenderweise nicht ganz ein Jahrzehnt nach Blakes amerikanischem Gegenstück in der Schweiz erschienen ist. Die gleichen Themen, die gleiche, stillschweigend akzeptierte Vorstellung, dass das Umweltdebakel im Grunde ein «moralisches» Problem sei, und der gleiche zornige Ruf nach einer inneren Umkehr — aber nun aufgetakelt in einem Ton, der ungefähr in der Mitte liegt zwischen dem Genre von BLICK-Schlagzeilen und der unfreiwilligen Komik einer Busspredigt vor Pfadfindern.[3]

S. von Moos

Déplacement de phases

1. On doit constater que le «nouveau monde» a considérablement vieilli depuis l'époque où l'on s'était accordé pour le considérer et l'imiter comme tel.
2. L'«architecture moderne» aux USA est restée une affaire touchant les constructions du big business, de certaines universités et de l'«urban renewal». En ce qui concerne l'habitat privé, la maison, le style ou le goût de la classe moyenne n'a que peu été influencé par le «moderne».
3. Enfin, si beaucoup d'architectes européens admirent la «générosité» de l'Amérique, c'est que là il peuvent espérer d'avoir «pleins pouvoirs» en matière de projets, dans une mesure qui est inimaginable en Europe, et notamment en Suisse — où s'exerce de manière pointilleuse le contrôle «démocratique» de comités et de commissions de toutes sortes.

Ces quelques considérations sur l'Amérique servent à l'auteur de prétextes pour aborder certains phénomènes de l'architecture suisse. Selon lui, les visions d'une «grande crise» de l'environnement, provoquée par de «faux» principes architecturaux ou résultant d'un manque de «qualité» architecturale, sont hors de propos — qu'elles soient avancées par un Peter Blake aux USA (1964) ou par un Rolf Keller en Suisse (1973). D'une part il est naïf et présomptueux de croire que les problèmes d'environnement sont avant tout des problèmes d'architecture; d'autre part il serait grand temps d'aborder enfin les vrais problèmes d'une théorie de l'architecture qui soit en rapport (peut être ironique) avec les réalités culturelles du public et qui respecte l'environnement existant au lieu de célébrer les vertus héroïques de la «forme pure» et d'une architecture romantico-brutaliste, crypto-militariste, comme le fait l'architecture «officielle» de nombre d'immeubles publics et d'églises suisses.

Gewiss: Kellers Buch war notwendig und nützlich, denn die Zustände, die es geisselt, sind alarmierend. Aber die Diskussion müsste eigentlich über das «Alarmschlagen» und das wichtigtuerische, beleidigte Zeter und Mordio hinausgehen. Wer wollte bestreiten, dass Blakes so gut wie Kellers Empörung gelegentlich ins Schwarze trifft; trotzdem wirkt sie streckenweise komisch und irgendwie irrelevant. Komisch ist — in Anbetracht der Realitäten — der gestelzte, heroische Habitus sowie der scheinbar unumstössliche Glaube daran, dass das Glück oder Unglück der Menschen von Architektur abhänge. Irrelevant aber ist eine Argumentation, die im Grunde gar keine ist, da sie auf groben Verallgemeinerungen und Gemeinplätzen beruht. Es ist schlichterdings zu einfach, das Bild irgendeines amerikanischen «Strip» (Blake, 1964) oder einer schweizerischen Strassenkreuzung (Keller, 1973) vorzuführen als Inbegriff visueller «Umweltverschmutzung» (5, 6). Man muss wirklich kein Touring-Club-Fan sein um zu wissen, dass Autobahnen nicht nur Landschaften und Siedlungen verschandeln, sondern auch Landschaften und Siedlungen erschliessen, und dass Signale am Strassenrand weder gut noch schlecht sind, dass sie vielmehr eine nützliche — was Verkehrssignale betrifft: sogar eine notwendige — Form von Organisation und Information im Verkehrsablauf darstellen.

Es ist ebenfalls zu einfach, eine Aufnahme von der Sprengung neuer Wohnblocks in St. Louis abzubilden als endgültigen Beweis für die «Verkehrtheit» moderner Planungsprinzipien (7).[4] Es braucht nicht mehr als ein Minimum von Unvoreingenommenheit, um zu sehen, dass das, was in Pruitt Igoe gescheitert ist, nicht architektonische Prinzipien sind, sondern die Fähigkeit der Administration, solche Prinzipien mit sozialpolitischen Massnahmen zu koordinieren. Würden Yamasakis Blöcke in einem europäischen Mittelklassvorort wie Schwamendingen stehen und nicht in einem besonders verwahrlosten schwarzen Ghetto in St. Louis, so gehörten sie wohl zu den sozial und architektonisch gelungeneren Aspekten der Zürcher Vorstadtlandschaft.

Man muss den Amerikanern zugutehalten, dass sie eine gesunde Skepsis gegenüber falschem Pathos haben. Sie sind auch nicht bei Blakes Katzenjammer von 1964 stehengeblieben, auch wenn sie nicht alle nach Las Vegas auszogen, um jene Landschaft zu studieren, die kurz zuvor in Architektenkreisen noch als Müllhaufen Amerikas galt. Viele gutgesinnte «progressive» Schweizer Journalisten dagegen stehen — seit Keller — noch immer ganz im Bann der bequemen Vorstellung, Empörung und Wut seien ausreichende Voraussetzungen für eine Diagnose unserer Umweltprobleme.

Wann werden auch sie sich die Zeit nehmen, die Augen aufzutun? Welches wird dann das schweizerische Las Vegas (das schweizerische «Spieglein an der Wand») sein? Wird es etwa der Bürgenstock sein, jenes helvetische Refugium für private Weekends und schöne Kongresse?[5]

«Architektur» und Architektur

Immerhin: zwei Dinge hat die Hotellandschaft des Bürgenstocks mit dem frivoleren Pendant in Nevada gemein (aber man könnte auch an Miami oder irgendeine amerikanische Ferienlandschaft denken): sie wird von einer Klientele aufgesucht, die ein hohes Durchschnittsalter aufweist, und sie verwöhnt diese Klientele mit Architekturen und Innendekors, die geeignet sind, ihren geheimen sozialen Aspirationen zu schmeicheln. Und sie tut dies umso erfolgreicher, je entschiedener sie jede outriert «moderne» Gestaltung vermeidet.

Die Autoren von *Learning from Las Vegas* haben zum Beispiel den «Caesar's Palace», eine der grossen Spielhöllen von Las Vegas, auf ihre architektonische Symbolik untersucht (8).[6]

↑ fig. 7   Saint Louis, Missouri: Demolition of residential blocks (Pruitt Igoe), 1972. From Rolf Keller op. cit.

↓ fig. 8   Caesar's Palace, Las Vegas;
from *Learning from Las Vegas*.   ↓ figs. 9–10   Bürgenstock Hotel, Lucerne, driveway.

Die Kolonnade, die sich in einer grossen, umarmenden Bewegung auf den Parkplatz hin öffnet, erinnert (im Grundriss) an Berninis Petersplatz in Rom und (im Aufriss) an Yamasaki. Der Hauptbau dahinter ist eine Art Gio Ponti-Barock. Die Skulpturen, die zwischen den Pfeilern aufgestellt sind, erinnern an den Canopus in Hadrians Villa in Tivoli, nur dass die Skulpturen (hier in Gips und papier maché) nicht antike, sondern Renaissance-Originale abbilden. Die vier Springbrunnen schliesslich scheinen den Petersplatz in Rom überbieten zu wollen (wo bekanntlich nur zwei solcher Brunnen zu finden sind). So ersteht, inmitten eines Meers parkierender Wagen, ein Bild spätrömischer Palastherrlichkeit mit Hilfe von eklektischen Anleihen an die Renaissance und an moderne Motel-Herrlichkeit.

Was hier vorliegt, ist eine Architekturlandschaft, die ihre Aufgabe nicht mit Hilfe abstrakter «Qualität», sondern mit Hilfe konkreter Symbolik erfüllt. Im Grunde geschieht im «Ehrenhof» der Bürgenstock-Hotels genau dasselbe (9, 10). Das Empfangsgebäude (die Bergstation der Zahnradbahn) prunkt mit einem Luzerner Scheunendach. Die Fenster darunter sind allerdings gross und modern, denn was in der Hotellerie zählt ist nicht der «antike» Rahmen als solcher, sondern seine Kombination mit modernem Komfort. Zu dieser Kombinatorik gehört dann auch die Bruchsteinmauer im Erdgeschoss. Bruchsteinmauern sind nicht nur Anleihen an Tessiner Folklore, sie sind teuer und sagen daher etwas aus über den Status des Etablissements. Und schliesslich die neckische, nierenförmige Rabatte mit dem Springbrunnen, der, eine etwas kümmerliche Anspielung an barocke Brunnenherrlichkeit, zum Verweilen einlädt. Diese Rabatte ist modern. Sie hat Teil an der Nierentisch-Mode der Fünfzigerjahre, aber sie erinnert auch an brasilianische Parklandschaften von Roberto Burle Marx. Gleichzeitig dienen ihre Aus- und Einbuchtungen dazu, dem im Auto vorfahrenden Besucher zu zwingen, im Schritt zu fahren; das wiederum erhöht den Reiz, überhaupt im Auto vorzufahren, denn man wird mit dem Wagen zusammen gesehen. Ist doch der Wagen, vorab im Ferienkontext, das Accessoire par exellence, er steigert, dramatisiert Persönlichkeit. (Freilich, wenn man keinen Lamborghini oder keinen Mercedes fährt, dann parkiert man besser ausserhalb des Hotelbezirks.)

Dass dieser «Kurplatz» gute Architektur sei, wird niemand behaupten (abgesehen vielleicht vom Besitzer des Bürgenstocks selbst). Er ist genauso langweilig wie irgendeine Fabrikantenvilla auf dem Zürichberg oder im Tessin. Jedoch erstens: unprätentiöse Langweile ist weniger ärgerlich als laute Wichtigtuerei. Und zweitens: es gibt keinen zwingenden Grund, warum eine komplexe und vielschichtige Ikonographie wie die hier vorliegende nicht auch zu einem formal überzeugenden Ganzen zusammengefügt werden könnte. Ein schweizerisches Beispiel für ein solches Vorgehen wüsste ich freilich (noch) nicht anzugeben. Vorderhand sind noch «saubere» Lösungen Trumpf, solche, die als reine Form erzwungen, ertrotzt sein wollen.

Die (nicht mehr ganz) «neue Monumentalität»
Beispiele von guten und sauberen Platzgestaltungen, die sich mit der zufälligen und «unsauberen» Situation auf dem Bürgenstock vergleichen lassen, gibt es viele in der Schweiz. Der Platz ist ein wichtiges Anliegen der

↓ fig. 11 Kallmann, McKinnell & Knowles, Boston City Hall (1963). ↓ fig. 12 Le Corbusier, La Tourette convent (1958).

Schweizer Architektur gewesen, insbesondere seit 1950, und das trifft auch auf Amerika zu. Sigfried Giedion (der Schweizer Architekturhistoriker, der seit 1938 von Harvard aus wirkte), hat in dem Büchlein *Architektur und Gemeinschaft* (1954) einige der Ideale beschworen, die dieser Faszination mit dem Platz zu Gevatter standen:

> Die Situation der Monumente muss geplant werden. Dies wird möglich sein, wenn die Neuplanung der Mittelpunkte unserer Städte im grossen Masstab vorgenommen und diese Neuplanung die Schaffung offener Räume in den jetzt chaotischen Zentren ermöglichen wird. In diesen offenen Räumen wird die monumentale Architektur den ihr gemässen Platz finden. Dann werden sich die monumentalen Bauten ausbreiten, denn, wie Bäume und Pflanzen, können sie nicht zusammengedrängt werden. Erst dann können neue Gemeinschaftszentren sich bilden.[7]

Das Zentrum von Boston mit seinem bereits postkartennotorischen Rathaus (von Kallmann, McKinnell und Knowles) kann als eine Art Apotheose jener «neuen Monumentalität» gelten, von der Giedion und andere einige Jahre zuvor im Rahmen der CIAM geschwärmt hatten. Freilich, um dieses heroische Bild urbaner Gemeinschaft realisieren zu können, musste in Boston zuerst ein Teil der realen städtischen Gemeinschaft aufgekündigt, ein ganzes Quartier zerstört werden. Solches war in der «knauserigen» Schweiz nicht ohne weiteres möglich, und so war denn die «Regeneration des Gemeinschaftslebens» ein Anliegen, das in bescheidenerem Format praktiziert wurde: in einigen reichen Städten und Dörfern (**16, 23**) — aber vor allem im Rahmen kirchlicher Zentren. Man findet hier in zahlreichen Abwandlungen Analoges zur Situation in Boston: die grosse, durch Pflästerung und Stufen «vermenschlichte» Piazza und im Hintergrund das gestreng herabblickende Architektur-Monument (**13** bis

↑ fig. 13 Boston City Hall Plaza. ↑ fig. 14 Dolf Schnebli, Catholic church, Oberentfelden, Aargau. ↑ fig. 16 Rolf Keller and Fritz Schwarz, Muttenz town center.

↑ fig. 15 Rolf Keller and Fritz Schwarz, Muttenz town center.

↓ fig. 17 Boston City Hall.

↓ fig. 18 Court building, Clayton, Missouri.

↓ fig. 21 R.+E. Guyer Stettbach school in Schwamendingen district of Zurich.

fig. 19 →
Töss-Zentrum, Winterthur.

fig. 20 ⇉
Ernst Gisel, School in Engelberg, 1965–67.

16). Nur dass die gigantischen Ausmasse dessen, was die Amerikaner «Civic Center», «Plaza» oder (exotisch) «Piazza» nennen, herabdimensioniert ist zum helvetisch-gemütlicheren Dorfplatz. Oder zur «Stätte der Begegnung», wie es die Cityvereinigungen und Shopping Centers neuerdings ausdrücken — denn diese haben das Thema Gemeinschaft inzwischen ebenfalls entdeckt.

Was diese architektonischen Monumente von dem Flickwerk auf dem Bürgenstock unterscheidet, das ist eben, dass sie relativ sauber sind, d. h. dass die eine Thematik abwandeln, die architektonisch ist und um die abstrakten Themen von Raum, Form, Konstruktion kreist. Es gibt äusserst sensible, differenzierte Lösungen, wie etwa der schöne Vorplatz einer Kirche in Oberentfelden AG (**14**), aber auch brutale, wie etwa das Obergericht in Aarau selbst, Mittelpunkt eines Mini-Civic-Centers. Hier wird etwa gezeigt, wie unerhört dramatisch es zugeht, wenn ein Betonpfeiler in die Schösse eines Curtain Walls hineinfährt. Auch das Rathaus von Boston ist zuallererst eine dramatische Schaustellung statischer Kräfte — immerhin eine formal kontrollierte (**22, 23**).

Beide Beispiele wandeln ein architektonisches Thema ab, das eigentlich wenig oder nichts mit der Funktion und der «Bedeutung» des Baus zu tun hat. Indem sie das tun, geraten auch sie — nolens volens — zum Symbol. Symbol zunächst für statische Leistung. Dann Symbol für das Bemühen, sich um jeden Preis vom historischen und topografischen Kontext abzuheben. Und schliesslich Symbol für eine architektonische Aesthetik, die den Kontakt mit den einfachen, undramatischen und freundlichen Aspekten des Alltags abgebrochen hat.

Fragwürdig an solchen Bauten ist nicht, dass sie «modern» sind. Das sind sie ohnehin nur im Hinblick auf einen fast antiquarischen Begriff von Modernität. Fragwürdig ist, dass sie sich à tout prix um Heroismus und Originalität bemühen — wo doch das mit Witz gewürzte Naheliegende gänzlich ausreichen würde. Das Naheliegende: das wäre etwa in einem Industrievorort wie Muttenz (**15, 16**) ein baslerisch-kultivierter Verwaltungsbau, und eben nicht ein Beton-Dörfli in einem brutalistisch aufgemöbelten Landi-Stil.

↑ fig. 22 Boston City Hall, detail.

↑ fig. 23 R. Meyer, Headquarters of an electric company, Aarau, detail.

tabloid genre that borrows its rhetoric from *BLICK* headlines.³

Indeed, Keller's book was necessary and useful. The situation it flags is alarming; it needs to be discussed. Often enough, Keller's observations hit the mark—as do Blake's. Nevertheless, in the end both authors' outrage sounds somewhat hollow. In hindsight, and measured against the real challenges at stake, the heroic posture and the apparently irrevocable belief that people's happiness or distress depends on architecture is simply grotesque. Granted the relevance of the issues raised, more often than not the arguments thrown into the debate are based on gross generalization and platitudes. To present a randomly chosen American "Strip" (Blake, 1964) or an ordinary Swiss road junction (Keller, 1973) as an epitome of "environmental pollution" is just too easy (figs. 5, 6). You don't have to be a Touring Club fan to know that freeways not only disfigure landscapes and settlements but also provide access to them. Similarly, road signs are neither good nor bad; as to traffic signs in particular, they are an indispensable means of organization and information along streets and freeways.

Nor are the famous pictures documenting the demolition of new housing blocks in St. Louis, Missouri, the decisive evidence of the "perversity" of modern planning principles (fig. 7).⁴ Anyone with a modicum of impartiality can see that what failed in Pruitt-Igoe was not so much architectural principles as the administration's ability to coordinate those principles with sociopolitical measures. Had Yamasaki's blocks been cut half in scale and erected in a European suburb such as Schwamendingen, rather than in an especially neglected black ghetto in St. Louis, who knows whether they might not be regarded as a particularly successful component of Zurich's cooperative housing program.

Luckily, Americans tend to treat false pathos with a healthy skepticism. And indeed, Blake's cry of alarm has by no means been this critic's last word. Nor did all his American colleagues choose to move out to Las Vegas to study the landscape that Blake had just labeled as America's junkyard. Meanwhile, in Switzerland, when it comes to architecture, "progressive" journalism still considers it appropriate to discuss its problems and challenges in terms of moral indignation and metaphysical disgust. When will reporters and critics take the time to open their eyes? What will be the Swiss Las Vegas, the Swiss "mirror on the wall"? Will it perhaps be the Bürgenstock, that elegant retreat for private weekends and well-sponsored congresses in the very heart of Switzerland?⁵

"Architecture" and Architecture

The hotel landscape of the Bürgenstock has at least two things in common with the entertainment resort in Nevada (though Miami or any other American leisure landscape might also serve as a paragon): it caters to a clientele with a high age profile, and it pampers its customers with architecture and interior decoration capable of pandering to their secret social aspirations. And it does so all the more successfully the more consistent it is in avoiding outré "modern" design. This is how the authors of *Learning from Las Vegas* investigated the architectural symbolism of Caesar's Palace, one of the major casinos in Las Vegas (fig. 8).⁶ In its ground plan, the colonnade, which opens out in a large, enveloping gesture toward the car park, recalls Bernini's St. Peter's Square in Rome. In elevation, however, it makes one think of Yamasaki. The main building behind it is a kind of Gio Ponti baroque. The sculptures standing between the columns are reminiscent of the Canopus in Hadrian's Villa in Tivoli, although in this case they are made of plaster and papier-mâché and represent imitations of Renaissance originals rather than examples from antiquity. The four fountains seem to want to outdo St. Peter's Square in Rome (where there are famously only two). Thus, amid a sea of parked cars, an image of late Roman opulence is created with the help of eclectic borrowings from both the Renaissance and modern motel glitz.

What we are dealing with is an architectural environment that fulfils its task not via abstract criteria of "quality" but based on figurative symbolism. The *cour d'honneur* at the core of the Bürgenstock hotel complex basically does the same thing (figs. 9, 10). The reception building (the top station of the funicular railway) flaunts a Lucerne barn roof. As to the windows beneath it, they are large and modern, because what counts in the hotel business is not the "antique" or the "local" as such but its combination with modern comfort. The quarry-stone wall on the ground floor is part of this architectural combinatorics. Quarry-stone walls do not merely refer to Ticino folklore. They are also expensive and therefore give us a clue as to the status of the establishment. Finally, the coquettish, kidney-shaped border with its fountain, surrounded by a pool—a somewhat meager echo of baroque garden art—invites the passers-by to linger. The border is modern. Its kidney shape, a 1950s cliché, recalls the Brazilian landscape gardens designed by Roberto Burle Marx. At the same time, its indentation and bulging force visitors driving past to travel at a pedestrian pace. That, in turn, increases the thrill of driving there to begin with—as it is only in this way that you are seen in your car. The car, after all, being the ultimate accessory, especially on holiday; it enhances and dramatizes personality (of course, if you are not driving a Lamborghini or a Mercedes, you are more likely to park outside the hotel precinct).

Nobody will claim that this "spa square" is good architecture (apart from perhaps the Bürgenstock's owner himself). It is as boring as any banker's villa on Zürichberg or in the Ticino region. But then, first, isn't unpretentious boredom less annoying than noisy bumbledom? Second (and more important): Why can't a complex, multifaceted iconography such as the one displayed here be brought together into a convincing formal whole?—To date, I (still) cannot name a single such Swiss example. Tidy solutions remain the trump cards. Such buildings want to be seen as a triumph of pure form over complex program and fuzzy symbolism.

The (No Longer Completely) "New Monumentality"

There are many examples in Switzerland of well-planned urban or village squares that can be juxtaposed to the arbitrary eclecticism of the Bürgenstock "plaza." Design and orchestration of public space enjoy a high status among Swiss architects, especially since the 1950s, and the same applies to the United States. In his small book *Architektur und Gemeinschaft* (1956) [published in English as *Architecture, You and Me* (1958)] Sigfried Giedion outlines a number of ideals that appear to have spawned a global fascination with squares:

> "Sites for monuments must be planned. This will be possible once replanning is undertaken on a large scale which will create vast open spaces in the now decaying areas of our cities. In those open spaces, monumental architecture will find its appropriate setting which now does not exist. Monumental buildings will then be able to stand in space, for, like trees and plants, monumental buildings cannot be crowded in upon any odd lot in any district. Only when this space is achieved can the new urban centers come to life."[7]

Boston City Hall and the huge public plaza at its foot are not merely an archetype of 1960s urban design but a key example of the "New Monumentality" that Giedion and others had launched as a concept in the 1940s (architects: Kallmann, McKinnell & Knowles). Unfortunately, the sacrifice to be made for this celebration of the idea of "community" was the de facto eradication of the *real* community that previously occupied this space—in fact, the ruin of an entire neighborhood. Such sweeping measures would be difficult to carry through in tiny Switzerland, given the grassroots culture of direct democracy practiced there. Hence it was in the format of small public spaces in some well-to-do Swiss towns and villages that the "regeneration of public life" was tested as an architectural theme (figs. 16, 23)—to be further refined in church centers, where Boston with its large piazza, "humanized" by cobblestone paving and steps, with a "monument" grimly peering down upon it from behind, is echoed in miniature format (figs. 13 to 16). Elsewhere, the American "civic centers"—or rather "plazas" and (exotic) "piazzas" have been downsized to the more congenial Swiss village square. Or into "Stätten der Begegnung" [sites for encounters], as developers of downtowns and shopping centers like to call them—now that they, too, have discovered the theme of community.

What distinguishes the ecclesiastic or civic "piazzas" just referred to from the Bürgenstock patchwork is the fact that they focus on abstract qualities of space, form, and construction. The spectrum goes from carefully scaled solutions —an example is Dolf Schnebli's beautiful church forecourt in Oberentfelden, Aargau (fig. 14)—

↓ fig. 24
Holiday Inn, sign.

↓ fig. 25 Dr. J. Dahinden,
Catholic church, Dielsdorf,
Canton of Zurich (1962).

↓ fig. 26 Polynesian restaurant on
an arterial road of Boston.

Schweizer Enten-Architektur

Die Schweizer Landschaft ist inzwischen angereichert mit Bauten der heroischen Art, häufig sogar sehr qualitätvollen. Unter ihnen gibt es viele, die ein vorkragendes Obergeschoss vorzeigen, von lamellenförmigen Stützen in die Höhe gehoben. Diese Form, welche die Entwerfer der Boston City Hall ihrerseits von Le Corbusier (La Tourette) übernommen haben, ist inzwischen zu einer Art international salonfähigem Imponierschema geworden. Ihre Botschaft ist beinah ebenso universal verständlich

↑ fig. 29   E. Rausser, Church in the Canton of Bern.   ↑ figs. 30–31   Gas station in Müstair, Graubünden.

33

↓ fig. 32 Walter M. Förderer, Catholic church, Bettlach, Solothurn.

↓ fig. 33 R. Venturi, "The Duck," from *Learning from Las Vegas*.

we should append the warning of Pugin: It is all right to decorate construction but never construct decoration.

wie diejenige des «Holiday Inn» Signals; sie heisst etwa «Achtung: hier war ein moderner Architekt». In solchen Bauten wird Konstruktion zum Ornament ihrer selbst. Wenn man, wie Venturi es getan hat, das Feld heutigen Bauens aufteilt in Bauten, die applizierte Dekoration aufweisen und solche, die selber plastisch inszenierte Dekoration sind, dazu fällt eben die entenförmige Entenrestaurant von New England plötzlich in dieselbe Kategorie wie ein brutalistischer Monumentalbau (33). Dass Venturis Skizze zahm ist verglichen mit Schweizer Betonkirchen ist vielleicht bedenkenswert. Kirchen als Enten? — Ist etwa vieles von dem, was im Schweizer Kirchenbau an Kreativität und Originalität produziert und (mit Hilfe dieser Begriffe) vermarktet wurde, eine religiöse Subspecies von Gaststätten — oder Ausstellungsarchitektur? Hat der gute alte Peter Meyer am Ende noch Recht:

> Technische Formen, Chichi der Ausstellungsarchitektur, Grafiker-Raffinement ist auf die Kirche übertragen, und jetzt ist diese ein Ausstellungspavillon des lieben Gottes, eine geschmackvolle Reiseagentur ins Jenseits — die Gratisprospekte liegen am Eingang auf. Das tobt in einem permanenten Veitstanz architektonischer Genialität und «Eigenwilligkeit», ausgestattet mit super-archaischen oder infantilen Skulpturen, Mosaiken, Gemälden...[8]

Natürlich hat er Recht, aber er sagt bloss die Hälfte. Denn nicht nur sehen Kirchen wie Ausstellungspavillons aus, die Rechnung klappt auch in umgekehrter Richtung: Einkaufszentren präsentieren sich als vorgeschichtliche Heiligtümer mit Götterthronen und Sakramentshäuschen in der Form gigantischer Menhire. Wohl gibt es katholische Gotteshäuser, die — stünden sie an der Route 2 nördlich von Boston — leicht mit einem polynesischen Restaurant verwechselt werden könnten (25, 26), und das ist auch gar kein Zufall, wo doch der hier fragliche Architekt vorab im Gaststätten- und Unterhaltungsressort renommiert ist. Doch andererseits gibt es z. B. in Graubünden Tankstellen, wo die gute Grenzlage und der damit zusammenhängende Benzinumsatz in einem säkularisierten Glockenturm seinen Ausdruck findet: Tank-Kapellen also, in deren Sakristeien Proviant feilgeboten wird (30, 31).

Nun ist es ja nicht so, dass die Bündner Tankstelle absichtlich als Sakralbau oder die Zürcher Landkirche als Nachtklub sich darstellen will. Gemeint ist in diesen Fällen eine abstrakte, semantisch unbelastete «künstlerische Qualität». Aber eben: die Absicht, in guter alter moderner Tradition Symbolik zu vermeiden, ist keine ausreichende Garantie dafür, dass die auch tatsächlich ausbleibt. Es würde sich also lohnen, einen Versuch zu machen, sie wieder in den Griff zu bekommen: zumindest sofern mit Architektur tatsächlich etwas die Benützer Betreffendes ausgedrückt werden soll.

Es könnte indes sein, dass heute die betonselige Imponiersakralität wie auch weniger pompöse Moden der Sechzigerjahre von viel trivialere Realitäten bedroht sind. Schon scheint das System eine deutlich straffere Gangart eingeschaltet zu haben. Die Stunde der Wahrheit schlägt vielleicht an Orten wie — Spreitenbach, grad ausserhalb Zürichs. Vor zehn Jahren entstand da ein grosses Einkaufszentrum, verpackt und verputzt in sehr viel Architektur: mit maurisch gekurvter Aussenform sowie Piazza und Plätscherbrunnen im Lichthof (35). Zehn Jahre später wird unmittel-

to examples of singular banality, such as the recent high court building in Aarau, which functions as the backdrop to a mini civic center. What a glorious spectacle that is: the boldness of a concrete pillar driven into the coattails of a curtain wall. Sure, Boston City Hall, too, is first of all a demonstration of static forces—a highly controlled one in comparison (figs. 22, 23).

Both examples play with architectural themes that are basically unrelated to the function of the given building and even more so to its "significance." In doing so, they, too, become symbols—whether intentionally or not: first, for dramatizing load-bearing performance; second, for celebrating an architectural aesthetics that has severed its ties to the simple, undramatic, and friendly aspects of everyday life.

What is questionable with buildings like these, however, is not that they are "modern" (whatever that may mean) but that they strive to achieve heroism and originality at any price, where a more obvious solution, perhaps laced with a little humor, would have sufficed. In an industrial suburb like Muttenz, the obvious might have been to highlight the town's smoothly running administration by way of an elegant curtain-wall office building as would be done in nearby Basel, rather than to drape it as a pepped-up post-Ronchamp-style concrete village (figs. 15, 16).

Swiss Duck Architecture

In the meantime, the Swiss landscape has been enriched with buildings of the heroic kind, some of considerable design quality. Many of them boast of a massive volume containing one or more floors and placed on supports that allow for generous public space below. Slatted profiles at times dramatize the spectacle, hanging from the upper floors like inverted crenellations. That order seems to have become a universal pathos formula for public buildings. The designers of Boston City Hall derived it from Le Corbusier (La Tourette). Its message is almost as universally understandable as a Holiday Inn sign: it says something like "Attention: Here comes serious architecture." In such buildings, construction itself becomes ornament. If, as Venturi has done, the field of contemporary building were divided into structures with applied decoration and ones that are themselves sculpturally staged decoration, then the legendary duck-shaped duck restaurant in Long Island can't help ending up in the same category as a brutalist monument — be it a city hall, a high school, or a church (fig. 33).

Churches as ducks? Could it be that much of the work produced in the name of creativity and originality in Swiss church building is ultimately to be ranked as a religious subspecies of restaurant and exhibition architecture?— Was good old Peter Meyer ultimately right?

> "Technical forms, the *chichi* of exhibition architecture and the *haut-goût* of the graphic designer are applied to the church, which has now become an exhibition pavilion of the Lord, a tasteful travel agency to the beyond—with free brochures presented at the entrance. It fidgets in a permanent St. Vitus dance of architectural geniality and 'waywardness,' equipped with super-archaic or infantile sculptures, mosaics, paintings ..." [8]

Of course, he is right, except for telling only half the truth. Not only do churches resemble exhibition pavilions; it works the other way around too: shopping centers present themselves as prehistoric sanctuaries with divine thrones and tabernacles in the form of enormous menhirs. Some Catholic churches in Switzerland, if they stood along Route 1 north of Boston, could easily be mistaken for a Polynesian restaurant (figs. 25, 26). Nor is that a coincidence, since the architect in question is famous for the magic of the gastronomic and entertainment resorts he designed. And there are gas stations in the Grisons where the benefits of their border location and the resulting high gas sales are transfigured into secularized bell towers: gas-station chapels, with tabernacles offering supplies for the journey (figs. 30, 31). Not that the Grisons gas station deliberately intends to resemble a sacred building, or that rural churches in the Zurich region mean to look like nightclubs. Clearly, the intention in these cases is nothing but semantically unburdened "artistic quality." However, the aim of avoiding symbolism does not prevent it from actually happening. Hence, it would be worth attempting to regain an element of control over that phenomenon—at least so long as architecture is thought to express values relevant to and shared by its users.

Granted that today, with the oil crisis, the luxury rhetoric of bunker sacredness and other less pompous fashions of the sixties may have to face much more trivial challenges. The system already appears to have initiated a much tougher approach to expenditures altogether. Spreitenbach, just outside Zurich, may be one of the locations where the moment of truth appears in its most naked fashion. Ten years ago, a large shopping center was built there, packed and plastered in a great deal of architecture: with a curved, Moorish envelope in concrete, a piazza as well as a fountain in the atrium (fig. 35). Ten years later, a new version of a shopping center is being erected directly beside it (fig. 36). Architectural packaging is no longer thought to be essential. In the days of discount retailing, design costs are radically skimmed down. A simple container will do—one of those boxes lying around along our freeways in all colors and sizes. The savings in architecture are canceled out by the additional energy costs: such boxes are completely sealed, both visually and climate-wise. And they are tidy (fig. 37). Architecture, design, form, and symbolism are suddenly reduced to the "cheerful" coloring of facades and the eclectic decor inside: the familiar folklore of good old Swiss graphics and the cool magic of neon light will do the job. The tone has been set: Switzerland is about to show its big brother how to do things better with "ducks and sheds."

ENDNOTES

1 Grumbling about Swiss "thriftiness," "lack of courage," and a general feeling of cultural gridlock as opposed to the dynamism of life and art in America is a recurrent theme in statements by returning "expatriates." See for instance Max Frisch, "Cum grano salis," *Werk* (October 1953): 325–29.

2 Robert Venturi, *Complexity and Contradiction in Architecture* (New York, 1966), 103; and R. Venturi, D. Scott Brown, and S. Izenour, *Learning from Las Vegas* (Cambridge, MA, 1972).

3 In the meantime, Blake himself has turned the tables on modern architecture, in whose name he castigated the vulgarity of the "Strip" in 1964. His article on "The Folly of Modern Architecture" was even published in *Reader's Digest* (May 1975) (orig. pub.: "The Folly of Modern Architecture," *Atlantic Monthly* (September 1974)).

4 The Pruitt-Igoe project is a 36-million-dollar social housing project consisting of 33 eleven-story housing blocks (architect: Minoru Yamasaki; construction began in 1955). In 1969, an average of one murder a week was committed in the new public housing project. As a result, four of the blocks were demolished by the Army Corp of Engineers, and the remaining buildings were evacuated.

5 Bürgenstock was chosen as an example after the present considerations were presented as a conference paper at an FSAI [Fédération Suisse des Architectes Indépendants] seminar held at the Grand Hotel Bürgenstock, June 1975.

6 *Learning from Las Vegas*, 48–51.— See also *archithese*, 13 (1975).

7 Sigfried Giedion, *Architecture, You and Me* (Cambridge, MA, 1958), 50.

8 Peter Meyer, "Lourdes-Grotten und Verwandtes," *Schweizer Monatshefte* (October 1974), 463ff. The art and architectural historian Peter Meyer was editor in chief of the Swiss architectural journal *Das Werk* from 1930 to 1942.

bar daneben die neue Version eines Shopping Centers realisiert (36). Auf architektonische Verpackung kann jetzt verzichtet werden. Im Zeichen des Discount-Geschäfts ist es die Architektur, die zuerst substrahiert wird; man kommt da rascher und müheloser zum Ziel mit einem schlichten Container, mit einer jener Schachteln, die bereits in allen Grössen und Farben entlang unserer Autobahnen herumliegen. Was man an Architektur einspart, das zahlt man an Energie: denn solche Boxen sind optisch wie klimatisch vollisoliert. Und sie sind

↓ fig. 34   E. Naef + G. Studer, Catholic Collegiate Church in Sarnen, Obwalden.
↓ fig. 35   Shopping center, Spreitenbach, Aargau (1965).
↓ fig. 36   Tivoli shopping center, Spreitenbach (1974).

sauber (**37**). Architektur, Design, Form und Symbolik schrumpfen da plötzlich zusammen auf die «fröhliche» Bemalung der Fassaden und das Dekor im Innern: auf die so populäre, gute Schweizergrafik und den kühlen Illusionismus von Neon-Licht. Die Weichen sind längst gestellt: die Schweiz ist daran, «mit Enten und Schuppen» dem grossen Bruder zu zeigen, wie man es besser macht.

[1]   Das Lob der «Grosszügigkeit» Amerikas und das Meckern über die schweizerische «Knauserigkeit», die «Mässigung» und den «Verzicht auf das Wagnis» ist ein Grundthema in den Aeusserungen von «Heimkehrern»; vgl. etwa Max Frisch, «Com grano salis», in *Werk*, Okt. 1953, S. 325–329.
[2]   Robert Venturi, *Complexity and Contradiction in Architecture*, New York, 1966, S. 103; R. Venturi, D. Scott Brown, S. Izenour, *Learning from Las Vegas*, Cambridge, Mass., 1972.
[3]   Blake selbst hat inzwischen den Spiess umgedreht wider die moderne Architektur, in deren Namen er 1964 gegen die Vulgarität des «Strips» wetterte. Seinem Beitrag über «Die Sünden der modernen Architektur» wurde sogar die Ehre zuteil, im *Reader's Digest* (Juli 1975) abgedruckt zu werden. (Erstausg.: «The Folly of Modern Architecture», in *The Atlantic Monthly*, Sept. 1974.)
[4]   Es handelt sich um das Sanierungsprojekt Pruitt-Igoe, ein 36 Mio-Unterfangen des sozialen Wohnbaus, bestehend aus 33 elfstöckigen Wohnblöcken (Arch.: Minoru Yamasaki; Baubeginn 1955). 1969 ereignete sich durchschnittlich ein Mord pro Woche im Neubauviertel. Infolgedessen wurden vier der Blöcke von amerikanischen Bundestruppen gesprengt und die restlichen evakuiert.
[5]   Die Wahl fiel auf den Bürgenstock, weil die vorliegenden Ueberlegungen zuerst im Rahmen eines FSAI-Seminars vorgetragen wurden, das auf dem Bürgenstock tagte (Juni 1975).
[6]   *Learning from Las Vegas*, S. 48–51. – Vgl. auch *archithese* 13.
[7]   *Architektur und Gemeinschaft*, S. 41.
[8]   Peter Meyer, «Lourdes-Grotten und Verwandtes», in *Schweizer Monatshefte*, Oktober 1974, S. 463 ff. Es spricht nicht für die Lebendigkeit der Schweizer Architekturdiskussion, dass Peter Meyer nach wie vor beinah der einzige ist, der sich kritisch und mit Verve über diese Zusammenhänge äussert.

↑ figs. 37–38   Container architecture near Zurich (horizontal) and in Manhattan (vertical).

Dolf Schnebli

Erfahrungen
mit einem Bauverlauf
•

Die Erweiterungsbauten der Washington-Universität in St. Louis, Mo. *

Architekten Schnebli Anselevicius Montgomery   Associates: W. Rupe, Robert Matter

1   SAM Architekten / architectes (Dolf Schnebli, George Anselevicius, Roger Montgomery): Erweiterungsbauten der Washington University, St. Louis, Mo. / extension de la Washington University, St. Louis, Mo. Wettbewerb / concours 1965; Ausführung / réalisation 1970. Aula und Bibliothek / Aula et bibliothèque.

Rosemarie Bletter

metropolis réduite

«Les gratte-ciel de New York sont trop petits.»
Le Corbusier, 1935
(d'après *Quand les cathérales étaient blanches*)

Lorsque l'on considère les réactions des architectes européens face au phénomène du gratte-ciel américain des années vingt, on a l'impression que les architectes américains acceptaient avec complaisance la prolifération de ce type de construction, qui — aux yeux de Le Corbusier par exemple — aurait pu être maîtrisé à son avantage. Bien sûr ces réactions datent d'une époque où l'Europe n'avait pas encore à faire face à cette réalité de la construction de gratte-ciel. Pour un Le Corbusier ou un Erich Mendelsohn le gratte-ciel américain devint un objet à la fois d'envie et de dérision, parce qu'il n'y avait rien de comparable en Europe et parce que les architectes européens avaient l'impression qu'ils auraient pu en faire quelque chose de mieux.

D'autre part les effets douteux et même pernicieux de la construction de gratte-ciel commençaient à se faire sentir pour les architectes américains. Même si ces derniers acceptaient et exécutaient des commissions pour des gratte-ciel, ils manifestaient une certaine ambivalence au sujet d'un développement apparemment inexorable, influencé plus par des facteurs économiques que par la planification architecturale. L'impression que l'architecture n'était plus contrôlée par la profession architecturale est reflétée dans le livre de Edwin Avery Park, *New Backgrounds for a New Age*, paru en 1927, dans lequel il déclare:

«L'architecte aurait pu tout aussi bien ne jamais avoir perdu son temps à apprendre à dessiner. Son travail est maintenant celui d'un ingénieur financier, il passe son temps à faire des coupes, à gratter et à manier le chausse-pied, essayant de produire quelque chose, sans avoir le temps de se soucier trop de quoi la chose aura l'air... L'art et l'architecture ne fonctionnent plus sur la base du mécénat. L'architecture est entrée dans la compétition moderne de la survie par l'adéquation.» [1]

L'idée que l'architecte n'est plus qu'un simple technicien au service du spéculateur foncier a été exprimée encore plus crûment par Sheldon Cheney, dans *The New World Architecture*, de 1930:

«Peut-être le ‚Commercialisme' est-il le nouveau Dieu — seulement trop puissant et trop séduisant — pour lequel les hommes construisent aujourd'hui leurs structures les plus larges, les plus coûteuses et les plus laudatives. Pour cette cause ils construisent de plus en plus haut, ils concentrent toujours plus d'activité dans un espace au sol toujours plus réduit, dérobant la lumière et l'air du voisin, enregistrant pieusement dans leurs structures l'exploitation, qui est la main droite du Commercialisme.»

Metropolis: verkleinert

Die Zwanzigerjahre bedeuteten für New York einen Boom, insbesondere was den Bau von Wolkenkratzern anbelangt, deren Dimensionen sich sprunghaft vergrösserten. Häufig zeigen diese Wolkenkrazter einen reichen Portalschmuck — entweder gemalt oder als Relief. Im allgemeinen wird hier ein verkleinertes Modell des betreffenden Baus angeordnet. Diese Modellwiedergabe soll offensichtlich dem Besucher ein klareres und fassbareres Bild des Baues vermitteln — dessen Form «in situ» aufgrund seiner Dimensionen unverständlich geworden ist, insbesondere unter den Bedingungen der New Yorker Zonenordnung, die eine stufenförmige Staffelung des Bauvolumens forderte.

Darüberhinaus sieht die Verfasserin hier einen Ausdruck des Zweifels und des Zögerns seitens der Architekten in Anbetracht eines Bauens, das sich ständig zu gigantischeren Ausmassen aufbläht — ja es scheint hier ein Versuch vorzuliegen, den menschlichen Massstab und die Natur in die neue Bauform herüberzuretten — nachdem diese Qualitäten aus ihm *de facto* eliminiert worden sind. Diese spezielle Bemühung der amerikanischen Architekten (für die es auch schriftliche Nachweise gibt) ist weder von den Filmregisseuren noch von den Fotografen der Epoche aufgegriffen worden. Diese haben ganz im Gegenteil die spektakulären und dramatischen Aspekte des Wolkenkratzers verherrlicht.

Shrunken Metropolis

Author:
Rosemarie Bletter

Translated by:
Brett Petzer

"New York's skyscrapers are too small."
Le Corbusier, 1935
(from *When Cathedrals Were White*)

When one considers the reactions of European architects to the American skyscraper phenomenon of the 1920s, one gets the sense that American architects looked on complacently as this new building typology proliferated. Others—for example, Le Corbusier—held that it might have benefited from further refinement. Of course, these reactions date from a time when Europe had yet to be confronted with the reality of skyscraper construction. For someone like Le Corbusier or Erich Mendelsohn, the American skyscraper became an object of envy and derision alike, because nothing in Europe compared to it, and because European architects felt they could have made rather more of it.

On the other hand, the questionable, perhaps even harmful effects of skyscraper construction were beginning to be felt by American architects. Although they accepted and carried out commissions for skyscrapers, they displayed a certain ambivalence toward what seemed like unstoppable growth influenced more by economic factors than by architectural planning considerations. The impression that architecture was no longer under the control of the architectural profession is reflected in Edwin Avery Park's 1927 book *New Backgrounds for a New Age*, in which he writes:

> "The architect might as well never have wasted his time learning to design. His job is now that of a financial engineer, his time spent cutting, scraping and shoe-horning, trying to produce something, without time to worry too much how that thing will look. ... Art and architecture no longer function upon a basis of patronage. Architecture is competing in the great modern struggle to survive through fitness."[1]

The idea that the architect had become a mere technician in the service of property speculators was expressed even more bluntly by Sheldon Cheney in *The New World Architecture* in 1930:

> "Perhaps Commercialism is the new God, only too powerful and alluring, to Whom men are building today their largest, costliest, and most laudatory structures. In this service they are building higher and ever higher, concentrating more and more activity in less ground space, stealing light and air from their neighbors, piously recording in their structures the exploitation that is [the] right-hand attribute of Commercialism.
> At any rate, the skyscraper is the typical building of the twentieth century. New York City, to be sure, ... sees the rise of scores of business buildings larger, more honest in methods of construction and in purpose ..., and more expressive of contemporary living. Business rules the world today, and as long as

business can best be served where many offices are concentrated in one small area, in buildings designed as machines for the efficient discharge of buying, selling, trading, banking, law disputes, gambling, and exploitation, business architecture will be supreme."[2]

American architects were caught between the realities of the market and a cultural mythology that favored agrarian ideals, the notion of a limitless countryside, and Rousseau's belief in the superiority of rural life over city living. The resulting uncertainty found its strongest expression not in the general appearance of the skyscraper but in its architectural ornamentation, an area more likely to escape the kind of control that owners exercised over the building's marketability.

For example, in William Van Alen's Chrysler Building (1928–30), the very elaborate painted ceiling just over the threshold of the lobby depicts a scaled-down Chrysler Building. The lobby of the Empire State Building, by Shreve, Lamb & Harmon (1930–31), includes a metal relief of the building (fig. 1). And above the entrance to 60 Wall Tower by Clinton & Russell and Holton & George (1930–32), one sees a sculpted model of the building itself (fig. 2).

The placement of these miniaturized replicas near street or lobby entrances has an obvious purpose: to give employees a clear understanding of the form of the building they are entering. This is because the general form of the large buildings erected in the 1920s could be appreciated only from a considerable distance. Seen up close, their silhouette is impossible to read due to the effects of foreshortenings and obstructions. From the sidewalk, moreover, everything above the first setback in the facade is generally lost to view. Architects were clearly also invested in maintaining the "legibility" of their buildings despite their immense size. This concern with making architecture tangible was articulated in the nineteenth century by John Ruskin and reworked for the American context by Louis Sullivan. However, while Ruskin's and Sullivan's intention had been to make the overall outline of a building more readily discernible, only in the New York building boom of the late 1920s was it deemed necessary to provide every skyscraper with a diminutive version of itself.

There may be a second reason for these efforts to diminish the scale of the building, one that has nothing to do with a concern for legibility. These scaled-down projections may well reflect the architect's true ideals. That is, this may be a curious reversal of the old convention by which a scale model served as a stand-in for the larger structure that was wanted. Here, the small-scale replicas of these buildings that seemed so colossal at the time may well be closer to the intentions of the architects, who were discomfited by the construction of buildings they saw as oversized.

The 500 Fifth Avenue Building (1930–31) by Shreve, Lamb & Harmon offers one more example of this reduction in scale. In a bas-relief above the entrance, a kneeling figure wearing a peplos presents a model of 500 Fifth Avenue, possibly serving as a kind of Tyche, or protector of the site (fig. 3).[3] In this example, where the architectural model appears alongside a human figure, the building's proportions are even more readily measurable, scaled down to less than human height. If Tyche were standing, 500 Fifth Avenue would reach to about the height of the reeds. The same can be said of the Fuller Building by Walker & Gillette (1928–29). In the presence of two athletic male figures, the stylized "skyline" is reduced to the dimensions of a small decorative balustrade (fig. 4).

These miniature replicas can thus be regarded as commentary on the buildings they decorate. They retain a sense of the human scale that no longer exists in the skyscrapers themselves. Many skyscraper architects seem to have shown some hesitation in taking on the design of mammoth office towers. However, the romantic power and visual drama of the skyline that was starting to emerge in the 1920s still made a deep impression on most American artists, photographers, and filmmakers. For example, in 1922 the artist Charles Sheller and the photographer Paul Strand made a film dramatizing the skyscrapers of Manhattan. Entitled *Manhatta*, after a poem by Walt Whitman, it almost never shows skyscrapers from street level. Instead, the camera is either aimed at the summit, or, for even greater dramatic effect, placed on the roof, plunging straight down to the streets below. Here, human beings are mere minutiae in the cityscape.[4] The exaggerated

↓ fig. 1   Shreve, Lamb & Harmon, 1930–31.
Empire State Building. Lobby.

↓ fig. 2   Clinton & Russell, Holton & George,
60 Wall Tower, 1930–32. Detail of the entrance.

De toute manière le gratte-ciel est la construction typique du vingtième siècle. La ville de New York . . . voit augmenter le nombre des immeubles commerciaux, toujours plus grands, toujours plus honnêtes dans leurs méthodes de construction et dans leurs buts . . . et plus expressifs de la vie contemporaine. Aujourd'hui ce sont les affaires qui dirigent le monde, et aussi longtemps qu'elles seront le mieux servies là où beaucoup de bureaux sont concentrés sur une petite surface, dans des constructions projetées comme des machines pour le débit efficace des achats, ventes, négociations, opérations de banque, disputes juridiques, jeux de hasard et exploitation, ce sera l'architecture commerciale qui sera reine.» [2]

Les architectes américains étaient pris entre les réalités du marché et une mythologie culturelle qui favorisait les idéaux agraires et la notion d'une campagne sans limites en même temps que la croyance rousseauiste en la supériorité de la vie rurale par opposition à l'habitation urbaine. L'incertitude provoquée par cette coupure trouva son expression la plus forte non pas dans l'aspect général du gratte-ciel, mais dans son ornementation architecturale, un domaine plus susceptible d'échapper au genre de contrôle que le propriétaire exerçait sur les chances de négociabilité de l'édifice.

Par exemple, dans le Chrysler Building de William Van Alen (1928—30), on peut observer dans une peinture très élaborée du plafond, juste à l'intérieur du hall d'entrée, une version à échelle réduite du Chrysler Building. Ou bien, dans le hall d'entrée de l'Empire State Building, de Shreve, Lamb & Harmon (1930—31), on peut voir un relief métallique illustrant l'Empire State Building (fig 1). Et au-dessus de l'entrée du 60 Wall Tower Building de Clinton & Russell et Holton & George (1930—32) on aperçoit un modèle sculpté de l'édifice qu'il décore (fig. 2).

Il y a une raison évidente qui explique cet emploi de répliques à échelle réduite près de la porte d'entrée ou dans le hall d'entrée, c'est qu'elles donnent aux employés une compréhension plus claire de la forme de l'édifice dans lequel ils pénètrent. Dans les larges structures érigées dans les années vingt la forme générale ne peut être appréciée qu'à grande distance

↓fig. 3   Shreve, Lamb & Harmon, 500 Fifth Avenue, 1930–31. Detail of the entrance.

car, vus de près, leur silhouette devient totalement incompréhensible à cause des effets de raccourcis et des obtructions; et en général du niveau du trottoir tout ce qui se trouve au-dessus du premier «set-back» (retrait) de la façade est perdu pour le regard. Il est également évident que les architectes avaient intérêt à ce que leurs constructions restent «lisibles» malgré les obstacles de la taille gigantesque. Cette préoccupation de rendre l'architecture tangible a été articulée de manière succincte au dix-neuvième siècle par John Ruskin et fut reprise et adaptée au contexte américain par Louis Sullivan. Cependant, alors que l'intention de Ruskin et Sullivan avait été de rendre la définition globale d'une construction plus facilement discernable, il semble que le besoin de pourvoir les gratte-ciel de leur propre version miniature n'ait pas été ressenti avant le boom de la construction à New York à la fin des années vingt.

Il peut y avoir une deuxième raison à cette tentative de réduire la taille de l'édifice, qui n'a rien à voir avec le souci de lecture. En fait, ces projections miniatures pourraient bien être des réflexions sur les vrais idéaux de l'architecte. En d'autres termes, on constate un curieux renversement des anciennes conventions, selon lesquelles le petit modèle était d'habitude un remplaçant pour la structure plus large qui était désirée. Ici les petites répliques de ces constructions, qui semblaient alors gigantesques, pourraient bien se rapprocher de l'intention idéale des architectes, qui étaient incommodés par l'exécution de structures qu'ils trouvaient trop larges.

Dans le 500 5th Avenue Building (1930 à 1931) de Shreve, Lamb & Harmon, on trouve un exemple de plus de cette réduction d'échelle. Dans un bas-relief au-dessus de l'entrée une figure à genoux, vêtue d'un peplos, présente un modèle de 500 5th Avenue — peut-être une sorte de Tyché protectrice des lieux[3] (fig. 3). Dans cet exemple-ci, dans lequel le modèle architectural est accosté avec une figure humaine, les proportions de l'édifice deviennent encore plus clairement mesurables — l'édifice étant réduit à une échelle inférieure à celle de l'homme. Si Tyché était debout, 500 5th Avenue atteindrait à peu près la hauteur des anches. On peut faire la même remarque au sujet du Fuller Building de Walker & Gillette (1928—29). Deux athlétiques figures masculines réduisent le

«skyline» stylisé aux dimensions d'une petite balustrade décorative (fig. 4).

On peut ainsi considérer ces répliques miniatures comme des commentaires sur les édifices-même qu'elles décorent. Elles conservent un sens de l'échelle humaine qui n'existe plus dans les gratte-ciel eux-mêmes. Cependant, alors que beaucoup d'architectes de gratte-ciel semblent avoir manifesté quelque hésitation dans leur conception d'une tour géante pour bureaux, la plupart des artistes américains, photographes et cinéastes, étaient encore très impressionnés par la puissance romantique et l'apparence dramatique offerte par le skyline qui commençait à émerger dans les années vingt. Par exemple en 1922 l'artiste Charles Sheller et le photographe Paul Strand firent un film de Manhattan, intitulé «Manhatta», basé sur un poème de Walt Whitman, dans lequel les gratte-ciel sont romantisés. Les édifices ne sont presque jamais montrés du niveau de la rue, mais la caméra est soit pointée vers les sommets, ou bien — avec un effet encore plus dramatique — placée sur le toit d'un gratte-ciel, plongeant abruptement vers l'abîme de la rue. Les êtres humains ne sont plus rien que de minuscules incidents dans le paysage urbain.[4] Les points de vue exagérés utilisés par Sheller et Strand ont été utilisés de manière encore plus écrasante dans le film de Fritz Lang

↓ fig. 4   Walker & Gillette, Fuller Building, 1928–29. Detail of the entrance.

Metropolis (1926—27), dont l'inspiration première est aussi le skyline de Manhattan. Lang arriva à New York en 1924, et alors qu'il était retenu à bord avant d'avoir l'autorisation de désembarquer — les Allemands étaient alors encore considérés comme des ennemis — il observa la ville de son bateau, ancré sur le Hudson River, et

«regarda dans les rues les lumières éblouissantes et les bâtiments élancés — et là . . . conçut *Metropolis*».[5]

Ce même point du vue à sensation, déshumanisant et mélodramatique, tel que l'ont employé Sheeler, Strand et Lang, est encore perceptible dans les photographies que Berenice Abbott fit de la ville de New York dans les années trente. Ainsi, pour tous ceux qui n'étaient pas directement impliqués dans leur construction — que ce soit les architectes européens ou les artistes et photographes américains — les gratte-ciel conservèrent leur image de puissance lyrique et spectaculaire jusque dans les années trente.

Il y a encore un autre élément de la décoration architecturale des constructions des années vingt, qui, de même que la réduction du gratte-ciel, jette un doute sur l'acceptation sans réserve par les architectes du boom de la construction. Par exemple le Lowell Building de Churchill & Lippmann (1926) possède au-dessus de son entrée une mosaïque octogonale qui montre un paysage de gratte-ciel parsemé de verdure, avec des arbres au premier plan (fig. 5). Cette image suggère une vue de Manhattan du beau milieu de Central Park, et l'on peut y voir une référence nostalgique à la nature car les gratte-ciel y sont représentés bien moins distinctement que les arbres. De même le large bas-relief au-dessus de l'entrée du Daily News Building de Raymond Hood (1929 à 1930), utilise un écran de nuages pour cacher un panorama de gratte-ciel qui serait sans cela fort impressionnant (fig. 6). Et de ces nuages surgissent, de façon tout à fait surréaliste, des joueurs de tennis et des cavaliers, comme si le nirvâna était une partie de plein air. L'ambivalence entre l'espace construit par l'homme et l'espace naturel est ici résolu par la collusion des deux.

De même on peut sentir cet élément de nostalgie pour une communauté pré-urbaine, ou du moins une incapacité de vouloir choisir entre la ville et la campagne, dans les pages dessinées par Hugh Ferriss dans sa *Metropolis of Tomorrow*, de 1929. Le skyline de Manhattan est souvent rendu de telle manière qu'on est porté à penser à des pics rocheux et à des hautes chaînes de montagnes, si bien que montagnes et gratte-ciel deviennent des images interchangeables, et le besoin de faire un choix entre les deux est ainsi éliminé. Le Rockefeller Center, commencé à la fin des années vingt mais pas achevé avant les années trente, prit part également dans les premières versions du projet à cette schizophrénie urbaine-ex-urbaine. Selon un des premiers projets des Associated Architects, les set-backs des niveaux inférieurs ainsi que le toit devaient être utilisés pour des jardins suspendus reliés par des ponts, et auraient dû être publics. Le plus grand complexe urbain de l'époque devait donc aussi avoir une place au paradis. Cet aspect de l'édifice, proposé par les architectes, fut toutefois rejeté par les promoteurs durant la dépression économique comme étant trop coûteux.[6]

Après les années vingt, quand les ornements architecturaux commencent à être utilisés de moins en moins fréquemment, le commentaire visuel sur le gratte-ciel et la ville continue principalement dans les films, qui suivent la voie engagée par les artistes et les photographes, en faisant une mythologie de ces représentations exagérément spectaculaires. Les scènes de New York dans les années trente sont rarement réalistes. Manhattan y apparaît comme le lieu des night clubs souterrains et des attiques de millionnaires. La ville au niveau de la rue, le niveau de l'expérience commune n'apparaît presque jamais. Au contraire beaucoup de films suggèrent une hyperbole dramatique et une fuite de la ville. Dans un film typique de 1930, *Madam Satan*, de Cecil B. de Mille, le point culminant est un bal masqué à bord d'un dirigeable qui plane au-dessus de Manhattan. Le scénario décrit l'intrigue en ces termes:

«La riche et mondaine Angela Brooks découvre qu'elle est en train de perdre l'amour de son mari, Bob, au profit d'une jeune actrice effrontée nommée Trixie . . . elle projette de reconquérir son mari en réincarnant la personnalité de la mystérieuse «Madame Satan». A un bal masqué à bord d'un dirigeable géant, Angela ravit son mari par une improvisation très à la mode, au milieu d'un spectaculaire ballet électrique dans lequel les personnages simulent toutes sortes de choses, des prises électriques jusqu'aux éclairs de foudre. Après qu'elle l'ait pris au piège avec succès, le dirigeable est touché par la foudre et les hôtes sont forcés de sauter

perspective used by Sheller and Strand became even more overwhelming in Fritz Lang's *Metropolis* (1926–27), for which the Manhattan skyline was also a primary inspiration. Lang arrived in New York in 1924, and, while waiting on board for permission to disembark—Germans were then still viewed as the enemy—he watched the city from his ship, at anchor in the Hudson River, and

> "looked out into the streets at the dazzling lights and the slender buildings—and there ... conceived *Metropolis*."[5]

The same dehumanizing, melodramatic perspective used by Sheeler, Strand, and Lang can still be seen in Berenice Abbott's photographs of New York City in the 1930s. For everyone not directly involved in their construction—whether European architects or American artists and photographers—the skyscrapers thus retained an image of lyrical and spectacular power into the 1930s.

One more element of the architectural decoration of buildings in the 1920s, in addition to the miniaturization of skyscrapers, raises doubts about architects' acquiescence to the building boom. For example, Churchill & Lippmann's Lowell Building (1926) has an octagonal mosaic above its entrance, depicting a landscape of skyscrapers dotted with greenery, with trees in the foreground (fig. 5). This image, suggestive of Manhattan seen from the middle of Central Park, is a nostalgic reference to nature, since the skyscrapers are much less distinctly rendered than the trees. Similarly, the large bas-relief above the entrance to Raymond Hood's Daily News Building (1929–30) employs a screen of clouds to obscure a skyscraper panorama that would otherwise be very striking (fig. 6). Moreover, tennis players and horse riders rise surreally from these clouds in a sort of Nirvana of outdoor pursuits. The ambivalence between the man-made and the natural environment is resolved here by superimposition [*collusion*].

One can likewise discern an element of nostalgia for a preurban community, or at least an inability to choose between town and country, in the drawings of Hugh Ferriss in *Metropolis of Tomorrow*, published in 1929. Here, the Manhattan skyline is often rendered in a way that evokes rocky peaks and high mountain ranges, so that mountains and skyscrapers become interchangeable images, obviating the need to choose between them. The Rockefeller Center, begun in the late 1920s but not completed until the 1930s, also featured in this urban/exurban schizophrenia, at least in its early incarnations. In one of the first models produced by Associated Architects, the setbacks on the lower levels, as well as on the roof, were to be used for hanging gardens connected by bridges and open to the public. The largest urban complex of its time was thus also intended to take up its place in paradise. However, this proposal by the architects was rejected by Depression-era developers as too costly.[6]

After the 1920s, when architectural ornament began to be used less and less frequently, visual commentary on the skyscraper and the city continued mainly in film. Filmmakers built on earlier work by artists and photographers to create a mythology around these exaggeratedly spectacular representations. As a result, depictions of New York in the 1930s are rarely realistic. Manhattan is presented as a place of underground night clubs and millionaires' lofts. The city is hardly ever shown at street level, at the level of everyday life. On the contrary, many films suggest dramatic hyperbole and escape from the city. A typical film from 1930, Cecil B. DeMille's *Madam Satan*, culminates in a masked ball aboard an airship hovering over Manhattan. The script summarizes the plot in these terms:

> "Wealthy socialite Angela Brooks finds she is losing the love of her husband, Bob, to a wild young showgirl named Trixie; ... she sets out to recapture her husband by taking on the personality of the mysterious 'Madam Satan.' At a costume party given aboard a giant dirigible, Angela entrances her husband by her modish vamping, amidst a spectacular electrical ballet in which characters simulate everything from sparkplugs to lightning bolts. After she has successfully ensnared him, the dirigible is struck by lightning, and the guests are forced to parachute from the ship, Angela giving hers to the distraught Trixie. Realizing his love for Angela, Bob gives her his parachute and dives from the ship, suffering only minor injuries by landing in the Central Park Reservoir."[7]

While the architects introduced an element of the human scale into the imagery of architectural ornament, filmmakers had developed a vision of New York as a place where you never have to come down to earth.

ENDNOTES

1 Edwin Avery Park, *New Backgrounds for a New Age* (New York, 1927), 141–42.

2 Sheldon Cheney, *The New World Architecture* (New York, 1930), 120.

3 This figure, although seemingly ancient in appearance, is not really Tyche, as it does not wear the usual mural crown; instead, it holds something resembling a winged solar disc. The figure therefore suggests the eclectic interests of architects educated in the Beaux Arts tradition more than any specific model.

4 The implications of Paul Strand's imagery are discussed in detail in an unpublished study of Paul Strand by Maria Morris, Department of Art History, Columbia University, 1975.

5 Peter Bogdanovich, *Fritz Lang in America* (New York, 1967), 15.

6 A good summary of the history of the Rockefeller Center and images of this project can be found in William H. Jordy, *American Buildings and Their Architects: The Impact of European Modernism in the Mid-twentieth Century* (New York, 1972).

7 *American Film Institute Catalogue of Feature Films 1921–1930* (Los Angeles, 1971), 471. This information comes from an unpublished study of American cinema in the 1930s by Maite Chaves, Department of Art History, Columbia University, 1975.

↓ fig. 5   Henry S. Churchill and Herbert Lippmann, The Lowell, 1926. Entrance.

↓ fig. 6   Howells & Hood, News Building, 1929–30. Detail of the relief above the entrance.

en parachute; Angela donne son parachute à Trixie prise de panique. Se rendant compte de son amour pour Angela, Bob lui donne le sien et plonge hors de l'aéronef. Au prix de quelques contusions mineures il atterrit dans le Réservoir de Central Park . . .»[7]

Alors que les architectes avaient introduit un élément à l'échelle humaine dans l'imagerie de l'ornement architectural, les cinéastes développèrent une vision de New York comme un lieu où il n'est pas nécessaire de descendre sur terre.

[1]   Edwin Avery Park, *New Backgrounds for a New Age*, New York, 1927, pp. 141–142.
[2]   Sheldon Cheney, *The New World Architecture*, Londres, New York, 1930, p. 120.
[3]   Cette figure, quoique d'apparence antique, n'est pas vraiment une Tyché, car, elle ne porte pas l'habituelle couronne murale, mais elle tient quelque chose qui ressemble à un disque solaire ailé. Cette figure suggère ainsi plus l'intérêt éclectique d'architectes éduqués aux Beaux-Arts que des modèles spécifiques.
[4]   Les implications de l'imagerie de Paul Strand sont discutées en détail dans l'étude non publiée sur *Paul Strand* de Marria Morris, département d'histoire de l'art, Columbia University, 1975.
[5]   Peter Bogdanovich, *Fritz Lang in America*, New York, 1967, p. 15.
[6]   On peut trouver un bon résumé de l'histoire du Rockefeller Center et des illustrations de ce projet dans William H. Jordy, *American Buildings and their Architects: The Impact of European Modernism in the Mid-Twentieth Century*, New York, 1972.
[7]   *American Film Institute Catalogue of Feature Films 1921–1930*, 1971, p. 471. Cette information provient d'une étude non publiée sur le cinéma américain des années trente, faite par Maite Chaves, département d'histoire de l'art, Columbia University, 1975.

Traduction: Irène von Moos

N.B.: Les illustrations sont toutes dues à des photographies de Cervin Robinson.

II REALISM AND AUTONOMY

123
From Idealism
to Disenchantment:
Realism in and
beyond *archithese*
    by Irina Davidovici

142
To Laugh in Order Not to Cry:
Interview with Robert Venturi
and Denise Scott Brown
    by Stanislaus von Moos

167
Rules, Realism, and History
    by Alan Colquhoun

177
Problems of Architecture
and Realism
    by Giorgio Grassi

188
A Realist Education
    by Aldo Rossi

194
On The Problem of
Inner Architectonic Reality
    by Bruno Reichlin
    and Martin Steinmann

From Idealism to Disenchantment

Realism in and beyond *archithese*

Irina Davidovici

Two issues of *archithese* published in the mid-1970s (number 13 / 1975 and number 19 / 1976) framed the agenda of architectural realism and autonomy that would shortly accompany the arrival of postmodernism. Under the shared title "Realismus in der Architektur" (Realism in Architecture) each issue had its own particular handle on the theme. Issue 13, subtitled "Las Vegas etc.," literally pink-tinted realism with reflective irony, connecting it to Robert Venturi's and Denise Scott Brown's forays into middle-class American popular culture. Issue 19, coedited with guests Martin Steinmann and Bruno Reichlin, had the explicitly theoretical ambition to provide a cogent, if synthetic, definition. Presenting a mainly European perspective focused on Italian neorationalism, the editors painted a pluralist overview of architectural realism as a theory whose general validity would transcend specific historical or cultural conditions. The differences between these two issues were partly explained by the make-up of the editorial boards. The first had been curated by the *archithese* editor in chief, Stanislaus von Moos, together with his two U.S. guest editors and Swiss historian Jacques Gubler. The second issue had been coedited by von Moos with Steinmann and Reichlin, both trained architects and researchers at the gta Institute of ETH Zurich, who brought an undertone of earnest theoretical density. The two issues were conceived as a diptych: the first, exploring an impressionistic understanding of realism through the lens of contemporary architecture; the second offering a systematic overview from historical and theoretical perspectives.[1]

Culled from both *archithese* issues, the texts selected for this section were penned partly by Swiss writers (von Moos, Steinmann, Reichlin) and partly by international figures (Venturi and Scott Brown, Giorgio Grassi, Aldo Rossi, Alan Colquhoun). Their range bears testimony to the journal's global perspective and explains the wider, indeed international, resonance the journal had by this time acquired. The historical legacy of the texts lies in their early exploration of ideas that later became defining components of architectural postmodernism, anticipating its explicit emergence in Charles Jencks's *The Language of Post-modern Architecture* (1977). Their curatorship betrays an editorial ambition to forego the immediate interests of the Swiss readership in favor of contributing to a wider theoretical discourse. Veering from the pragmatic aim of the journal's funders—to present the latest architectural developments worldwide to the local professional audience— issues 13 and 19 were intended as an international contribution, demonstrating the journal's relevance beyond its immediate context. Subsequently, the concepts of architectural realism and autonomy were woven together into a hybrid design method that gained traction in the Swiss architecture of the 1980s and 1990s, influencing and resonating in various contextual architectural productions in Europe and beyond.

This text provides commentaries for the selected articles, integrating them into a partial overview of the established discourse on architectural realism and autonomy. In the decades since the selected articles first appeared, a perceptible sense of transformation occurred in the oscillations between the theories and practices associated with these notions. Historically, even when intended to express a critical view of a nominal "real," realism was grounded in the search for an underlying order. In its societal dimensions, the disenchantment of architectural realists concealed an ultimately idealist belief in the existence and necessity of meaning. Today, overtaken by other priorities, that perspective is tinged with the nostalgia usually reserved for certitudes that no longer matter.

An Imperfect Reality

The conversation "To Laugh in Order Not to Cry"[2] between von Moos, Venturi, and Scott Brown, recorded in October 1974 in Philadelphia, posits the notion of realism as the precondition for socially engaged architecture. In opposition to the modernists' attempts to bend reality to suit their vision, Venturi and Scott Brown acknowledge existing constraints and contradictions as generators of form.[3] This position is reflected in the issue's editorial, which states,

> Today, the renunciation of bold building alternatives, the acceptance of reality and what is possible within its framework is an important concern of socially committed architects. ... It is not just a matter of escaping into a sociological and planning empiricism, but also to challenge the architect to take a closer look at the rich store of traditional and folkloric images and forms that history has left us.[4]

Realism, that is, is a political matter, informed by the specificity of socioeconomic conditions. Conversely, the attempt to conceal or suppress them to bring into being an alternative reality—procedures associated with the modernist project and manifest since the late 1960s in U.S. advocacy planning—is seen as a withdrawal from reality:

> [I]t seems to us that the usual rhetoric of modern architecture about "building for the poor," and so on, is not an approach to reality but a flight from it. And as soon as one tries to keep a lookout for opportunities to get closer to the reality, one finds that there is simply no option other than to work within the system—or to give up and design utopias.[5]

This critique of modernist design procedures, however, contains a paradox that hinges upon architecture's social engagement. Both modes of practice—the former aiming at the production of transformative utopias, the latter at the analysis and interpretation of the realities on the ground—claim a sense of social conscience. At the same time, both are defeatist: whether by engaging in knowingly quixotic attempts at challenging the hegemonic system or by subverting it from within. The realist approach of Venturi and Scott Brown consisted of studying "what cities actually look like and ... understand why it is that they look the way they do—without all too many aesthetic and moral expectations."[6] Nevertheless, this critical acceptance resulted in a misalignment of design aims and procedures. Venturi and Scott Brown used irony as a critical device to distance themselves from the imperfect reality they were attempting to make sense of:

> Our answer is that we try as best we can to get closer to the realization of our social concerns—specifically, in the immediate future and with the aid of instruments that the society around us makes available. As artists, we use irony. … We see irony as a means to help the individual to survive in a culturally multicolored, thrown-together society. We believe that the role of a socially committed artist or architect in our society does not have to be so far removed from that of a jester.[7]

The title of the interview, "To Laugh in Order Not to Cry," indicates the true cost of adjusting to an imperfect reality. If, by using irony, Venturi and Scott Brown found they could address the lack of ideological content and the potential generalization of postwar capitalism, they also acknowledge that the conclusions thus reached are incomplete.

The Right to Architecture
The shift in tone of the second *archithese* issue on "Realism in Architecture" is largely explained by the influence of its guest coeditors. Unlike the art historian von Moos, Steinmann and Reichlin had trained as architects at the ETH during the 1960s, part of a politicized generation that closely followed the debates of Italian neorationalism. Both men had conducted research at the gta Institute in the chair of Adolf Max Vogt. The Ticinese Reichlin had assisted, together with his partner in practice, Fabio Reinhart, Rossi's teaching studio at ETH from 1972 to 1974. In 1973 they had been actively involved in the Fifteenth Triennale in Milan, "Architettura Razionale," and in 1976, alongside Eraldo Consolascio, had collaborated with Rossi on his Venice Biennale exhibit, the collage *Città analoga (The Analogous City)*. A researcher at the gta Institute from 1968 and until 1978, in 1975 Steinmann curated the ETH exhibition *Tendenzen—Neuere Architektur im Tessin*, which theoretically reframed the recent Ticinese architecture as an illustration of architectural autonomy.[8] The collaborative editorship of *archithese* 19 followed a similar agenda to the *Tendenzen* exhibition, exploring the potential of realism to enact a "critical revision of the notion of architecture itself."[9] To this end, the editors invited contributions from

architects Colquhoun, Grassi, Rossi, and Scott Brown, Marxist philosopher Hans Heinz Holz, and architectural historian Otakar Mácel.

Steinmann and Reichlin's definition of *realism* was relative to the notion of architectural autonomy. Rather than consider the role of architecture within wider cultural, political, and social structures, they proposed an interpretation of realism pertaining, first, to intradisciplinary reflections on the history of architecture and, second, to its material presence. Their essay "On the Problem of Inner Architectonic Reality" examines how the conceptual category of realism could be applied to architecture. In the article, Steinmann and Reichlin reject both the purely ideological and purely functional understandings of realism, focusing instead on its rhetorical potential. This vision of realism amalgamated Rossi's interest in formal typological analogy with Venturi and Scott Brown's appreciation of everyday environments.

For Steinmann and Reichlin, the inherent reality of architecture is generated in dialogue with its own history. Quoting Rossi's hermetic formulation "l'architettura sono le architetture [architecture is architectures]," they argue that "the fundamental dimension of meaning *lies in the relatedness of architectural language to itself* (self-reflexivity)."[10] On the other hand, echoing Scott Brown's contribution, they posit architecture's inherent reality in an empirical understanding, ultimately aimed at the experience of its constructed, material existence. This grounding of architectural production in readings of reality—cultural baggage, rules, habits, and customs derived from personal and collective experiences—established ideological connections with both neorationalism and structuralism. Realism in architecture is thus understood in a double sense in which its reflections on social reality are ultimately subsumed under its own, sensuous nature.

> The repression of architecture's own concrete reality has brought with it its reduction to an "object of daily use." This is in keeping with a general trend to separate contemplative life from practical life and to restrict it to a compensatory, consolatory function. Practical life permits only desire (*désir*), which is the driving force of the capitalist process of valorization, but it precludes self-satisfying pleasure (*plaisir*).... The pleasure of architecture is one of these deprived pleasures. The goal is to demand in the name of realism the right to the pleasure of architecture.[11]

Delivered with the confidence of a manifesto, this final statement nevertheless opens more questions than it answers. It posits the aesthetic pleasure of architecture as a counterpart to its utility and outward desirability, both equally subject to capitalist consumption. Freeing the aesthetic experience from the same predicament, however, implies an autonomy of architecture without recourse: its ultimate isolation as artwork. The intellectual legacy of the article is cemented at its midpoint, where it addresses the question of architectural intelligibility: "Understanding the significance of a work means determining its position within a dense network of relationships. The denser this network is, the more numerous the examples, and the more concrete the knowledge, the more structured the field of architecture seems to the observer, no matter his preferences."[12] According to the authors, this density of meanings renders architecture legible—presumably as symbol but also in the concrete entanglements of form, material, construction, typology, and relations to site. In this legibility—that is, in the architectural work's connections to embodied experience—the work is able to lay claim to its realism. In hindsight, this statement can be read as an incipient form of a design method that situates every architectural object in a network of relationships—from its inner-architectural, typological history to the history of its site. This vision had profound implications for the subsequent Swiss and international discourse.

Between Autonomy and Heteronomy

For British architect and critic Colquhoun, realism represented an entry point to the issue of architectural autonomy. His essay "Rules, Realism, and History" examines the tension between architecture as "self-referential system" with its own traditions and value systems, and architecture as a "social product" shaped by wider social and economic circumstances.[13] Colquhoun is more skeptical of its aesthetic dimensions. He argues that historical attempts in art to circumvent stylistic norms by defining realism as a universal, unmediated language had been doomed, since the understanding and the representation of "reality" were different categories to begin with. Conversely, architecture retained a double condition—as part of the real world and as representation of that world—which the modern movement had "radically" conflated. The overlap between the (supposed universally intelligible) classical rule systems and the actual circumstances of architecture had resulted in a fundamental misalignment of form and content. Colquhoun resolves this tension in a dialectic manner, arguing that any substantive change in architectural norms must take into account "two variables—the socio-economic system and the aesthetic rule system—[that] can only be accounted for dialectically."[14] Paradoxically, architecture's attempts to achieve realism by evading stylistic norms resulted in a new dominant style. Its disconnection from the ideological or symbolic meanings attached to certain forms had resulted in an eclecticism even more arbitrary than that of the nineteenth century, of which Rossi's "purely self-reflective" Gallaratese housing block is a prime example.[15] Given the proven futility of the search for an unmediated, primordial language, Colquhoun argues that the rethinking of realism must take into account the constant modification of cultural conventions by external socio-economic pressures. The emergent synthetic, contingent realism "would gain its validity both from existing aesthetic structures and from a reality which would affect and alter these structures."[16]

The text "Problems of Architecture and Realism," also included in *archithese* 19, is the transcription of a lecture delivered by Italian architect Grassi at ETH on June 2, 1976. Its point of departure is Georg Lukács's aesthetic theory describing the architectural work as simultaneously fulfilling a function and expressing this function symbolically. Grassi proposes the notion of "appropriateness" as the framework for architecture's responsibilities as an inherently collective work. "Thus the notion of 'suitability' must always include the generalizing tendency that characterizes the historical experience of architecture; that is, the sense common to all the solutions of a particular problem that architecture poses to itself over time, be it the house, the public place, the street, and so on."[17]

Architecture's collective intelligibility is illustrated through a gamut of aspects: the correspondence of formal articulations and methods of construction, the relation to handicraft, the durability of meanings attached to forms, the necessity of professional "discipline" as guarantor of its communicability. Its potential as cultural superstructure is inextricably tied to its contribution to wider societal goals. In the end, "while architecture is linked to an immediate use, it is also the 'world' that most directly bears witness to the collective desire to leave a trace for the future."[18] Grassi's argument is thus aligned with Colquhoun's dialectic of architecture as artistic and social product, yet stops short of advancing a more proactive agenda.

Rossi's contribution, "A Realist Education," came at a pivotal moment in his career. In the same year, he exhibited at the Venice Biennale the collage *La città analoga*, created with his Zurich assistants Reichlin, Reinhart, and Consolascio, and published the related article "An Analogical Architecture" in *A+U*.[19] Through these outlets, Rossi unveiled a new design method based on "a different sense of history, conceived of not simply as fact but rather as a series of things, of affective objects to be used by the memory or in a design."[20] Analogical architecture is inherently subjective, articulating forms through the processing of personal experiences, sources, and decisions. Rossi's reorientation toward an individual poetics effectively supplanted the rationalism of his earlier typological and morphological method, which he had deployed during his teaching at ETH from 1972 to 1974 and which his ETH devotees still zealously followed.

Contrary to Reichlin and Steinmann, in his article Rossi is skeptical about architecture's connection to "realism," a category usually pertaining to art, literature, and film: "However, unless for some academic purpose, it is silly to make realism into a category of architecture. Otherwise, it will end up like rationalism, or symmetry, or so many other names that are useful for expressing a certain idea."[21] He argues that architecture could be realist only inasmuch as built artifacts have the capacity, with admittedly limited means, to produce genuine emotion. The title "A Realist Education" refers to early formative experiences carrying emotive reactions that, in time, had become personal resources for his own projects: the "distant, fascinating, grandiose" reality of socialist realist art, the "everyday and antique" realism of Roman construction and Lombard houses. These references built up a multifaceted concept of "reality," blurred by personal reflections and analogies so as to acknowledge its own subjectivity.[22]

Dialectical Realisms

The two *archithese* issues on architectural realism bring together a wide range of disciplinary and methodological approaches. The collection of critical essays is arranged around a set of dialectical tensions, sampling—as Ákos Moravánszky argues—Rossi's existential listlessness and Scott Brown's unedited reality as an ideological polarity.[23] This is due not only to the use of opposite referential frames, socialist-realist and liberal-capitalist, but also to procedural differences. Rossi's insistence on formal autonomy and Venturi Scott Brown's nonjudgmental acceptance of the everyday—Rossi emphasizing the formal aspects of architecture; Venturi Scott Brown, its sociopolitical reality—rendered a dialectical rereading inevitable. Colquhoun, Grassi, Steinmann, and Reichlin seem to concur that such a dialectic is centered on the constantly renegotiated tension between the aesthetic and functional attributes of architecture. Colquhoun rephrases the dichotomy of architectural autonomy versus its social origins and responsibilities as a "dialectical process, in which aesthetic norms are modified by external forces to achieve a provisional synthesis."[24] Accordingly, the "traditional" realism that sought to read "real" conditions by rejecting stylistic choice could be superseded by a dialectical reading that considered both the actual conditions explored and the aesthetic dimensions they generate. Steinmann's and Reichlin's affirmation of architecture's concrete reality sought to resist the excessive intellectualization of architecture, a reiteration of its material presence. Subsequent developments in the actual architectural production of northern Switzerland over the following two decades offer several illustrations of such syntheses.

Realism and Postmodernism in Swiss Architecture

The *archithese* realism issues illustrate the debt of Swiss architecture to a double theoretical import, Anglo-Saxon and Italian, widely associated with postmodernism. The weight and significance ascribed in Switzerland to this discourse is all the more remarkable since, in the 1980s, the highly heterogeneous architectural profession almost monolithically rejected postmodernism as an architectural proposition. The collective attitude is neatly summarized by Ticinese practitioner Flora Ruchat-Roncati, who dismisses it as "a purely pictorial, superficial dimension."[25] Across regional and generational categories, the Swiss voiced their rejection of formal arbitrariness, their contempt for frivolous irony, their suspicion of elaborate theories, and their abhorrence of shoddy construction—all seen as postmodernist motifs. Above all, however, postmodernism challenged Swiss architecture's uninterrupted, if constantly probed, relation to architectural modernism as a form of cultural habituation.

As a rallying cry in 1980s and 1990s Swiss architecture, opposition to the postmodern discourse paved the way to its own self-definition. And yet, along ideological and intellectual lines, this resistance became both more nuanced and more partial. An older generation, cast in a firmly rationalist mold, would not accept the masking of rational structures behind stylized historicist elements—a procedure seen, in the modernist mindset, less as ironic than blasphemous. Even those who openly grappled with the impossibility of a total correspondence of form and construction balked at the idea of an arbitrary, seemingly haphazardly applied, classicist scenography.

In contrast, the younger generation of Swiss architects born around 1950, several of whom had studied at ETH under Rossi, were well attuned to the reevaluation of history as an instrument for design. Whether rejecting a historicist-formalist set or a constructional Potemkin village, they relied, to a great extent knowingly, upon the conceptual foundations of postmodernism, showing a keen interest in its design procedures. This cohort instrumentalized the conceptual and methodological principles of postmodernism to carve out a position distinct from the somewhat dogmatic, limited, and dated modernism of their older peers. This Oedipal impulse manifested itself in the amalgamation of motifs derived equally from the work of Rossi and Venturi Scott Brown. Rossi's melancholy appreciation of postindustrial landscapes merged with Venturi's and Scott Brown's fascination with a vital popular culture, finding new expressions in the local situation. By virtue of economic and political conjectures (the import of U.S. material values, the palpable effects of the transition from industrial manufacture to a service economy), both motifs reverberated deeply in postwar Switzerland. The proliferation of peripheral rust belts and the emergence of a new entropic (sub)urbanization, amplified by the economic slumps of the 1970s and early 1990s, represented a main category of the "real" that architects felt bound to address. As Herzog & de Meuron compellingly asked,

> What else can we do but carry within us all these images of the city, or pre-existing architecture and building forms and building materials, the smell of asphalt and car exhaust and rain and to use our pre-existing reality as a starting point and build our architecture in pictorial analogies? The utilization of these pictorial analogies, their dissection and recomposition into an architectural reality is a central theme in our work.[26]

This translation of "pre-existing reality" into "an architectural" one lies at the crux of architectural realism. In the Swiss case, realism sided strongly with Rossian melancholy, whereas Venturi's and Scott Brown's distancing use of irony was collectively met with a blank stare. If, throughout the 1970s, the fascination with Rossi's discourse led to experiments with the stark geometries of neorationalism, by 1980 this latter-day Italianate style had been abandoned — and with it, much of the formal vocabulary of a developing postmodernism.[27] The reason was the collective recognition that the resulting architecture barely resonated in the Swiss popular imagination. As Marcel Meili wrote, "it was impossible simply to graft rationalistic Italian typologies onto our existing cities."[28] Instead, Meili and his contemporaries advocated an architecture that retrieved its meaning "from the fabric of customary activities secreted by actual modes of life in Switzerland, rather than from a typological tradition."[29] One of the most literal adaptations of the Rossian discourse to the Swiss context was pursued over many years in the ETH Analogue Architecture Studio, originally set up by Reinhart, Rossi's former assistant. The architecture of the "analogues" was redefined through the "oldnew" (*altneu*) architecture of Miroslav Šik, a contemporary of Meili and a fellow student in Rossi's studio at ETH in 1977–78.[30]

I have discussed elsewhere the multiple meanings ascribed by Swiss architects to the idea of realism.[31] The varied positions of architects such as Herzog & de Meuron, Šik, Meili Peter, Burkhalter Sumi, and other contemporaries signals the range and heterogeneity of Swiss realism. Alternate categories—the sensory presence of material, the reconstruction of everyday environments or practices, the pragmatism of construction, the adoption and abstraction of typical forms, and so on—could all be seen as realist design strategies. Little else connects, ideologically or referentially, the synthetic modernism of Diener & Diener's knowingly anonymous buildings in Basel; the timber grammar of Burkhalter and Sumi's forestry stations; the didactic tectonic experiments of Meili Peter; Gion Caminada's exacting reinterpretations of vernacular in his native Vrin; or the deployment of local gneiss in Peter Zumthor's Therme in Vals. And yet, all these take as a point of departure a generalized design method, based on the objective, nonsentimental appraisal of existing situations. Whether inspired by local modernisms in a minor key, the pathos of suburbia, or abstractions of alpine vernaculars, this common method drew its meaning from the analysis, interpretation, and reconstitution of typical, culturally recognizable "preexisting" realities.

Realism in Translation

The *archithese* explorations of architectural realism in the mid-1970s created a nexus of connections between Swiss architecture and international theory. Their trajectory is easier to identify closer to the time, most notably in the republication and translation of selected *archithese* themes, articles, and authors. These contributions propelled a wider discussion around the operative role of history as architectural tool, subsequently incorporated into postmodernist design procedures. Bernard Huet, who edited the thematic issue of *L'architecture d'aujourd'hui* "Formalisme-Réalisme," translated three texts from the 1976 *archithese* issue "Realismus in der Architektur": Rossi's and Steinmann and Reichlin's texts in full, and excerpts of Grassi's ETH lecture "Architekturprobleme und Realismus."[32] Huet placed Italian neorealism—and Manfredo Tafuri's theorization of early twentieth-century realism—in the *archithese* trajectory of Ernst Bloch, Bertolt Brecht, Soviet socialist art, and Mácel. His editorial presents realism as a counterpart to a "political," "technocratic," and ultimately "irrational" formalism that had raised the specter of architecture's dissolution into economic or technical operations.[33] Conversely, Huet argues that realism in architecture does not consist merely in "accepting reality, but of using it in order to transform it politically."[34] This attitude echoes Brecht's plea for a politicized realist writing capable of "discovering the causal complexes of society / unmasking the prevailing view of things as the view of those who are in power / writing from the standpoint of the class which offers the broadest solutions for the pressing difficulties in which human society is caught up."[35]

In 1989, the issue of realism reemerged as the appeal of postmodern irony unraveled. Liane Lefaivre locates the "Dirty Realism" of emerging European architects away from the populist projections of Venturi and Scott Brown and in the urban grittiness of corroding industrial neighborhoods:

> Whereas the pop contextualists of the 1960s were "learning" from the vital popular culture, these architects of the late 1980s appear to be "learning" from the frayed, abandoned, once-thriving industrial edges of cities and from their ransacked centres; from the Docklands in London, La Biccoca in Milan, the Péripheriques in Paris and Lyon, Kreuzberg and Moabit in Berlin. Reality is seen as harsher, and consequently the mood is on the whole confrontational. [36]

This "harsher" actuality was equivalent to the urban discontinuities that Herzog and Meili had acknowledged and felt compelled to address in their own design. Lefaivre illustrates her notion of "Dirty Realism" with a different and diverse coterie, including Jean Nouvel, Rem Koolhaas, Laurids Ortner, Carel Weeber, Kees Christiaanse, Hans Kollhoff, and Zaha Hadid. Their inclusion is argued based on a common method, extracted from the confrontation with the context of a European everyday—described in the article as "Reaganomic, Thatcherite, postindustrial."³⁷ These architects grounded their designs in common strategies of estrangement, which Lefaivre connects with the procedure of *ostranenie*, or defamiliarization, coined by Russian formalist Viktor Shklovsky.³⁸ There is no clear reason to exclude from Lefaivre's account the design operations of Swiss contemporaries, who also engaged within the immediate context by incorporating its fragments into their designs, submitting them to degrees of abstraction, reductivism, and recomposition. These common strategies, rather than the specific cultural context of the architects, rendered "dirty realism" an artistic strategy for its moment in time.

A Less Innocent Realism
The notions of architectural realism and autonomy that *archithese* had explored in 1976 came back to the fore in the early 2000s in the context of the postmodernism reviews that began, in earnest, at the end of its implicit statute of limitations. The architectural discourse trailed, as it often does, cultural criticism. Art historian Tomás Llorens distinguishes realism as a critical category—not merely as the faithful representation of a given reality but as giving formal expression to otherwise unexpressed social realities.³⁹ As early as 1996, Hal Foster had located "The Return of the Real" in the attempts of artistic neo-avant-gardes to ground artistic production in societal critique.⁴⁰ Foster theorized art-historical realism in terms of cultural trauma, itself based on the Lacanian theoretical model of "the traumatic as a missed encounter with the real."⁴¹ Following the cultural imprint left by the tragic apocalyptic reality of 9/11, this theme was then forcefully reprised in U.S. discourse, which has rewritten the notion of realism into an altogether less stable and objectivity-affirming construct than ever before. This indefinite pluralism is made explicit in *The Real Perspecta* (2010), in which the newer, less innocent realism is loosely framed by the lens of "the physical, the imaginary, and the traumatic."⁴² In comparison with the equivalent project of *archithese*, this heterogeneous collection of essays no longer offers a comprehensive framework for a recognizable realism.

In the architectural discourse of the last two decades, realism and autonomy have been revisited in the context of major reevaluations of 1960s, 1970s, and 1980s theory. These reviews did not merely position these notions historically but also pondered their continued impact.[43] K. Michael Hays circumscribes the peculiarity of architectural realism by arguing that "the 'real' represented by architectural realism is a real that architecture itself has produced."[44] In *Architecture's Desire* (2010), he reiterates architecture's capacity to comment critically on—rather than merely depict—the realities that be.[45] In *The Project of Autonomy* (2008), Pier Vittorio Aureli sites autonomy in the context of the politicized debates of 1960s Italian architecture, in which Rossi played a central role. Realism in an era of postcriticality is addressed in *Utopia's Ghost* (2010), Reinhold Martin's reframing of postmodernism as a discursive formation. Martin returns to a central dilemma of realism, architecture's dual condition as both the representation of reality and an actual component thereof: "a cipher in which is encoded a virtual universe of production and consumption, as well as a material unit, a piece of that universe that helps to keep it going."[46] Martin had earlier addressed the paradox of realism by announcing the notion of "utopian realism" as a "style with no form ... utopian not because it dreams impossible dreams, but because it recognized 'reality' itself as—precisely—an all-too-real dream enforced by those who prefer to accept a destructive and oppressive status quo."[47]

Thanks to its relativism, realism is the gift that keeps on giving. While its exhaustive review is not the objective here, certain common themes are worth highlighting. In *The Antinomies of Realism* (2013), Fredric Jameson revisits nineteenth-century realist literature as the synthesis of "narrative impulse" (the *récit* as the context and the act of narration) and "the realm of affect" (in which the story is elaborated to achieve a scenic affective quality).[48] Mary Lou Lobsinger applies this antinomic character to her analysis of postwar Italian housing. By confronting the intrinsic paradox of realism with the ideological and typological trajectory of housing projects, from Tiburtino to Corviale, she acknowledges not only the bewildering variety of positions included in the theoretical notion but also the necessity of grounding it at all times in the (relative) reality of the architectural project.

In the mid-1970s, *archithese* merely reopened the debates on realism; it could not bring them to an ordered conclusion. Its international contributions were later credited in K. Michael Hays's anthology *Architecture Theory since 1968* (1998) and historicized in Beatriz Colomina's *Clip Stamp Fold* (2010).[49] And yet, the newer reconsiderations of realism make few, if any, explicit references to the *archithese* discourse. On the one hand, the *archithese* realism issues are themselves reflections of an international discourse into which they were quite naturally reassimilated. On the other hand, this process of assimilation should not stop us from acknowledging their momentous impact on a constellation of related agents and protagonists who were key drivers of subsequent developments in Swiss architecture. As with Italian theory in the late 1960s and early 1970s, realism and autonomy were connected in *archithese* with a renewed understanding of historical study as retaining a certain operativity.[50] Within this mindset, history—and, indeed, its emanations in present-day reality: types, landscapes, the city—could be used to clarify architectural problems and define new design strategies. Its consequences for Swiss practice have been discussed, and the effects still reverberate today.[51]

The notion of realism in architecture is, as in art, subject to an unresolvable oscillation between its double ontology as artifact in the world and as representation of that world. Architecture, moreover, locates the paradox of realism in the impossibility of any number of subjective dispersed realities being summed up as one nominal "reality" or being adequately represented by any one, static building.[52] The dispersed realities of the twenty-first century preclude even the remote possibility of a cogent synthesis like that formulated in the *archithese* issues decades ago. Revisiting their notion of realism today brings attention, more than anything else, to its idealism.

1   Editorial, "'Realismus' in der Architektur," *archithese* 13 (1975): 3.

2   "'To Laugh in Order not to Cry' Interview with Robert Venturi and Denise Scott Brown," Interview by Stanislaus von Moos, 142–64 in this publication. First published in *archithese* 13 (1975): 17-32.

3   Stanislaus von Moos, "Las Vegas etc.," *archithese* 13 (1975): 16.

4   Editorial, "'Realismus' in der Architektur," *archithese* 13 (1975): 2–3. Translation by the author.

5   "'To Laugh in Order not to Cry'" (see note 2), 142–64.

6   Ibid., 155.

7   Ibid.

8   K. Michael Hays, ed., *Architecture Theory since 1968* (Cambridge MA: MIT Press, 1998), 246.

9   Stanislaus von Moos, "Realismus in der Architektur," *archithese* 19 (1976): 2. Translation by the author.

10 Bruno Reichlin and Martin Steinmann, "On the Problem of Inner Architectonic Reality," 194–209, 205 in this publication; emphasis in original. First published in *archithese* 19 (1976): 3–11. This argument repeats an identical statement in Bruno Reichlin and Fabio Reinhart, "Die Historie als Teil der Architekturtheorie: Anmerkungen zu neuen Projekten für Zürich, Bellinzona, Modena und Muggiò," *archithese* 11 (1974): 20–29, here 21.

11 Reichlin and Steinmann, "On the Problem" (see note 10), 206; emphasis in original.

12 Ibid., 205.

13 Alan Colquhoun, "Rules, Realism, and History," 166–75 in this publication. First published in *archithese* 19 (1976): 12–17, here 14. First English publication in Alan Colquhoun, *Collected Essays in Architectural Criticism: Modern Architecture and Historical Change* (Cambridge, MA: MIT Press, 1981), 67–74.

14 Colquhoun, "Rules, Realism, and History" (see note 13), 173.

15 Ibid., 174.

16 Ibid.

17 Giorgio Grassi, "Problems of Architecture and Realism," 176–87, 178 in this publication. First published in *archithese* 19 (1976): 18–24, here 20.

18 Ibid., 184.

19 Aldo Rossi, "An Analogical Architecture," trans. David Stewart, *Architecture and Urbanism* 56 (May 1976): 74–76.

20 Ibid.

21 Aldo Rossi, "A Realist Education," 188–93 in this publication. First published in *archithese* 19 (1976): 25–26. Republished in *L'architecture d'Aujourd'hui*, 190 (1977): 38.

22 Ibid., 193.

23 Ákos Moravánszky, "Formen exaltierter Kälte: Rossis Rationalismus und die Deutschschweizer Architektur," in *Aldo Rossi und die Schweiz: Architektonische Wechselwirkungen*, ed. Judith Hopfengärtner and Ákos Moravánszky, 209–22 (Zurich: gta Verlag, 2011), 220.

24 Colquhoun, "Rules, Realism, and History" (see note 13), 174.

25 Tibor Joanelly and Flora Ruchat-Roncati, "Erfahrung und Zufall: Gespräch mit Flora Ruchat-Roncati, der einzigen, nun scheidenden ordentlichen Professorin des Departements Architektur der ETH Zürich," *Tec21* 128 (2002): 7.

26 Jacques Herzog, "The Hidden Geometry of Nature" (1988), trans. Claire Bonney, in *Herzog & de Meuron*, ed. Wilfred Wang (Zurich: Artemis Verlag, 1992), 143.

27 Rossian formal motifs can be identified in the projects of his students at ETH in 1973 and 1974, as well as in their early buildings; for example, Herzog & de Meuron's Blue House (Oberwil, 1979–80). See Pia Simmendiger, "Entwurfsarbeiten aus Rossis Jahreskursen an der ETH Zürich," in *Aldo Rossi und die Schweiz* (see note 23), 55–68; Philip Urspung, "Die Rückkehr des Realen," in *Aldo Rossi und die Schweiz* (see note 23), 197–208.

28 Marcel Meili, "A Few Remarks Concerning Swiss-German Architecture," *a+u Architecture and Urbanism* 309 (1996): 24–25, here 24.

29 Marcel Meili, "Ein paar Bauten, viele Pläne," in *Architektur in der Deutschen Schweiz 1980–1990*, exh. cat., ed. Peter Disch (Lugano: ADV, 1991), 22. Free translation from the German text.

30 See Eva Willenegger, Lukas Imhof, and Miroslav Šik, *Analogue Oldnew Architecture* (Lucerne: Quart, 2019).

31 For a more extensive discussion of realism in Swiss architecture, see Irina Davidovici, "The Paradox of Realism," in *Forms of Practice: German Swiss Architecture 1980–2000* (Zurich: gta Verlag, 2018), 293–303.

32 *L'architecture d'aujourd'hui* 190 (April 1977).

33 Bernard Huet, "Formalisme-réalisme," in *L'architecture d'aujourd'hui* 190 (April 1977): 35–36.

34 Ibid., 36.

35 Bertolt Brecht, "Popularity and Realism" (1938), in *Modern Art and Modernism: A Critical Anthology*, ed. Francis Frascina and Charles Harrison, 227–32 (New York: Harper and Row, 1982), 231.

36 Liane Lefaivre, "Dirty Realism in European Architecture Today: Making the Stone Stony," in *Design Book Review* 17 (Winter 1989): 17–20, here 18.

37 Ibid., 17.

38 Ibid., 18.

39 Tomás Llorens, *Mimesis: Realismos modernos, 1918–45* (Madrid: Fundación Caja Madrid, 2005), 260, quoted in Maria Gonzalez-Pendas, "Realism under Construction: Manfredo Tafuri's Other Road to Criticism," in *99th ACSA Annual Meeting Proceedings: Where Do You Stand* (Washington, DC: ACSA, 2011).

40 Hal Foster, *The Return of the Real: The Avant-Garde at the End of the Century* (Cambridge, MA: MIT Press, 1996).

41 Ibid., 132.

42 Matthew Roman and Tal Schori, "Editors' Preface," *Real Perspecta*, 42 (2010): 9.

43 Charles Rice, "The Project of Autonomy: Politics within and against Capitalism; Architecture's Desire: Reading the Late Avant-garde; Utopia's Ghost: Architecture and Postmodernism, Again; First Works: Emerging Architectural Experimentation of the 1960s and 1970s," *Journal of Architecture: Architecture and Conflict* 16, 1 (2011): 155–63, here 155.

44 Hays, *Architecture Theory since 1968* (see note 8), 254.

45 K. Michael Hays, *Architecture's Desire: Reading the Late Avant-Garde* (Cambridge MA: MIT Press, 2010).

46 Reinhold Martin, *Utopia's Ghost: Architecture and Postmodernism, Again* (Minneapolis: University of Minnesota Press, 2010), xi.

47 Reinhold Martin, "Critical of What? Toward a Utopian Realism" (2005), in *The New Architectural Pragmatism: A Harvard Design Magazine Reader*, ed. William S. Saunders, 150–61 (Minneapolis: University of Minnesota Press, 2007), 160.

48 Fredric Jameson, *The Antinomies of Realism* (London: Verso, 2013), 8, 10, 26. "We now have in our grasp the two chronological end points of realism: its genealogy in storytelling and the tale, its future dissolution in the literary representation of affect. A new concept of realism is then made available when we grasp both these terminal points firmly at one and the same time" (10).

49 In Hays, *Architecture Theory since 1968* (see note 8), 246–47, the *archithese* realism issue edited by Steinmann and Reichlin is obliquely mentioned in a network of related contemporary publications, including Steinman's article in the Tendenzen catalog and its reproduction in *A+U* in 1976 and *L'architecture d'aujourd'hui* in 1977. Beatriz Colomina and Marie Theres Stauffer, "Interview with Stanislaus von Moos, Archithese Editor in Chief 1970–1980, Zurich, October 27, 2007," in *Clip Stamp Fold: The Radical Architecture of Little Magazines, 196X to 197X*, ed. Beatriz Colomina and Craig Buckley (Barcelona: Actar, 2010), 483–88. When queried about realism, von Moos defined it as "acknowledging the reality of the built environment as a context for architectural work, as opposed to inventing utopian concepts that were not likely to work" (485).

50 Ruth Hanisch and Steven Spier, "'History Is Not the Past but Another Mightier Presence': The Founding of the Institute for the History and Theory of Architecture (gta) at the Eidgenössische Hochschule (ETH) Zurich and Its Effects on Swiss Architecture," *Journal of Architecture* 14, 6 (2009): 655–86, here 674–75.

51 See Irina Davidovici, "Reiterations: Cliché and Interpretation in Contemporary Swiss Architecture," *Project Journal* 6 (2017): 34–43.

52 Davidovici, "The Paradox of Realism" (see note 31), 293–303.

To Laugh in Order Not to Cry

Interview with Robert Venturi and Denise Scott Brown

Authors:
Stanislaus von Moos
Denise Scott Brown
Robert Venturi

First published in:
archithese, 13 (1973): 17–32

Translated by:
Steven Lindberg

1. On Eclecticism, Irony, and Several Functionalist Myths

S.v.M.: Much of what you have planned and built in recent years smacks of eclecticism. Architects perceive that as somehow frivolous, as confusing. Because they assume that quality in architecture is first and foremost a question of originality, that, in other words, a building is good if it refers as neatly as possible and without further ado to the requirements of the program. But when planning you are not ashamed to adopt models of very different origins, historical as well as popular and commercial models—including Las Vegas.

R.V.: First, a general remark: Every architect, every artist learns from numerous different sources and role models, consciously or unconsciously and in different phases of his creative life, and I don't believe that one can say or assume that certain sources are "right" and others not. As far as I am concerned, I believe that an architecture will be that much richer and more diverse the more sources an architect has, and I would never establish in advance that one source is better than another. Admittedly, for us certain sources were more important than others in certain phases of our creative work. In the years around 1960, when we were designing my mother's house (figs. 29, 30), we were very heavily influenced by Italian architecture, especially by mannerist architecture, but the "Shingle Style"[1] also played a role—more in the background. We found inspiration in so many different buildings, such as the Villa Barbaro in Maser (I especially love the rear wall of the *giardino segreto*: a curved gable with no substructure [fig. 28]), in the Porta Pia (fig. 27), and also in the Villa Savoye—a building that is, despite its austere shell, extraordinarily complex (fig. 22). I addressed that in my book *Complexity and Contradiction in Architecture*. We have learned more since then. The ordinary and folklore have increasingly entered our field of vision, and today anonymous commercial architecture is one of our most important sources.

Admittedly, we are still sufficiently orthodox "modern architects" of the old school to keep us from copying a certain style all too literally and completely. That is one of the reasons for our mistrust of the so-called White School.[2] These architects copy Le Corbusier

Lachen, um nicht zu weinen

Interview mit Robert Venturi und Denise Scott Brown

1. Ueber Eklektizismus, Ironie und einige funktionalistische Mythen

S.v.M.: Vieles von dem, was Sie in den letzten Jahren projektiert und gebaut haben, hat einen eklektischen Beigeschmack. Architekten empfinden das irgendwie als frivol, als verwirrend. Denn sie gehen davon aus, dass Qualität in der Architektur zuallererst eine Frage der Originalität sei, dass, mit anderen Worten, ein Bau dann gut ist, wenn seine Form möglichst ohne Umschweife auf die Anforderungen des Programms Bezug nimmt. — Sie aber schämen sich nicht, beim Projektieren auf zahlreiche Vorbilder verschiedenster Herkunft zurückzugreifen, historische ebensogut wie volkstümliche oder kommerzielle Vorbilder — bis hin zu Las Vegas.

R.V.: Zunächst eine allgemeine Bemerkung: jeder Architekt, jeder Künstler lernt von zahlreichen verschiedenen Quellen und Vorbildern, bewusst oder unbewusst und in verschiedenen Phasen seines Schaffens, und ich glaube nicht, dass man sagen kann oder dass man davon ausgehen kann, dass gewisse Quellen «richtig» seien und andere nicht. Was mich betrifft, so glaube ich, dass eine Architektur umso reicher und vielfältiger sein wird, je mehr Quellen ein Architekt hat, und ich würde niemals zum vornherein festlegen, dass eine Quelle besser sei als eine andere. Freilich, für uns waren bestimmte Quellen in bestimmten Phasen unseres Schaffens wichtiger als andere. Als wir — in den Jahren um 1960 — das Haus meiner Mutter projektierten (Abb. 29, 30), standen wir sehr stark unter dem Einfluss italienischer Architektur, besonders der Architektur des Manierismus; aber auch der «Shingle Style»[1] spielte — mehr hintergründig — eine Rolle. Wir liessen uns anregen von so verschiedenen Bauten wie der Villa Barbaro in Maser (ich liebe ganz besonders die Rückwand des *giardino segreto:* ein geschwungener Giebel ohne Unterbau; Abb. 28), von der Porta Pia (Abb. 27) und auch von der Villa Savoie, einem Bau, der trotz seiner strengen Hülle ausserordentlich komplex ist (Abb. 22). Ich habe davon in meinem Buch *Complexity and Contradiction in Architecture* gehandelt. Seither haben wir dazugelernt. Das Gewöhnliche und die Folklore ist immer stärker in unseren Gesichtskreis getreten, und heute gehört die anonyme kommerzielle Architektur zu unseren wichtigsten Quellen.

Freilich, wir sind nach wie vor genügend orthodoxe «moderne Architekten» vom alten Schlage, um uns zu hüten, einen bestimmten Stil allzuwörtlich und vollumfänglich zu kopieren. Das ist einer der Gründe für unser Misstrauen gegenüber der sogenannten «White School»[2]. Diese Architekten kopieren Le Corbusier (den Le Corbusier der Zwanzigerjahre) noch wörtlicher als je ein eklektischer amerikanischer Architekt um 1900 beim Bau eines Wohnhauses oder einer Bank Bauernhäuser der Normandie oder italienische Palazzi kopiert hat. Ich glaube — auf die Gefahr hin, dogmatisch zu sein — dass die Einflüsse verschiedenartiger und weniger direkt sein müssen, um wirkliche und intensive Kunstwerke hervorzubringen.

S.v.M.: Mit anderen Worten: die Quellen selbst und die Werte, die sie verkörpern, scheinen Ihnen weit weniger wichtig als die Verarbeitung dieser Quellen zu etwas Neuem.

R.V.: Das ist richtig. Und das ist auch der Grund, warum wir Pop Art lieben: dem Pop Künstler kommt es nicht sosehr auf die gewöhnliche Realität an, derer er sich bedient, als auf ihre Verarbeitung — indem er den Kontext, den Masstab, die Proportionen verändert.

S.v.M.: Ist es das, was Sie im Auge haben, wenn Sie von Ironie sprechen?

R.V.: Nun, ist das zum Teil ein bisschen als Spiel, als Scherz zu verstehen. Das heisst: wir arbeiten nicht wie jene «Battle-of-the-Styles»-Architekten, die Stile für propagandistische Zwecke gebrauchten. Die Beobachtung von Stilen ist eine Art, über Architektur nach-

↓ fig. 27 Michelangelo, Porta Pia, Rome.
↓↓ fig. 28 Andrea Palladio, Villa Barbaro in Maser, "giardina segreta."

zudenken, die uns besonders anregend scheint, das heisst, die unser Schaffen stimuliert.

D.S.B.: In unserem Buch über Las Vegas haben wir auf einen Aufsatz von Richard Poirier hingewiesen³, der davon handelt, dass in Joyce's *Ulysses* beinahe keine Stimme ertönt, die nicht irgendeine andere Stimme nachahmt. Die Summe dieser verfremdeten Stimmen *ist* Joyce. Joyce benützt ein Amalgam, eine Collage von Mimikry, um sich auszudrücken. Trotzdem käme es wohl niemandem in den Sinn, zu sagen, *Ulysses* sei nicht Joyces eigenes Werk, bloss weil es seiner Struktur nach «eklektisch» ist.

R.V.: Wissen Sie, wir sind gerade erst dabei, zur Symbolik in der Architektur zurückzukehren. Es ist sehr schwierig für uns, und neu. Wir wissen noch gar nicht, wie wir Symbolik in der Architektur handhaben sollen. Wir wurden als moderne Architekten im traditionellen Sinne ausgebildet: d. h. wir lernten, Symbolik und Ornament tunlichst zu vermeiden. So tasten wir im Dunkeln.

In meinem Falle spielt vielleicht die Tatsache eine Rolle, dass ich meine Ausbildung als Architekt in den Vierzigerjahren in Princeton bekommen habe – und nicht etwa in Harvard. In Princeton spielte Kunstgeschichte eine wichtige Rolle. Die Architekturabteilung war dem Fach Kunstgeschichte untergeordnet. Ich hatte ein natürliches Interesse an Kunstgeschichte. Aber zu jener Zeit herrschte an anderen Architekturschulen die Bauhaus-Methode, das heisst man schenkte historischen Bauten nicht allzuviel Aufmerksamkeit – abgesehen vielleicht von jenen, die Giedion als Vorfahren der Moderne legitimiert hatte.

S.v.M.: Als Kunsthistoriker fühle ich mich natürlich angesprochen durch das, was Sie sagen. Wäre ich ein Architekt mit einer traditionell modernen Ausbildung, so hätte ich vielleicht mehr Schwierigkeiten. Unter zahlreichen Architekten und Theoretikern herrscht heute ein geradezu ikonoklastischer Puritanismus, ein tiefes, grundsätzliches Misstrauen gegenüber Bildern schlechthin. Vor allem in Deutschland kann man etwa Dinge hören wie: Form lügt immer, Kunst lügt immer: sie ist Vorspiegelung, Verschleierung, und insofern Symbol – vielmehr: Instrument – der Unfreiheit. In einer solchen Perspektive bedeuten formale Spielereien in der Architektur nichts anderes als einen Versuch, den Fortschritt in Richtung auf

ein Endziel sozialen Glücks aufzuhalten, eines Zustandes, wo die Menschen nackt sein werden und weder Kunst noch Rhetorik benötigen werden.

R.V.: Ich habe keine besonderen Kenntnisse auf dem Gebiet der Psychologie, aber es scheint mir doch ein unmöglicher menschlicher Zustand zu sein, in einer Umwelt zu leben, die keine Bezüge zu vergangenen Erfahrungen aufweist. Menschen scheinen ein grosses Verlan-

(the Le Corbusier of the twenties) more literally than any eclectic American architect around 1900 would have done when borrowing elements of Norman farmhouses or Italian palazzi for a house or a bank. I believe—at the risk of being dogmatic—that the influences must be more diverse and less direct in order to produce real and intense works of art.

S.v.M.: In other words, the sources themselves and the values they embody seem far less important to you than how those sources are turned into something new.

R.V.: That's right. And that's also the reason we love pop art: the pop artist is interested not so much in the ordinary reality on which he draws as he is in its reworking—by changing the context, the scale, the proportions.

S.v.M.: Is that what you have in mind when you speak of irony?

R.V.: Well, all of that should be understood, in part, a little as a game, as a joke. That is, we do not work like the "Battle of the Styles" architects, who used styles for propagandistic purposes. Observing styles is one way to think about architecture that seems especially exciting to us; that is to say, it stimulates our work.

D.S.B.: In our book on Las Vegas we referred to an essay by Richard Poirier,[3] which is about how hardly any voice is heard in Joyce's *Ulysses* that is not imitating some other voice. The sum of these defamiliarized voices *is* Joyce. Joyce uses an amalgam, a collage of mimicry, to express himself. Nevertheless, it would never occur to anyone to say that *Ulysses* is not Joyce's own work, just because it is "eclectic" in its structure.

R.V.: You know, we are only just beginning to return to symbolism in architecture. That is very difficult for us, and new. We don't even know how we are supposed to treat symbolism in architecture. We were trained as modern architects in the traditional sense: that is, we learned to avoid symbolism and ornament as much as possible. So we are groping around in the dark.

In my case, it perhaps plays a role that I was trained as an architect in the forties at Princeton —and not, say, at Harvard. In Princeton, art history played an important role. Architecture was part of the Department of Art and Archaeology. I had a natural interest in art history. Other architecture schools followed the Bauhaus method at the time—that is to say, not too much attention was paid to historical buildings —apart, perhaps, from those that Giedion had legitimized as precursors of modernism.

S.v.M.: As an art historian, of course, what you are saying speaks to me. If I were an architect with a traditional modern training, perhaps I would have more difficulties. Among many architects and theorists today, an almost iconoclastic puritanism dominates, a fundamental mistrust of images per se. In Germany especially, you can hear things like: Form always lies, art always lies. It is a pretense, an obfuscation, and in that sense a symbol— or rather, an instrument—of oppression. From such a perspective, formal games in architecture represent nothing other than an attempt to prevent progress in the direction of a final goal of social happiness, a state in which people will be naked and will need neither art nor rhetoric.

R.V.: I do not have any particular knowledge in the field of psychology, but for me it seems like an impossible human condition to live in an environment that has no connections to past experiences. People seem to have a strong desire for security, for pleasure, and for comfort that comes from things that are not absolutely essential. More than that, everything you learn, you learn from imitation. Look at a small child. What is sometimes too funny and comical about the behavior of children is the way they understand the form more quickly and immediately than the content. They understand the form but not the content, and the lack of a correspondence between form and content is what fascinates us and makes us laugh.

If imitation were not such an important element in human coexistence, then every generation would be absolutely primitive—in the unpleasant sense of the word.

D.S.B.: That is also why we think Alan Colquhoun's essay is so good.[4] He is trying to show that architects who believe they can derive form directly from function—perhaps with a little aid from intuition—are very naive. Because that's just not how the brain works. Not only are we anything but free of associations with our experiences of the past, we would also cripple an important dimension of our creativity if we wanted to free ourselves from these associations. All that can be added to that is that the architects who believe they are free and independent of influence from existing forms and formal languages are in reality all but tyrannized by formal languages that they adopt unthinkingly—formal languages that are perhaps not especially suitable in light of the functional tasks with which these architects see themselves confronted.

2. On Pop Art, Consumerism, and Advocacy Planning

S.v.M.: You have mentioned your historical sources and also talked about how important the anonymous sphere of commercial architecture has become for your work in recent years. Can you go into more detail about your sources in the twentieth century? Who are the contemporary artists you consider especially important for your work?

R.V.: You mean artists working today we admire?

S.v.M.: Yes, or those working between 1950 and 1970 whose work has somehow proved important for your own work.

R.V.: We have learned a great deal from the masters, of course: Aalto, Mies, Le Corbusier, Kahn. We have also learned from many of the pop artists: Warhol, Oldenburg, Johns, Rosenquist, Lichtenstein. It took some time before I "discovered" pop art myself. But when I had, I learned a great deal. Their world of motifs was particularly important to me, the ordinary element and its relationship to our sensibility. On the other hand, we have not learned a great deal from the abstract expressionists, in contrast to the neo-realists, whom we find very interesting. The conceptual artists, in turn, do not interest me, in my creative field. But I am not trying to be a critic here: we observe these artistic movements very much for our own ends and use them as part of our personal learning environment.

D.S.B.: To name a few more names: there are the architectural pictures of John Bader— painted from photographs. We have assembled a collection of old postcards, and he in turn borrowed from Steve Izenour a series of old original photographs of White Towers on which to base a series of paintings.[5] I should also mention Mahaffey, a painter from Philadelphia, who bases his paintings on beautiful architectural postcards; for example, a postcard of the Art Deco insurance palace opposite the museum in Philadelphia. And above all Ed Ruscha from Los Angeles, whose vision und whose interest in commercial art is very close to ours (figs. 31–33).

S.v.M.: One could conclude from all of that that you are more interested in the American status quo as such than in exploring the possibility of changing that status quo. The opulently designed Las Vegas book conveys that impression as well. From a European perspective, however, it seems that anyone who goes to Las Vegas and spends time studying the commercial Strip must already have a strange, decidedly erotic relationship to consumer society, to the world of commodities. Ulrich Franzen—to mention only him—called this relationship "Nixonite."[6] To him and many other modern architects who declare that it is the task of the architect to build for a better, more humane, et cetera, world, you seem to be exponents of a system-stabilizing intelligentsia. Do you see yourselves in that role?

D.S.B.: That is a very long question and much more difficult to answer because it makes us aware of so many thoughts at once. We believe that our ideas are rooted in the social and aim at social improvement. In our book, in the context of a detailed discussion of this question, I said, "Don't bug us for lack of social concern; we are trying to train ourselves to offer *socially relevant skills*." But our critics cite only the first half of that observation: "Don't bug us for lack of social concern." Moreover, our entire argumentation that supports this observation and lends it meaning is simply ignored.

To answer your question, it is important first to recollect that the American context is very different from the European one. We believe that our—let's call it—neo-populist stance is a left-wing position in the American context rather than a right-wing one. On the other hand, the arguments of our critics sound like left-wing arguments in Europe, but within the situation in the United States they are not really left-wing arguments. In truth, they represent an escape from reality, because America quite simply completely lacks the social and technical

Stanislaus von Moos,
Denise Scott Brown, and Robert Venturi

↓ figs. 29–30 Venturi & Rauch, Venturi House, Chestnut Hill, Philadelphia, 1963.

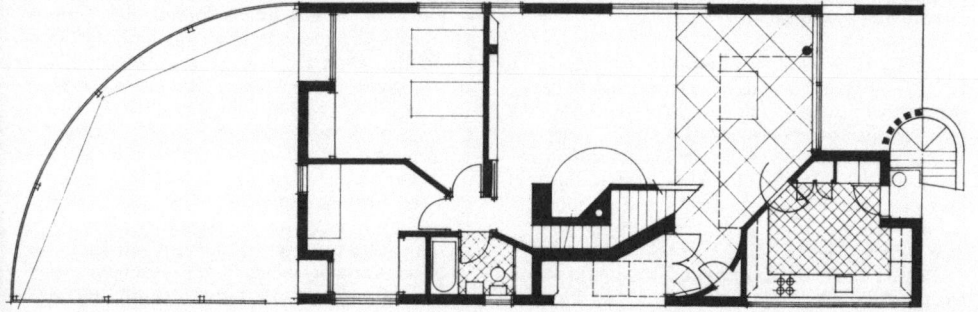

gen nach der Sicherheit, dem Vergnügen und der Annehmlichkeit zu haben, die von Dingen ausgehen, die nicht absolut wesentlich sind. Das ist es doch, was zu einem Teil den Sinn von Kunst ausmacht, und was das Leben erträglich macht. Ueberdies: alles, was man lernt, lernt man durch Nachahmung. Schauen Sie einem kleinen Kinde zu. Was bisweilen so lustig und komisch ist im Verhalten von Kindern, das ist, dass sie die Form rascher und unmittelbarer verstehen als den Inhalt. Sie kapieren die Form, aber nicht den Inhalt, und die fehlende Korrespondenz zwischen Form und Inhalt ist es, was fasziniert und was uns lachen macht.

Wäre nicht Nachahmung ein so wichtiges Element im Zusammenleben der Menschen, so wäre jede Generation absolut primitiv — im unerfreulichen Sinne des Wortes.

D.S.B.: Das ist auch, warum wir den Aufsatz von Alan Colquhoun so gut finden.[4] Ihm geht es darum, zu zeigen, dass Architekten, die glauben, sie könnten die Form unmittelbar von der Funktion ableiten – vielleicht mit einem kleinen Zustupf an Intuition – dass solche Architekten sehr naiv sind. Denn das Gehirn arbeitet ganz einfach nicht so. Um es mit seinen Worten zu sagen: Nicht nur sind wir alles andere als frei von Assoziationen an unsere Erfahrungen der Vergangenheit, wir würden auch eine wichtige Dimension unserer Kreativität lahmlegen, wollten wir versuchen, uns von diesen Assoziationen zu befreien. Dazu ist bloss zu sagen, dass Architekten, die glauben, sie seien tatsächlich frei und unabhängig vom Einfluss bestehender Formen und Formensprachen in Wirklichkeit geradezu tyrannisiert werden von Formensprachen, die sie unreflektiert übernehmen; Formensprachen, die vielleicht gar nicht besonders geeignet sind im Hinblick auf die funktionellen Aufgaben, denen sich diese Architekten gegenübergestellt sehen.

2. Ueber Pop Art, Warenwelt und «Advocacy Planning»

S.v.M.: Sie haben einige Ihrer historischen Quellen erwähnt und auch davon gesprochen, wie wichtig in den letzten Jahren die anonyme Sphäre des kommerziellen Bauens für Ihre Arbeit geworden ist. Können Sie noch etwas näher auf Ihre Quellen im zwanzigsten Jahrhundert eingehen? Welches sind die zeitgenössischen Künstler, welche Sie im Hinblick auf Ihre Arbeit als besonders wichtig erachten?

R.V.: Sie meinen Künstler, die heute arbeiten, und die wir schätzen?

S.v.M.: Ja, oder solche, die zwischen 1950 und 1970 arbeiteten und deren Werk sich als irgendwie bedeutsam für Ihr eigenes Schaffen erwiesen hat.

R.V.: Wir haben natürlich sehr viel von den Meistern gelernt: Aalto, Mies, Le Corbusier, Kahn. Ueberdies haben wir sehr viel von den Pop Künstlern gelernt: Warhol, Oldenburg, Johns, Rosenquist, Lichtenstein. Es hat einige Zeit gedauert, bis ich Pop Art für mich «entdeckte». Als es aber soweit war, lernte ich sehr viel. Besonders wichtig war mir ihre Motivwelt, das gewöhnliche Element und seine Beziehung zu unserer Sensibilität. – Andererseits haben wir von den abstrakten Expressionisten nicht viel gelernt, im Gegensatz zu den Neo-Realisten, die uns sehr interessieren. Die Konzeptkünstler wiederum interessieren mich nicht, in meinem schöpferischen Bereich. Aber ich versuche hier nicht, ein Kritiker zu sein: wir beobachten diese künstlerischen Bewegungen ganz eigennützig und benützen sie als Teil unserer persönlichen Lern-Umwelt.

D.S.B.: Um ein paar weitere Namen zu nennen: da sind die – nach Fotografien gemalten – Architektur-Bilder von John Bader. Wir haben zusammen eine Sammlung alter Ansichtskarten angelegt und er hat seinerseits von Steve Izenour eine Reihe alter Originalaufnahmen von «White Towers» ausgeliehen, als Vorlagen für eine Reihe von Bildern.[5] Ich sollte auch Mahaffey erwähnen, ein Maler aus Philadelphia, der schöne Architektur-Ansichtskarten als Vorlagen für seine Gemälde benutzt, z. B. eine Ansichtskarte nach dem Art Déco-Versicherungspalast gegenüber dem Museum in Philadelphia. Und vor allem Ed Ruscha aus Los Angeles, dessen Vision und dessen Interesse an kommerzieller Kunst dem unseren sehr nahekommen (Abb. 31–33).

S.v.M.: Aus alledem könnte man schliessen, dass Sie mehr interessiert sind am amerikanischen Status Quo als daran, Möglichkeiten zu erproben, diesen Status Quo zu verändern. Auch von dem opulent aufgemachten Las Vegas-Buch geht dieser Eindruck aus. Aus europäischer Sicht will es nun doch scheinen, dass wer nach Las Vegas geht und Zeit darauf verwendet, den kommerziellen «Strip» zu studieren, schon ein merkwürdiges, ausgesprochen erotisches Verhältnis zur Konsumgesellschaft, zur Warenwelt haben muss. Ulrich Franzen – um nur ihn zu nennen – hat dieses Verhältnis «Nixonite» genannt.[6] Ihm und vielen anderen modernen Architekten, die verkünden, dass es die Aufgabe des Architekten sei, für eine bessere, humanere, usw. Welt zu bauen, erscheinen Sie als Exponenten einer systemstabilisierenden Intelligenzia. Wie fühlen Sie sich in dieser Rolle?

D.S.B.: Das ist eine sehr lange Frage, umso schwerer zu beantworten, als sie so viele Gedanken auf einmal ins Bewusstsein ruft. Wir glauben, dass unsere Ideen im Sozialen verwurzelt sind und auf soziale Besserung abzielen. In unserem Buch sagte ich, im Rahmen einer ausführlichen Diskussion dieser Frage: «Werft uns nicht Mangel an sozialer Gesinnung vor. Wir versuchen, sozial wirklich relevante

Kenntnisse und Fähigkeiten zu erlernen.» — Aber unsere Kritiker zitierten nur die erste Hälfte dieser Feststellung: «Werft uns nicht Mangel an sozialer Gesinnung vor.» Ueberdies wurde unsere gesamte Argumentation, die diese Feststellung unterstützt und ihr ihren Sinn gibt, einfach ignoriert.

Um Ihre Frage zu beantworten: es ist zunächst einmal wichtig, sich zu vergegenwärtigen, dass der amerikanische Kontext sehr verschieden ist vom europäischen. Wir glauben, dass unsere sagen wir neo-populistische Position innerhalb des amerikanischen Kontexts eher eine linke Position ist als eine rechte. Andererseits tönen die Argumente unserer Kritiker wie linke Argumente in Europa — aber innerhalb der Situation in USA sind es nicht wirklich linke Argumente. In Wirklichkeit stellen sie eine Flucht vor der Realität dar, denn hier in Amerika fehlt ganz einfach die soziale und verwaltungstechnische Organisation, die dazu notwendig ist, um die vielen europäischen Ideen zur Sozialreform mit Hilfe von Architektur zu realisieren. In den Fünfziger- und Sechzigerjahren wurden in den Vereinigten Staaten im Durchschnitt ungefähr 20 000 Wohnungen pro Jahr im Sozialen Wohnbau gebaut. In den Siebzigerjahren liegt dieser Durchschnitt wahrscheinlich noch tiefer. In Anbetracht dieser Tatsache scheint uns die übliche moderne Architektur-Rhetorik über das «Bauen für die Armen» usw. als ein Umgehen der Realität, als eine Flucht. Und sobald man versucht, Ausschau zu halten nach Möglichkeiten, näher an die Realität heranzukommen, stellt man fest, dass es einfach nichts anderes gibt als innerhalb des Systems zu arbeiten — oder aber aufzugeben und Utopien zu entwerfen. Aber wenn man versucht, hier und jetzt Verbesserungen zu erzielen, so tönt das nach konservativer Politik, besonders wenn man versucht, mit Hilfe privaten Unternehmertums soziale Ziele zu erreichen. Es ist eine komplexe Situation, die wenig zu tun hat mit dem erhobenen Zeigefinger der neo-linken Architektur-Elite.

S.v.M.: Man könnte also sagen, dass die Aesthetik und die Ethik der modernen Bewegung direkt abhängt von der Möglichkeit, oder zumindest von der Hoffnung auf die Möglichkeit, unter einer Bürokratie arbeiten zu können, die imstande ist, umfangreiche Aufträge auf dem Gebiete des sozialen Wohnbaus zu vergeben. Da aber diese Möglichkeit in den Vereinigten Staaten nicht existiert, ist der soziale Reformismus der modernen Bewegung in Amerika auf weite Strecken irrelevant.

D.S.B.: Nicht nur irrelevant: er wird vom Establishment dazu missbraucht, sozial repressive Bauprogramme zu rechtfertigen. Ich kann Ihnen dazu ein Beispiel geben. Als wir von den Bewohnern eines ziemlich ärmlichen Stadtteils in Philadelphia (South Street; Abb. 34) aufgefordert wurden, ihnen bei dem Versuch zu helfen, den Bau einer Expressstrasse zu verhindern, sagte man uns: wenn Ihnen Las Vegas gefällt, so vertrauen wir auch darauf, dass Sie nicht versuchen werden, South Street auf unsere Kosten zu «sanieren». Wir wurden beigezogen, weil die Leute den Eindruck hatten, dass wir zunächst einmal daran interessiert sind, wie Städte tatsächlich aussehen, und dass wir verstehen möchten, woran es liegt, dass sie so und nicht anders aussehen — ohne allzuviele ästhetische und moralische Wunschvorstellungen. Diesen Leuten schien dies zumindest ein guter Anfang zu sein. Aber für viele Architekten ist das natürlich grundfalsch. Sie finden, der Architekt müsse «hingehen und dem Volk» kühne, saubere, moderne Wohnungen hinstellen. Nun haben wir ja gesehen was passiert ist in den Vereinigten Staaten, wo diese kühnen, neuen Wohnungen aufgrund der entsprechenden sozialen Rhetorik gebaut wurden — nur leider nicht für die richtigen Leute. In der Tat spielte sich das ja im allgemeinen so ab, dass die Bewohner eines armen Stadtteils das Feld räumen mussten, während ein vermöglicheres Publikum in neue, nach CIAM-Grundsätzen aufgestellte Wohnblöcke einzog. Sosehr die Moderne Bewegung sich dafür einsetzte, arme und benachteiligte Bevölkerungsgruppen in guten Wohnungen unterzubringen, so selten hat sie das auch tatsächlich zustandegebracht — und daher versuchen einige von uns, andere Methoden auszuprobieren. Wir haben Las Vegas studiert unter anderem weil die Leute (zumindest Leute, die dem Mittelstand und den unteren Schichten angehören) Las Vegas zu schätzen scheinen, jedenfalls mehr als sie jene Architektur schätzen, von der ihnen die Architekten sagen, dass sie sie eigentlich schätzen sollten. Eine sehr konfuse Antwort auf Ihre Frage . . .

S.v.M.: Vielleicht eine konfuse Frage . . .

D.S.B.: Nein, nicht Ihre Frage, die Sache selbst ist konfus. Unsere Antwort darauf ist,

dass wir versuchen, so gut wir können der Verwirklichung unserer sozialen Anliegen näherzukommen, und zwar in der unmittelbaren Zukunft und mit Hilfe der Instrumente, die uns die Gesellschaft, die uns umgibt, zur Verfügung stellt. Als Künstler benützen wir im Hinblick auf diese Situation Ironie — vielleicht in einem ähnlichen Sinne wie jenem, den Poirier in seinem bereits erwähnten Artikel im Auge hatte, als er schrieb, dass der Künstler das Material für seine Kunst jener Welt entnimmt, die ihn umgibt. Wenn der Künstler mit seiner Welt im Einvernehmen ist, dann benützt er dieses Material geradeheraus und unmittelbar; wenn nicht, dann ironisch. Wir glauben, dass wir es ironisch verwenden: wir lachen, um nicht zu weinen. Wir sehen Ironie als ein Mittel, das dem Einzelnen helfen kann, in einer kulturell bunt durcheinandergewürfelten Gesellschaft zu überleben. Wir glauben, dass die Rolle eines sozial engagierten Künstlers oder Architekten in unserer Gesellschaft gar nicht so weit entfernt zu sein braucht von derjenigen eines Spassmachers.

Da haben Sie nochmals unser zwiespältiges Verhältnis gegenüber der Gesellschaft. In vieler Hinsicht ist sie entsetzlich, in vieler Hinsicht wunderbar — und dieser Zwiespalt schlägt sich in unserer Arbeit nieder als Ironie.

S.v.M.: — Also eine Art Galgenhumor, wie es ein deutscher Kollege, Michael Müller, in seiner Erwiderung auf Ihren Vortrag in Berlin [7] ausdrückte?

D.S.B.: Ja, aber es ist zärtlicher, weniger böse als Galgenhumor. Wir sind nicht ganz und gar gegen diese Gesellschaftsform. Wir glauben, dass nicht nur unsere Position als amerikanische Architekten eine kompromittierte Position ist, sondern dass die Position der gesamten industrialisierten Welt kompromittiert ist — gegenüber der restlichen Welt. Daher sind wir gegen viele Aspekte unserer Gesellschaft . . .

S.v.M.: . . . aber Sie sind nicht apokalyptisch.

D.S.B.: Nein, schon aus Veranlagung nicht.

3. Ueber Monumentalität heute — oder: Probleme einer alternden Revolution

S.v.M.: Woran liegt es, dass die moderne Architektur mehr und mehr zu einem heroischen Habitus neigt? Wie kommt es, dass so viele neue Bauten, insbesondere in den Vereinigten Staaten, in Charakter und Tonart immer deutlicher an die Monumentalität, die Theatralik und den Pomp der Architektur der «City Beautiful»-Bewegung erinnert (Abb. 35) — trotz der anti-Beaux-Arts Theorie, die sie immer noch mit sich schleppt? Wie erklären Sie dieses Phänomen? — Ich stelle Ihnen diese Frage, weil mir scheint, dass Sie innerhalb der heutigen Archi-

↑↓ figs. 31–33 Ed Ruscha, Three gasoline stations, photographs
(from Ed Ruscha, *Twentysix Gasoline Stations* [Alhambra, CA, 1962])

tekturszene eine dem post-brutalistischen Heroismus extrem entgegengesetzte Position vertreten.

D.S.B.: Ich glaube, dass das, was wir heute zum Teil beobachten können, mit zwei Dingen zusammenhängt: mit dem revolutionären Eifer der modernen Bewegung einerseits und mit der Stosskraft einer Revolution, die in die Reaktion umkippt andererseits. Das heisst: der Eifer ist geblieben, aber die Revolution selbst ist zur Reaktion geworden. Ich glaube, das ist einer der Gründe für den heroischen Habitus der Moderne. Ich erinnere mich z. B. an das, was der italienische Architekt Albini einmal gesagt hat: dass die moderne Architektur das strahlende Licht gewesen sei, das ihm während der faschistischen Periode und während des Krieges am Leben erhalten habe. Nun, die Glut, die diesem Gefühl zugrundeliegt, wurde nun während mehreren Generationen weitergegeben, aber die Revolution selbst ist alt geworden und ins Lager des Establishments übergegangen.

Ausserdem ist die Architekturausbildung ausserordentlich autoritär, speziell in Amerika mit seinem Beaux-Arts-Hintergrund — mehr so als zum Beispiel England, wo es Schulen wie etwa die Architectural Association gibt. Architekten werden dazu ausgebildet, Führerfiguren zu werden. Sie haben soziales Prestige und halten sich für Gurus der Gesellschaft. Insofern sind sie genau so schlimm wie die Psychiater, jene andere grosse, autoritäre Berufsgruppe. *Wir* sind informiert, und *Du* kannst das nicht verstehen. Wenn du glaubst, dass du autofahren willst und draussen in der Vorstadt wohnen willst, so beweist das nur, dass du nichts verstehst: du solltest zu Fuss gehen und in einer Megastruktur wohnen. Das ist weitherum die typische Attitüde eines Architekten. Dazu kommt noch etwas anderes: in Amerika war Architektur von alters her eine Angelegenheit der Oberklasse, und eine Angelegenheit der Männer; das hängt zum Teil damit zusammen, dass, wer ein eigenes Architekturbüro eröffnen will, über ein zweites Einkommen verfügen muss. Es scheint uns auch, dass Gropius, als eine Art Preusse unter den modernen Architekten, sehr gut zu den Brahmins von Boston passte; dass hier eine Allianz von zwei verwandten Typen vorliegt. Und in der Tat hat sich die moderne Architektur in und um Harvard herum besonders fest etabliert und wurde auch von dort aus über das Land verbreitet.

Ein weiterer Grund für die gegenwärtige Arterienverkalkung in der Architektur liegt darin, dass sich die Architektenausbildung mehr und mehr vom Erlernen handwerklicher Fähigkeiten entfernt hat. Amerikanische Hochschulen haben keine Zeit mehr für eine sorgfältige Grundschulung in Baukonstruktion und Bauhandwerk; und eine Folge davon ist, dass wir eine moderne Architektur ohne traditionelle konstruktive Finesse und ohne Details bekommen. Ein Mann wie Mies aber war durch und durch Handwerker. Die nächste Generation hat dann diesen Sinn für das Handwerk bereits weitgehend eingebüsst; in der darauffolgenden Generation ist fast nichts mehr davon übriggeblieben. Es scheint mir, dass dieser Verlust der Grundlage im Handwerklichen ziemlich aufgeblasene Architekten und eine ziemlich aufgeblasene Architektur zur Folge hat.

S.v.M.: Ich verstehe Ihre Kritik an Gropius nicht ganz. Ich sehe ihn eigentlich nicht als den grossen, autoritären «Preussen» (ganz abgesehen davon, dass er wahrscheinlich dem, was Sie über den Verlust des Handwerks sagen, beipflichten würde). Er sagte einmal, dass die Farbe, die er am meisten liebe, «bunt» sei. Das ganze Bauhaus wäre undenkbar gewesen ohne seine im Grunde unautoritäre, pluralistische Einstellung.

D.S.B.: Ich spreche natürlich nicht von Gropius als Person, ich spreche von seinen Ueberzeugungen als Architekt.

R.V.: Seine Vorschriften für eine «totale» und «objektive» Umweltgestaltung [8] haben einen stark puritanischen Zug; sie zielen auf eine Welt, in der architektonische Führerfiguren die «totale Landschaft» entwerfen, um eine totale Einheit zu erreichen, und zwar eine Einheit, die von oben, vom Experten her für die restliche Menschheit verordnet wird.

Ich bin ganz einverstanden mit dem, was Denise über die progressive, aber in Wirklichkeit rückläufige revolutionäre Glut gesagt hat. Es ist heroisch, ein Revolutionär zu sein; man riskiert sein Leben damit. Mir scheint, dass dieses heroische Gefühl irgendwie noch immer fortlebt, diese rhetorische Qualität, das Dogma einer Revolution. Wir leben in einer expressionistischen Periode, ich weiss eigentlich nicht warum; aber es ist eine Periode, die sich zum Teil in Form von Uebertreibungen früherer Dogmas ausdrückt.

S.v.M.: Es scheint mir neben alledem noch etwas anderes eine Rolle zu spielen. Die Menschen scheinen sich wohlzufühlen in einer Umgebung, in der es auch Monumente gibt, die an heroische Ereignisse und Auseinandersetzungen erinnern. Das ist zum Teil der Sinn jener Tradition klassizistischer Formen in der amerikanischen «Staatsarchitektur» — oder zumindest der Tradition klassizistischer Strenge in der Architektur: sie will den Triumph von Ordnung und Gesetz, von staatlicher Kontrolle über Unordnung und Laissez-faire symbolisieren und zwar vom 18. Jahrhundert bis hinauf zum Rathaus von Boston (Abb. 4).

R.V.: Was Sie über Monumentalität sagen scheint mir richtig zu sein. Die Menschen wollen Rhetorik, sie wollen Ausdruck, sowohl in ihrem Leben als auch in ihrer Umwelt, und sie wollen die grosse, zur übersichtlichen Form zusammengefasste Aussage. Und das ist auch durchaus richtig so. Aber es könnte sein, dass heute, in dieser speziellen Epoche, niemand so ganz sicher weiss, was diese grosse Aussage sein könnte. Vielleicht sind die Grosskonzerne ihrer Sache ganz sicher gewesen — zumindest

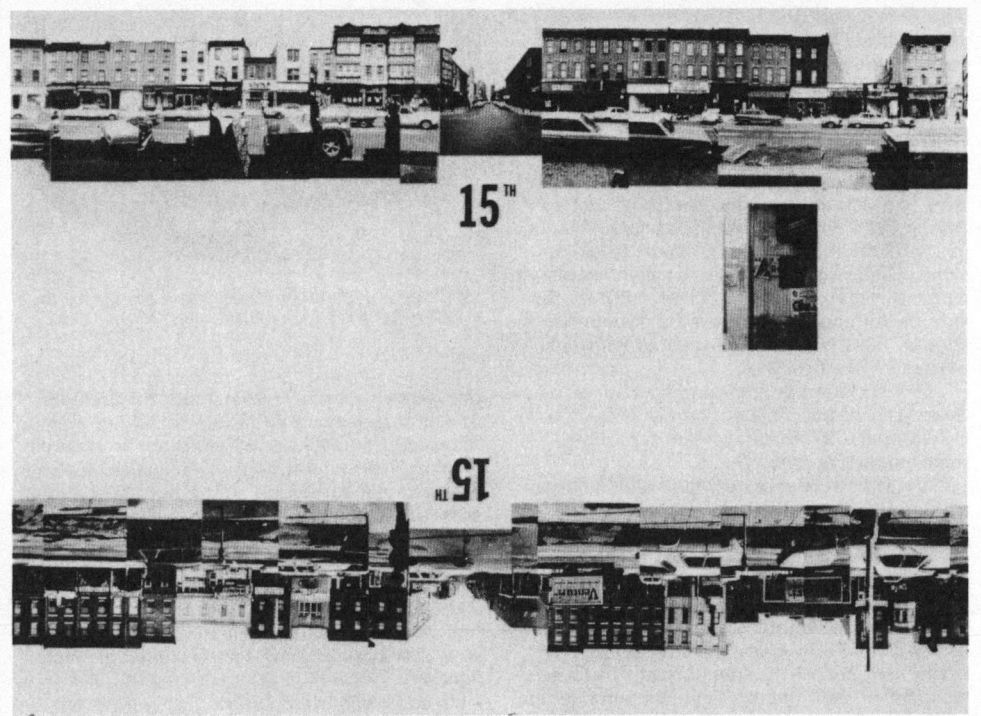

bis vor ein paar Monaten. Aber selbst sie sind etwas diskreter geworden; oft bemühen sie sich sogar, nicht allzusehr aufzufallen.

Ich bin mit Ihnen einverstanden, dass die Gesellschaft immer wieder grosse öffentliche Aussagen in Form von Architektur machen wollte – aber ich weiss ganz einfach nicht, was *unsere* grossen Aussagen in Amerika, heute, sein könnten. Es gibt eigentlich bloss zwei Arten von volkstümlichen, leichtverständlichen Aussagen: Einerseits die architektonischen Bilder der Grosskonzerne, des Big Business, andererseits die Freizeit-Bilder, à la Las Vegas. Ich würde nicht sagen, dass wir heute dermassen verwirrt sind, dass wir darüberhinaus keine öffentlichen Aussagen – grosse, rhetorische Aussagen – haben können. Das wäre etwas zu einfach. Ich würde nicht so weit gehen, obwohl es klar ist, dass wir heute keine grosse, zur Form zusammengefasste architektonische Aussage machen können wie etwa diejenige von Chartres im 12. Jahrhundert. Das können wir aus verschiedenen Gründen hier in Amerika nicht haben. Schon deshalb nicht, weil wir nicht alle katholisch sind; wir haben eine extrem heterogene Gesellschaft, und wir befinden uns in einer Zeit der Verwirrung, wir sind in einer Art manieristischen Periode. So oder so: ich vermute, dass das Medium unserer öffentlichen Aussagen in Zukunft nicht Architektur sein wird. Unsere grossen öffentlichen Statements werden nicht im gleichen Sinne architektonisch sein wie etwa in Chartres, auf der Akropolis oder in Versailles – und auch nicht im gleichen Sinne wie das etwa noch in der amerikanischen Stadt des 19. Jahrhunderts möglich war, mit

↓ fig. 35 Daniel H. Burnham, Civic Center project for Chicago, 1909.

ihren Bahnhöfen und Rathäusern. Ich weiss nicht, wie sie tatsächlich aussehen werden — vielleicht werden es gewaltige öffentliche Plakatwände sein, oder gewaltige, 100 Meter hohe Skulpturen, à la Oldenburg, entsprechend dem neuen räumlichen Masstab und der Geschwindigkeit in unseren Städten. Jedenfalls glaube ich, dass die Lösung des Problems nicht mehr reine Architektur sein wird (natürlich war es auch in der Vergangenheit nicht reine Architektur). — Und ich glaube auch, dass die Monumente der Grosskonzerne irgendwie irrelevant sind. Ich glaube, dass sehr vieles auf dem Gebiet unserer heutigen Architektur-Monumentalität leere Pose ist, im Gegensatz zu wirklich wirksamer Rhetorik.

D.S.B.: Man hat jahrelang nach einer «Aussage» gesucht für die amerikanische Zweihundertjahrfeier (1976): aber man hat nichts Ueberzeugendes gefunden.

S.v.M.: Wird es eine Multi-Media-Veranstaltung werden?

R.V.: Nun, das ist eine interessante Art, das Problem anzugehen — denn in den vergangenen hundert Jahren waren Weltausstellungen eher Mono- als Multi-Media-Veranstaltungen, nicht wahr? Jedenfalls waren es Veranstaltungen, welche die industrielle Revolution verherrlichten, mit Hilfe einer fortschrittlichen, technischen Architektur — wie sie von Giedion beschrieben wurde. Heute ist das nicht mehr so: wir haben keinen Kristallpalast, keine Galerie des Machines und keinen Eiffelturm. Heute sind auch Buckminster Fuller und Frei Otto ziemlich langweilig. Die wirklich interessanten Dinge an unseren Weltausstellungen ereignen sich auf dem Gebiete des Films und des Fernsehfilms; demgegenüber sollte die Architektur nichts weiter sein als ein zurücktretender Hintergrund für die nationalen und internationalen Darbietungen einer derartigen Messe. Die Architektur sollte das, was sie ausdrücken will, nicht mit Hilfe ihrer Formen ausdrücken, sondern mit Hilfe ihrer Zeichen. Die Zeichen und die Botschaften sollten ein «Appliqué» sein. Sie konstituieren eine Umgebung, die aus Mitteilungen, und nicht aus «reiner» Architektur besteht. Die verspätet heroischen Architektur-Monumente, die wir zuvor erwähnt haben, sind nicht mehr als die letzten Züge der reinen Form, die überaus langweiligen letzten Atemzüge.

D.S.B.: Die grossen öffentlichen Aussagen oder Bekenntnisse könnten Dinge sein wie z. B. der Versuch, endlich einmal das Problem der Armut anzupacken. Philadelphia schlug im Hinblick auf die Zweihundertjahrfeier vor, dass ein grosser Teil der städtischen Ausgaben Sozialprogrammen zufliessen sollte, um die schlimmsten Missstände in der Stadt zu beseitigen. Aber Washington wollte davon nichts wissen. Seither herrscht hier ein Gefühl, dass es 1976 nicht besonders viel zu feiern geben wird, sofern nicht zuerst diese sozialen Massnahmen ergriffen werden. Unsere eigenen Vorschläge für eine Zweihundertjahrfeier-Ausstellung, bestehend aus Ausstellungsschuppen und Zeichen, sind vor diesem Hintergrund zu verstehen (Abb. 38—41).   (Philadelphia, Oktober 1974)

[1] «Shingle-Style»; der Begriff charakterisiert eine Reihe entwicklungsgeschichtlich wichtiger amerikanischer Wohnhäuser des späten 19. Jahrhunderts, die in der Tradition der «Arts and Crafts»-Bewegung stehen. (Vgl. Vincent Scully, *The Shingle Style*, New Haven, 1955).
[2] Oder: die sog. «New York Five»: Peter Eisenmann, Michael Graves, Charles Gwathmey, John Hejduk, Richard Meier; vgl. versch. Autoren, *Five Architects*, New York, 1972.
[3] Richard Poirier, «T. S. Eliot and the Literature of Waste», in *The New Republic*, 20. Mai 1967.
[4] Alan Colquhoun, «Typology and Design Method», in *Arena*, Juni, 1967, S. 11—14; abgedr. in Charles Jencks und George Baird, *Meaning in Architecture*, New York, 1969.
[5] Vgl. Paul Hirshorn und Steven Izenour, «Learning From Hamburgers», in *Architecture Plus*, Mai 1973.
[6] Ulrich Franzen, «Letter to the Editor», in *Progressive Architecture*, April, 1970, S. 8.
[7] «Functionalism Yes, But . . .». Vortrag im Rahmen eines vom Internationalen Design Zentrum *(IDZ)* Berlin veranstalteten Symposions zum Thema «Das Pathos des Funktionalismus», Sept. 1974.
[8] Vgl. Walter Gropius, *Scope of Total Architecture*, New York, 1943 ff.

organization necessary to realize the many European ideas of social reform with the aid of architecture. In the United States in the fifties and sixties, on average around 20,000 apartments were built per year as public housing. In the seventies, this average was probably even lower. In view of that fact, it seems to us that the usual rhetoric of modern architecture about "building for the poor," and so on, is not an approach to reality but a flight from it. And as soon as one tries to keep a lookout for opportunities to get closer to the reality, one finds that there is simply no option other than to work within the system—or to give up and design utopias. But if one tries to achieve improvements here and now, that sounds like conservative politics, especially if one tries to achieve social goals with the help of private entrepreneurship. It is a complex situation that has little to do with the wagging finger of the neo-leftist architectural elite.

S.v.M.: So, one could say that the aesthetics and the ethics of the modern movement is directly dependent on the possibility—or at least the hope for a possibility—of working under a bureaucracy that is able to hand out substantial contracts in the area of public housing construction. Because this possibility does not exist in the United State, the social reformism of the modern movement in America is largely irrelevant.

D.S.B.: Not just irrelevant: it is abused by the establishment to justify socially repressive architectural programs. I can give you an example. When we were asked by the residents of a rather poor neighborhood in Philadelphia (South Street; fig. 34) to help their effort to stop the construction of an expressway, they said to us: If you like Las Vegas, then we trust you not to try to "revitalize" South Street at our expense. We were called in because people felt that we were first and foremost interested in what cities actually look like and that we could understand why it is that they look the way they do—without all too many aesthetic and moral expectations. To these people, that at least seemed like a good start. But for many architects, of course, that is fundamentally wrong. They find the architect "has to go to the people" and put up bold, clean, modern apartments. Now we have seen what happened in the United States, where these bold new apartments were built based on the corresponding social rhetoric —but unfortunately not for the right people. In fact, in general what happened is that the residents of a poor neighborhood had to clear the field while a wealthier public moved into the residential blocks built according to CIAM principles. However much the modern movement worked to put poor and disadvantaged groups of the population in good apartments, the more rarely it actually happened—and for that reason several of us are trying out other methods. We studied Las Vegas, among other reasons, because people (at least people who belong to the middle and lower classes) seem to appreciate Las Vegas, at least more so than they appreciate the architecture that the architects tell them they should really appreciate. A very confused response to your question …

S.v.M.: A confused question, perhaps …

D.S.B.: No, not your question: the issue itself is confused. Our answer is that we try as best we can to get closer to the realization of our social concerns—specifically, in the immediate future and with the aid of instruments that the society around us makes available. As artists, we use irony when looking at this situation— perhaps in a similar sense to that which Poirier had in mind in his article when he wrote that the artist takes the material for his art from the world around him. If the artist is in agreement with his world, then he uses this material openly and directly; if not, then ironically. We believe that we use it ironically: we laugh in order not to cry. We see irony as a means to help the individual to survive in a culturally multicolored, thrown-together society. We believe that the role of a socially committed artist or architect in our society does not have to be so far removed from that of a jester.

There, once again, you have our divided relationship to society. In many respects, it is horrible; in many respects, wonderful—and this split is expressed in our work as irony.

S.v.M.: So, a kind of gallows humor, as a German colleague, Michael Müller, expressed it in his response to your recent lecture in Berlin?[7]

D.S.B.: Yes, but it is kinder, less nasty, than gallows humor. We are not at all against this form of society. We believe not only that our position as American architects is a compromised position but also that the position of the whole industrialized world is compromised — compared to the rest of the world. For that reason, we are against many aspects of our society …

S.v.M.: … but you are not apocalyptic.
D.S.B.: No, not even by inclination.

3. On Monumentality Today; or, Problems of an Aging Revolution

S.v.M.: Why is it that modern architecture tends more and more to a heroic temper? Why are so many new buildings, especially in the United States, increasingly reminiscent of the monumentality, the theatricality, and the pomp of the architecture of the City Beautiful Movement, both in character and in tone (fig. 35), despite the anti-Beaux Arts theory it is still burdened with? How do you explain this phenomenon? I ask you because it seems to me that within today's architecture scene you represent a position extremely opposed to post-brutalist heroism.

D.S.B.: I believe that what we can observe in some cases today is connected to two things: to the revolutionary zeal of the modern movement, on the one hand, and to the impetus of a revolution that is suddenly turning reactionary, on the other. That means the zeal remains but the revolution itself has become reactionary. I believe that is one of the reasons for the heroic temper of modernism. I recall, for example, what the Italian architect Albini once said: that modern architecture had been a beacon that kept him alive during the fascist period and during the war. Now the ardor underlying this feeling was passed down through several generations, but the revolution itself has gotten old and gone over to the establishment camp.

Moreover, education in architecture is extraordinarily authoritarian, especially in America with its Beaux Arts background — more so than in England, for example, where there are schools such as the Architectural Association. Architects are trained to become leader figures. They have social prestige and consider themselves society's gurus. In that sense, they are just as bad as psychiatrists, this other large, authoritarian professional group. *We* are informed, and *you* cannot understand that. If you think you want to drive a car and want to live out in the suburbs, that only proves that you don't understand anything: You should walk and live in a megastructure. That is the typical attitude of an architect. Then there is something else: In America, architecture has long since been a concern of the upper class, and a concern of men; that is in part because anyone who wants to open up his own architectural office has to have a second income. It also seems to us that Gropius, as a kind of Prussian among the modern architects, was very well suited to the Boston Brahmins; that it was a kind of alliance of two related types. And, in fact, modern architecture established itself particularly well at and around Harvard and also spread from there across the country.

Another reason for the current hardening of the arteries in architecture is that architectural education has moved farther and farther from learning craft skills. American universities no longer have time for a meticulous basic education in construction and the building trades; and one consequence of that is that we get a modern architecture without traditional constructional finesse and without details. But a man like Mies was a craftsman through and through. The next generation had already largely lost this sense of the craft, and in the generation that followed almost nothing more of it remained. It seems to me that this loss of the foundation in the craft has resulted in rather conceited architects and a rather conceited architecture.

S.v.M.: I don't entirely understand your criticism of Gropius. I don't really see him as the great, authoritarian "Prussian" (leaving aside the fact that he would probably agree with what you say about the loss of the sense of craftsmanship). He once said that the color he likes most is "colorful." The whole Bauhaus would have been inconceivable without his essentially nonauthoritarian, pluralist attitude.

D.S.B.: I am, of course, not speaking of Gropius as a person; I'm speaking of his convictions as an architect.

R.V.: His prescriptions for a "total" and "objective" design of the environment[8] have a strong puritanical streak; they aim at a world in which leading architectural figures design

Rire pour ne pas pleurer

Interview avec Robert Venturi et Denise Scott Brown

1. Eclecticisme, ironie et quelques mythes fonctionnalistes

S.v.M.: Une grande partie de ce que vous avez construit et projeté pendant ces dernières années a un certain parfum éclectique, ce qui n'est pas pour plaire aux architectes, qui très souvent jugent cela frivole ou déconcertant. Pour eux, la qualité en architecture est avant tout une question d'originalité, et par ailleurs une construction est jugée satisfaisante dans la mesure où sa forme est une réponse directe au programme donné.
— Tout au contraire, vous ne craignez pas de puiser à différentes sources, autant historiques que vernaculaires ou commerciales — y compris Las Vegas.

R.V.: D'abord une remarque générale: n'importe quel architecte tire son savoir d'un grand nombre de sources variées — qu'il en soit conscient ou non; et ses sources changent avec son dévelopement artistique. Ceci n'implique pas — à mon avis — qu'une source soit plus valable qu'une autre. En ce qui me concerne, il me semble que plus l'architecte a des sources, plus son architecture sera riche, et je ne voudrais en aucune façon indiquer une source comme meilleure qu'une autre. Selon les monuments une source a pu nous apporter plus qu'une autre. Par exemple quand nous faisons la maison de ma mère (Fig. 29, 30), autour de 1960, nous étions très influencés par l'architecture italienne, surtout l'architecture maniériste, alors que le «shingle style»[1] a certainement joué un rôle d'arrière-plan important. Nous avons été influencés par des constructions aussi diverses que la villa Barbaro à Maser (j'adore le fond du giardino segreto, qui n'est qu'un grand fronton incurvé avec rien en-dessous) (Fig. 28), la Porta Pia (Fig. 27), et la villa Savoie (Fig. 22) — qui sous une enveloppe sévère a des aspects très complexes. Je traite de ces choses dans mon livre *Complexity and Contradiction in Architecture*. Plus récemment nous avons ajouté parmi nos sources celles qui viennent de l'ordinaire et du folklore, et en particulier l'architecture commerciale.
Toutefois nous apportenions encore suffisamment à la vieille école de «l'architecture moderne» orthodoxe pour nous garder de copier littéralement un style particulier dans sa plénitude. C'est une des raisons pour lesquelles nous avons des doutes sur ce qu'on appelle la «White School»[2]. Ces architectes copient Le Corbusier (celui des années 20) plus littéralement que ne l'ont fait les architectes éclectiques américains du début du siècle avec la ferme normande ou le palais italien pour dessiner des banques et des maisons. Je suis persuadé, presque au point d'en être dogmatique, que les influences doivent être plus variées et plus indirectes si l'on veut obtenir des œuvres réussies et intenses.

S.v.M.: En d'autres termes: les sources et les valeurs qu'elles peuvent représenter sont moins importantes pour vous que l'acte de transformation de ces sources en quelque chose de neuf.

R.V.: C'est exact. C'est pourquoi nous aimons le Pop Art: l'artiste Pop prend la réalité ordinaire et la transforme de différentes manières — en changeant le contexte, l'échelle ou la proportion.

S.v.M.: Est-ce cela que vous voulez dire quand vous parlez d'«ironie»?

R.V.: Eh bien, il faut prendre cela un peu comme une plaisanterie. Ce que je veux dire c'est que nous ne sommes pas comme ces architectes «Battle of the Styles» qui emploient les styles dans un but de propagande. Pour nous, regarder les styles est une façon de méditer sur l'architecture qui nous semble stimulante pour notre imagination.

D.S.B.: Dans notre livre sur Las Vegas nous avons cité un article de Richard Poirier[3] qui attire l'attention sur le fait que dans l'*Ulysse* de Joyce, il n'y a presque pas seule voix qui ne soit une parodie. La somme de toutes ces parodies *est* Joyce. Joyce s'exprime lui-même à travers un amalgame, un collage de parodies. Et pourtant personne n'aurait l'idée de dire que l'*Ulysse* n'est pas l'œuvre de Joyce parce qu'elle est «éclectique».

R.V.: Nous sommes juste en train de revenir au symbolisme. C'est très difficile pour nous, c'est une chose qui nous est toute nouvelle. Nous ne savons pas encore comment employer le symbolisme. Nous avons été éduqués dans la tradition moderne — c'est-à-dire éduqués à éviter tout symbolisme et ornement. C'est pourquoi maintenant nous tâtonnons.
Dans mon cas, le fait que l'aie reçu mon éducation à Princeton — dans les années 40 — plutôt qu'à Harvard, est peut-être significatif. A Princeton l'histoire de l'art avait une place importante. Le département d'architecture était sous le contrôle d'un département d'histoire de l'art très puissant. J'étais porté naturellement vers l'histoire de l'art. Mais à cette époque l'approche du Bauhaus prédominait dans l'enseignement de l'architecture, ce qui signifiait qu'en général on ne s'intéressait pas à des bâtiments historiques — sauf à ceux que Giedion avait légitimés comme précurseurs de l'architecture moderne.

S.v.M.: Etant moi-même historien d'art, ce que vous dites ne me met nullement mal à l'aise. Mais si j'étais un «vrai» architecte, éduqué dans la tradition moderne, j'aurais plus de difficulté. Parmi beaucoup d'architectes et de théoriciens il existe une sorte de puritanisme iconoclaste, une méfiance envers les images. On entend souvent dire, spécialement en Allemagne: la forme est trompeuse, l'art est trompeur, il ne tient pas ce qu'il prétend; c'est du camouflage, et par conséquent un symbole, et même un instrument de répression. Dans une telle perspective tout jeu formel en architecture ne signifie rien d'autre que la tentative de retarder le progrès vers l'ultime phase du bonheur social, où l'homme sera nu et n'aura plus aucun besoin d'art ni de rhétorique.

R.V.: Je ne m'y entends pas beaucoup en psycho-

logie, mais cela me semble une condition humaine
insupportable que de vivre dans un environnement où il
n'y a pas de référence à l'expérience passée. Il semble
que les êtres humains sont très attirés par la sécurité,
le plaisir et l'aménité que leur procurent des choses
qui ne sont pas absolument essentielles. Et c'est en
quelque sorte ce qu'est l'art et ce qui rend la vie supportable. D'autre part, on apprend tout par imitation. Regardez le petit enfant qui apprend! C'est si amusant de
regarder les enfants parce qu'ils appréhendent la forme
bien avant de comprendre le contenu. L'effet comique
vient d'un manque de correspondance fascinant entre
forme et contenu. S'il n'y avait pas cette imitation,
chaque génération serait complètement primitive.

D.S.B.: C'est pourquoi nous trouvons si bien l'article d'Alan Colquhoun [4]. Il dit que les architectes qui
ont cru pouvoir passer directement de la fonction à la
forme — avec, peut-être, un coup de main de l'intuition
— étaient très naïfs. Le cerveau ne travaille pas de cette
manière. Non seulement nous ne sommes pas libres des
associations de nos expériences passées, dit-il, mais
si nous essayons de nous en libérer, nous nous privons
d'une large partie de notre créativité. A cela nous ajoutons que les gens qui se croient libres de l'influence
des formes existantes et des vocabulaires formels sont
les plus tyrannisés par l'adoption irréfléchie de vocabulaires formels pas forcément adéquats à la tâche
fonctionnelle à laquelle ils sont confrontés.

2. Pop Art, consommation et «advocacy planning»

S.v.M.: Vous avez mentionné quelques-unes de vos
sources historiques et parlé de l'importance qu'a prise
l'architecture commerciale dans votre travail de ces
dernières années. Pourriez-vous citer plus précisémment
quelques-unes de vos sources contemporaines? Quels
sont les artistes contemporains que vous considérez
comme significatifs pour votre travail?

R.V.: Vous voulez dire les gens qui travaillent
maintenant que nous apprécions?

S.v.M.: Oui, ou bien qui travaillaient entre 1950 et
1970 et dont l'œuvre a été significative pour votre
propre travail.

R.V.: Nous avons naturellement beaucoup appris
des maîtres: Aalto, Mies, Le Corbusier, Kahn. D'autre
part nous avons aussi appris des grands artistes Pop:
Warhol, Oldenburg, Johns, Rosenquist, Lichtenstein.
Quand le Pop Art a surgi il a fallu quelque temps pour
que je m'y intéresse, mais alors j'en ai beaucoup profité.
Les motifs du Pop Art, les éléments ordinaires et leur
relation avec notre sensibilité ont été très fructueux
pour moi. En revanche, nous n'avons pas appris beaucoup des expressionnistes abstraits. Les néo-réalistes
nous intéressent beaucoup. Les conceptualistes ne sont
pas intéressants dans notre domaine. Mais je ne veux
pas être un critique: nous regardons ici ces différents
mouvements artistiques d'un point de vue purement
égoïste, comme faisant partie de notre environnement
éducatif.

D.S.B.: Il y a aussi les photographies architecturales et les peintures de John Bader. Nous avons fait
avec lui des échanges de vieilles cartes postales, et il a
utilisé pour une série de peintures les photographies
originales des White Towers qu'a faites Steve Izenour [5].

↓ figs. 36–37   Venturi & Rauch (with Gerod Clark),
"Bill-Ding-Board" for the National Football Hall
of Fame. Project, 1967.

Et puis il y a Mahaffey, de Philadelphie, qui peint
d'après de magnifiques cartes postales architecturales,
entre autres une vue du palais art déco abritant une
compagnie d'assurance en face du musée de Philadelphie; et enfin Ed Ruscha, de Los Angeles, dont la vision
et l'intérêt dans la publicité et l'art commercial sont
très proches des nôtres (Fig. 31–33).

S.v.M.: A voir votre livre si opulent sur Las Vegas
on pourrait avoir l'impression que vous adorez les panneaux publicitaires et le monde de la consommation,
et que par conséquent vous vous intéressez plus au statu
quo américain qu'aux manières de le changer. Pour un
intellectuel européen il semble bien que des gens qui
vont passer quelques temps à Las Vegas pour y étudier
le «strip» commercial doivent avoir un attachement
assez trouble et érotique à la société de consommation
et ses images. Ulrich Franzen a employé le mot de
«nixonité».[6] Pour lui, comme pour beaucoup d'architectes
modernes, il y a un profond accord sur le fait qu'à la
base de l'engagement de l'architecte il doit y avoir
l'idée de créer un monde meilleur, plus humain, etc. . . .
Pour ces gens vous représentez une intelligentsia qui
renforce le système. Comment ressentez-vous ce rôle
qu'on vous attribue?

D.S.B.: C'est une très longue question, et difficile
à répondre parce qu'elle fait venir à l'esprit toutes sortes
de pensées. Nous croyons que nos idées ont une base

↓ fig. 38–39   Murphy, Levy, Wurmann, Venturi & Rauch (with Steven Izenour), Billboards along a Philadelphia highway. Project, 1974 (Schuylkill River Corridor Study).

sociale et un intérêt pour une amélioration sociale. J'ai dit dans notre livre — dans une longue discussion sur cette question: «Ne nous reprochez pas notre manque de conscience sociale. Nous essayons de nous entraîner pour offrir des connaissances et des capacités socialement significatives.» Mais nos critiques n'ont cité que la premières partie de cette déclaration: «Ne nous reprochez pas notre manque de conscience sociale.» D'autre part, toute l'argumentation qui supporte et justifie cette déclaration a été simplement ignorée.

Pour répondre à votre question la première chose à dire est que le contexte américain est nettement différent du contexte européen. Nous pensons que notre position pour ainsi-dire néo-populiste est dans le contexte américain plus une position de gauche que de droite. D'autre part, si les arguments de nos critiques peuvent paraître de gauche en Europe, il n'en va pas de même aux Etats-Unis. En fait, ils marquent plutôt une fuite de la réalité, car ici, en Amérique, il n'existe simplement pas l'organisation sociale et gouvernementale indispensable pour réaliser les théories européennes dans le domaine de l'architecture. Dans les années 50 et 60 la moyenne des logements publics construits aux Etats-Unis a été de 20 000 unités par année. Le compte pour les années 70 est probablement encore plus bas. Cet état de choses étant connu, toute l'habituelle rhétorique de l'architecture moderne sur la construction pour les classes pauvres et défavorisées apparaît comme une fuite de la réalité, un faux problème. Mais dès que vous commencez à chercher les moyens de vous approcher de la réalité, vous découvrez qu'il vous faut travailler avec le système tel qu'il est — ou bien renoncer et échaffauder des utopies. Mais si vous essayez d'apporter des améliorations dans la situation présente, alors vous paraissez réactionnaires, surtout si vous essayez d'utiliser les entreprises privées pour atteindre des buts sociaux. C'est une situation très complexe, qui a peu à faire avec les discours moralisateurs de la nouvelle élite architecturale progressiste.

S.v.M.: Autrement dit: une grande partie de l'esthétique et de l'éthique du mouvement moderne a quelque chose à faire avec la possibilité de travailler (ou l'espoir de pouvoir travailler) dans le cadre d'une bureaucratie capable d'entreprendre de grands travaux dans le domaine du logement social. Etant donné que cette possibilité n'existe pas dans ce pays, une bonne part du réformisme social du mouvement moderne est, dans ces conditions, plutôt futile.

D.S.B.: Pas seulement futile! Ces théories sont utilisées par la classe dirigeante pour justifier des programmes de construction socialement coercitifs. En voici un exemple: dans un quartier pauvre de Philadelphie (South Street, Fig. 34), un groupe d'habitants nous a demandé de les aider dans leur lutte pour empêcher la construction d'une autoroute. Ils nous dirent: si vous pouvez aimer Las Vegas nous vous faisons confiance que vous n'allez pas «assainir» South Street à nos dépens. Les gens nous ont invités parce qu'ils ont compris que nous regardons les villes existantes comme elles sont et que nous essayons de comprendre pourquoi elles sont comme cela, sans faire intervenir toutes sortes d'impératifs esthétiques ou moraux. Pour ces gens cela semblait un bon départ. Mais pour beaucoup d'architectes c'est totalement faux. Ils croient que le devoir de l'architecte est d'«apporter au peuple» un bon logement tout propre et tout neuf. Eh bien, nous avons vu ce qui est arrivé aux Etats-Unis lorsque ces beaux logements tout neufs ont été construits, avec toute la rhétorique sociale appropriée, mais seulement pas pour la clientèle appropriée. En fait, il est souvent arrivé que les habitants de quartiers pauvres ont été délogés pour faire place à de nouveaux immeubles, de style CIAM, dans lesquels a été accueilli un public appartenent à des catégories aisées. En dépit du dévouement du mouvement moderne à la cause de l'amélioration du logement pour les classes défavorisées, très peu a été fait dans ce domaine — et c'est pourquoi certains parmi nous essaient une autre méthode. Nous avons étudié Las Vegas en partie parce que les gens (middle et lower class) semblent l'aimer bien plus qu'ils n'aiment l'architecture qu'ils devraient aimer au gré des architectes . . . C'est une réponse plutôt confuse . . .

S.v.M.: Peut-être la question est-elle confuse . . .

D.S.B.: Non, ce n'est pas votre question mais le

↓ fig. 40   Venturi & Rauch, Study for bicentennial celebrations in Philadelphia, 1972.

problème qui est confus. Dison que nous faisons tout notre possible pour servir nos objectifs sociaux dans un proche futur, en utilisant le matériel disponible dans la société où nous vivons. Comme les artistes confrontés avec cette situation nous utilisons l'ironie, peut-être de la même manière dont en parle Poirier dans l'article que nous avons déjà cité: il dit que l'artiste pour faire son art tire son matériel du monde qui l'entoure. Si ce monde lui convient, l'artiste l'utilise tel qu'il est; sinon il (ou elle) l'utilise ironiquement. Nous croyons que nous l'utilisons ironiquement: nous utilisons l'ironie comme en moyen de rire pour ne pas pleurer. Nous voyons l'ironie comme une manière d'aider les membres d'une société multiculturelle à vivre ensemble. Nous pensons que dans notre société un artiste ou un architecte socialement conscient peut devenir une sorte d'amuseur public.

Ceci de nouveau montre notre ambivalence vis-à-vis de la société. Sous certains aspects elle est terrible, sous d'autres elle est magnifique — notre ambivalence se manifeste dans notre œuvre sous forme d'ironie.

S.v.M.: . . . alors une sorte d'humour noir, comme le suggérait un collègue allemand, Michael Müller, dans sa réponse à votre récente conférence à Berlin ? [7]

D.S.B.: Oui, sauf que c'est plus gentil que l'humour noir. Nous ne sommes pas entièrement contre cette société. Nous pensons que notre position comme architectes américains est une position compromise, mais que la position de tout le monde industriel vis-à-vis du reste du monde l'est tout autant. Ainsi nous sommes contre beaucoup d'aspects de notre société . . .

S.v.M.: Mais vous n'êtes pas apocalyptiques.
D.S.B.: Non, par tempéramment.

3. La monumentalité aujourd'hui — ou les problèmes d'une révolution qui vieillit

S.v.M.: Comment se fait-il que l'architecture moderne a un penchant toujours plus marqué vers l'hé-

roïque ? Comment se fait-il qu'un si grand nombre de constructions nouvelles, spécialement en Amérique, est si proche, de caractère et de tempérament, de la «City Beautiful» (Fig. 35) et de la monumentalité classique, de l'effet théâtral et de la pompe qui caractérisent ce mouvement — en dépit de l'idéalisme anti-Beaux-Arts qu'elle traîne avec elle? Comment expliquez-vous ce phénomène? — Je vous pose cette question parce que je trouve que sur la scène architecturale actuelle vous êtes à l'extrêmité opposée de ce nouvel héroïsme post-brutaliste.

D.S.B.: Je crois que le phénomène auquel nous assistons aujourd'hui est à mettre en rapport avec d'une part la ferveur révolutionnaire du mouvement moderne, et d'autre part avec la force de la révolution lorsqu'elle devient réaction. C'est-à-dire que la ferveur est restée, mais la révolution elle-même est devenue réaction. Je pense que c'est là une des raisons de cette attitude héroïque. Je me souviens par exemple que l'architecte italien Albini a une fois dit que l'architecture moderne était la lumière éclatante qui l'avait soutenu pendant la période fasciste et la guerre. Eh bien, l'ardeur que recouvre ce sentiment s'est transmise à travers plusieurs générations, mais la révolution est maintenant vieille et est passée dans le camp de l'establishment.

D'autre part, l'éducation architecturale est fortement autoritaire, particulièrement aux Etats-Unis à cause de ses origines Beaux-Arts — bien plus que, par exemple en Angleterre, où il y a des écoles comme l'Architectural Association. Les architectes sont éduqués pour devenir des leaders. Ils ont un grand prestige social et se considèrent eux-mêmes comme des gurus pour la société. En cela ils sont aussi mauvais que les psychiâtres, autre grande profession autoritaire. Ce sont eux qui savent, et vous, pauvre idiot, qui ne voulez jamais comprendre. Si vous voulez conduire une voiture et vivre dans un suburb, cela prouve simplement que vous n'avez rien compris: vous devriez marcher et vivre dans une mégastructure. Cette attitude est très fréquente parmi les architectes. En plus, il faut considérer encore une

30

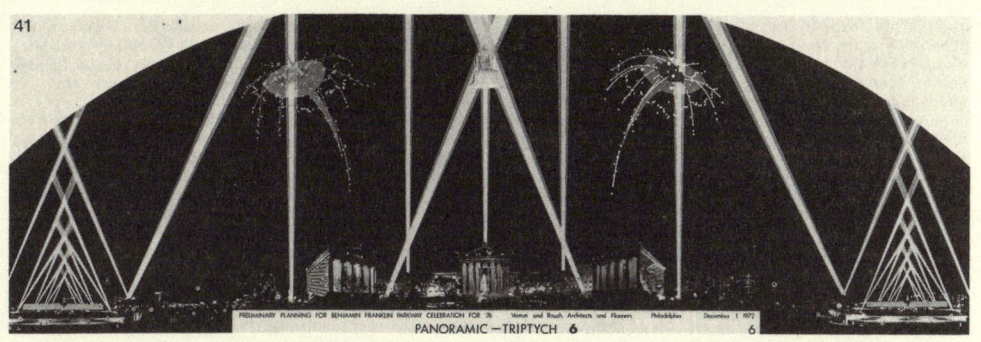

fig. 41 Venturi & Rauch, Study for bicentennial celebrations in Philadelphia, 1972.

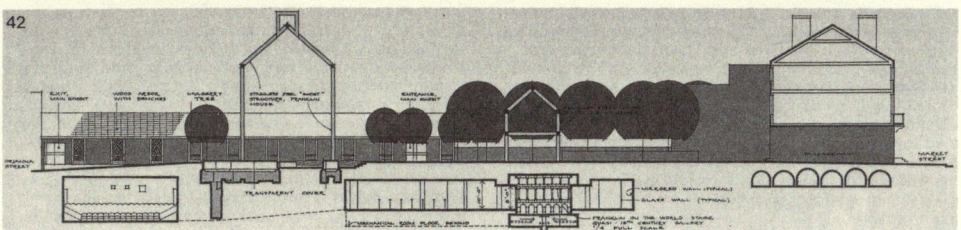

chose: l'architecture américaine a été dès l'origine une profession de la classe supérieure et une profession purement masculine. Cela tient en partie au fait que pour mettre en train votre propre atelier vous avez besoin d'un second revenu.

Il nous semble aussi que Gropius, espèce de prussien architectural, s'est accordé très bien avec les brahmanes de Boston, qu'il y a là une alliance de deux types similaires. Et, en fait, l'architecture moderne a très bien pris autour de Harvard, et de là elle s'est disséminée dans le pays.

Une autre cause de la sclérose architecturale actuelle est à chercher dans le fait que l'éducation architecturale a progressivement abandonné toute exigence dans les qualifications artisanales. Les universités américaines n'ont plus le temps d'enseigner les connaissances de base de la construction et de la pratique artisanale, et la conséquence en est que nous avons une architecture moderne sans les finesses constructives traditionnelles et sans détails. Un homme comme Mies était un artisan jusqu'au bout des ongles. La première génération après Mies a commencé à perdre ce sens du métier artisanal, et à la seconde génération il n'en restait plus rien. Ainsi je pense qu'avec la perte d'une base artisanale et technique on obtient des architectes gonflés et une architecture ampoulée.

S.v.M.: Je ne comprends pas bien votre critique de Gropius. Je ne peux vraiment pas l'imaginer comme le type du prussien autoritaire (mis à part le fait que je suis persuadé qu'il aurait approuvé entièrement ce que vous dites au sujet de l'habileté artisanale). Il a dit une fois que sa couleur préférée était «multicolore». Toute l'expérience du Bauhaus serait — je crois — impensable sans sa perspective anti-autoritaire et pluraliste.

D.S.B.: Je ne voulais évidemment pas parler de Gropius en tant que personne, mais de ses vues comme architecte.

R.V.: Ses prescriptions pour une planification totale et objective [8] ont un caractère fortement puritain. Elles visent à un monde où des leaders architecturaux projettent un «urbanisme total» pour atteindre une unité totale, mais cette unité est imposée par en-haut, par des experts, sur le reste du monde.

Je suis tout à fait d'accord avec ce que dit Denise

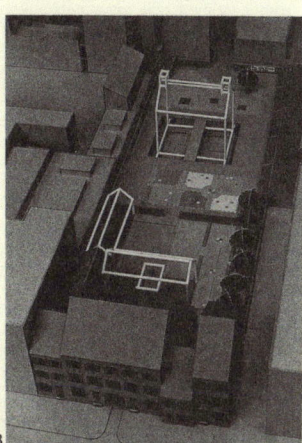

←fig. 42

Venturi & Rauch (with David Vaughan), Reconstruction of the outlines of the home of Benjamin Franklin in Philadelphia, with underground exhibition spaces. Under construction.

←fig. 43

au sujet de l'ardeur révolutionnaire progressiste en apparence mais en réalité rétrograde. C'est héroïque d'être révolutionnaire; on risque sa vie. Il me semble que ce sentiment héroïque est toujours vivant, cette qualité rhétorique, le dogme d'une révolution. Nous sommes dans une époque expressionniste — pouquoi, je n'en sais rien — mais c'est une époque qui implique des exagérations d'anciens dogmes.

S.v.M.: Il me semble qu'en plus de tout cela il y a encore autre chose qui joue un rôle. Il semble que les gens se sentent à l'aise dans un environnement comportant des monuments commémoratifs de combats et de faits héroïques. C'est en partie le sens de toute une tradition dans l'architecture étatique américaine — depuis le 18ième siècle jusqu'à l'hôtel de ville de Boston — de classicisme ou de rigidité classique, symbolisant le triomphe de l'ordre et de la loi, du contrôle de l'état sur le chaos et le laissez-faire.

R.V.: Ce que vous dites au sujet de la monumentalité me paraît vrai. Les gens veulent de la rhétorique, ils veulent de l'expression aussi bien dans leurs vies que dans leur environnement, et ils veulent de grandes déclarations, claires et univoques. Il n'y a rien de mal à cela. Mais il se pourrait qu'aujourd'hui, dans cette époque-ci, personne ne sache vraiment quoi dire. Il se peut que les grands trusts aient été très sûrs de leur affaire — du moins jusqu'à il y a quelques mois. Mais maintenant les grands trusts eux-mêmes se font plus discrets, et quelquefois ils s'efforcent même de n'être pas trop en vue.

Je suis d'accord avec vous que la société a toujours voulu faire des déclarations publiques — mais je ne sais pas en quoi ces déclarations pourraient consister actuellement en Amérique. Il existe, en fait, deux sortes de déclarations populaires et facilement compréhensibles: d'une part les images architecturales des grands trusts, du big business, et d'autre part les images de la vie de loisirs du type Las Vegas. Je ne voudrais pas dire que nous sommes aujourd'hui confus au point de ne pas pouvoir avoir de grandes déclarations publiques, de grandes déclarations rhétoriques. Il serait trop facile de dire cela. Je ne voudrais pas aller si loin quoiqu'il semble évident que nous ne pouvons pas faire aujourd'hui de déclaration architecturale univoque comme celle de Chartres au 12ième siècle. Cela n'est pas possible maintenant en Amérique pour plusieurs raisons. D'abord nous ne sommes pas tous catholiques; nous avons une société extrêmement hétérogène, et nous sommes dans une période très troublée, nous sommes dans une sorte d'époque maniériste. J'ai l'impression que dans le futur, nos grands monuments ne seront pas des morceaux d'architecture, comme à Chartres, sur l'Acropole ou à Versailles — ni même comme ils l'étaient dans la ville américaine du 19ième siècle avec ses gares et des hôtels de ville. Je ne sais pas ce que seront ces monuments, peut-être d'énormes panneaux publics, ou de gigantesques statues de 100 mètres de haut — comme celles de Oldenburg — qui s'accordent avec notre nouvelle échelle spatiale et nos grandes vitesses. Mais j'ai l'impression que la réponse n'est plus dans l'architecture pure (bien sûr, autrefois cela n'était pas non plus de l'architecture pure). Et je crois vraiment que les monuments des grands trusts n'ont pas vraiment de signification. A mon avis, une large partie de la monumentalité de l'architecture actuelle est de la pose gratuite plutôt que de la rhétorique effective.

D.S.B.: Depuis plusieurs années on cherche quelque chose de spécial à faire pour la célébration du bi-centennaire américain (1976): on a encore rien trouvé.

S.v.M.: Est-ce que cela sera un spectacle «multi-media»?

R.V.: Eh bien, c'est une manière intéressante d'envisager ce problème, car dans les 100 dernières années les expositions mondiales ont été des événements «mono-media» plutôt que «multi-media», n'est ce pas? Il s'agissait d'événements célébrant la révolution industrielle et sa technologie à travers l'architecture technique et progressive décrite par Giedion. Il n'en est plus ainsi. Nous n'avons pas de Crystal Palace, de Galerie des Machines, ni de Tour d'Eiffel. Aujourd'hui Bucky Fuller et Frei Otto sont plutôt ennuyeux. Les événements vraiment intéressants de nos expositions mondiales sont maintenant les films de cinéma et de télévision. L'architecture devrait fournir un arrière-plan pour les messages nationaux et internationaux de la foire. L'architecture ne devrait pas être expressive à travers ses formes, mais à travers ses signes. Les signes et les messages devraient être «en appliqué», formant un environnement de messages, et non plus de pure architecture. Les monuments d'architecture héroïque que nous venons de mentionner ne sont que les derniers soubresauts de la forme pure, les derniers soubresauts désespérément ennuyeux.

D.S.B.: Les grandes déclarations publiques du futur seront peut-être d'un tout autre ordre, comme par exemple des mesures pour attaquer sérieusement le problème de la pauvreté. Philadelphie a proposé pour le bi-centennaire qu'large portion de ses dépenses soit employée dans un programme social de première urgence. Cette proposition a été refusée à Washington. On a l'impression ici qu'il n'y aura pas beaucoup à célébrer en 1976, à moins que ses mesures sociales ne soient prises. Notre proposition pour une exposition du bi-centennaire consistant de panneaux et de signes, doit être comprise dans ce contexte (Fig. 38–41).

---

[1]   «Shingle style»: ce terme désigne une série historiquement importante de maisons de la fin du 19ième siècle aux USA, qui se placent dans la tradition du mouvement «Arts and Crafts». (Cf. Vincent Scully, *The Shingle Style*, New Haven, 1955.)
[2]   Egalement appelée «New York Five»: Peter Eisenmann, Michael Graves, Charles Gwathmey, John Hejduk, Richard Meier; cf. différents auteurs, *Five Architects*, New York, 1972.
[3]   Richard Poirier, «T. S. Eliot and the Literature of Waste», in *The New Republic*, 20 mai 1967.
[4]   Alan Colquhoun, «Typology and Design Method», in *Arena*, juin 1967, pp. 11–14; reproduit dans Charles Jencks et George Baird, *Meaning in Architecture*, New York, 1969.
[5]   Cf. Paul Hirshorn et Steven Izenour, «Learning from Hamburgers», in *Architecture Plus*, mai 1973.
[6]   Ulrich Franzen, «Letter to the Editor», in *Progressive Architecture*, avril 1970, p. 8.
[7]   «Functionalism Yes, But . . .» Conférence dans le cadre d'un symposium organisé par les Internationales Design Zentrum (IDZ), Berlin, sur le thème «Le pathos du fonctionnalisme», septembre 1974.
[8]   Cf. Walter Gropius, *Scope of Total Architecture*, New York, 1943 ss.

the "total landscape" in order to achieve a total unity, and specifically a unity that is regulated from above, by the experts for the rest of humanity.

I am in complete agreement with what Denise said about the progressive revolutionary ardor that is in reality reactionary. It is heroic to be a revolutionary; you risk your life doing it. It seems to me that this heroic feeling still lives on, somehow, this rhetorical quality, the dogma of a revolution. We live in an expressionist period, I don't really know why, but it is a period that is expressed in part in the form of exaggerations of earlier dogmas.

S.v.M.: It seems to me that something else plays a role in addition to all that. People seem to feel comfortable in an environment in which there are monuments that recall heroic events and conflicts. That is in part the sense of the tradition of classicist forms in American "state architecture"—or at least the tradition of classicist austerity in architecture: it wants to symbolize the triumph of law and order, of state control over disorder and laissez-faire, from the eighteenth century right up to Boston City Hall (fig. 4).

R.V.: What you are saying about monumentality seems right to me. People want rhetoric; they want expression, both in their lives and in their environment, and they want the big message summed up in a manageable form. And that is how it should be. But it may be that today, in this special era, no one is entirely sure what this big message could be. Perhaps the big corporations were entirely sure of themselves—at least until a few months ago. But even they have become somewhat more discreet; often they even try not to stand out too much.

I agree with you that now and again society wanted big public messages in the form of architecture, but I simply don't know what our big messages could be in America today. There are really just two kinds of popular, easy-to-understand messages: On the one hand, the architectural images of the big corporations, of big business, and, on the other hand, the leisure images à la Las Vegas. I wouldn't say that we are so confused today that we cannot have any public messages—big, rhetorical messages—beyond that. That would be too simplistic. I would not go that far, although it is clear that today we cannot make any big architectural message summed up in a form, like that of, say, Chartres in the twelfth century. We cannot have that here in America for various reasons. If only because we are not all Catholic; we have an extremely heterogeneous society, and we find ourselves in a time of confusion; we are in a kind of mannerist period. Be that as it may, I suspect that in the future the medium of our public messages will not be architecture. Our big public statements will not be architectural in the same sense as, say, in Chartres, on the Acropolis, or in Versailles—nor in the same sense that was still possible in the American city of the nineteenth century, with its train stations and city halls. I don't know what it will look like, in fact—perhaps they will be enormous public billboards or enormous three hundred-feet-tall sculptures à la Oldenburg, in keeping with the spatial scale and speed in our cities. In any case, I believe that the solution to the problem will no longer be pure architecture (it was not pure architecture in the past either, of course). And I also believe that the monuments of the big corporations are somehow irrelevant. I believe that a great deal in the area of our architectural monumentality today is an empty pose, in contrast to a rhetoric that has a real effect.

D.S.B.: People searched for years for a "message" for the American bicentennial (1976), but they never found anything convincing.

S.v.M.: Will it be a multimedia event?

R.V.: Well, that's an interesting way to approach the problem, because in the past hundred years world's fairs were mono- rather than multimedia events, right? In any case, they were events that glorified the Industrial Revolution, with the help of progressive, technological architecture—of the kind described by Giedion. That's no longer true today: We have no Crystal Palace, no Galerie des Machines, and no Eiffel Tower. Today, even Buckminster Fuller and Frei Otto are rather boring. The truly interesting things at our world's fairs happen in the area of film and the television movie. In such a situation, architecture is not supposed to be anything more than a receding backdrop for the national and international offerings at such a fair.

Architecture should express what it has to express not by means of its forms but by means of symbols. The symbols and messages should be an "appliqué." They constitute an environment that consists of messages and not of "pure architecture." The belated heroic architectural monuments that we mentioned earlier are nothing other than the last gasp of pure form, the quite boring last gasp.

D.S.B.: The big public messages or confessions could be things like, for example, the effort to finally address the problem of poverty. Philadelphia proposed for the bicentennial that a large part of the municipal expenditures should go to social programs in order to eliminate the worst deficiencies in the city. But Washington didn't want to hear about it. Ever since, the feeling here has been that there won't be a lot to celebrate in 1976 if these social measures are not taken up first.

Our own proposals for a bicentennial exhibition composed of exhibition sheds and symbols should be understood against that backdrop (figs. 38–41). (Philadelphia, October 1974)

[Ed. Note: "[...] the Art Deco insurance palace opposite the museum in Philadelphia" referred to above are the Fidelity Mutual Life Insurance Company Building (today the Ruth and Raymond G. Perelman Building), ca. 1927, designed by Zantzinger, Borie, and Medary; and the Philadelphia Museum of Art.]

ENDNOTES

1 "Shingle Style": this term describes a series of American homes of the late nineteenth century in the tradition of the Arts and Crafts Movement that were important for the history of the evolution of architecture. See Vincent Scully, *The Shingle Style* (New Haven, 1955).

2 Or the so-called New York Five: Peter Eisenman, Michael Graves, Charles Gwathmey, John Hejduk, and Richard Meier. See various authors, *Five Architects* (New York, 1972).

3 Richard Poirier, "T.S. Eliot and the Literature of Waste," *New Republic*, May 20, 1967.

4 Alan Colquhoun, "Typology and Design Method," *Arena*, June 1967, 11–14, reprinted in Charles Jencks and George Baird, *Meaning in Architecture* (New York, 1969).

5 See Paul Hirshorn and Steven Izenour, "Learning from Hamburgers," *Architecture Plus* 1, 5 (June 1973).

6 Ulrich Franzen, "Letter to the Editor," in *Progressive Architecture*, April 1970, 8.

7 "Functionalism Yes, but ...," lecture as part of a symposium on "Das Pathos des Funktionalismus" [The pathos of functionalism], organized by the Internationales Design Zentrum, Berlin, September 1974.

8 See Walter Gropius, *Scope of Total Architecture* (New York, 1943).

Stanislaus von Moos, Denise Scott Brown, and Robert Venturi

Alan Colquhoun

Regeln, Realismus und Geschichte

Eines der Probleme, die im heutigen Architekturgespräch im Vordergrund stehen, betrifft die Beziehung der Architektur zur gesamtgesellschaftlichen Kultur: ist Architektur ein auf sich selber verweisendes System, das seine eigene Tradition und seine eigenen Werte besitzt, oder ist sie vielmehr ein gesellschaftliches Produkt, das erst dann zu einem Wesen wird, wenn das System durch äussere Kräfte rekonstituiert wird?

Es gibt heute unzweifelhaft eine starke Meinungsströmung, die zu der ersten dieser Alternativen neigt. Sie scheint hervorgetreten zu sein als eine Reaktion auf die schwache theoretische Position, in die die Architektur im Lauf der letzten 15 oder mehr Jahre gedrängt wurde. Während dieser Zeit waren nämlich ihre Verteidigungslinien den aufeinanderfolgenden Angriffswellen von Operationalismus, System-Methodologie, poetischer Technologie, sozialem Realismus und sogar einer gewissen Semiologie-Diskussion ausgesetzt, die alle zu ihrem obersten Ziel hatten, die «architektonischen Werte» abzubauen, die Banham einmal die «kulturelle Bagage» nannte. Auf der einen Seite wurde die architektonische Schöpfung zurückgestellt bis ein scheinbar endloser Prozess von Induktion und Untersuchung zu Ende geführt war, auf der anderen wurde ästhetischer Eifer ermuntert, vorausgesetzt dass seine Wurzeln expressionistisch oder populistisch waren und das Vorhandensein irgend eines gültigen Systemes von Regeln, die der Tradition der «hohen» Architektur angehörten, zurückgewiesen wurde. Sofern eingeräumt wurde, dass Architektur eine Sprache ist, dann ist sie nach dieser Auffassung eine Sprache, die der Intuition entspringt, unbehindert von irgend einem ihr vorausgehenden Wissen — eine Sprache also, die natürlicher wäre als die natürliche Sprache selber, da sie nicht gelernt zu werden brauchte.

Diese Auffassung — die immer noch wirksam ist — ergibt sich in einem gewissen Sinn aus einer der stärksten Triebkräfte der avantgardistischen Kunst seit der Mitte des 19. Jahrhunderts: dem Bemühen um «Realismus» oder

Règles, réalisme et histoire

L'architecture est-elle un système qui se refère à lui-même ou bien un système qui ne se constitue qu'à la base de forces extérieures? — On a récemment tenté à plusieurs reprises de nier l'existence d'un système valable de règles dérivées de l'architecture «haute». Ceux qui admettaient l'architecture comme un langage ont pourtant ajouté qu'il s'agissait d'un langage qui est basé sur l'intuition, sans savoir préétabli. Cette idée résulte en quelques sorte d'une des plus fortes composantes de l'art d'avant-garde depuis le 19ième siècle: la recherche d'un «réalisme». Si un des buts de cette recherche était d'éliminer le style pour découvrir l'essence, elle devait confronter enfin nécessairement le fait que la façon de comprendre la réalité et la façon de la reproduire dans l'art sont deux choses différentes.

Il existe donc nécessairement des lois de construction esthétique mais celles-ci ne sont pas immuables, elles sont sujettes à des changements qui ne surgissent pas du système esthétique même mais sont provoquées par des faits extérieurs. On pourrait penser à un processus contenant deux variables — le système socio-économique et le système esthétique — un processus qui ne peut être compris que dialectiquement.

Le vieux «réalisme», selon lequel il s'agit de trouver un langage fondamental qui exclut la médiation par le style devrait être remplacé par un nouveau «réalisme», qui respecte aussi bien ces structures esthétiques qu'une réalité qui les influence et les modifie.

Rules, Realism, and History

Author:
Alan Colquhoun

Sources:
archithese, 19 (1976): 12–17
Alan Colquhoun, *Essays in Architectural Criticism: Modern Architecture and Historical Change* (Cambridge, MA: MIT Press, 1981), 67–74 (EN)

Captions translated by:
Steven Lindberg

Perhaps the most crucial problem in architecture today is that of its relationship with the culture of society as a whole. Is architecture to be considered as a self-referential system, with its own traditions and its own system of values, or is it rather a social product which only becomes an entity once it has been reconstituted by forces external to it?

There is undoubtedly today a strong current of opinion which tends toward the first of these alternatives. These ideas seem to have appeared as a reaction against the weak theoretical position forced on architecture during the last fifteen years or so, during which its defenses have been attacked by successive waves of operationalism, systems methodology, poetic technology, social realism, and even certain semiological discussions, all of which have had as their chief aim the dismantling of "architectural values"—what Reyner Banham has called the "cultural baggage." On the one hand, architectural creation has been postponed until an apparently endless process of induction and analysis (whether technical or social) has been completed; on the other, aesthetic fervor has been encouraged, provided that its roots were either expressionistic or populist, and the existence of any valid system of rules or norms belonging to the tradition of "high architecture" has been denied. If it has been admitted that architecture is a "language," then it is a language which springs from intuition, unhampered by any previous knowledge of the subject—a language more natural than natural language itself, since it does not have to be learned.

These tendencies—which are still very strong—are, in one sense, the result of one of the most powerful motives of avant-garde art since the mid-nineteenth century—the drive toward "realism" or "naturalism." The successive artistic revolutions of the last 150 years have all been attempts to "get behind" the "stylistic" representation of ideas, to destroy the artificial rules which not only mediate between the representation and the reality but also give this representation a particular ideological coloring. It is true that this search for a primordial language with which to express man's relation to reality eventually took a form which seems almost the antithesis of realism, when, instead of imitating structures which were immediately given, it attempted to discover hidden and underlying structures. This turn toward formalism, which sought to create analogues of the real world, not only affected painting and literature as "imitating" arts but also architecture and music, where the humanizing and reassuring elements of style belonging to the "classical" repertoire were rejected in favor of more elementary structures.

But if the aim of this revolutionary force was to eliminate style and to discover essences, it was in the end bound to come up against the fact that our mode of understanding "reality" and our mode of "representing" reality artistically are separate things.

Already in the 1920s Boris Tomashevsky drew attention to the infinite regress in which the avant-garde found itself in literature:

> "In general the nineteenth century abounded in schools whose very names hint at realistic techniques of motivation—'Realism,' 'Naturalism,' 'the Nature School,' 'Populism,' and so on. In our time the Symbolists replaced the Realists in the name of some kind of transnaturalism … a fact which did not prevent the appearance of Acmeism … and Futurism. … From school to school we hear the call to 'Naturalism.' Why, then, has a 'completely naturalistic school' not been founded…?—because the name 'Realist' is attached to each school (and to none)… . This explains the ever present antagonism of the new school for the old—that is, the exchange of old and obvious conventions for new, less obvious ones within the literary pattern. On the other hand, this also shows that realistic material in itself does not have artistic structure and that the formation of an artistic structure requires that reality be reconstructed according to aesthetic laws. Such laws are always, considered in relation to reality, conventional."[1]

The facts stated here, though clearly admissible in the case of the "nonutilitarian" arts, might be questioned in relation to architecture, which has to embrace both the real and the representational—the work of architecture being part of the real, "usable" world, as well as a representation of that world. It could be argued that the Modern Movement radically confused these two aspects, attributing to the need for practical buildings a representational function or, conversely, burdening the representational function with the responsibility for solving practical building problems. But if it did this, the reason must lie in the fact that these two aspects of architecture, which are independent from a logical point of view, are never independent experientially, and that the search for the "essence" of the building has an aesthetic motivation, embracing a certain idea of utility and its representation—one in which the transparency of the form was symbolic of a reality which could be totally described and manifested.

Thus the "materialism" of modern architecture was just as "metaphysical" as architecture had ever been, and this seems to show that when we are talking of architecture, we are referring to a system of representation of essentially the same kind as that found in the other arts. It is no more possible in architecture than any other system of representation to arrive at the ne plus ultra in which the representation and the represented coincide; the need for aesthetic laws of construction must be admitted. Such laws are not like the laws established on the basis of hypothesis and experiment in the physical sciences—laws which, according to Karl Popper, have to be capable of falsification. If we are to make a scientific analogy, we should rather say that they are like the "paradigms" which, in Thomas Kuhns's analysis, determine the area of scientific discourse. They are norms, and a complete description of the phenomenon of architecture could no more neglect to include them than could a description, say, of football omit to include those rules which alone render the game intelligible. In Tomashevsky's terms, they are "conventional."[2]

But however much the necessary existence of such laws may justify a view of architecture as a self-referential system, it does not support a view which would regard such a system as dependent on laws which are absolute and unchanging. The laws regulating aesthetic construction are subject to change, and this change comes about not from inside the aesthetic system but from outside.

That this is true can be seen even in a system so apparently independent of technical and economic conditions as music. The change in musical language which came about in the eighteenth century, when a contrapuntal gave way to a homophonic method, can only be explained by a change in the social function of music. What took place was, of course, a purely musical change, and it can be completely explained in terms of rules which belong to music alone. Nonetheless, the motivation for the change was external to music.

Up until the nineteenth century, the external pressures on architecture were no more than on the other arts, but since the Industrial Revolution, and with increasing intensity in the twentieth

«Naturalismus». Die seit damals aufeinanderfolgenden künstlerischen Revolutionen waren alle Versuche, «hinter» die «stilistische» Darstellung von Ideen zu gelangen, die mit einem Stil verbundenen Regeln zu zerstören, die nicht nur zwischen der Wirklichkeit und der Darstellung vermitteln, sondern dieser Darstellung auch eine besondere ideologische Färbung verleihen. Freilich nahm diese Suche nach einer Ur-Sprache, mit der die Beziehung des Menschen zur Wirklichkeit auszudrücken wäre, gelegentlich eine Form an, die fast das Gegenteil von Realismus zu sein scheint: wenn sie, statt die Strukturen nachzuahmen, die unmittelbar gegeben waren, darunter liegende verborgene Strukturen zu finden trachtete. Diese Wendung zum Formalismus, die Analoga der wirklichen Welt zu schaffen suchte, wirkte sich nicht nur auf die «nachahmenden» Künste wie die Malerei und die Literatur aus, sondern auch auf die Architektur und die Musik, indem die vermenschlichenden und versichernden Elemente des Stils, die zum «klassischen» Repertoire gehören, zugunsten von elementareren Strukturen verworfen wurden.

Doch wenn es das Ziel dieser revolutionären Kraft war, Stil auszuschliessen, um Essenz zu entdecken, so stiess sie am Ende notgedrungen auf die Tatsache, dass unsere Weise, Wirklichkeit zu verstehen und die Weise, Wirklichkeit künstlerisch darzustellen, zwei verschiedene Dinge sind.

Schon in den Zwanzigerjahren lenkte Tomasevskij die Aufmerksamkeit auf das endlose Zurückweichen, in dem sich die literarische Avantgarde befand:

«Im Allgemeinen wimmelte das 19. Jahrhundert von Schulen, die in ihren Namen schon auf die realistische Motivierung anspielen: Realismus, Naturalismus, Natur-Schule, Populismus undsoweiter. (...) Von Schule zu Schule hören wir den Ruf nach «Naturalismus». Warum denn wurde eine vollständig naturalistische Schule nie gegründet? Weil der Name «Realismus» mit allen Schulen (und mit keiner) verbunden wird. Das erklärt den immer vorhandenen Antagonismus der neuen Schule gegen die alte, das heisst, das Auswechseln von alten und offensichtlichen Konventionen gegen neue, weniger offensichtliche innerhalb der literarischen Muster. Das zeigt aber auch, dass das Material der Wirklichkeit selber keine künstlerische Struktur aufweist und dass die Schaffung einer künstlerischen Struktur verlangt, die Wirklichkeit nach ästhetischen Gesetzen zu rekonstruieren. In Beziehung zur Wirklichkeit betrachtet sind derartige Gesetze immer konventionell.»

Diese Feststellungen, die sicher annehmbar sind für den Fall der Künste, die keine Gebrauchsgegenstände schaffen, könnten in Frage gestellt werden, wenn sie bezogen werden auf die Architektur, die das Wirkliche und das Darstellende gleichermassen umfassen muss, indem ein Werk der Architektur Teil der wirklichen Welt, der Welt des Gebrauchs ist, wie auch eine Darstellung dieser Welt. Es liesse sich beweisen, dass die Moderne Bewegung diese beiden Seiten vollständig durcheinander brachte, indem sie der Notwendigkeit, zweckdienliche Bauwerke zu schaffen, eine darstellende Funktion zuschrieb oder umgekehrt, indem sie der Darstellungs-Funktion die Verantwortung auflud, praktische Bauprobleme zu lösen. Wenn sie das aber tat, dann muss der Grund darin zu suchen sein, dass diese beiden Seiten der Architektur von einem logischen Standpunkt aus zwar unabhängig voneinander sind, nicht aber unabhängig voneinander erfahren werden. Die Suche nach dem Wesen eines Bauwerkes hatte eine ästhetische Begründung, indem sie eine bestimmte Idee von Nützlichkeit und deren Darstellung gleichermassen umfasste, eine Darstellung, in der die Transparenz der Form Symbol war für die Wirklichkeit, die sich vollständig beschreiben und manifestieren liesse.

Insofern war die «materialistische» Architektur des Neuen Bauens genauso metaphysisch, wie es die Architektur immer war. Das scheint zu zeigen, dass wir uns, wenn wir von Architektur sprechen, auf ein Darstellungs-System beziehen, das wesentlich das gleiche ist wie in den anderen Künsten. Nicht mehr als in irgend einem anderen Darstellungs-System ist es in der Architektur möglich, zu einem «nec plus ultra» zu gelangen, in dem die Darstellung und das Dargestellte sich decken. Die Notwendigkeit ästhetischer, konstruktiver Gesetze muss eingestanden werden. Diese Gesetze gleichen nicht den Gesetzen, die die Naturwissenschaft auf der Grundlage von Annahmen und Experimenten aufstellt und die sie nach Popper falsifizieren können muss. Wenn wir eine Analogie zur Wissenschaft herstellen wollten, dann sollten wir sagen, dass diese Gesetze wie die Paradigmen sind, die nach der Analyse von Thomas Khun das Feld des wissenschaftlichen Gespräches bestimmen. Sie sind Normen und eine vollständige Beschreibung des Phänomens der Architektur könnte sie ebensowenig vernachlässigen wie beispielsweise eine Beschreibung von Fussball die Spielregeln weglassen könnte, die das Spiel erst verständlich machen. Nach

↓fig. 1   Le Corbusier,
Villa, Vaucresson, 1922.
Street facade.

↓fig. 2   Le Corbusier,
Palais des Nations, 1927.
Axonometric drawing.

den Begriffen von Tomasevsij sind sie konventionell.

Wie immer aber das notwendige Bestehen solcher Gesetze eine Auffassung rechtfertigen mag, die die Architektur als ein auf sich selber verweisendes System sieht, es stützt dennoch nicht die Meinung, ein solches System hänge von unveränderlichen, absoluten Gesetzen ab. Die Gesetze, die die ästhetische Konstruktion regeln, sind Veränderungen unterworfen und diese Veränderungen gehen nicht vom ästhetischen System selber aus, sie kommen von aussen.

Dass diese Feststellung zutrifft, lässt sich sehen an einem System, das so unabhängig ist von technischen und wirtschaftlichen Bedingungen wie die Musik. Die Veränderung der musikalischen Sprache, die im 18. Jahrhundert eintrat, als die kontrapunktische Methode einer homophonen Platz machte, kann nur erklärt werden aus einer veränderten gesellschaftlichen Funktion der Musik. Was stattfand war selbstverständlich eine rein musikalische Veränderung, und sie kann vollständig erklärt werden in der Sprache der Regeln, die allein der Musik zugehören. Die Gründe für die Veränderung indessen lagen ausserhalb der Musik.

Bis zum 19. Jahrhundert war der von aussen auf die Architektur wirkende Druck nicht stärker als der auf die anderen Künste; seit der industriellen Revolution aber, und in steigendem Grad im 20. Jahrhundert, war die Architektur einem sozialen und technischen Druck von einer unmittelbareren Art ausgesetzt als diese. Veränderungen in den Formen von Niederlassung und Arbeit, technische Veränderungen, die die Verwendung neuer Materialien mit sich brachten, wirtschaftliche Veränderungen, die sich aus der ungeheuren Steigerung der Bodenprofite ergaben, Veränderungen in der Methode, Menschen und Güter zu verteilen – sie alle stellten die architektonische Infrastruktur vollständig auf den Kopf. Keine dieser Veränderungen hatte ihren Ausgangspunkt in der Architektur selber, sie alle aber machten eine Veränderung in den Architektur-Regeln notwendig.

Ein derartiger Prozess, der zwei variable Grössen enthält – das sozio-ökonomische System und das System der ästhetischen Regeln – kann nur dialektisch betrachtet werden.

Als Beispiel für diesen in Gang befindlichen Prozess wollen wir das nehmen, was sich als das «Fassaden-Problem» an der modernen Architektur bezeichnen lässt. In der ersten Zeit der Modernen Bewegung wurde dieses Problem weitgehend für nicht-bestehend gehalten. Aufgrund der organischen Analogie galt die äussere Form eines Bauwerkes als das Ergebnis seiner inneren Organisation; Fassaden-Architektur wurde mit einer Architektur von falscher Rhetorik gleichgesetzt. Dennoch behielten bestimmte Architekten die Fassade und die damit verbundene Funktion der Frontalität als ein Bestandteil ihrer Architektur-Sprache bei. Das gilt namentlich für Le Corbusier. Das Problem der Frontalität ist nicht einfach das Problem der äusser-

↓ fig. 3   Le Corbusier, Armée du Salut (Salvation Army), Paris, 1932–33.

↓ fig. 4   Le Corbusier, Secretariat building, Chandigarh, 1958.

lichen Erscheinung des Bauwerkes, obschon dieses an sich verbunden ist mit dem gesamten Problem des Bauwerkes als einer Darstellung und darum nicht oberflächlichen rhetorischen Bedürfnissen zugeschrieben werden darf. Es steht ebenso in Verbindung mit dem Problem der Schicht zwischen öffentlichem und privatem Bereich und dem des Ueberganges von «aussen» nach «innen». In diesen Begriffen ist es ein rein architektonisches Problem – ein Problem, das nicht verschwinden wird, wie sehr sich auch die Bedingungen ausserhalb der Architektur verändern.

Das Problem aber kann nicht dadurch gelöst werden, dass Zuflucht zu irgend einem unveränderlichen System von Architektur-Regeln genommen wird. Es gelingt nur dann, wenn wir die bestehenden Regeln nehmen, sie den neuen Bedingungen anpassen und so einen abgeänderten Satz von Regeln gewinnen. In allen seinen grösseren Werken können wir sehen, wie Le Corbusier sich dem Fassaden-Problem mit unerreichter Erfindungskraft stellte: die Drehung der Treppe um 90 Grad in der Villa in Vaucresson (Abb. 1), das System von ihrem Wesen nach frontalen Ebenen im Völkerbunds-Palast (Abb. 2), das sorgfältig ausgearbeitete Eingangs-System im Heilsarmee-Gebäude (Abb. 3), die Brise-Soleil (Abb. 4), um nur einige wenige Fälle zu nennen. Als ein Gegenbeispiel könnten wir einen von Hertzbergers späteren Entwürfen nehmen (Abb. 5). In seinem Versuch, den Grundriss als ein System zu entwickeln (das sich vermutlich von einem Computer ausarbeiten liesse), hat Hertzberger das Problem der Fassade unbeachtet gelassen. Seine Entwürfe lassen sich nur verstehen als innerlich entwickelt, sie verweisen nicht auf das Problem des Bauwerkes als einer Darstellung oder auf das der Annäherung von aussen. Das Bauwerk ist gesehen als Fragment des «wirklichen» Raumes, dessen Ausdehnungsgesetze in seiner inneren Organisation zu suchen sind, während das spezifische architektonische Problem des Raumes zwischen den Bauwerken nicht beachtet wird. Diese kritischen Feststellungen sind objektiv. Die Mängel, die sie blosslegen, sind die Folge der Ueberzeugung, es könne Architektur geschaffen werden ohne dass dafür ästhetische Normen festgelegt zu werden brauchen.

Ein Beispiel für neue Architektur-Regeln finden wir wieder bei Le Corbusier. Die augenfälligsten unter diesen sind die «fünf Punkte». Mit diesem Beispiel stellen wir ein Merkmal der Moderne fest, in dem sie sich von der Vergangenheit unterscheidet; Systeme von Regeln neigen dazu, von einzelnen Architekten erfunden zu werden und nur einen beschränkten Grad von Geltung zu erlangen. Was in vorausgehenden Zeiten ein Teil von «langue» war, ist zu «parole» geworden. Das von Mies van der Rohe erfundene Netz einer über den curtainwall gelegten virtuellen Struktur ist ein anderes derartiges System. Das System von Regeln kann sich sogar auf das Verhalten der Menschen in einem Gebäude erstrecken, wie das in den Zeichnungen von Le Corbusier zu erkennen ist – etwas mit dem Bereich der Architektur verbindend, das in früheren Perioden zu einem äusseren System von Regeln gehörte (Regeln des sozialen Verhaltens – Abb. 6).

Die Tatsache, dass Systeme von Regeln die Erfindung einzelner Architekten sind, führte oft dazu, dass Gebäude in Uebereinstimmung mit einem gegensätzlichen System von Regeln umgestaltet wurden. Eines der auffälligsten Beispiele dafür sind die nach den Grundsätzen der «fünf Punkte» errichteten Häuser in Pessac, die mit der Zeit so verändert wurden, dass sie

↓ fig. 5 Hertzberger, Centraal Beheer administration building, Apeldoorn, 1971–72.

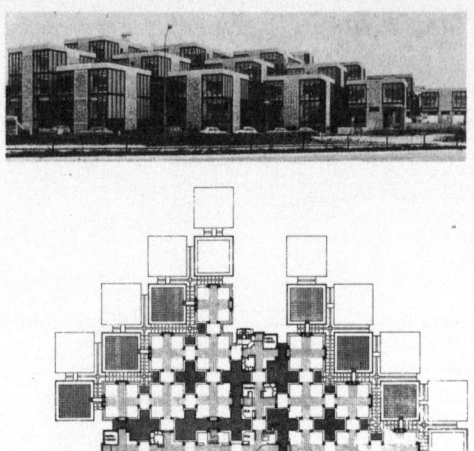

Grundriss eines Obergeschosses

don kleinbürgerlichen Normen entsprachen, die kleine Fenster, Fensterläden, Giebeldächer undsoweiter verlangten (Abb. 7).

Der Vorschlag, Architektur als ein auf sich selber verweisendes System aufzufassen, war begleitet von einer «Aufweichung» des Systemes von Regeln, das in den Zwanzigerjahren entwickelt wurde und das, wenn auch mit wichtigen Verschiebungen des Standpunktes, die architektonische Praxis bis vor kurzem leitete.

Aufgrund der oben erwähnten Tatsache, dass die Systeme von Regeln in der Moderne von einzelnen oder bestenfalls von kleinen Gruppen aufgestellt wurden, die für sich eine besondere Beziehung zum Zeitgeist beanspruchten, lässt sich nicht sagen, dass es im Rahmen des Neuen Bauens irgendeine feste Grundlage gibt, um alternative Systeme von Regeln auszuschliessen. Die Normen des Neuen Bauens haben kein «Recht auf Ausschliesslichkeit» und gerade der Eifer, mit dem die Moderne auf den unauflösbaren Verbindungen zwischen der Architektur und der kommenden «Welt-Kultur» bestand, bedeutete, dass mit dem Verblassen dieser grossen ideologischen Vision auch die Regeln der architektonischen Form erschlafften, die diese stützten.

Es ist deswegen möglich, den neuen Hang zum Historismus so zu verstehen, dass er nicht eine Alternative zu einer monolithischen Moderne bildet, sondern eine latent vorhandene Fliehkraft aufdeckt, die nie sehr tief unter der Oberfläche lag.

Nichtsdestotrotz weist diese Entwicklung ihre paradoxen Züge auf. Soviel die Architektur ihre Geschichtlichkeit auch aus ihrer eigenen verinnerlichten Tradition ableiten mag, für ihre Verwirklichung bleibt sie doch abhängig von der «Gelegenheit». Und die Gelegenheiten sind selten, die das moderne gesellschaftliche Leben für jenen Symbolismus bietet, der den Systemen von Regeln der klassischen Architektur eigen ist! Es scheint also eine Trennung stattzufinden, und zwar nicht nur zwischen der Architektur und den umfassenderen ideologischen Grundmustern, sondern auch zwischen der Architektur und gerade den «Gelegenheiten», die eine realistische Architektur anerkennen müsste. Aus einer Situation, in der «Stil» schliesslich überwunden werden sollte, sehen wir uns in eine andere versetzt, in der alles «Stil» ist, die Formen des Neuen Bauens mit eingeschlossen. Diese Art von Eklektizismus ist launenhafter als der des 19. Jahrhunderts, denn damals beruhte die Wahl des Stils auf dessen Eignung, bestimmte politische, philosophische oder religiöse Ideen darzustellen.

Ein Beispiel dafür liefert vielleicht der Gallaratese-Entwurf von Aldo Rossi, dessen Elemente — die grossen Säulen, eine «klassische» Anordnung der Fenster — sich weniger auf das Bauprogramm beziehen als auf eine Art von «abwesender» Architektur. Weit davon entfernt, diesen Elementen die «Bedeutungen» zuzuschreiben, die für den Historismus des 19. Jahrhunderts wesentlich waren, stützt sich der Gebrauch, den Rossi von ihnen macht, auf ihre

century, architecture has been subject to social and technological pressures of a more direct kind than in the other arts. Changes in patterns of settlement and work, technical changes involving the use of new materials, economic changes due to a vast increase in the profitability of land development, changes in the method of distributing people and goods, have radically altered the architectural infrastructure. None of these changes has originated from inside architecture; all of them have necessitated a change in architectural rules.

Such a process, involving two variables—the socioeconomic system and the aesthetic rule system—can only be accounted for dialectically.

As an example of this process in operation, let us look at what might be called the "facade problem" in modern architecture. In the early days of the Modern Movement this problem was widely held to be nonexistent. According to the organic analogy, the external form of a building was supposed to be the result of its internal organization; "facadism" was identified with an architecture of false rhetoric. Yet certain architects, notably Le Corbusier, retained the facade and the related function of frontality as part of their architectural language. The problem of frontality is not simply the problem of the outside appearance of the building, though this in itself is bound up with the whole problem of the building as a representation in the public realm and cannot be attributed to superficial rhetorical needs. It is also connected with the problem of the interface between public and private and the transition from "outside" to "inside." In these terms it is a purely architectural problem—a problem that will not dissolve however much the conditions external to architecture change.

But the problem cannot be solved by recourse to any unalterable system of architectural rules. It can only come from taking the existing rule system, adapting it to the new conditions, and laying down a revised set of rules. In all his major buildings, we see Le Corbusier facing this problem with unrivaled inventiveness: the turning of the staircase through ninety degrees at the Villa in Vaucresson (fig. 1), the system of virtual frontal planes in the League of Nations building (fig. 2), the elaborate entrance system in the Salvation Army hostel (fig. 3), the invention of the *brise-soleil* (fig. 4), to mention only a few cases. As a counter-example we might take one of Herman Hertzberger's projects (fig. 5). In his attempt to generate the plan as a system, Hertzberger has ignored the problem of the facade. His buildings can only be comprehended as internally generated, and no reference is made to the problem of the building as a representation or to the approach to the building from outside. The building is seen as a fragment of "real" space, whose laws of extension lie in the building's internal organization, and the space between buildings as a specifically architectural problem is ignored. These criticisms are objective. The faults which they expose are the result of the belief that architecture can be created without the establishment of aesthetic norms.

It is also to Le Corbusier that one must turn for an example of new architectural rules. The most obvious of these are the "Five Points," and with this example one notices a characteristic of the modern situation which differs from the past; rule systems tend to be invented by individual architects and tend to attain only a limited degree of acceptance. What in previous epochs was part of the *langue* has become a function of the *parole*. Mies's invention of a network of virtual structure superimposed on the curtain wall is another such rule system. The rule system can even extend to the behavior of people within a building—as can be seen in Le Corbusier's drawings—thus annexing to the architectural sphere something which, in earlier periods, belonged to an external rule system (rules of social behavior) (fig. 6).

The invention of rule systems by individual architects has often resulted in the transformation of buildings in accordance with a contradictory rule system. One of the most striking examples of this is the modification of Pessac, where the organization of homes according to the principles laid down in the "Five Points" has been altered to conform to petit-bourgeois norms requiring small windows, shutters, pitched roofs, and so on (fig. 7).

The proposition that architecture is a self-referential system has been accompanied by a "softening" of the rule system which was developed during the 1920s and which has, albeit with important developments and shifts in viewpoint, governed architectural practice until recently.

Owing to the fact, mentioned above, that the rule systems of modern architecture were made

by individual architects, or, at most, by small groups claiming to stand in some special rapport with the *Zeitgeist*, there cannot be said to exist, within the framework of the Modern Movement, any firm basis for excluding alternative rule systems. The norms of modern architecture have no "right of exclusion," and the very fervor with which the Modern Movement insisted on the inextricable links between architecture and the approaching "world culture" meant that, once that great ideological vision had faded, the rules of architectural form supporting it would also tend to weaken.

It is therefore possible to see the modern tendencies toward historicism, not as constituting an alternative to a monolithic Modern Movement but simply as acting out a centrifugal tendency which was never far beneath the surface.

But this development nonetheless has its paradoxical side. However much architecture derives its historicity from its own internalized tradition, it still depends for its realization on the "occasion." And the occasions which are provided by modern social life for the symbolism inherent in the rule systems of classical architecture are very rare. In this way we seem to see a separation taking place, not only between architecture and the broader ideological patterns, but also between architecture and those very occasions which a "realistic" architecture should accept. From a situation in which "style" was finally to be superseded, we find ourselves in a situation in which everything is "style"—including the forms of the Modern Movement itself—a type of eclecticism more arbitrary than that of the nineteenth century, since at that time the choice of a style was based on its ability to represent certain political, philosophical, or religious ideas.

An example of this can perhaps be seen in Aldo Rossi's Gallaratese, where the "virtual" elements—giant pilotis, a "classical" arrangement of windows—refer less to the program than to some kind of "absent" architecture. The function of the rule system seems less to establish an architecture of meaning than to bring architecture back from the verge of an empty garrulousness, where reality is reflected in endless functional episodes each more banal than the last—those stair towers and service shafts which so often form the lexicon of modern buildings. Whatever one may say in defense of such an architecture of polemic, there is a danger that the belief in an architecture which is purely self-reflective might lead to a devaluation of the building program and to an architecture which would no longer need to be built.

The dichotomy posed earlier (architecture as an internally or externally referential system) should be replaced by a less simplistic concept—that of a dialectical process in which aesthetic norms are modified by external forces to achieve a partial synthesis.

The kind of realism according to whose tenets a fundamental language can be disclosed, and which rejects the mediation of style, should be replaced by a new realism which would gain its validity both from existing aesthetic structures and from a reality which would affect and alter these structures—a realism which accepts the fact that it is not possible to foresee a society whose unity is fully reflected in the forms of its art.

ENDNOTES

1 "Thematics," in *Russian Formalist Criticism: Four Essays*, trans. Lee T. Lemon and Marion J. Reis (Lincoln: University of Nebraska, 1965), 82–83.

2 I am not concerned here with the question of whether the norms of art have any basis in nature. This problem, which belongs to epistemology, has a long and complex history, and, as a problem, it appears in different guises at different historical periods. In the Renaissance the laws of art were considered to be divinely ordained. With the rise of the bourgeoisie and the development of empiricism, artistic norms began to be considered as residing in the link between sensation and mind (that is to say, in the subject rather than in the object) and their universality as being due to social customs. But from the eighteenth century, and increasingly with the development of mass culture and consumerism, social customs lost their de jure force, and the resulting incoherence (expressed in eclecticism) was certainly one of the reasons for the attempt by avant-garde art to rediscover archetypes and to reduce the subject to psychological, and even physiological, laws. At the same time an opposite tendency emerged—the study of the sign as a social function. The sign was not studied, as it had been in the eighteenth century, as the natural reflection of normative social customs but, in the generalized form in which it appears in any society whatsoever, as constituting a de facto rather than a de jure system, and as being essentially arbitrary and conventional. This essay, by stressing the de facto, conventional, and ludic aspects of the architectural sign, creates, perhaps, an unbalanced picture. It leaves out the extent to which the sign is always, in an ideological sense, motivated and therefore the extent to which meanings are historically limited.

↓ fig. 6   Le Corbusier, Drawing of a "hanging garden," 1928–29 (design for Wanner, Geneva).

«Neutralität». Er begründet nicht eine Architektur der Bedeutung, sondern holt die Architektur vom Abgrund einer leeren Geschwätzigkeit zurück, wo «Wirklichkeit» sich in endlosen funktionalen Episoden spiegelt, eine banaler als die andere. Denken wir nur an die «Treppenhaus-Türme» und «Versorgungs-Schächte», die so oft das Wörterbuch moderner Bauwerke bilden. Was immer sich sagen lässt zur Verteidigung einer solchen Architektur der Polemik, es besteht Gefahr, dass der Glaube an eine rein autoreflexive Architektur zu einer Abwertung des Bauprogrammes und zu einer Architektur führen könnte, die nicht mehr gebaut zu werden braucht.

Die eingangs aufgestellte Dichotomie — Architektur als ein System, das auf sein Inneres oder auf ein Aeusseres verweist — sollte ersetzt werden durch eine weniger simplistische Vorstellung, nämlich die eines dialektischen Prozesses, in dem ästhetische Normen durch äussere Kräfte verändert werden, um eine teilweise Verbindung zustandezubringen.

Der alte «Realismus», nach dem eine Grundsprache gefunden werden kann, die die Vermittlung durch Stil zurückweist, sollte durch einen neuen «Realismus» ersetzt werden, der sowohl aus sich selber entwickelte ästhetische Strukturen gelten lässt wie auch eine Wirklichkeit, die auf sie einwirkt und sie verändert. Und dies unter Berücksichtigung der Tatsache, dass es bisher nicht möglich ist, eine Gesellschaft vorauszusehen, deren Einheit vollkommen widerspiegelt ist in den Formen ihrer Kunst.

(Uebersetzung: Martin Steinmann)

↑ fig. 7   Le Corbusier, Gratte-ciel residence, Pessac, 1925.

↑ fig. 8   The same house as altered by its users, photograph, 1968. From: P. Boudon,

↑ fig. 9   Aldo Rossi, Apartment building, Gallaratese.

Giorgio Grassi

ARCHITEKTUR-PROBLEME UND REALISMUS

Ich versuche, diesen Gegenstand vom Gesichtspunkt meiner Arbeit, das heisst vom Gesichtspunkt des Entwerfens aus zu diskutieren.

Ich denke, dass die Architektur auf das Problem des Realismus vor allem dann eine konkrete Antwort gibt, wenn sie ohne Umweg sich selbst ist, ihre eigene Konkretheit ausweist; das heisst, wenn sie Mal für Mal ihre eigene «raison d'être» erneuert.

Das mag offensichtlich scheinen, ist es aber nicht allzusehr, wenn man z. B. den Experimentalismus bedenkt, dem wir heute begegnen; die Architektur hingegen findet, so meine ich, ihre realistische Bestimmung dann, wenn sie sich auf ihre Grundlagen, ihren Tradition besinnt. Aufgrund des Gesagten erlangt die Frage des Realismus in der Architektur wegen der Eigenart der Architektur selbst spezifisches Gewicht. Eine Eigenart ist für die Architektur zweifellos entscheidend: ich meine die «Wirklichkeit» des architektonischen Raumes. Da Darstellung und dargestellter Gegenstand in der Architektur zusammenfallen, stellt sich das Problem des Realismus in diesem Falle tatsächlich in ganz besonderen Begriffen. Es ist beispielsweise augenfällig, dass die evokative Qualität der Architektur nie die Formen von Negation oder offenem Widerspruch anzunehmen vermag. Nur wer sich eine gebaute Architektur vorstellen kann, die sich gleichzeitig aufzuheben vermag (das ist nur von einer auseinanderfallenden, unbrauchbaren Architektur denkbar), kann eine Architektur der Anklage

Problèmes d'architecture et réalisme

La question du réalisme en architecture se pose en termes spécifiques étant donné qu'il n'y a pas dans ce cas de décalage entre l'objet empirique et sa représentation. C'est ce que Lukacs a clairement mis en évidence dans son *Esthétique* quand il affirme que l'architecture crée un espace réel adéquat et évoque visuellement l'adéquatesse.

Le contenu réaliste de l'architecture appartient aux deux moments mis en évidence par Lukacs, lesquels sont inséparables dans le sens où l'un ne se définit que par le moyen de l'autre. Le réalisme d'un pilier consiste moins dans sa fonction que dans la notion d'adéquation que sa forme suscite à son apparition et dans le temps, et dans cette notion apparaît de nouveau la fonction de soutien du pilier.

Si par «espace adéquat» nous entendons par exemple la correspondance empirique à la donnée fonctionnelle, à l'élément technique, aux lois statiques, etc. . . . alors la fonction, la technique de construction, la science de la construction, etc. . . . manifestent leur qualité spécifique et leur rôle uniquement dans le projet, en rapport avec l'observation qu'il connaît, et il tend à évoquer le monde particulier de la représentation architecturale. Ceci signifie que dans le projet la définition d'«espace adéquat» devra beaucoup au degré d'approfondissement atteint dans la notion même d'adéquation, qui est l'objet spécifique de l'évocation.

Le monde des formes possibles, le domaine des projets, montre des innombrables liens avec le passé, à travers les images construites dans le temps. Il se dévoile seulement en comparaison avec ce passé et devient réalité seulement à condition d'une «imitation» concrète et positive. Une imitation comprise non comme une ré-évocation nostalgique mais comme une compréhension et dépassement, comme continuité et unité des objectifs plus généraux, et finalement comme le moment par excellence de la transmission positive du «métier». Ceci incarne pour ainsi dire la transmissibilité même de l'architecture. Dans le métier convergent en fait l'observation et la connaissance, l'habileté acquise par les expériences innombrables, le savoir faire «manuel» et enfin ce qui est le moment même du travail intellectuel: l'imagination et les choix synthétiques.

Problems of Architecture and Realism

Author:
Giorgio Grassi

Sources:
archithese, 19 (1976): 18–24
Original typescript courtesy of the author (IT)

Translated by:
Shanti Evans
Steven Lindberg

I will try to discuss this subject from the viewpoint of my work; that is, from the viewpoint of the architectural project.

I think that the concrete response architecture can give to the question of realism lies above all in its being itself without going astray, in expressing its own necessity and pragmatism; that is, in renewing its raison d'être on each occasion.

While this may even seem obvious, in reality it is not, if we think for example of the experimentalism we see in this field today; whereas, I believe, architecture renews its propensity for realism at the moment in which it rediscovers its fundamentals, its tradition. Having said that, the question of realism in architecture takes on specific relevance as a result of the characteristics of architecture itself. Among the typical characteristics of architecture, one is undoubtedly decisive: I am referring to the "reality" of architectural space. There being no discernible gap between representation and object represented, the question of realism is posed in this case in highly unusual terms. For example, that the distinctive evocative quality of architecture can never be expressed through its forms as negation or as open contradiction is evident. Only someone who can imagine a built architecture capable simultaneously of negating itself (an architecture that is incoherent, useless, that does not stand up, etc.) can postulate an architecture of denunciation or protest; for instance, an "expressionist" architecture in the current sense of the term. In reality the architecture of expressionism is a marginal experience; where it has entered the history of architecture, its character derived in the majority of cases from superficial elements, often scenic or decorative ones. This characteristic mode of forcing architectural figuration, distorting or shattering it on the plane of the image, can also be found in the architecture of the past. There, too, since such works never display elements of contradiction within the process of construction, what stand out are the stratagems of an essentially "pictorial" nature (from Laon Cathedral to Borromini's Sant'Andrea, and so on). Which means, for example, that architecture may even be ambiguous (*ambigua*), but it cannot express—that is, evoke—ambiguity (*ambiguità*); and this is its peculiar fate. The fact is that architecture cannot be make-believe without paying a high price.

For this reason architecture appears not only to be stable (*stabilita*), necessary—that is, affirmative in and of itself—but also and always essentially approbatory (*approvativa*). And just as architecture's range of expression is limited by this thematic renunciation, the sphere of critical interpretation is greatly reduced for aesthetic inquiry as well. (See the inapplicability of the canonical distinction between critical realism and socialist realism and other forms of realism.)

In his *Ästhetik* [Aesthetics] Lukács gives a definition of the particular nature of architecture, and it is one that I find very important. He says something like this: architecture creates a real and appropriate space that visually evokes its suitability.

The crux of the question of realism is entirely contained within this definition. Obviously, the realistic content of architecture pertains to both these moments highlighted by Lukács. However, the two moments are inseparable, in the sense that one can be defined only through the other and vice versa. The realism of a pillar consists of course in its function, but also in the sensations that its form evokes; and within this perception the pillar's support function is contained anew. That is, in design, the definition of "suitable space" will owe a great deal to the extent to which the notion of "suitability" itself has been analyzed—a suitability that is precisely what is being evoked. Whence the reciprocal, inevitable link between different works of architecture over time.

If by appropriate space we can understand, for example, its unequivocal conformity with functional, technical, structural, and other requirements, then this sense of appropriateness, as well as its special quality and role in the project, becomes accessible only through an observation that is aimed at evoking the particular world of architectural representation: the world of forms.

The eye that intends to share and thus evoke, the evocative eye, has a particular way of looking at the historical experience. It judges, seeks the truth of the object, recognizes the moments when it repeats itself. And, in contrast to the nostalgic eye that likes to linger, it shuns models. In other words, it does not rely on first appearances but looks for confirmation, attentive only to the logical and progressive thread that binds works of architecture together over time. Thus, it will be very difficult, for example, to force the notion of "function" to remain within the limits of immediate necessity or those of relevance to the present. And it will also be very difficult to turn it into an ideology. If by *function* is meant conformity to the use made of architectural forms, I believe that when all is said and done necessity has by now fixed those forms. It suffices to observe that, up until the bourgeois city of the end of the last century, the connection with function had never been a problem for architecture. The extreme functional specification of the parts of the dwelling, for example, is a typical product of the bourgeois culture that attained its definitive form at the end of the century; but the same is true for the layouts of buildings in general: it is a false problem that has been passed off as new content (it is in this sense that the ideologization of function should be understood).

We can say the same thing about the technical aspect. This can never be overruled by the aesthetic conception, but neither can it become an aesthetic in its own right, as some still accredited tendencies would have us believe (the Bauhaus must take some responsibility for this). Instead it has always been the specific task of the technical element to demonstrate its necessity directly.

Thus the notion of "suitability" must always include the generalizing tendency that characterizes the historical experience of architecture; that is, the sense common to all the solutions of a particular problem that architecture poses to itself over time, be it the house, the public place, the street, and so on. In other words, suitability cannot disregard the element of universality that is evident in each work, and therefore the irrepressible progressive propensity that such solutions display.

This is the domain of the typical forms of architecture, of its elements of permanence, of those forms that seem more than others to present themselves as definitive solutions to particular questions. Let us give some examples: Filarete's Ospedale Maggiore in Milan, Piermarini's University of Pavia, Le Corbusier's Unité d'habitation, and Mies van der Rohe's Convention Hall are buildings remote from one another in time, and yet they are in fact

oder des Protestes fordern, z. B. eine dem geläufigen Sprachgebrauch nach «expressionistische» Architektur. In Wirklichkeit ist die Architektur des Expressionismus eine Randerscheinung; wo sie in die Architekturgeschichte eintrat, rührte ihre Eigenart meist von oberflächlichen, häufig kulissenhaften Elementen ab. Diese bezeichnende Art, der architektonischen Gestaltung Gewalt anzutun, indem man sie auf der Ebene des Bildhaften entstellt, ist auch der Architektur der Vergangenheit eigen. Da derartige Werke niemals innere konstruktive Widersprüche zeigen, sind auch hier die hervorstechenden Kunstgriffe wesentlich «malerischer» Art (die Kathedrale von Laon, die Kirche S. Andrea von Borromini, usw.). Das besagt beispielsweise, dass die Architektur dahin gelangen kann, doppelsinnig zu sein (ambigua), aber nie vermag, Doppelsinn (ambiguità) auszudrücken, d. h. zu evozieren; dies gehört zu ihrem besonderen Status. In der Tat kann die Architektur nicht Fiktion sein, ausser zu einem sehr hohen Preis.

Aus diesem Grunde erscheint die Architektur nicht nur als feststehend (stabilita) und notwendig, das heisst von sich aus affirmativ, sondern auch als wesentlich positiv (approvativa), ausnahmslos. Damit schränkt sich das Feld des architektonischen Ausdruckes gleichermassen ein wie für die ästhetische Untersuchung das Feld der kritischen Interpretationen. (Daraus folgt beispielsweise die Nichtanwendbarkeit der kanonischen Unterscheidung zwischen kritischem und sozialistischem Realismus).

Lukacs gibt uns in seiner *Aesthetik* eine meiner Meinung nach sehr wichtige Definition von der Besonderheit der Architektur. Er sagt grosso modo: die Architektur schafft einen wirklichen angemessenen Raum, der visuell Angemessenheit evoziert.

Der ganze Knoten des Realismusproblems ist in dieser Definition enthalten. Der realistische Gehalt der Architektur gehört offensichtlich diesen beiden Momenten an, die Lukacs erläutert hat. Jedenfalls sind diese beiden Momente in dem Sinne untrennbar, als sich das eine nur mittels des anderen definieren lässt und umgekehrt. Der Realismus eines Pilasters besteht gewiss in seiner Funktion, aber auch in den Empfindungen, die von seiner Form ausgelöst werden; in diesen Empfindungen ist von neuem die Stützfunktion des Pilasters enthalten. Das heisst: die Definition des «angemessenen Raumes» hängt stark vom Vertiefungsgrad des Begriffs der «Angemessenheit» ab; diese aber ist der spezifische Gegenstand der Evokation. Hieraus folgt der wechselseitige unaufhebbare Bezug, der die Architekturen in der Zeit miteinander verbindet.

Wenn wir unter der Angemessenheit eines Raums zum Beispiel dessen eindeutige Antwort auf die funktionellen, technischen, statischen und anderen Forderungen verstehen können, dann erschliesst sich diese in ihrer besonderen Qualität und ihrer Rolle im Entwurf nur einer Betrachtung, die darauf gerichtet ist, die besondere Welt der architektonischen Darstellung zu evozieren: die Welt der Formen.

Das Auge, das teilhaben und deswegen evozieren will, das evokative Auge kennt eine besondere Art, die geschichtliche Erfahrung in Betracht zu ziehen. Es urteilt, sucht die Wahrheit des Gegenstandes, erkennt dessen repetitive Momente. Und im Gegensatz zum nostalgischen Auge, das zu verweilen liebt, verfällt es nicht den Modellen, traut nicht dem ersten Zeugnis, sucht Bestätigungen, richtet sich nur auf die logische und progressive Spur, die die Architekturen in der Zeit verbindet. Es wird dann sehr schwierig sein, beispielsweise den Begriff der Funktion in die Schranken der unmittelbaren Notwendigkeit zu pressen, oder in die Grenzen der Aktualität. Es wird auch schwerfallen, ihn zu ideologisieren. Versteht man unter Funktion die Entsprechung auf den Gebrauch der architektonischen Formen, dann, denke ich, hat die Notwendigkeit im Ganzen gesehen ihre Formen festgesetzt. Die Bemerkung genügt, dass bis zur bürgerlichen Stadt des ausgehenden 19. Jahrhunderts der Bezug zur Funktion für die Architektur nie ein Problem darstellte. Die äusserste funktionelle Spezifikation der Wohnungselemente z. B. ist ein typisches Produkt der bürgerlichen Kultur, so wie sie sich am Ende des Jahrhunderts stabilisierte; dasselbe lässt sich für die distributiven Merkmale der Gebäude im Allgemeinen sagen: es handelt sich um ein falsches Problem, das als neuer Gehalt ausgegeben wurde. (Die Ideologisierung der Funktion ist in diesem Sinne zu verstehen.)

Mit dem technischen Aspekt verhält es sich ebenso. Von der ästhetischen Konzeption darf er nie übersehen werden, aber er darf auch nicht von sich aus ästhetisch werden, wie dies einige immer noch im Kurs stehende Richtungen haben möchten (es ist hier auf die Verantwortlichkeit des Bauhauses hinzuweisen). Hingegen ist es seit je spezifische Aufgabe des Technischen gewesen, in direkter Weise die eigene Notwendigkeit zu zeigen.

Der Begriff der «Angemessenheit» muss immer auch den verallgemeinernden Zug umfassen, der die geschichtliche Erfahrung der Architektur charakterisiert, also den Sinn, der allen Lösungen eines Problems gemeinsam ist, das sich die Architektur in der Zeit selbst stellt: das Haus, der öffentliche Ort, die Strasse usw... Angemessenheit kann also nicht von jenem Moment der Allgemeinheit absehen, das in jedem einzelnen Werk zutage tritt, und deshalb auch nicht von jenem nicht zu unterdrückenden progressiven Zug, den diese Lösungen manifestieren.

Dies ist das Feld der typischen Formen der Architektur: jener permanenten Formen also, die sich mehr als andere als endgültige Lösungen bestimmter Probleme anbieten. Einige Beispiele: das Ospedale Maggiore von Filarete in Mailand, die Universität von Piermarini in Pavia, die Unité d'habitation von Le Corbusier, die Convention Hall von Mies van der Rohe. Es sind zeitlich weit auseinanderliegende Architekturen, aber dennoch sind sie in Wirklichkeit gleichzeitig, weil ihnen die Tendenz gemeinsam ist, sich vor allem als «Typus», d. h. als im wesentlichen endgültige Antworten zu setzen.

Gewiss erschöpft der Verweis auf die spezifischen Bedingungen der Architektur den Begriff der «Angemessenheit» nicht, doch gibt er eine definitive methodische Entscheidung für das Entwerfen an. Der Rest gehört zum Feld der Bedeutungen architektonischer Formen. Die gebaute Stadt, die vom Menschen bearbeitete Landschaft — allgemein alles, was die Herrschaft des Menschen über die Natur bezeugt — drücken kollektive Inhalte aus. Die Architektur ist in weitgehendem Mass deren Spiegel, und auf diese Weise erhalten die Formen feste Bedeutungen.

Im Begriff der «Angemessenheit» ist die Widerspiegelung auch jener kollektiven Inhalte eingeschlossen, die, wie immer sie sich in der Aktualität auch manifestieren, der Linie des Fortschrittes angehören. Dieses Prinzip des Fortschritts, das einer bestimmten Interpretation des geschichtlichen Prozesses (als einheitlicher Verlauf in der vielfältigen Welt der Kulturen) entspricht, ist Gegenstand einer exakten Analyse von Ernst Bloch. Ich führe hier einen Abschnitt aus seinem berühmten Essay *Differenzierungen im Begriff Fortschritt* von 1955 an. Bloch schreibt:

«... Es gibt überall den Fortgang von einer Urkommune über Klassengesellschaften bis schliesslich zur Reifung des Sozialismus; und es gibt überall, in allen Ensembles gesellschaftlicher Verhältnisse, das Menschenhafte (...) das diese Ensembles so wechselnd färbt wie einheitlich zusammenfasst. (...) So gibt dies immer noch im Schwung befindliche Humanum mit den vielen versucherischen und beitragenden Wegen zu ihm hin —

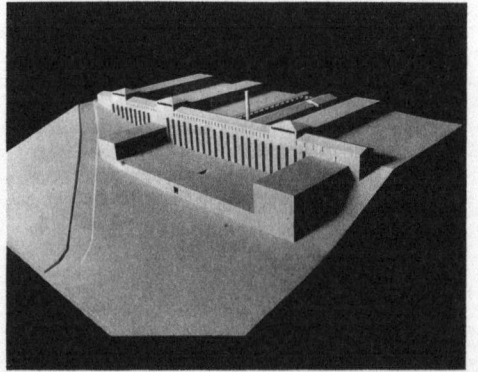

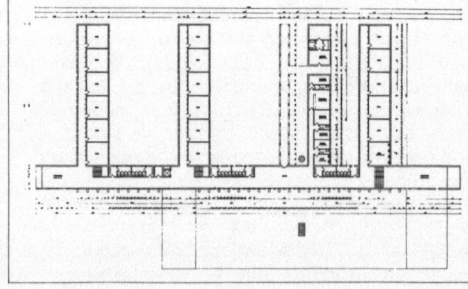

↑ fig. 1 Project for a secondary school in Tollo, Chieti, Italy, 1975, with A. Monestiroli. Photograph of model.

↑ fig. 2 Plan of the ground floor.

den einzig echt toleranten, nämlich utopisch-toleranten Zielpunkt. Und je mehr Nationen, Nationalkulturen zum sozialistischen Lager gehören werden, desto breiter und sicherer wird auch die Zieleinheit für die Multiversa in der neuen Kulturgeschichte wirksam, also fassbar sein.»
(Sitzungsberichte der deutschen Akademie der Wissenschaften zu Berlin, Nr. 5. Berlin 1956, S. 23 f.)

Die Architektur ist der designierte Interpret dieser kollektiven Inhalte, die sich jenseits der Bedingungen der Geschichte stellen und die dennoch fest in den geschichtlichen Prozess eingeschlossen sind. Diese positive Tendenz, diese progressive Linie, die Bloch in der Geschichte zu erkennen einlädt, stellt vielleicht das letzte dar, was wir vernünftigerweise zum evokativen Moment der Architektur wiederholen können. Alles, was wir zur «raison d'être» dieser besonderen und notwendigen Welt der architektonischen Formen erwähnen können, ist, dass sie ihrer Beschaffenheit nach keine doppelsinnige oder zufällige Inhalte ausdrücken kann.

Hier zeigt die Welt der möglichen Formen – das Feld des Entwerfens – durch die in der Zeit hervorgebrachten Bilder, ihre zahllosen Verbindungen mit der Vergangenheit. Sie enthüllt sich nur auf dem Hintergrund dieser Vergangenheit und wird Wirklichkeit nur unter der Bedingung einer konkreten, positiven «Nachahmung». Diese nicht als nostalgische Beschwörung verstanden, sondern als Aneignung und Ueberwindung; als Kontinuität und Einheit der allgemeinsten Ziele; schliesslich als das Moment einer positiven Vermittlung des Metiers selbst.

So wie man den besonderen Eigenschaften der Architektur Rechnung tragen muss, sind auch die spezifischen Bedingungen der «Disziplin» in Betracht zu ziehen; denn diese verkörpern sozusagen die Vermittelbarkeit der Architektur selbst. Sie stehen natürlich in direkter, feststehender Beziehung zu den ersteren. Da wir diese Bedingungen nur erkennen, weil sie das Ergebnis unzähliger Versuche und Erfahrungen sind, geben sie die Sicherheit von Mitteln und Entscheidungen, die aus den Notwendigkeiten heraus entstanden und ihnen angemessen sind: so wie das Werkzeug die selbstverständliche und feste Form des Gebrauchs darstellt.

Hierin kommt die «Disziplin» der Architektur

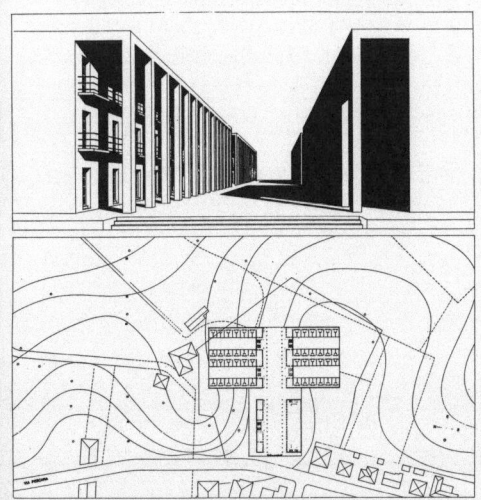

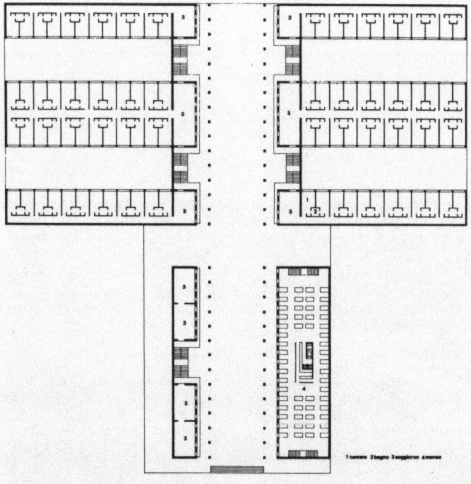

↑fig. 3   Competition project for a student dormitory, Chieti, Italy, 1975, 1976, with A. Monestiroli. Perspective and site plan.

↑fig. 4   Plan of the ground floor.

der handwerklichen Arbeit sehr nahe. Tessenow kommt das Verdienst zu, den Bezug zwischen Architektur und handwerklicher Arbeit vom richtigen Gesichtswinkel der Tradition aus gesehen zu haben. Damit entzog er einer Reihe von Scheinproblemen den Boden, die sich die Moderne stellte. Aber Tessenow geht fehl, wenn er die handwerkliche Arbeit als eine Bedingung versteht, die der architektonischen Arbeit vorausgeht. Die Annahme dieser These hiesse in der Tat, einen Bruch anzuerkennen zwischen dem Moment der erworbenen Sicherheit und Geschicklichkeit, der «Handfertigkeit», ferner der Beobachtung und Erkenntnis einerseits und dem Moment der Imagination und der synthetischen Entscheidungen andererseits, d. h. dem eigentlichen Moment der geistigen Arbeit. Dieser Bruch (der in Tessenows Schaffen nicht vorhanden ist) bedeutet, den Entwurf bewusst von der Erfahrung, die Architektur von ihrer eigenen Wirklichkeit zu trennen. Dasselbe liesse sich vom berühmten Axiom Loos' sagen:

«Nur ein ganz kleiner Teil der Architektur gehört der Kunst an: das Grabmal und das Denkmal.»

Diese Einheit der Erfahrung zu brechen kann für bestimmte zeitbedingte Probleme förderlich sein, wie das bei Loos und Tessenow selbst der Fall ist, erweist sich aber stets gleicherweise verhängnisvoll. Es bedeutet, die Architektur von ihrer eigenen Grundlage zu trennen, ihre ständige Bemühung einzustellen, die darin besteht, in ihrer Darstellung die Widersprüche der Wirklichkeit aufzuheben. Bei der handwerklichen Arbeit stellen sich Probleme des Realismus nicht, wie sich auch nicht das Problem der Erfindung oder der Kopie stellt. An der handwerklichen Arbeit ist das Modell stets das Werk selbst, und dieses kennt keine Modifikation. Nicht so beim Entwurf. Die besonderen Bedingungen des Entwurfs enthalten immer einen hohen Grad an Unsicherheit und Problematik; je zahlreicher die einschränkenden Bedingungen sind, umso mehr gewinnt der Entwurf an Sicherheit; deswegen handelt es sich um notwendige Bedingungen. Und da sie im Verlaufe der Arbeit selbst auftauchen und sich definieren, definiert sich auch das Werk stets im Verlaufe seiner Vollendung. Auch hier ist das Werk das Modell, aber es verändert sich: entwerfen heisst auch, die «Bilder» auf das Werk, das im Entstehen ist, abzustimmen; dergestalt, dass der Schöpfer immer zum Teil auch Zuschauer ist.

Die Architektur muss also stets die handwerkliche Arbeit beachten, freilich im Bewusstsein, dass sich die Bedingungen handwerklichen Schaffens nur zum Teil mit denen architektonischen Schaffens decken. Sonst könnten wir in Umkehrung von Tessenows These sagen, dass die handwerkliche Bedingung die Utopie der architektonischen Arbeit sei. Dies ist wahr und zeigt sich gerade in den Momenten grösster Einheit, formaler Stabilität in der Geschichte; in jenen Momenten, in denen evozierte Form, wirkliche Form, Mittel und Technik in die Einheit des Stils zusammenfallen: gerade die Momente grosser formaler Stabilität sind in

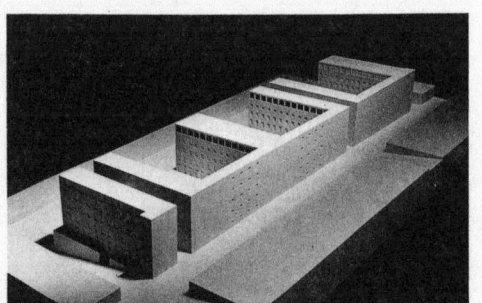

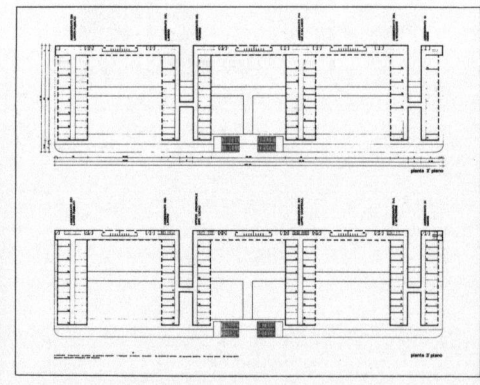

↑ fig. 5 Competition project for the regional administration in Trieste, on the Corso Miramare, 1975. Photograph of model.

↑ fig. 6 Plan of the upper floor.

"contemporary," because they have in common the tendency to establish themselves first of all as "types"; that is, as essentially definitive responses.

To be sure, reference to the specific conditions of architecture does not exhaust the notion of "suitability," but it does indicate a definite choice of method for design. The rest belongs to the sphere of the meanings of architectural forms. The built city, the layouts and forms of the rural landscape, and in general everything that reflects human domination of the natural element express collective contents. Architecture is to a great extent their mirror, and this is how forms take on stable meanings.

So the notion of "suitability" also embraces the reflection of those collective contents that belong to a line of progress, regardless of how they manifest in the present. This principle of progress, which corresponds to a well-defined interpretation of the historical process (seen as a unified course in the multifaceted world of cultures), is the subject of precise analysis by Ernst Bloch. I quote here a passage from his famous 1955 essay *Differentiations in the Concept of Progress*. Bloch writes:

> "Everywhere there is an advance from a primitive commune, through class societies, to the ultimate maturity of socialism; and everywhere, in all ensembles of social relations, there is the human element—from the anthropological to the *humanum*—which colors these ensembles so variously and holds them in a uniform embrace. … Therefore this *humanum* (still in process) … provides the only genuinely tolerant (i.e., utopian-tolerant) point of time. And the more nations and cultures belong to the humanist camp, the larger and surer will be the reality and therefore the conceivability of a single goal for the multiverses in the new history of culture."
> (*Sitzungsberichte der deutschen Akademie der Wissenschaften zu Berlin* [Berlin], no. 5. [1956]: 23–24)

Architecture is the designated interpreter of these collective contents that place themselves above the conditions of history and yet are included so permanently in the historic process. This, in any case, positive trend, this line of progress that Bloch invites us to recognize in history, represents perhaps the last thing we can reasonably repeat on the subject of the evocative quality of architecture. All that we might say about the raison d'être of this particular, necessary world of architectural forms is that, by its nature, it cannot express ambiguous or random contents.

And so it is that the world of possible forms, the realm of design, shows its innumerable ties with the past through images that have been constructed over time. It is revealed only in the comparison with this past, and it becomes reality only through a concrete, positive "imitation." Imitation understood, that is, not as nostalgic reminiscence but as comprehension and surmounting, as continuity and unity of more general objectives; finally as the moment par excellence for a positive transmission of the elements of the discipline.

Just as we must reckon with the peculiar characteristics of architecture, we also must consider the specific conditions of the "discipline"; for these embody, so to speak, the transmissibility of architecture. Naturally they are directly connected with the former, and this connection is fixed in time, but since we are able to recognize such conditions precisely because they are the product of innumerable experiments and trials, they offer the assurance that they provide suitable means and solutions stemming from unchanging needs: just as a utensil represents the undisputed form and stability of a use.

In this the "discipline" of architecture is very close to handicraft. Tessenow deserves credit for having approached, at that particular moment, the relationship between architecture and handicraft from the correct angle of tradition. His intervention was decisive for a series of false problems that the modern movement was debating. But Tessenow got it wrong when he saw handicraft as a condition that preceded the work of architecture. Accepting this version would mean recognizing a de facto fracture between the moment of confidence in the skills acquired, of "manual ability" in addition to that of observation and knowledge, and the moment of imagination and of succinct choices; that is, the moment when intellectual qualities are brought to bear. This split (which is not present in Tessenow's work) means consciously distancing design from experience, architecture from its reality. We could say the same thing of Loos's famous axiom:

> "Only a very small part of architecture belongs to art: the tomb and the monument."
> (Adolf Loos, "Architecture," in *On Architecture* [Riverside, CA: Ariadne Press, 2002][1])

Breaking up this unity of experience may meet the needs of contingent questions, as in the case of Loos and Tessenow himself, but it invariably proves pernicious. It means detaching architecture from the reason for its existence. It means nullifying its state of constant effort to overcome the contradictions of reality in its representation, which is the condition of that existence. When dealing with handicraft, we do not raise questions of realism, just as we never pose the problem of invention or imitation. The model in handicraft is always the work itself, and this is not modified. It is not the same in architectural design. The specific conditions of the project always maintain a high degree of uncertainty and complexity; the more numerous the conditions limiting the design prove to be, the more it gains confidence, and so these conditions are necessary. And since they arise and are defined in the course of the work, the work is also always defined as it is carried out. Here, too, the model is the work itself, but it is modified: designing also signifies adjusting the "images" to the work that is being shaped, in such a way that the person who is creating is always also in part a spectator.

So architecture must always be attentive to handicraft while clearly bearing in mind that the conditions of craft and architectural labor only partially correspond. If anything, we might say, turning Tessenow's hypothesis on its head, that the condition of craft is the utopia of architectural work. And this is true and manifest precisely in the moments of greater unity, of stability of form in history; in those moments in which image, evoked form, real form, means, and techniques coincide perfectly in the unity of the style: in fact, moments of great formal stability are precisely those that bring architecture closest to the state of a craft.

Finally, another aspect of the question of realism regards the special relationship that exists between the work of architecture and the public. In fact, architecture is a public work, a collective work par excellence. This is why we should give careful consideration not only to those tendencies that seek to exclude architecture from the field of art, but also, for example, to the fact that today there is a general lack of interest in architecture, which again signifies exclusion of architecture as such from the realm of common goods.

The fact is that architecture must first come to terms with itself; that is, with its specific characteristics. At the same time, however, it has to face up to its social responsibility. From this point of view, the question of its relationship with the public cannot be ignored. This is why the language of architecture is—or indeed ought to be—a direct language. Moreover, since architecture enters directly into life—for instance, through the functionality that takes it outside the domain of art—this creates a permanent bond that offers the public a basis from which to pass irrevocable judgment.

Yet another less obvious, but equally strong link that derives from architecture's particular evocative purpose has already been mentioned. It is the link between architecture and society and its grand collective aims; it is the characteristic conceptual tension that manifests in style, which in turn is destined to embody those aims (see, for example, the architecture of the bourgeois revolution). A link capable, therefore, of performing a well-defined historical function in the domain of cultural superstructure. This tension can be recognized in all the great architecture of the past: in the most significant moments in the history of cities, in their buildings, and in their dominant forms. This tension is maintained as historical conditions change; this is due not only to the fact that forms become part of collective memory but also, and above all, because these forms represent very long-term goals (see again Bloch's concept of progress). The forms themselves do not lose their efficacy with respect to these aims over time. This is the precise meaning of the question that Hannes Meyer asked at the end of his 1942 essay "The Soviet Architect":

> "Shall we, the architects of the democratic countries, be found ready to hand over the pyramids to the society of the future?"

Above and beyond the symbolic meaning Meyer assigned to the pyramids, he also affirmed the destiny of architectural forms to serve as a concrete, perennial testimony. In fact, while architecture is linked to an immediate use, it is also the "world" that most directly bears witness to the collective desire to leave a trace for the future. Let us take the same examples as before:

der Tat diejenigen, die einer handwerklichen Bedingung für die Architektur am nächsten kommen.

Ein weiterer Aspekt des Realismusproblems betrifft schliesslich den besonderen Bezug, der zwischen architektonischem Werk und Oeffentlichkeit besteht. In der Tat ist die Architektur kollektives, öffentliches Werk par excellence. Deswegen müssten nicht nur jene Strömungen aufmerksam beobachtet werden, die die Architektur aus dem Feld der Kunst auszuschliessen suchen, sondern z. B. auch der Umstand, dass heute ein verbreitetes Desinteresse an der Architektur besteht, was wiederum den Ausschluss der Architektur aus dem Bereich der gesellschaftlichen Güter bedeutet.

In der Tat rechnet die Architektur vor allem mit sich selbst, d. h. mit ihrer Eigenart, zugleich aber auch mit der ihr eigenen sozialen Aufgabe. Von diesem Gesichtspunkt aus ist das Problem des Bezugs zur Oeffentlichkeit unumgänglich. Deswegen ist die Sprache der Architektur unmittelbar — oder müsste es doch sein. Da ferner die Architektur direkt ins Leben eindringt — z. B. durch ihre ausserkünstlerische Funktionalität — schafft sie eine dauernde Verbindung zur Oeffentlichkeit und liefert ihr unanfechtbare Elemente für ein Urteil.

Es war bereits die Rede von einer anderen, weniger offensichtlichen aber nicht weniger hartnäckigen Verbindung, die sich aus der besonderen evokativen Bestimmung der Architektur ableitet. Es ist die Verbindung der Architektur mit der Gesellschaft und ihren grossen Zielen, die charakteristische gedankliche Spannung, die sich im Stil niederschlägt, der zur Verkörperung dieser Ziele bestimmt ist (siehe zum Beispiel die Architektur der bürgerlichen Revolution). Eine Verbindung also, die eine bestimmte geschichtliche Funktion im Feld des kulturellen Ueberbaus zu entwickeln vermag. Diese Spannung ist in der gesamten grossen Architektur der Vergangenheit erkennbar: in den bedeutungsvollsten Momenten der Geschichte der Städte, in der Gestalt ihrer Gebäude und in den vorherrschenden Formen. Diese Spannung bleibt erhalten im Wandel der geschichtlichen Bedingungen; nicht nur, weil die Formen kollektive Erinnerung werden, sondern auch und vor allem, weil diese Formen Ziele interpretierren, die lange Zeiträume besetzen (siehe auch hier den Begriff des Fortschritts bei Bloch). Angesichts dieser Ziele verlieren die Formen ihre Wirksamkeit in der Zeit nicht. Dies ist gemeint in der Frage von Hannes Meyer am Schluss seiner Schrift *Der sowjetische Architekt* von 1942:

«... werden wir, demokratische Architekten, bereit sein, der zukünftigen Gesellschaft die Pyramiden weiterzugeben?»

Jenseits der symbolischen Bedeutung, die in diesem Satz den Formen zugeschrieben wird, anerkennt er das Schicksal der architektonischen Formen, dauernde konkrete Zeugnisse zu sein. In der Tat ist die Architektur zwar an einen unmittelbaren Gebrauch gebunden, doch ist sie auch jene «Welt», die den kollektiven Willen unmittelbarer bezeugt, Wegmarken in

↑ fig. 7 Photograph of model of the Corso Miramare.

der Zukunft zu setzen. Nochmals dieselben Beispiele: das Ospedale Maggiore von Filarete in Mailand, die Universität in Pavia von Piermarini, die Unité d'habitation von Le Corbusier, die Convention Hall von Mies sind zeitlich weitauseinanderliegende Bauten, geeignet zur Demonstration dieses Anspruchs und dieses Schicksals. Es handelt sich um Architekturen, die bestimmten Kulturen entsprechen, die aber in der gemeinsamen Tendenz, sich vor allem als «Typen» zu fixieren, allgemein und progressiv, das heisst im richtigsten Sinne archetypisch werden — im Sinne der «Pyramiden» Meyers, um uns richtig zu verstehen. Mehr als einer Erwartung der Gegenwart zu entsprechen interpretieren diese Architekturen die Utopie, das heisst sie evozieren «Angemessenheit».

In Wirklichkeit sind die mittelalterliche Stadt, die Kathedrale und das Schloss die Elemente der monarchischen oder der neoklassischen Stadt, sind die Paläste und Plätze in ihren Formen immer mehr als die wirkliche Stadt, obwohl sie diese tatsächlich konstituieren.

In diesem Sinne darf der Realismus nicht davon absehen, diesem besonderen Schicksal des formal-architektonischen Zeugnisses Rechnung zu tragen. Wenn die Architektur diese ihre Aufgabe ausser Acht lässt, verfehlt sie den Sinn ihrer «Dauer» selbst.

Dies gilt auch für die persönlichere Untersuchung. Deswegen hält es schwer, einen grossen Teil des heutigen Experimentalismus hinzunehmen, obschon sich dieser der Architektur gegenüber affirmativ verhält. Damit meine ich jene Untersuchungen über geometrische Komposition und Dekomposition, die am stärksten ihre abstrakte und radikale Grundlage zeigen; oder jene offen und programmatisch «unvollendeten» oder «vorläufigen»; oder dann jene Untersuchungen, die sich auf die Erfahrung einer anderen Tätigkeit wie Bildhauerei oder Malerei stützen (für diese letzteren Fälle gilt immer noch die von Michelangelo ausgesprochene Meinung; dieser ist nie davon abgegangen, der Architektur den Vorrang einzuräumen).

Vom gleichen Gesichtspunkt aus müssen wir auch jene Erfahrungen beurteilen, die sich programmatisch am Problem des Realismus gemessen haben: ich beziehe mich, abgesehen von der entscheidenden und komplexen Erfahrung der Sowjetunion und der sozialistischen Länder, beispielsweise auf den architektonischen Neorealismus der Nachkriegszeit in Italien — aber es ist auch jener viel weniger diskutierte «pragmatische» Weg eines Grossteils der nordeuropäischen Architektur in Betracht zu ziehen. Ich denke an das grobe Missverständnis, das zu einer zugleich paradoxen und degradierenden Nachahmung des Bildes der gotisch-bürgerlichen Stadt führte. Die Architektur kann diesem ihrem Schicksal nicht entgehen, im weitesten Sinne kollektives Werk zu sein; ebenso wenig kann sie die besondere Welt ihrer Darstellung umgehen, indem sie beispielsweise thematische Probleme missachtet, die ihr seit je eigen waren (siehe die Frage des «Monumentalen» und der absurde Streit über «Monumentalismus»).

Nur wenn sie sich mit den Themen ihrer eigenen geschichtlichen Erfahrung auseinandersetzt, kann sie sich mit dieser von neuem auf rationale Weise messen und danach streben, im alltäglichen Leben ein konkreter Bezug zu sein.

Uebers. H. Helfenstein, B. Reichlin und M. Steinmann

Zum Problem der innerarchitektonischen Wirklichkeit (Fortsetzung von Seite 11)

Vgl. Bruno Reichlin und Fabio Reinhart, «Die Historie als Teil der Architekturtheorie», in: *archithese*, Heft 11, 1974.

Theodor W. Adorno, *Aesthetische Theorie*, Frankfurt am Main, 2. Auflage, 1974, S. 71–72.

Karl Marx, *Oekonomisch-philosophische Manuskripte*, in: *MEW* Erg.-Bd. I, Berlin (DDR), 1968, S. 541.

Robert Venturi in: Heinrich Klotz und John W. Cook, *Architektur im Widerspruch*, Zürich, 1974, S. 254.

Vgl. Wolfgang Fritz Haug, *Kritik der Warenästhetik*, Frankfurt am Main, 1971.

Vgl. Robert Venturi, Denise Scott Brown, Steven Izenour, *Learning From Las Vegas*, Cambridge, Mass. and London, 1972, S. 65 ff.

Theodor W. Adorno, *Aesthetische Theorie*, Frankfurt am Main, 2. Auflage, 1974, S. 16.

Roland Barthes, *Le plaisir du texte*, Paris, 1973, S. 74.

Filarete's Ospedale Maggiore in Milan, Piermarini's University of Pavia, Le Corbusier's Unité d'habitation, and Mies's Convention Hall are buildings remote from one another in time and thus suited to demonstrating this aspiration and this destiny. They are works of architecture that correspond to well-defined cultures, but through the common tendency to establish themselves first of all as "types," they become universal and progressive; that is, archetypal in the truest sense—namely, in the sense of Meyer's "pyramids." Rather than meeting an expectation for the present, these buildings interpret utopia; that is, they evoke "appropriateness."

In reality, the medieval city, the cathedral and the castle, the elements of the monarch's city or of the neoclassical one, townhouses and squares always go beyond the real city in their forms, even though they are the very constituents of that city.

In this sense realism cannot avoid reckoning with the particular destiny of architectural forms to serve as testimony. If architecture shirks this task, then we can say that the very sense of its "durability" is lost.

This is true even for personal exploration. That is why it is difficult to accept much of today's experimentalism, even when it affirms architecture. I am referring to those attempts at geometric composition and decomposition that most clearly display their abstract and radical basis; or those explicitly and programmatically "unfinished" or "makeshift" works of architecture; or, finally, those explorations that are based on experiences in another practice, such as sculpture or painting (for these last cases what holds good, in my view, is the opinion expressed by Michelangelo, who, trusting solely in architecture, also assigned it a permanent preeminence).

We must also judge those experiences that have programmatically tackled the question of realism from this same point of view: apart from the decisive and complex experience of the Soviet Union and the socialist countries, I am referring, for example, to the architectural neorealism of postwar Italy—but it is also necessary to consider the far less widely debated "pragmatic" choices of much of Northern European architecture. I am thinking here of the gross misunderstanding that has led to the equally paradoxical and degrading imitation of the image of the Gothic-bourgeois city. Architecture cannot escape its fate of being a collective work in the broadest sense; just as it cannot evade the particular world of its representation by neglecting, for instance, thematic questions that have always been peculiar to it (such as the question of the "monumental" and the absurd controversy over "monumentalism").

Only by confronting the themes of its own historical experience can architecture reasonably hope to vie with it and aim to be a concrete point of reference in daily life.

ENDNOTE

1 German original: Adolf Loos, "Architektur," *Der Sturm*, 15. Dezember 1910.

A Realist Education

Author:
Aldo Rossi

Source:
archithese, 19 (1976): 25–28

Translated by:
Brett Petzer

"They called me Pablo because I played the guitar." With this sentence, Cesare Pavese begins *The Comrade*, his most personal novel, and also the work most closely based on a specific program —realism. From the first sentence, realism is interwoven with personal drama, in language that blends García Lorca with Piedmontese. Italian neorealism rediscovered the Paduan countryside with new realist principles that come as much from the Americans—Hemingway, Faulkner— as from distant memories of picaresque novels. The landscape of Italian neorealism is that of Luchino Visconti's *Obsession*. An incredible Clara Calamai wanders, sunglasses on, through the gardens of Ferrara, looking for the love and the blame entangled in her everyday reality. Reality emerges here from a singular composition of monuments and emotions that envelop the characters, with a sublime and ridiculous mélange of the music of Verdi. An aria from *La Traviata* fades into ditties of the time, "Ma [sic] il tuo vecchio genitor" [But your old parent] and "Fiorin Fiorello / L'amore è bello" [Love is beautiful], while the Castle of Ferrara strips itself of de Chirico's metaphysics to present itself as a heap of bricks, a shed, or a wood-fired oven made by a long-gone peasant civilization.

In Roberto Rossellini's *Paisà*, realism is more straightforwardly aggressive. However, the black children of America, the ladies of the night, the boarding rooms beyond belief, the body sold for a packet of *Américaines* under a scorching sun—today, all of these look almost archaeological, like evidence of an impossible Italy. Fellini could use them in a new *Satyricon*.

These are, perhaps, my memories of realism; at that time, one could find it in the grand cinemas and in small outlying ones, in Aristarco's *Cinema* magazine, and in the pages of the Politecnico. With these examples we tried to translate reality; perhaps we simply discovered it.

Later, in films, we met the Soviets again. Pudovkin and Eisenstein seemed identical: an unknown world was discovering reality— a distant, fascinating, grandiose reality.

As a young student, wandering the immense streets of Moscow, this reality seemed incredible to me, as I had an interest in architecture. The provocative, incredible, gentle architecture of the time of metro stations and the university on the Lenin Hills.

Was this realism?

Aldo Rossi

Une éducation réaliste

«On m'appelait Pablo parce que je jouais de la guitare», c'est avec cette phrase que Cesare Pavese commence ‚Le camarade', le roman le plus personnel qu'il ait écrit, et aussi celui qui se base le plus sur un programme précis: le réalisme. Dès la première phrase le réalisme se mêle au drame personnel, à une géographie autobiographique, à un langage où Garcia Lorca se fond dans le dialecte piémontais. Le néoréalisme italien a redécouvert la campagne de Padoue avec de nouveaux principes de réalisme, principes qui lui viennent autant des Américains — Hemingway, Faulkner — que de lointains souvenirs de roman picaresque. Le paysage du néoréalisme italien est celui de «Obsession» de Luchino Visconti. Une incroyable Clara Calamai parcourt, avec ses lunettes de soleil, les jardins de Ferrare, cherchant l'amour et la faute enchevêtrés dans sa réalité quotidienne; et la réalité en sort dans une composition singulière de monuments et de sentiments qui enveloppent les personnages, avec en plus un mélange sublime et ridicule de musique de Verdi. Un air de la Traviata se mêle aux chansonnettes de l'époque, «Ma il tuo vecchio genitor» avec «Fiorin Fiorello / L'amore è bello», tandis que le château de Ferrare se dépouille de la métaphysique de De Chirico et se présente comme un monceau de briques, hangar ou four à pain d'une civilisation paysanne désormais révolue.

Avec «Paisà» de Roberto Rossellini, le réalisme présente une agressivité plus directe. Cependant, ces enfants noirs de l'Amérique, les «demoiselles», les incroyables chambres de pension, le corps vendu pour un paquet d'«américaines» sous un soleil de plomb, tout cela apparaît aujourd'hui comme des témoignages presque archéologiques d'une Italie impossible. Ils pourraient servir à un nouveau Satyricon de Fellini.

Voilà peut-être mes souvenirs du réalisr.ie; on le trouvait alors dans les cinémathèques, les cinémas de périphérie, dans la revue «Cinéma» de Aristarco, dans les feuilles du Politecnico. Nous cherchions à partir de ces exemples à traduire la réalité: mais peut-être simplement on découvrait la réalité.

Plus tard, de nouveau au cinéma, nous avons connu les soviétiques. Pudovkin et Eisenstein semblaient identiques; un monde inconnu découvrait la réalité, une réalité lointaine, fascinante, grandiose.

Jeune étudiant, par les immenses rues de Moscou, cette réalité me semblait incroyable; avec quelque intérêt pour l'architecture. L'architecture provocatrice, incroyable et douce au temps des stations de métro et de l'université sur les collines de Lénine.

Etait-ce cela le réalisme?

D'abord j'ai vu le réalisme comme une solution de rechange: avant tout il combattait avec supériorité l'aspect gris et pénitenciaire de l'architecture moderne.

Je le répète, ce n'est pas l'architecture qui m'intéressait particulièrement — et il en est de même maintenant — mais c'est toute émotion que — *entre autres* — l'architecture, malgré ses limites, semblait me donner.

C'est pourquoi le réalisme socialiste en architecture a été pour moi un épisode glorieux, et beaucoup de débats que j'ai suivis proviennent de ce noeud. Mais il est idiot — à moins que cela ne serve à quelque exercice acadé-

25

mique — de faire du réalisme en architecture une catégorie. Sinon il lui arrive ce qu'il est arrivé au rationalisme, à la symétrie, à tant d'autres choses, qui sont utiles pour exprimer une certaine idée.

Le réalisme peut être d'une manière ou d'une autre un problème social ou politique — mais le blanchissement des os peut l'être aussi. Quel manuel de statistique a-t-il étudié la résistance constructive du corps humain dans la muraille de Chine ou dans d'autres constructions antiques ou mythologiques? Ce sont les gestes, les douleurs, les hontes d'une cité inconnue.

Je cherchais un réalisme quotidien. Et antique. A l'étude des schémas typologiques du mouvement moderne j'opposais les longs couloirs des maisons de la Lombardie; et à partir des émotions je remontais à quelque certitude. Les grandes cours représentaient l'*insula*, éléments locaux de l'antique colonisation latine. Les constructions romaines avaient accepté cette civilisation, en lui donnant une forme universelle, et ceci était le rapport le plus authentique avec la réalité. C'est pour cela que le réalisme — ou la réalité — s'entremêlaient d'analogies, de références, de réflexions, de relations — licites ou illicites. Mais je commencais à penser *aussi* à l'architecture avec liberté: l'amour et la faute de Clara Calamai dans «Obsession» pouvait parcourir tranquillement les couloirs et les corridors de mes projets, alors que finalement le David de Tanzio da Varallo offre la signification imprévue à la «cité analogue».

Le réalisme est-il donc seulement pédagogique et didactique? Non, certainement pas. Mais il est certain qu'il n'est pas académique et qu'il fuit les académies et les thèses de doctorat, les professeurs et leurs élèves, avec son incroyable, merveilleuse, oblique vitalité — ou bien, justement, sa réalité.

(Traduction: I. von Moos)

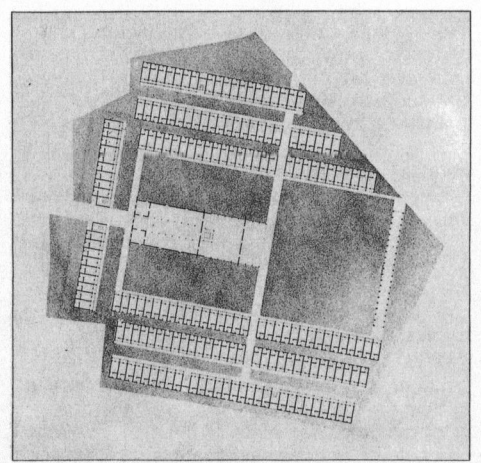 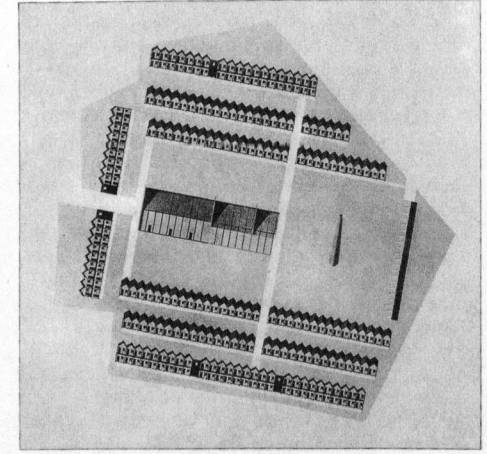

↑ figs. 1–2 Aldo Rossi, competition project for a student residence in Chieti, Italy; 1976. Plan (1); facades (2).

figs. 3–4 Aldo Rossi, the "portone" in Bellinzona, 1974, with Bruno Reichlin and Fabio Reinhart. Plan (3); elevation (4).

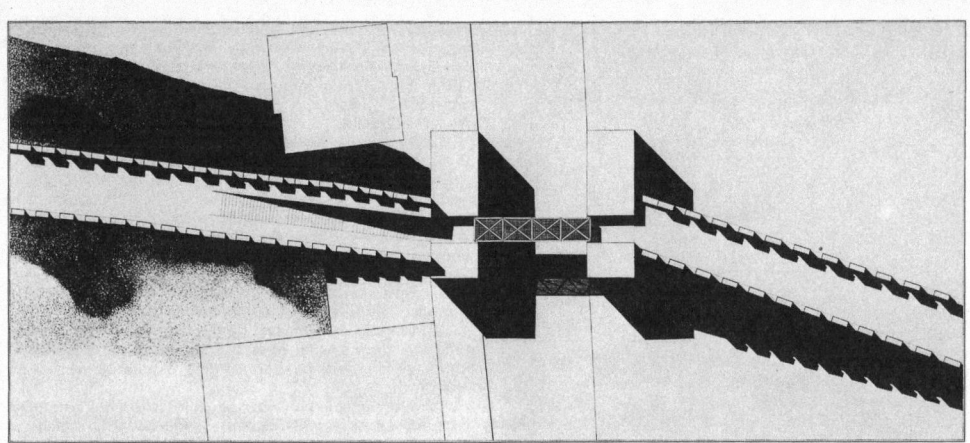

Aldo Rossi

Realismus als Erziehung

«Sie nannten mich Pablo, weil ich die Gitarre spielte», mit diesem Satz beginnt Cesare Pavese seinen ebenso programmatischen wie persönlichen Roman «Il compagno»: das Programm war der Realismus, der sich vom ersten Satz an vermischt mit dem persönlichen Schicksal, mit einer autobiographischen Beschreibung der Landschaft, mit einer Sprache, in der Garcia Lorca aufgeht im Dialekt des Piemont. Nach den Regeln des Realismus, wie sie aus den Werken der Amerikaner, Hemingways wie Faulkners, und aus fernen Erinnerungen an den pikarischen Roman gewonnen wurden, suchte der italienische Neorealismus die Poebene auf; er fand seine Landschaft im Film «Ossessione» von Visconti. Eine unwahrscheinliche Clara Calamai, mit Sonnenbrille, geht durch die Gärten von Ferrara auf der Suche nach Liebe und Sünde, die sich in der Wirklichkeit ihres Alltages vermengen; die Wirklichkeit erscheint merkwürdig durchsetzt mit den Bauwerken und den Gefühlen, die, auch noch auf lächerliche und zugleich erhabene Weise gemischt mit Motiven von Verdi, die Personen einhüllen. Die Arie der Traviata geht in zeitgenössische Schlager über, «Ma il tuo vecchio genitor»

fig. 5   Aldo Rossi, "Städtische Landschaft mit Schnitt"/
"paysage urbain avec coupe," 1970.

in «Fiorin Fiorello, l'amore è bello», während das Schloss von Ferrara De Chirico's metaphysische Hülle abwirft und sich als eine Anhäufung von Ziegelsteinen zeigt, Hof- und Ofenanlage einer vergangenen bäuerlichen Kultur.

Im Film «Paisà» von Rossellini griff der Realismus entschiedener zu: Aber die schwarzen «Gls», die «Segnorine», die unwahrscheinlichen Hotelzimmer, die Körper, die für eine Schachtel von «Amerikanischen» verkauft werden unter einer weissen Sonne, sie erscheinen uns heute als gewissermassen archäologische Zeugnisse eines unmöglichen Italien. Sie könnten für ein neues Satyricon von Fellini dienen.

Das sind vielleicht meine Erinnerungen an Realismus; schon in den Filmklubs, in den Vorstadtkinos, in der Zeitschrift «Cinema» von Aristarco, in «Politecnico». Durch diese Filme versuchten wir, die Wirklichkeit zu erkennen . . . damit waren wir vielleicht schon dabei, sie zu entdecken.

Später lernten wir die Russen kennen, immer noch im Film; Pudovkin und Eisenstein waren für uns das gleiche, eine unbekannte Welt enthüllte die Wirklichkeit, eine ferne, faszinierende, grossartige Wirklichkeit.

Als Student in den unabsehbaren Strassen von Moskau schien mir diese Wirklichkeit unglaublich; mit einigem Interesse für Architektur. Die herausfordernde, unglaubliche und doch auch liebliche Architektur der Metro-Stationen und der Universität auf den Lenin-Hügeln: War das der Realismus?

Anfänglich sah ich den Realismus als eine Alternative: vor allem war er eine überlegene Antwort auf die graue, gefängnishafte Erscheinung der zeitgenössischen Architektur.

Ich war nicht sonderlich an der Architektur interessiert, ich muss es wiederholen — wie sie mich heute nicht interessiert — aber an den Empfindungen, die mir auch die Architektur, trotz ihrer Grenzen, zu vermitteln scheint.

Darum bleibt für mich der Sozialistische Realismus in der Architektur eine glanzvolle Zeit; viele spätere Auseinandersetzungen gehen von ihm aus. Aber es ist unsinnig, oder dient nur akademischer Uebung, aus dem Realismus eine Kategorie zu machen. Es geht damit wie mit dem Rationalismus, wie mit verschiedenen Dingen, die einem dazu dienen, eine Idee auszudrücken.

Der Realismus kann in gewisser Weise ein politisches oder soziales Problem sein, oder auch die Farbe von gebleichten Knochen: welches Handbuch hat einmal den statischen Widerstand der menschlichen Körper ausgerechnet, die in der Chinesischen Mauer oder in anderen antiken und mythologischen Bauwerken eingemauert wurden?

Es geht um Handlungen, Schmerz und Schande einer unbekannten Stadt.

Ich suchte einen alltäglichen Realismus, einen sehr alten. Den typologischen Schemen des Neuen Bauens stellte ich die langen Laubengänge des lombardischen Hauses gegenüber; und von meinen Empfindungen gelangte ich zu einigen Gewissheiten. Die grossen Höfe wiederholten die Insula, die alte lateinische Besiedlung und örtliche Elemente. Die römischen Bauwerke übernahmen diese Kultur und gaben ihr eine allgemeine Form, und das war ihre tiefe Beziehung zur Wirklichkeit. Darum war der Realismus, oder die Wirklichkeit, mit Analogien, Anspielungen, Beziehungen, erlaubten oder unerlaubten, durchsetzt.

Ich fing an, *auch* über Architektur frei zu denken: so könnte Clara Calamai im Film «Ossessione» ihrer Liebe und ihrer Sünde genausogut in den Gängen und Hallen meiner Entwürfe nachgehen. Und so fügt schliesslich der David von Tanzio di Varallo in grossen Bild der «Città Analoga» die unerwartete Bedeutung hinzu.

So käme dem Realismus lediglich pädagogischer und didaktischer Wert zu? Sicher nicht. Er ist nicht akademisch, er entzieht sich den Akademien mit seiner unglaublichen, wunderbaren, unfassbaren Lebenskraft oder, eben, Wirklichkeit.

(Uebers.: B. Reichlin und M. Steinmann)

At first, I saw realism as an alternative: more than anything, it seemed to triumph over the gray, carceral aspect of modern architecture.

I repeat, it was not architecture specifically that interested me then (and that is still true); it was rather the emotion that architecture (among other things), and despite its limits, seemed to give me.

That is why, for me, socialist realism in architecture was a glorious chapter. Many of the debates I have followed flow from this issue. However, unless for some academic purpose, it is silly to make realism into a category of architecture. Otherwise, it will end up like rationalism, or symmetry, or so many other names that are useful for expressing a certain idea.

Realism can, in some ways, be a social or political issue—so can bone bleaching. What statistics textbook has studied the structural stability of human bodies interred in the Great Wall of China or in other ancient or mythological structures?

These are the gestures, the sorrows, the shames of an unknown city.

I was looking for an everyday realism. It had to be ancient too. I countered the study of typological schemas of modern movement with the long hallways of houses in Lombardy, and from the emotions I returned to a degree of certainty. The great courtyards represented the *insula*, the local elements of Latin colonization in antiquity. What the Romans had built accepted this civilization and gave it a universal form: this was the most authentic relationship with reality. That is why realism—or reality—was riddled with analogies, references, reflections, and relationships—licit and illicit. But I was also increasingly free in my thinking about architecture: Clara Calamai's love and blame in *Obsession* could wander calmly through the hallways and corridors of my projects, while Tanzio de Varallo's *David* offers up the unforeseen meaning of the "analogous city."

Is realism, then, only pedagogical and didactic? No, certainly not. But it is certainly not academic; it flees from academics and doctoral theses, from professors and their students, with its incredible, marvelous, oblique vitality—or, more precisely, its reality.

On the Problem of Inner Architectonic Reality

Authors:
Bruno Reichlin
Martin Steinmann

Source:
archithese, 19 (1976): 3–11, 24

Translated by:
Steven Lindberg

"We are like sailors who have to rebuild their ship on the open sea, without ever being able to dismantle it in dry-dock and reconstruct it from the best components."

Otto Neurath

Around 1950, when socialist realism (which had been worked out as a theory or method in the period before World War II) was monopolizing that concept with its own interpretation of it, various attempts were made to counter it with a materialist standpoint taken from Neues Bauen [New Building]. That is true, for example, of Georg Schmidt, for whom this view was confirmed by the fact that *Sachlichkeit* [objectivity/functionalism] is the German word for "realism" ("Realismus und Naturalismus"). The proposition of his brother, Hans Schmidt, that building was by its nature technology—that is, a matter of necessity—describes the foundation of this realism: building is the technology that

"everywhere where it does not have to take anything alien to its nature into account is … *calculating with specific* laws, the laws of forces that apply in nature." ("Die Technik baut," 1930)

This realism aims to exchange the laws of style or, more generally, of form, for "more natural" laws (precisely the laws of nature), with which reality could be grasped directly. (Alan Colquhoun addresses this question in more detail elsewhere in this issue.)

(It is characteristic of the seriousness of his view that, for a time after the Great Depression, under transformed conditions of production, Hans Schmidt rejected as formalism the forms of Neues Bauen; that is, as a style in the nineteenth-century sense that was not grounded in the reality of the construction site.)

In the Dessau-Törten housing development (1926–27), Gropius adopted precisely the approach of the technological way of thinking and working, which

"clearly designs outward from the materials, from the building processes, and from the requirement for the finished building,"

as Schmidt wrote. But: the forms are not simply the consequence of the construction processes; they illustrate them (on a scale of mechanization that was not employed at all). Another building by Gropius in Dessau, the Arbeitsamt [Employment Office], makes clear how the form was determined on the level of organization, as laid out by Karel Teige: the organization of spaces, levels, paths, and fixtures that serve the procedures in a building and constitute its content.

Bruno Reichlin und Martin Steinmann

Zum Problem der innerarchitektonischen Wirklichkeit

«Wie Schiffer sind wir, die ihr Schiff auf offener See umbauen müssen, ohne es jemals in einem Dock zerlegen und aus besten Bestandteilen neu errichten zu können.»
Otto Neurath

Als um 1950 der Sozialistische Realismus (der als Theorie oder Methode in der Zeit vor dem Zweiten Weltkrieg ausgearbeitet worden war) mit seiner Auslegung den Begriff mit Beschlag belegte, wurde verschiedentlich versucht, ihm gerade von einem materialistischen Standpunkt aus das Neue Bauen als realistisch entgegenzustellen. Das gilt beispielsweise für Georg Schmidt, für den sich diese Auffassung darin bestätigte, dass «Sachlichkeit» das deutsche Wort für «Realismus» ist *(Realismus und Naturalismus)*. Der Satz seines Bruders Hans Schmidt, demzufolge Bauen seinem Wesen nach Technik, also eine Sache des Notwendigen sei, beschreibt die Grundlage dieses Realismus: Bauen sei Technik, die

«überall dort, wo sie keine wesensfremden Rücksichten zu nehmen hat, ein (...) *Rechnen mit bestimmten Gesetzen*, den Gesetzen der Kräfte, die in der Natur wirksam sind» *(Die Technik baut,* 1930).

Dieser Realismus richtet sich darauf, die Regeln des Stils oder allgemeiner der Form gegen «natürlichere» Gesetze (eben die Gesetze der Natur), auszutauschen, mit denen die Wirklichkeit unmittelbar zu erfassen wäre. (Im Rahmen dieses Heftes behandelt Alan Colquhoun diese Frage ausführlicher.)

(Es bezeichnet den Ernst seiner Auffassung, dass Hans Schmidt nach der Wirtschaftskrise die Formen des Neuen Bauens unter den veränderten Bedingungen der Produktion zeitweise

Au sujet de la réalité immanente de l'architecture

En architecture comme dans les arts en général la question du réalisme est d'habitude posée au niveau de la fonction expressive d'un œuvre qui, elle, n'existe qu'en relation avec une réalité *autre* que celle de l'architecture: les conditions matérielles et techniques, le système de production, la fonction sociale ou l'idéologie.

Cette idée de la réalité n'arrive pas à reconnaître dans les œuvres le travail qui les a produit. Mais si l'on néglige ce travail qui se réalise en elles, elles se présentent dans une «naturalité» illusoire, ne disant rien sur les processus qui déterminent le fonctionnement du fait poétique. Comme les autres arts, l'architecture ne reflète pas uniquement une réalité sociale. Elle possède sa propre réalité, qui est de nature formelle. D'où le postulat d'une théorie immanente à l'architecture, qui élabore des catégories capables d'identifier les méthodes poétiques réalisées dans les œuvres.

Le concept de réalisme ici proposé vise à la «nature» de l'architecture comme la somme de ses possibilités immanentes, en partie déterminées par le métier. La nature ou l'essence d'une chose ne peut être reconnue qu'à travers le changement. Le lieu de ce changement est l'histoire: c'est là que la «nature» de l'architecture se révèle.

Comme les autres arts, l'architecture est liée à l'expérience immédiate, autrement elle ne serait pas différente par exemple de la science. Renoncer à sa propre réalité conceptuelle et sensuelle (ne serait-ce au nom d'un engagement social) signifierait priver notre sensualité d'une expérience fondamentale. Vis-à-vis des tendances qui veulent éliminer le plaisir de l'architecture, il faut donc revendiquer le droit à ce plaisir.

↓ fig. 1 Walter Gropius, Dessau-Törten housing development, construction scheme, 1926.

↓ fig. 2 Walter Gropius, Employment Office, Dessau, 1928–29, plan of ground floor, "Arrangement of the main facility on ground level to avoid congestion on the steps."

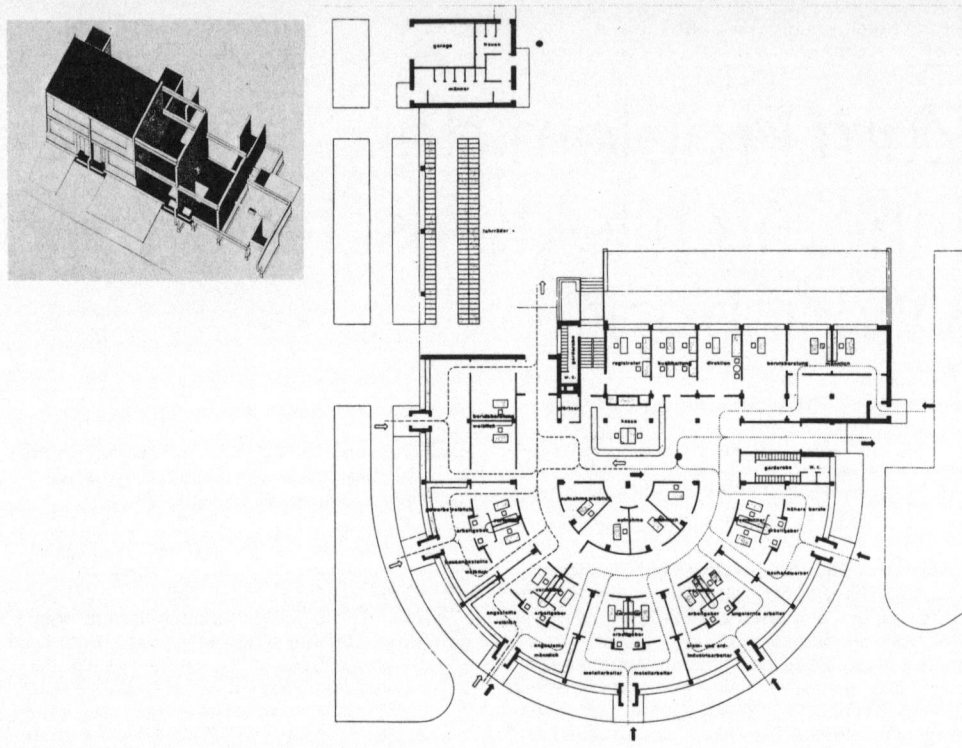

als Formalismus ablehnte, das heisst als Stil im Sinne des 19. Jahrhunderts, der nicht in der Wirklichkeit der Baustelle begründet war.)

In der Siedlung Dessau-Törten (1926–1927) übernahm Gropius genau die Denk- und Arbeitsweise der Technik, die

«eindeutig aus dem Material, aus den Bauvorgängen und aus den Anforderungen an das fertige Bauwerk heraus gestaltet»,

wie Schmidt schrieb. Aber: *die Formen sind nicht einfach die Folge der Bauvorgänge, sie verbildlichen diese, sie inszenieren diese* (in einem Mass an Mechanisierung, wie es gar nicht zur Anwendung kam). Ein anderes Bauwerk von Gropius in Dessau, das Arbeitsamt, veranschaulicht die Bestimmung der Form auf der Ebene der Organisation, wie sie Karel Teige gibt: sie sei die Organisation der Räume, Flächen, Wege und Einrichtungen, die den Vorgängen in einem Bauwerke dienen, die seinen Inhalt ausmachen.

Diese vereinfachende Auslegung von Realismus zog bestimmte Anforderungen vor auf Kosten von anderen, bemühte sich um die messbaren Werte wie «Licht, Luft, Oeffnung» und vernachlässigte die nicht-messbaren wie beispielsweise die «Werte des Interieurs» (die stärker an die Form gebunden sind und durch Mimesis weitergegeben werden). Der Bereich der Form wurde auf den des «Rechnens» eingeschränkt und das aus ihm ausgeschlossen, was mit dessen ärmlichen Kriterien nicht erfassbar war. (In der Wissenschaft würde das gleiche Verhalten bedeuten, neue Fakten, die in einer Theorie nicht vorgesehen sind, gar nicht wahrzunehmen.)

Solange es die einzige Aufgabe der Form ist, den messbaren Werten zu entsprechen, bleibt sie weit unterdeterminiert. Le Corbusier wies auf diesen Umstand hin, als er Stellung bezog gegen die genannte Auslegung:

«Un ingenieur calcule la section d'une poutre; l'examen des efforts qu'elle subit lui fournit le moment de flexion, le moment de résistance et enfin le moment d'inertie. Mais le moment d'inertie est un produit dans lequel à sa volonté jouent la hauteur et la largeur de la poutre. Il choisit alors une hauteur qui souvent n'a que la raison de lui plaire, et la largeur en découle.» *(Urbanisme.)*

In der Tat besitzt eine Architektur, deren einziger Inhalt die Gesetze der Natur, der Konstruktion und der Distribution sind, keine gesicherten Kriterien für die Bestimmung der Form, indem alle formalen und kulturellen Motivierungen als «arbiträr» aus ihr verbannt werden. In Wirklichkeit kehren sie, mangels Gesetzen der Form, erst recht als arbiträr in sie zurück! Das erklärt die Vielfalt der Formen in der postfunktionalistischen Architektur.

Die Auffassung, die den Funktionalismus als Realismus versteht, bestreitet die wechselseitige Beziehung zwischen Form und Inhalt, in der Meinung, auf diese Weise die gesellschaftliche Wirklichkeit unmittelbar zu erfassen. In Wahrheit stehen sich die gesellschaftlichen, ausserarchitektonischen und die innerarchitektonischen Momente nicht als «entweder – oder» gegenüber: sie sind voneinander verschieden und sie werden durch einander vermittelt. Aus diesem Grund brandmarkte Lukacs die Auffassung von Realismus, die die Kunstwerke als einfache gesellschaftliche Erscheinungen zu begreifen sucht, ohne ständig auch ihre besondere ästhetische Beschaffenheit mit einzubeziehen: *sie verfalle einem platten Soziologismus.*

Die Architektur gehört der «Welt der Gebrauchsgegenstände» an und wird von den jeweiligen gesellschaftlichen Bedürfnissen bestimmt. Die Architektur schafft zu deren Befriedigung bestimmte materielle-technische Gebilde, sie wandelt aber diese als Wirklichkeit «für sich» seienden Gebilde in einer zweiten Widerspiegelung so um, dass sie von ihr *Wirklichkeit «für uns»* werden. (Georg Lukacs hielt dem Funktionalismus gerade das vor: dass er die zweite Widerspiegelung, die gewissermassen aus dem Bauwerk «für sich» ein Kunstwerk «für uns» macht, mit der ersten Widerspiegelung, die das Bauwerk «für sich» hervorbringt, gleichsetzt und damit die «Anschaulichkeit» der Architektur aufhebt.)

Diese Bestimmung der architektonischen Wirklichkeit ist richtig, sie entgeht aber nicht der Gefahr, als «inhaltistisch» aufgenommen zu werden, solange diese Wirklichkeit von «aussen» untersucht wird, solange nicht von ihrem Inneren ausgegangen wird. Es ist das Verdienst der russischen Formalisten, *die Frage des Realismus* (in der Literatur) *von «innen» gestellt* zu haben. So bezieht sich der Aufsatz von Roman Jakobson, 1921, auf die Verfahren, die der Realismus verwendet. Der Grund für einen Realismus ist in der gesellschaftlichen Entwicklung zu suchen, die Verfahren aber, die ihn ästhetisch verwirklichen, gewinnen ihre Bedeutung im Inneren der literarischen Strukturen selber. (Realistisch ist die Verwendung der Volkssprache, beispielsweise, nicht durch ihren «Populismus», sondern durch ihren Antagonismus zur «hohen» Sprache: durch den Normbruch, den sie darstellt und der seine Bedeutung erlangt im Verhältnis zur gebrochenen Norm.)

Von dieser Ebene – der *Ebene der innerarchitektonischen Wirklichkeit*, die oft gar nicht wahrgenommen wird in der Frage des Realismus in der Architektur – werden wir im weiteren sprechen, auf die Gefahr hin, einseitig zu erscheinen.

In der realistischen Annäherung wird Kunst gerne auf Ideologie eingeschränkt oder darauf, ein «Bild» der Gesellschaft zu geben. Darin finden auch die Philosophen, Soziologen und soweiter ihre Grenze, die der Kunst eine blosse Ausdrucksfunktion zuschreiben, die sich nur bestimmt in der Beziehung zu etwas von ihr unterschieden. Wenigstens *eine der Wurzeln dieses «inhaltistischen» Hindernisses,* das auch bei einem marxistischen Aesthetiker wie Lukacs bestehen bleibt, wurde von Walter Siti in seinem Buch *Il realismo dell'avanguardia* klar erkannt, nämlich wo er schreibt, dass der Inhaltismus

«sich genau genommen aus einer Sünde idealistischer Herkunft ableitet, indem es ihm nicht gelingt, im Werk die richtige Arbeit zu erkennen, die es hervorgebracht hat.»

Es ist diese Einsicht, die uns dazu führt, bei unserer Untersuchung von der Arbeit auszugehen.

«Der Kunst liegt ein Können zugrunde, und es ist ein Arbeitskönnen. Wer Kunst bewundert, bewundert eine Arbeit. Und *es ist nötig, etwas von dieser Arbeit zu wissen,* damit man sie bewundern und ihr Ergebnis, das Kunstwerk, geniessen kann.» (Bertolt Brecht: *Betrachtung der Kunst und Kunst der Betrachtung.)*

Auf diese Weise verstanden als eine Arbeit, die aufgrund des dialektisch aufgefassten pro-

↓ figs. 3a+b Le Corbusier, Residence near Cherchell, 1942. Analyzed for "transparency" in Rowe and Slutzky, ed. Bernhard Hoesli, *Transparency*.

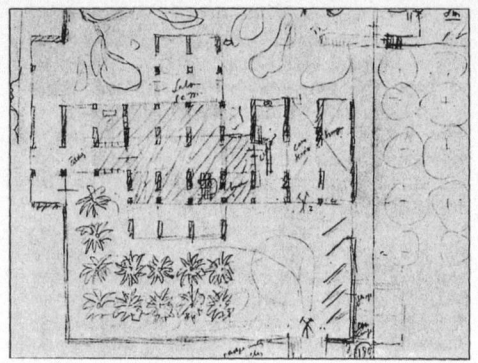
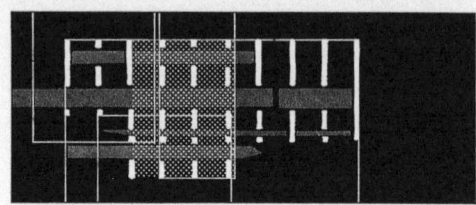

im additiven Gefüge der aufgereihten Citrohan-Raumschnitten entstehen durch die Fluchten der seitlichen Wanddurchbrüche räumliche Beziehungen quer zur primären Richtung der Raumabschnitte. Grundriss und Raum sind transparent.

Transparenz erlaubt Flexibilität innerhalb einer Formordnung.

duktiven Prozesses bestimmt werden kann, den sie darstellt, erweist sich die Architektur als eine besondere Form der Erkenntnis, die sich selber zum Gegenstand hat als Materie, die schon ausgearbeitet ist

«précisément par l'imposition de la structure complexe (sensible-technique-idéologique) qui la constitue comme objet de connaissance, même la plus fruste — comme objet qu'elle va transformer, dont elle va modifier les formes, au cours de son processus de développement, pour produire des connaissances sans cesse transformées, mais qui ne cesseront jamais de porter sur son objet, au sens d'objet de connaissance.» (Louis Althusser und Etienne Balibar: *Lire le capital*.)

Es gibt also keinen archimedischen Punkt ausserhalb der architektonischen Arbeit, von dem aus gelingen würde, den «teleologischen» Sinn, das Wesen, die «Natur» der Architektur zu begreifen. Wenn man absieht von der Arbeit, die sich in einem Werk vergegenständlicht, dann erscheint dieses in einer trügerischen «Natürlichkeit», die seine Künstlichkeit verschleiert: die Tatsache, dass es das Produkt von bestimmten Arbeitsgängen und Techniken ist, die *das Funktionieren des poetischen Faktums* festlegen. Mit anderen Worten widerspiegelt die Architektur nicht nur eine gesellschaftliche Wirklichkeit, sondern weist eine eigene Wirklichkeit der Form auf.

«Une masse architecturale, un rapport de tons, une touche de peinture, un trait gravé existent et valent d'abord en eux-même, (...) *le contenu fondamental de la forme est un contenu formel*» (Henri Focillon: *La vie des formes*).

Daraus ergibt sich die Forderung einer architekturimmanenten Theorie, die diese Wirklichkeit untersucht, indem sie die Kategorien ausarbeitet, die geeignet sind, die Gleichartigkeit und Verschiedenartigkeit aller Werke und die in ihnen auffindbaren poetischen Verfahren (die rhetorischen Figuren, deren Aktualisierung, undsoweiter) zu erfassen.

Wenn Bernhard Hoesli «Transparenz» so beschreibt, dass sie im Raum Stellen schaffe

«die zwei oder mehreren Bezugssystemen zugeordnet werden können, wobei die Zuordnung unbestimmt und die Wahl einer Zuordnungsmöglichkeit frei bleibt» (Kommentar zu Colin Rowe und Robert Slutzky: *Transparenz*),

dann kennzeichnet er eine dieser rhetorischen Figuren, die in der modernen Kunst ihre vielschichtigste Verwirklichung gefunden hat, die aber in der Kunstgeschichte immer wieder nachweisbar ist. Das unvermittelte Aneinanderstossen von Teilen («pezzi e parti») im Entwurf von Aldo Rossi für Scandicci (1968) als Fall von Parataxe, die Inflektion im Haus in Chestnut Hill (1962) von Robert Venturi, die verschiedenen Formen von Symmetrie, sie alle sind solche *rhetorische Figuren*. In den Formen ihrer Aktualisierung machen sie die Poetik der Werke aus. So wird die spiegelbildliche Symmetrie von Le Corbusier systematisch in Frage gestellt: «nicht-symmetrisches Gleichgewicht»

This simplifying interpretation of realism preferred certain demands at the cost of others, striving for quantifiable values such as "light, air, openness" and ignoring unquantifiable ones such as the "values of the interior" (which are more closely tied to form and are passed on through mimesis). The realm of form was limited to that of "calculation," and that which could not be captured by these impoverished criteria was excluded from it. (In science, the same approach would mean not perceiving at all new facts not predicted in a theory.)

As long as the only task of form is to conform to measurable values, it remains far underdetermined. Le Corbusier pointed to this fact when he took up a position against the aforementioned interpretation:

> "An engineer works out the section of a beam; the inquiry into the strain it will bear gives him the coefficients of tension, resistance and inertia. But the coefficient of inertia is the product of the height and breadth of a beam chosen by himself. Therefore he can choose a beam height for his beam whose only justification may be his own pleasure; the breadth is a necessary consequence of that height."
> (*The City of To-morrow and Its Planning*)

Indeed, an architecture whose only content is the laws of nature, of construction, and of distribution has no assured criteria for the determination of form, as all formal and cultural motivations are banned from it as "arbitrary." In reality, for lack of laws of form, they return to it as all the more arbitrary! That explains the diversity of forms in postfunctionalist architecture.

The view that understands functionalism as realism disputes the reciprocal relationship between form and content, believing it can grasp social reality directly in this way. In truth, the social, extra-architectural, and inner-architectural aspects do not relate to one another as an "either-or": they are different from one another and are conveyed by one another. For that reason, Lukács denounced the view of realism that tries to understand works of art as simple social phenomena without also constantly integrating their particular aesthetic constitution: *they decline into a trite sociologism*.

Architecture belongs to the "world of commodities" and is determined by particular social needs. To satisfy these needs, architecture creates certain material-technical structures, but, in a second reflection [*Widerspiegelung*], it transforms these structures that exist as a reality "for themselves" such that they become a *reality "for us."* (This is exactly what Lukács charges functionalism with: that, in a sense, it equates the second reflection, which turns the building "for itself" into a work of art "for us," with the first reflection that produces the building "for itself," and thus sublates the "vividness" of architecture.)

This definition of the architectural reality is correct, but it does not avoid the risk of being perceived as "contentist," so long as this reality is studied from "outside" and one does not proceed from within it. The Russian formalists deserve credit for having asked the *question of realism* (in literature) from "*inside*." Roman Jakobson's essay of 1921 refers to the processes that realism employs. The reason for realism should be sought in the development of society, but the processes that realize it aesthetically obtain their significance inside literary structures themselves. (The use of popular language, for example, is not realistic because of its "populism" but because of its antagonism to "high" language: by means of the violation of norms that it represents and from which obtains its significance in relation to the violated norm.)

Concerning this level—the level of inner-architectural reality, which is often not perceived at all in the question of realism in architecture—we will speak below, at the risk of seeming one-sided.

In the realistic approach, art is often reduced to ideology or to offering a "picture" of society. The philosophers, sociologists, and so on who find themselves restricted by this idea are those who attribute to art merely an expressive function and who differ from it only in relation to something other. At least one of the roots of this *"contentist" obstacle*, which persists even in a Marxist aesthetician such as Lukács, was clearly recognized by Walter Siti in his book *Il realismo dell'avanguardia* [The realism of the avant-garde]; namely, when he writes that contentism

> "is derived, strictly speaking, from a sin of idealist origin; the work cannot be considered a phenomenon because one cannot find in it the mechanism of work."

This insight leads us to starting out from work in our study.

"Art is based on an ability, and it is an ability to labor. Anyone who admires art admires labor. And *it is necessary to know something about this labor* in order to be able to admire it and enjoy its result, the work of art." (Bertolt Brecht, "Betrachtung der Kunst und Kunst der Betrachtung" [Contemplation of art and the art of contemplation])

Understood in this way as labor that can be determined based on the dialectically conceived productive process that it represents, architecture turns out to be a special form of knowledge that is its own object, as material that is always worked out

"precisely by the imposition of the complex (sensuous-technical-ideological) structure which constitutes it as an *object of knowledge*, however crude, which constitutes it as the object it will transform, whose *forms* it will change in the course of its development process in order to produce knowledges which are constantly *transformed* but will always apply to its *object*, in the sense of *object of knowledge*."
(Louis Althusser and Étienne Balibar, *Lire le capital* [*Reading Capital*])

There is therefore no Archimedean point outside the architectural work from which one could understand the "teleological" meaning, the essence, the "nature" of architecture. If one disregards the labor that is concretized in a work, it appears in a deceptive "naturalness" that conceals its artificiality: the fact that it is the product of certain labor processes and techniques that establish the *functioning of the poetic fact*.

In other words, architecture not only reflects a social reality but points to its own reality of form.

"An architectural mass, a relationship of tones, a painter's touch, an engraved line exist and possess value primarily in and of themselves …, the fundamental content of form is a *formal* content." (Henri Focillon, *La vie des forms* [*The Life of Forms in Art*])

From this derives the call for a theory immanent to architecture that studies this reality by working out the categories suited to grasping the similarity and difference of all works and the poetic approaches that can be found in them (the rhetorical figures, their updating, and so on).

When Bernhard Hoesli describes "transparency" as creating locations in space

"which can be assigned to two or more systems of reference—where the classification is undefined and the choice between one classification possibility or another remains open" (commentary on Colin Rowe and Robert Slutzky, *Transparency*)

he is characterizing one of these rhetorical figures that has found its more multilayered realization in modern art but can be traced again and again in the history of art. The immediate collision of parts (*pezzi e parti*) in Aldo Rossi's design for Scandicci (1968) as a case of parataxis, the inflection in the house in Chestnut Hill (1962) by Robert Venturi, the various forms of symmetry—they are all such *rhetorical figures*. In the forms of their actualization, they constitute the poetics of the works. For example, mirror symmetry is systematically called into question by Le Corbusier: "non-symmetrical balance" (Klee) of the northern facade in Garches (1925–27), a certain kind of chiasma in the first design for Carthage (1928), and so on.

It is illuminating for the rhetorical status of architecture that Rossi also included the aqueduct of Segovia among the points of reference for his design in Milan-Gallaratese (1970–72). The difference in time and the difference in purpose separating Roman engineering and a residential complex confirm that for him it has to do with *an analogy of purely formal values*. In the aqueduct, Rossi saw the mastering of large scale by a strict rhythmic articulation (of particular importance in this respect is the theoretical work written by Ginzburg in 1923: *Rhythm in Architecture*!).

When Rossi says of analogy that it is

"a way to understand the world of forms and things so directly that it can hardly be expressed other than through other new things" ("Analoge Architektur" [Analogous architecture], lecture in Zurich in 1976)

he is calling for anything but an irrational approach to the world of forms; rather, he is drawing the logical and necessary conclusion from the insight that the special, also sensory experience of space, form, materials (and the associated pleasure) originates in the most appropriate way from comparison.

The tradition of the métier itself proves the effectiveness and necessity of this kind of architectural knowledge: the provision of evidence as usual in the treatises, with their very different comparative plates based entirely on a structured, ordered inventory of variations; the traditional teaching of architecture founded on the copy, imitation, the building survey, working in the studio, and, finally, also on study journeys (the stay in Rome and the *voyage d'Orient*).

↓ fig. 4   Aldo Rossi, Competition entry for the town hall of Scandicci, 1968, photograph of a model.

(Klee) der Nordfassade in Garches (1925–27), eine bestimmte Art von Chiasma im ersten Entwurf für Karthago (1928), undsoweiter.

Für den rhetorischen Status der Architektur ist es erhellend, dass Rossi unter den Bezugspunkten für seinen Entwurf in Mailand-Gallaratese (1970–1972) auch den Aquaedukt von Segovia aufzählt. Gerade der zeitliche Unterschied und der Unterschied des Zweckes, die den römischen Ingenieurbau und die Wohnanlage trennen, bestätigen, dass es ihm um *eine Analogie von rein formalen Werten* zu tun ist. Im Aquaedukt sah Rossi die Meisterung der grossen Dimension durch eine strenge rhythmische Gliederung. (Von besonderer Bedeutung ist in dieser Hinsicht das 1923 von Ginzburg verfasste theoretische Werk über *Rhythmus in der Architektur!)*

Wenn Rossi von der Analogie sagt, sie sei

«eine Art, die Welt der Formen und der Dinge so unmittelbar zu verstehen, dass sie kaum anders ausgedrückt werden kann als durch andere neue Dinge» *(Analoge Architektur*, Vorlesung in Zürich 1976),

dann fordert er alles andere als einen irrationalen Zugang zur Welt der Formen; er zieht vielmehr den logischen und notwendigen Schluss aus der Einsicht, dass die besondere, auch sinnliche, Erfahrung von Raum, Form, Material (und das damit verbundene Vergnügen) auf angemessenste Weise dem Vergleich entspringt.

Die Tradition des Metiers selber beweist die Wirksamkeit und Notwendigkeit dieser Art von architektonischer Erkenntnis: die Beweisführung, wie sie in den Traktaten üblich ist mit ihren verschiedensten vergleichenden Tafeln, die ganz auf einem gegliederten, geordneten Inventar von Varianten beruhen; die traditionelle Architekturlehre, die sich auf die Kopie, die Nachahmung, die Bauaufnahme, die Arbeit im Atelier und schliesslich auch auf die Studienreise stützt (den Romaufenthalt wie den «voyage d'orient»).

Nach unserer Meinung gilt auch für die Architektur-Produktion, was Jacques Derrida über die Produktion von Text schreibt:

«Soit dans l'ordre du discours parlé, soit dans l'ordre du discours écrit (das gilt auch für den architektonischen Diskurs), *aucun élément peut fonctionner comme signe sans renvoyer à un autre élément* qui à son tour n'est pas seulement présent comme tel. Cette concatenation fait que chaque élément, phonème ou graphème (oder Archem, um einen Begriff zu verwenden, der in der Semiologie der Architektur eingeführt wurde) se constitue à partir de la trace d'autres éléments présente en lui. Cette concatenation, ce tissu est alors le texte qui ne se produit que par la transformation d'autres textes« *(Sémiologie et grammatologie;* in *Social Science Information,* Juni 1968).

Der Ort dieser Veränderungen ist die Geschichte. Nach Karl Popper aber sind Geschichte, das heisst die Beschreibung der Veränderung, und Wesen «Natur», das heisst das, was während der Veränderung unverändert bleibt, korrelative Begriffe. Noch mehr: die «Natur» einer Sache setzt Veränderung geradezu voraus, denn diese bringt die verschiedenen Seiten der Sache zum Vorschein, also ihre «Natur». Sie kann aufgefasst werden als die Summe der einer Sache innewohnenden Möglichkeiten und die Veränderung als die Aktualisierung ihrer «Natur». Daraus zieht Popper den *Schluss, dass die Natur einer Sache nur durch ihre Veränderung erkannt werden* kann und dass die Begriffe zu ihrer Beschreibung historische sein müssen (Das Elend der Historismus). Das ist der ge-

7

↓ fig. 5 Robert Venturi and John Rauch, House in Chestnut Hill, Philadelphia, 1962.

↓ fig. 7 Le Corbusier, Villa in Garches, 1927, entry facade.

naue Sinn des scheinbar hermetischen Satzes von Rossi:

«l'architettura sono le architetture».

Und das führt weiter zum Schluss, dass sich die Bedeutung der Architektur nur in der Beziehung zu sich selber, zu ihrer Tradition bestimmt, wobei Tradition die Werke und die Vorstellungen, die wir von diesen haben, gleichermassen umfasst. Mit anderen Worten, dass die grundlegende Dimension der Bedeutung in der *Bezogenheit der architektonischen Sprache auf sich selber* liegt (Autoreflexivität). Die Geschichte der Architektur ist somit nicht einfach eine grosse Deponie von schon gemachten Erfahrungen, sie ist vielmehr der Ort, an dem sich die Bedeutung der Architektur bildet. Das garantiert den intersubjektiven, also relativ objektiven Charakter der mit ihr verbundenen begrifflichen und sinnlichen Erfahrung.

Die Bedeutung eines Werkes verstehen heisst, seine Lage in einem dichten Netz von Beziehungen zu bestimmen. Je dichter dieses Netz ist, je zahlreicher die Beispiele und je konkreter das Wissen, desto strukturierter erscheint das Feld der Architektur für den Betrachter, gleichgültig welches seine Vorlieben sind. Für den Architekten bestimmt sich dieses Wissen als *Metier:* dieses

«setzt die Grenze gegen die schlechte Unendlichkeit in den Werken; es bestimmt, was mit einem Begriff der Hegelschen Logik die abstrakte Möglichkeit der Kunstwerke heissen dürfte, zu ihrer konkreten (Theodor W. Adorno: *Aesthetische Theorie*).

Architektur ist der Gegenstand einer besonderen, auf ihre eigene Wirklichkeit bezogenen Erkenntnis. *Das macht sie zu einem unverzichtbaren Faktum.* Diese Wirklichkeit und ihre Probleme aufzugeben im Namen einer Unmittelbarkeit des Ausdruckes (die sich oft als gesellschaftliches Engagement versteht) bedeutet, sich zur architektonischen Aphasie zu verurteilen, unsere Sinnlichkeit einmal mehr um grundlegende Erfahrungen zu betrügen. Denn nur der platteste Naturalismus mag sich einbilden, es gebe spontane Sinneserlebnisse, die nicht von einem gesellschaftlich-geschichtlichen Wissen vermittelt sind. Auch die Bildung der fünf Sinne ist, wie Marx bemerkte,

fig. 6 →
Le Corbusier,
Villa in Carthage,
1928, first project.
Analytical drawing
from a study
by R. Reichlin

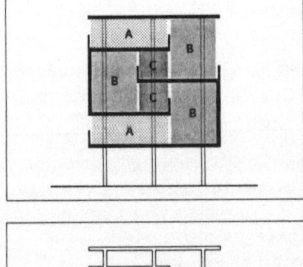

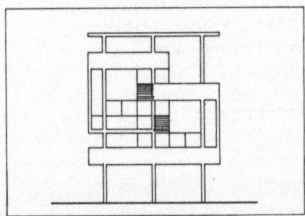

↓ fig. 8 The Roman aqueduct of Segovia.

↓ fig. 9 Aldo Rossi, Residential unit in Gallaratese, Milan, 1970.

«eine Arbeit der ganzen bisherigen Weltgeschichte»
(Oekonomisch-philosophische Manuskripte).

Unsere obigen Gedankengänge legten das Schwergewicht auf die autonome Entstehung der Architektur. In ihrer Entwicklung eignet sich die Architektur aber auch ständig neue Wirklichkeiten an, Techniken und Materialien, Probleme und Erfindungen, undsoweiter. *Ihre Entstehung ist sowohl autonom wie heteronom.* Die besten Werke von James Stirling bilden einen eigentlichen Diskurs über dieses «both-and». So eignet sich die Ingenieurschule in Leicester (1959–1963) Materiale, Mittel und Konstruktionen des Ingenieurbaues (des 19. Jahrhunderts) an, teilweise unmittelbar, teilweise vermittelt durch die Werke des Russischen Konstruktivismus, also einer Bewegung, die ihrerseits diese Aneignung zu ihrem Programm gemacht hatte. Die heteronome Entstehung scheint beim gleichen Stirling, im Olivetti-Gebäude in Haslemere (1968–1972), an eine Grenze gestossen zu sein: in den Klassentrakten reproduziert die Architektur ganz die Formensprache des Industrial Design, auf die sich Stirling in einem Vergleich bewusst beruft. Statt in den Begriffen der Architektur über die Sprache des Design zu sprechen, über ihre Mechanismen, wird die Architektur dieser Trakte sozusagen von ihr «gesprochen».

Eine besondere Form der heteronomen Entstehung findet sich in den Werken von Venturi und Rauch. Ihre Aufmerksamkeit gilt der «ge- wöhnlichen» Architektur von Suburbia, die sie zum Ausgangspunkt ihrer eigenen «hohen» Architektur machen.

«Wir sagen, unsere Bauten seien gewöhnlich (...). Aber unsere Bauten sind natürlich auch aussergewöhnlich, ausser-gewöhnlich. Obwohl sie gewöhnlich ausschauen, sind sie es doch überhaupt nicht, sondern sind, wie wir hoffen, anspruchsvolle Architektur, die vom Kleinen bis ins Grosse sehr sorgfältig durchgearbeitet wurde. Literaturkritiker kennen dieses Stilmittel schon seit langem, den Gebrauch von gewöhnlicher alltäglicher Sprache, von Klischees — was die Werke von Eliot und Joyce zum Beispiel auszeichnet und ausser-gewöhnlich macht. In allen Künsten ist das eine weitverbreitete Methode, die auch jedermann bekannt ist, offenbar nur den Architekten nicht» *(Architektur im Widerspruch).*

Die Theorie des «decorated shed», die die Venturis aufstellen, «learning from what's there», scheint die Architektur zur Warenhülle zu erklären. Sie scheint auf diese Weise eine grundlegende Erfahrung, die der «Mann auf der Strasse» in der Warenwelt macht, im Freud'schen Sinn zu rationalisieren: den Widerspruch von Warenschein und Gebrauchswert. Indem sie die Architektur auf das reine Zeichen beschränkt, bedeutet sie obendrein einen nicht leicht zu nehmenden Verzicht auf sinnliche Erfahrungen. (Die Venturis bemängeln an der «hohen» Architektur gerade, dass man durch sie hindurchgehen müsse, um sie zu geniessen.) Dass die aus der Theorie des «decorated shed» hervorgegangenen Werke aber eine klare Widerspiegelung des genannten Widerspruches sind, verdanken sie der List, die den Kunst-

9

↓fig. 10   Venturi and Rauch, Fire Station No. 4,
Columbus, Indiana, 1965.

werken eigen ist, das heisst dem *Umstand, dass die Antagonismen der Wirklichkeit als Gegenstand der Poetik in ihnen wiederkehren* und als Probleme der Form:

«Form ist das an den Kunstwerken, durch das diese sich als kritisch in sich selbst erweisen» (Adorno: *Aesthetische Theorie*).

In diesem Sinn ist die Architektur von Venturi und Rauch auf gleiche Weise realistisch, wie es die Romane von Balzac sind.

Die Verdrängung der eigenen konkreten Wirklichkeit der Architektur hat ihre Reduktion auf den «Gebrauchsgegenstand» mit sich gebracht. Diese fügt sich ein in die allgemeine Tendenz, das kontemplative Leben vom praktischen zu trennen und es einzuschränken auf eine kompensatorisch-konsolatorische Funktion. Das praktische Leben lässt nur das Verlangen (désir) zu, das der Motor des kapitalistischen Verwertungsprozesses ist, es schliesst aber das sich selbst genügende Vergnügen (plaisir) aus. Für den Ausschluss des Vergnügens aus der Architektur gilt, was Roland Barthes in seiner herausfordernden Schrift *Le plaisir du texte* schreibt:

«Un Français sur deux, parait-il, ne lit pas; la moitié de la France est privée, se prive du plaisir du texte. Or on ne déplore jamais cette disgrâce nationale que d'un point de vue humaniste, comme si, en boudant le livre, les Français renonçaient seulement à un bien moral, à une valeur noble. Il vaudrait mieux faire la sombre, la stupide, la tragique histoire de tous les plaisirs auxquels les sociétés objectent ou renoncent: il y a un obscurantisme du plaisir.»

Das Vergnügen an der Architektur ist eines dieser aufgegebenen Vergnügen. *Es gilt, im Namen des Realismus das Recht auf das Vergnügen an der Architektur zu fordern.*

Quellen

Georg Schmidt, «Naturalismus und Realismus» (1959), in: *Umgang mit Kunst – Ausgewählte Schriften 1940–1963*, Basel, 1976, Zweite unveränderte Auflage 1976, S. 36.
Hans Schmidt, *Die Technik baut*, in: *Das Wohnen*, 1930, Heft 6, S. 120–121.
Vgl. Martin Steinmann, *Hans Schmidt. Zur Frage des Sozialistischen Realismus*, in: Werk, Heft 10, Oktober 1972.
Karel Teige, s. den Beitrag von O. Macel in diesem Heft.
Le Corbusier, *Urbanisme*, Paris, 1925, S. 47–48.
Georg Lukacs, *Aesthetik. Teil I*, Neuwied und Berlin, 1972, S. 402 ff.
Roman Jakobson, «Realismus», in tschechischer Sprache publiziert in: *Cerven, IV*, 1921, S. 300–304.
Walter Siti, *Il realismo dell'anvanguardia*, Torino, 1975, S. 7.
Bertolt Brecht, «Betrachtungen der Kunst und Kunst der Betrachtung», in Bertolt Brecht: *Ueber Realismus*, Frankfurt am Main, 2. Auflage, 1971, S. 80.
Vgl. Marcelin Pleynet, *L'enseignement de la peinture*, Paris, 1971.
Louis Althusser, Etienne Balibar, *Lire le Capital*, Paris, 1971, S. 49–50.
Henri Focillon, *Vie des Formes*, Vendôme, 6. Auflage, 1970, S. 5.
Rowe und Slutzky, Bernhard Hoesli, *Transparenz*, Basel und Stuttgart, 1968, S. 49.
Aldo Rossi, «Analoge Architektur», Vorlesung an der ETH-Zürich, Juli 1976.
Jacques Derrida, «Sémiologie et grammatologie», in: *Social Science Information*, Juni 1968.
Vgl. Karl Popper, *Das Elend des Historizismus*, Tübingen, 4. Auflage, 1974, S. 26.

Fortsetzung Seite 24

fig. 11 →
Olivetti Divisumma-18.

fig. 12 ⇉
James Stirling, Olivetti Training Center, Haslemere, 1969.

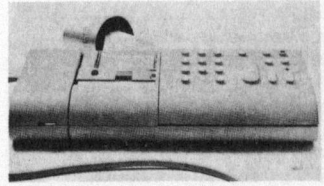 

In our view, what Jacques Derrida writes on the production of text also applies to the production of architecture:

> "Whether in the order of spoken or written discourse [this also applies to architectural discourse], *no element can function as a sign without referring to another element* which itself is not simply present. This interweaving results in each "element"—phoneme or grapheme [or *archeme*, to use a term that has been introduced into the semiology of architecture]—being constituted on the basis of the trace within it of the other elements of the chain or system. This interweaving, this textile, is the *text* produced only in the transformation of another text." ("Sémiologie et grammatologie" [Semiology and Grammatology], *Social Science Information*, June 1968)

The site of these changes is history. According to Karl Popper, however, history (i.e., the description of change) and essence, "nature" (i.e., what remains unchanged during the change) are correlative concepts. More than that: the "nature" of a thing all but presumes change, since the latter brings the different sides of the thing to the fore; that is, its "nature." It [history] can be grasped as the sum of the possibilities inherent in a thing and change as the updating of their "nature." From this Popper draws the conclusion that *nature can only be known through its change* and that the concepts to describe it must be historical (The Poverty of Historicism). That is the precise meaning of this seemingly hermetic sentence from Rossi:

> "the architectures are the architecture."

And that leads to the conclusion that the significance of architecture is determined only in relation to itself, to its tradition, whereby tradition comprises in equal measure both the works and the ideas we have of them. In other words, the fundamental dimension of meaning *lies in the relatedness of architectural language to itself* (self-reflexivity). The history of architecture is thus not simply a great repository of experiences gained; rather, it is the place where the meaning of architecture is formed. That guarantees the intersubjective—that is, relatively objective—character of the terminological and sensory experience associated with it.

Understanding the significance of a work means determining its position within a dense network of relationships. The denser this network is, the more numerous the examples, and the more concrete the knowledge, the more structured the field of architecture seems to the observer, no matter his preferences. For the architect, this knowledge is determined as métier: this

> "sets boundaries against the bad infinity in works. It makes concrete what, in the language of Hegel's *Logic*, might be called the abstract possibility of artworks." (Theodor W. Adorno, *Aesthetic Theory*)

Architecture is the object of a special knowledge related to its own reality. That makes it an undeniable fact. Abandoning this reality and its problems in the name of an immediacy of expression (which is often understood to be social engagement) means condemning oneself to architectural aphasia, once again deceiving our senses concerning fundamental experiences. For only the tritest naturalism can imagine there could be spontaneous sensory experiences that are not mediated by a social, historical knowledge. The forming of the five senses is also, as Marx noted,

> "a labor of the entire history of the world." (*Ökonomisch-philosophische Manuskripte* [Economic-philosophical manuscripts])

Our thought processes above placed the main emphasis on the autonomous creation of architecture. Over its evolution, architecture has, however, also continually acquired new realities, techniques and materials, problems and inventions, and so on. *Its creation is both autonomous and heteronomous.* The best works of James Stirling represent a genuine discourse on this "both-and." For example, his engineering school in Leicester (1959–63) adapts materials, means, and structural engineering techniques (from the nineteenth century)—sometimes directly, sometimes mediated by the works of Russian constructivism, a movement that had for its part made this kind of adaptation its program. Heteronomous creation seems to have reached a limit in the same Stirling's work; namely, in the Olivetti building in Haslemere (1968–72): in the classroom wings, the architecture reproduces completely the formal language of industrial design, to which Stirling deliberately appeals in an analogy. Rather than speaking with the terms of architecture about the language of design, about its mechanisms, the architecture of these wings is, as it were, "spoken" by the latter.

One special form of heteronomous creation is found in the works of Venturi and Rauch.

They pay attention to the "ordinary" architecture of suburbia, which they make the point of departure for their own "high" architecture.

> "We say our buildings are 'ordinary'.... But, of course, our buildings in another sense are extraordinary, *extra*-ordinary. Although they look ordinary, they are not ordinary at all, but are, we hope, sophisticated architecture designed very carefully, from each square inch to the total proportions of the building. Literary critics have known about this all along, that is, about the use of clichés, the use of common, everyday language which makes the literature of Eliot and Joyce, for instance, *extra*-ordinary. This is a widely-used method in all art, and it is well-known, except, apparently, to architects." (*Conversations with Architects*)

The theory of the "decorated shed" that the Venturis propose, "learning from what's there," seems to declare architecture to be the packaging of a commodity. In this way, it seems to rationalize in the Freudian sense a fundamental experience that the "man on the street" has in the world of commodities: the contradiction between commodity appearance and use value. By restricting architecture to pure drawing, moreover, it represents a not-easy-to-accept renunciation of sensory experiences. (The Venturis criticize "high" architecture precisely because one has to walk through it in order to enjoy it.) But the fact that the works that emerged from the theory of the "decorated shed" are a clear reflection of the aforementioned contradiction is indebted to the trick inherent in works of art; that is, to the *fact that the antagonisms of reality reappear in them as the object of poetics* and as problems of form:

> "Form ... is that through which artworks prove self-critical." (Adorno, *Ästhetische Theorie* [Aesthetic Theory])

In that sense, the architecture of Venturi and Rauch is realistic in the same way that the novels of Balzac are.

The repression of architecture's own concrete reality has brought with it its reduction to an "object of daily use." This is in keeping with a general trend to separate contemplative life from practical life and to restrict it to a compensatory, consolatory function. Practical life permits only desire (*désir*), which is the driving force of the capitalist process of valorization, but it precludes self-satisfying pleasure (*plaisir*). What Roland Barthes writes in his challenging book *Le plaisir du texte* [*The Pleasure of the Text*] applies to the exclusion of pleasure from architecture:

> "One out of every two Frenchmen, it appears, does not read; half of France is deprived—deprives itself of the pleasure of the text. Now this national disgrace is never deplored except from a humanistic point of view, as though by ignoring books the French were merely forgoing some moral good, some noble value. It would be better to write the grim, stupid, tragic history of all the pleasures which societies object to or renounce: there is an obscurantism of pleasure."

The pleasure of architecture is one of these deprived pleasures. *The goal is to demand in the name of realism the right to the pleasure of architecture.*

fig. 4 Aldo Rossi, Residential unit in Gallaratese, Milan, 1970. The portico.

der Zukunft zu setzen. Nochmals dieselben Beispiele: das Ospedale Maggiore von Filarete in Mailand, die Universität in Pavia von Piermarini, die Unité d'habitation von Le Corbusier, die Convention Hall von Mies sind zeitlich weitauseinanderliegende Bauten, geeignet zur Demonstration dieses Anspruchs und dieses Schicksals. Es handelt sich um Architekturen, die bestimmten Kulturen entsprechen, die aber in der gemeinsamen Tendenz, sich vor allem als «Typen» zu fixieren, allgemein und progressiv, das heisst im richtigsten Sinne archetypisch werden — im Sinne der «Pyramiden» Meyers, um uns richtig zu verstehen. Mehr als einer Erwartung der Gegenwart zu entsprechen interpretieren diese Architekturen die Utopie, das heisst sie evozieren «Angemessenheit».

In Wirklichkeit sind die mittelalterliche Stadt, die Kathedrale und das Schloss die Elemente der monarchischen oder der neoklassischen Stadt, sind die Paläste und Plätze in ihren Formen immer mehr als die wirkliche Stadt, obwohl sie diese tatsächlich konstituieren.

In diesem Sinne darf der Realismus nicht davon absehen, diesem besonderen Schicksal des formal-architektonischen Zeugnisses Rechnung zu tragen. Wenn die Architektur diese ihre Aufgabe ausser Acht lässt, verfehlt sie den Sinn ihrer «Dauer» selbst.

Dies gilt auch für die persönlichere Untersuchung. Deswegen hält es schwer, einen grossen Teil des heutigen Experimentalismus hinzunehmen, obschon sich dieser der Architektur gegenüber affirmativ verhält. Damit meine ich jene Untersuchungen über geometrische Komposition und Dekomposition, die am stärksten ihre abstrakte und radikale Grundlage zeigen; oder jene offen und programmatisch «unvollendeten» oder «vorläufigen»; oder dann jene Untersuchungen, die sich auf die Erfahrung einer anderen Tätigkeit wie Bildhauerei oder Malerei stützen (für diese letzteren Fälle gilt immer noch die von Michelangelo ausgesprochene Meinung; dieser ist nie davon abgegangen, der Architektur den Vorrang einzuräumen).

Vom gleichen Gesichtspunkt aus müssen wir auch jene Erfahrungen beurteilen, die sich programmatisch am Problem des Realismus gemessen haben: ich beziehe mich, abgesehen von der entscheidenden und komplexen Erfahrung der Sowjetunion und der sozialistischen Länder, beispielsweise auf den architektonischen Neorealismus der Nachkriegszeit in Italien — aber es ist auch jener viel weniger diskutierte «pragmatische» Weg eines Grossteils der nordeuropäischen Architektur in Betracht zu ziehen. Ich denke an das grobe Missverständnis, das zu einer zugleich paradoxen und degradierenden Nachahmung des Bildes der gotisch-bürgerlichen Stadt führte. Die Architektur kann diesem ihrem Schicksal nicht entgehen, im weitesten Sinne kollektives Werk zu sein; ebenso wenig kann sie die besondere Welt ihrer Darstellung umgehen, indem sie beispielsweise thematische Probleme missachtet, die ihr seit je eigen waren (siehe die Frage des «Monumentalen» und der absurde Streit über «Monumentalismus»).

Nur wenn sie sich mit den Themen ihrer eigenen geschichtlichen Erfahrung auseinandersetzt, kann sie sich mit dieser von neuem auf rationale Weise messen und danach streben, im alltäglichen Leben ein konkreter Bezug zu sein.

Uebers. H. Helfenstein, B. Reichlin und M. Steinmann

Zum Problem der innerarchitektonischen Wirklichkeit (Fortsetzung von Seite 11)

Vgl. Bruno Reichlin und Fabio Reinhart, «Die Historie als Teil der Architekturtheorie», in: *archithese*, Heft 11, 1974.
Theodor W. Adorno, *Aesthetische Theorie*, Frankfurt am Main, 2. Auflage, 1974, S. 71–72.
Karl Marx, *Oekonomisch-philosophische Manuskripte*, in: MEW Erg.-Bd. I, Berlin (DDR), 1968, S. 541.
Robert Venturi in: Heinrich Klotz und John W. Cook, *Architektur im Widerspruch*, Zürich, 1974, S. 254.

Vgl. Wolfgang Fritz Haug, *Kritik der Warenästhetik*, Frankfurt am Main, 1971.
Vgl. Robert Venturi, Denise Scott Brown, Steven Izenour, *Learning From Las Vegas*, Cambridge, Mass. and London, 1972, S. 65 ff.
Theodor W. Adorno, *Aesthetische Theorie*, Frankfurt am Main, 2. Auflage, 1974, S. 16.
Roland Barthes, *Le plaisir du texte*, Paris, 1973, S. 74.

SOURCES

[Otto Neurath, "Protocol Statements," in *Philosophical Papers 1913–1946*, ed. and trans. Robert S. Cohen and Marie Neurath with Carolyn R. Fawcett (Dordrecht: 1983), 92.]

Georg Schmidt, "Naturalismus und Realismus" (1959), in *Umgang mit Kunst: Ausgewählte Schriften, 1940–1963*, 2nd ed. (Basel, 1976), 36.

Hans Schmidt, "Die Technik baut," *Das Wohnen*, 6 (1930): 120–21.

Martin Steinmann. "Hans Schmidt: Zur Frage des Sozialistischen Realismus," *Werk*, 10 (October 1972).

Karel Teige. See the essay by O. Macel in this issue.

Le Corbusier, *Urbanisme* (Paris, 1925), 47–48. [Le Corbusier, *The City of To-morrow and Its Planning*, trans. Frederick Etchells (New York, 2013), 49–50.]

Georg Lukács, *Ästhetik*, pt. 1 (Neuwied and Berlin, 1972), 402ff.

Roman Jakobson, "Realismus" [in Czech], in *Cerven* 4 (1921): 300.

Walter Siti, *Il realismo dell'avanguardia* (Turin, 1975), 7.

Bertolt Brecht, "Betrachtungen der Kunst und Kunst der Betrachtung," in *Über Realismus*, 2nd ed. (Frankfurt am Main, 1971), 80.

Marcelin Pleynet, *L'enseignement de la peinture* (Paris, 1971).

Louis Althusser and Étienne Balibar, *Lire le Capital* (Paris, 1971), 49–50. [Louis Althusser, "From *Capital* to Marx's Philosophy," in Louis Althusser and Étienne Balibar, *Reading Capital*, trans. Ben Brewster (New York, 1997), 43.]

Henri Focillon, *Vie des formes*, 6th ed. ([Paris:] Vendôme, 1970), p. 5. [Henri Focillon, *The Life of Forms in Art*, trans. Charles Beecher Hogan and George Kubler with S.L. Faison (New York, 1989), 35.]

Bernhard Hoesli, in Colin Rowe and Robert Slutzky, *Transparenz* (Basel and Stuttgart, 1968), 49. [Bernhard Hoesli, "Commentary," trans. Jori Walker, in Colin Rowe and Robert Slutzky, *Transparency* (Basel, 1997), 61.]

Aldo Rossi, "Analoge Architektur" (lecture at the ETH Zürich, July 1976).

Jacques Derrida, "Sémiologie et grammatologie," *Social Science Information*, June 1968. [Jacques Derrida, "Semiology and Grammatology: Interview with Julia Kristeva," in *Positions*, trans. Alan Bass (Chicago, 1972), 26.]

Karl Popper, *The Poverty of Historicism* (London, 1957), 33.

Bruno Reichlin and Fabio Reinhart, "Die Historie als Teil der Architekturtheorie," *archithese,* 11 (1974).

Theodor W. Adorno, *Aesthetische Theorie*, 2nd ed. (Frankfurt am Main, 1974), 71–72. [*Aesthetic Theory*, ed. and trans. Robert Hullot-Kentor (Minneapolis, 1997), 44.]

Karl Marx, *Oekonomisch-philosophische Manuskripte*, in *Marx-Engels-Werke*, suppl. vol. 1 ([East] Berlin, 1968), 541. [Karl Marx, *Economic and Philosophic Manuscripts of 1844*, trans. Martin Milligan (New York, 1988), 109.]

Robert Venturi in "Robert Venturi and Denise Scott Brown," in John W. Cook and Heinrich Klotz, *Conversations with Architects* (New York, 1973), 248.

Wolfgang Fritz Haug, *Kritik der Warenästhetik* (Frankfurt am Main, 1971). [Wolfgang Fritz Haug, *Critique of Commodity Aesthetics*, trans. Robert Bock (Minneapolis, 1986).]

Robert Venturi, Denise Scott Brown, and Steven Izenour, *Learning from Las Vegas* (Cambridge, MA, 1972), 65ff.

Theodor W. Adorno, *Aesthetische Theorie*, 2nd ed. (Frankfurt am Main, 1974), 16.

Roland Barthes, *Le plaisir du texte* (Paris, 1973), 74. [Roland Barthes, *The Pleasure of the Text*, trans. Richard Miller (New York, 1975), 46.]

III URBANISM AND CONSUMPTION

213
Between Crisis and Myth:
The City at the
End of Modernity
    by Torsten Lange

232
Questions for Henri Lefèbvre
    by Jean-Claude Widmer

242
Three Warnings against
a Mystical Rebirth of Urbanism
    by Superstudio

252
Collective Housing:
Theories and Experiments
of the Utopian Socialists Robert
Owen (1771–1858) and
Charles Fourier (1772–1837)
    by Franziska Bollerey
    and Kristiana Hartmann

273
"New Babylon": The New
York of the 1920s and
the Search for Americanism
    by Manfredo Tafuri

296
Roxy, Noah, and
Radio City Music Hall
    by Rem Koolhaas

Between Crisis and Myth

The City at the End of Modernity

Torsten Lange

The 1970s marked a critical juncture in the discourse surrounding city planning and architecture. The period was characterized by a pervasive sense of crisis that underscored the limitations of modernist approaches to urban development. This notion of crisis also found expression on the pages of *archithese*. Significantly, after the journal's relaunch as a series of thematic monographs in 1972, the inaugural issue was dedicated to the "crisis of city planning" and put a question mark behind the word *urbanism* in its title. "Most new cities," Stanislaus von Moos remarked in the issue's editorial, "still give the impression that city planning, urbanism, is a matter of composing volumes in space."[1] Nevertheless, for more than a decade, word had been out that architects' urban plans, no matter how ambitious and well-crafted, played a relatively subordinate role in city-making processes that were chiefly determined by economic and social factors.[2] This admission—that design endeavors were inherently subservient to these intricate forces—represented a seismic shift in perspective, highlighting the limited authority architects exerted in shaping the urban milieu. Von Moos's barb against architects: plan-makers were not necessarily good planners. Furthermore, "a good architectural plan might even get in the way of sound planning development."[3] While this predicament had haunted the profession for at least a century as architects shifted their attention from erecting monuments for those in power to more quotidian challenges, the sentiment that experts in building design may not have all the answers to people's ever-changing needs was now more acutely felt—first among those affected by architectural solutions, city residents and users, and later by architects and planners.[4] Because of its scale of intervention, city planning, more than other design tasks, causes unforeseen consequences, often with far-reaching ecological, material, and socioeconomic ramifications. In their 1973 essay "Dilemmas in a General Theory of Planning," Horst Rittel and Melvin Webber put a name (and theory) to the frequently perceived "wickedness" of the problems confronted by design and planning professionals.[5] Planning problems, they argued, due to their uniquely complex and open-ended character, resist being reduced to a set of general principles and therefore defy definitive and static solutions in favor of temporary resolutions. Arguably, precisely this recognition of architecture's relatively restricted influence on the urban scale threw the profession and its long-held beliefs into crisis—with ripple effects lasting to this day. This is not to deny that, during the 1970s, cities underwent genuine crises that were symptoms of more significant ecological, economic, and social upheavals.

A sense of disenchantment with modernist urban planning had already set in during the 1960s. Until then, professionals were widely in agreement not only in their assessment of the condition of the "industrial city"—an ideal type in the Weberian sense—but also concerning the broader aims, analytical methods, and instruments with which planning sought to overcome the perceived common ills of the modern metropolis: its uncontrolled growth and resulting formlessness, congestion, pollution, poor housing, and segregation. From the start of the decade, the clash between city planners' idealized visions and urban realities on the ground increasingly received critical attention; moreover, existing urban forms and their qualities became objects of analysis and reappraisal.[6] In 1961, Jane Jacobs warned of the imminent death of North American cities at the hands of "modern, orthodox city planning and rebuilding."[7] Only a few years later, across the Atlantic, Berlin-based journalists Wolf Jobst Siedler and Gina Angreß together with photographer

Elisabeth Niggemeyer announced the "murder" of the historic European city (in contrast to Jacobs, however, they refrained from declaring modern planning guilty of the crime, instead noting that the historic city had become the victim of new social conditions).[8] Preceding the historic preservation movement, which gained traction in the run-up to the European Architectural Heritage Year 1975, the authors mourned not the loss of the city's material fabric per se but rather the disappearance of a sense of "urbanity" that, they claimed, had persisted over time and enabled affective experiences of the city and its "dwelling figures" (*Wohnfiguren*).[9] In 1965, psychologist Alexander Mitscherlich diagnosed modern cities as increasingly "inhospitable" environments that caused human isolation and alienation.[10] The growing interest in urban patterns and their experiential qualities was mirrored in the architectural and planning disciplines through studies informed by Gestalt psychology, like those of Kevin Lynch.[11] Furthermore, Aldo Rossi championed a renewed understanding of the continuity of urban form and memory through adaptation, in contrast to the rupture and loss resulting from large-scale urban reconstruction and other drastic interventions in the city.[12]

While this historical sketch is far too brief and schematic to properly delineate the contours of what might be called the postmodern turn in urbanism, it must suffice to set the scene for how the discussion on urbanism and the city played out across the twenty-four issues of *archithese* published from 1971 to 1976. Overall, this discussion followed the broader perception that the crisis of city planning was indicative of a larger crisis of modernity—its promises, enduring faith and confidence in technical solutions, and the overstated agency of experts. Furthermore, it reflected vital characteristics of the shifting urban discourse of the time; above all, the growing interdisciplinarity of knowledge, combining insights from sociology, anthropology, psychology, economics, political theory, and the nascent cultural and media studies. Crucially, it also reflected the turn to history within urbanism. This not only left its mark on the face of the city itself through a revaluation of the historic urban fabric, including the hitherto reviled nineteenth-century city; it also involved growing awareness of both the city and urban planning's historicity. Because cities were subject to change over time, historically distinct ways of conceiving and making cities became connected to different economic conditions, technological transformations, and shifting ways of life. Finally, the role of architects in urban processes was profoundly interrogated and reformulated in response to an influx of critical theory, particularly the analysis of "architectural ideology" by the influential Italian architectural historian Manfredo Tafuri.[13]

The original contributions to *archithese* chosen to accompany this essay as primary sources to support its core arguments embody the abovementioned characteristics. Their authors reflect a relatively broad spectrum: among them are a sociologist (Henri Lefèbvre), three historians (Franziska Bollerey, Kristiana Hartmann, and Tafuri), one architect (Rem Koolhaas), and a design collective (Superstudio). The articles have been culled from volumes one, two, three, and six of the journal. Urbanism and the city are explicit themes in only five of the issues—two from the early phase of *archithese* (nos. 1 and 3, 1972) and three from its late period immediately preceding the merger with *Das Werk* (nos. 17, 19, and 20, 1976, dedicated to the theme of "Metropolis"). In the interim years, planning and the city remained essential concerns. However, they were folded into such topics as "Anfänge des sozialen Wohnbaus" (Origins of Social Housing; no. 8), "'Spontane' Architektur" ("Spontaneous" Architecture; no. 9), "Das Kollektivwohnhaus (1900–1930)" (The Collective Dwelling; no. 12), "Realismus in der Architektur: Las Vegas etc." (Realism in Architecture: Las Vegas etc.; no. 13), and "Grosshaushalt" (Communal Household; no. 16). The five years from 1971/72 to 1976 are characterized by a noticeable shift in approaching the topic of urbanism, from an engagement with present-day concerns to a more clearly delineated historical outlook that aims to uncover pervasive and unquestioned truths about the links between modernity and the making of the early twentieth-century American metropolis.

Crisis and myth thus form the two brackets between which the discourse on the city in *archithese* unfolds. While the former bears witness to the waning of modernity, the latter seems to foreshadow developments and debates that would crystallize about a decade later with the emergence of the postmodern city as a vehicle for "flexible accumulation"—already embryonic in both historical and speculative analyses of Manhattan and the skyscraper as a distinct building type.[14] In contrast to the modern city as a site for industrial production, the postmodern city with culture and consumption at its heart is simultaneously a financial asset and economic factor.[15] Revisiting these 1970s urban discourses is worthwhile not only because their questions persist to this day, but also because the articles hold several unfulfilled lessons. Today, many architects remain fixated on object making and continue to show little interest in grasping the social and economic dynamics of cities, let alone in developing systematic strategies to intervene in these dynamics. In architectural education, the socioeconomic factors of design continue to be a sidenote too. While knowledge about the dynamics of space production has multiplied and deepened within the social sciences and cultural studies, this interest is not matched by architects, many of whom still refuse to engage meaningfully with this "external" knowledge.[16] Moreover, large parts of the profession cling to the enduring ideal of autonomy, to which critical theory could not provide a fix but could at least offer a necessary corrective.

The Crisis of the City
When we delve into the issues of *archithese*, the theme of crisis is present from the outset. Whether "we are currently in the midst of a crisis in urban planning" was the opening question that the journal's coeditor, Jean-Claude Widmer, a journalist from Geneva, posed to the renowned French Marxist philosopher and sociologist Lefèbvre in their conversation published in issue two of the inaugural volume. The latter's resolute answer: "We have been in one for a very long time! To the extent that architecture has tried to solve the contemporary world's problems, it has very plainly subordinated itself to a certain number of economic requirements, such as the requirement for industrial growth."[17] In Lefèbvre's view, the fundamental challenge of the

present lies in overcoming this growth paradigm. In contrast to the past, when architecture supplied the forms required for industrial expansion, the present need to change course (already urgent in 1971 and still unresolved today!) called for the invention of "something profoundly novel, but that something cannot be isolated, architecturally speaking, from issues that are political in nature."[18] One of Lefèbvre's fundamental tenets, that architecture is a heteronomous discipline enmeshed in a web of ideologies, practices, laws, regulations, and institutions, all of which shape its field of action, shines through here. That is, architecture constitutes a social practice that does not operate in isolation but is one among many actors engaged in the production of space, typically through the medium of the plan/drawing. Hence, any critique—and potential reconception—of its operations must begin with this recognition. The extent to which the conditions of architectural production could be reflected upon and ultimately changed from within the discipline thus remained a highly controversial question —indeed, one over which Lefèbvre quarreled with the other influential Marxist position on architecture and the city presented in the journal, that of Tafuri.[19] But more on that later.

The fact that Lefèbvre was interviewed for *archithese* not only testifies to its interdisciplinary and international scope—a red thread that runs through its early years. It also speaks to Lefèbvre's position as a central figure in urban discourse in France and internationally, primarily through his leadership of the Institut de sociologie urbaine (ISU) from 1962 to 1973. Łukasz Stanek resituates Lefèbvre's key theoretical contributions on "everyday life" (1947, 1961, 1981), "the right to the city" (1968), and "the production of space" (1974) by showing that these concepts were shaped in dialogue with the empirical studies the French sociologist conducted at various public research institutions over his decades-long career, thus pointing to the intersections between "his critical reflections on the general condition of modernity, his research on the process of urbanization, and his project of spaces for a transforming society."[20] Owing to his rich oeuvre, unconventional thinking, and political commitment, also expressed in his close involvement with the journal *utopie* (1967–1978), Lefèbvre became a transformative force within the urban planning discourse and practice of his time.[21] His conceptualization of space as a material construct and a sociopolitical arena engendered an especially profound reevaluation of urban studies. His triadic formulation of "perceived, conceived, and lived" space in *The Production of Space* instigated a conceptual shift, challenging abstract functionalist perspectives on the city as championed by members of the Congrès internationaux d'architecture modern (CIAM) and foregrounding the dynamic interplay between spatial configurations, lived experiences, and societal power structures instead.[22] Notably, Lefèbvre also advocated for a participatory and inclusive approach that recognized the agency of city dwellers in shaping their environments.[23]

Lefèbvre's interview for *archithese*—which runs through his critical positions on industrial modernity, the agency of city residents, the link between urban planning and capitalist production (he did not distinguish between state-managed capitalism and socialism in producing modern abstract space), architecture's role in representing political ideologies and embodying bureaucratic rule, the disillusionment with technocratic utopias, reforms in the education of architects and city planners, and alternative forms of practice—introduced a Swiss readership not yet familiar with Lefèbvre to his complex thinking.[24] Many of the interview's central theses resonate with the third *archithese* issue, "Zürich & Co.," published in 1972. This issue focuses entirely on Switzerland's largest city, where some of the dynamics Lefèbvre had described played out directly on the lead editor's doorstep. Von Moos and the issue's contributors, including Max Bill, Lucius Burckhardt, Martin Fröhlich, Martin Steinmann, and Sibylle Schroeder-Keller (the last three working at the Institute for History and Theory of Architecture (gta institute), ETH Zurich), were representative of the growing population that had become weary of growth and development for profit's sake. "Enough of the shiny showcases, spicy business advertisements presented in the form of pop facades, and musically accompanied pedestrian passages," von Moos wrote.[25] Since the mid-1960s, the editorial summarized, the restoration of Zurich's city center had pushed out residents; zoning plans had been drawn in the shadow of institutions using dubious methods; car-friendly transport planning had torn up the urban fabric; and banks, department stores, insurance companies, and hotels had shot out of the ground—all in the name of "progress," "prosperity," and "pride."

In 1969, Richard Allemann, chief executive of the City Vereinigung Zürich (Zurich City Association), the umbrella organization of downtown businesses founded in 1967, publicly presented his visions—propelled by the optimism of the economic boom years—for the development of Zurich into a "European metropolis."[26] In the preceding years, several speculative proposals had fired the imagination. For instance, authors dreamt of expanding the city into the lake basin, beginning with Werner Müller's "Seepark" proposal (1956), followed by Andre E. Bosshard's "City im See" (1961) and Hugo Wandeler's megastructural "Seebrücke" (1969), a multistory inhabitable bridge connecting the western and eastern lake shores.[27] Many of these projects sought to tackle the problems of densification and congestion simultaneously. One such example was the "counterproposal for the configuration of expressways and layout of the Sihl area" along the western side of the city center between the central rail station and Selnau offered by the Zürcher Arbeitsgruppe für Städtebau ZAS (the Zurich Working Group for Urban Planning) founded in 1959 as an initiative of eighteen young architects, including Benedikt Huber, Eduard Neuenschwander, and Beate Schnitter, to promote their vision of a better city.[28] Nevertheless, the growing public awareness of the "limits of growth"—the Club of Rome report was published in 1972, the same year as the Zurich issue of *archithese*—spelled an end to these visions as disillusion with dreams of linear progress set in. The population's rejection of the city's plans to construct an underground railroad in the 1973 cantonal referendum was a decisive turning point.[29] Lefèbvre's critique of architecture and urban planning in the service of capital spoke through many articles that renounced large-scale urban reconstruction for profit not people, as did his disdain for the architect-expert as the embodiment of state bureaucracy.[30]

Disenchanted Utopias

Without a direct link to the situation in Zurich, yet in dialogue with Lefèbvre's disavowal of abstract and technocratic utopias (though he nonetheless maintained that the construction and interrogation of what he called "concrete utopias" was crucially important), was an article by the Italian radical architecture collective Superstudio published in the 1971 "Urbanismus?" issue.[31] Conceived initially by group member Piero Frassinelli as a total of "twelve cautionary tales," each describing a vision of an ideal city turned dystopian nightmare due to the hyperbolic exaggeration of prevailing concepts of modern urbanism, such as users' needs, dwelling cells, or production, the complete project was simultaneously launched in various international architecture outlets, including *AD Architectural Design* and *Casabella*.[32] For the *archithese* spinoff version, only three narratives of "ideal cities" were chosen, all of which heavily drew from popular science fiction both in content and narrative style: "First city: 2,000-Ton City," "Second City: Temporal Cochlea-City," and "Third City: Continuous Production Conveyor Belt City" (the seventh city in the *AD* version). They were accompanied by a sinister epilogue in the form of a personality test that would reveal to readers whether they embodied a (designated) "head of state," "an element of the system," "a worm," or someone who had not "understood that the descriptions represent cities now," depending on how many of the portrayed visions one hoped would come true—from three to none.[33]

Superstudio employed a deliberately prophetic tone to depict prevailing trajectories of the time and amplified them through a lens of profound irony and corrosive commentary, offering a dramatic and scathing interpretation of urban realities and their repressive and inhumane character. In the collective's eyes, the (post)industrial city was a thoroughly rational apparatus shot through with totalitarian control that threatened the destruction of nature and caused the alienation of its inhabitants. People's needs and behaviors were entirely subordinated to the primacy of the system's self-preserving mechanism, tolerating no dissent.[34] Their work was informed by critical theorists like Herbert Marcuse and his notion of the "end of utopia" in advanced capitalist society, presented in 1967, where ideas pose as utopian while, in truth, being no more than the negation of existing realities. Rather than offering a means of liberation, utopian ideals had been co-opted and neutralized by the prevailing system, becoming a form of social control. A reinvigorated and subversive form of critical thinking should thus challenge the existing system's domination and conformity. At the same time, Superstudio's "projects" were informed by the strategy of refusing work championed by the Italian labor theorist Mario Tronti and members of the Operaismo (Workerist) movement. Against this backdrop, Superstudio renounced the creation of utilitarian items, the act of building, or pragmatic urban planning and engaged instead in communicative strategies, perception, and the construction of subjectivity.[35]

In presenting a negative form of utopia, or "counter-utopia," Superstudio also eschewed the work of many leading architectural historians—in particular, those charged by Tafuri with operative criticism; that is, distorting their reading of the past by conforming to the needs of the present—who recounted the involvement of architects imbued with a sense of moral duty in pursuit of "utopia" and social betterment through meticulous and rational urban planning.[36] This is where the contribution of the German and Swiss urban historians Bollerey and Hartmann lies. The pair sought to create an alternative to this established historiography by excavating the "theories and experiments of the utopian socialists Robert Owen and Charles Fourier."[37] Their article, published in *archithese* 8 (1973; guest edited by art historian Kurt W. Forster), drew heavily from Bollerey's PhD dissertation submitted at TU Berlin.[38] Hartmann had completed her doctoral thesis on the German garden city movement, cultural politics, and social reform at Freie Universität Berlin at the same time.

For Bollerey and Hartmann, Owen's proposals for ideal workers' communities and their corresponding social infrastructures and Fourier's Phalanstère, a palatial building to achieve collective luxury, presented an ambiguous heritage. On the one hand, their work stood out against other reform models of the period as it offered "overall conceptions for a new urban organism" while "at the same time anticipat[ing] new social conditions" based on the recognition that, "in the bourgeois order, ... true misery is and cannot be eradicated."[39] Projecting the past into the present, Owen's and Fourier's "ideally conceived housing schemes"—shunned as ideological by later proponents of scientific socialism—were therefore viewed as an antidote to the technocratic operations of urban planning in the postwar era. On the other hand, the authors concluded that "the complexity of their planning, which is today interpreted as progressive, ... condemned all pragmatic approaches to failure. The complexity was not planned for a restructured society but was supposed to contribute to the restructuring. Idealism operating in isolation failed because of its existence as a foreign body within the society."[40] Nevertheless, Owen and Fourier were of interest to historians of architecture precisely because they lent concrete forms to social and urban ideas—even if, according to Bollerey and Hartmann, they differed in how they approached the status of the formal solution vis-à-vis the social vision. Owen interpreted the "transformed architectural environment [as] the precondition for the socialization process," while Fourier held that "architecture should be adapted to the psychological and physical conditions of human beings."[41] That said, the authors also stress how, in the case of Owen, formal and aesthetic expression were secondary concerns behind the suitability of the proposed infrastructures for their intended social purpose, not least because architects at the time were skeptical of these projects, so actors from outside the discipline ended up planning them. In contrast, the graphic rendering of Fourier's Phalanstère by Victor Considerant (1840) is, in its deployment of lavish classical ornament on the exterior facades, interpreted as a marketing stunt that sought to play to prevalent bourgeois tastes in order to secure funding for the ambitious project. In closely attending to the historical conditions from which the urban models of these two utopian socialists emerged and by tracing their historical trajectory over the nineteenth century until they eventually became subsumed by bourgeois society, Bollerey and Hartmann sought to instill a historical consciousness in the often uncritical present-day search for planning concepts, a project of demystification to counter the commonplace ahistorical citation of precedent.[42]

Metropolitan Myths

This ambition to dispel "myths" through rigorous historical analysis, shared by most if not all members of the editorial board of *archithese*, also defined the work of Tafuri, the Italian Marxist architect turned historian based at the Istituto Universitario di Architettura di Venezia. He contributed an article titled "'New Babylon': The New York of the 1920s and the Search for Americanism"—his second for the journal—to the third monograph on the theme of "Metropolis."[43] This essay was an early draft version of a lengthier chapter published four years later as part of his *La sfera e il labirinto: Avanguardie e architettura da Piranesi agli anni '70* (*The Sphere and the Labyrinth: Avant-Gardes and Architecture from Piranesi to the 1970s*).[44] It reframed, as Joan Ockman highlights, Tafuri's earlier work on the American city conducted as part of a decade-long collaborative research program, beginning in 1968, with "[t]he aim ... to study twentieth-century architecture and cities in relation to the three 'great systems' that had shaped them: Soviet communism, American capitalism, and European social democracy."[45] With its ambition to construct a multidimensional picture of New York as an enigmatic symbol of modernity and the embodiment of Americanism, the effort by the editors of *archithese* may have taken inspiration from the research project that Tafuri had launched shortly before. Indeed, as the editorial of the first of the three "Metropolis" issues confirms, he was involved in the issue's conception alongside Claude Lichtenstein, Werner Oechslin, Andreas Adam, and Rosemarie Bletter as part of a team of guest editors spanning three countries and two continents.[46] The first issue focused on European representations of the American city that oscillated between admiration and revulsion, while the second issue focused more intensely on the architecture of the city: "the traffic machinery, stylized to the essence of the metropolis"; "the lighthouse as 'model' of the modern skyscraper"; "the battle for the tangibility of the metropolitan skyscraper as a single form"; "the looming divergence of large architectural form and decorative-theatrical infill, tasked with the communication of meanings on a human scale."[47] The third and final "Metropolis" issue, edited by Oechslin, continued the focus on the skyscraper, and here is where Tafuri's article was placed.[48]

In hindsight, the editors' interest, in the mid-1970s, in the theme of Americanism may seem surprising, perhaps even slightly anachronistic. Undoubtedly, the United States exercised huge geopolitical, economic, and (pop) cultural influence throughout postwar Europe, mainly through the proliferation of consumer goods and mass media ("soft power"). However, the country's influence as an aspirational role model had faded after the U.S. involvement and atrocities in the Vietnam War. In this context, the widespread perception by the European public and intellectual elites of the United States as a "laboratory of modernity" and its blanket association with "everything considered modern" gradually became questioned, a process of deconstruction and demystification that continues today as scholars on both sides of the Atlantic undo these monolithic constructs with postcolonial and other readings that shed light on the multifaceted and incoherent experience of modernity in the United States, including its dark aspects and historical oversights (settler colonial violence, slavery, and racism).[49] In a way, this shifting assessment is already somewhat palpable in the three "Metropolis" issues, even though some of the contributions repeat more than deconstruct the "fictions of the European avantgarde" about New York and the United States.[50]

As Ockman notes, the capitalist metropolis was difficult to pin down. Was it "an exceptional phenomenon, unique to the special circumstances that gave birth to it, or was it an unconscious anticipation of what was to come everywhere?"[51] At least when it came to understanding the role of the skyscraper within this constellation, Tafuri's verdict was clear: it was less a unique typological invention insofar as its volumetric form, dramatically staged in the renderings of Hugh Ferriss, sprang from zoning legislation introduced in the 1910s. Likewise, the eclectic and loose reinterpretation of Indigenous motifs in its decorative treatment was chiefly aimed at providing a "consumable image."[52] The skyscraper, a mythical construction, therefore presented "an (ultimately futile) effort by technocratic architects and planners to resist urban formlessness by means of a singular, monumental building."[53] In this sense, it shared the same fate as the architecture designed and built in the other socioeconomic systems Tafuri studied—communism and social democracy—because a joint trajectory of modernity and capitalist development shaped it.

In this assessment, Tafuri differed drastically from the last position presented in the *archithese* "Metropolis" monographs to be discussed here—that of Koolhaas. For Tafuri, the skyscraper type proved an unsuitable model for future urban invention because it demonstrated, in historical retrospect, that possibilities for control on the urban scale had run aground under American capitalism. He ended his 1973 essay "The Disenchanted Mountain" by noting that "the realism that characterized the creation of the Rockefeller Center—to the point of cynicism—marked the end of any utopian ideal of comprehensive public control over the urban structure."[54] Koolhaas, in contrast, perceived Manhattan as the starting point for further speculation, "a germinal moment, the dawn of a new world of possibilities for architecture and architects."[55] The skyscraper and urban grid became the chief characters in his "retroactive manifesto for Manhattan." After graduating from London's Architectural Association at the beginning of the 1970s, the young Koolhaas, captivated by the enduring myth of New York like so many modern architects and artists before him, moved across the Atlantic to continue his studies at Cornell University. A few years later, he was one of two designers researching the hidden creative potentials of Manhattan's past and present at the Institute of Architecture and Urban Studies in New York, next to the French-Swiss architect Bernard Tschumi.[56] The result of this investigation was his 1978 book *Delirious New York*, of which his article for *archithese* "Roxy, Noah, and Radio City Music Hall," is an early fragment.[57]

Koolhaas's short text, later woven into the book's significant fourth chapter on the Rockefeller Center, focuses on the episode of the conception around 1930 of Radio City Music Hall, the gigantic (yet empty) performance machine dreamt up by theater director Samuel Lionel "Roxy" Rothafel and installed in the center's belly. In condensed form, the article rehearses some of the book's core arguments regarding the unconscious production of architectural and urban form without a mastermind, largely "automatic" and without any conventional—that is, professional—design intent. Koolhaas says, "In Roxy the Music Hall has a planner whose vision is the laughingstock of his fellow men, or at least of his architects."[58] Moreover, using the metaphor of Noah's Ark, Koolhaas claims that, in anticipation of impending (economic or ecological) catastrophe, each single Manhattan block contained an entire city able to reproduce itself. The blueprint for this thinking, which reveals Koolhaas's doubts about the potential of planning and prediction, can be found in his close collaboration with Oswald Mathias Ungers on their 1977 study "Berlin—A Green Urban Archipelago." With its embrace of loosely connected urban islands, or nuclei, surrounded by urban greenery, Koolhaas gave up on previous modernist theories of comprehensive urban development.[59] This is why he hailed Manhattan (and the Rockefeller Center as its main achievement) as "the result of a feverish dream, a phantasmagoric delirium freed from any rational control." It had "evolved without a script or master plan, in a space void of theory, unconsciously and at breathtaking speed."[60]

Conclusion:
From the Industrial City to the City of Flexible Accumulation
The discussion of urbanism and the city in *archithese* from 1971 to 1976 encompassed an impressive array of positions, from the emergence of critical urban theory in response to the crisis of city planning (Lefèbvre), to debates concerning the exhaustion of utopia and the presentation of counter-utopias, as well as utopia's demystification (Superstudio, Bollerey and Hartmann), to the deconstruction and reactivation of the myth of the metropolis (Tafuri, Koolhaas). As a representative of the younger generation, Koolhaas, despite sharing with Tafuri the impetus for revising modernist historiography and similar methods,

had a significantly different outlook on planning compared to the other voices discussed here. Furthermore, the view in the rear mirror discloses a process of departure from the industrial city, with its corresponding scientific and comprehensive urban planning approaches, toward the gradual emergence of the postmodern city of flexible accumulation and its concomitant abandonment of overarching theories for reshaping urban realities. For Harvey, postmodernism in the urban context marks a "break with the idea that planning and development should focus on large-scale ... design, and that vernacular traditions, local history, and specialized spatial designs ranging from functions of intimacy to grand spectacle should be approached with much greater eclecticism of style."[61] Such new forms of postmodern urbanism deliberately seek to promote new cultural values and practices in line with the regime of flexible accumulation. Transitory spectacle, play, and festivities have become core features of this new urban reality. Work on the "generic city" today, to refer to one of Koolhaas's dictums, is piecemeal and happens through individual objects that are supposed to act as catalysts for urban change.[62] At the same time, the forces shaping contemporary urban dynamics and its challenges have steadily grown, provoking the question anew whether it is time to rethink the accepted truths about urban planning.

1   Stanislaus von Moos, "Urbanismus?," *archithese* 1 (1972): 2.

2   In the Swiss context, the sociologist Lucius Burckhardt had been a crucial voice in urbanistic debates since the mid-1950s and advocated process-based thinking. At the 1961 meeting of the Federation of Swiss Architects focusing on transport planning at the national scale, he cautioned professionals in a talk titled "The Crisis of the City" that the factor of time presented a challenge to planning decisions. Referring to Martin Wagner, Burkhardt argued that city planning had to consider the "never-ending development of the city," which meant planning with economic factors and the life of the city itself. Lucius Burckhardt, "Die Krise der Stadt," *Das Werk* 48, 10 (1961): 336–37.

3   Von Moos, "Urbanismus?" (see note 1), 2.

4   See the essay by Gabrielle Schaad, 311–26 in this publication.

5   Horst W.J. Rittel and Melvin M. Webber, "Dilemmas in a General Theory of Planning," *Policy Sciences* 4, 2 (1973): 155–69, http://www.jstor.org/stable/4531523. For further background to Rittel's work and its resonance in architecture and urban planning since the 1970s, see Torsten Lange, "Rittel's Riddles: Design Education and 'Democratic' Planning in the Age of Information," in *Re-scaling the Environment: New Landscapes of Design, 1960–1980*, ed. Ákos Moravánzsky and Karl R. Kegler (Basel: Birkhäuser, 2017), 61–80.

6   Angelus Eisinger, *Die Stadt der Architekten: Anatomie einer Selbstdemontage* (Basel: Birkhäuser, 2005), 101–2.

7   Jane Jacobs, *The Death and Life of Great American Cities* (New York: Random, 1961).

8   Wolf Jobst Siedler, Elisabeth Niggemeyer, and Gina Angreß, *Die Gemordete Stadt: Ein Abgesang auf Putte und Straße, Platz und Baum* (Berlin: F.A. Herbig, 1964).

9   Ibid., 7.

10   Alexander Mitscherlich, *Die Unwirtlichkeit unserer Städte: Anstiftung zum Unfrieden* (Frankfurt am Main: Suhrkamp, 1965).

11   Kevin Lynch, *The Image of the City* (Cambridge, MA: MIT Press, 1960).

12   Aldo Rossi, *The Architecture of the City* (Cambridge, MA: MIT Press, 1984). The first edition, in Italian, was published in 1966.

13   Manfredo Tafuri, *Architecture and Utopia: Design and Capitalist Development* (Cambridge, MA: MIT Press, 1976). The first edition, in Italian, was published in 1973.

14   David Harvey, "Flexible Accumulation through Urbanization: Reflections on 'Post-modernism' in the American City," *Perspecta* 26 (1990): 251–72. See also David Harvey, *The Condition of Postmodernity: An Enquiry into the Origins of Cultural Change* (Oxford, UK: Blackwell, 1990). Recently this debate has been revisited and expanded with a focus on the skyscraper. See Mariano Gomez Luque, "The Late Capitalist Skyscraper Theoretically Considered" (PhD diss., Harvard University, 2019).

15   See Andreas Reckwitz, "Die Selbstkulturalisierung der Stadt: Zur Transformation moderner Urbanität in der 'creative city,'" in *Kreativität und Soziale Praxis: Studien zur Sozial- und Gesellschaftstheorie* (Bielefeld: transcript, 2016), 155–84; Ash Amin and Nigel Thrift, "Cultural-Economy and Cities," *Progress in Human Geography* 31, 2 (2007): 143–61, https://doi.org/10.1177/0309132507075361.

16   Eisinger, *Die Stadt der Architekten* (see note 6), 7.

17   Henri Lefèbvre, "Questions for Henri Lefèbvre," interview by Jean-Claude Widmer, 232 in this publication. First published in *archithese* 2 (1971): 11–15.

18   Ibid.

19   Łukasz Stanek, *Henri Lefebvre on Space: Architecture, Urban Research, and the Production of Theory* (Minneapolis: University of Minnesota Press, 2011), 165–66.

20   Ibid.

21   Craig Buckley and Jean-Louis Violeau, *Utopie: Texts and Projects, 1967–1978* (Los Angeles: Semiotext(e), 2011).

22   Henri Lefèbvre, *The Production of Space* (Oxford, UK: Blackwell, 1991). The first edition, in French, was published in 1974.

23   See the chapter by Gabrielle Schaad, 311–26 in this publication.

24   Swiss professionals may already have been familiar with Lefèbvre's critique of modern city planning through his commentary on the SNF-funded project for a new city near Otelfingen in the Furttal Valley developed by a team around Ernst Egli, professor for urbanism at ETH Zurich. See Stanek, *Henri Lefebvre on Space* (see note 19), 93–99.

25   Stanislaus von Moos, "'keinerlei Proportion,'" *archithese* 3 (1972): 2–3, here 3.

26   For an account of Zurich's resistance to *Großstadt* thinking until the mid-twentieth century, its brief embrace of metropolitan visions, and the rapid disillusionment with dreams of progress from the start of the 1970s, see Thomas Schneider, "Die Grossstadt—Des Schweizers Wunsch oder Albtraum?," *Medienheft Dossier*, 17 (2002): 38–43. In the "Zürich & Co." issue of *archithese*, Fröhlich and Steinmann looked at the unbuilt Zurich. Martin Fröhlich and Martin Steinmann, "Zürich, das nicht gebaut wurde," in "Zürich & Co.," special issue, *archithese* 3 (1972): 25–33.

27   Christina Gubler, "Versunkene Ideen," *Hochparterre: Zeitschrift für Architektur und Design* 29, 1–2 (2016): 34–37.

28   "Gegenvorschlag für die Expreßstraßenführung und die Gestaltung des Sihlraumes in Zürich," *Das Werk: Architektur und Kunst* 48, 10 (1961): 348–53. On the thirty-year history of the ZAS, see Benedikt Huber, "Die Stadtvisionen der ZAS und ihre Bedeutung für Zürich: Zürcher Arbeitsgruppe für Städtebau, 1959–1989: Eine Dokumentation," *Schweizer Ingenieur und Architekt* 118, 20 (2000): 432–44.

29   Ulrich Pfammatter's article in the "Zürich & Co." issue formulated a stinging critique of the underground railway project from a class perspective. Ulrich Pfammatter, "Die Zürcher U-Bahn," in "Zürich & Co.," special issue, *archithese* 3 (1972): 22–24.

30   Another contemporaneous example of this broader shift is the exhibition

Profitopoli$ oder Der Mensch braucht eine andere Stadt (Profitopoli$, or another city for human being), curated by the architect Josef Lehmbrock and the art historian Wend Fischer, on display from November 1971 to February 1972 at Die Neue Sammlung in Munich.

31   Superstudio, "Three Warnings against a Mystical Rebirth of Urbanism," 242–51 in this publication. First published in *archithese* 1 (1972): 3–6, 36.

32   Superstudio, "Twelve Cautionary Tales for Christmas: Premonitions of the Mystical Rebirth of Urbanism," *Architectural Design* 41, 12 (1971): 737–42; Superstudio, "Premonizioni della parusia urbanistica," *Casabella*, 361 (1972): 45–55.

33   Superstudio, "Three Warnings," 251 in this publication. The test was also part of the extended version published in the December 1971 issue of *AD*.

34   Daniela N. Prina, "Superstudio's Dystopian Tales: Textual and Graphic Practice as Operational Method," *Writing Visual Culture* 6 (2015): 88–102, here 93.

35   Ross K. Elfline, "Superstudio and the 'Refusal to Work,'" *Design and Culture* 8, 1 (2016): 55–57, https://doi.org/10.1080/17547075.2016.1142343.

36   Prina, "Superstudio's Dystopian Tales" (see note 33).

37   Franziska Bollerey and Kristiana Hartmann, "Collective Housing: Theories and Experiments of the Utopian Socialists Robert Owen (1771–1858) and Charles Fourier (1772–1837)," 252–71 in this publication. First published in *archithese* 8 (1973): 15–26.

38   This was later published as Franziska Bollerey, *Architekturkonzeption der utopischen Sozialisten: Alternative Planung und Architektur für den gesellschaftlichen Prozeß* (Munich: Heinz Moos Verlag, 1977).

39   Bollerey and Hartmann, "Collective Housing," 252 in this publication.

40   Ibid., 268.

41   Ibid., 259.

42   Bollerey, *Architekturkonzeption der utopischen Sozialisten* (see note 38), 168.

Fourier was simultaneously being reread by Lefèbvre, among others, for his work's potential use in fusing the two opposing concepts of "unitary architecture" and differential space. See Stanek, *Lefebvre on Space* (see note 19), 170–79.

43   Manfredo Tafuri, "'New Babylon': The New York of the 1920s and the Search for Americanism," 272–94 in this publication. First published in *archithese* 20 (1976): 12–24, 51.

44   Manfredo Tafuri, "The New Babylon: The 'Yellow Giants' and the Myth of Americanism," in *The Sphere and the Labyrinth: Avant-Gardes and Architecture from Piranesi to the 1970s* (Cambridge, MA: MIT Press, 1987), 171–89.

45   Joan Ockman, "Russia, Europe, America: The Venice School between the U.S.S.R. and the U.S.A.," in *Re-framing Identities: Architecture's Turn to History, 1970–1990*, ed. Ákos Moravánszky and Torsten Lange (Basel: Birkhäuser, 2017), 121–48. For an earlier account that emphasizes Tafuri's reception in the United States more than his perception of the country, see Joan Ockman, "Venice and New York," *Casabella* 59, 619/620 (1995): 57–71. Tafuri's earlier work culminated in a collectively authored volume: Giorgio Ciucci, Francesco Dal Co, Mario Manieri-Elia, and Manfredo Tafuri, eds., *The American City from the Civil War to the New Deal* (Cambridge, MA: MIT Press, 1979). The first edition, in Italian, was published in 1973.

46   Stanislaus von Moos, "Metropolis I," *archithese* 17 (1976): 2–3.

47   Stanislaus von Moos, "Metropolis II," *archithese* 18 (1976): 2–3.

48   According to von Moos, a later, unrealized plan was developed to assemble all the contributions in a book, prefaced by an introduction written by Reyner Banham.

49   Thomas Welskopp and Alan Lessoff, "Fractured Modernity—Fractured Experiences—Fractured Histories: An Introduction," in *Fractured Modernity: America Confronts Modern Times, 1890s–1940s*, ed. by Andreas Wirsching (Munich: R. Oldenbourg Verlag, 2012), 1–17. The issue of "race" in Tafuri's work on the American city (and indeed the other contributions to *archithese*, "Metropolis I–III"), suffers from a similar

weakness, inherited from Lewis Mumford, who is a standard reference, despite the presence of the civil rights movement at the time. See Charles L. Davis II, Mabel O. Wilson, and Irene Cheng, *Race and Modern Architecture: A Critical History from the Enlightenment to the Present* (Pittsburgh: University of Pittsburgh Press, 2020). An important corrective is Adrienne Brown, *The Black Skyscraper: Architecture and the Perception of Race* (Baltimore: Johns Hopkins University Press, 2017).

50   On the significance of Americanism, particularly in German modernist circles, see M. David Samson, "'Unser New Yorker Mitarbeiter': Lewis Mumford, Walter Curt Behrendt, and the Modern Movement in Germany," *Journal of the Society of Architectural Historians* 55, no. 2 (1966): 126–39.

51   Ockman, "Russia, Europe, America" (see note 45), 137–38.

52   Tafuri, "'New Babylon,'" 285 in this publication.

53   Ockman, "Russia, Europe, America" (see note 45), 138.

54   Manfredo Tafuri, "The Disenchanted Mountain," in *The American City* (see note 45), 484.

55   On Tafuri's and Koolhaas's shared material and method but opposed views, see Marco Biraghi, "Games, Jokes, Masked Balls," in *The Project of Crisis: Manfredo Tafuri and Contemporary Architecture*, 145–72 (Cambridge, MA: MIT Press, 2013), 165.

56   Martino Stierli, "Montage and the Metropolis Unconscious: Rem Koolhaas's Delirious New York," in *Montage and the Metropolis: Architecture, Modernity, and the Representation of Space*, 228–67 (New Haven, CT: Yale University Press, 2018), 245.

57   Rem Koolhaas, *Delirious New York: A Retroactive Manifesto for Manhattan* (London: Thames and Hudson, 1978); Rem Koolhaas, "Roxy, Noah, and Radio City Music Hall," 296–307 in this publication. First published in *archithese* 18 (1976): 37–43. Another partial publication that appeared prior to the release of *Delirious New York* is Rem Koolhaas, "'Life in the Metropolis' or 'The Culture of Congestion,'" *Architectural Design* 47, 5 (1977): 319–25.

58 Koolhaas, "Roxy, Noah, and Radio City Music Hall," 296–307 in this publication. The article does not mention Raymond Hood, and the Associated Architects (designers of the Rockefeller Center) are a mere footnote. The story centers on Roxy and his "dream" as the project's origin—hardly the traditional narrative of the execution of an architectural brief.

59 Stierli, "Montage and the Metropolitan Unconscious" (see note 56), 240–41. See also the critical reedition of Ungers's manifesto: Oswald Mathias Ungers et al., *The City in the City: Berlin, a Green Archipelago: Manifesto* (1977) (Zurich: Lars Müller Publishers, 2013).

60 Stierli, "Montage and the Metropolitan Unconscious" (see note 56), 235.

61 Harvey, "Flexible Accumulation through Urbanization" (see note 14), 253.

62 Eisinger, *Die Stadt der Architekten* (see note 6), 20.

Questions for Henri Lefèbvre

Authors:
Jean Claude Widmer
Henri Lefèbvre

Source:
archithese, 2 (1971): 11–15

Translated by:
Brett Petzer

In our present moment, while it is not the case that everything is changing, some of the most central problems are transforming quite rapidly. A few decades ago, urban and town-planning problems were not the center of attention. I think that there has been a shift in focus, in the scientific as well as the political sense, and that that shift has gained ground with exceptional speed. Over the last two or three years, urban planning issues that were already well defined have been moving into the mainstream, but they have done so in a very strange way, by means of minor and indirect aspects. For example, we start talking about the environment or about pollution when, in reality, the central problem lies elsewhere. But little by little, we arrive at that problem by following its edges and adjacencies.

Can we say that we are currently in the midst of a crisis in urban planning?

We have been in one for a very long time! To the extent that architecture has tried to solve the contemporary world's problems, it has very plainly subordinated itself to a certain number of economic requirements, such as the requirement for industrial growth. Architecture has simply provided the morphology that industrial expansion requires, such as low-cost housing and bedroom communities: places for the workforce to rest from their labors. And even a certain architect—you know who I'm talking about; it's Le Corbusier—who was considered a creative genius among architects, has in fact provided this society with both state capitalism and state socialism. He provided the places such a society needed, which were only pseudo-inventions. Today, now, we have our backs against the wall; we have been put on notice to invent something profoundly novel, but that something cannot be isolated, architecturally speaking, from issues that are political in nature.

The fundamental problem, in my opinion, is this: For how long will the major industrialized countries, of which we are a part, persist in maintaining growth patterns that subordinate everything else to industrial growth? When will they realize that industrial growth cannot continue indefinitely and that we need to adopt different development patterns, starting right now? That means thinking about a society, indeed a civilization, in which the growth imperative is not the measure of all things,

Questions à Henri Lefèbvre

J.-C. Widmer

A notre époque, bien que tout ne change pas, les problèmes centraux se déplacent assez vite. Il y a quelques dizaines d'années, les problèmes urbains et urbanistiques n'étaient pas au centre des préoccupations. Je pense que le déplacement du centre d'intérêt, dans l'acception scientifique mais aussi dans l'acception politique, ce centre d'intérêt se déplace avec une rapidité extraordinaire. Depuis deux ou trois ans, les problèmes urbanistiques qui en réalité étaient déjà des problèmes concrets passent au centre des préoccupations, mais d'une manière tout à fait étrange, par des côtés mineurs et dérivés. On se met à parler de l'environnement par exemple ou des pollutions et en réalité le problème central est ailleurs. Mais il est peu à peu cerné à travers ces alentours, cet entourage.

Henri Lefèbvre, peut-on dire que nous sommes actuellement dans une période de crise de l'urbanisme ?

Nous y sommes depuis très longtemps, dans la mesure où l'architecture a tenté de résoudre les problèmes du monde contemporain, elle s'est tout simplement subordonnée à un certain nombre d'exigences d'ordre économique. Celles de la croissance industrielle. Elle a simplement fourni à la croissance industrielle la morphologie dont elle avait besoin, c'est-à-dire des H.L.M., des habitations à bon marché, des cités-dortoir, des endroits où se récupérait la force de travail et même, tel ou tel architecte, vous savez qui je vise, c'est Le Corbusier, dont on a cru qu'il était un génie inventif en architecture, a, en fait, fourni à cette société aussi bien le capitalisme d'Etat que le socialisme d'Etat d'ailleurs, les lieux dont elle avait besoin et ce n'était qu'une pseudo-invention. Aujourd'hui, maintenant, nous sommes mis au pied du mur, mis en demeure d'inventer quelque chose de profondément nouveau, mais qui ne peut pas, d'ailleurs, être isolé, architecturalement parlant, de problèmes qui sont d'ordre politique.

Le problème fondamental, à mon avis, est le suivant: jusqu'à

Während eines Interviews mit J.-C. Widmer weist Henri Lefèbvre darauf hin, dass jetzt der Moment gekommen ist, von Grund auf neue Prinzipien des Urbanismus zu erarbeiten, welche nicht von den politischen Grundlagen getrennt werden können.
Das Hauptproblem von Lefèbvre:
« Wie lange werden die industrialisierten Mächte an den nur auf die technologische Entwicklung ausgerichteten Schematas festhalten, und zu welchem Zeitpunkt werden sie einsehen, dass wir nicht ausschliesslich die industriellen Interessen fördern können, sondern ganz andere, übergeordnete Entwicklungsschematas anwenden müssen? Es gibt, mit anderen Worten, eine Gesellschaft und eine Zivilisation anzustreben, die nicht allein den Gesetzen des industriellen Fortschrittes unterliegt. »
Ist der Urbanismus in den westlichen Ländern von den kapitalistischen Interessen abhängig? Ja! Es ist aber erstaunlich, wie die urbanen Probleme in den sozialistischen Ländern keineswegs verschieden sind.
Es sind die Bedingungen der ökonomischen Interessen, welche hier wie dort die Raumgestaltung diktieren.

quand les grands pays industriels dont nous faisons partie vont-ils maintenir des schémas de croissance en subordonnant tout à la croissance industrielle, à quelle date s'apercevront-ils qu'on ne peut pas poursuivre indéfiniment la croissance industrielle et qu'il faut dès maintenant adopter d'autres schémas de développement. C'est-à-dire envisager une société, une civilisation qui ne soit plus simplement subordonnée aux impératifs de la croissance, mais qui passe à une certaine organisation, à une production, ou à une gestion consciente de l'espace. Voilà le problème fondamental de notre époque, ce problème émerge peu à peu, mais il devient crucial.

Mais ne croyez-vous pas, en fait, que les populations, les citadins, ont l'architecture qu'ils méritent ?

Votre appréciation est un peu dure. Les peuples ont les gouvernements qu'ils méritent, les peuples ont les lieux et la morphologie sociale qu'ils méritent, mais les peuples non plus ne sont pas entièrement passifs. S'ils acceptent, s'ils se résignent, à un certain moment peut-être que leur résignation et leur passivité ont des limites. Et à ce moment-là, il y a des rebondissements que l'on peut dire spectaculaires de la spontanéité sociale et politique.

S'il vous fallait donner un exemple d'architecte ou de chercheur intéressant à l'heure actuelle, lequel choisiriez-vous ?

Votre question m'embarrasse un peu parce que dans les études que j'ai faites dans beaucoup de pays, j'ai surtout vu des chaos indescriptibles. Je ne me lasserai pas de décrire quelques chaos urbanistiques en Amérique du Nord ou au Japon. S'il fallait parler d'un endroit particulièrement réussi je parlerais peut-être de Stockholm, mais surtout de Montréal qui est une ville que j'aime beaucoup, je sais très bien pourquoi d'ailleurs: elle est au croisement de plusieurs cultures, de plusieurs civilisations. Elle est française, elle est américaine. Elle est très industrialisée et il y a pourtant un noyau urbain qui date du 16e et du 17e siècle et alors, dans le centre de Montréal qui a été pensé et réorganisé par des architectes et des urbanistes extrêmement intelligents, il y a la Place qui est l'un des très beaux endroits du monde. C'est une place entourée de très grands bâtiments à la manière américaine qui est libérée de la circulation et où l'on trouve des cafés, des cinémas, avec un urbanisme souterrain tout à fait adapté à la circulation et aux rassemblements des gens pendant les mois d'hiver. La Place Ville-Marie dans le cadre d'un urbanisme capitaliste, j'insiste bien sur cette restriction qui est extrêmement importante, dans le cadre d'un urbanisme capitaliste et d'un pays hautement urbanisé et riche, c'est une réussite assez remarquable.

Mais l'urbanisme, dans les pays occidentaux est toujours aux mains des capitalistes ?

Oui. Mais ce qu'il y a de plus étonnant, c'est que l'urbanisme, dans les pays socialistes n'est pas tellement différent. Qu'il s'agisse du capitalisme pur ou du capitalisme d'Etat ou encore du socialisme d'Etat, ce sont les impératifs de la croissance économique qui commandent l'organisation de l'espace. Et c'est dans

Und in Zukunft? Wir müssen auf dem Bestehenden aufbauen. Es kann nicht die Rede sein, den Weg zum Neuen mittels totaler Zerstörung zu ebnen. Ausserdem können wir aus der Geschichte der historischen Architektur der alten Städte in gewissem Masse Lehren für die Zukunft ziehen.

ce cadre que la subordination aux simples impératifs de la croissance, que l'occupation de l'espace arrive à ce chaos extraordinaire que l'on peut constater dans ces agglomérations que l'on baptise pompeusement « Mégalopolis », ou encore « Œcuménopolis ». En réalité ce sont des espaces qu'il faudrait complètement réorganiser de fond en comble, à partir d'une prise de conscience des problèmes nouveaux.

Et Brasilia que la « critique » internationale s'est plue à louer, à l'époque ?

Brasilia, je dois dire que j'en ai une horreur particulière. J'ai une horreur particulière pour les œuvres de Monsieur Niemeyer. Monsieur Niemeyer est peut-être un grand architecte mais c'est celui qui a incarné dans une conception architecturale la bureaucratie d'Etat.

Ce qu'il est en train de faire ailleurs, par exemple les plans de l'Alger nouveau qu'on m'a montrés, il n'y a pas très longtemps, m'ont l'air indescriptiblement abominable. C'est même de la folie. La nouvelle Alger va être une cité bureaucratique de 500.000 habitants, sur le cap Matifou, sous prétexte de la recherche d'un cadre architectural prodigieux avec la baie d'Alger. Mais imaginez ce que c'est que de mettre une cité de 500.000 habitants, uniquement des bureaucrates sur un cap. Le moindre bon sens dit que les communications seront bloquées. L'urbanisme et l'architecture de Monsieur Niemeyer sont totalement bureaucratiques et à mon avis, cela résume tout ce que l'on peut dire de pire d'une tentative architecturale.

Mais pourtant, les régimes politiques brésilien et algérien me paraissent assez éloignés ? pour ne pas dire diamétralement opposés ?

Je crains que la bureaucratie d'Etat ait des caractères communs quel que soit le régime. Cette appréciation pourra choquer certains, mais je la maintiens. Le pouvoir d'Etat, bureaucratie d'Etat, le compromis entre la bureaucratie et la technocratie d'une grande quantité de pays met entre eux une espèce de dénominateur commun. Même si le régime s'intitule capitalisme ou socialisme. Il y a des différences par ailleurs, mais en ce qui concerne le rôle et la fonction sociale de la bureaucratie, il y a de singulières homologies et précisément ces homologies transparaissent à travers l'architecture. Nous pouvons prendre l'architecture et par exemple celle de Niemeyer comme symptomatique d'un rapprochement singulier entre les Etats et les bureaucraties d'Etat qu'elles s'intitulent socialistes ou capitalistes. En Algérie, il y a un certain socialisme. Au Brésil c'est un capitalisme assez dur, même surveillé par une autorité militaire assez forte, eh bien il se trouve qu'il y a des éléments communs, que l'on ne trouve pas seulement à Alger ou à Brasilia mais aussi à Paris où Monsieur Niemeyer est en train de construire un immeuble d'une importance particulière qui n'est autre que le siège du parti communiste français.

Henri Lefèbvre, jusqu'ici nous avons plutôt été pessimistes. Alors que peut-on attendre de positif ?

Une poussée d'invention, de créativité qui à mon avis n'a pas encore trouvé sa percée, mais qui de tous les côtés se fait jour.

Faites-vous ici allusion à ceux que l'on appelait les « Utopiques » il y a encore dix ans, des gens comme Yona Friedman ou d'autres ?

Je fais quelques réserves en ce qui concerne l'utopie technocratique. Les utopies technocratiques comme celles de Friedman réduisent la société à un schéma d'une simplicité vraiment exorbitante. Un espace découpé à la manière d'une construction mécanique serait le seul espace social ? Je ne suis pas du tout de cet avis. Mais on voit de tous les côtés des tentatives. Je pense à Ricardo Boffil en Espagne. Je pense à Constant à Amsterdam et je pense aussi à des quantités de formations sociales peut-être un peu sommaires et spontanées et peut-être qui n'iront pas très loin mais qui peuvent créer des morphologies. Je pense aux communautés telles que les communautés Hippies ou encore des communautés d'étudiants qui se constituent de différents côtés. Et je pense à toutes sortes de tentatives de création d'espaces.

Imaginez que quelqu'un étudie des bidonvilles. Imaginez que quelqu'un étudie tous les abris souterrains que les combattants du Vietnam ont faits pour échapper aux bombardements terribles de l'aviation américaine. Imaginez que l'on étudie toutes ces créations d'espace; est-ce que vous ne croyez pas que l'on arriverait à des notions nouvelles de l'espace ?

Pensez-vous que la formation que l'on donne actuellement aux futurs architectes est suffisante ?

Non, je ne le crois pas. Seulement, c'est en pleine gestation que se trouve cette transformation de la pédagogie architecturale. A mon avis, cette pédagogie architecturale ne peut pas se dissocier d'une théorie de l'espace. Je défends un peu ici mes affaires et ce dans quoi je m'estime peut-être un peu compétent. C'est cette théorie de l'espace que j'essaie d'élaborer et qui serait la théorie d'un espace nouveau, d'un espace tel que sa production serait complètement en toute connaissance de cause, en tenant compte de tous les éléments, sociaux, politiques, technologiques et formels de sa constitution. Par exemple, j'insiste beaucoup sur le fait que l'informatique et le téléinformatique sont des éléments tout à fait importants de la constitution et de la création de l'espace à l'échelle mondiale.

Mais pour y parvenir, il faudrait que les architectes ou les chercheurs en architecture deviennent des hommes politiques ?

La question est en effet extrêmement difficile, parce que l'on pourrait exiger de l'architecte qu'il soit une espèce d'encyclopédie des connaissances en démographie, en sociologie parce qu'il y a des gens concrets, réels, qui doivent occuper ce qu'il construit, en psychologie, parce que ces gens ont des tendances, des désirs, en psychanalyse, puisqu'après tout, il y a un inconscient de la réalité urbaine. Il devrait connaître les mathématiques, l'anthropologie, et en plus, il devrait être politique. Alors, c'est là la grande difficulté. Nous sommes amenés à faire des programmes d'enseignement véritablement encyclopédiques et ensuite, après avoir fait ces programmes énormes à les rétrécir, à les réduire à des niveaux accessibles à des étudiants qui ont entre vingt, vingt-cinq ans, qui

but in which we can start organizing, producing, and managing space conscientiously. This is the fundamental issue of our time. It's emerging bit by bit, but it is becoming crucial.

But don't you believe that people—that is, city residents—get the architecture they deserve?

Your assessment is a little harsh. Yes, people get the governments they deserve, and they get the places and the social morphology they deserve, but people are not entirely passive either. They may accept things, they may resign themselves to the way things are, but that acceptance and resignation have their limits. Once that limit is reached, you will see what might be called spectacular repercussions that are socially and politically spontaneous.

If you had to give an example of an interesting architect or researcher at this point in time, who would it be?

Your question puts me in a bit of a delicate position, because in my research across many different countries, most of what I've seen is indescribable chaos. I will never tire of talking about some of the urban chaos I have seen in North America or Japan. If I had to name a place that has been particularly successful, I could mention Stockholm, but most of all, Montreal, a city that is very close to my heart, and I can tell you exactly why. It lies at the crossroads of several cultures and civilizations. It is at once French and American. It is highly industrialized, but its old town dates back to the sixteenth and seventeenth centuries. And in the heart of Montreal, which was designed and redeveloped by very smart architects and urban planners, you have the Place Ville Marie, one of the most beautiful places in the world. It's a traffic-free square framed by vast American-style buildings where you can find cafés and cinemas, with access to an underground city that is perfectly suited to pedestrian movement and crowds in the winter months. Place Ville Marie, seen in the context of capitalist urban planning—and I must insist on that very important qualification—is, as capitalist urban planning in a highly urbanized, wealthy country, an altogether remarkable achievement.

But urban planning in Western countries is still in the hands of capitalists?

Yes, but the most surprising thing is that urban planning in socialist countries is not so different. Whether it's pure capitalism or state capitalism or state socialism, it's the imperatives of economic growth that govern how space is organized. And it is within this framework of subordination to the growth imperative that the way in which space is occupied leads to the extraordinary chaos of the kind of city region that we rather grandly term a "megalopolis" or even "ecumenopolis." In reality, these spaces need a complete reorganization from top to bottom, beginning with an acknowledgment of new challenges.

And what about Brasília, which was roundly praised by international "critics" in its time?

I must confess that I have a particular aversion to Brasília. I have a particular aversion to the works of Oscar Niemeyer. Niemeyer may be a great architect, but he has come to embody state bureaucracy in architectural design.

The work he is doing elsewhere—for example, the plans for the new Algiers that I was shown not long ago—look indescribably appalling. You might even call it madness. The new Algiers is to be a bureaucratic complex of 500,000 residents on Cape Matifou, created under the pretext of a search for a colossal architectural gesture to complement the Bay of Algiers. Imagine what it means to set down a city of 500,000 residents—nothing but bureaucrats—on a rocky promontory. The most basic common sense tells you that access is going to be difficult. Niemeyer's town planning and architecture are utterly bureaucratic, and that, to me, is the worst thing you can say of an architectural project.

At the same time, it seems to me that the political contexts of Brazil and Algeria are quite far apart, if not diametrically opposed.

I'm afraid that state bureaucracies have certain features in common, regardless of the regime. That assessment may shock some people, but I stand by it. State power, state bureaucracy, and the compromise between bureaucracy and technocracy in many countries:

all of these impose a kind of common denominator, whether the regime styles itself a capitalist or socialist one. There may be differences elsewhere, but as far as the role and social function of the bureaucracy is concerned, there are common elements, and they come to light through architecture. We can take architecture—and, for example, Niemeyer's architecture—as symptomatic of a unique rapprochement between states and state bureaucracies, whether they call themselves socialist or capitalist. Algeria has a particular kind of socialism. Brazil has a fairly hard-nosed strain of capitalism, it is even overseen by a rather strong military authority. And yet, they share common elements, which we find not only in Algiers or Brasília but also in Paris, where Mr. Niemeyer is putting up a building of especial importance—in fact, it is none other than the headquarters of the French Communist Party.

So far we have been rather pessimistic. What positive outcomes can we expect?
We can expect to see a burst of invention and creativity that, I think, hasn't yet broken through but is taking shape on all sides.

Are you referring here to those who were called "Utopians" ten years ago, people like Yona Friedman, or to someone else?
I have some reservations about technocratic utopias. Technocratic utopias like Friedman's reduce society to a schema of truly excessive simplicity. A space cut out like a piece of rough construction is supposed to be the only social space? I don't think so at all. But attempts are being made on all sides. I'm thinking of Ricardo Bofill in Spain. I'm thinking of Constant in Amsterdam, and I'm also thinking of a number of social formations that may be a little rough and spontaneous, and perhaps won't go very far, but which can create morphologies. I am thinking of communities such as hippie communities or communities of students that form in different contexts. And I am thinking of all kinds of attempts to create spaces.
Imagine someone studying slums. Imagine someone studying all the underground shelters that Vietnamese fighters made to escape the terrible bombings of the American air force. Just think what would be possible if we studied all of these kinds of space creation—don't you agree that surely we would come up with new notions of space?

Do you think that the training currently being given to future architects is sufficient?
No, I don't think so. But I think that a transformation of architectural teaching is underway; it's still in the making. In my view, this approach to teaching architecture cannot be separated from a theory of space. Here I am advocating for my own work a little; an area in which I think I'm somewhat competent. It is this theory of space that I am trying to develop further, and it would be a theory of a new kind of space, a space produced in full cognizance of the facts, taking into account all the elements—social, political, technological, formal—of which it consists. For example, I emphasize the fact that information technology is a very important element in the constitution and creation of space on a global scale.

But in order to achieve this, wouldn't architects or architectural researchers have to become politicians?
This is an extremely difficult question to answer, because one could demand of architects that they develop an encyclopedic knowledge of many fields. For example, demography and sociology, because real, actual people must inhabit what the architect builds; or psychology, because these people have tendencies and desires; or psychoanalysis, because urban reality, after all, has a subconscious of its own. The architect should be conversant in mathematics and anthropology, and, in addition, the architect should be political. So that's the great difficulty. We are called upon to create truly encyclopedic syllabi. And then, once we've created these enormous course loads, we must trim them and bring them down to a level accessible to students between twenty and twenty-five years old who need to be prepared to work in a challenging profession and within fairly narrow limits. And I must say in all honesty that this problem has not been solved.

And yet, there is still the option of working in teams?
Yes. So, in this area, we have tried to build collectives, teams. I must say that, thus far,

ont besoin d'être préparés à l'exercice d'une profession difficile et dans les limites assez étroites, et je dois le dire honnêtement, le problème n'est pas résolu.

Il resterait tout de même une possibilité, celle de travailler en « team » ?

Oui. Alors dans ce domaine, nous avons essayé de constituer des collectifs, des équipes. Je dois dire que cela n'a pas été jusqu'à maintenant une réussite. Il est bien connu que le travail interdisciplinaire se heurte à des barrières qui sont d'abord et tout simplement des barrières de langage, on ne parle pas le même langage, et alors, pour orienter et condenser des gens appartenant à des disciplines différentes, sur une construction déterminée, correspondant à une commande sociale, en général très étroitement déterminée, soit par les pouvoirs publics, soit par les intérêts financiers, soit par les promoteurs, et bien il y a une espèce de disproportion entre tous les termes du problème. Jusqu'à maintenant, il faut le dire honnêtement, le problème n'est pas résolu, malgré les efforts que nous faisons depuis quelques années en France.

L'architecture du passé n'est plus applicable à notre société, mais l'architecture d'aujourd'hui ou de demain est encore à faire ?

C'est bien là l'intérêt de la situation. Si les problèmes étaient résolus, ils ne seraient pas intéressants, s'il fallait simplement tracer une croix sur le passé, cela ne serait pas très intéressant non plus. Il faut tenir compte de ce qui s'est fait jusqu'à maintenant. Il ne peut pas être question de partir en faisant table rase et après tout l'histoire, l'architecture historique, les villes historiques, nous pouvons aussi les consulter dans une certaine mesure. Et d'autre part, les problèmes de l'avenir sont immenses et presque démesurés. A mon avis c'est toute une époque qui va être confrontée à ces problèmes et je ne pense pas du tout qu'on puisse les résoudre à court terme. En ce qui me concerne, je parie à long terme et je pense que c'est pendant des dizaines, peut-être des centaines d'années que les usagers d'un côté, de l'autre les constructeurs et les théoriciens vont être confrontés à des problèmes profondément nouveaux. C'est toute une période nouvelle qui s'annonce, celle que j'appelle la société urbaine par opposition avec la société industrielle dont nous commençons à sortir et par opposition encore plus à la société agraire dont nous sommes déjà, dans une large mesure, sortis.

Nous serions alors la génération des sacrifiés ?

Toutes les générations sont sacrifiées à l'avenir. Mais aucune génération n'est complètement sacrifiée. Elle mène sa vie comme elle le peut, elle s'affirme. Je ne crois pas appartenir à une génération sacrifiée. On a fait ce qu'on a pu. On s'est affirmé, quelquefois assez fortement. Dans d'autres occasions, notamment politiques on a été assez énergiquement contrecarré par les gouvernements, mais de tout cela, il faut dire qu'à travers les heurts, les conflits, ce que l'on appelle dans mon langage marxiste le processus dialectique, il s'ensuit tout de même quelque chose qui a une certaine orientation et un certain sens.

this has not been successful. Everyone knows that interdisciplinary work means bumping up against barriers, first and most simply those of language. We do not share a common language. Yet we have to bring together and orient people from different disciplines, working on a given project, conforming with a public mandate, that is also generally very narrowly defined, either by the authorities, or by financial interests, or by developers. And, you know, there is a kind of lack of proportionality between the terms we use to describe this problem. To date, to be very honest, this problem has not been resolved, despite the efforts we have made in France over several years.

So, the architecture of the past is no longer applicable to our society, but the architecture of today, or that of tomorrow, must still be created?

Yes, those are the stakes of the situation. If problems had been solved, they wouldn't be interesting. If it was only a question of drawing a line under the past, that wouldn't be very interesting either. We have to take stock of what has been done up to now. There can be no question of setting out with a clean slate. After all, to some extent, we can also draw on history and historic architecture and historic cities. On the other hand, the problems of the future are immense, almost limitless. In my opinion, a whole era will face these problems, and I don't think they can be solved at all in the short term. As far as I'm concerned, it is possible only in the long term, and I think that for decades, maybe centuries, users, on the one hand, and builders and theorists on the other, will be confronted with profoundly new problems. This is the start of a whole new period, one I call the urban society, as opposed to the industrial society from which we are beginning to emerge and, even more so, the agrarian society from which we have already, to a large extent, emerged.

Would ours then be the generation that gets sacrificed?

All generations are sacrificed to the future. But no generation is completely sacrificed. They live their lives as they can; they assert themselves. I don't think I belong to a generation that has been sacrificed. We did what we could. We've asserted ourselves, sometimes quite strongly. On other occasions, particularly political ones, we have been rather vigorously thwarted by governments. But it must be said that, through the clashes and the conflicts and what in my Marxist terms is called the dialectical process, you can trace a thread of something that has a certain orientation and a certain meaning.

Three Warnings against a Mystical Rebirth of Urbanism

Author:
Superstudio

Sources:
archithese, 1 (1972): 3–6, 36
"Twelve Cautionary Tales for Christmas," *Architectural Design* 42 (December 1971): 737–42 (EN)

Translated by:
Steven Lindberg

Here follow visions of three ideal cities: apotheosis of humanity after twenty thousand years of blood, sweat, and tears. They show Man, having arrived at the goal of his dreams, in possession of the Truth, finally freed from contradiction, equivocation, and indecision. Totally and forever subsumed in the abundance of his own PERFECTION.

First City
2,000-Ton City

Even and perfect, the city lies amid green lawns, sunny hills and wooded mountains; slim, tall sheets of continuous buildings intersect in a rigorous, square mesh, one league apart. The buildings, or rather the single, uninterrupted building consists of cubic cells 5 cubits each way; these cells are placed one on top of another in a single vertical stack, reaching a height of a third of a league above sea-level, so that the relative height of the building varies in relation to the level of the ground on which it rises. Each cell has two external walls. Cell walls are of opaque material, porous to air, rigid, but light. The wall facing north (or if this is an external wall, the wall facing west) is capable of emitting 3D images, sounds and smells. Against the opposite wall is a seat capable of moulding perfectly to the human body, even of enclosing it completely. Incorporated in this seat is an apparatus for satisfying all physiological needs. When not in use, this membrane and all apparatus withdraw and the wall reforms. The floor is a simulator, and can evoke all sensations of living things. The ceiling is a brain-impulse-receiver.

In each cell is an individual whose brain impulses are continually recorded by a ceiling panel and forwarded to the central electronic analyzer. This analyzer, a complex system of apparatuses, is located at the top of the building, beneath a continuous semicylindrical vault. It selects, compares, and mediates between the needs of the individuals, programming the life of the entire city moment by moment with the aid of the broadcast wall, the material simulator (floor), and the reflexes of the automatic "housing wall." In this way, all citizens possess at every moment the same preconditions of equality.

Death no longer exists. Sometimes someone indulges in absurd thoughts of rebellion against the perfect and eternal life granted to him.

Drei Warnungen vor einer mystischen Wiedergeburt des Urbanismus

Hier folgen die Visionen von drei Idealstädten: Apotheose der Menschheit, nach zwanzigtausend Jahren des Blutvergiessens, des Schweisses und der Tränen. Sie zeigen den Menschen, am Ziel seiner Träume angelangt, im Besitz der Wahrheit, endlich von seinen Widersprüchen, Zweifeln, Missverständnissen und Unentschlossenheiten erlöst. Endgültig und vollständig aufgehoben in der Fülle seiner eigenen VOLLKOMMENHEIT.

1. Die 2000-Tonnen-Stadt

Die Stadt, vollkommen in ihrer Ordnung, dehnt sich über grüne Felder, besonnte Hügel und bewaldete Bergrücken. Dünne und hohe Scheiben von zusammhängenden Gebäuden kreuzen sich in einer Weise, dass sich streng quadratische Maschen von je einer Meile Seitenlänge ergeben. Die Bauten, vielmehr der einzige, ununterbrochene Baukomplex besteht aus kubischen Zellen von fünf Ellen Seitenlänge. Diese Zellen sind nach einem durchgehenden Prinzip übereinandergeschichtet, und zwar bis zu einer Höhe von einem Drittel einer Meile über Meereshöhe; und zwar so, dass die relative Höhe des Baus sich verändert je nach der Höhe des Terrains, auf dem er sich befindet. Jede Zelle besitzt demnach zwei gegenüberliegende Wände, die sie gegen Aussen abschliessen. Ihre Wände sind in einem undurchsichtigen Material er-

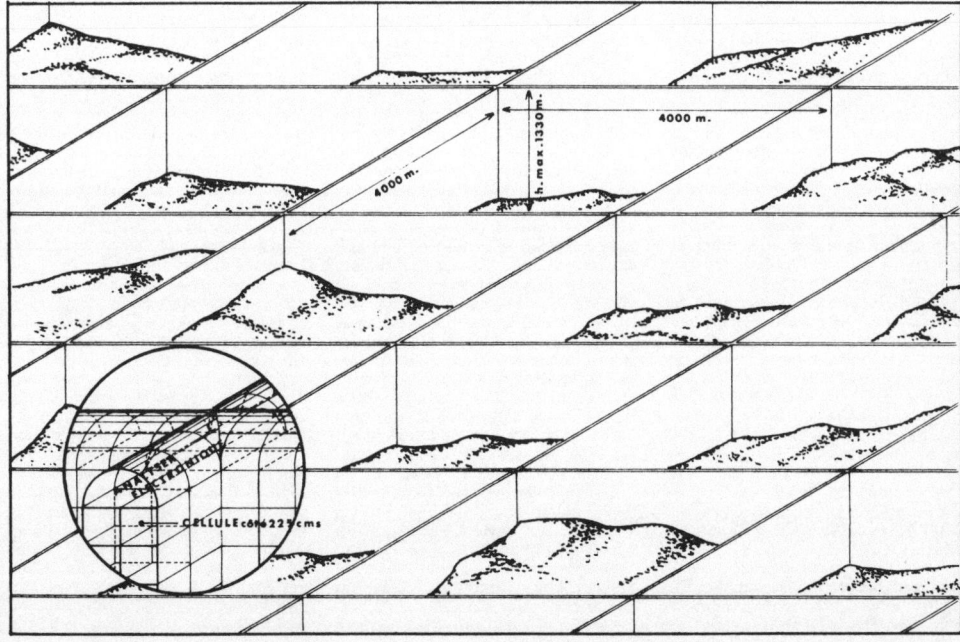

←fig. 1
2,000-Ton City

richtet, das indes luftdurchlässig ist; sie sind zwar steif, aber weich. Die Nordwand ist in der Lage, dreidimensionale Bilder zu entsenden, überdies auch Geräusche und Düfte. Die gegenüberliegende Wand ist von einem Stuhl eingenommen, der sich jedem menschlichen Körper vollständig anschmiegen und ihn einhüllen kann. In diesem Stuhl wurden die Apparate angeordnet, die jedes physiologische Bedürfnis — Nahrungsaufnahme, Darmentleerung, Geschlechtsleben — befriedigen können. Wenn sie sich nicht in Funktion befindet, so zieht sich die Membrane, die diesen Apparat konstituiert, mit ihren Accessoires zurück und die Wand ist wiederhergestellt. Der Boden ist ein Materie-Simulator und kann alle sensorielle Parameter einer grossen Anzahl organischer Stoffe wiedergeben. Wesentliches Element der Zelle ist hingegen die Decke: sie besteht aus einer einzigen Platte, die die cerebralen Impulse empfängt.

In jeder Zelle lebt ein Individuum, dessen cerebrale Impulse kontinuierlich vom Deckschirm aufgenommen und an den zentralen elektronischen Analysator weitergeleitet werden. Dieser Analysator, ein komplexes System von Apparaten, befindet sich zuoberst im Gebäude, unter einem durchgehenden, halbkreisförmigen Tonnengewölbe. Er wählt aus, vergleicht und vermittelt zwischen den Bedürfnissen der Individuen, indem er Sekunde für Sekunde das Leben der ganzen Stadt programmiert mit Hilfe der Sendewand, dem Materie-Simulator (Boden) und den Reflexen der automatischen «Wohnwand». Auf diese Weise sind sämtliche Bürger in jedem Augenblick im Besitz derselben Voraussetzungen der Gleichheit.

Hier gibt es keinen Tod mehr. Es kommt vor, dass sich jemand von der absurden Idee einer Rebellion gegen das vollkommene und ewige Leben hinreissen lässt, das man ihm geschenkt hat. Beim ersten Mal übersieht der Analysator das Verbrechen, aber falls sich dieses wiederholt, so beschliesst die Stadt, jenem den Lebensraum zu verweigern, der sich ihrer so unwürdig erweist. Die Deckplatte senkt sich mit einer Kraft von 2000 Tonnen, bis sie den Boden berührt.

Es ist dies der Augenblick, wo in der wunderbaren Oekonomie der Stadt neues Leben entsteht. Während der Deckenschirm wieder zu seiner ursprünglichen Position aufsteigt, spenden sämtliche Individuen, welche die Zellen bewohnen, die in einem Umkreis einer Viertelmeile um die leere Zelle angeordnet sind, ein Ei oder eine Serie von Spermatozoen. Diese werden in eigens für sie eingerichteten Kanälen transportiert, und zwar so, dass sie sich so rasch wie möglich gegen den leergewordenen Stuhl bewegen. Dort wird nun ein Ei befruchtet, und der Stuhl verwandelt sich in einen Uterus, um während neun Monaten, bis zur Morgendämmerung seines glücklichen Schicksals, den neuen Sohn der Stadt zu beschützen.

2. Die diesseitige Schnecken-Stadt

Die Stadt ist eine gewaltige, unendliche Schraube, deren äussere Form einem Zylinder von 4,5 km entspricht, und die sich langsam bewegt, indem sie alljährlich eine Umdrehung vollzieht.

Wie ein Raumschiff, so bewegt sich die Stadt in der Lithosphäre mit einer Winkelgeschwindigkeit von 2'28''/sec.; die perimetrale Geschwindigkeit beträgt 3584 mm/h. Ihr unteres Ende, welches der Erdmitte zustrebt, besteht aus einer Bohranlage, einer Art Turbine, die mit gewaltigen Klingen ausgerüstet ist, welche, indem sie sich dreht, den Felsen abbault und das Material zum Mittelpunkt des Zylinders bewegt. Von dort wird es mit Hilfe eines Abzugsschachts nach Aussen befördert. Oberhalb der Turbine befinden sich die Antriebsmaschinen, die Atomzentrale (die 10 000 Jahre lang automatisch arbeitet) und die Computers, die die Stadt regieren.

Ihr äusseres Ende wächst in einer Weise, dass es immer auf der Höhe des Bodens bleibt. Dieses Wachstum wird erreicht, indem ständig neue Stadtteile gebaut werden, und zwar von einem automatischen Bauplatz, der wie eine Brücke zwischen der Mittelachse und dem äusseren Rand der Stadt gespannt ist. Hier werden die Gesteinsreste, welche von den Bohrarbeiten im Erdinnern stammen, als Baumaterialien verwendet.

Die Stadt besteht aus Wohnzellen, die in konzentrischen Kreisen angeordnet sind, und zwar in je zwei Reihen. Die Wand jeder Zelle ist gleich hoch wie die Zelle tief: 280 cm. Zwischen den einzelnen Kreisen, die aus den zusammengefügten Zellen bestehen, ist eine 280 cm breite Strasse angeordnet. 1440 Radialstrassen verbinden die Kreisstrassen untereinander. Jede Zelle besitzt nur eine Oeffnung, nämlich eine Tür zur nächstliegenden Kreisstrasse. Die restlichen Wände zwischen den Zellen sind vollständig undurchsichtig und schalldicht. Der Niveauunterschied zwischen zwei Stockwerken beträgt 330 cm.

Der Boden der Zellen ist weich, und sämtliche Installationen, die zur Befriedigung der Lebensbedürfnisse des Individuums nötig sind, sind in der Decke verborgen und ihre Aktivität ist ferngesteuert. Die ganze Stadt ist konstant klimatisiert: 25° Celsius und 60 % Feuchtigkeit. Jede Zelle ist konstant erleuchtet, und zwar mit einer Intensität von 500 Lux. Das Licht enthält den gesamten Wellenbereich des sichtbaren Spektrums; in den Strassen enthält es zusätzlich kleine Dosen von ultravioletten Strahlen. Als Lichtquelle dient die gesamte Oberfläche der Decken, sowohl in den Zellen als auch in den Strassen, was die Schaffung von Schatten- und Halbschattenzonen verunmöglicht.

Die Zellen besitzen keinerlei Schliessvorkehrungen; die Sicherung der Türen ist unmöglich.

Die Bewohner der Stadt leben allein in ihrer Zelle, sie besitzen weder Kleider noch Gegenstände, weil die Stadt für die vollkommene Befriedigung aller ihrer Bedürfnisse aufkommt. Sie sind vollkommen frei, was die Organisation ihres individuellen und gemeinschaftlichen Lebens betrifft; frei, Versammlungen zu veranstalten, sich Gesetze oder Regeln zu geben. Die einzige Beschränkung besteht darin, dass sie ihre Stadt nicht verlassen können, da ja die oberen Enden der Kreisstrassen — die in Wirklichkeit spiralförmig angelegt sind und von unten nach oben führen — durch den automatischen Bauplatz, den die Stadt baut, abgeschlossen sind. Unter den Einrichtungen, mit denen jede Zelle versehen ist, befindet sich ein «automatischer Gebärapparat», der nach Wunsch in Funktion tritt. Er wird vom Abdomen der Schwangeren appliziert und befreit den Foetus ohne jede Schmerzempfindung. Das Kleinkind wird dann durch Schächte in eine neuen Zellen geführt, wo es automatisch ernährt und aufgezogen wird. Nur während dieser Phase wird die Zellentür

↓ fig. 2 Temporal Cochlea-City.

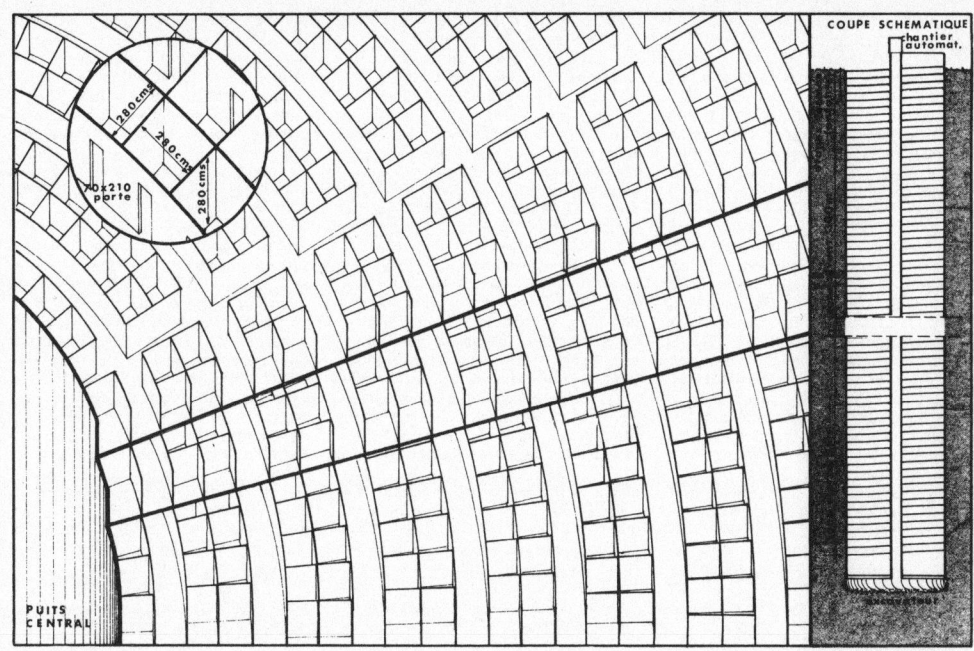

durch eine Stahlplatte verschlossen, so dass sie weder von innen noch von aussen geöffnet werden kann. Während vier Jahren bleibt das Kind in seine Zelle eingeschlossen, und während dieser Zeit wird es die ethischen Prinzipien und das Funktionieren seiner Stadt erlernen. Sobald die vierte Umdrehung seit dem Bau der Zelle abgeschlossen ist, gleitet der Metallverschluss zur Seite und verschwindet vollkommen in der Wand.

Die Materialien, mit deren Hilfe die Stadt gebaut wird, haben eine Lebensdauer von einem Jahrhundert. Während dieser Zeit benötigen sie keinen Unterhalt; anschliessend beginnen sie, langsam zu verderben. Das gilt ebenso für die Installationen und die Einrichtungen, aber selbstverständlich nicht für die tragenden Bauteile und die allgemeinen Erschliessungen.

Die Bewohner der Stadt verbringen einen grossen Teil ihrer Zeit in den Strassen im Umkreis ihrer Zelle; oft steigen sie, in Gruppen oder einzeln, die Spiralstrassen empor, bis zu der Zone der Kinder oder, noch weiter, bis zu den vier letzten, verlassenen und einsamen Türmen, in denen die Neugeborenen leben. Häufig versuchen sie, Hände und Ohren an die warme, vibrierende Metallwand des Bauplatzes gepresst, das Geheimnis der Aussenwelt zu erlauschen. Aber andererseits dringt nur sehr selten jemand in die andere Richtung vor, bis hinab in die Zonen des hohen Alters und, noch weiter, in die Türme, wo Gegenstände und Menschen der Auflösung und der Fäulnis anheimfallen. Oder, noch weiter, bis in die Zone, die nur mehr von schwachem Licht und von Hitze erfüllt ist: wo die Wohnkreise angefüllt sind von Abfällen, von Staub und von Knochenresten. Finsternis, überhitzte und vibrierende Stadtteile, die sich im Kreise drehen, hinab in unendliche Tiefen.

3. Die Bandstadt, die sich kontinuierlich produziert

Die Stadt marschiert, sie rollt voran wie eine majestätische Schlange durch sich ständig verändernde Landschaften, indem sie ihre acht Millionen Einwohner über Ebenen, Täler und Hügel, an Bergen und Meeresküsten entlang spazieren führt, von Generation zu Generation.

Der Kopf der Stadt ist die Grosse Fabrik von 4 Meilen Breite — wie die Stadt selbst, die sie ohne Unterbruch produziert — und von einer Viertelmeile Tiefe. In ihrer Mitte besitzt sie eine Höhe von 100 Yards. Die Grosse Fabrik baut das Terrain und den Untergrund ab, auf dem sie sich voranbewegt, und sie entnimmt ihm auf wunderbare Weise alles, was für den Bau der Stadt nützlich ist. Die Grosse Fabrik verzehrt die Fetzen einer unnützen Natur und die formlosen Mineralien durch ihren Vorderteil und sie scheidet an ihrem

Ende vollkommen ausgerüstete und gebrauchsfertige Stadtteile aus. Die Grosse Fabrik schreitet mit einer Geschwindigkeit von 1 Fuss und 2,5 Inches pro Stunde voran. Der Plan der Stadt ist gekennzeichnet durch einen Schachbrettgrundriss von Strassen, die senkrecht und parallel zur Grossen Fabrik verlaufen. Die Strassen sind 29 Yards breit und unterteilen die Stadt in quadratische Zonen von 261 Yards Seitenlänge. Die längsgerichteten Strassen sind, ausgehend von der Mittelachse, fortlaufend numeriert, wobei der Buchstabe «D» oder «S» beigefügt wird, je nachdem ob sie sich zur Rechten oder zur Linken der Hauptachse befinden, die zur Grossen Fabrik führt. Die Parallelstrassen hingegen sind nach dem Monat und dem Jahr ihrer Entstehung benannt. In der Tat produziert die Grosse Fabrik eine Kolonne von Wohnsektoren in 27 Tagen und die dazugehörige Parallelstrasse in drei Tagen. Da die Herstellung der Strassen vollkommen automatisiert ist, bleibt die Fabrik während dieser drei Tage geschlossen. Diese Pause innerhalb der nie abbrechenden Arbeit wird «month end» oder, im Volksmund, «street holiday» genannt.

Das hauptsächliche Bestreben der Bewohner ist, möglichst häufig in ein neues Haus umzuziehen, weil die neu produzierten Häuser durch den Verwaltungsrat der Stadt beständig erneuert zum Nutzen des Bewohner und mit ständig perfektionierten Bequemlichkeiten ausgerüstet werden. Stellen Sie sich vor: die Notabeln der Stadt, die «grandes familles», die es sich leisten können, ziehen jeden Monat um in die Häuser, die eben fertiggestellt wurden; sie folgen gewissermassen dem Produktionsrhythmus der Grossen Fabrik auf dem Fuss. Die übrigen Bürger versuchen, es ihnen gleichzutun; nur die Dandies und die Faulenzer warten vier Jahre, bis sie sich dazu entschliessen, ihr Haus zu wechseln. Glücklicherweise ist es gar nicht möglich, länger als vier Jahre im gleichen Haus zu wohnen, denn nach dieser Zeitspanne beginnen die Einrichtungsgegenstände, ja sogar die tragenden Bauteile der Häuser, sich aufzulösen. Sie werden unbenützbar und fallen alsobald dem Zerfall anheim. Nur der Ausschuss der Gesellschaft, verrückte oder verrufene Individuen, wagen es, zwischen diesen Ruinen, Abfällen und Müllhaufen umherzuirren, welche die Stadt hinter sich lässt, damit sich Ratten und andere Parasiten darum streiten.

Gerade um zu verhindern, dass sich die Bürger zu einem derart bedauernswerten Zustand herabwürdigen, wird ihnen seit der zarten Kindheit die Idee eingeimpft, wonach ein jeder zuallererst nach einem neuen Haus zu streben habe. Aus demselben Grund machen die Zeitungen, die TV und alle anderen Medien kontinuierlich Propaganda für die wunderbaren Neuheiten in den frischgebauten Häusern; technische Neuerungen, nie nie dagewesene Bequemlichkeiten, usw.

Gibt es etwas Schöneres und etwas Sittigerendes als der Anblick von Familien, die Tag für Tag in den gelben Bussen, die ihnen der Verwaltungsrat zur Verfügung stellt, der Grossen Fabrik zustreben, wo die neuen Häuser entstehen? Gibt es etwas Stimulierenderes als der kontinuierliche Wettlauf der Bürger, die alle in jener Parallelstrasse wohnen wollen, welche gerade das jüngste Datum trägt? Gibt es einen glücklicheren Tag als denjenigen des Umzugs in das neue Haus, wenn Ihnen der Direktor einen Freitag gewährt und Sie persönlich beglückwünscht? Gibt es eine seligere Stunde als die, während der Sie in das neue Heim eintreten und Ihre neuen technischen Einrichtungen, Ihre neuen Kleider entdecken und sich innewerden, dass Ihnen das alles durch die Grosse Fabrik bereitgestellt wurde? Bewundern Sie die Stadt von oben: mit ihrem grossen, schwarzen Kopf, umwölkt vom Rauch aus Tausenden von Kaminen, mit ihrem gepflegten Körper von 8 Meilen Länge und, im Zentrum, ihren grandiosen Wolkenkratzern, begleitet von Volkshäusern, neben denen sich weite Gärten hinziehen. Und, dahinter, die nicht endenwollende Schleife von Abfällen, die Zeugnis ablegt für den zurückgelegten Weg. Betrachten Sie diese vollkommene Stadt, autonom im Hinblick auf ihre sämtlichen Bedürfnisse, in ihren kleinen Fabriken mehr Exportartikel als jede andere Stadt produziert. Betrachten Sie die langen Prozessionen von Lastwagen, die leer ankommen, aber voll beladen wieder wegfahren, um die Prosperität unseres grossen Landes und die Vermögen unserer geliebten Aktionäre ständig zu mehren.

(Auszug aus: *Happy birthday, Grand Factory — our town is two hundred years old;* hrsg. von dem «Public Relations Office» der Stadt.

Epilog

Nun haben Sie also drei * Beispiele für die Ueppigkeit von Träumen vorgeführt bekommen, wie sie der Schlummer unserer Zivilisation produziert. Drei: eine magische, versöhnende Zahl. Eine Art Hommage von uns Städtern an die Völker einer entfernten Zeit, welche die Städte erfinden werden.

Der Augenblick ist gekommen, wo es gilt, die wahre Bedeutung dieser Schilderungen zu enthüllen. Es handelt sich um einen Test, nicht weniger sorgfältig zusammengestellt als jene Tests, wie sie die Illustrierten häufig veröffentlichen. Wie üblich, so finden Sie auch hier die Resultate.

LESEN SIE SIE AUFMERKSAM UND SIE WERDEN WISSEN, WER SIE SIND. DIE ENTHUELLUNG IST NAHE.

Frage: «Wieviele von diesen drei Städten, deren Beschreibungen Sie eben gelesen haben, erwecken in Ihnen den Wunsch, dass sie Wirklichkeit werden? Oder: sind sie der Meinung, dass ihr Zustandekommen der Menschheit förderlich sein wird?»

Resultate auf Seite 36

* in der von Superstudio zusammengestellten, vollständigen Fassung sind es zwölf Idealstädte — vgl. *Casabella*, No 361.

At first the analyser ignores the crime; but if it is repeated. the man who has shown himself unworthy is rejected. The ceiling panel descends with a force of two thousand tons until it reaches the floor.

At this point, in this marvellous economy, another life is initiated. The panel returns to its original height, and all the individuals living in cells within a distance of a quarter of a league from the empty cell donate an ovum or a group of spermatozoa, which are transported in channels created for this purpose in a mad race to the now-empty seat. Here, an ovum is fertilized and the seat is transformed into a uterus, protecting the new son of the city for nine months, until his happy dawn.

Second City
Temporal Cochlea-City

The city is an endless screw, 4.5 Km. in diameter, completing one revolution a year.

Like a spaceship, the city moves in the lithosphere with an angular velocity of 2' 28"/sec.; the perimetral velocity is 3,584 mm/hr. Its lower extremity, facing the centre of the earth, consists of an excavating apparatus (a kind of turbine, with blades) that, in revolving, crushes rock, forcing all matter towards the centre of the cylinder and through a duct up to the ground. Above the turbine is the propulsion apparatus, an atomic power centre set to last 10,000 years and the automatic plant and electronic computers that control the city.

The upper extremity grows gradually, remaining constantly at the level of the ground outside. Growth is realized through the continuous construction of new sections of city by means of an automatic building-site placed like a bridge between the centre and the perimeter. On this site, rock detritus from the excavations at the bottom is used as building material.

The city is composed of living-cells arranged in a double row of concentric circles. The wall of each cell is as tall as it is deep: 280 cm. Between the two contiguous circles of cells is a roadway 280 cm across. 1,440 radial roadways connect the circular streets. Each cell has a single opening, a door giving on to the circular roadway; the other walls backing onto other cells are totally opaque and soundproof. The difference in levels between two floors is 330 cm.

The floor of the cells is soft, all apparatus required for the satisfaction of individual living needs are hidden in the ceiling and are tele-controlled. The entire city is climatized at a constant 25°C, with 60% humidity. Each cell is constantly lit to an intensity of 150 lux; the roads are illuminated to an intensity of 500 lux; this light contains all the wavelengths of the visible spectrum; that of the roads also contains small quantities of ultra-violet light. The entire ceiling surface serves as a light source, both in the cells and on the streets, making it impossible to create zones of shade or semishade.

The cells have no system for closing or screening.

Inhabitants live one to a cell, and possess no clothes or other objects because the city provides for their every need. They are absolutely free to act and organize their lives, both as individuals and as a community; to be alone; to gather in groups; to create laws or regulations; the only restriction is that they cannot go outside the city because the upper ends of the circular roads are closed by the automatic building-site. Each cell contains an "automatic obstetrician" which, applied to the abdomen of the future mother, extracts the foetus painlessly. The baby is transported by pipeline to a cell in the newly-built section, where it is fed and looked after automatically. Only in this phase is the door of the cell sealed by a steel panel. For four years the child remains in his cell, during which time he learns the ethics and working of his city. Thereafter the metal door slides away and disappears forever into the wall.

Materials used for building the city remain unaltered for a century, without maintenance; then they begin to degenerate; this is also true of the equipment and machinery. Naturally, load-bearing structures and the general equipment of the city are an exception.

The inhabitants spend a lot of time in the roads near their cells; often, in groups or alone, they climb the spiral roads until they reach the children's zone and beyond, into the last four deserted and silent spirals where the newborn babies live. Often, placing their hands and ears against the warm, vibrating metal walls of the building-site, they try to penetrate the mystery of the outside world. But it is rare for someone to go down the road beyond the zone of extreme old age, into the spirals of decay and putrefaction of things and men, and yet further into the uncertain light and the heat, into the spirals scattered with detritus, dust, bones, until they reach the dark, suffocating and vibrant zones spiralling towards indefinite depths.

Third City
Continuous Production Conveyor Belt City

The city moves, unrolling like a majestic serpent, over new lands, taking its 8 million inhabitants on a ride through valleys and hills, from the mountains to the seashore, generation after generation.

The head of the city is the Grand Factory, four miles wide and 100 yards high, like the city it continuously produces. The Grand Factory exploits the land and the underground materials of the territory it crosses, and from these marvellously extracts all that it requires for the construction of the city. The Grand Factory devours shreds of useless nature and unformed minerals at its front end and emits sections of completely formed city, ready for use, from its back end. The Grand Factory moves forward at a speed of 1 ft. 2½ in. per hour. The plan of the city is based on a chequerboard of roads perpendicular and parallel to the Grand Factory; the roads separate square blocks, 261 × 261 yards, and are 29 yards wide. The perpendicular roads are numbered progressively, starting from the central axis of the city adding the letter L or R to the number according to whether it is on the left or the right of the axis; the parallel roads however are called by the name of the month and year of their construction. The Grand Factory produces a series of blocks (including the segments of perpendicular roads between them) in 27 days and the parallel road next to them in 3 days. Because the production of the streets is completely automated, the factory remains closed during these 3 days. This break in the incessant work is called "month end" or, popularly, "street holiday."

The greatest aspiration of every citizen is to move more and more often into a new house because the houses produced are continually modernized and equipped with the yet more perfect commodities that the Administrative Council invents for the joy of the citizens. The Great Families move monthly into the houses just built, following the rhythm of the Grand Factory. The other citizens do their best and only those with little willpower and the laziest wait for four years before moving house. Luckily, it is not possible to live in the same house for more than four years after its construction; after this period, objects, accessories and the structure of the houses themselves decay, become unusable and soon after collapse. Only society's rejects, mad or insane individuals, still dare to wander amongst the ruins, the detritus and rubble that the city leaves behind it.

It is in order to prevent the citizens being reduced to such a desperate state that from their earliest age they are inculcated with the concept that everyone's greatest desire must always be a new house, and it is for this reason that the newspapers, TV and all other media continually advertise the marvellous novelties of the new houses, the technical innovations, the never-before-seen comforts.

What could be more fascinating and reassuring than the spectacle of the families that daily drive up the perpendicular roads in the little yellow buses put at their disposal by the Administrative Council, in the direction of the Grand Factory, towards their new houses? What could be more stimulating than the continual rivalry between all citizens in trying to live on parallel streets with the most recent dates? What day could be happier than when you move into your new house, and your Director gives you a day off on special grounds and congratulates you? What hour could be happier than when you enter your new home and discover all your new things, your new equipment, your new clothes and everything else that the Grand Factory has prepared for you? Admire the city from above, with its great black head, plumed with the smoke of thousands of factory chimneys, with its tidy body eight miles long, with at its centre the grandiose crest of skyscrapers, flanked by great blocks

↓ fig. 3 Continuous Production Conveyor Belt City.

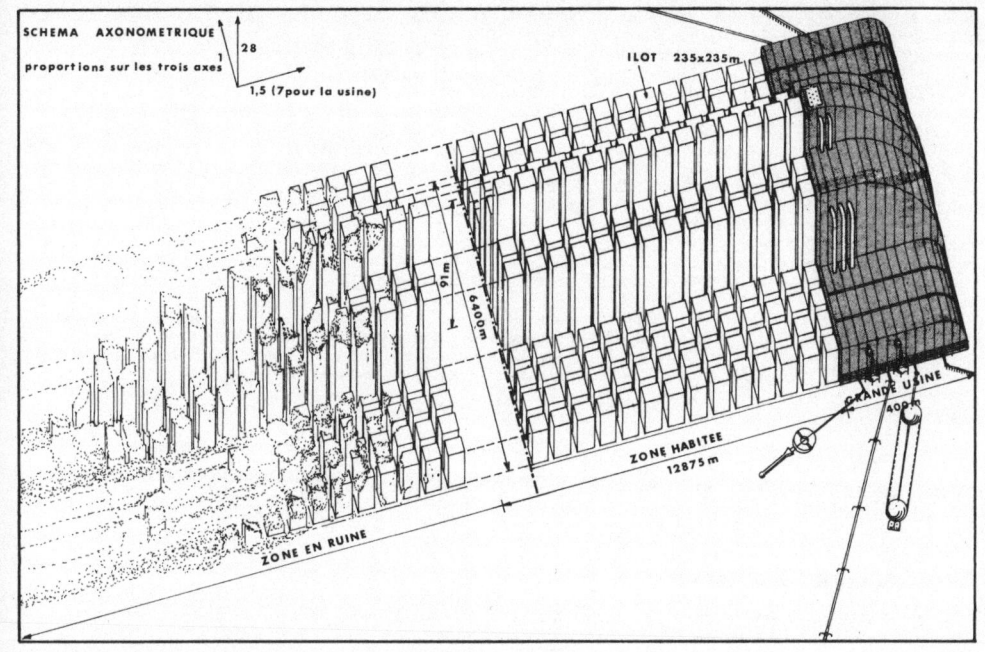

N. J. Habraken

Das Ende des Wohnbauprojektes

Nikolaas J. Habrakens Alternative zur heutigen Praxis des sozialen Wohnbaus ist zugleich radikal und pragmatisch. 1961 erschien sein Buch «De Dragers en de Mensen». Es forderte das Ende des Wohnbauprojektes im traditionellen Sinn — ähnlich wie, später, Yona Friedman, die japanischen Metabolisten und andere Gruppen. Aber mit einem — entscheidenden — Unterschied: der Gedanke wurde als solcher in die Welt gesetzt, und nicht durch konkrete Projekte ästhetisch (und damit stilgeschichtlich) fixiert. Er blieb «Konzept». Die Folge ist, dass er seit 1961 nichts von seiner Frische eingebüsst hat. Heute steht eine englische Ausgabe des Buches von Habraken bevor; wir drucken daraus einen Teil des deutschen Erstdrucks.

Die Redaktion

Das Ende des Wohnbauprojektes

1918 erschien in Rotterdam eine Broschüre von weniger als 50 Seiten. Sie trug den Titel «Normalisierung des Wohnbaus. Ein Vortrag von Dr. H. P. Berlage. Mit 30 Illustrationen und einem Vorwort von Ing. J. van der Werden. Zum Wohnbau-Kongress in Amsterdam, Februar 1918».

Aus dieser Broschüre erfährt man, dass Mr. van der Waerden am oben genannten Kongress eine Ansprache hielt, in der er eine Reihe von drastischen Massnahmen vorschlug, um mit dem Wohnungsmangel fertigzuwerden. Er plädierte in erster Linie für eine rigorose Normalisierung der Planung sowie für ein zentrales Verteilersystem von Baumaterialien und Bauarbeiten. Offensichtlich entzündeten sich an diesen

cédera à l'authentique, mais par l'expérience intérieure d'une dimension autre, qui révèle brusquement, au moyen de ce que les historiens des religions appellent un changement de niveau, l'irréalité du kitsch.

[26] Pour une «lecture» récente, voit Le centre du monde se trouve aussi à Mulhouse, de L. Burckhardt et Ch. Hunziker in «Moebius international», no 6—7/1969, pp. 5—20; sur les circonstances de cette opération, cf. R.-H. Guerrand, Les origines du logement social en France, Les Editions Ouvrières, Paris 1966, pp. 122—125; sur le fond, cf. aussi P. Riboulet, Eléments pour une critique de l'architecture, in «Espaces et Société», no 1, novembre 1970, p. 35: «Le résultat (...) que souhaitaient Dollfuss à Mulhouse ou Siegfried au Havre, celui que dénonçait Engels en 1872: attacher l'ouvrier à son capitaliste».

[29] «Chaque maison sera construite pour une seule famille, sans communication» (Article premier des statuts de la Société mulhousienne des Cités ouvrières, cit. in Guerrand, p. 123); «La société disposait d'un terrain de 8 hectares sur lequel on implanta des pavillons groupés de trois façons: adossés deux à deux, par bloc de quatre au milieu d'un jardin, entre cour et jardin» (ibid. p. 123); «le pot-au-feu (...) est en définitive une des pierres angulaires de la famille et il serait très fâcheux de voir des ouvriers y renoncer pour se donner les vaines distractions d'une table commune» (opinion d'un philanthrope local, ibidem, p. 125); «les ménages devaient vivre repliés sur eux-mêmes et se consacrer exclusivement à l'aménagement de leur intérieur, visité chaque année par un jury qui décernait des primes en argent et des mentions honorables à ceux qui se distinguaient par ,l'ordre, la propreté et en général la bonne tenue'» (ibid. p. 125). Ce paternalisme fait apparaître clairement le kitsch comme la seule soupape légitime au besoin de créativité.

[30] Cf. p. ex. M. Ragon, Où vivrons-nous demain? Laffont, Paris 1963, p. 178: «Liberté de mouvement, d'emplacement, soit (...), mais non n'importe quel baroquisme» — et ce qui précède.

Resultate des Tests von Seite 7

Drei: Sie sind ein Staatschef oder hoffen, einer zu werden; auf jeden Fall bringen Sie alle Voraussetzungen mit, einer zu werden. Sie haben die Logik und die Mechanismen des Systems vollkommen assimiliert. Sie sind ein Teil von ihm, ja Sie sind identisch mit ihm. Sie sind nichts als eine leere Muschel, eine feuchte und dunkle Mulde, in die das System eingedrungen ist wie die Wurzelranken der Kürbisse, welche in die Spälte des Erdreichs eindringen und diese vollkommen ausfüllen. Sie sind eine entsetzliche Vision der Hölle, ja Sie sind der personifizierte Horror.

Sie sind kein menschliches Wesen, Sie sind bloss ein «Zombie».

Zwei: Sie sind ein Teil des Systems, ein vollkommen funktionelles Zahnrädchen innerhalb des Ganzen. Geölt und geschmiert durch die Logik der Kultur und infolgedessen ohne jede Reibung, vollziehen Sie Ihre regelmässigen Umdrehungen, Synchron und in vollkommenem Einklang mit Ihren Artgleichen. Sie sind das vollkommne Produkt Ihres Schöpfers: halluziniert und sadistisch, verbreiten Sie Schrecken. Auch Sie sind kein menschliches Wesen, sondern ein kleiner und krüppeliger «Golem».

Eine: Sie sind eine Art Wurm. Sie haben zwar verstanden, aber Sie wollen es Ihnen nicht eingestehen. Ihre Beine, Arme und Zähne wurden Ihnen amputiert, weil Sie sich sogar davor gefürchtet haben, zu fliehen. Und im Augenblick halten Sie sich in dunklen Winkeln versteckt, die Schnauze in den Dreck gesteckt, um nicht hören und sehen zu müssen. Wenn Sie sich selber anekeln, so liegt das daran, dass Sie weniger Angst haben möchten, um wie die anderen sein zu können. Sie sind ein Schreckgespenst. Sie sind zwar ein menschliches Wesen, aber es wäre weniger schlimm, wenn Sie keines wären. Sie sind ein obszöner «Mutant».

Gar keine: Gut, Sie fühlen sich also erleichtert. OK, mein Freund, aber Sie sollten es nicht sein, denn Sie haben überhaupt nichts verstanden. Sie haben nicht verstanden, dass die Beschreibungen gar keine imaginären Städte wiedergeben, sondern unsere Stadt, in diesem Augenblick, und alle Städte. Gleichfalls haben Sie möglicherweise nicht einmal gemerkt, dass noch viel halluzinierendere Vorstellungen als die, die wir in diesen armseligen Dörfchen zu beschreiben versuchten, Wirklichkeit werden können, sobald einmal die Logik des Systems noch etwas logischer ist. Passen Sie auf: die Strasse ist frei, die «technisch fortgeschrittenen» Länder eilen schon in voller Geschwindigkeit auf dieser Strasse voran und nähern sich zusehends ihrem Ziel. Und die «Entwicklungsländer» folgen ihnen auf dem Fuss. Es tut mir leid, aber es kann für Sie nur eine Definition geben: «Idiot».

Nur WENN SIE DAS SPIEL VERSTANDEN HABEN, von Anfang an, können Sie das Heil erwarten. Die «Offenbarung» kann das Resultat des Schreckens sein, den wir über uns selbst und unsere Umgebung empfinden. Dann aber, gehen Sie hin und suchen Sie den Alten des Berges und seien Sie seine Söhne. Verbringen Sie die Zeit damit, die Haare seines weissen Bartes zu liebkosen, und kommen Sie, neugeboren, zurück, die Haschischpille unter der Zunge, das Messer zwischen Ihrer Weste und Ihrer Brust, um die Geister, die Gespenster, die Monstren und die Dämonen, welche die Erde verpesten, zu tilgen. Und dann, von Wasser und Weihrauch gereinigt, können Sie die Fundamente der neuen Stadt mit ihren Weissen Mauern vorbereiten.

Uebersetzung: S. v. M.

of popular housing estates, and stretches of villas with gardens at the edges; with its interminable wake of rubble indicating the ground covered. Look at the perfect city that produces more goods for export than any other city. Look at the rows of lorries arriving empty and going away loaded with goods to contribute to the greater prosperity of our great country and the better fortunes of our well-loved shareholders.

(Excerpt from "Happy Birthday, Grand Factory: Our Town Is Two Hundred Years Old," published by the public relations office of the city).

Epilogue

Now you have been presented with three* examples of the lavishness of the dreams produced by the slumber of our civilization. Three: a magic, reconciling number. A kind of homage by us city dwellers to the people of a remote time who will invent the cities.

The moment has come in which to reveal the significance of these descriptions. It is a test, no less meticulously compiled than the tests glossy magazines often publish. As usual, here, too, you will find the answers.

READ THEM CAREFULLY, AND YOU WILL KNOW WHO YOU ARE. THE REVELATION IS NIGH.

Question: "How many of these three cities whose descriptions you have just read awaken in you the desire that they become reality? Or: Are you of the opinion that their coming about would benefit humanity?"

Results on page 36

* The complete version compiled by Superstudio has twelve ideal cities; see *Casabella*, no. 361 [(1972): 44–55].

Results of the Test on Page 7

Three: You are a head of state or hope to become one, or at any rate you are suited to be one. You have completely assimilated the logic and the mechanism of the system. They are part of you—indeed, you are identical with them. You are but an empty shell, a dark and humid cavity into which the system has penetrated like tendrils of pumpkin plants into earthy crevices, completely filling them. You are a horrid vision of hell—indeed, you are horror personified. You are not a human being. You are simply a zombie.

Two: You are an element of the system, a cog functioning perfectly within the whole. Oiled and lubricated by the logic of the culture and thus free from friction, you turn smoothly, perfectly synchronized with other members of your species. You are the perfect product of your creator: hallucinating and sadistic, you disseminate terrors. You are not a human being, either, but a small and crippled "golem."

One: You are a worm. You have got the idea, and you don't want to admit it even to yourself. You have amputated your legs, arms, and teeth because you're scared even to run away. And now you're hidden away in a dark corner with your snout in the mud so as not to see or hear. But the disgusting thing about you is that you'd like to be less frightened so as to be like everyone else. You are a bogeyman. You're a human being, but perhaps it wouldn't be as bad if you weren't. You are an obscene "mutant."

None at all: So, you feel self-satisfied, but you shouldn't. Because you have not caught on: you haven't understood that the descriptions represent cities now. Is it possible that you didn't realize that it is enough to carry forward the logic of the system until it becomes rigorous logic, to concretize many more hallucinating fantasies than those described here? Hold on, the way is broad, the "technologically advanced" countries are running rapidly along it (ever nearer their goal), and the "developing countries" are following close. You are an "idiot."

Only IF YOU UNDERSTOOD THE GAME from the beginning can you hope to be saved. From the horror of us and our surroundings, "revelation" could spring. Ascend, then, up to the Old Man of the Mountain and be of his children. Observe time through the white hairs of his beard, and when you have been reborn, descend with a pill of hashish beneath your tongue and a knife under your shirt, to exterminate the spirits, monsters, and demons that infest the Earth, and finally, purified with water and incense, you can prepare the foundations for the new City of the White Walls.

Collective Housing

Theories and Experiments of the Utopian Socialists Robert Owen (1771–1858) and Charles Fourier (1772–1837)

Authors:
Franziska Bollerey
Kristiana Hartmann

Source:
archithese, 8 (1973): 15–26

Translated by:
Steven Lindberg

Utopian designs for collective housing developments reflect the urban planning practice of their time and at the same time anticipate new social conditions. It is in keeping with the self-image of the utopians not to present their architectural ideas in an isolated space; their planning concepts are instead part of general proposals to restructure the entire society. The urbanistic reflections of the advocates of utopian socialism—Owen and Fourier—differ from those of the utopians and planners of ideal cities of antiquity and the Renaissance in their relationship to the changed conditions of production. Owenite activity and the theoretical and practical models of architecture to be described here fell in the era of the Industrial Revolution and the establishment of the industrial bourgeoisie. The concepts of Fourier and his disciples emerged against the backdrop of postrevolutionary events, the Napoleonic era, the Restoration, and the period after the July Revolution.[1]

The proposals for reform resulted from analyzing contemporaneous sociopolitical deficiencies. In the effort to redress those ills, two possibilities stood out. On the one hand, in the urbanist sector the old cities were countered with new forms of living together; on the other hand, there was an effort to resolve partial aspects of the problem in a kind of pseudo-redevelopment. In the process, however, they lost sight of the connections and, unlike the utopian socialists, did not come up with overall conceptions for a new urban organism.

Robert Owen (1771–1858) and Charles Fourier (1772–1837) shared with the utopians of antiquity and the Renaissance an opposition to the apologists for existing conditions and the insight that in the bourgeois order, despite the liberation of the individual from feudal society, true misery is not and cannot be eradicated.[2] Like the former, they assumed that the society they designed could be established at any time and in any place. This overestimate of the field of influence of ideally conceived housing developments provoked the critique of the representatives of scientific socialism. For the utopian socialists, therefore, it was "necessary, then, to discover a new and more perfect system of social order and to impose this upon society from without by propaganda, and, wherever it was possible, by the example of model experiments."[3]

"Periods of development that are supposed to redesign what exists from the ground up [are]

↓ fig. 1   Robert Owen, Lithograph after an undated sketch by J. Comerford.   ↓ fig. 2   Portrait of Charles Fourier.

Franziska Bollerey und Kristiana Hartmann

Kollektives Wohnen
Theorien und Experimente der utopischen Sozialisten Robert Owen (1771-1858) und Charles Fourier (1772-1837)

Habitat collectif
Théories et expériences des socialistes utopiques Robert Owen (1771—1858) et Charles Fourier (1772—1837)

Les théories et propositions de formes d'habitat collectif développées par Owen et Fourier ne sont pas d'abord architecturales mais sociales et utopiques. Mais elles s'avancent quand même dans les domaines concrets de l'architecture et mènent à des concepts de planification d'une actualité remarquable.

Les projets de Owen répondent aux exigences de la révolution industrielle, alors que ceux de Fourier ont pour arrière-plan l'aire napoléonienne, la restauration et l'époque qui suivit la révolution de Juillet.

Après avoir participé à la réforme d'une usine de tissage de coton en Ecosse, dont il était directeur associé, Owen projeta un établissement où devaient s'intégrer production et consommation. En 1824 il émigra en Amérique, pour y créer une ville modèle, New Harmony, dans l'Indiana. Pour la première fois une ville était planifiée en tenant compte des critères sociaux, et offrait tous les avantages techniques connus.

Fourier basa son concept de Phalanstère sur l'analyse du développement social de l'humanité, concept qu'il expose dans le *Nouveau Monde Industriel* (1829). Ses idées furent en partie réalisées à Guise par Victor Considérant.

Malgré les réalisations partielles, les concepts d'habitat de Owen et Fourier restent en large mesure utopiques, car ils visent à la planification d'une société dont les structures seraient déjà changées.

Utopische Entwürfe kollektiver Siedlungen reflektieren die städtebauliche Praxis ihrer Zeit und antizipieren gleichzeitig neue gesellschaftliche Zustände. Dem Selbstverständnis der Utopisten entspricht es, architektonische Vorstellungen nicht in einen isolierten Raum zu stellen; ihre Planungskonzepte sind vielmehr Teil gesamtgesellschaftlicher Umstrukturierungsvorschläge. Die urbanistischen Ueberlegungen der Vertreter des utopischen Sozialismus, Owen und Fourier, unterschieden sich von denen der Utopisten und Idealstadtplaner der Antike und der Renaissance durch ihr Verhältnis zu den veränderten Produktionsbedingungen. Die Owensche Tätigkeit und die hier darzustellenden architekturtheoretischen und pragmatischen Modelle fallen in die Zeit der Industriellen Revolution und der Etablierung des Industriebürgertums. Die Konzepte Fouriers und seiner Schüler entstanden vor dem Hintergrund postrevolutionärer Ereignisse, der Aera Napoleon, der Restauration und der Zeit nach der Julirevolution.[1]

Die Reformvorschläge resultierten aus der Analyse zeitgenössischer gesellschaftspolitischer Mängel. Beim Versuch, den Uebeln abzuhelfen, zeichneten sich zwei Möglichkeiten ab. Einerseits stellte man auf dem urbanistischen Sektor den alten Städten neue Formen des Zusammenlebens gegenüber; anderseits versuchte man, in einer Art Pseudosanierung Teilaspekte des Problems zu lösen. Dabei verlor man die Zusammenhänge aus den Augen und kam, im Gegensatz zu den utopischen Sozialisten, nicht zu Gesamtkonzeptionen für einen neuen Stadtorganismus.

Robert Owen (1771—1858) und Charles Fourier (1772—1837) teilten mit den Utopisten der Antike und der Renaissance die Opposition gegen die Apologeten des Bestehenden und die Erkenntnis, dass in der bürgerlichen Ordnung, trotz der Befreiung des Einzelnen aus der Leibeigenschaft, das wirkliche Elend weder aufgehoben ist, noch aufgehoben werden kann.[2] Sie gingen wie diese davon aus, dass die von ihnen entworfene Gesellschaft jederzeit und allerorten einzurichten wäre. Diese Ueberschätzung des Wirkungsfeldes ideal konzipierter Siedlungen provozierte die Kritik der Vertreter des wissenschaftlichen Sozialismus. Für die utopischen Sozialisten handelte es sich darum, «ein neues, vollkommenes System der gesellschaftlichen Ordnung zu erfinden und es der Gesellschaft von aussen her, durch Propaganda, womöglich durch das Beispiel von Musterexperimenten aufzuoktroyieren».[3]

«Entwicklungsperioden, die Bestehendes von Grund auf umgestalten sollen, (werden) nie durch noch so scharfsinnig und detailliert ausgedachte, fertige (auch architektonisch konzipierte) Pläne von einer Idealgesellschaft herbeigeführt, (sie vollziehen sich im dialektischen Prozess), wenn die Bedingungen einer neuen Gesellschaftsformation vorhanden sind.»[4]

Das «Kommunistische Manifest» erhellte zwar die Widersprüche der vorausgegangenen Bewegungen, trug aber dazu bei, dass die politische Theorie alle stadtplanerischen Bewegungen und Experimente unterschätzte, «da sie alle Vorschläge für Teilreformen restlos in einer Generalreform der Gesellschaft aufgehen lassen möchte. Abgelöst von der politischen Diskussion wird die Stadtplanung ihrerseits immer mehr zur reinen Technik im Dienste der herrschenden Klasse.»[5]

Für Owen wie für Fourier war die Siedlung, d. h. der in Reaktion auf die existenten Wohnverhältnisse der untersten Gesellschaftsklassen (Abb. 4) entwickelte architektonische Behälter, nur Bestandteil eines neuen gesamtgesellschaftlichen Systems. Die Divergenz innerhalb der architektonischen Planung bei Owen und bei Fourier, die Interpretation der Architektur als einer Trägerin der Emanzipation schlechthin, resultiert aus der unterschiedlichen Auseinandersetzung mit dem Menschen. Für den Pragmatiker Owen war die veränderte architektonische Umwelt Voraussetzung für den von ihm intendierten Sozialisationsprozess. Fourier hingegen ging davon aus, dass die Architektur den psychischen und physischen Bedingungen des Menschen anzupassen sei.

Die Metamorphose der Umwelt ist in beiden Fällen als ein emanzipatorischer Akt geplant. Ort dieser Emanzipation ist nicht das Einfamilienhaus, nicht die isolierte Kleinfamilie, sondern die Grosswohneinheit.

1. Das Owensche Siedlungsparallelogramm als Ort der Sozialisation

Robert Owen (Abb. 1) leitete von 1800 bis 1824 als dirigierender Associé die Baumwollspinnerei in New Lanark (Abb. 5). Hier hatte er die Möglichkeit, seine theoretischen Erwägungen in die Tat umzusetzen. Er verkürzte die Arbeitszeit, erhöhte die Löhne, schuf menschenwürdigere Wohnungen, liess eine Schule, ein

↓ fig. 3   Illustration of a schoolroom in the New Institute. Dance lesson before visitors. The dancers wear dresses designed by Owen. On the walls are illustrated panels on natural history and geography.

←fig. 4
Cottages in the Southwark working-class district of London.

←fig. 5
New Lanark, title page of a Russian book on the settlement. The "New Institute" is the building in the center with a portico.

Krankenhaus, ein Konsumgeschäft und 1816 die «*Institution for the Formation of the Human Character*» errichten. Von der Erziehung ausgehend, trachtete Owen danach, dem bisherigen Desintegrationsprozess entgegenzuwirken und die Arbeiter in einer idealen Gemeinschaft neu zu integrieren. Dieses «Neue Institut» war das zentrale Kommunikationszentrum New Lanarks und wurde in ähnlicher Form in allen späteren Idealplanungen und praktischen Versuchen wieder aufgenommen (Abb. 3). New Lanark wurde zum vielbesuchten Musterbeispiel der paternalistischen Fürsorge des frühen aufgeklärten Industriemanagements.

Von der Idee getragen, sein Experiment auf breiter Basis zu verwirklichen, verfeinerte Owen seine architektonischen Konzeptionen zum Bau von Siedlungen. Die «*Villages of Unity & Mutual Co-operation*» sollten 1817 dazu beitragen, das nach den Napoleonischen Kriegen aufgetretene Problem der Arbeitslosigkeit zu bewältigen.

In seinem «*Report to the Committee of the Association for the Relief of the Manufacturing Poor*» von 1817 und, nach einer weiteren Wirtschaftskrise, im «*Report to the County of Lanark*» von 1820 erläuterte Owen sein geometrisches Siedlungsmodell (Abb. 6). Es handelt sich um denselben architektonischen Entwurf, der 1817 zum ersten Mal graphisch dargestellt und erst 1824 durch den Architekten Thomas Stedman Whitwell differenziert und erweitert wurde.

Owensche Siedlungseinheiten für ca. 1200 Personen auf einem Terrain von 485 ha sollten nach und nach das ganze Land überspannen. Die zweigeschossigen Wohnarme eines Parallelogramms umschliessen einen viereckigen Platz (Square), auf dem die zentral angeordneten Gemeinschaftsgebäude (Gemeinschaftsküche, Speiseräume, Schule, Kindergarten, Lese- und Klubräume, Bibliothek usw.) stehen.

Drei der Wohnflügel dienen den Wohnbedürfnissen der (meist) verheirateten Erwachsenen (Wohneinheiten zu vier Zimmern). Zwei der überhöhten Mittelrisalite dieser Trakts sind für die Wohnungen des Oberaufsehers, des Geistlichen, der Lehrer, des Arztes vorgesehen. Der dritte Mittelrisalit dient als Lagerhaus. Der vierte Flügel enthält Schlafräume für Kinder über drei Jahren und deren Aufsichtspersonal. In den beiden kurzen Aussenflügeln dieses Traktes sind eine Krankenstation und ein Gästetrakt untergebracht.

Hinter den Häusern, ausserhalb des Quadrates, liegen von Strassen umgebene Gärten. An einer Seite schliessen sich Kraftanlagen und Produktionsstätten an, die sowohl wie die Ställe und das Schlachthaus von der Siedlung durch Baumpflanzungen getrennt sind. Auf der gegenüberliegenden Seite befinden sich die Wäscherei, die Bleiche und in einiger Entfernung die Landwirtschaftsgebäude mit der Brauerei und der Mühle.

Die erste und wichtigste Funktion des Owenschen Parallelogramms war es, Produktions- und Konsumtionsmöglichkeiten für die Bewohner zu gewährleisten. Dieser Anspruch, zusammen mit der Bereitstellung ökonomischer Folgeeinrichtungen, machte eine begrenzte Einwohnerzahl auf einem beschränkten Territorium notwendig. Owens Berechnungen bezogen sich auf Einwohnerzahlen zwischen 300 und 2000 und auf ein Gelände von 808 ha für die obere Einwohnergrenze (485 ha für 1200 Personen).[7]

Das Siedlungsparallelogramm war als Modell der Selbsthilfe organisiert. Die Bewältigung sozialer Probleme stellte gleichzeitig den Versuch dar, über die Trennung von Stadt und Land hinauszukommen. Die Konstituierung von Owenschen Siedlungen wirkte der Zersiedelung des Landes und der chaotischen Explosion der Städte entgegen. «Villages of this extent, in the neighbourhood of others of a similar description, at due distances, will be found capable of combining within themselves, all the advantages that city and country residences now afford, without any of the numerous inconveniences and evils which necessarily attach to both those modes of society.»[8]

Die formale Aussage der Architektur war vorerst ein sekundäres Problem. Owen interessierte vor allem die soziale Zweckgebundenheit der von ihm konzipierten Anlagen. Das Hauptinteresse der zeitgenössischen Architekten galt dem privaten und staatlichen Repräsentativbau im Georgian Style. Mit der Industriellen Revolution stellte sich ihnen das Problem der Industrie-Architektur und des damit verbundenen Wohnungsbaus. Den neuen Konstruktionsproblemen begegneten sie mit Skepsis. So zeichneten als Planer nicht Architekten, sondern Ingenieure, Erfinder und Unternehmer.[9]

2. Der Idealentwurf für New Harmony

In Grossbritannien blieb Owens Vorschlägen die praktische Verwirklichung versagt. Der europäischen Erfahrung überdrüssig und dennoch dem europäischen Trend folgend, in der Neuen Welt zu versuchen, was in Europa unmöglich war, ging er 1824 nach Amerika. Hier erwarb er von den Rappisten, die neben den Shakern zu den erfolgreichsten Siedlern gehörten, 8100 ha Land, Steinhäuser für ca. 700 Personen und einige Produktionsstätten in Harmony, Indiana.

Das Management der am 5. Juni 1825 gegründeten Siedlungskommune *New Harmony* überliess Owen seinem Sohn William. Er selbst widmete sich der Propagierung seines Ideals.

↓ fig. 6 View of a settlement based on designs by Owen, 1817.
Published as an offprint with a descriptive text in a print run of 30,000.

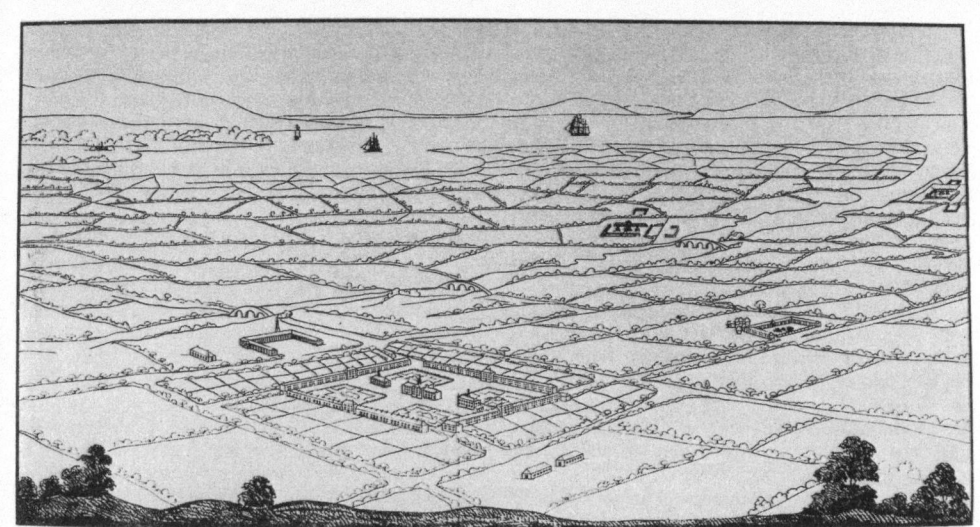

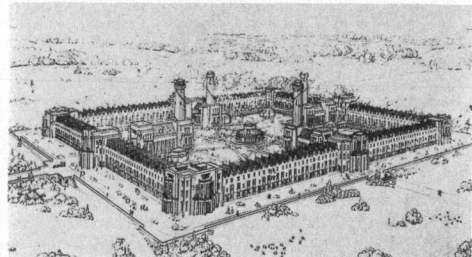

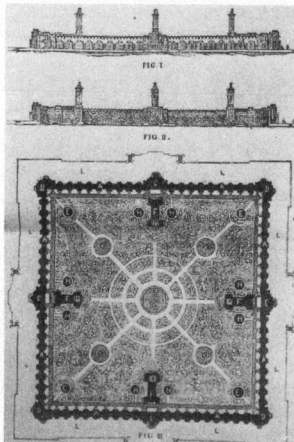

← fig. 8
Drawing of the
floor plan of the
same design.

In einer Rede vor dem amerikanischen Kongress am 7. März 1825 definierte er sein Konzept für *New Harmony*, wie es Thomas Stedman Whitwell in einem Plan zusammengefasst hatte (Abb. 7 und 8).[10]

Das Gesamt-Gelände sollte 16,5 ha betragen, der engere Wohnbereich auf einem Baugrund von 11 ha errichtet werden, was etwa der dreifachen Fläche des Londoner Russell Square entspricht. Die Aussenseiten, der an die «georgian terraces» erinnernden spitzgiebeligen Hausreihen waren in einer Länge von 305 m geplant. Einer der vorgesehenen diagonalen Wege sollte nach Möglichkeit mit einem Meridian übereinstimmen und auf einen markanten Punkt in der Landschaft hinweisen. So war auch eine gleichmässige Besonnung aller Gebäude gewährleistet.

↑ fig. 7 Ideal design for New Harmony
from a bird's-eye view. Drawn by
Thomas Stedman Whitwell in 1825.

Der Aufriss der Musterkolonie, die nicht leugnet, ihre theoretische Existenz auch den Ideen eines Plato, eines Lord Bacon und eines Sir Thomas Moore zu verdanken, hat beim ersten Anblick nur wenig Aehnlichkeit mit dem Entwurf für ein «village of unity» von 1817. Der Erfindungsboom der industriellen Revolution hatte kaum nachgelassen, und da die Siedlung mit allen «advantages of scientific discoveries down to the present»[11] versehen sein sollte, wies sie mehr technischen Komfort auf als die embryonale Konzeption.

Das Whitwell-Modell erhebt sich, wie auf einem Tablett, über künstlich aufgeschüttetem Land. Die sehr breite Esplanade (o), eine Abart des Boulevards mit Grünanlagen und asphaltierten Wegen (p), passt sich dort, wo sie sich von der Landschaft abhebt in ihrer Umrandung den Eck- und Mittelbetonungen der Square-Bebauung an. Die Umgehungs-Allee ist an den Ecken und vor den Mittelbetonungen durch Treppen (s) erreichbar. Der Promenaden-Highway ist von einem Geländer (t) umgeben und an einer Seite durch eine befahrbare Rampe mit der Landschaft verbunden. Darunter ist ein Zufahrtsweg für das unterirdische Versorgungssystem angelegt (r). Das Ganze soll sich in einer paradiesischen Landschaft von Bäumen, Spalierobst und kultiviertem Land erheben. Das achsensymmetrisch angelegte Wohnquadrat wird von flach gedeckten, mit gotisierenden Elementen versehenen Eckbauten (e) verklammert, während der frühe Owensche Entwurf die vier Square-Begrenzungen nur lose aneinander stellte (Abb. 6).

Die dem «Georgian Style» entlehnten Mittelrisalite der Owenschen Planung übernimmt Whitwell, indem er sie, stilistisch den Eckbauten vergleichbar, zugleich mit den verschiedenen Dienstleistungs- und Nachfolgeeinrichtungs-Trakten (f, g, h, i), die in die Squaremitte hineinragen, verband. Diese haben, obwohl sie verschiedene Funktionen übernehmen, denselben Aufbau. Mit dem Mitteltrakt durch die umlaufende innere Terrasse und einen Arkadengang (q) verbunden, erhebt sich ein ebenfalls flachgedeckter Gebäudeteil auf fast quadratischem Grundriss. Der dem Square-Zentrum zugewandte Bauteil ist Sockel für die kannelierten, 61 m hohen Rundtürme mit den spiralförmigen Aussentreppen (I) — eine Turmkonstruktion, die an Boullée erinnert. Die eigentlichen Wohnräume befinden sich in langen Gebäudetrakten, die zwischen die flachgedeckten Mittel- bzw. Eckbauten eingespannt sind. Erker, unterschiedliche Fenstergrössen und Giebelhöhen rhythmisieren die langgestreckten Fassaden (m, n).

Die Wohnhäuser haben im Parterre und im ersten Stock Wohnungen mit je einem Zimmer und einem «sitting room» (m). Separate Eingänge befinden sich an der Aussenseite zur Promenade und im Innenhof in den Arkadengängen. Treppen gewährleisten den Zugang zur Terrasse. Im zweiten Stock der Wohnhaustrakte befinden sich Schlafsäle für Unverheiratete und Kinder (n), die durch Treppenanlagen in den Eck- und Zentralbauten zu erreichen sind. Das Besondere dieser Säle ist ihre Variabilität. Sie können nach Belieben in grosse Wohnungen oder kleine Zimmer verwandelt werden.

Die Zentral- (f, g, h, i) und Eckbauten (e) sind weniger symbolische Wehrtürme eines Kastells, als Haupteingänge zum botanischen Binnengarten und Angelpunkte des öffentlichen Lebens. Hier sind Büchereien, Museen, Theater, Ausstellungshallen, Ball- und Konzertsäle, Kommunikationsräume jeder Art und Grösse untergebracht. Im Innenhof liegen vier weitere Gebäudekomplexe. Die «Speise-Kathedrale» (d) ist ein bis unter das Dach gezogener hell beleuchteter, stattlicher Saal. Man erreicht ihn von den Arkadengängen über ein Vestibül. Diese Vorhalle wird von den Speisesälen der Kinder und Jugendlichen flankiert (k). Der Service ist von äusserster Funktionalität. Speiselifte verbinden das Refektorium mit der darunter liegenden Küche.

Bäder sind in den kleinen oktogonalen, mit den Gymnasien (b) formal identischen Zentralbauten (c) untergebracht. Um die Türme sind die Brauereien, die Bäckereien und die Wäschereien angesiedelt (j). Einer exotischen Blume gleich erhebt sich inmitten der Anlage das polygonale Konservatorium (a). Ein Heizungs- und Ventilationssystem ist sowohl für den Privatbereich der Wohnungen, als auch für den öffentlichen Bereich der Trakte geplant. Aus allen Wasserhähnen fliesst warmes und kaltes Wasser, Reparatur- und Reinigungsbetriebe sind durchgehend geöffnet.

Ein weitverzweigtes unterirdisches System von Fliessbändern und Schienen verbindet alle Teile des Siedlungsquadrats. Es führt zu den verschiedenen Lagerräumen und Küchen und dient der mechanischen Abfallbeseitigung. Dieses unterirdische Netz ist mit den Geschossen

never produced by finished (even architecturally conceived) plans of an ideal society, however astutely and thoroughly thought out (they occur in the dialectical process), if the conditions for a new formation of society are present."[4]

The Communist Manifesto shed light on the contradictions of the earlier movements but also contributed to political theory underestimating all urban planning movements and experiments, "since they would like to have all proposals for partial reforms subsumed entirely under a general reform of society. Separated from the political discussion, urban planning increasingly becomes for its part purely a technology in the service of the ruling class."[5]

For Owen as for Fourier, the housing development—that is, the architectural vessel developed for the existing living conditions of the lowest classes of society (fig. 4)—is merely a component of a new general social system. The divergence within architectural planning in Owen and in Fourier—interpreting architecture as the principal agent of emancipation—results from the different ways they engage with the human being. For the pragmatist Owen, the transformed architectural environment was the precondition for the socialization process he intended. Fourier, by contrast, presumed that architecture should be adapted to the psychological and physical conditions of human beings.

In both cases, the metamorphosis of the environment is planned as an emancipatory act. The site of this emancipation is not the single-family home, not the isolated small family, but the large housing unit.

1. The Owenite Parallelogram Settlement as the Site of Socialization

Robert Owen (fig. 1) ran, as acting partner, the cotton mill in New Lanark from 1800 to 1824 (fig. 5). There he had the opportunity to put into practice his theoretical reflections. He shortened the work week, increased wages, created more humane housing, and built a school, a hospital, a cooperative store, and, in 1816, the Institution for the Formation of the Human Character. Setting out from education, Owen sought to counter the existing process of disintegration and to reintegrate workers in an ideal community.

This "new institute" was the central communication center of New Lanark and was adopted in similar form in all the later ideal plans and practical experiments (fig. 3). New Lanark became the oft-visited model example of the paternalist charity of early enlightened industrial management.

Borne by the idea of realizing his experiment on a broad basis, Owen refined his architectonic concepts for the building of housing developments. The "Villages of Unity and Mutual Cooperation" were designed in 1817 as a solution to the problem of unemployment that had arisen after the Napoleonic Wars.

In his "Report to the Committee of the Association for the Relief of the Manufacturing Poor" of 1817 and, following another economic crisis, his "Report to the County of Lanark" of 1820, Owen explained his geometric model for housing developments (fig. 6). This architectural design, first rendered graphically in 1817, was then refined and expanded by the architect Thomas Stedman Whitwell in 1824.[6]

Owenite housing developments, each for circa 1,200 people on 1,200 acres, were supposed to gradually cover the entire country. The two-story residential wings of a parallelogram surround a square on which the common buildings are arranged around its center (public kitchen, dining halls, school, kindergarten, reading and clubrooms, library, and so on).

Three of the residential wings serve the housing needs of the (mostly) married adults (housing units of four rooms). Two of the elevated central avant-corps of these wings are reserved for the apartments of the general superintendent, the clergyman, the teachers, and the physician. The third central avant-corps serves as a storeroom. The fourth wing has dormitories for the children above the age of three and the staff that supervises them. The two short outer wings of this section house an infirmary and a wing for guests.

Behind the buildings, outside the square, lie gardens surrounded by streets. Adjacent on one side are power plants and production facilities, which, like the stables and the slaughterhouse, are separated from the settlement by trees. On the opposite side are the laundry, bleachery, and at some distance the farm buildings along with the brewery and mill.

The first and most important function of the Owenite parallelogram was to offer opportunities for production and consumption to the residents. That ambition, along with the provision of economical social infrastructure for the community, made it necessary to limit the number of residents on a circumscribed territory. Owen's calculations were based on populations of between 300 and 2,000 and on 2,000 acres for the upper limit of population (and 1,200 acres for 1,200 people).[7]

The parallelogram was organized on a model of self-help. Addressing social problems also represented the effort to overcome the separation of city and countryside. The Owenite communities were constituted to counter urban sprawl in the countryside and the chaotic explosion of the cities. "Villages of this extent, in the neighbourhood of others of a similar description, at due distances, will be found capable of combining within themselves, all the advantages that city and country residences now afford, without any of the numerous inconveniences and evils which necessarily attach to both those modes of society."[8]

The formal statement of architecture was, at first, a secondary problem. Owen was primarily interested in the social suitability of the facilities he had conceived. Contemporaneous architects were primarily interested in designing stately buildings in the Georgian style for private and public clients. The Industrial Revolution presented them with the problem of industrial architecture and the associated housing construction. They approached these new construction problems with skepticism. Consequently, the planners of these projects were not architects but engineers, inventors, and entrepreneurs.[9]

2. The Ideal Design for New Harmony

In Great Britain, Owen's proposals were never implemented. Tired of his European experiences but nevertheless following the European trend of attempting in the New World that which was impossible in Europe, he went to America in 1824. There he acquired from the Rappites, who along with the Shakers were some of the most successful settlers, 20,000 acres of land, stone buildings for circa 700 people, and several production facilities in Harmony, Indiana.

Owen entrusted management of the New Harmony community, founded on June 5, 1825, to his son William. He devoted himself to propagating his ideal. In a speech before the American Congress on March 7, 1825, he defined his concept for New Harmony, as summarized in a plan by Thomas Stedman Whitwell (figs. 7 and 8).[10]

The overall grounds were planned to be built on forty acres with the narrower residential area on a lot of twenty-seven acres, corresponding roughly to three times the size of Russell Square in London. The exterior, whose gabled fronts resemble Georgian terraces, was planned to be one thousand feet long. One of the planned diagonal lines was supposed to coincide, if possible, with a meridian and point to a striking feature in the landscape. This would also ensure that all of the buildings received uniform sunlight.

The elevation of the model colony, which does not deny that its theoretical existence is also indebted to the ideas of the likes of Plato, Lord Bacon, and Sir Thomas More, has at first glance little similarity to the design for a "village of unity" from 1817. The boom of inventions during the Industrial Revolution had scarcely slowed, and the community should have all the "advantages of scientific discoveries down to the present";[11] this pointed more to technological comfort than to the embryonic conception.

The Whitwell Model is raised above ground, as if on a platter, on artificially elevated land. The very broad esplanade (o), a variation on the boulevard with green spaces and paved roads (p), is adapted, where it stands out in its bordering, to the accents on the corners and centers of the square structure. The bypass boulevard can be accessed at the corners and in front of the accents in the middle via stairs (s). The promenade highway is surrounded by a terrace (t) and connected to the landscape on one side by a ramp for vehicles. Built underneath it is an access way to the subterranean supply system (r). The whole is intended to rise in a paradisiacal landscape of trees, espaliers of fruit, and cultivated land. The symmetrical square of residences is flanked by flat-roof corner buildings with neo-Gothic elements (e), while the early Owenite design related only loosely the four boundaries of the square (fig. 6).

fig. 9 Caricature by G. Cruikshank of the failure of the American experiment. The bust on a pedestal is of R. Owen. (*The Comic Almanac*, 1848.)

über der Erde durch eine grosse Zahl von Liften verbunden.

Einem Kreuzgang ähnliche und ihm wohl auch nachgebildete Arkaden ermöglichen den geschützten Zugang zu den Wohnungen, Schulen, Theatersälen, Bädern, den Speisesälen. Hier wie auch auf der darüber liegenden Terrasse und auf den Gartenwegen stehen Bänke.

Die vier Türme übertreffen den Urentwurf bei weitem und setzen funktionale und stilistische Akzente. Ihre Basis bilden die inneren Zentralgebäude, von denen man über bequeme Wendeltreppen zu Observatorien emporsteigen kann. Ungefähr in der Mitte jedes Schaftes sind Uhren angebracht. Mit Gaslicht beleuchtet und von jeder Seite sichtbar konnte man auch nachts die Uhrzeit ablesen. In einem Ring unterhalb jeder Turmgalerie hatte Whitwell ein mit Reflektoren versehenes Gasscheinwerfer-System untergebracht, dessen Leuchtkapazität die gesamte Anlage erhellen sollte.

In unserer Interpretation wird Whitwell nicht durch seine formal-phantastischen Spielereien bedeutend, sondern durch seine gesellschaftsbezogenen Planungskriterien. Er hat unter Einbeziehung der neuesten technischen Errungenschaften für die Owenschen Sozial- und Gesellschaftslehren ein architektonisches Gehäuse geschaffen.

Als Gegenstück zu den später auch von Engels kritisierten Cottages[12] entstand die Grosswohneinheit. An die Stelle von Isolation, aufreibender Arbeit, enger, unhygienischer Bebauung und Einfamilienhaushalt sollten weiträumige, hygienische, durchgrünte Bebauung, Grossküche, Service-Haus, Kommunikation und mehr Freizeit treten. Dieses von Engagement und ungebrochenem Optimismus getragene Architekturmodell blieb Theorie. New Harmony scheiterte als Siedlungsexperiment (Abb. 9).

Die Siedlungsexperimente, die in den USA und in England (u. a. Orbiston, Ralahine, Harmony Hall) von Owens Vorschlägen inspiriert waren, scheiterten an ihrem Inseldasein. Eine isolierte Gruppe, mögen ihre Mitglieder einen noch so hohen Grad an Idealismus besitzen, ist nicht in der Lage, die Gesellschaft, von der sie sich abgekapselt hat, zu verändern.

3. Palastarchitektur in sozialen Diensten

Fouriers (Abb.10) Vorstellungen zum sozialen Siedlungsbau sind in ein verwobenes sozialpsychologisches und philosophisches System eingebettet. Innerhalb eines von ihm erdachten «Schemas des Verlaufs der sozialen Bewegungen» entwirft er für die 6. und die 7. von insgesamt 32 Perioden präzise architektonische Modelle. Ausgehend von der Ablehnung der «Zivilisation» (5. Periode) mit ihren Widersprüchen strebt er die «universale Harmonie» an. Die von Fourier entwickelte neue Gesellschaftsform, die «Assoziation der Menschheit», unterwirft sich einer doppelten Kausalität, der wirtschaftlichen und der psychologischen. Im wesentlichen geht die Fouriersche Philosophie davon aus, dass alle sozialen Reformen der Menschheit durch das Wesen des Menschen determiniert seien, und alles soziale Wissen nur dann von Wert sei, wenn ihm die Erkenntnis der menschlichen Psyche zugrunde liegen. Fouriers Zielvorstellungen richten sich auf die Institutionalisierung von Kollektiven. Hier wird der Hingabe des Individuums an die Allgemeinheit — ohne Aufgabe der Individualität oder gar der Identität — und damit indirekt die Ablehnung des Egoismus als Organisationsprinzip angesprochen. Schon in der für die 6. Periode entworfenen Stadt steht die kollektive Wohneinheit im Vordergrund. Sie ist in Grünzonen, Industrie- und Wohnbezirke aufgeteilt und erinnert an Howards Gartenstadt-Diagramm (1898).

In der 1808 veröffentlichten «*Théorie des quatre mouvements*» geht Fourier zum ersten Mal ausführlicher auf diese Wohnform ein. In

21

fig. 10   Facsimile of a *phalanstère* design from *Le nouveau monde industriel* (Paris, 1829).

«*Nouveau Monde Industriel*» (1829) wird die Idealarchitektur der 7. Periode, das *Phalanstère*, im Detail geschildert. Fourier weist immer wieder darauf hin, «dass sich in einer völlig neuen Gründung die theoretischen Ansätze erst in Relation zu ihrer Praktikabilität verwirklichen können».[13]

Formal scheint sich der Citoyen Fourier vom Glanz einer absolutistischen Schlossanlage wie Versailles oder Meudon — vom Ernst einer Klosteranlage vom Range des Escorial leiten zu lassen, obwohl er sich ausdrücklich gegen derartige Vergleiche ausspricht. Funktional steht die Fouriersche Grosswohneinheit den monarchischen und klösterlichen Gewohnheiten entgegen.

Der Sozialpalast ist das architektonische Zentrum der 1620 Siedler, einer Phalange. Die Siedlungsgemeinschaften, von denen sich Fourier auf der Erde insgesamt 2 985 984 vorstellt, schwanken in der Mitgliederzahl zwischen 900 bis 2000. Sie sollen sich nach Möglichkeit hügeliges und von einem Fluss durchzogenes, eine Quadratmeile umfassendes Terrain aussuchen und bei der Anlage der Kulturen darauf achten, den Charme der Landschaft nicht zu zerstören, um den Arbeitsgruppen eine abwechslungsreiche Arbeit zu ermöglichen.

Das zentrale Gebäude der einen grossen Ehrenhof umspannenden Flügelbaus beherbergt die Speisesäle, die Bibliothek, Studiensäle, den Tempel, das Telegraphenamt, das Observatorium, usw. Der eine Flügel ist für die «lärmerzeugenden Werkstätten», die Zimmerei, die Schmiede, usw. reserviert, hier soll auch die Kinderkrippe untergebracht werden. Der andere Flügel beherbergt die Karawanserei, die Begegnungsstätte für Fremde und Besucher (Abb. 10).

Das Phalanstère bietet unterschiedliche Wohnungsgrundrisse und -grössen für die verschiedenen Bewohnerschichten in 18 Preisklassen an. Obwohl Qualität und Preis der Wohnungen zum Mittelbau hin zunehmen, soll eine Mischung des Angebots stattfinden.

Die Idee der Grosswohneinheit, der organisierten kollektiven Konsumptions- und Produktionsgemeinschaft auf der Grundlage der Fourierschen hedonistischen Theorie, sollte durch die «*Rue-Galerie*» oder den «*Perystile continue*» in besonderer Weise gekrönt werden (Abb. 11). Die Rues-Galeries, die es dem Phalangisten erlauben, unbehelligt von Witterungseinflüssen seinen Standort zu wechseln, befin-

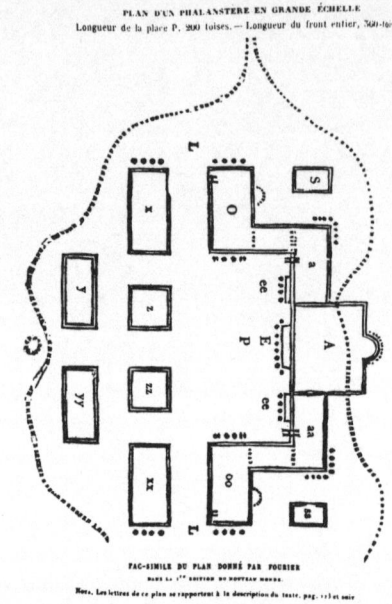

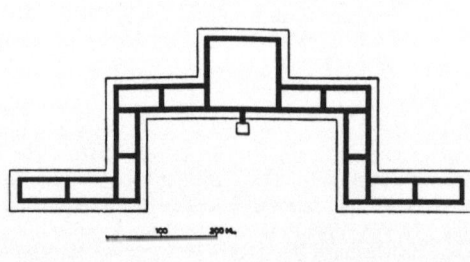

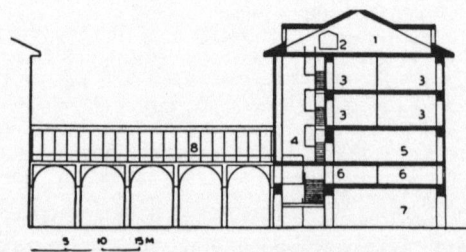

fig. 11   Course of the street-galleries. Reconstruction by Leonardo Benevolo.
fig. 12   Elevation of a *phalanstère*.

Whitwell adopts the central avant-corps of the Owenite plan, borrowed from the "Georgian style," by directly integrating them, stylistically analogously to the corner buildings, with the sections with the various service and social infrastructure facilities (f, g, h, i), which extend into the center of the square. Although they perform different functions, the latter have the same structure. Connected to the central section by the continuous interior terrace and an arcaded walkway (q), a section of the building, also with a flat roof, looms up from the nearly square ground plan. The section of the building that faces the center of the square is the base for the 200-foot-tall fluted round towers with exterior spiral stairs (l)—a tower construction that resembles Boullée. The living spaces proper are located in long wings extending between the flat-roofed central and corner buildings. Bay windows and variations in window size and gable height lend rhythm to the elongated facades (m, n).

The residential buildings have apartments on the ground floor and second floor, each with one room and a "sitting room" (m). Separate entrances are located on the outer side of the promenade and in the arcaded walkways of the interior courtyard. Stairs provide access to the terrace. The third floor of the residential wings houses dormitories for the unmarried and for children (n), which are reached via stairs in the corner and central buildings. The special feature of these halls is their variability. They can be converted at will into large apartments or small rooms.

The central (f, g, h, i) and corner buildings (e) are not so much the symbolic defensive towers of a fortified castle as they are the main entrances to the interior botanical garden and the linchpins of public life. They house libraries, museums, theaters, exhibition halls, ballrooms and concert halls, communication spaces of all kinds and sizes. There are four more building complexes in the interior courtyard. The "Dining Cathedral" (d) is a brightly lit, stately hall that extends up to the ceiling. It is accessed from the arcades via a vestibule. This entry hall is flanked by the dining rooms for the children and teenagers (k). The service is extremely functional. Dumbwaiters connect the refectory to the kitchen below it.

Baths are located in the small octagonal central buildings (c), which are identical in form to the gymnasiums (b). The breweries, bakeries, and washrooms are located around the towers (j). Rising like an exotic flower in the middle of the grounds is the polygonal conservatory (a). A heating and ventilation system is planned for the private areas of the apartments and for the public area of the wings. Hot and cold water flows from all the taps; repair and cleaning services are open nonstop.

A broadly ramified subterranean system of conveyor belts and rails connects all the parts of the settlement's square. It leads to various storerooms and kitchens and provides mechanical waste disposal. This subterranean network is connected to the aboveground floors via numerous elevators.

Arcades resembling a cloister—and presumably also modeled on one—offer covered access to apartments, schools, theaters, baths, and dining halls. There are benches here, on the terrace above, and on the garden paths.

The four towers far exceed the original design and add functional and stylistic accents. Their base is formed by the central buildings inside the perimeter, from which one can climb comfortable spiral stairs to observatories. Clocks are installed approximately in the middle of that shaft. Lit with gas lamps and visible from every side, the time can be seen even at night. In a ring under every tower gallery, Whitwell installed a system of gas spotlights with reflectors that was intended to be capable of lighting the entire grounds.

In our interpretation, Whitwell is important not for his formally imaginative gimmicks but for his society-based planning criteria. He created an architectural housing for the Owenite social and societal theories that integrates the latest technological achievements.

As a counterpart to the cottages that also were later criticized by Engels,[12] he created the large residential unit. Isolation, exhausting work, crowded, unhygienic construction, and the single-family household were to be replaced by the spacious, hygienic, well-planted construction, the shared kitchen, the service house, communication, and more leisure time. This architectural model born of social commitment and unbroken optimism remained a theory.

New Harmony failed as an experimental settlement (fig. 9).

The experimental settlements in the United States and Great Britain (e.g., Orbiston, Ralahine, Harmony Hall) inspired by Owen's proposals failed because of their insular existence. An isolated group—however much idealism its members might have—is not in a position to change the society from which it has closed itself off.

3. Palace Architecture in Social Services

Fourier's ideas for the construction of social housing (fig. 10) are embedded into an interwoven sociopsychological and philosophical system. Within the "Schema of the Course of the Social Movements" he conceived, he designed precise architectural models for the sixth and seventh of thirty-two periods. Setting out from the rejection of "Civilization" (fifth period) and its contradictions, he strove for "universal harmony." The new form of society developed by Fourier—the "association of humanity"—subjects itself to the dual causality of the economic and the psychological. In essence, Fourier's philosophy assumes that all social reforms of humanity are determined by the essence of the human being and that social knowledge is of value only if it is based on knowledge of the human psyche. Fourier's objectives are aimed at institutionalizing collectives. He addresses the individual's devotion to the universal—without abandoning individuality or even identity—and hence indirectly the rejection of egoism as a principle of organization. Already in the city designed for the sixth period, the collective housing unit is in the foreground. It is divided into green zones and industrial and residential areas and recalls Howard's garden city diagram (1898).

In *Théorie des quatre mouvements* [Theory of the Four Movements], published in 1808, Fourier goes into the details of this form of housing for the first time. In *Le nouveau monde industriel* [The new industrial world] (1829), the ideal architecture of the seventh period—the Phalanstère—is described in detail. Fourier repeatedly points out "that the theoretical approaches can only be realized in relation to their practicality in a completely new founding."[13]

Formally, the Citoyen Fourier seems to have been guided by the splendor of an absolutist palace grounds such as Versailles or Meudon—and by the austerity of a monastic grounds of the stature of the Escorial—although he explicitly speaks out against such comparisons. In terms of function, the Fourieresque large housing unit counteracts monarchical and monastic habits.

The societal palace is the architecture center of the 1,620 residents, a phalanx. The settlement communities, of which Fourier imagines a total of 2,985,984 on earth, are supposed to have from 900 to 2,000 members. They are supposed to seek out, if possible, one square mile of hilly terrain with a river running through it and to take care not to destroy the charm of the landscape when establishing cultures, in order to offer the work groups varied work.

The central building of a large winged structure around a *cour d'honneur* houses the dining halls, the library, study halls, the temple, the telegraph office, the observatory, and so on. One wing is reserved for the "noise-producing workshops"—the carpentry workshop, the smithy, and so on—as well as the nursery. The other wing houses the caravansary: the meeting place for outsiders and visitors (fig. 10).

The Phalanstère offers apartments with different floor plans and sizes in eighteen price classes for residents of different strata. Although the quality and price of the apartments was supposed to increase as one moved toward the central building, there should be a mix of offerings.

The idea of the large housing unit, of an organized collective community of consumption and production on the basis of Fourier's hedonistic theory, was supposed to be crowned in a particular way by the "rue-galerie" or "perystile continue" (fig. 11). The *rues-galeries*, which enable the *phalangistes* to change their location unhindered by the influences of weather, are located on the second story. Fourier imagines the architecture of the street-galleries as follows: "The street-galleries of a Phalanx wind along just one side of the central edifice and stretch to the end of each of its wings. All of these wings contain a double row of rooms. Thus one row of rooms looks out upon the fields and gardens and the other looks

fig. 13 Victor Considerant's depiction of the social palace, 1840.

den sich im 1. Stock. Architektonisch stellt sich Fourier die Galeriestrassen folgendermassen vor: «Die Rues-Galeries einer Phalange erhalten nicht von beiden Seiten Tageslicht, sondern schliessen unmittelbar an den Wohntrakt an. In diesem Wohntrakt liegen zwei Reihen von Zimmern, von denen die einen in die Landschaft, und die anderen auf die Rue-Galerie hinausgehen. Die Rue-Galerie sollte deshalb die Höhe aller drei Stockwerke haben... Die Eingangstüren aller Wohnungen des 1., 2. und 3. Stockwerks gehen auf die Rue-Galerie hinaus; in gewissen Abständen befinden sich Treppen, um in den 2. und 3. Stock zu gelangen... Die Fenster der Galerie können denen der Kirchen ähnlich sein, ,de forme haute et ceintré (cintré)'. Es ist nicht notwendig, dass die Galerie den drei Stockwerken entsprechend auch drei Fensterreihen an der Aussenfassade aufweist.»[14]

Die Galeriestrassen gehören zu den wichtigsten architektonischen Aspekten. Sie sind zentrales Planungsmerkmal des Funktionsablaufes innerhalb des Phalanstère, werden jedoch von Fourier in ihrer Wirkung überschätzt. «Die Rues-Galeries... stellen Kommunikationsmöglichkeiten dar, die ausreichen, um die Paläste und schönen Städte der Zivilisation zu degradieren. Wer die Rues-Galeries einer Phalange gesehen hat», so hofft Fourier, «wird den schönsten ,zivilisierten' Palast als ein Exil ansehen, einen Wohnsitz von Idioten, die nach 3000 Jahren Studium der Architektur, nicht einmal in der Lage sind, sich gesund und bequem unterzubringen...»[15]

Fourier greift mit dem Konzept dieser Kommunikationswege auf die von ihm bewunderte frühe *unité d'habitation*, das Palais Royal zurück. Es entspricht durchaus dem Charakter eines utopischen Entwurfes, bei Antizipation neuer gesellschaftlicher Zustände zeitgenössische oder auch vorausgegangene städtebauliche Praxis aufzunehmen, wobei die formalästhetische Aussage dann oft konventionell bleibt.

4. Die graphische Konkretisierung des Phalanstère

Fourier hatte in Paris eine Anzahl von Schülern um sich versammelt. Der Fourierist und Polytechniker Victor Considérant veröffentlichte in seiner 1840 erschienenen «*Description du Phalanstère*», die die verstreuten architektonischen und soziographischen Ideen seines Meisters Fourier systematisieren und klären sollte, eine dem sozietären Konzept entsprechende Ideal-Ansicht (Abb. 13). Obwohl Considérant versichert, dass sein formaler Vorschlag keinerlei Absolutheitsanspruch hat, wirkt sein der Humanität gewidmetes Phalanstère sehr determiniert. Der klassizistische Flügelbau ruft erneut die Assoziation Schlossarchitektur, die Assoziation Versailles hervor. Der breitgelagerte Wohnpalast, das Phalanstère, liegt — hier übernimmt Considérant die Vorschläge Fouriers — einem Industrie- und Landwirtschaftskomplex gegenüber in einer Gartenlandschaft. «Betrachten wir das Panorama, das sich vor unseren Augen entfaltet. Ein wunderbarer Palast erhebt sich aus dem Mutterleib des Gartens, aus beschatteten Beeten und Rasenplätzen, wie eine marmorne Insel in einem Kräuterozean. Das ist der königliche Aufenthaltsort einer regenerierten Bevölkerung.»[16]

Das mit einem Turm ausgestattete Mittelcarré wird von Flügelbauten flankiert, an die sich rechtwinklig — einen grossen Ehrenhof umfassend — wiederum Flügelbauten anschliessen. Diese knicken parallel zur Hauptfront nach beiden Seiten hin nochmals ab. Um eine möglichst grosse Anzahl Menschen (bis zu 2000) aufnehmen zu können, wird diese Gebäudebewegung in einer doppelten Reihe gezeichnet.

Die nach aussen (zum Ehrenhof, zur Strasse, zur Landschaft) gerichteten Fassadenteile zeigen einen dreistöckigen Aufriss, während die in die Innenhöfe blickenden Gebäudeteile 4, resp. 5 übereinanderliegende Fenster aufweisen. Considérant übernimmt auch hier das Grundrisskonzept Fouriers, dessen Rues-Galeries zum Innenhof und dessen Wohnräume zur Landschaft, resp. zur Strasse hin gerichtet sind.

Es kann angenommen werden, dass der ganze Komplex drei Stockwerke (ein Erdgeschoss und zwei Obergeschosse) hat. Die niedrigere Fensterhöhe zu den Innenhöfen hin resultiert nicht aus einer anderen Geschosshöhe, sondern aus der Konstruktion der Rues-Galeries (oder Cirsum-Galeries). «*La rue-galerie d'un Phalanstère de haute Harmonie est au moins aussi large et aussi somptueuse que la galerie du Louvre. Elle sert pour les grands repas et les réunions extraordinaires. Parées de fleurs comme les plus belles serres, décorées des plus riches produits des arts et de l'industrie les galeries et les salons des Phalanstères ouvrent aux artistes d'Harmonie d'admirables expositions permanentes. Il est probable que, souvent, elles seront construites entièrement en verre.*»[17]

Die unterschiedliche architektonische Ausstattung der Aussen- und Innenfassade ist demnach funktional zu erklären. Während die Strassen- und Platzfassaden des Phalanstère architektonisch gegliedert sind, die verschiedenen Gebäudeteile Eck- und Mittelrisalite aufweisen, vermeiden die Hoffassaden diese klassizistischen Akzente.

Die klassizistischen Zitate könnten als ein Propagandamittel interpretiert werden. Schliesslich sollte ja jemand gefunden werden, der die geplante Grossanlage finanziert. Considérant räumt ein, dass im Phalanstère prächtige und bescheidenere Wohnungen eingerichtet werden (*«pour que chacun puisse s'y caser suivant ses goûts et sa fortune»*[18]). So kann die architektonisch-dekorative Aussage seines Phalanstère-Entwurfes als ein Zugeständnis an die ästhetischen Ansprüche der Bourgeoisie verstanden werden. Das Mittelcarré ist — wie bei Fourier — den luxuriösen Wohnungen vorbehalten und wird besonders betont. Eine Häufung der Risalite gegen das Zentrum hin ist unübersehbar; der geplante Ordnungsturm konzentriert ebenfalls die Blicke des Betrachters auf sich.

Der gesamte Gebäudekomplex findet seinen oberen Abschluss in einer durchlaufenden Balustrade. Die den Wirtschaftsgebäuden zugekehrte Front trägt einen den Risaliten entsprechenden Figurenschmuck, der auf der Gartenfront in kleineren Abständen wiederholt wird. Aus Considérants Entwurf lässt sich nicht genau ablesen, ob Gartenfront und Paradehof-Front eine unterschiedliche Ausbildung erfahren. Trotz einiger durch die perspektivische Verkürzung auftretender Ungenauigkeiten drängt sich dem Betrachter eine reichere Gestaltung der Hoffassade auf. Die flache Gebäudebedachung weist dort, wo die Risalite erhöht sind, Treppen auf. Diese begehbare Dachzone denkt sich Considérant als eine weitere Kommunikationsebene. Das kommunikative Dach wird u. a.

out upon the street-gallery. The street-gallery, then, will be three stories high with windows on one side. The entrance to all the apartments of the second, third, and fourth stories is located in the street-gallery. Flights of stairs are placed at intervals to ascend to the upper stories. … The windows of the gallery can be, like those of churches, *de forme haute et ceintrée* [*cintrée*] [long-arched]. It is not necessary that there be three levels of windows like the three floors."[14]

The street-galleries are among the most important architectural aspects. They are a central planning feature of the sequence of functions within the Phalanstère, but Fourier overestimated their effect. "The street-galleries are a mode of internal communication which would alone be sufficient to inspire disdain for the palaces and great cities of civilization. Once a man has seen the street-galleries of a Phalanx, he will look upon the most elegant civilized palace as a place of exile, a residence worthy of fools who, after three thousand years of architectural studies, have not yet learned how to build themselves healthy and comfortable lodgings."[15]

In his concept for these paths of communication, Fourier takes up the early *unité d'habitation* he admired, the Palais Royal. It certainly corresponds to the character of a utopian design to take up contemporaneous or even earlier urban planning practice when anticipating new social conditions, although the resulting formal-aesthetic statement then often remains conventional.

4. The Graphic Concretizing of the Phalanstère

Fourier had assembled several disciples around him in Paris. The Fourierist and graduate of the École Polytechnique Victor Considerant published in his *Description du Phalanstère* of 1840, which was intended to systematize and clarify the scattered architectural and sociographic ideas of his master, Fourier, an ideal view that corresponds to the societal concept (fig. 13). Although Considerant assures us that his formal proposal has no claim to absoluteness whatsoever, his Phalanstère dedicated to humanity seems highly determined. The classicistic winged structure evokes once again the association of the architecture of palaces, the association of Versailles. The broad housing palace, the Phalanstère, is located— Considerant adopts Fourier's proposals in this respect—in a garden landscape opposite an industrial and agricultural complex. "Consider the panorama that unfolds before our eyes. A splendid palace rises out of the bosom of the garden, out of shaded beds and lawns, like a marble island bathing in an ocean of greenery. That is the royal sojourn of a regenerated population."[16]

The central square with a tower is flanked by wings of buildings that connect in turn at right angles—framing a large cour d'honneur—to other wings of buildings. The latter bend again toward both sides parallel to the main facade. To accommodate as many people as possible (up to 2,000), this movement of the buildings occurs in two rows.

The sections of the facade that point outward (toward the cour d'honneur, the street, and the landscape) have an elevation of three stories, whereas the sections of the building facing the interior courtyards have four or five windows one above the other. Here, too, Considerant adopts Fourier's concept for the floor plan, in which the *rues-galeries* are oriented toward the interior courtyard and the living spaces toward the countryside or the street.

It can be assumed that the entire complex has three floors (a ground floor and two upper floors). The lower height of the windows facing the interior courtyards results not from a difference in floor height but from the construction of the *rues-galeries* (or *cirsum-galeries*). "The gallery-street of a Phalanstère (phalanstery) imbued with the high Harmony is at least as wide, and as sumptuous, as the gallery of the Louvre. It is host to large meals and extraordinary meetings. Adorned with flowers in the manner of the most beautiful greenhouses, decorated with the richest products of art and industry, the galleries and salons of the Phalanstères offer admirable permanent exhibitions to the artists of Harmony. It is likely that, more often than not, they will be built entirely of glass."[17]

The differences in the architectural design of the exterior facade and the interior one can accordingly be explained functionally. Whereas the facades of the Phalanstère facing the street and the square are articulated architecturally and the different parts of the building have central and corner avant-corps, these classicistic accents are absent from the courtyard facades.

The classicistic citations could be interpreted as a means of propaganda. After all, the goal was to find someone who would finance the large complex being planned. Considerant admits that both stately and more modest apartments are furnished in the Phalanstère ("pour que chacun puisse s'y caser suivant ses goûts et sa fortune" [to each according to their taste and ability to pay]).[18] The architectural-decorative statement of his Phalanstère design can therefore be understood as a concession to the aesthetic ambitions of the bourgeoisie. The central square building is—as in Fourier's design—reserved for luxury apartments and is particularly emphasized. It is impossible to overlook that the avant-corps are more numerous as one moves toward the center; the planned Tour d'Ordre also draws the viewer's eyes to itself.

The overall complex of buildings has a continuous balustrade as its upper termination. The facade facing the farm buildings is decorated with figures that correspond to the avant-corps and are repeated at smaller intervals on the garden facade. It is not possible to determine precisely from Considerant's design whether the garden facade and the facade facing the cour d'honneur differ in form. Despite some of the imprecisions resulting from the perspective foreshortening, the viewer cannot help but notice that the design of the courtyard facade is more lavish. The flat roof of the building has stairs where the avant-corps are elevated. Considerant conceives this walk-on roof zone as another level of communication. The accessible roof is later again taken up by, among others, Le Corbusier in his *unité*.

Fourier's theoretical design and Considerant's graphic concept are nearly identical. Considerant placed greater weight on the technological developments of his time in terms of glass construction and further refined the system of heating and ventilation already planned by Fourier.

5. Paternalistic Fourierism in Guise

Just ten years after the revolution of 1848, the idea of the societal palace was realized in an experiment in France. From 1859 to 1885, the Fourierist and industrialist Jean-Baptiste-André Godin constructed a complex of housing and production facilities in Guise on the Oise.[19]

The complex known as the Familistère is subdivided into three self-contained blocks of buildings totaling 180 meters in length. (The facade of the largest Phalanstère by Fourier was 1,200 meters!) The interior courtyards of the three residential blocks are covered with glass in a wooden truss construction. These interior courtyards are accessed by galleries that lead to 465 housing units of different sizes (figs. 14, 15).

The social infrastructure (e.g., a nursery, a kindergarten, a school, a theater, restaurants, showers, and swimming pools) of Godin's Familistère overshadows other contemporaneous settlements based on the system of the single-family home (e.g., the Cité Ouvrière in Mulhouse). Compared to Fourier's ideal, however, the paternalist experiment lost a great deal of ground. Perhaps, however, it was precisely the securing of the seed of the nation—the family—that resulted in so much applause from the bourgeois side for the Fourierist experiment in Guise.

Owen and Fourier designed new forms of cohabitation for the masses. For the scientific socialists, their restlessness and theoretical anticipation of new social conditions downgraded them to utopian socialists. It is, however, precisely their lending concrete form to urbanist ideas—the flaw of the utopian—that makes them interesting for scholarship on the history of architecture. "Only where heterogeneity itself has an activating influence can a social life result and a socially autonomous form, in the sense of a settlement, a village, or a city, obtain content and structure. But that is the precondition for a society living together in a limited space."[20] It is above all the social ambition and the integrative character of the designs by Owen and Fourier that produce fascination. But it was precisely the complexity of their planning, which is today interpreted as progressive, that condemned all pragmatic approaches to failure. The complexity was not planned for a restructured society but was supposed to contribute to the restructuring. Idealism operating in isolation failed because of its existence as a foreign body within the society.

fig. 14   Site plan of the Familistère: (A) Interior courtyard; (B) Nursery and day care; (C) School; (D) Farms and outbuildings; (E) Washroom, bathtubs, and swimming pool; (F) Gasworks.

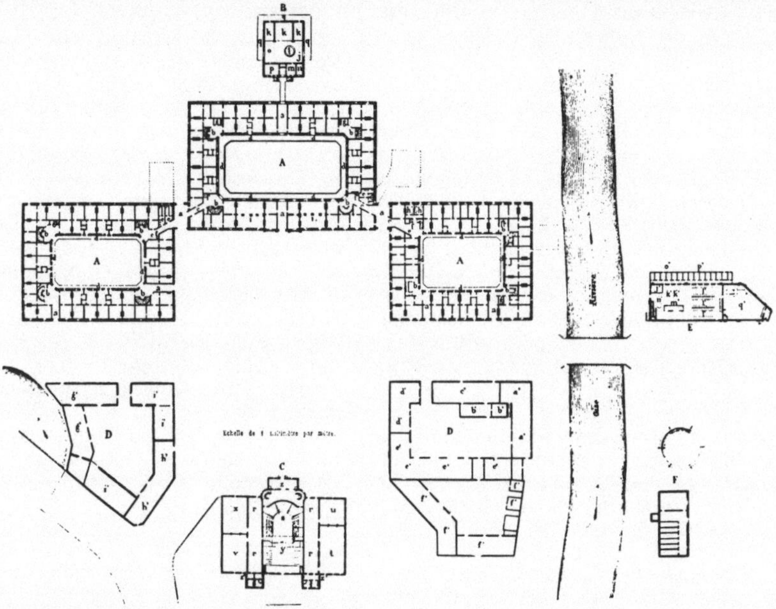

bei Le Corbusier in seiner *unité* wieder aufgenommen.

Der theoretische Entwurf Fouriers und das graphische Konzept Considérants sind annähernd identisch. Considérant hat der technischen Entwicklung seiner Zeit entsprechend der Glaskonstruktion grösseres Gewicht verliehen und hat das schon bei Fourier vorgesehene Heizungs- und Lüftungssystem weiter ausgebaut.

5. Paternalistischer Fourierismus in Guise

Erst zehn Jahre nach der Revolution von 1848 wurde in Frankreich die Idee von einem Sozialpalast in einem Experiment verwirklicht. Von 1859 bis 1885 errichtete der Fourierist und Fabrikant Jean-Baptiste-André Godin in Guise an der Oise eine Wohn- und Produktionsstätten umfassende Anlage.[19]

Der als *Familistère* bezeichnete Komplex ist in drei geschlossene Baublöcke mit insgesamt 180 m Länge aufgeteilt. (Die Front des grössten Phalanstère betrug bei Fourier 1200 m!) Die Innenhöfe der drei Wohnblöcke sind glasüberdacht in einer hölzernen Sprengwerkkonstruktion. Diese Innenhöfe werden durch

25

fig. 15   Cross section of the Familistère.

Galeriewege erschlossen, die zu den 465 unterschiedlich grossen Wohneinheiten führen (Abb. 14, 15).

Die sozialen Folgeeinrichtungen (z. B. Kinderkrippe, Kindergarten, Schule, Theater, Restaurationsbetriebe, Dusch- und Schwimmbäder) von Godins *Familistère* stellen andere zeitgenössische, fast nur auf dem Einfamilienhaussystem basierende Siedlungen (z. B. Cité Ouvrière Mühlhausen) in den Schatten. Im Vergleich mit dem Fourierschen Ideal büsst der paternalistische Versuch jedoch sehr viel Terrain ein. Vielleicht war es aber gerade die Sicherstellung der Keimzelle der Nation, der Familie, welche das fourieristische Experiment in Guise von bürgerlicher Seite mit Applaus aufnehmen liess.

Owen und Fourier entwarfen neue Formen des Zusammenlebens für die Masse der Menschheit. Ihre Unruhe und die theoretische Vorwegnahme neuer gesellschaftlicher Bedingungen deklassierten sie für den wissenschaftlichen Sozialismus zu utopischen Sozialisten. Aber es ist gerade die Konkretisierung urbanistischer Vorstellungen, der Makel des Utopischen, der die architekturhistorische Forschung interessiert. «Nur wo Heterogenes sich aktivierend zu beeinflussen vermag, kann soziales Leben entstehen, kann ein sozial eigenständiges Gebilde im Sinne einer Siedlung, eines Dorfes oder einer Stadt Inhalt und Struktur gewinnen. Das aber ist die Voraussetzung für soziales Zusammenleben in einem abgegrenzten Raum.»[20] Es sind vor allem der soziale Anspruch und der integrative Charakter der Entwürfe von Owen und Fourier, von denen eine Faszination ausgeht. Aber gerade die heute als progressiv interpretierte Komplexität der Planung verurteilte alle pragmatischen Ansätze zum Scheitern. Die Komplexität war nicht für eine umstrukturierte Gesellschaft geplant, sondern sollte zur Umstrukturierung beitragen. Der Idealismus aus der Isolation scheiterte an seinem gesellschaftlichen Fremdkörperdasein.

---

[1] Auf eine extensive Behandlung des historischen Hintergrundes muss hier verzichtet werden. Vgl. dazu: F. Bollerey und K. Hartmann: *Beiträge zur urbanistischen Diskussion im 19. und 20. Jahrhundert.* Phil. Diss. FU-Berlin, 1973.
[2] Max Horkheimer, *Anfänge der bürgerlichen Gesellschaftsphilosophie*, Stuttgart, 1930, p. 87.
[3] Friedrich Engels, *Herrn Eugen Dührings Umwälzung der Wissenschaft*, 3. Aufl., Stuttgart, 1894, p. 274.
[4] August Bebel, *Charles Fourier*, Stuttgart, 1907, p. 23.
[5] Leonardo Benevolo, *Le origini dell'urbanistica moderna*, Bari, 1968, p. 9.
[6] Eine ausführliche Liste der Veröffentlichungen Robert Owens findet sich bei J. F. C. Harrison: *Robert Owen and the Owenites in Britain and America*, London, 1969.
[7] Alle späteren Reaktionen auf die chaotische Stadt haben das zu überbauende Territorium und die Einwohnerzahl genau festgelegt. Howard sah z. B. 1898 für die Garden-City 150 ha für 2000 Bewohner vor (2400 ha für 32 000 Personen). Die erste deutsche Gartenstadt Hellerau hatte auf einem Gelände von 140 ha 2000 Einwohner angesiedelt.
[8] R. Owen, *The Life of Robert Owen. Written by Himself*, Bd. 1A, London, 1858, p. 281.
[9] Vgl. William Harvey, Pierson, Jr.: «Notes on Early Industrial Architecture in England», in: *Journal of the Society of Architectural Historians*, VIII, 1—2, (1949).
[10] Vgl. Stedman Whitwell: *Description of an Architectural Model from a Design by Stedman Whitwell Esq. for a Community upon a principle of united interests, as advocated by Robert Owen, Esq.*, London, 1830.
[11] Vgl. Erklärungen Whitwells zu seiner Zeichnung. Abb. 6a.
[12] Vgl. Friedrich Engels, *Die Lage der arbeitenden Klasse in England*. Nach eigener Anschauung und authentische Quellen, 1845, in: MEW, Bd. 2, Berlin 1970, pp. 229—506.
[13] Charles Fourier, *Œuvres complètes*, 12 Bde. (Paris 1841), Repr. Paris 1966, IV, p. 455 ff.
[14] Ebda., pp. 465 ff.
[15] Ebda., p. 462 f.
[16] Victor Considérant, *Destinée sociale*, Paris 1847 (2. Aufl.), p. 421.
[17] Ebda., p. 425.
[18] Ebda., p. 419 f.
[19] Zu Godins Familistère vgl. u. a.: J.-B.-A. Godin, *Solutions sociales*, Bruxelles und Paris, 1871; F. Bernardot, *Le Familistère de Guise; Etude faite au nom de la société du Familistère de Guise . . .*, Exposition universelle de 1889, Guise 1889; *Le Familistère illustré.* Résultat de vingt ans d'association 1880—1900, Paris 1900; Hans Honegger, *Godin und das Familistère von Guise.* Ein praktischer Versuch der Verwirklichung von Fouriers Utopie. Ein Beitrag zum Problem der industriellen Demokratie und zum Problem der Organisierung von Arbeitersiedlungen, Phil. Diss., Zürich, 1919.
[20] Friedrich Spengeli, «Gedanken zum Wohnungsbau», in: *Bauen und Wohnen*, 9 (1972), p. 399.

ENDNOTES

1 The historical background could not be treated in detail here. On that, see F. Bollerey and K. Hartmann, "Beiträge zur urbanistischen Diskussion im 19. und 20. Jahrhundert," PhD diss. FU [Freie Universität] Berlin, 1973.

2 Max Horkheimer, *Anfänge der bürgerlichen Gesellschaftsphilosophie* (Stuttgart, 1930), 87. [Max Horkheimer, "Beginnings of the Bourgeois Philosophy of History," in *Between Philosophy and Social Science: Selected Early Writings*, trans. G. Frederick Hunter, Matthew S. Kramer, and John Torpey (Cambridge, MA, 1993), 370.]

3 Friedrich Engels, *Herrn Eugen Dührings Umwälzung der Wissenschaft*, 3rd ed. (Stuttgart, 1894), 274. [Friedrich Engels, *Anti-Dühring: Herr Eugen Dühring's Revolution in Science*, trans. Emile Burns, in Karl Marx and Friedrich Engels, *Collected Works*, vol. 25 (New York, 1987), 246.]

4 August Bebel, *Charles Fourier* (Stuttgart, 1907), 23.

5 Leonardo Benevolo, *Le origini dell'urbanistica moderna* (Bari, 1968), 9.

6 A detailed list of the publications of Robert Owen can be found in J.F.C. Harrison, *Robert Owen and the Owenites in Britain and America* (London, 1969).

7 All of the later reactions to the chaotic city precisely determined the territory to be built up and the number of residents. For example, in 1898 Howard planned 370 acres for 2,000 residents (6,000 acres for 32,000 people). The first German garden city, Hellerau, had 2,000 residents on 140 hectares (350 acres).

8 R. Owen, *The Life of Robert Owen, Written by Himself*, vol. 1A (London, 1858), 281.

9 See William Harvey, Pierson, Jr., "Notes on Early Industrial Architecture in England," *Journal of the Society of Architectural Historians* 8, 1–2 (1949).

10 See Stedman Whitwell, *Description of an Architectural Model from a Design by Stedman Whitwell Esq. for a Community upon a Principle of United Interests, as Advocated by Robert Owen, Esq.* (London, 1830).

11 See Whitwell's key to his drawing in figure 6a.

12 See Friedrich Engels, "Die Lage der arbeitenden Klasse in England, nach eigener Anschauung und authentische Quellen" (1845), in Karl Marx and Friedrich Engels, *Werke*, vol. 2 (Berlin, 1970), 229–506. [Friedrich Engels, *The Condition of the Working-Class in England: From Personal Observation and Authentic Sources*, trans. Florence Kelley-Wischnewetzky, in Karl Marx and Friedrich Engels, *Collected Works*, vol. 5 (New York, 1975), 295–583.]

13 Charles Fourier, *Œuvres complètes d'association, 1880*, 12 vols. (Paris, 1966; reprint of Paris, 1841), 4:455ff.

14 Ibid., 4:465ff. [Charles Fourier, *The Utopian Vision of Charles Fourier: Selected Texts on Work, Love, and Passionate Attraction*, ed. and trans. Jonathan Beecher and Richard Bienvenu (Columbia, MO, 1983), 244. The final two sentences of this quotation are omitted in the published translation.]

15 Ibid., 4:462–63. [Fourier, *The Utopian Vision of Charles Fourier*, 242–43.]

16 Victor Considerant, *Destinée sociale*, 2nd ed. (Paris, 1847), 421.

17 Ibid., 425.

18 Ibid., 419–20.

19 On Godin's Familistère, see, among others, J.-B.-A. Godin, *Solutions sociales* (Brussels and Paris, 1871); F. Bernardet, *Le Familistère de Guise: Étude faite au nom de la société du Familistère de Guise …, Exposition universelle de 1889* (Guise, 1889); *Le Familistère illustré: Résultat de vingt ans d'association, 1880–1900* (Paris, 1900); and Hans Honegger, "Godin und das Familistère von Guise: Ein praktischer Versuch der Verwirklichung von Fourier Utopie; Ein Beitrag zum Problem der industriellen Demokratie und zum Problem der Organisierung von Arbeitersiedlungen," Phil. diss. (Zurich, 1919).

20 Friedrich Spengelin, "Gedanken zum Wohnungsbau," *Bauen und Wohnen* [26], 9 (1972), 399.

Manfredo Tafuri

«NEU-BABYLON»

das New York der Zwanzigerjahre und die Suche nach dem Amerikanismus

Wie schon in früheren Artikeln,[1] unterstreicht Harvey Wiley Corbett 1923 in der Zeitschrift *Pencil Points* die neuen formalen Möglichkeiten und die funktionellen Vorteile des 1916 erlassenen «Zoning Law» von New York. Ihn interessiert dabei nicht so sehr die grundsätzliche Bedeutung des «zoning», auch wenn er flüchtig die Auswirkung auf die Stabilisierung der Bodenpreise erwähnt,[2] als vielmehr der szenische Apparat, der suggeriert wird: in diesem Artikel werden denn auch — auf Angaben von Helmle & Corbett beruhend — die vier berühmten Schemen der zurückgestuften Wolkenkratzer wiedergegeben, in der emphatischen Ueberhöhung des «rendering» von Hugh Ferriss. Trotz einiger Bedenken ökonomischer und funktioneller Natur zum zweiten dieser Schemen — mit regelmässiger, zwei Stockwerke umfassender Stufung im rechten und unbegrenzter Höhe im linken Block — gibt Corbett dazu eine bezeichnende Beschreibung:

"(. . .) vertical part of the distance sloping the rest of the way, and with the tower, which would be the ideal of Biblical days, actually reaching to the heavens, a veritable tower of Babel".[3]

Das Spektrum des Turms von Babel hält somit seinen Einzug in die architektonische Kultur New Yorks: die apokalyptischen Bezüge verbinden sich dabei aufs engste mit dem neuen Optimismus, der in Manhattan besonders nach

«La nouvelle Babylone» et la recherche de l'américanisme

A la recherche des mythes dominant l'architecture des gratte-ciel de la New York des années vingt, l'auteur voit dans la reconstruction du Temple et de la Citadelle de Salomon, projet de Helmle & Corbett (1925), un symbole clé de la «New Babylon» frappée par un boom spéculatif sans précédent. En confrontant des œuvres telles que le Barclay-Vesey Building (1925, projet de Ralph Walker) et le Park Avenue Building (1927, de Ely Jacques Kahn) avec les écrits de Louis Mumford, de E. Kahn et de Francisco Mujica, l'auteur tente d'expliquer les raisons qui conduisirent à chercher dans les cultures anti-européennes — la Perse, les styles moresques, l'architecture maya et pré-colombienne — les racines d'une architecture «Neo-american». L'aspiration à une culture autochtone se révèle ainsi complémentaire des intérêts des forces de la spéculation foncière new yorkaise. Le vitalisme de la «New Babel», de la Manhattan qui précède la grande dépression, apparaît ainsi comme un masque sans épaisseur, qui cache la course irresponsable vers un écroulement économique fatal. Dans le film de Busby Berkeley, *Gold Diggers of 1935*, l'individu et la métropole sont représentés comme indissolublement liés: mais une telle relation est mortelle. Le music-hall gigantesque de la Manhattan chantée par les gratte-ciel de Walker, Ely Kahn, Hood. etc. . . . est donc une dernière célébration du laissez-faire à son déclin.

"New Babylon"

The New York of the 1920s and the Search for Americanism

Author:
Manfredo Tafuri

Sources:
archithese, 20 (1976): 12–24, 51
Manfredo Tafuri, *The Sphere and the Labyrinth: Avant-Gardes and Architecture from Piranesi to the 1970s* (Cambridge, MA: MIT Press, 1987), 171–89 (EN)

Translated by:
Steven Lindberg

Writing in *Pencil Points* in 1923, Corbett exalts—as he had already done in previous articles[1]—the new formal possibilities and the functional advantages of the New York Zoning Law. Corbett is not as interested in the structural significance of zoning, even though he points out in passing its effect on the stabilization of land prices,[2] as he is in the new scenic apparatus that it suggests: precisely in that article are reproduced the four famous schemes for setback skyscrapers, made emphatic in the perspective renderings by Hugh Ferriss that illustrate the results of Helmle & Corbett's zoning envelope studies. Corbett, while holding reservations of an economic and functional nature regarding the second scheme—with its upward thrusts arranged in levels of two floors in the tower on the right side, and with its tower of an indefinite height on the left—comments on it in a most significant way:

> "with the vertical part inclining up to the top and with the tower that, like the ideal of the Biblical epoch, touches the sky: an authentic tower of Babel."[3]

The specter of the tower of Babel thus begins to circulate in New York architectural culture; the apocalyptic allusions perfectly coincide with the new optimism that in Manhattan, especially after 1925, follows the upsurge in building and the new boom in tertiary structures. It is not accidental that a few years after the publication of Corbett's article, Fritz Lang films, in his *Metropolis*, the very reconstruction of the myth of Babel.[4] The setback skyscrapers, determined by the zoning law, come to be read as carriers of two complementary symbolic meanings. The confusion of tongues resulting from the undertaking of Babel merges with the reference to the city as "New Babylon": the project for the system of roof gardens and bridges suspended over the streets in Rockefeller Center is only a belated result of this widespread identification.[5] But, meanwhile, it becomes necessary to compensate for such a disquieting reading with a cathartic interpretation. Babel is the prelude to new knowledge, to the division of language, the triumph of "difference"—but only as the premise of a new globality. If Claude Bragdon could interpret the renderings by Ferriss as Piranesian prisons, in which man is swallowed up by a machine that is infernal because it is irrational,[6] Helmle & Corbett do not hesitate to elaborate in 1925 an ideal restoration of King Solomon's Temple and Citadel, in a plan sent, along with others, to the Berlin exhibition of American architecture opened in 1926 at the Akademie der Künste.[7]

It would be an error to consider the pastiche designed by Helmle & Corbett as simply a divertissement of kitsch derivation. The rationality of Solomon is not an antithesis to the "differences" institutionalized by the chaos of Babel; on the contrary, the latter is the very foundation of that rationality. The paroxysmal competition that invades mid-Manhattan along with the new commercial skyscrapers does not need to rationalize interventions coming from outside the market. The new laissez-faire has built into itself adequate potential for *self-planning*: this is the unexpressed ideology that makes the rounds of New York architectural culture during the 1920s. The zoning law, precisely for its "restrictive" characteristics, for its capacity to project the status quo into the future, for its use as an instrument for stabilizing the economy, can be accepted as a tranquilizing measure; the same does not apply, however, to the reports prepared by Henry Wright and Clarence Stein for Governor Al Smith, which were seen as destructive of a *self*-correcting equilibrium.

The orgy of forms deposited on the skyscrapers of New York, between the resumption of building activity after the First World War and the crash of 1929, cannot be interpreted monolithically as a simple optimistic merging of the influences of late-romantic European culture and Hollywood taste. That art deco, expressionist, Viennese, and Dutch influences had shaped this orgy of forms is indubitable, as has been recently underlined by Rosemarie Bletter. But nothing as yet has been said about the structural reasons that pushed for such a widespread adoption of the "jazz style," for such a deliberate mediation of mechanization and allegories that are immediately understandable, for such an indifference to matters of linguistic coherence (every language is permitted in the "great theatre" of the metropolis).

Certainly, the "New Babylon" is invited to participate joyously in the world of commerce: the commodities themselves, here, tend to hide the abstractions of their exchange value, to exalt the "gratuitous," to present themselves as pure use-value. The refined lobbies of the Chanin Building, the Chrysler Building, and the Film Center Building are composed as true and proper *boîtes à surprises* [surprise boxes]: the conventional naturalism of the exteriors (the decorated walls of the Chanin Building come to mind) or their fragmentariness are exalted in spaces that absorb into themselves the only "social" values possible in the new metropolis. Yet the fragment, isolated as it is, celebrates its own provisionality: the elevator lobby designed by Ely Jacques Kahn for the Film Center Building (1928–29) is merely an accumulation of plastic objects in syncopated rhythm, unstable, ready to change form in a mechanically controllable metamorphosis.

There is no celebration of the irrational in such an ostentatious fragmentation of objects. The cute remark that Benjamin made in "Zentralpark" is quite valid. Referring to Nietzsche's well-known metaphor, he writes:

> "For the idea of eternal recurrence, most important is the fact that the bourgeoisie no longer dared to face the next phase in the development of the order of production which it had set into motion. Zarathustra's idea of an eternal recurrence and the motto on the antimacassars covering the cushions [of the divans of the bourgeois salon] 'Just a quarter hour' are complementary."[8]

Thus the unstable surfaces hollowed out and dotted with denticles and the graded, slanted ceilings of Ely J. Kahn's Film Center elevator lobby, and the spiral tangles of the radiator grills in the lobby of Sloan and Robertson's Chanin Building and the polychrome backgrounds of that building's elevators, though through different devices, express the same allegorical meaning: the exaltation of the temporary. "The eternal recurrence" is banalized, but rendered totally enjoyable; "the bad infinity of time" is exorcized in a triumph of the transitory, of the flowing without pause, of the "inessential" play of forms. "Just a quarter hour": the entire metropolis calls for the ceaseless acceleration of movement, of velocity, of exchange. Within the metropolis, it must be made impossible "to stop," impossible to perceive the laws of its own productive order. "The New Babylon" must present itself as a variety theatre, through which eccentricity becomes an institution, a mode of collective behavior.

↓ fig. 1   Helmle & Corbett, Reconstruction of the temple district and Solomon's temple; general view.

↓ fig. 2   Helmle & Corbett, Reconstruction of Solomon's temple and citadel; rendering by Hugh Ferriss.

1925 zur Zunahme der Bautätigkeit und zum neuen Boom des tertiären Sektors führt. Nicht zufällig bezieht Fritz Lang, drei Jahre nach dem erwähnten Artikel Corbetts, die eigentliche Rekonstruktion des Turms von Babel in seinen Film «Metropolis» ein.[4] Die «set-back»-Wolkenkratzer, bedingt durch das «zoning law», werden somit lesbar als Träger zweier sich ergänzender symbolischer Momente. Das Sprachgewirr Babels vereinigt sich mit der Assoziation der Metropolis als «Neues Babylon»: das Projekt eines Systems von Dachgärten und Strassenbrücken für das Rockefeller Center ist nur eine späte Konsequenz dieser verbreiteten Identifikation.[5] Gleichzeitig setzt sich aber auch die Notwendigkeit durch, dieses beunruhigende Bild mit einer reinigenden Deutung zu kompensieren: Babel ist Voraussetzung der Neuen Weisheit, ist Sprachentrennung, Triumph des Unterschieds; aber nur als Vorläufer einer neuen Synthese. Wenn Claude Bragdon nachträglich die Zeichnungen Ferriss' im Sinne der «Carceri» Piranesis interpretiert, in denen der Mensch in einer irrationalen Höllenmaschine eingefangen ist,[6] so versäumen es anderseits Helmle & Corbett nicht, 1925 eine ideale Rekonstruktion des Tempels und der Festung Salomons auszuarbeiten, die im übrigen an die 1926 eröffnete Ausstellung amerikanischer Architektur in der Berliner Akademie der Künste gesandt wurde.[7]

Es wäre falsch, dieses von Helmle & Corbett projektierte «pastiche» als Kitschvergnügen abzutun. Die salomonische Vernunft steht nicht im Widerspruch zu den vom babelischen Chaos eingeführten Unterschieden; im Gegenteil, das Chaos begründet erst jenes vernünftige System. Der auf hohen Touren laufende Wettbewerb, der über Mid-Manhattan mit seinen Geschäftswolkenkratzern hereinbricht, bedarf nicht der von ausserhalb des Marktes herkommenden Rationalisierungsvorschläge. Das neue «laissez-faire» trägt in sich die Kraft der Eigengesetzlichkeit: dies ist die unausgesprochene, innerhalb der architektonischen Kultur aber bekannte Ideologie New Yorks der Zwanzigerjahre. Gerade wegen seines «restriktiven» Charakters, wegen seiner Fähigkeit, den status quo in die Zukunft zu projizieren und aufgrund seiner Eigenschaft als Instrument ökonomischer Stabilisierung kann das «zoning law» als beruhigende Massnahme gelten: im Gegensatz zu den von Henry Wright und Clarence Stein für den Gouverneur Al Smith ausgearbeiteten *Reports*, die als Störung eines in sich *selbst* zu vervollkommnenden Gleichgewichts empfunden werden.

Die formale Orgie, die sich zwischen dem

fig. 3 Ely Jacques Kahn, Elevator lobby of the Film Center Building, New York, 1928/29.

Aufschwung des Bausektors nach dem Ersten Weltkrieg und dem Bruch von 1929 auf die Wolkenkratzer New Yorks niederlässt, darf deshalb nicht einfach als optimistische Vermengung von Anregungen der spätromantischen europäischen Kultur und dem Hollywood-Geschmack gesehen werden. Dass Art Déco-Einflüsse sowie Reminiszenzen des Expressionismus aus Wien und Holland diese formale Orgie begünstigten, steht ausser Zweifel — wie kürzlich von Rosemarie Bletter unterstrichen worden ist. Aber über die eigentlichen Gründe, die zu einer solch verbreiteten Aufnahme des «jazz style», zu einer derart ausgeklügelten Vermittlung von Mechanismus und unmittelbar assimilierten Allegorien und zu einer solchen Indifferenz gegenüber linguistischer Kohärenz führen — jede Sprache ist in diesem «grossen Theater» Metropolis zugelassen! — ist noch nichts gesagt.

Sicherlich bedeutet «Neu-Babel» eine Einladung, am Universum der Waren fröhlich teilzuhaben: die Waren selber neigen dazu, die Abstraktheit ihres Tauschwertes zu verbergen, die Billigkeit hervorzustreichen und sich als reinen Gebrauchswert darzustellen. Die raffinierten *lobbies* des Chanin Building, des Chrysler Building, des Film Center Building entpuppen sich so als eigentliche Wundertüten: der konventionelle Naturalismus des Aeussern (man denke nur an die Mauerdekoration des Chanin Building) oder ihr Fragmentarismus werden somit in Räumen überhöht, die in sich die einzig möglichen «sozialen» Werte der neuen Metropolis aufnehmen. Und trotzdem zeigt das Fragment, als solches enthüllt, die eigene Vorläufigkeit: die von Ely Jacques Kahn für das Film Center Building (1928–29) projektierte «elevator lobby» ist schliesslich nichts anderes als eine Vereinigung plastischer und in synkopischen Rhythmus angehäufter Objekte, die, unstabil, sich anzuschicken scheinen, in einer mechanisch gelenkten Metamorphose ihre Form zu verändern.

Keine Verherrlichung also des Irrationalen in dieser offensichtlichen Aufsplitterung des Gegenständlichen. Viel eher trifft die scharfe Beobachtung Benjamins in seinem *Zentralpark* zu:

«Für den Gedanken der ewigen Wiederkunft hat die Tatsache ihre Bedeutung, dass die Bourgeoisie der bevorstehenden Entwicklung der von ihr ins Werk gesetzten Produktionsordnung nicht mehr ins Auge zu blicken wagte. Der Gedanke Zarathustras von der ewigen Wiederkunft und die Devise des Kissenschoners ‚Nur ein Viertelstündchen' sind Komplemente.»

In diesem Sinne besitzt die Unstabilität der ausgehöhlten und mit Zackenmustern versehenen Oberflächen, der schiefen und gestuften Decke der *lobby* von Ely J. Kahn — oder jene der wirren Spiralformen der Radiatoren der *lobby* im Chanin Building von Gloan und Robertson oder der polychromen Musterung der Aufzüge desselben Gebäudes — einen einzigen allegorischen Inhalt: die Verherrlichung des Provisorischen. Die «ewige Wiederkunft» ist banalisiert, aber mit Erfolg nutzbar gemacht: «die schlechte Unendlichkeit der Zeit» wird in einem Triumph des Vergänglichen exorziert, des Fliessens ohne Pose, des «unwesentlichen» Spiels der Formen. «Nur ein Viertelstündchen»: die ganze Metropole lädt zur Beschleunigung ohne Stillstand, der Beweglichkeit und des Wechsels ein. In ihr muss es verunmöglicht werden, «anzuhalten»: es muss verhindert werden, dass die Gesetze seines Produktionsablaufes eingesehen werden. Und deshalb muss sich «Neu-Babylon» darbieten als Theater der Attraktionen, wo Exzentrizität eine Institution, ja kollektive Verhaltensweise geworden ist.

Ausserhalb dieser Ueberlegung ist die dauernd wiederholte Verbindung von der Entwicklung der Wolkenkratzer und des Amerikanismus in den Zwanziger- und frühen Dreissi-

↓ fig. 4   McKenzie, Voorhees & Gmelin (Ralph Walker, designer), Barclay-Vesey Building, New York, 1923–26. Schematics of floor plan and elevation of the technical installations.

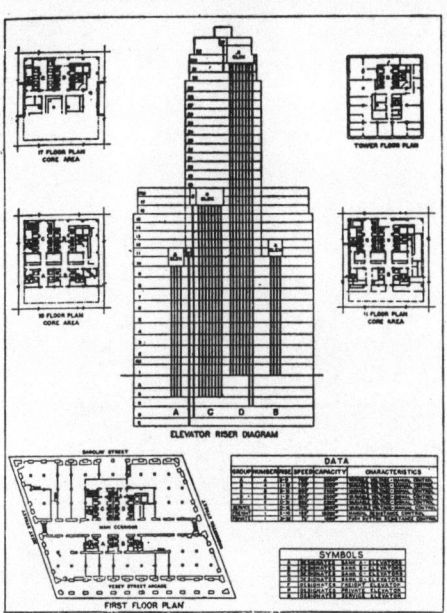
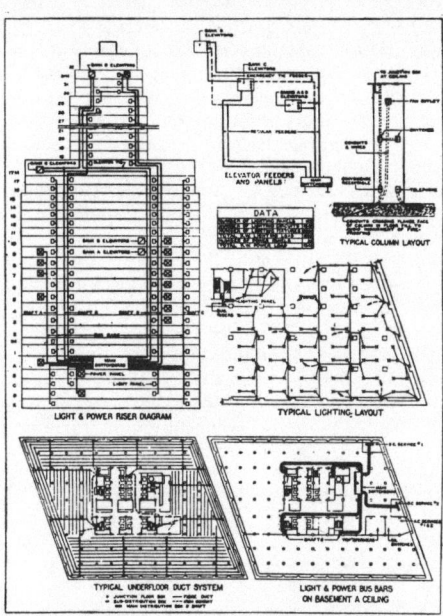
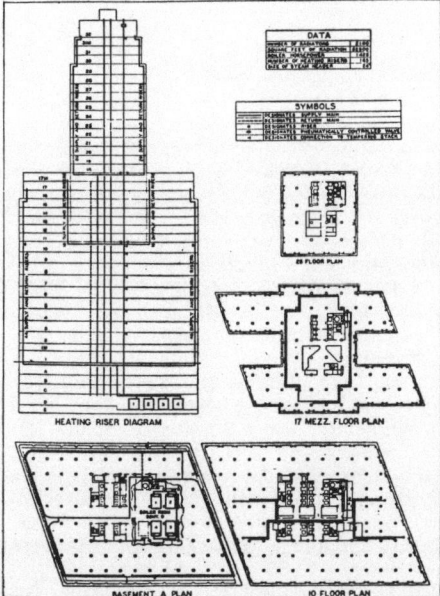
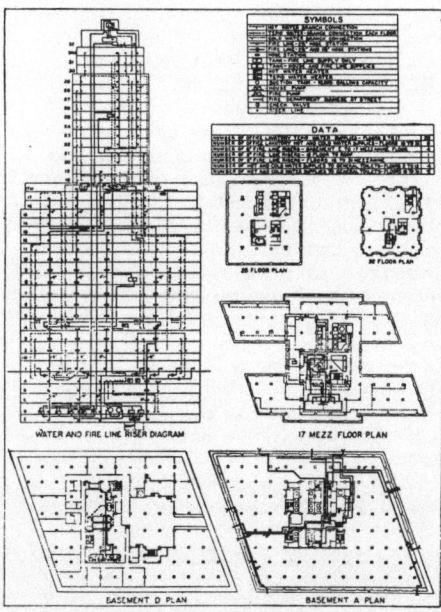

fig. 5   Barclay-Vesey Building, New York, partial view.

gerjahren nicht verständlich. Nicht mehr Struktur, sondern szenisches Spielzeug, reich an spielerischen Momenten, negiert der Wolkenkratzer das ihm von einem George B. Post oder einem Ernest Flagg grundgelegte Strukturprinzip. Sein Vitalismus ist gleichzeitig das Resultat eines ungezügelten Spekulationslaufs, der schnurgerade auf die Katastrophe der grossen Depression hingeht, und dessen eigene «Maske».

In einem Artikel von 1930 in *The Architectural Forum* unterstreicht Paul Robertson, Präsident der «National Association of Building Owners and Managers», den engen Zusammenhang zwischen der Entwicklung des Wolkenkratzers und dem «american way of life», indem er mit den damals in Spekulantenkreisen üblichen Argumenten die Verdichtung durch Tertiärkonzentrierungen in der Höhe verharmloste. Die wirklichen Feinde, die Robertson damit angreifen wollte, sind die restriktiven Vorschriften, die — wie er sagt — von der gleichen Mentalität geprägt seien, mit der man vormals die mit 20—30 Std./km fahrenden Züge bekämpfte: Robertson zögert nicht festzuhalten, dass unter Berücksichtigung der Boden- und Gebäudewerte die Investitionssumme im Bereich der Bauwirtschaft sieben Billionen Dollars übersteige, und somit der Wolkenkratzer zu einer Industrie angewachsen sei, die diejenige der Autofabrikation, des Stahls, der Eisenbahnen — gemessen am investierten Kapital — übertreffe.[9] Er bemerkt im weiteren die Benachteiligung dieser Kategorie im Rahmen eines Steuersystems, das die Gebäude der Central Business Districts belastet: nach seiner Analyse sieht es so aus, als wären die inflationistischen Folgen, verursacht durch die Ausbreitung der Wolkenkratzer im gesamtstädtischen Rahmen, nirgends mehr anzutreffen, und als gäbe es keine paradoxe Situation des Baumarktes der Stadt New York, die in Tat und Wahrheit um 1926 durch eine Ueberproduktion von Büroräumen gekennzeichnet war — wie übrigens Untersuchungen von Frederic A. Delano festhalten, bestätigt (wohlgemerkt) von niemand anderem als der «Building Owners and Managers Association of New York».[10]

Wenn schon — entgegen allem Anschein — der Wolkenkratzer im Zusammenhang der Weltwirtschaftskrise als unumgängliches «Schicksal» auftritt, so werden anderseits die Anfänge dieses ökonomischen Kreislaufes, der das Gesicht New Yorks gänzlich verändert, von den Architekten auf recht verschiedene Weise erlebt. Das Kapitel «Art Déco in New York» mit dem Barclay-Vesey Building (1923—26) von Mc Kenzie, Voorhes & Gmelin (Ralph Walker designer) zu beginnen, wie dies üblicherweise geschieht, kann deshalb irreführen. Betrachten wir dessen Struktur: auf einem Sockel über trapezoidalem Grundriss (entsprechend der Ausdehnung des Grundstücks) erhebt sich der für die New York Telephone Company errichtete Wolkenkratzer kompakt über zehn Geschosse, um dann die Form eines H mit — immer noch von der trapezoidalen Grundform bestimmten — kürzeren Aesten anzunehmen. Unabhängig von dieser Struktur türmt sich jedoch der zentrale Kern des Gebäudes: frei über 19 Geschosse und bekrönt von drei Triumphbogen und gegen den Himmel gestaffelten Hochrechtecken «à la manière de Saarinen». Die Typologie des Wolkenkratzers mit geöffneten Höfen — 1880 von Post eingeführt — wird somit von jener des Turmes überlagert. Und

Outside of this framework, the link, continually reaffirmed in the twenties and the early thirties, between the development of the skyscraper and Americanism is incomprehensible. No longer a structure but a scenic toy rich with ludic valences, the skyscraper negates the structural matrix imposed upon it by George B. Post and by Ernest Flagg. Its vitalism is both a response to the unrestrained course of financial speculation that leads directly to the catastrophe of the Great Depression and, at the same time, a "mask" superimposed on that course.

Writing in 1930 in *The Architectural Forum*, Paul Robertson, President of the National Association of Building Owners and Managers, reaffirms the tenacious bond between the development of the skyscraper and the American way of life, contesting, with the usual arguments addressed to the forces governing the financial speculation of the epoch, the relation between congestion and tertiary concentrations. The real enemies that Robertson intends to strike are the restrictive regulations conceived, as he writes, by the same mentality that in the good old days would have been frightened by the thought of trains proceeding at the speed of fifteen to twenty miles per hour. Robertson, having taken into account the values of the lands and buildings, does not hesitate to affirm that the total investment in the commercial building sector is in excess of seven billion dollars, making the skyscraper, at least in terms of invested capital, into an industry larger than the auto, steel, and railroad industries.[9] Moreover, he expresses disappointment on behalf of his own group in the system of taxation that hits the buildings of the central business districts: in his analysis, the inflationary effects provoked, on an urban scale, by the proliferation of skyscrapers are made to disappear, along with any consideration of the paradoxical situation of the building market in New York City—afflicted already around 1926 by an overproduction of office spaces, according to investigations by Frederick A. Delano and confirmed (note well) by the New York chapter of the Building Owners and Managers Association.[10]

While even during the depression, the skyscraper, against all evidence, could be reaffirmed as an ineluctable component of an urban "destiny" already marked out, the initial stages of the economic cycle that reshapes the face of the tertiary aspects of New York were experienced in an exactly opposite manner by the architects. To begin the chapter on New York art deco—as is usually done—with the Barclay-Vesey Building (1923–26) by McKenzie, Voorhees & Gmelin, with Ralph Walker as designer, can, from the viewpoint of the previous sentence, send us off in the wrong direction. If we examine the structure of this skyscraper, which was constructed for the New York Telephone Company, we find that its base takes the form of a parallelogram, coinciding with the shape of its lot. The building rises compactly to the tenth floor, where it assumes the planimetric form of an H, with the short sides still determined by the basic shape of the parallelogram. Independent of this structure, however, the central core of the building rises for another nineteen stories, culminating in three large triumphal arches and a series of recessions in the form of parallelepipeds descending in tiers against the sky "à la manière de Saarinen." The typology of the skyscraper with an open courtyard—introduced by Post in 1880—is thus replaced by one with a single tower. And since we are dealing with an assemblage, what is emphasized is the effect of torsion, produced by the divergent orientation of the geometric coordinates of the central core and of the volume articulated by the form of the parallelogram. The dramatization of structure is further accentuated by the prevalence of the continuous vertical bands of brickwork that "liberate" themselves from their functional constrictions once they reach the level of the crown with its varying heights: a "liberation" that is underlined by, among other things, the heightened density of the decorative motifs—interwoven plants and exotic animals—at the levels of the shopping arcade and the upper stories.

Louis Sullivan had perceived correctly; Eliel Saarinen's project for the *Chicago Tribune* concluded a formal experiment that Sullivan had left incomplete. The Barclay-Vesey Building is entirely within such a tradition. The struggle of structure to reaffirm its own coherence assumes here an epic tone: only formal distortion guarantees to the tension of volumes an organicity regained by means of a dialectic. Thus the tragic quality inherent in the very condition of the skyscraper—a typological event sundered from every morphological support on the urban level—is assumed and sublimated: the organicity of the building is not guaranteed by the givens upon which it is based but by their deformation, by the imposition of a structurality obtained by means of "heroic" disarticulations. The distance from the fragmentariness of the Film Center Building could not be greater.

Nevertheless, three years after its opening, the Barclay-Vesey Building would be hailed by Mujica as a work marking the triumph of the Modern School, as opposed less to the neo-Gothic already in decline than to the classicism advocated by Hastings.[11] Yet even Lewis Mumford, writing in 1928 his first article dedicated to the review of new tendencies in American architecture,[12] having argued against every connection between the zoning envelope and the aesthetic treatment of the skyscraper, cites the Barclay Vesey Building as one of the signs of a cultural renaissance, placing it alongside Hood's Radiator Building, the Graybar Building, and the Alabama Power Company Building. Mumford, however, sees the work of Ralph Walker not as a unified organism, but rather as a split, dualistic structure:

> "The building as a whole has a feeling of dark strength, but in the stone work of the lower stories and in the interior the designer introduces a delicate, naturalistic carving, heightened within by the use of gold. When one enters the main hall, one almost forgets its purpose: it is as gaily lighted and decorated as a village street in a strawberry festival. Mr. Walker, in other words, accepts the contrast between structure and feeling: he does not attempt to reconcile them... . In Mr. Walker's design decoration is an audacious compensation for the rigor and mechanical fidelity of the rest of the building; like jazz, it interrupts and relieves the tedium of too strenuous mechanical activity."[13]

It is significant that Mumford does not comprehend the structural aspects of the Barclay-Vesey Building, which, with its shopping arcade on Vesey Street, among other things, takes into account the principle of multilevel traffic, even though it is confined to the restricted ambit of a single passage. What interests the American critic is the juxtaposing of the elementaristic terrorism of the European avant-gardes against the principle of synthesis at the heart of the tradition of Sullivan and Wright; to Walker's work, he opposes the Park Avenue Building by Ely Jacques Kahn, which he interprets as a reconciliation of the two poles that, in his opinion, the Barclay-Vesey Building keeps apart.

And yet, from the structural point of view, Raymond Hood, Corbett, and Kahn are in accord in advancing proposals antithetical to the regionalism that was advocated by the RPAA and that Mumford himself will defend against the bland hypotheses of decentralization suggested by the Regional Plan of New York drawn up by Thomas Adams. Hood and Corbett more explicitly, and Kahn more generally, propose concentrations of high density in the large areas of the central business district to create a vertical integration of residences, services, offices, industries, and social spaces, in single and completely equipped blocks.[14] However, Kahn arrives at the solution of the Park Avenue Building only after a Beaux-Arts education, an experience as a painter, researches in vernacular style, buildings in New York that are still ambiguous, such as the John Thorpe Building (1921), the Arsenal Building (1925), the 550 Seventh Avenue Building (1925), the International Telephone and Telegraph Building (1927). Only with the triad of skyscrapers built in 1927—the Insurance Building, the Park Avenue Building, the Broadway and Thirty-seventh Street Building does a Kahnian "style" become definitive: exactly the personal style that triumphs in the Film Center discussed above, in the Allied Arts Building of 1929, and in the Bricken Casino Building of 1931.

It is evident that Mumford praises the formal continuity of the Park Avenue Building for its vague resemblance to some of Wright's formulas. But the decomposition of Buchman & Kahn's skyscraper, on the whole a traditional organism, effected by its ornamental and colored projections, designed in collaboration with Leon Solon, belongs to a composite poetics, which departs from European experiments only to confront them critically with openly anti-European traditions. The abstract silhouettes that torment the surfaces of the Park Avenue Building alternate, and enter into dialogue, with a gamut of colors and materials ranging from masonry, to terracotta, to ochre, to magenta red, to blue, with gradations dimensioned according to their distance from the observer's eye. Presenting the building in 1928, Leon Solon speaks of a scientific approach to

↓ fig. 6 Buchmann & Kahn, Park Avenue Building, New York, 1926. Floor plan and volume computation.

↓ fig. 7 Park Avenue Building, New York. Detail study of the upper part of the building, taking into account the choice of colors and materials.

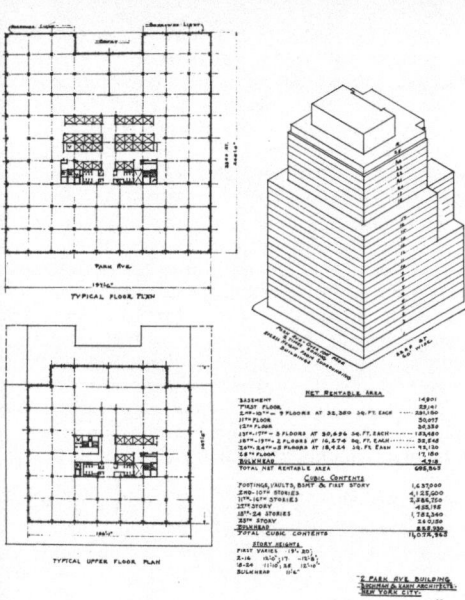

← figs. 8–9
Ely Jacques Kahn
2 Park Avenue
Building,
New York.
Partial views.

dass es sich dabei um eine Assemblage handelt, unterstreicht der Torsionseffekt, der sich aus der ungleichen Orientierung der trapezoidalen Grundform und des Gebäudekerns ergibt. Die Dramatisierung der Struktur wird zudem durch die dominierenden vertikalen Mauerbänder unterstrichen, die sich auf den verschiedenen Absätzen der Bekrönungen von ihrem funktionellen Zwang «befreien»: eine «Befreiung», die durch zunehmende Verwendung dekorativer Motive — in Form verschlungener exotischer Tiere und Pflanzen — unter anderm das Geschoss der «shopping arcade» und des Gebäudeabschlusses auszeichnet.

Louis Sullivan hatte recht gesehen: Eliel Saarinens Projekt für die «Chicago Tribune» beschloss eine von ihm eingeleitete, dann aber unterbrochene formale Angelegenheit. Das Barclay-Vesey Building steckt mitten in dieser Tradition. Der Kampf der Struktur um ihre eigene Kohärenz nimmt hier eine epische Tonalität an: nur die formale Drehung verleiht der Gespanntheit der Volumen auf dialektischem Wege organischen Charakter. Dies bedeutet, dass das tragische Moment, durch den Wolkenkratzer selbst bedingt als ein von der morphologischen Umgebung der Stadt unabhängiges typologisches Phänomen, aufgenommen und sublimiert wird: der organische Charakter des Gebäudes liegt nicht in den Ausgangsbedingungen, sondern in deren Deformation begründet, im Aufsetzen einer durch «heroische» Artikulierungen erwirkten Struktur. Der Abstand zum Fragmentarismus des Film Center Building könnte nicht grösser sein.

Trotzdem wird das Barclay-Vesey Building drei Jahre nach seiner Einweihung von Mujica als Werk bezeichnet, das den Triumph der «modern school» darstellt— nicht so sehr im Gegensatz zu der nun im Rückgang begriffenen neogotischen Formgebung als zu dem von Leuten wie Hastings vertretenen Klassizismus.[11] Auch Mumford zählt in einem ersten den neuen Tendenzen der amerikanischen Architektur gewidmeten Aufsatz von 1928[12] das Barclay-Vesey Building zu den Symptomen einer kulturellen Erneuerung — zusammen mit Hoods Radiator Building, mit dem Grayar Building und dem Alabama Power Company's Building: nicht ohne zuvor jeden Zusammenhang zwischen *zoning law* und ästhetischer Behandlung des Wolkenkratzers geleugnet zu haben. Aber das Werk Ralph Walkers wird von ihm nicht als einheitlicher Organismus, sondern als verdoppelte, dualistische Struktur gelesen. Mumford schreibt:

"The building as a whole has a feeling of dark strenght; but in the stonework of the lower stories and in the interior the designer introduces a delicate naturalistic carving, heightened within by the use of gold. When one enters the main hall one almost forgets its purpose: it is as gaily lighted and decorated as a village street in a strawbery festival. Mr. Walker, in other words, accepts the contrast between strucure and feeling: he does not attempt to reconcile them (...). In Mr. Walker's design, decoration is an audacious compensation for the rigor and mechanical fidelity of the rest of the building; like the jazz, it interrups and relieves the tedium of too strenuous mechanical activity."

Es ist bezeichnend, dass Mumford nicht auf die strukturellen Aspekte des Barclay-Vesey Building eingeht, das ja im übrigen mit seiner an der Vesey Street gelegenen «shopping arcade» — trotz der Begrenzung auf die einzelne Parzelle — dem Prinzip der Trennung der Verkehrsebenen Rechnung trägt. Was hingegen den amerikanischen Kritiker interessiert, ist eine Gegenüberstellung des elementaren Terrorismus der europäischen Avantgarden mit dem Prinzip einer der Tradition Sullivans und Wrights innewohnenden Synthese: dem Werk Walkers hält er Ely Jacques Kahns Park Avenue Building entgegen, gelesen als Vereinigung der beiden Pole, von der — immer nach Mumfords Meinung — das Barclay-Vesey Building getrennt bleibt.

Und trotzdem sind sich sowohl Raymond Hood als auch Corbett und Ely J. Kahn auch in struktureller Hinsicht einig und äussern zu dem vom RPAA propagierten Regionalismus antithetische Vorschläge. Ebenso nimmt Mumford gegenüber der beabsichtigten Dezentralisierung Stellung, wie sie der Regional Plan of New York von Thomas Adams vorsieht. Deutlich setzen sich Hood und Corbett, etwas allgemeiner auch Kahn für die Konzentration und hohe Dichte in weiten Bereichen des Central Business District ein: im Zeichen einer vertikalen Integration von Wohnung, Dienstleistung, Büro, Industrie und öffentlichem Raum in einzelnen Baukörpern.[14] Anderseits gelangt Kahn zum Resultat des Park Avenue Building nach einer Beaux-Arts Ausbildung, nach einer Tätigkeit als Maler, nach der Auseinandersetzung mit English Domestic Style und einigen noch zwiespältigen New Yorker Bauten wie dem John Thorpe Building (1921), dem Arsenal Building (1925), dem 550-7th-Avenue Building (1925) und dem International Telephone und Telegraph Building (1927). Erst mit den drei Wolkenkratzern von 1927 — Insurance Building, Park Avenue Building, Brodway-37th-Street Building — äussert sich deutlich eine kahn'sche «Manier»: jene, die in dem erwähnten Film Center, im Allied Arts Building von 1929 und im Bricken Casino Building von 1931 ihren Höhepunkt erreichen wird.

Es ist offensichtlich, dass Mumford die formale Kontinuität des Park Avenue Building auf Grund einiger vager Anspielungen an Wright' sche Formeln lobt. Aber die Zusammensetzung des Wolkenkratzers von Buchmann & Kahn, als Organismus durchaus traditionell und mit seiner farbigen, in Zusammenarbeit mit Leon Solon studierten Ornamentik, gehört zu einer Poetik, die von den europäischen Erfahrungen nur ausgeht, um sie kritisch mit antieuropäischen Elementen zu vergleichen. Die abstrakten Silhouetten, die die Oberfläche des Park Avenue Building bestimmen, variieren und stützen sich gegenseitig in Farbe und Material:

↓ fig. 10 Helmle / Corbett & Harrison and Sugarman & Berger, Master Building, New York, 1928–29.

vom Mauerwerk zur Terrakotta, von Ocker zu Magentarot und Blau in Abstufungen, die auf das Auge des Betrachters und die Distanz berechnet sind. Solon, der das Gebäude 1928 vorstellt, spricht von einer wissenschaftlichen Behandlung der Form, im Gegensatz zu einem stilistischen Zugang.[15] In diesem Zusammenhang ist der Hinweis interessant, dass gerade 1928 Kahn zusammen mit Hood, Walker, Saarinen, John Root und Schoen eine Architekturausstellung im Metropolitan Museum New York organisiert, die die neuen Strömungen innerhalb der «Architectural League» dokumentiert und in einem gewissen Sinn eine Antwort auf die von Kahn eingehend studierte Pariser Ausstellung von 1925 darstellt. Dabei ist allerdings zu bemerken, dass der gegenüber den europäischen Avantgarden so aufgeschlossene Kahn[16] die Farbigkeit der griechischen Tempel bemüht, um die entsprechende Ausschmükkung des Park Avenue Building zu rechtfertigen. «We are thinking of Greek primary colors» – schreibt er in einem unveröffentlichten, kurz vor seinem Tod verfassten (ca. 1972) autobiographischen Manuskript[17] – «and that is exactly what we tried to produce». (Ein interessantes Detail: ein detailliertes Modell des Gebäudes wird Hood der Beurteilung vorgelegt, der ihm zustimmt.)

Farbe und Materialbeschaffenheit werden somit als neue formale Instrumente in den Vordergrund gerückt. Derselbe Kahn schreibt 1928[18]:

"The dream of a colored city, buildings in harmonious tones making great masses of beautiful patterns, may be less of a vision in the enterprising city developer suspects the result. There is evident economy of effort in the application of color in lieu of carved decoration that cannot be seen, and the novelty of a structure that can be distinguished from its neighbours has a practical value that must appeal without question to the designer and his public."

Die «colored city» ist somit eine Struktur der Eigenpropaganda, ein System, das die Oeffentlichkeit der Metropole anzieht, und – wie im Fall der neuen Wolkenkratzer der 42th Street oder der Park Avenue – ein wirksames Instrument einer als Pioniertat, als Herausforderung und Gewinnung neuer Bereiche für das besungene «Abenteuer» der Wolkenkratzer selbst gelesenen Spekulation. Nicht zufällig ist die Organisation im Büro Kahns eisern: die Firma ist nicht nur in der Lage, ihren Kunden neue Formen der Reklame anzubieten, sondern berät auch mit sicherer Hand bei der Lokalisierung von Unternehmungen – dank einem mit wissenschaftlicher Akribie angelegten Archiv zur Entwicklung der Bodenpreise auf dem Schachbrett Manhattan.[19]

Auf diese Beziehung design-Spekulation lässt sich nun eine auf die Suche der autochtonen Werte der «American Civilisation» ausgerichtete Poetik herab. Nicht zufällig besass Kahn eine in New York einzigartige Bibliothek mit Schriften der klassischen Archäologie, zu Aegypten und dem Orient und zudem eine Sammlung von Maiolika- und Porzellangegenständen Persiens. Sein Interesse für die primitiven Dekorationsformen Chinas und der Maya-Kultur, für die persische Kunst und die maurischen Stilvarianten wird unmittelbar wirksam, aber hat auch in seinem Grunde ein ideologisches Gesicht: der Aufstieg des türkischen Reichs und der Niedergang der byzantinischen und europäischen Zivilisation wird

↓ fig. 11   Francisco Mujica, Reconstruction of the pyramids of Papantla, Mexico.

↓ fig. 12   Francisco Mujica, Reconstruction of the pyramids of Tikal, Guatemala.

von ihm als Folge der endgültigen Zersetzung einer überfälligen Tradition gesehen, während die Berufung auf die präkolumbianische Kunst einem «Kult der Ursprünge» zugehört, die ihn in die Nähe von Wrights Suche nach dem — auf dem amerikanischen Kontinent durch die «korrupte» europäische Rationalität unterbrochenen — roten Faden bringt.[20]

Hatte nicht schon Rose Henderson 1923 die Künstlerkolonien gelobt, die sich nach 1903 in Taos und Santa Fé in Mexiko auf der Suche nach dem Leben und der Kultur der Pueblos niedergelassen hatten, mit der Bemerkung: "the Indians were the first Cubists in this country?"[21]

Die einheitlichen Massen der Wolkenkratzer Ely J. Kahns — ergänzt von einem Fragmentarismus, der sich erst 1930 im Squibb Building niederschlägt — sind viel weniger von der Rekonstruktion des Tempels von Jerusalem von Helmle & Corbett entfernt, als es auf den ersten Blick erscheinen mag. Auch das Park Avenue Building, das Allied Arts Building und das Holland Plaza Building (1930) stellen Monumente der «Weisheit» dar: nur, dass sich in ihnen der Kult des Archaischen mit der «Monumentalität des Exzentrischen und Veränderbaren» vereinigt, der der formalen Strukturierung — nun befreit vom Zwang eines direkten Bezuges — eines Wolkenkratzers wie Helmle & Corbett's Master Building (1928—29) abgeht.

Das schnell aufnehmbare Bild mit seinen dynamischen Artikulierungen — man denke nur an den extremen Virtuosismus Kahns bei der Gestaltung der Obergeschosse des Bricken Casino Building — sucht somit seine Wurzeln in Kulturen, die fern der Geschichtlichkeit der europäischen Tradition liegen. Auf seiner Suche nach dem Autochtonen begegnet Kahn weder Emerson noch Whitman, vielmehr scheinbar «ahistorischen», stabilen Kulturen und Künsten, die bereitstehen, um aufgenommen zu werden als neue «sources of inspiration» in einem Umkreis, der das Vergängliche als Monstrum erkoren hat, das überwunden werden muss, dem aber auch Opfer darzubringen sind.

Man merke wohl: sowohl für Richardson, als auch für Kahn und Wright sind die «Wurzeln» einer neuen amerikanischen Kultur in der Andersartigkeit begründet. Was zählt, ist die Gleichsetzung des Archaischen — als Symbol, und nur als Symbol unberührter Wahrheiten — mit dem Sieg über atavistische Minderwertigkeitskomplexe gegenüber Europa. Neu ist, verglichen mit der Neoromantik des «Golden Age», dass jetzt, zu Ende der Zwanzigerjahre, der organische Charakter der Architektursprache der zu schlagende Feind zu sein scheint. Ja, die Wolkenkratzer des «neuen» Manhattan, da sie sich als vollzogene «Synthese» weder darstellen können noch wollen, erscheinen als Komparsen eines gigantischen Ballets: die Subjektivität, die das System des «big business» dem molekularen Gefüge der von ihr beherrschten Masse — den Individuen! — entzieht, wird so von den «neuen Subjekten» der Stadt in einer Art kompensatorischen Ritus' wieder eingefangen: festgelaunt betreten sie die Rampe

form as opposed to a stylistic approach:[15] one should note that in this same year Kahn, together with Hood, Walker, Saarinen, John Root, and Schoen, organizes an architectural exhibition for the Metropolitan Museum of New York, which testifies to the ferments raging within the Architectural League and which is in some way a response to the Paris Exposition of 1925, thoroughly studied by Kahn. And one should further note that Kahn himself, so attentive to the debate of the European avant-garde,[16] cites the use of color in ancient Greek temples to justify the formal artifices of the Park Avenue Building. In an unpublished autobiographical manuscript composed shortly before his death (around 1972), he writes: "We were thinking of the primary colors of Greek antiquity. It is exactly those that we have attempted to reproduce."[17] (Particularly interesting, the detailed model of the building was submitted to the judgment of Hood, who approved its erection.)

Thus the color and the texture of materials come to be exalted as new formal instruments. Kahn also writes in 1928:

> "The dream of a colored city, buildings in harmonious tones making great masses of beautiful patterns, may be less of a vision if the enterprising city developer suspects the result. There is evident economy of effort in the application of color in lieu of carved decoration that cannot be seen and the novelty of a structure that can be distinguished from its nondescriptive neighbors has a practical value that must appeal without question to the designer and his public."[18]

The "colored city" is therefore a self-advertising structure, a system intended to involve the metropolitan public, and, as in the case of the new skyscrapers on 42nd Street and on Park Avenue, the efficient instrument of a speculation perceived as pioneering, an attack upon and conquest of new areas for the "adventure" sung by the skyscrapers themselves. It is not coincidental that the professional organization of Kahn's studio is ironbound: the firm can offer its clients not only new forms of publicity but also accurate advice on the suitability of locations, thanks to a scientifically kept up-to-date archive monitoring the state of land prices on the chessboard of Manhattan.[19]

It is upon such a relation between design and speculation that a poetics aimed at a search for the autochthonous values of "American Civilization" is based. Kahn possessed, not by chance, a library containing texts on classical, Egyptian, and Oriental archaeology and a collection of objects, majolica, and porcelains from ancient Persia that were unique in New York. His interests in Chinese primitive decorations, Mayan architecture, Persian art, Moorish styles directly influenced his work, but they also have a deeper ideological meaning: Kahn saw the ascendancy of the Turkish Empire and the decadence of the Byzantine and European civilizations as consequences of the definite deterioration of an obsolete tradition, whereas his recourse to pre-Columbian art belongs to a "cult for roots" that places him close to the free wanderings of Wright in search of the red thread that was broken, in the American continent, by the "corrupting" rationality of Europe.[20]

Besides, had not Rose Henderson, already in 1923, exalted the colonies of painters who had installed themselves after 1903 at Taos and Santa Fe, in New Mexico, near the anthropological sites of the Indians and the remaining Pueblo tribes, affirming that "the Indians were the first Cubists in this country"?[21]

The unitary masses of Kahn's skyscrapers, commented upon by a fragmentism that becomes appeased only in the Squibb Building (1930), are not as remote from Helmle & Corbett's reconstruction of Solomon's Temple as appears at first sight. The Park Avenue Building, the Allied Arts Building, and the Holland Plaza Building (1930) are also monuments to "knowledge": even if in them the cult of the archaic merges with a celebration of the "monumentality of the eccentric and the transitory," unknown to the formal disjointedness—by now lacking any will to reintegration—of a skyscraper like the Master Building (1928–29) by Helmle & Corbett.

The immediately consumable image, despite its articulation by dynamic trajectories (one thinks immediately of the flagrant virtuosity exhibited by Kahn in the ultimate designs for the Bricken Casino Building), seeks roots in a culture that ignores the historicity of the European tradition. In the quest for the autochthonous, Kahn encounters neither Emerson nor Whitman, but rather arts and cultures apparently "ahistorical," stable, capable of being absorbed as new "Sources of Inspiration," in a context that makes the transitory into a monster to be exorcized but to which, nevertheless, sacrifices must be dedicated.

Note well: whether for Richardson, Kahn, or Wright, the "roots" sought for a new American culture are embedded in the *other*. What counts is the equation between the archaic—symbol, and only symbol, of an uncontaminated truth —and the victory over the atavistic inferiority complex vis-à-vis Europe. But with a new feature, which emerges alongside the neoromanticism of the Golden Age: now, at the end of the twenties, the enemy to defeat appears to be the organicity of language. In fact, being neither able nor willing to offer themselves as complete "syntheses," the skyscrapers of the "new" Manhattan pose as spectators at a gigantic collective ballet. The subjectivity that the system of big business transfers to the molecules of the crowd—the individuals —it dominates is thus recuperated, in a sort of propitiatory rite, by the "new subjects" of the city, who advance joyously to the front of the stage of the metropolis transformed into a music hall. The ludic installs itself in the metropolis with masks that lack thickness; the vitalism that emanates from it knows not the desperation of Fitzgerald, but rather the "foolish" vanities of Zelda.

Yet the vitalism of the parade, denounced by critics like Croly or Murchison,[22] is deeply characteristic of the search for the Americanism of which we are attempting to reconnect the threads. The "New Babel" is the innocence that accepts every language, but also the ability to single out collective myths to follow, conscious of their provisionality. It is not surprising that one of the first systematic histories of the skyscraper—that of the Chilean Francisco Mujica—works out organically some of the hypotheses that Ely Kahn had formulated empirically and with the taste of a collector.

The binding together of the search for a truly American architecture and the "American" typology par excellence, that of the skyscraper, is for Mujica a straightforward operation. In this sense, his interpretation of the reasons for the "downfall" of the so-called Chicago School, after the Chicago World's Fair of 1893, is symptomatic: the neoromanticism of Root and Sullivan was "un-American."[23] Moreover, the search for "roots," obstinately pursued by Mujica, is the legacy of the tradition of the American Renaissance. That compounding of transcendental subjectivity and the naturalistic refounding of civil society had as its objective a "frontier" folded back on itself: the metropolis of the skyscrapers was an instrument at the national level, the brain of a complex organization, that, especially in the twenties, aspired to a self-control, to an automatic healing of its institutional wounds. (In fact, such an aspiration to capitalist self-planning, in the absence of interventions by the public administrators was the goal of the regional plan for New York financed and organized by the Russell Sage Foundation, from 1923 onward.)

It is exactly to such a "miraculous" compounding of irrepressible differences that the search for the roots of a "pure" Americanism, liberated from the mortgages fixed by European culture and founded on a neo Rousseauean naturalism of the "noble savage," attempts to offer a contribution. Mujica writes:

> "In these latter days a new tendency has appeared that does not accept the preconceived patterns of the classical and the Gothic styles, but strives to express spontaneously a rational and sincere decoration of the structure employing for this purpose the most modern lines… . The characteristic qualities of these new lines and proportions present great resemblance with the elements of primitive American architecture. As to cornices it has not been possible to apply to skyscrapers any of the hitherto known proportions. The new architecture has had to find an element which only marked the limit of the wall-surface. By this quality and by the fact that its principal decorative elements are brought out in large surfaces, the new style strikingly recalls the Pre-Columbian architecture with its palaces and pyramids with small cornices, and magnificent decorations carved in big dominating surfaces."[24]

That the first illustrations in Mujica's book are ideal reconstructions of the Mexican pyramids of Papantla and Teopantepec and that of Tikal, in Guatemala, has therefore a polemical significance. The "new" draws its guarantees of validity by fastening itself to the primitive —even though the examples used by Mujica do not appear innovative with respect to the practice of designing within the circle of the Architectural League of New York. But let us allow the author to continue:

> "After a profound study of the ruins it is possible to conceive a *new* line in which only the sentiment of the American forms subsists. It appears to me correct to call this new type of architecture Neo-American.

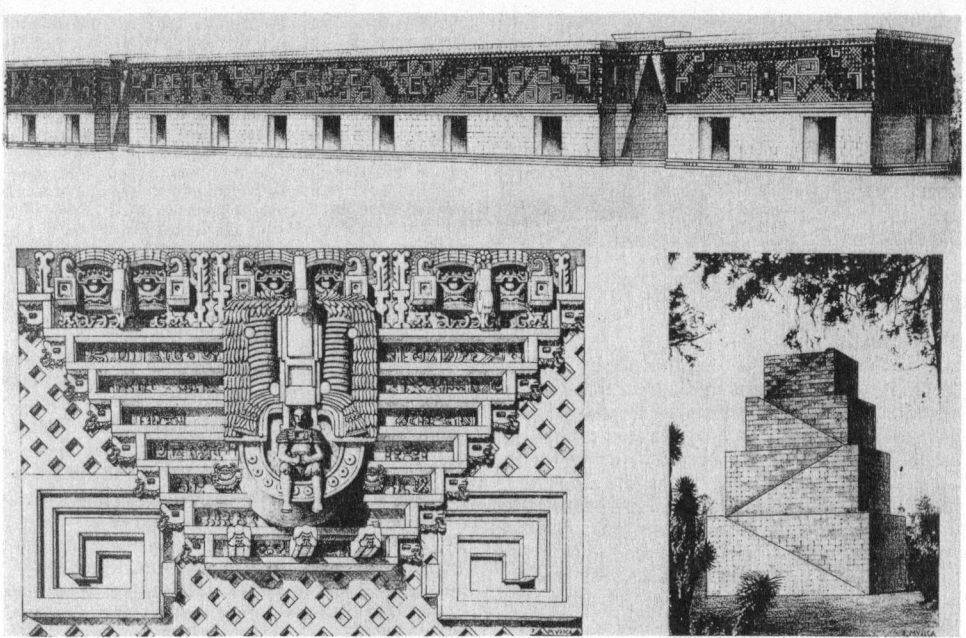

↓ fig. 13   Francisco Mujica, top and left: Reconstruction of the House of the Governor, Uxmal, Mexico; lower right: Reconstruction of the pyramid of Teopantepec, Mexico.

der in eine Music-Hall verwandelten Metropole. Das Spielerische lässt sich nieder mit einer Maske ohne Untergrund: der Vitalismus, der davon ausgeht, kennt nicht die Verzweiflung Fitzgeralds, aber die «verrückten» Eitelkeiten Zeldas.

Und trotzdem gehört dieser von Kritikern wie Croly und Murchison [22] verurteilte Paradevitalismus zum innern Kern der Bemühungen um den Amerikanismus, dessen Zusammenhang wir zu erschliessen suchen. «Neu Babel» bedeutet Offenheit in der Aufnahme jeglicher Sprache, aber auch Verwirklichung der zu verfolgenden und in ihrer Vorläufigkeit erkannten kollektiven Mythen. Es ist kein Zufall, dass eine der ersten systematischen Geschichten des Wolkenkratzers — nämlich jene des Chilenen Francisco Mujica — einige der empirisch formulierten und mit dem Geschmack des Sammlers Ely Kahn vorgebrachten Hypothesen auf organische Weise aufnimmt.

Die Suche nach einer «truly American architecture» mit der Typologie «amerikanisch» schlechthin zu verbinden, stellt bei Mujica eine willkürliche Operation dar. In diesem Sinn ist seine Analyse der Gründe der «Niederlage» der sog. Chicago-School nach der Ausstellung von 1893 symptomatisch: die Neoromantik von Root und Sullivan war «un-american».[23] Trotzdem ist die von Mujica so offensichtlich betriebene Suche nach den «Wurzeln» ein typisches Erbe der Tradition der «American Renaissance». Nur besitzt nun jene Zusammensetzung von Subjektivität und naturalistischer Neubegründung der Gesellschaft als Ziel eine «innere Front»: die Metropole der Wolkenkratzer ist auf nationaler Ebene Tertiärinstrument, das Gehirn einer weitgespannten Organisation, die gerade in den Zwanzigerjahren die Selbstkontrolle anstrebt, um selbständig die eigenen institutionellen Fehlstellen auszumerzen. (Nichts anderes als ein solches Bemühen um

fig. 14   Michel Dupré, Residential high-rise mentioned by Mujica.

"After a profound study of the ruins it is possible to conceive a *new* line in which only the sentiment of the American forms subsists. It appears to me correct to call this new type of architecture Neo-American. The difference between Renaissance and the Neo-American architecture is fundamental: the Renaissance works with a model before it. The Neo-American architecture is a new creative work which requires profound study of the primitive American architecture and of the geometrical and mechanical elements of the regional nature. When all the forms peculiar to us have germinated in our minds and can follow the summons of our immagination, we will be prepared to create this new architecture and to produce designs and plans embodying reminiscences of their primitive origins, but at the same time revealing their modern character clearly and powerfully."

eine kapitalistische Planung in eigener Regie — unter Ausschaltung der Einflüsse der öffentlichen Hand — stellt die von der Russell Sage Foundation ab 1923 finanzierte und organisierte Planung für New York und Umgebung dar.) Und zu diesem «wunderbaren» Zusammenschluss unüberwindbarer Gegensätze will nun die Suche nach den Wurzeln des «reinen», von den Hypotheken europäischer Kultur befreiten und auf einem neo-rousseau'schen Naturalismus des «bon sauvage» aufgebauten Amerikanismus etwas beitragen. Mujica schreibt [24]:

"In these later days a new tendency has appeared that does not accept the preconceived patterns of the classical and the Gothic styles, but strives to express spontaneously a rational and sincere decoration of the structure employing for this purpose the most modern lines (...). The characteristic qualities of these new lines and proportions present great resemblance with the elements of primitive American architecture. As to cornices it has not been possible to apply to skyscrapers any of the hitherto known proportions. The new architecture has had to find an element which only marked the limit of the wall-surface. By this quality and by the fact that its principal decorative elements are brought out in large surfaces, the new style strikingly recalls the Pre-Columbian architecture with its palaces and pyramids with small cornices, and magnificent decorations carved in big dominating surfaces."

Der Umstand, dass die ersten Illustrationen im Buche Mujicas Idealrekonstruktionen der mexikanischen Pyramiden von Papantla und Teopantepec und derjenigen von Tikal in Guatemala darstellen, hat somit polemische Bedeutung. Das «Neue» zieht seine Gültigkeitsgarantie aus der Verbindung mit dem Primitiven, auch wenn die von Mujica bemühten Beispiele im Vergleich zu der im Umkreis der «Architectural League» von New York gültigen Praxis der Projektierung nichts Neues beinhalten. Lassen wir Mujica weiterreden [25]:

Wie man sieht, beschränkt sich Mujica darauf, einige im New Yorker Milieu zirkulierende Auffassungen zu rationalisieren. Es ist klar, dass ausserhalb des subjektiven Mystizismus eines Frank Lloyd Wright Apelle an die «neo-American-architecture», an den Stilismus des Art Déco, an einen assimilierten und zum Kitsch neigenden Maschinismus — man denke ans Chrysler Building, aber auch an die Wohnwolkenkratzer der Firma Chanin — nur dazu dienen, ein allgemeines Verständnis der nun paradoxen, durch die eigenen Gesetze des Wachstums eingeengten städtischen Struktur zu vereiteln.[26] Die Umfrage zur Bewertung des Systems der Wolkenkratzer unter den Architekten New Yorks, die Mujica im fünften Kapitel seines Buches publiziert, ist bezeichnend. Der absolut gegen die hohen Geschäftshäuser gerichteten Meinung Thomas Hastings schliesst sich diejenige des Mayor Henry Curran an, der in seiner am Meeting von 1927 des «Civic Development Department of the Chamber of Commerce of the United States» gehaltenen Rede die fehlende Wirtschaftlichkeit der baulichen Konzentration unterstreicht:

"Is it good sense not to have a dollar for any other city need, to pour it all into more traffic facilities to take care of a coagulated bunch of skyscrapers, is that sense? Is that city planning? Is that good business? Is it good for your individual business? That is where we are headed." [27]

Anderseits zeigen sich John Sloane, Wiley Corbett und Mujica selbst bereit aufzuzeigen, dass der Wolkenkratzer ein Instrument des «good business» sein kann: das Problem läge in der Begrenzung des Central Business District — durch die Konzentration ja gerade ermöglicht! —, in der Handhabung eines dem Handel angepassten Steuersystems und in der Verwen-

↓ fig. 15   Sequence from the film *Gold Diggers of 1935*, by Busby Berkeley, 1935.

dung des so gewonnenen Kapitals für die Restrukturierung des Strassensystems durch die öffentliche Hand unter Berücksichtigung der seit Jahrhundertbeginn in Vorschlag gebrachten Modelle der Verkehrstrennung, schliesslich in der Anwendung des Prinzips der «ville radieuse» Le Corbusiers.[28] Die Utopie reicht hier dem beruflichen Opportunismus die Hand: Corbett, Sloan, Hood, Mujica verleihen dem Drängen Paul Robertsons eine disziplinierte Form.

Wenn wir ausserhalb solcher Ueberlegungen — die sich das «Big Business» Amerikas auch nach der grossen Depression nicht zu eigen macht — die Wirkungen des «Neu Babels» der Zwanzigerjahre auf das allgemeine Bewusstsein untersuchen wollen, so müssten wir neben Zeugnissen wie dem von R. Bletter [29] zitierten Film *Madam Satan* noch ein weiteres filmisches Dokument heranführen. In der Film *Gold Diggers of 1935* zeigt Busby Berkeley eine beinahe völlig unabhängige Sequenz, «a film within the film»: «Lullabay Broadway»[30]. Die Kamera beginnt mit einer Aufnahme der Sängerin Wini Shaw aus Distanz, deren Gesicht auf schwarzem Hintergrund abgehoben erscheint. Während Wini mit ihrem «song» fortfährt, schwenkt die Kamera um 90 Grad in die Höhe und zeigt die Sängerin von oben. Mittels eines Auflösungseffektes reduziert sich Winis Kopf auf die Umrisse, innerhalb deren eine Luftaufnahme Manhattans auftaucht. Die Metropole der Wolkenkratzer ist also enthalten im Unbewussten des Individuums, und demzufolge sind der Teil und das Ganze nicht getrennt, sondern in einer Beziehung ohne Ausschluss verbunden. Aber dieses Verhältnis ist tödlich: nach einer meisterhaften Darstellung des «Chors der Stadt» — eine musikalische Sequenz, die hunderte von Tänzern in einem gigantischen Night-Club zeigt — stürzt Wini aus der Höhe des Wolkenkratzers, während die Kamera sich in Manhattan bewegt und ihre eigene Existenz lustlos weiterführt: noch einmal überlagert sich die Metropole dem Gesicht Winis, während die letzten Akkorde des Chors dieses hervorragende filmische Fragment beschliessen.

Berkeley zeigt auf diese Weise, dass die geliebt-gehasste «big-city» konkrete Reformen erwartet, um «authentisch» das kollektive Fest des «musical» erleben zu können, aber auch, dass alle Suche nach «Wurzeln», die wir anhand einiger Beispiele der Zwanzigerjahre beobach-

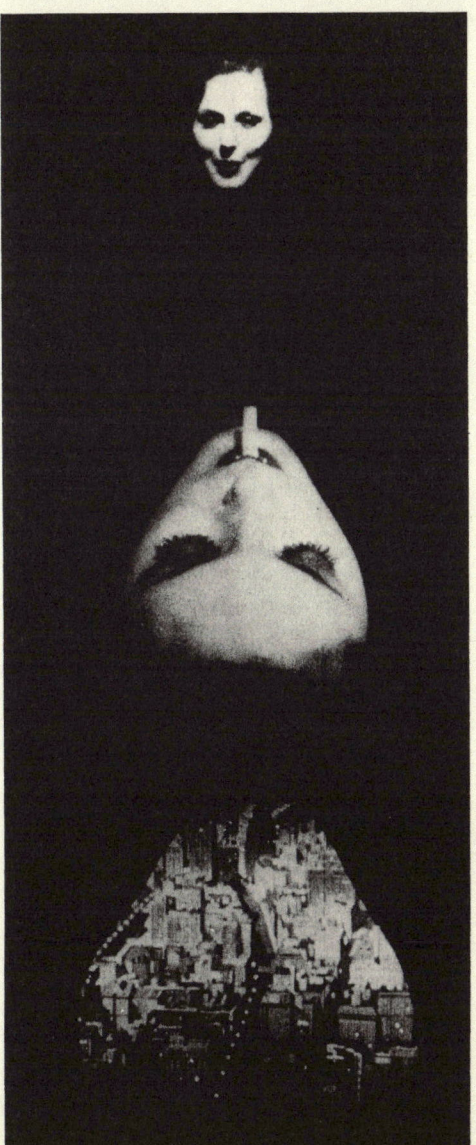

23

tet haben, überflüssig ist. Das Individuum hat in sich selbst schon längst die «Werte» der Stadt-Maschine inkorporiert: diese aber sind tödlich. Es überlebt der Traum: der Tanz und der Chorgesang des musical. Aber es handelt sich nicht mehr um die «gaiety» des Chrysler Building oder der Park Avenue Building. «Neu Babylon» bedarf nicht mehr der «Formen», sondern der Reformen. Die vom New Deal Roosevelts geweckten Hoffnungen stehen noch bevor: aber auch sie werden schnell zerstört werden. Die «Dynosaur City» wird sich ihrer annehmen, indem sie die unauflösliche Beziehung mit dem Triumphzug des «urban-industrial America» hin zum imperialistischen Expansionismus bekräftigt, dessen Schicksal — trotz allem — bereits in der amerikanischen Ideologie eines Helmle & Corbett, eines Ely Kahn und eines Mujica aufleuchtet.

(Uebersetzung: Werner Oechslin)

1 Cf. Harvey Wiley Corbett, «The Influence of Zoning in New York's Skyline», in The American Architect and the Architectural Review, 1923, vol. CXXIII, n. 2410, S. 1—4: Corbett erinnert hier an die 1908 von David Knickerbacker Boyd gemachten Vorschläge (cf. The American Architect, November 18, 1908). — Id., «Zoning and the Envelope of the Building», Pencil Points, 1923, vol. VI n. 3, S. 15—18. — Id., «Effect of the New York Zoning Resolution on Commercial Buildings», The American Architect, 1920, vol. CXXV, n. 2448, S. 547—551.
2 Zur strukturellen Bedeutung der «Zoning Law» siehe den gut dokumentierten Aufsatz von Franco Manuso, «Lo zoning: l'esperienza di New York», L'urbanistica del riformismo. USA — 1890—1940 (hrsg. von Pier Luigi Crosta), Milano, S. 89 ff.
3 H. W. Corbett, «Zoning and the Envelope of the Building», zit. in Anm. 1, S. 18.
4 Cf. Giusi Rapisarda, «Die Stadt und ihr Doppelgänger». Von «Metropolis» zu «King Kong», archithese, 1976, n. 17, S. 29—35.
5 Cf. «The Rockefeller Building Project in Mid-Town New York», Pencil Points, 1931, vol. XII, n. 10, S. 776—777. — William H. Jordy, American Buildings and their Architects, IV. The Impact of European Modernism in the Mid-Twentieth Century, New York, 1972, S. 1—85. — Manfredo Tafuri, «La montagna disincantata. Il grattacielo e la City», in La città americana dalla guerra civile al New Deal, Bari, 1973, S. 496 ff.
6 Claude Bragdon, «Skyscrapers», The Arch Lectures (1940), New York, 1942, S. 103—115.
7 Cf. «Dr. John Wesley Kelchner's Restoration of King Solomon's Temple and Citadel, Helmle & Corbett Architects», Pencil Points, November 1925, VI, n. 11, S. 69—86. — Cervin Robinson / Rosemarie Haag Bletter, Skyscraper Style. Art Deco New York, New York, 1975, S. 11—12. — Das Projekt von Helmle & Corbett wurde auch anlässlich der 41. Ausstellung der Architectural League von New York ausgestellt: cf. The American Architect, February 20, 1926.

8 Walter Benjamin, Zentralpark, Gesammelte Schriften, I, 2, Frankfurt a. M. 1974, S. 677. — Der Passus Benjamins ist zurecht mit dem Aphorismus 105 von Adornos Minima Moralia (ed. Frankfurt a. M., 1975, S. 217) in Beziehung gebracht worden: «Das Menschenleben wird zum Augenblick, nicht indem es Dauer aufhebt, sondern indem es zum Nichts verfällt, zu seiner Vergeblichkeit erwacht im Angesicht der schlechten Unendlichkeit von Zeit selber. Im überlauten Ticken der Uhr vernimmt man den Hohn der Lichtjahre auf die Spanne des eigenen Daseins. Die Stunden, die als Sekunden schon vorbei sind, ehe der innere Sinn sie aufgefasst hat, und ihn fortreissen in ihrem Sturz, melden ihm, wie er samt allem Gedächtnis dem Vergessen geweiht ist in der kosmischen Nacht. Dessen werden die Menschen heute zwangshaft gewahr.» Cf. Elvio Facchinelli, Minima (im)moralia, L'Erba voglio, 1974, n. 26, S. 16—17.
9 Paul Robertson, «The Skyscraper Office Building», The Architectural Forum, 1930, vol. II, n. 6, S. 879—880.
10 Cf. Frederic A. Delano, «Skyscrapers», The American City, January 1924. — Id., Journal of the Real Estate Board of New York, August, 1930.
11 Francisco Mujica, History of the Skyscraper, Paris, 1929, S. 33. Es ist aufschlussreich festzustellen, dass der von Mujica (ibid.) zitierten Hastings in seinem Modern Architecture Sozialismus und künstlerische Avantgarde identifiziert, um beide klar abzulehnen: «Surely modern architecture should not be the deplorable creations of the would-be style inventors, the socialists who have penetrated the world of art farther than they have the world of politics, who are more concerned in promulgating an innovation than in establishing a real improvement — so-called Futurists, New Thinkers, Cubists, ‚art nouveau' followers, all unrelated to the past without thought of traditions.»
12 Lewis Mumford, «American Architecture to-day, 1», Architecture, 1928, vol. LVIII, n, 4, S. 181—188. Man bemerke, dass sich durch den ganzen Aufsatz Mumfords eine Polemik gegen die Thesen von Helmle & Corbett und gegen Ferriss' «rendering» zieht: die zentrale Hypothese lautet, dass nach dem Halbschlaf der Jahre 1890—1920 die neuen Hoffnungen an der grossen Strömung Root, Sullivan und Frank Lloyd Wright anknüpfen sollen.
13 Mumford, op. cit., S. 185.
14 Cf. Ely Jacques Kahn, «On New York. Past, Present and Future» (1926), in: Arthur Trappan North (ed.), Ely Jacques Kahn, New York/London, 1931, S. 25—27. — Raymond Hood, «A City under a Single Roof», Nation's Business, 1929, n. 12, S. 18—20 und 206—209. — H. W. Corbett, «Design in Office Building», The Architectural Forum, June 1930, n. 52, S. 779.
15 Leon V. Solon, «The Park Avenue Building, New York City», The Architectural Record, 1928, vol. 63, n. 4, S. 289—297.
16 Cf. E. J. Kahn, «Schools of Europa and America», Design in Art and Industry, New York, 1935, S. 173 bis 204. Der Autor untersucht hier den Beitrag der Pariser Ausstellung von 1920, derjenigen von Turin 1902, die Arbeiten der Wiener Werkstätte, von Otto Wagner, Hoffmann, Klimt, Behrens, des Werkbundes und des Dessauer Bauhauses. Gemäss einem späten Zeugnis hatte Kahn in seiner Jugend auch das russische Ballett

Fortsetzung Seite 51

> The difference between the Renaissance and the Neo-American architecture is fundamental: The Renaissance worked with a model before it. The Neo-American architecture is a new creative work which requires profound study of the primitive American architecture and of the geometrical and mechanical elements of the regional nature. When all the forms peculiar to us have germinated in our minds and can follow the summons of our imagination we will be prepared to create this new architecture and to produce designs and plans embodying reminiscences of their primitive origin, but at the same time revealing their modern character clearly and powerfully."[25]

As you can see, Mujica manages merely to rationalize the ideas widely circulating in the New York milieu. Beyond the subjective mysticism of a Frank Lloyd Wright, it is very clear that the appeals to a "Neo-American architecture," to the art deco style, to a domesticated machinism tending toward kitsch—I am thinking of the Chrysler Building, but also of the residential skyscraper by the Chanin firm—are merely instruments to seize a general consensus for an urban structure that is paradoxical and increasingly shackled by its own laws of growth.[26] The opinion poll of New York architects that addressed the convenience of the skyscraper system, which Mujica published in the fifth chapter of his book, is indicative. The opinion of Thomas Hasting, who is absolutely opposed to the tall commercial building, is coupled with that of Mayor Henry Curran, who, in his speech delivered at the meeting in 1927 of the Civic Development Department of the Chamber of Commerce of the United States, confirms the uneconomicalness of the tertiary concentrations, posing these questions:

> "Is it good sense not to have a dollar for any other city need, to pour it all into more traffic facilities to take care of a coagulated bunch of skyscrapers, is that sense? Is that city planning? Is that good business? Is it good for your individual business? That is where we are headed."[27]

But John Sloan, Wiley Corbett, and Mujica himself are ready to demonstrate that the skyscraper can be an instrument of good business: the problem is to limit the central business district, possible because of the high tertiary concentration; to apply taxes compatible with the market; to use the resulting fiscal yield for a reconstruction of the streets, supervised by a public administration capable of taking into account the proposals for the separation of traffic advanced since the first years of the century; and to adopt Le Corbusier's model for the *ville radieuse*.[28] Here utopia extends its hand to professional optimism: Corbett, Sloan, Hood, Mujica merely put into the form of their own discipline the demands of Paul Robertson.

If, going beyond such considerations—with which American big business will not come to terms even after the Great Depression—we attempt to consider the effects the "New Babel" had upon the collective consciousness of the 1920s, we must place, alongside documents like the film *Madam Satan*, cited by Bletter,[29] one more illuminating cinematic sequence. In the film *Gold Diggers* of 1935, Busby Berkeley inserts a practically independent segment, a film within the film: *Broadway Lullaby*.[30] The camera begins with a long shot of the singer Wini Shaw, isolating her face against a black background. While Wini performs her song, the camera executes a perpendicular movement, framing the protagonist from above. After a dissolve, Wini's face remains only in profile, within which appears an aerial view of Manhattan. The metropolis of the skyscrapers is completely contained in the unconscious of the individual, as it were: the whole and its parts are no longer distinguishable, bound as they are in a relationship of complete correspondence. But here we are dealing with a mortal relationship. After an exceptional representation of "urban chorality"—a musical sequence that assembles a hundred dancers in a gigantic nightclub—Wini falls from the top of a skyscraper, while the camera moves within a Manhattan that continues indifferently its own existence. Once again, the metropolis is superimposed upon the face of Wini.

In this way, Berkeley demonstrates that the loved-hated big city requires concrete reform in order for the collective festival of the musical to be experienced "authentically"; but he also shows that the entire search for "roots," which we have attempted to characterize by isolating some examples from the 1920s, is completely superfluous. The individual has already internalized the "values" of the urban machine—and they are mortal. The dream will survive: the dance and the choral song of the musical. We are no longer dealing with the gaiety of the Chrysler and Park Avenue buildings. The hopes raised by Roosevelt's New Deal remain as yet unfulfilled; the "Dinosaur City" will see to their destruction all too soon, reaffirming its own indissoluble connection with the triumphal march of urban-industrial America toward imperialist expansion, the destiny of which—in spite of everything—the Americanist ideology of Helmle & Corbett, of Ely Kahn, of Mujica had celebrated.

ENDNOTES

1   See Harvey Wiley Corbett, "The Influence of Zoning in New York's Skyline," *The American Architect and the Architectural Review* 123, 2410 (1923): 1–4, in which Corbett recalls the proposals formulated in 1908 by David Knickerbocker Boyd (*The American Architect*, November 18, 1908); and "Zoning and the Envelope of the Building," *Pencil Points* 6, 3 (1923): 15–18. See also Corbett, "Effect of the New York Zoning Resolution on Commercial Buildings," *The American Architect* 125, 2448 (1920): 547–51; and Carol Willis, "Zoning and Zeitgeist: The Skyscraper City in the 1920s," *Journal of the Society of Architectural Historians* 45, 1 (1986): 47ff.

2   On the structural significance of the Zoning Law, see Franco Mancuso's well documented essay, "Lo zoning: L'esperienza di New York," in *L'urbanistica del riformismo: Usa, 1890–1940*, ed. Pier Luigi Crosta (Milan, 1975), 89 ff.; and Willis, "Zoning and Zeitgeist."

3   Corbett, "Zoning," 18.

4   See Giusi Rapisarda, "Die Stadt und ihr Doppelgänger: Von 'Metropolis' zu 'King Kong,'" *archithese* 17 (1976): 29–35.

5   See "The Rockefeller Building Project in Mid-town New York," *Pencil Points* 12,10 (1931): 776–77; William H. Jordy, *American Buildings and Their Architects*, vol. 4: *The Impact of European Modernism in the Mid-twentieth Century* (New York: Doubleday, 1972), 1–85; and Tafuri, "La montagna disincantata," 496ff.

6   Claude Bragdon, "Skyscrapers," in *The Arch Lectures* (1940) (New York, 1942), 103–15.

7   See "Dr. John Wesley Kelchner's Restoration of King Solomon's Temple and Citadel, Helmle & Corbett Architects," *Pencil Points* 6, 11 (November 1925): 69–86; and Robinson and Haag Bletter, *Skyscraper Style*, 11–12. Helmle and Corbett's project was also exhibited at the forty-first show of the Architectural League of New York. See *The American Architect*, February 20, 1926.

8   Walter Benjamin, "Zentralpark," in *Gesammelte Schriften* (Frankfurt am Main: Suhrkamp Verlag, 1972), vol. 1, pt. 2, 677. The passage by Benjamin has been justly compared to aphorism 105 of Adorno's *Minima Moralia*: "Man's life becomes a moment, not by suspending duration but by lapsing into nothingness, waking to its own futility in face of the bad eternity of time itself. In the clock's over-loud ticking we hear the mockery of light-years for the span of our existence. The hours that are past as seconds before the inner sense has registered them, and sweep it away in their cataract, proclaim that like all memory our inner experience is doomed to oblivion in cosmic night. Of this people are today made forcibly aware." *Minima Moralia: Reflections from Damaged Life* (London: Verso, 1974), 165. See Elvio Facchinelli, "Minima (im)moralia," *L'Erba voglio* 26 (1974): 16–17.

9   Paul Robertson, "The Skyscraper Office Building," *The Architectural Forum* 2, 6 (1930): 879–80.

10   See Delano, "Skyscrapers"; and the *Journal of the Real Estate Board of New York*, August 1930. An outline of the historical reconstruction of the economic significance of the skyscraper in relation to the phenomena of concentration of financial capital can be found in Heinz Ronner's article, "Skyscraper: A propos Oekonomie," *archithese* 18 (1976): 44–49, 55.

11   Mujica, *History of the Skyscraper*, 33. It is interesting to note, incidentally, that Hastings himself, cited by Mujica (ibid.), identifies in his *Modem Architecture* artistic socialism and avant-gardes, totally rejecting both: "Surely modern architecture should not be constituted by the deplorable creations of aspiring inventors of styles, the socialists who have penetrated the world of art more than that of politics, who are more interested in promulgating some innovation or other than in achieving a concrete improvement, the so-called futurists, the new thinkers, the cubists, the followers of art nouveau, all of them lacking in ties with the past, without any knowledge of tradition."

12   Lewis Mumford, "American Architecture To-day, I," *Architecture* 58, 4 (1928): 181–88. Note that Mumford's entire essay refutes the above-mentioned theses of Helmle and Corbett as well as Ferriss's rendering; his main hypothesis is that, after the dormant period from 1890 to 1920, the new experiments were linked to the great tradition of J.W. Root, Louis Sullivan, and Frank Lloyd Wright. Perceptive passages on Mumford's position with respect to the "original values" of the American experience are contained in Francesco Dal Co's essay, "La forza della tradizione," the introduction to the Italian edition of L. Mumford's *The Brown Decades* (New York: Harcourt Brace, 1931), entitled *Architettura e cultura in America dalla guerra civile all'ultima frontiera* (Venice, 1977), 7–21.

13   Mumford, "American Architecture To-day," 185.

14   See Ely Jacques Kahn, "On New York: Past, Present and Future (1926)," in Arthur Tappan North, *Ely Jacques Kahn* (New York and London: McGraw-Hill, 1931), 25–27; Raymond Hood, "A City under a Single Roof," *Nation's Business* 12 (1929): 18–20, 206–9; and H. W. Corbett, "Design in Office Building," *The Architectural Forum*, 52 (June 1930): 779.

15   Leon V. Solon, "The Park Avenue Building, New York City," *The Architectural Record* 63, 4 (1928): 289–97.

16   See E.J. Kahn's essay, "Schools of Europe and America," in *Design in Art and Industry* (New York, 1925), in which the author examines the contribution of the Paris Exposition of 1900 and that held in Turin in 1902, and the research of the Wiener Werkstätte, of Otto Wagner, Hoffmann, Klimt, Behrens, the Werkbund, and the Dessau Bauhaus. According to his later recollections, Kahn, as a youth in Paris, had learned to appreciate Leon Bakst's Russian ballets and the collections of paintings of Matisse and Picasso, by striking up a friendship with Gertrude Stein. See the unpublished manuscript by E. Kahn in the Avery Library of Columbia University, New York, ch. 3.

Fortsetzung von Seite 24
unter Leon Bakst und die Bildersammlungen mit Werken Matisse's und Picassos — beides in Beziehung mit Getrude Stein — schätzen gelernt. Cf. das unveröffentlichte Ms. von E. Kahn, Avery Library, New York, Kapitel 3.
[17] Cf. Ms. Avery Library, cit., Kapitel 2, S. 4—5.
[18] E. J. Kahn, «On the Use of Color» (1928), in A. T. North, zit. in Anm. 14, S. 24.
[19] Cf. Henry H. Saylor, «Ely Jacques Kahn», *Architecture*, 1931, vol. LXIV, n. 2.
[20] Cf. E. J. Kahn, «Sources of Inspiration», *Architecture*, 1929, vol. LX, n. 5, S. 249—256. — Id., Ms. Avery Library cit., Kapitel 11.
[21] Rose Henderson, «A Primitive Basis for Modern Architecture», *The Architectural Record*, 1923, vol. 54, n. 2, S. 189—196. (Zitat von S. 189.)
[22] Cf. H. Croly, «The Scenic Function of the Skyscraper», *The Architectural Record*, 1928, vol. 63, S. 77—78. — Kenneth M. Murchison, «The Spires of Gotham», *The Architectural Forum*, 1930, n. 52, S. 786 und 878.
[23] F. Mujica, *History of Skyscraper*, op. cit., S. 32.
[24] *Ibidem*, S. 19.
[25] *Ibidem*, S. 20.
[26] Cf. M. Tafuri, «La dialectique de l'absurde. Europa—USA: les avatars du gratte-ciel (1918—1974)», *L'Architecture d'aujourd'hui*, 1975, n. 178, S. 1—19.
[27] F. Mujica, *op. cit.*, S. 47.
[28] *Ibidem*, S. 49—53.
[29] R. Bletter, «Metropolis réduite», *archithese*, 1976, n. 18, S. 26—27.
[30] Cf. Tony Thomas / Jim Terry, *The Busby Berkeley Book*, Greenwich, Conn., 1973, S. 88—90.

Fortsetzung von Seite 40
[7] Lewis Mumford, «Architecture and the Machine», *American Mercury*, September 1924, S. 77.
[8] W. Francklyn Paris, «The International Exposition of Modern Industrial and Decorative Art in Paris», *Architectural Record*, Oktober 1925, S. 376.
[9] Marrion Wilcox, «Crane Company Exhibit Building, Atlantic City, New Jersey», *Architectural Record*, February 1926, S. 101.
[10] Irwin S. Chanin, Interview mit dem Verfasser, New York, 27. December 1972.
[11] Paul Frankl, *Form and Re-Form: A Practical Handbook of Modern Interiors*, New York, 1930, S. 43.
[12] Paul Frankl, *New Dimensions*, New York, 1928, S. 17.
[13] Raymond Loewy, *Never Leave Well Enough Alone*, New York, 1951, S. 210.
[14] Walter Dorwin Teague, *Design this Day, The Technique of Order in the Machine Age*, New York, 1940, S. 64.
[15] Paul Frankl, *Space for Living*, New York, 1938, S. 14.
[16] Alvin Johnson, «A Building for Adult Education», *T-Square Journal*, Oktober 1931, S. 19.

Illustrationen:
Die Bewilligung zum Abdruck der Abb. 3, 5 und 7 wurde freundlicherweise erteilt durch die Bel Geddes Collection, University of Texas; Mrs. Edith Lutyens Bel Geddes.

17   See the above-cited unpublished manuscript by Kahn, ch. 2, 4–5.

18   E.J. Kahn, "On the Use of Color (1928)," in North, *Ely Jacques Kahn*, 24.

19   See Henry H. Saylor, "Ely Jacques Kahn," *Architecture* 64, 2 (1931).

20   See E.J. Kahn, "Sources of Inspiration," *Architecture* 9, 5 (1929): 249–56; and ch. 11 of Kahn's unpublished manuscript.

21   Rose Henderson, "A Primitive Basis for Modern Architecture," *The Architectural Record* 54, 2 (1923): 189–96 (the citation is on p. 189).

22   See H. Croly, "The Scenic Function of the Skyscraper," *The Architectural Record* 63, 4 (1928): 77–78; and Kenneth M. Murchison, "The Spires of Gotham," *The Architectural Forum* 52 (1930): 786, 878. The "scenic function" of the skyscraper was carried to its extreme at the ball at the Astor Hotel in New York on 23 January 1931, at which the most prominent architects of the city represented "The New York Skyline," with costumes and headgear evoking their own works: Leonard Schultze appeared dressed as the New Waldorf Astoria, Ely J. Kahn as the Squibb Building, William Van Alen as the Chrysler Building, Ralph Walker as One Wall Street, and so forth. Architecture expresses itself as theatre; its creators unconsciously close the cycle opened by the expressionist and Dadaist cabarets. On the 1931 ball, see Rem Koolhaas, "The Architect's Ball: A Vignette, 1931," *Oppositions* 3 (1974): 92–96. Two symbolic interpretations of the American skyscraper are presented in the articles by Diana Agrest, "Le ciel est la limite," *L'architecture d'aujourd'hui* 178 (1975): 55–64; and by Dolores Hayden, "Skyscraper Seduction, Skyscraper Rape," *Heresies* 2 (1977): 108–15.

23   Mujica, *History of the Skyscraper*, 32.

24   Ibid., 19.

25   Ibid., 20.

26   Cf. M. Tafuri, "La dialectique de l'absurde: Europa—USA: les avatars du gratte-ciel (1918–1974)," *L'Architecture d'aujourd'hui* 178 (1975): 1–19.

27   Mujica, *History of the Skyscraper*, 47.

28   Ibid., 49–53.

29   R.H. Bletter, "Metropolis réduite," *archithese* 18 (1976): 26–27.

30   See Tony Thomas and Jim Terry, *The Busby Berkeley Book* (New York: A&W Visual Library, 1975), 88–90.

Roxy, Noah, and Radio City Music Hall

The New York of the 1920s and the Search for Americanism

Author:
Rem Koolhaas

Sources:
archithese, 18 (1976): 37–43
Rem Koolhaas, *Delirious New York: A Retroactive Manifesto for Manhattan* (London: Thames and Hudson, 1978), 170–71; 177–87 (EN)

Translated by:
Steven Lindberg

"I grow so sentimental when I see how perfect perfection can be …"
Top Hat

"What are those little mice doing on the stage?"
—"Those aren't mice. Those are horses!"
Visitors to Radio City Music Hall

Dream

"I didn't conceive of the idea, I dreamed it. I believe in creative dreams. The picture of Radio City Music Hall was complete and practically perfect in my mind before architects and artists put pen on the drawing paper."
Roxy

In the congestion of hyperbole that is Manhattan, it is relatively reasonable for Roxy, the animator of Radio City Music Hall, to claim a crypto-religious revelation as inspiration for his amazing theater. The parthenogenesis of architecture—that is, the creation of buildings without the assistance or intervention of architects—is one leitmotiv in the history of the architecture of Manhattan.

Roxy—real name Samuel Lionel Rothafel of Stillwater, Minnesota—is the most brilliant showbiz expert in the hysterical New York of the twenties. After abandoning the ideal of the new Metropolitan Opera as cultural epicenter of his complex, John D. Rockefeller, Jr., buys Roxy away from Paramount and gives him carte blanche to create instead a "Showplace of the Nation" at the Center.

Five Layers

Against the background of an unwritten theory of Manhattanism, the conceptual organization of Rockefeller Center (and the secret of its success) would have to be traced back to the overlapping of five layers, each of which embodies a different architectural philosophy. Indeed, Rockefeller Center consists of five different projects that somehow coexist at the same address, provisionally held together by such infrastructure as elevators, heating and ventilation shafts, and so on.

The O level of the present Rockefeller Center, dominated by the RCA lobby and Radio City Music Hall, is a drastically reduced version of much more daring alternatives that were projected and even almost built. Although plans for the new Metropolitan Opera had been discarded, the Associated Architects continue to consider theaters. They design versions of a fantastic ground floor entirely occupied by more and more theaters: a three-block ocean

Rem Koolhaas

ROXY, NOAH UND DIE RADIO CITY MUSIC HALL

"I grow so sentimental when I see how perfect perfection can be . . ."
Top Hat

"What are those little mice doing on the stage?" — "Those aren't mice. Those are horses!"
Besucher der Radio City Hall

Traum
«Ich habe die Idee nicht konzipiert; ich habe sie geträumt. Ich glaube an schöpferische Träume. Das Bild der Radio City Music Hall war in meiner Vorstellung vollständig perfekt lange bevor Architekten und Künstler zur Feder griffen . . .»
Roxy

← fig. 1
Model of
Rockefeller Center
View from the
northwest;
the RKO Building
(foreground /
premier plan) and
the RCA Building
(from behind).

In Anbetracht der Anhäufung linguistischer Hyperbeln, welche Manhattan darstellt, ist es beinah logisch dass Roxy, der Animator von Radio City Music Hall, die Geburt seines erstaunlichen Theaters in Begriffen schildert, die an die jungfräuliche Empfängnis Mariens anspielen. Die «Parthenogenese» von Architektur — d.h. die Entstehung von Bauwerken ohne Mithilfe oder Dazwischentreten von Architekten — das ist ein Leitmotiv in der Baugeschichte von Manhattan.

Roxy — sein ganzer Name lautet Samuel Lionel Rothafel und sein Herkunftsort ist Stillwater, Minnesota — war der intelligenteste und glamouröseste Bonz im New Yorker Show Business der hysterischen Zwanzigerjahre. Rockefeller hatte Roxy von Paramount weggekauft und gab ihm «carte blanche», um innerhalb des Rockefeller Centers den «Showplace of the Nation» zu schaffen — nachdem der Bau einer neuen «Metropolitan Opera», welche die ursprüngliche *raison d'être* des Centers gewesen war, angesichts der Depression fallengelassen werden musste.

5 Schichten
Vor dem Hintergrund einer noch ungeschriebenen Theorie des «Manhattanism» müsste man die konzeptuelle Organisation des Rockefeller Centers (und das Geheimnis seines Erfolges) auf die Ueberlagerung von 5 «Schichten» zurückführen, die eine je verschiedene architektonische «Philosophie» verkörpern. In der Tat besteht das Rockefeller Center aus fünf verschiedenen Projekten, die irgendwie an derselben Adresse koexistieren, notdürftig zusammengehalten durch Infrastrukturen wie Lifte, Heizungs- und Lüftungsschächte, usw.

Das 0-Niveau des heutigen Rockefeller Centers ist eine drastisch verkleinerte Version von weit kühneren Alternativen, die jahrelang ausgearbeitet wurden und beinah auch verwirklicht worden wären. Obwohl der Plan einer neuen «Metropolitan Opera» fallengelassen

37

↓ fig. 2   The Rockettes embodying "Stars and Stripes."

worden war, dachten die für das Projekt verantwortlichen Associated Architects weiterhin daran, im Erdgeschoss des Centers Theatersäle anzuordnen. Zahlreiche Versionen wurden ausgearbeitet, die alle darauf abzielten, das Erdgeschoss voll und ganz mit Theatern zu besetzen: ein Ozean von Plüschsesseln, über drei Blöcke hin, Hektaren von Bühnen und Kulissendepots, Quadratmeilen von Kinoleinwänden ... Ein Teppich von hochmoderner Technologie im Dienste von professioneller «Showbusiness» aller Art, wo sieben oder acht Spektakel gleichzeitig über die Bühne gehen können – wie widersprüchlich auch immer deren «Message» sein mochte. Ein gigantisches aufgehängtes Foyer, die 49. und 50. Strasse überbrückend, würde als Bindeglied zwischen allen diesen Theatern funktionieren und den verschiedenen «events» den Charakter von Simultaneität mitteilen. Eine Art metropolitanischer Wohnraum, welcher die verschiedenen Publikumsgruppen in einen einzigen, dem Phantasiekonsum hingegebenen Körper verwandeln würde – in eine «hypnotisierte» Gemeinschaft auf Zeit.

Voraussetzungen

Das Modell für einen solchen «Teppich» von Installationen, die imstande sind, einen permanenten Theaterbetrieb zu gewährleisten, liegt in der Geschichte von Coney Island. Seit 1890 waren dort nicht weniger als drei Pärke (Steeplechase, Luna Park und Dreamland) mittels einer speziellen Form von «phantastischer Technologie» erschlossen worden – d. h. mittels einer Technologie, die dazu dient, die menschliche Imagination zu erreichen und zu unterstützen, d. h. «synthetische Spektakel» zu produzieren. Mit audiovisuellen und kinetischen Mitteln, auch mit Hilfe von Luftströmen, Düften und Dämpfen aller Art wurde das Publikum dieser Darbietungen in eine «andere Welt» versetzt. Das projektierte O-Niveau des Rockefeller Centers und sein «Theater-Teppich» stellt den Versuch dar, ein ganzes Fragment von Coney Island ins Herz von Manhattan zu verpflanzen. Eine Vergnügungslandschaft sollte entstehen – und zwar mitten in der Grosstadtsituation selbst, die den Hunger nach Erholung geweckt hat. Wenn auch die Ausmasse dieses

of red velvet chairs, acres of stage and backstage, square miles of projection screens ... A carpet of ultramodern technology in the service of all kinds of professional show business, where seven or eight spectacles can unfold at the same time—however contradictory their messages may be. An enormous suspended lobby, bridging 49th and 50th streets, will connect all these theaters, reinforcing the simultaneity of clashing performances. This metropolitan lounge will turn the separate audiences into a single fantasy-consuming body—a temporarily hypnotized community.

Antecedents

The model for such a carpet of installations capable of achieving a constant theatrical operation lies in the history of Coney Island. Since 1890, no fewer than three parks (Steeplechase, Luna Park, and Dreamland) had been created there using a special form of Fantastic Technology—that is, by means of a technology that serves to reach and support the human imagination; that is, to produce synthetic spectacles. With audiovisual and kinetic means and with the aid of currents of air, scents, and gases of all kinds, the audience of these performances was transported to another world. The planned O level of Rockefeller Center and its theatrical carpet represents the effort to transplant an entire fragment of Coney Island into the heart of Manhattan. An amusement landscape was to be created—and it was to be situated in the center of the metropolis itself, which had awakened the hunger for relaxation. Even if the scale of this carpet was reduced in the process of its realization, Radio City Music Hall offers a measure of its original ambition.

New York—Moscow

In this venture—"the greatest theatrical adventure the World has ever known"—Roxy cannot expect much enthusiasm from the Center's Associated Architects, who want to be sober and modern; as far as the traditions of Fantastic Technology that fascinate Roxy are concerned, they remain virtually without effect on the architects. They even convince Roxy to join them on a study tour of Europe, where they want him to see with his own eyes the advances modern architecture has made in theater construction.

Summer 1931: the consummate showman Roxy, two businessmen-architects, Harrison and Reinhard, and a delegation of technical experts make the transatlantic journey. The mission opposes Roxy, expert in the production of illusions in sufficient quantity and density to satisfy the metropolitan masses, to the European architects, puritanical enemies of the tradition of showbiz that Roxy embodies. In fact, the European architects move in a direction precisely opposed to Roxy's interests. They are interested in how theatrical processes can be placed in objective envelopes; traditional theater, by contrast, represents for them an unacceptable form of mass production by which a bad audience is fed trivial acting.

Roxy is bored in France, Belgium, Germany, and Holland; his architects even force him to take the train to Moscow so that he can inspect and experience firsthand the Constructivist clubs and theaters built there since the mid-twenties. Somewhere in mid-ocean during his return to New York, a revelation strikes a melancholy Roxy. Staring at a sunset. he receives the "Annunciation" of his theater: it is to be an incarnation of this sunset.

Back in New York, this quasi-pregnancy is then translated by the team of architects and designers of Radio City Music Hall into one of those fusions of opposites that characterize the history of Manhattan; the stage becomes a completely mechanized artificial environment, the auditorium becomes the largest visual metaphor in the world.

Sunrise and Sunset

From the beginning, Roxy insists on the literalness of his metaphor. Within the rectangular section and plan of the Hall's external envelope, the sunset theme is established through a series of consecutive plaster semicircles that diminish toward the stage to create a vaguely uterine hemisphere whose only exit is the stage itself.

This exit is "masked by the beautiful contour curtain" made of a specially developed synthetic fabric whose reflectivity makes it an acceptable

substitute for the sun. The "rays" from the curtain continue along the plaster arches, reaching around the entire auditorium. The arches are covered in gold to better reflect the purple of the setting sun and the glow of the red velvet which Roxy insists on for the chairs.

The consequence of Roxy's dream is that, while the effect of a sunset is successfully achieved when the lights of his auditorium are dimmed, the return of electricity in the intermissions and at the end of each performance corresponds to a sunrise. In other words, the twenty-four-hour cycle of day and night is repeated several times during a single performance at Radio City Music Hall. Day and night are drastically reduced, time accelerated, experience intensified, life—potentially—doubled, tripled …

Chill

Roxy's understanding of Fantastic Technology inspires a further intensification of his metaphor: questioning the conventional use of the air-conditioning system—ventilation and cooling—he realizes that this would only add chill to the sunset. With the same maniacal logic that characterized his earlier visions, Roxy then considers adding hallucinogenic gases to the atmosphere of his theater, so that synthetic ecstasy can reinforce the fabricated sunset. A small dose of laughing gas would put the 6,200 visitors in a euphoric mood, hyper-receptive to the activity on the stage. His lawyers dissuade him, but for a short period Roxy actually injects ozone—the therapeutic O_3 molecule with its "pungent refreshing odor" and "exhilarating influence"—into the air-conditioning system of his theater.

Combining super-time with super-health, Roxy defines the definitive formula of the metropolitan resort with his slogan

"A visit to Radio City Music Hall is as good as a month in the Country."

Mutations

The perfection and metaphorical stringency of Roxy's artificial paradise—the "ultimate countryside"—sets off a chain reaction of further, unforeseen cultural mutations. On the night of the official opening of Radio City, the exhausted remnants of a stale and spent vaudeville tradition—a tradition that peaked 20 years earlier in Coney Island—fall flat into Roxy's sparkling new apparatus. The old histrionics do not survive the test. People sitting 200 feet from the footlights cannot follow the grimaces on the comedians' faces as they embark on their tired routines; the size of the theater alone precludes reliance on conventional use of the human voice or even the human body; the gigantic stage—wide as a city block—denies the meaning of mise-en-scène, where suggested vastness can always rely on actual intimacy. On this stage, "atmosphere" is atomized.

"In grandeur of conception, in glory of planning, in perfection of fulfillment nothing like Radio City has ever been dreamed,"

claims its creator, with justice; but the container is so perfect that it ridicules its imperfect contents.

"Much of it [writes a critic on the first night] seemed sadly second-rate stuff, out of place amid such triumphs of architecture and mechanics."

Unintentionally, Radio City represents a more radical break with the past than any consciously revolutionary theater has managed so far. Light years separate the technology of Roxy's theater from the actual activity on its stage: it is—still—a space without a performance.

Particles

In the early thirties only Hollywood is producing the kind of scenarios that equal Roxy's fantastic landscape in anti-authenticity. Hollywood has developed a new dramatic formula—*isolated human particles floating weightlessly through a magnetic field of fabricated pleasure, occasionally colliding*—that can match the artificiality of Radio City Music Hall and fill it with abstracted, formalized emotions of sufficient density. The production of the Dream Factory is nowhere more at home than in Roxy's brainchild.

Noah

After the first-night fiasco, humanity—in the form of superannuated vaudeville—is abandoned, and the Music Hall becomes a movie

↓ fig. 3   RKO Building; entrance to Radio City Music Hall.

↓ figs. 4–5   Radio City Music Hall; plans of the main floor (4) and of the balcony level (5).

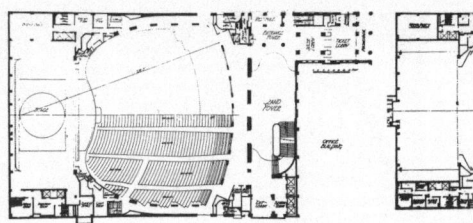
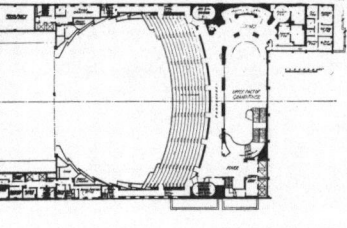

«Teppichs» im Verlaufe der Realisierung zusammengeschrumpft sind, so gibt die *Radio City Music Hall* doch in etwa das Mass der ursprünglichen Ambition.

New York — Moskau

Mit seiner Absicht, «the greatest theatrical adventure the world has ever known» zu verwirklichen, konnte Roxy nicht mit viel Enthusiasmus seitens der Architekten des Rockefeller Centers rechnen. Diese bemühten sich um Nüchternheit und Modernität; was die Traditionen «phantastischer Technologie» anbelangt, die Roxy faszinierten, so waren sie praktisch ohne Wirkung auf die Architektenschaft geblieben. Die Architekten brachten es sogar fertig, Roxy auf eine Studienreise nach Europa mitzunehmen, wo sie mit eigenen Augen die Fortschritte begutachten wollten, welche die

← fig. 6
Edward Stone, Rendering of the interior of Radio City Music Hall. The future Edward Durrell Stone was then an employee of Associated Architects.

Roxy, Noé et le Radio City Music Hall

Le «showplace of the Nation» et «le plus grand théâtre du monde» fut conçu non pas par des architectes, mais par Samuel Lionel Rothafel («Roxy»), le roi du «showbiz» des années vingt. Il s'agit d'un véritable tissu d'installations destinées à créer un environnement hallucinant, illusioniste et fantastique. On enviseagea même l'utilisation de gaz hallucinogènes — inspiration directe de Coney Island. Parmi les équipements des coulisses on trouvait le dortoir des danseuses du Music Hall (les «Rockettes»), des étables pour animaux sauvages (ainsi que des ascenseurs capables de transporter des éléphants sur les pâturages installés sur les toits du Rockefeller Center), et, finalement l'appartement de Roxy, «Noé» de cette arche placée au cœur de New York, «Nouvelle Jérusalem» du business américain.

L'auteur discute des intérêts contradictoires des architectes et de Roxy, de l'impossibilité de monter des spectacles conventionnels dans une salle immense comme celle du Music Hall, et surtout des allusions bibliques, voire apocalyptiques du programme, qui font du *Radio City Music Hall* un paradigme de «manhattanisme».

↓ fig. 7 Radio City Music Hall, view.
↓ figs. 8–9 Model of the proscenium. With curtain closed (8) and with a view of the separately mobile parts of the stage (9).

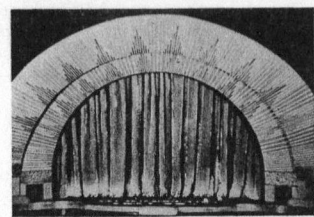
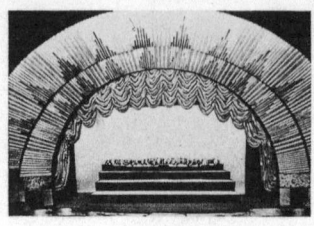

moderne Architektur dort im Theaterbau erzielt hatte.

Im Sommer 1931 machten sich Roxy, der Showman, sowie Harrison und Reinhard, zwei geschäftstüchtige Architekten, zusammen mit einer Delegation von technischen Experten auf die transatlantische Fahrt. Die wenig erfolgreiche Mission spielte Roxy, der mühelos imstande war, Illusionen in genügender Quantität und Dichte herzustellen, um die Grosstadtmassen damit abzufüttern, gegen die europäischen Architekten aus: denn diese waren puritanische Erzfeinde der Idee von «Showbiz», wie sie Roxy verkörperte. In der Tat bewegten sich die europäischen Architekten in einer Richtung, die Roxy's Interessen genau entgegengesetzt war. Sie interessierten sich dafür, wie theatralische Vorgänge in «objektive» Gehäuse untergebracht werden können; das traditionelle Theater hingegen stellte für sie eine unannehmbare Form von Massenabfertigung dar, mittels der ein schlechtes Publikum mit belangloser Schauspielerei gefüttert wird.

Nachdem er gelangweilt Frankreich, Belgien, Deutschland und Holland durchreist hatte, wurde Roxy sogar genötigt, den Zug nach Moskau zu nehmen, um die konstruktivistischen Klubhäuser und Theater zu begutachten, die dort seit der Mitte der Zwanzigerjahre gebaut worden waren. Schliesslich, auf seiner Rückreise nach New York, irgendwo draussen im Atlantik, erlebte der erschöpfte Roxy eine Offenbarung. Während er einen melodramatischen Sonnenuntergang anstarrte, ereignete sich die «Verkündigung» seines Theaters: es wird die Fleischwerdung dieses Sonnenunterganges sein.

Zurück in New York wird dann diese Scheinschwangerschaft durch das Team von Architekten und Dekorateuren von *Radio City Music Hall* in eine jener Fusionen von Gegensätzen übersetzt, die die Geschichte von Manhattan kennzeichnen; die Bühne wird zu dem am vollständigsten mechanisierten künstlichen «environment», das Auditorium wird zur grössten optischen Metapher der Welt.

Sonnenauf- und -untergang

Roxy bemühte sich nach Kräften, seinen widerspenstigen Architekten die Metapher des Sonnenuntergangs aufzudrängen, und zwar in möglichst «buchstäblicher» Umsetzung. In völliger Missachtung von Plan und Aufriss des rechteckigen Baus der *Radio City* wird das Thema des Sonnenuntergangs in der Form einer Reihe von konzentrisch angeordneten, halbkreisförmigen Gipsprofilen festgelegt, die sich gegen die Bühne hin verjüngen. Das Resultat ist eine Art Gebärmutter, deren einziger Ausgang die Bühne selbst ist: d. h. «fantasy».

Dieser Ausgang ist maskiert durch den prachtvollen Bühnenvorhang, bestehend aus einem speziell entwickelten synthetischen Stoff, der dank seiner Reflexivität und unerhörten Geschmeidigkeit als akzeptabler Ersatz für die Sonne selbst gelten kann. Seine «Strahlen» werden von den Gipsbögen aufgefangen und setzen sich in der Decke fort; sie erreichen so die gesamte Tiefe des Auditoriums. Die Bögen sind in Goldfarbe übermalt, um den Purpurglanz der untergehenden Sonne zu reflektieren, wie auch den roten Samt der Sessel, auf den Roxy – wiederum entgegen dem Rat der aufgeklärten Architekten – grossen Wert gelegt hatte.

So wird denn, im Endeffekt, die Wirkung eines Sonnenuntergangs in dem Augenblick erreicht, wo die Saalbeleuchtung erlischt; das

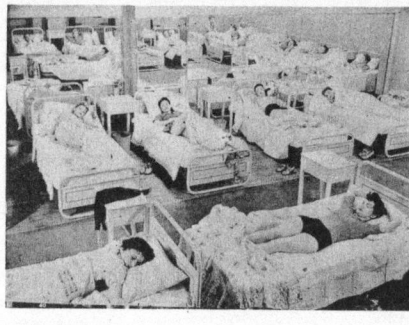

↓ fig. 10   The Rockettes resting (?) in their mirrored dormitory.

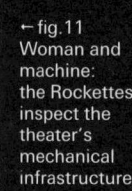

← fig. 11
Woman and machine: the Rockettes inspect the theater's mechanical infrastructure

Wiedereinschalten der Lichter am Ende jeder Vorstellung hingegen bewirkt einen Sonnenaufgang. Es wiederholt sich, mit anderen Worten, der 24-Stunden-Zyklus von Tag und Nacht mehrere Male während eines einzigen Abends in *Radio City Music Hall*. Tag und Nacht sind drastisch verkürzt, die Zeit ist beschleunigt, die Wahrnehmung intensiviert, die Lebensdauer — potentiell — verdoppelt, verdreifacht ...

Schauer

Roxy's Verständnis von «phantastischer Technologie» führt schliesslich zu einer weiteren Eskalation der Metapher. Mittels einer leichten Neudefinition der konventionellen Rolle von *air condition* — Ventilation und Kühlung — wird es möglich, so argumentiert er, im Augenblick des Sonnenuntergangs Kühle im Saal zu verbreiten. Mit derselben manischen Objektivität, die seine früheren Kaprizen kennzeichnen, spielt Roxy auch mit dem Gedanken, der Atmosphäre seines Theaters halluzinogene Gase beizumischen, so dass der fabrizierte Sonnenuntergang noch durch eine synthetisch erzeugte Ekstase unterstützt wird. Eine kleine Dose Lachgas würde die 6200 Besucher — *Radio City* ist noch immer das grösste Theater der Welt — in einen euphorischen Zustand versetzen, hyper-rezeptiv für die Darbietungen der Bühne. Entgegen dem Rat seiner Rechtsanwälte spies Roxy für eine kurze Zeit die Lüftungskanäle seines Theaters mit Ozon — dem therapeutischen O_3-Molekül mit seinem «stechend erfrischenden Duft» und «erheiternden Einfluss».

Roxy kombiniert so «Super Time» mit «Super Health» und prägt schliesslich die endgültige Formel für die Flucht aus der Metropolis:

«Ein Besuch in der *Radio City Music Hall* ist genausogut wie ein Monat auf dem Lande.»

Mutationen

Die Vollkommenheit und metaphorische Stringenz von Roxy's künstlichem Paradies bewirkt nun eine Kettenreaktion weiterer, unvorhergesehener kultureller Mutationen. Am Abend der offiziellen Eröffnung von *Radio City* — dem ersten Teilstück des Rockefeller Centers — füttert Roxy die glitzernde neue Maschine seines krypto-jungianischen Labors mit den erschöpften Resten einer abgestandenen und erloschenen Vaudeville-Tradition, einer Tradition, die zwanzig Jahre früher in Coney Island ihre Sternstunden erlebt hatte. Aber die altmodischen Darbietungen überleben die «Prüfung» nicht. Zuschauer, die 200 Fuss vom Rampenlicht entfernt sitzen, sehen sich ausserstande, die Grimassen der Schauspieler im Ablauf ihrer müden Routine zu verfolgen. Allein die Grösse des Theaters macht jede konventionelle Form des Einsatzes der menschlichen Stimme, ja selbst des menschlichen Körpers unmöglich; die verletzlichen Kanäle humoristischer Kommunikation werden denn auch über das erträgliche Mass hinaus strapaziert. Die gigantische Bühne — so breit wie ein ganzer Häuserblock — unterminiert den Sinn jeder «mise-en-scène», wo die Suggestion von Raum und Weite immer eine fiktive Erweiterung der tatsächlichen räumlichen Intimität darstellt. Auf dieser Bühne wird Atmosphäre atomisiert.

«Was die Grösse der Konzeption, die Glorie der Planung, die Vollkommenheit der Ausführung anbelangt, so wurde noch nie etwas mit der *Radio City* Vergleichbares erträumt»,

behauptet der Initiator mit Recht, doch der «container» ist in der Tat so vollkommen, dass

sich jeder Inhalt darin lächerlich ausnimmt. Um einen Kritiker der Eröffnungsvorstellung zu zitieren:

«Viele von den Darbietungen erwiesen sich als jämmerliches zweitrangiges Zeug, fehl am Platz inmitten solcher Triumphe von Architektur und Mechanik.»

Ob mit Absicht oder nicht, Radio City stellt einen weit entschiedeneren Bruch mit der Vergangenheit dar als so viele bewusst revolutionäre Theaterräume jener Zeit. Lichtjahre liegen zwischen der Technik von Roxy's Theater und dem tatsächlichen Geschehen auf der Bühne: es ist — noch — ein Raum ohne Aufführung.

Partikel

In den frühen Dreissigerjahren produzierte einzig der Film — d. h. Hollywood — eine Form von Szenarios, die der Künstlichkeit und Anti-Authentizität von Roxy's Theaterlandschaft entgegenkommt. Hollywood hat eine neue dramatische Formel entwickelt: *isolierte menschliche Partikel, gewichtslos durch ein magnetisches Feld von fabriziertem Vergnügen schwebend, gelegentlich kollidierend* — eine Formel, die der Künstlichkeit sowie dem Masstab der *Radio City Music Hall* angemessen ist und sie auch mit abstrakten, formalisierten Emotionen von ausreichender Dichte zu füllen vermag. Die Produktion der «Dream Factory» ist denn auch nirgends besser zuhause als in Roxy's Theater.

Noah

Nach dem Fiasko des ersten Abends wird «menschliche Authentizität» — dieser überalterte Vaudeville — fallengelassen und das Theater wird zum Kino. Ein Kino benötigt bloss eine Projektionskabine, einen Saal und eine Leinwand; aber hinter der Leinwand von *Radio City* gibt es noch eine andere Domäne: «eine vollkommen durchorganisierte Einheit von 700 Seelen»: *Backstage*. Die Einrichtungen dieser Domäne hinter den Kulissen umfassen Schlafsäle, ein kleines Hotel, Proberäume, eine Sporthalle, eine Kunstabteilung, Kostümateliers. Hier befindet sich die *Radio City Symphony* und eine permanente Truppe von 64 Tänzerinnen — die Rockettes, alle zwischen 1,62 und 1,69 m gross — eine scriptlose Kolonne von Revuetänzerinnen, deren Auftritte keine spezifische Handlung zum Gegenstand haben. Ueberdies befindet sich hier auch eine Menagerie — Pferde, Kühe, Ziegen und andere Tiere. Sie leben in ultramodernen Stallungen, künstlich belichtet und belüftet; ein Tieraufzug — gross genug, um Elefanten aufzunehmen — deponiert diese Tiere je nachdem auf der Bühne oder auf einer speziellen Weide auf dem Dach der *Radio City*. Und schliesslich ist hier auch Roxy selbst zu finden — gewissermassen Noah — in einem Appartement, das zwischen den Stahlträgern, die das Dach seines Sonnenuntergangs tragen, angeordnet ist. Nun schien es, nach der Umfunktionierung der *Music Hall* zum Kino, als wäre diese extravagante Domäne insgesamt zur Zwecklosigkeit verurteilt. Aber der Gedanke, dass sie auf immer hinter dem Hymen der Kinoleinwand verschwinden könnte, war unerträglich.

Unter dem vielfältigen Druck der Verhältnisse, angesichts frenetisch aufeinanderfolgender Sonnenauf- und -untergänge, angesichts des Vaudeville-Desasters, der brachliegenden «vollständigsten mechanischen Einrichtungen der Welt», auch angesichts der ständig verfügbaren «Rockettes», der grossstädtischen Publikums-Ressourcen, angesichts von Roxy selbst, ratlos in seinem Ei, gibt es nur eines: eine neue Show muss auf die Beine gestellt werden, eine Show, die in einem Minimum an Zeit ein Maximum an Möglichkeiten dieser kopflastigen Infrastruktur der Illusion auszuwerten vermag.

Unter diesen kritischen Bedingungen erfindet Roxy zusammen mit Leon Leonidoff, dem obersten Produktionsleiter, sowie mit dem Direktor der Rockettes ein erstaunliches Ritual. In genauer Entsprechung zur Krise besteht die neue Routine der Rockettes in einer systematischen Abwandlung des Themas von der «fehlenden Inspiration». Grundlage der völlig inhaltslosen Darbietung ist ein Prozess entfesselter Synchronisierung, eine Präsentation unmenschlicher Koordination, eine atemberaubende Aufopferung menschlicher Individualität auf dem Altar eines automatisierten synthischen Frühlingsrituals.

Essenz der Darbietung ist das simultane Vorzeigen der weiblichen Sexualregion, eine Einladung zu deren Inspektion. Aber das vollzieht sich in einem Masstab, der dem Spektakel den Charakter einer privaten Provokation nimmt; Adressat ist hier offensichtlich eine andere, noch nicht existierende Gattung von Liebhabern. Die Rockettes erscheinen als neue

theater. A movie theater needs only a projection booth, an auditorium, and a screen; but behind Radio City's screen still exists another realm, "a perfectly organized entity of 700 souls" backstage. Its elaborate facilities include dormitories, a small hospital, rehearsal rooms, a gymnasium, an art department, costume workshops. There is Radio City Symphony and a permanent troupe of 64 female dancers—the Roxyettes, all between 5' 4" and 5' 7"—a scriptless chorus line without any action to sustain. Furthermore, there is a menagerie—horses, cows, goats, and other animals. They live in ultramodern stables, artificially lit and ventilated; an animal elevator—dimensioned to carry even elephants—not only deposits them on the stage but also on a special grazing ground on Radio City's roof. And, finally, Roxy can be found here too—Noah, in a sense—in an apartment fitted in between the steel roof trusses bearing his sunset. Now it seems, after repurposing the music hall into a cinema, as if that entire extravagant domain were condemned to uselessness. But the idea that it could disappear forever behind the hymen of the projection screen was unacceptable.

Under the multiple pressures of the frenetic sunsets and daybreaks, combined with the vaudeville disaster and the inactivity of the "most complete mechanical installation in the world," in view of the permanent availability of the Roxyettes and the cosmopolitan livestock, and in view of Roxy himself, helpless in his egg, there is only one thing to do: a new show has to be launched that can exploit in the shortest possible time the maximum capacities of this top-heavy infrastructure of illusion.

Under these critical conditions Roxy, general director of production Leon Leonidoff, and the director of the Roxyettes (their name soon streamlined to Rockettes) invent a stunning ritual: a new routine that is, in a sense, a record of the crisis: a systematization of the concept of "lack of inspiration"; variations on the theme of "no content," founded on a *process*, a display of inhuman coordination that relies on frenzied synchronization, an exhilarating surrender of individuality to the automatism of a synthetic year-round rite of spring.

The essence of this performance is a mass high-kick: a simultaneous display of sexual regions, inviting inspection but on a scale that transcends personal provocation. The Rockettes are a new race, exhibiting their superior charms to the old one. Thus Roxy's Theater, itself the fruit of an immaculate conception, produced its own race.

Only the Rockettes' abstract movement can generate completely plotless theatrical energy commensurate with the theater Roxy has created. The Rockettes = the chorus line as main protagonist, the *lead*, a single personage made up of 64 individuals, filling the gigantic stage, dressed in Suprematist costumes: flesh-colored bodystockings marked with a series of black rectangles that shrink toward the waist to end in a small black triangle—living abstract art that denies the human body.

With the development of its own race, its own mythology, its own time, its own rituals, the container of Radio City Music Hall has finally generated a worthy content.

Ark

"Rockefeller Center itself, (is) the New Jerusalem, within whose walls Radio City is but the broadcasting and dramatic Ark." FORTUNE

Roxy, the dancers, and the animals are the only residents of Rockefeller Center. The fact that Radio City Music Hall contains ultrasophisticated accommodation for selected wild animals and the apparatus to dispatch them throughout the structure; the fact that, in the Rockettes, the Music Hall has its own race, luxuriating in its mirror-clad dorm—a kind of gigantic maternity ward whose inmates reproduce ad infinitum without sex, strictly through the effects of architecture—and, finally, the fact that in Roxy the Music Hall has a planner whose vision is the laughing stock of his fellow men, or at least of his architects: all of that supports the thesis that, in the completeness of its equipment, every block of Manhattan was conceived, designed, and built to survive the Flood—or its modern equivalent. Every block harbors a Noah's Ark.

If a Flood-like disaster should indeed befall humanity, and if only a single block, a single center were spared, both the animal kingdom and civilization could indeed be revived simply by reproducing its contents. In view of the glamorous crew of Radio City, such an interpretation seems inevitable; it testifies to the constant expectation of the Apocalypse as the basic underlying theme of all of Manhattan's enterprises. Radio City Music Hall is the most fanatic institution ever conceived to cope with this expectation. To cite Roxy again:

"In Radio City Music Hall the fun never sets."

↓ fig. 12 Part of the menagerie "onstage" during a performance of "Roman Plays."

← fig. 13
The Rockettes in their "Suprematist costumes.

Menschenrasse, die ihre überlegenen Reize der alten Rasse vorzeigt. So hat Roxy's Theater, selbst Frucht einer Jungfernzeugung, sein eigenes Geschlecht hervorgebracht.

Die abstrakte Bewegung der Tänzerinnen kann nun absolut inhaltslose theatralische Energie produzieren, die dem gigantischen Masstab des Auditoriums adäquat ist. Die Rockettes, d. h. die Kolonne von Revuetänzerinnen, werden zur Leitfigur: ein Hauptdarsteller, der sich aus 64 Individuen zusammensetzt, welche die riesige Bühne anfüllen. Sie tragen suprematistische Kostüme: fleischfarbene Trikots, markiert mit schwarzen Rechtecken, die sich in der Lendengegend zu einem kleinen schwarzen Dreieck zuspitzen — lebende abstrakte Kunst, Verneinung des Unbestreitbaren, d. h. des menschlichen Körpers.

So hat *Radio City Music Hall* durch die Hervorbringung ihres eigenen Geschlechts, ihrer eigenen Geschichte, ihres eigenen Rituals — kurz: ihrer eigenen Kosmogonie — einen ihr adäquaten Inhalt entwickelt.

Arche

«Rockefeller Center itself, (is) the New Jerusalem, within whose walls Radio City is but the broadcasting and dramatic Ark.»

«Das Rockefeller Center selbst, (ist) das Neue Jerusalem, und *Radio City* innerhalb seiner Mauern ist nichts anderes als die Arche der Medien und des Theaters.» *FORTUNE*

Roxy, die Tänzerinnen und die Tiere sind die einzigen Bewohner des Rockefeller Centers. Die Tatsache, dass *Radio City Music Hall* eine hochraffinierte Unterkunft für ausgewählte wilde Tiere bereitstellt sowie eine Maschinerie, die ihren vertikalen Transport von Niveau zu Niveau gewährleistet; die Tatsache, dass die *Music Hall* in Gestalt der Rockettes ihr eigenes Geschlecht hat, das es sich in seinem spiegelbeschlagenen Schlafsaal wohlergehen lässt — einer Art gigantischer *Maternité*, deren Insassen sich ohne Sex, vielmehr aufgrund der blossen Imprägnierung der Architektur ad infinitum vermehren — und schliesslich die Tatsache, dass die *Music Hall* in Roxy einen Planer hat, dessen «Vision» zum Gespött seiner Mitmenschen, oder doch zumindest seiner Architekten wird: das alles kann die These bekräftigen, dass jeder Häuserblock Manhattans dank der Komplettheit seiner Ausrüstung ersonnen, entworfen und gebaut wurde, um die Sintflut — oder ihr modernes Aequivalent — zu überleben. Jeder Häuserblock ist eine Arche Noah.

Sollte tatsächlich ein sintflutartiges Unheil über die Menschheit hereinbrechen, und würde dann nur ein einziger Häuserblock, ein einziges «Center» verschont bleiben, so könnte in der Tat sowohl das Tierreich wie die Zivilisation wiedererstehen aufgrund einer simplen Fortpflanzung seines Inhalts. Angesichts der glamourösen «Crew» der *Radio City* erweist sich eine solche Interpretation als unausweichlich; sie bezeugt die beständige Erwartung der Apokalypse als unterschwelliges Grundthema aller Unternehmungen Manhattans. *Radio City Music Hall* war die fanatischste Institution, die je ersonnen wurde, um mit dieser Erwartung fertigzuwerden. Um noch einmal Roxy zu zitieren:

"In Radio City Music Hall the fun never sets."

(Uebers. S. v. M.)

IV USE AND AGENCY

311
Whose Agency?
Impact of User, Appropriation,
and Consumerism in the
Built Environment
    by Gabrielle Schaad

329
Project-Based Learning
at the ETH: Critical Rather
Than Technocratic
    by Seminar Janssen [AA.VV]

339
Citizens' Action Groups:
How, Where, Why?
    by Marianne Günter
    and Roland Günter

350
Group Portraits and
Self Portraits: Some Remarks
on Recent Approaches
to Town-Planning
    by David P. Handlin

364
Atelier 5, 1955–1975:
Experiments in
Communal Living
    by Jacques Blumer

378
Signs of Life: Symbols
in the American City
    by Denise Scott Brown

Whose Agency?

Impact of User, Appropriation, and Consumerism in the Built Environment

Gabrielle Schaad

The question of how architecture might learn from social science, specifically sociology, created and continues to generate, well beyond the 1970s, significant frictions in practice and academic discourse. The original texts gathered in the "Use and Agency" section of this volume show the extent to which their authors deemed the architects' position within their more extensive field of practice to be relatively weak and subject to dynamics beyond their control. The texts implicitly negotiate a larger debate between the quantitative, system-oriented social sciences and the sociological deconstruction of meaning- and taste-making that marked the 1970s. All authors featured here —the building preservation activists Marianne (Janne) Günter and Roland Günter, architectural historian David P. Handlin, architect Jacques Blumer, architect Denise Scott Brown, and the AA.VV editorial collective—critically weigh in their texts, which span a five-year period from 1971 to 1976, the use of both sociocultural, anthropological analysis and specific (activist) tools to gain a better understanding of the building industry, the design process, the use-value of architecture, and class-related issues of taste by investigating and even resolutely blurring the boundaries between high-brow and low-brow (i.e., popular) culture.

The cybernetically inspired systems-theory-driven approaches to urban planning and architecture of the 1950s and 1960s helped to establish technocratic top-down planning on a large scale by quantitatively analyzing the environment beyond the boundaries of East and West.[1] As a result, the supposed "user-adapted" flexibility of megastructures petrified, especially in the case of government-funded social housing in buildings and infrastructures that either cut into vital urban tissues or were not planned at all. In some cases, the spaces produced by the architects of postwar welfare societies in Western Europe and the United States seemed to turn against the people they were supposed to shelter. Charles Jencks provocatively regarded the example of the social housing complex Pruitt-Igoe in St. Louis, Missouri, built by Minoru Yamasaki in 1951–1955 and demolished in 1972–1976, as ushering in the death of modern architecture.[2] The "soft" factors of architecture beyond the building, such as policy decisions, ownership models, and cuts to infrastructure and maintenance budgets gave way to criminal activities and decay in the built structures, which lacked identification and adaptability. In retrospect, they were a far more destructive force than the actual building. Nevertheless, Swiss design critic Rolf Keller included Pruitt-Igoe as a material witness in his early lampoon demonizing building with concrete because of its resulting "monotony."[3]

The understanding of built "ecologies" as self-regulating systems (i.e., environments) oscillated between the poles of top-down control (i.e., surveillance) and bottom-up "participation."[4] Frustrated by the limited capacity of architecture to better the environment and under pressure to achieve profitability amid soaring land prices, leading architects in the early and mid-1970s turned their attention away from social issues and back to form, claiming architecture's autonomy.

On questions of form, they not only valued the autonomy of the quantitative social sciences but showed a renewed interest in cultural-historical building types and their embeddedness in society through the centuries. The architect was reestablished as a solitary ingenious author able to read these cultural traces. The interdisciplinary designer of social processes collaborating with linguists, sociologists, and engineers alike to understand environments cybernetically belonged to the past. Analysis of form could also take various shapes through the lenses of sociocultural and anthropological methods and semiotics. With these the architects would focus on class-related constructions of taste tied to specific cultural artifacts and their dispersion throughout consumer culture. Practitioners of architecture and architectural theory framed both approaches during the 1970s as investigations into reality, or as "realism."[5]

Another thread of history, one concerned with quantitatively rather than qualitatively based investigations in the field of architecture, led to the normalized, "neutral," unmarked (male, white) user—a projection popularized by interwar twentieth-century European modernism. Architects reassured themselves that they were enabling users through their designs because their anthropocentric, anthropometric design process relied on idealized models borrowed from Ernst Neufert's building design theory "Bauentwurfslehre" (Architect's data, 1936), Le Corbusier's "Le Modulor" (1942–1955), Henry Dreyfuss's characters "Joe and Josephine" (1960), and Alexander Kira's bathroom ergonomics (1966).[6] Kira's manual featured a genuinely "user-centered" approach, based on meticulous observations and measurements of people's behaviors and diverse needs in bathroom settings. Architectural historian Anna-Maria Meister reminds us, however, that "for Neufert, man was never the measure of all things; man needed to fit the system."[7] And, even if the civil rights protests of the 1960s had led American industrial design pioneer Dreyfuss to publish a revised edition of *The Measure of Man* (1967) after becoming critically "aware that normate figures representing statistical averages were often [mis]taken as real bodies," not all architects using his manual were likewise in the know.[8] As the (post-)Foucauldian assessment of architecture as a "political technology" of the body demonstrates, architecture's concern with the idealized abstraction of a normative, nongendered, nondisabled user has not only shaped our behavior and physiques, but it operates through the bodies it claims to shelter and house and creates exclusions.[9] A design process exclusively concerned with form—or even with formal deconstruction—will consistently fail to deconstruct these ingrained biases of architecture toward its subjects when the body as an idealized abstraction precedes all construction. Philosopher and sociologist Henri Lefèbvre became convinced toward the end of the 1970s that the term *user*, initially suggesting an orientation toward the "use-value" of space, instead dehumanized inhabitants, discounting their agency by turning them into passive, functional objects.[10] What about socio-anthropologically inspired observation and study of the inhabitants' actual performance of "use" instead?

Architectural historian Kenny Cupers states in his collection *Use Matters* (2013) that "the interest in the agency of the user across many creative disciplines today delivers new promises for the social role of design." He goes on to point out that "the user is both a historical construct and an agent of change, too often relegated to the margins of architectural history."[11] However, understanding everyday use, and hence the production of users, simply as a function of planning and design does not go far enough. Even though "the user" has to be recognized and traced as a historical construct, it also proves fruitful to think about how users—precisely in the very diversity that the term tries to homogenize—transform and actively constitute "building," understood here as both a noun and a verb.

Projecting a user brings up, if only implicitly, the question of "agency" within the built environment. But whose agency? The question is partly tackled by Isabelle Doucet and Cupers, who notice that the term is difficult to pin down: "Are we talking about the agency of the architect, and if so the agency to do what: to act in service of the client or to guide society to a better end? Or do we mean instead the power of the architectural project or the building itself, to convince its users about the virtuous lifestyle it hopes to instill, or its spectators about the beauty of its form?"[12]

Cupers suggests that participation be considered over a longer historical period that does not isolate it as an approach tied to 1960s/1970s politics of empowerment and democratization but instead understands it as "enmeshed" with "the bureaucratic development of the welfare state and burgeoning culture of leisure and mass consumption."[13] If Italian architect Giancarlo de Carlo (1919–2005) called for citizen or "user" participation in all relevant design processes of public space in the early 1980s, the editors of the volume *Participation in Art and Architecture* (2015), Mechtild Widrich and Martino Stierli, remind us that the process of participation has not only been theorized on a political level by authors like Jacques Rancière, Lefebvre, and Jürgen Habermas since the 1960s but also has been actualized in the discourse around (public) art by proponents of relational aesthetics in the 1990s, such as Nicolas Bourriaud, and contested by art historian and critic Claire Bishop.[14] The paternalism detected in functionalist ideas of "participation"—for example, Le Corbusier's modernist *promenade architecturale* as a sequential progression of inhabitants through their built environs—was dropped by feminist initiatives toward the end of the 1970s. Their participatory workshops catered to community-oriented public buildings such as the London-based architectural design cooperative MATRIX's (1981–1994) Jagonari Educational Resource Center for Asian Women (1984–1987) and the Dalston Children's Center (1984–1985).[15] Political theorist Nancy Fraser's feminist reassessments of Habermas's thoughts on the public sphere after the fall of the Iron Curtain also shed a new light on "subaltern counterpublics," complicating the debate around who is allowed to participate in and hence constitute the public sphere.[16] Queer theorists Lauren Berlant and Michael Warner later extended this concept to the marginalization of queer sexuality in urban public space.[17]

The interest shown by theory, history, and design criticism in the "use" of architecture has only further increased. From the late 1980s onward, paradigms and theoretical approaches from science and technology studies—for example, Actor-Network Theory—helped put the architect's central role into perspective.[18] Understanding planners and designers as actors in a network of interdependent human and nonhuman relationships expanded architectural discourse to include various material, social, economic, and political actors within and beyond the built environment.[19] At least in history and theory the myth of a universal user has come under scrutiny, because more recent, decolonial accounts, following Donna Haraway's work in the late 1980s, increasingly draw on "situatedness," specificity, and "partial perspective."[20] Not least has the recent criticism of an anthropocentric perspective allowed for the ecological sustainability of building practices to take center stage.[21] The term *spatial agency* has in turn helped to decenter the agency of architects in the production of architectural space, allowing the "more-or-less formal and more-or-less welcome actors that produce, inhabit, maintain and destroy architecture in different ways" to enter the discourse.[22]

Cohabitation and Processes of Adaptation

In his 1975 contribution to *archithese*, "Atelier 5: 1955–1975: Experiments in Communal Living," Swiss architect Blumer looks back on two housing projects completed by the collaborative firm Atelier 5 (founded by Erwin Fritz, Samuel Gerber, Rolf Hesterberg, Hans Hostettler, and Alfredo Pini), where he worked from 1955 to 1963 and where he reintegrated in 1970 after a professorship at the University of Illinois Chicago.[23] Blumer exemplifies the promises and pitfalls of understanding the architect as an orchestrator of the social process through form by looking at the Thalmatt housing project (a 1974 follow-up to Atelier 5's earlier Halen settlement of 1957–1960) near Bern and the Wertherberg housing project (1966–1968) near Münster (then part of West Germany).[24] He argues that the entrepreneurial social utopists Robert Owens and Charles Fourier in the early nineteenth century, as well as communal housing in general, tried to establish new rules and new people by proposing new forms of intertwining productive and reproductive labor in reorganized domesticities.[25] In contrast, Blumer frames Atelier 5's approach as less ambitious because, while the firm offered playful variants to established living patterns, it did not expect new ways of cohabitation to emerge thanks to architecture. Aware that architects always work within the constraints of the capitalist, increasingly profit-oriented building industry, Blumer proposes that, despite these circumstances, architects should be able to create livable environments if they abide by a few hypotheses, among which: Free space within a settlement needs to be discernable as common public space and ideally co-owned by the inhabitants;

The inhabitants decide for themselves how individual/shared space is organized or transformed; Threshold-areas mediate between public and private; The building structure houses different social groups, allows for communal uses other than housing, and satisfies different economic ambitions.[26] Even though both of the projects discussed in Blumer's self-critical essay followed these axioms in the planning process, resulting in comparable if slightly different layouts, they differ in approach and with respect to their levels of "user participation."

In Blumer's view, 1960s consumer culture heavily influenced ideas about living and, more specifically, the representative character of the domestic setting. Beyond interior design magazines, he denounces then emerging DIY shops as players in an aesthetic economy of aspiration. By selling ready-to-use building elements, they cater to homeowners' desire for an individualistic lifestyle, allowing them to transform their housing entities into their own small, personalized utopias. As Blumer muses, a fake-brick cladding glued to a "poor looking" architect-designed *béton brut* structure embodies the lower middle classes' striving toward an aesthetics of higher economic standing—the aesthetic of the free-standing, suburban, nuclear family house. On the one hand critical of architects who tend to impose their choices of style and taste on inhabitants, Blumer on the other hand regrets the outcome of user-based retro-transformations. Being cosmetic rather than structural, the interventions miss increasing the use-value of individual entities and the overall settlement. While welcoming the inhabitants' engagement with their living environment, he finds a grain of sand in the aesthetic outcome. Nevertheless, Blumer eventually dismisses as naive any attempt to use architecture to control or guide broader efforts to emancipate society from capitalism.

Self-Portraits; Or the Symbolism of Idealized Individual Homeownership

A different take—involving a different scale and geographic focus—is found in architect and architectural historian David P. Handlin's "remarks on recent approaches to town-planning" in his contribution "Group Portraits and Self-Portraits."[27]

Nevertheless, we find an intersection with Blumer's observation of how the social aspirations of class tie in with user-initiated adaptations of built structures, which Handlin compares to the more homogeneous town structures of precapitalist societies and cultures. He doubts whether settlements and towns can be analyzed extensively through or give real insights into their inhabitants' customs and culture, since such analysis tends to homogenize what always is and needs to be heterogeneous and diverse. Even if his preference is for a "situated" approach over universalist, unifying, and eventually dehumanizing architectural proposals—he cites Le Corbusier's Ville Radieuse (1933), for example—he doubts the adequacy of social anthropology as a valuable tool for architectural planning processes. He underpins his argument by bringing up what he deems the shortcomings of Herbert J. Gans's pioneering study in urban ethnography, *The Urban Villagers*.[28] Gans based his study on an analysis of parts of a Boston community in the West End district where "Italian-Americans made up the largest group, about forty percent, but the area also had [among others] sizeable contingents of Jewish-, Polish-, Albanian-, Ukrainian- and Greek-Americans." Gans argues that the so-called urban villagers' buildings and their use were proof of an overall, more or less consistent design resistance to modernism. The inhabitants, Gans concludes, were rejecting consumer culture because they wished to reproduce their "rurally based ancestors' living patterns."[29] If one would today denounce Gans's reductive view of an Italian-American community as rurally marked and hence "behind" in general, at the time it was published Gans's text offered a nuanced view of the community's dynamics, countering the simplistic portrayals often found in media and popular culture.

Handlin, on the other hand, points out that Gans cut short the diversity within the larger group of "urban villagers" when he overlapped and identified the community with a homogenous building "style": "There is a compelling temptation to claim that the community speaks with a single voice. It makes good rhetoric, especially if that rhetoric emphasizes the difference between 'insiders' and oppressive 'outsiders.'"[30] Handlin is convinced that sociological "group images" do not provide an adequate and generalizable basis for planning. In his view, only an approach that assumes people primarily strive to express themselves rather than their membership in a collective would do justice to diversity and repetition. Handlin elaborates that even the dense and heterogenous urban population studied here remained committed to homeownership and individual expression. However, despite all the individualism in the mass, the houses often resembled one another like peas in a pod. When his text appeared in *archithese*, Handlin was an associate professor of architecture at the Harvard Graduate School of Design (1973–1978). In the text, he makes a culturally specific and ideologically marked diagnosis by stating that "the dream of homeownership" still broadly pervaded American households. He dismisses attempts at flexibilization and personalization of housing units (e.g., with movable wall partitions) as "accommodating the self-portrait in the collectivist ideal" and eventually amounting to nothing more than an expression of the childish playfulness of architectural students.[31] His polemic hence dismisses both "group and self-portraits." He aims to devalue—or at least to call into question—the contemporaneous architectural discourse's emerging investigative interest in the shantytowns of South American cities or so-called squatter architecture as models for future urban development.[32]

Handlin draws alternative urban patterns and so-called spontaneous architecture into the picture not only to contextualize his reasoning but to distance himself from such an approach.[33] When he argues that, in American society, the mobile home promised, despite its utopian mobility, customized specimens increasingly resembling the shape of individual houses, he quotes from an advertisement for a mobile home producer while blowing a poisoned kiss at Archigram's 1960s radical utopias.[34] One wonders whose aspirations Handlin has in mind. In his view, a white, American, middle-class "user"—even more so if that person hails from a lower stratum of society that has evaded stereotyping because of its diversity—would continue to idealize individual homeownership and build accordingly, which would not negatively affect the practice of community-building beyond domestic borders. His criticism of group portraits as reductive in their aim at specificity might be justified. Rounding his argument off, however, he mistakes individual homeownership for an almost preconscious, "innate" universal aspiration of large parts of the society, rather than denouncing it as the commodity it was ideologically advertised to be by state housing policies and the building industry in the United States.

The notion of "self-portrait" reappears in Scott Brown's analysis under changed auspices as "the physical elements of suburbia—the roads, houses, roofs, lawns, and front doors —[that] serve practical purposes such as giving access and shelter, but they also serve as means of self-expression for suburban residents."[35] That Gans's work—although criticized by Handlin—informed Scott Brown's approach may be less of a surprise.[36] Scott Brown complemented her studies in planning at the Department of City Planning at the Graduate School of Fine Arts of the University of Pennsylvania with social sciences courses, among them lectures by Gans. To study the Levittown settlements in Philadelphia, Gans had created a classic participant-observer framework that allowed him to portray working-class and lower-middle-class life in America.[37] Scott Brown took a particular interest in his nonjudgmental viewpoint, or the "new objectivity" of his urban sociological understanding, which brought together "social life, popular culture, and planning."[38] Referring to Peter Smithson, she calls her own method an "active socioplastics."[39] In the format of a "letter to the editors," Scott Brown makes clear from the beginning of her essay that her exhibition project *Signs of Life* targets the matter of (American) taste.[40] In 1976, the French philosopher Pierre Bourdieu was still writing his pathbreaking, statistically based *La distinction* (Distinction, 1979)—an empirical, socio-anthropological analysis of class-related differentiation processes in the formation, performance, and embodiment of taste in the French middle-class bourgeois culture.[41] Scott Brown was thus untouched by this contemporaneous European push to deconstruct the category of taste as a symbolic system in which minute distinctions become the basis for social judgment. She nevertheless consciously sheds light on everyday phenomena and realities and contextualizes her notion of "realism" in the editorial framing of her letter as "deriv[ed] theor[y] from specific examples and not the other way around."[42] With "the other way around," she seems to disagree with and gesture toward contemporaneous protagonists who affiliated themselves with Aldo Rossi when applying a theory knitted around archaic, seemingly universal building types as "realist" on specific urban contexts instead.[43] Focusing on the American suburb and commercial urban settings—for example, with a case study of the aesthetics of Levittown housing types, which she classifies as "Colonial," "Jubilee," "Levittowner," "Rancher," and "Country Clubber"—Scott Brown carves out the continuity and transformations of visual languages that signify and symbolize specific socially constructed meanings. Her method of iconographic analysis or "taxonomy" of the symbols of different housing types is empirically inductive and based in visual culture and vocabularies.

In her consideration and in contrast to Handlin, Scott Brown highlights the influence of advertisements produced by a housing industry seeking to plant style aspirations in the heads of its lower-middle-class consumers even as it reflects their subconscious desires and nostalgia.[44] Her dissection of space in *Signs of Life* can be considered another attempt at reconstructing vectors of agency in the built environment.

Activist Impacts—Formats of Education and Participation
If the contributions of Blumer, Handlin, and Scott Brown make clear that their authors were shifting attention away from an idealized, abstracted mechanical user figure to a socially constructed inhabitant with desires and aspirations raised by consumer culture, cultural identification processes, and social standing, they still did not attribute to users much agency vis-à-vis the built environment or their impact on its planning. Authors like Handlin questioned whether assuming architects who promoted the concepts of flexibility or mobility had collective needs in mind or reflected their own privileged and playful perspective.[45] At the other end of the debate spectrum, we find an article by the couple Marianne Günter and Roland Günter.

Married since 1963, Marianne (Janne) Günter, a pharmaceutical graduate of the University of Bonn, worked during her secondary studies in sociology alongside her husband on citizens' initiatives fighting for the preservation of approximately one thousand workers' settlements in the Ruhr area.[46] Their *archithese* contribution, which concerns the impact of grassroots movements taking on architecture and urban planning projects, not only summarizes past initiatives in which they had been involved but also shares suggestions for how to make an impact; for example, by filing complaints. Their activist field guide forgoes the DIY activism of late-1960s counterculture "cookbooks" that argue for abandoning urban settings altogether in favor of building alternative (dome) communes.[47] Instead, the Günters cite the massive urban redevelopment projects throughout Europe and the United States in the late 1960s that turned old towns and derelict city centers into business hubs. While politicians and other decision-makers primarily supported these decisions with arguments about wanting to increase standards of safety and hygiene, renewal, and beautification, the Günters justifiably denounce such notions of "care" as a pretext for authorizing the clearing of cities' unwelcome populations (read: low-income and/or immigrant). This process often went hand in hand with the displacement of specific demographics and the erection of massive complexes (e.g., the Jordaan neighborhood in Amsterdam or the destruction of the Bonn Südstadt quarter) to either house the offices or staff of increasingly international corporations; for example, from the pharmaceutical and chemical industries.[48] The comforts such complexes offered to their inhabitants or to the neighborhood more broadly were reduced to a bare minimum so as to build "rationally" or more "economically." Often the town planners' and investors' interest in "mobility" meant new expressways to accommodate individual traffic rather than the interests of all inhabitants, especially pedestrians. The authors see the sprouting grassroots initiatives they describe as a symptom not only of the malfunction of town and urban planning processes but of mistrust in political representatives, who prove to be insufficiently critical of the interests of developers and the construction industry generally—or, worse, prove to be biased toward the interests of investors and building enterprises. In weighing the effectiveness of grassroots initiatives, the authors suggest the use of such proven tactics as involving children or other figures with whom the public can easily identify. However, they warn that exposure can result in block lists, since interest groups in cities are often intertwined, and targeted corporations have little to lose by sharing the names of opponents with third parties. Recognizing that marginalized individuals are already precariously situated and that activism would only further compound their exposure, the authors suggest that protagonists embrace multiplicity and diversity by working across groups and employing a variety of tactics so as to share responsibilities broadly within the collective. Better-earning citizens of higher social standing are summoned to join the efforts in a "mosaic" approach, thus presenting a unified front of constituents capable of putting pressure on policymakers.[49]

That denouncing processes of capitalization within the building industry can backfire is demonstrated by architect Janssen's dismissal as a guest lecturer from ETH Zurich after he completed his project seminar (1971).[50] The self-organized, bottom-up learning entity understood itself as a (Marxist) collective, investigating the means and conditions of production in architecture under capitalism. More precisely, it scrutinized recent building projects by the Swiss private developer Ernst Göhner AG and the political and economic mechanisms and power-related frameworks at stake. In its contribution to one of the first *archithese* issues, the so-called editorial collective of students from the experimental seminar looked back on its case study of the Göhner housing estate in Volketswil, Switzerland. In a later interview, Janssen pointed out that his motivation for the seminar lay in the observation that "architects do not play the central role they attribute to themselves; instead, they are the interpreters of developments in the construction industry."[51] By asking basic questions—"How does the hypothecary market influence city planning in Zurich? How are land prices and traffic planning intertwined?"—the collective geared its analytical instruments toward "Göhnerswil," a particularly instructive case because it involved a conglomerate. "Belonging to this conglomerate was a factory for prefabricated components for residential development and various buyers whose task it was to acquire land without sellers being aware that the different brokers were connected. Today it's called 'short selling.' Göhner purchased these properties not as sites zoned for building but as agricultural land. That is a capitalist trick."[52] For allowing the seminar to be partly organized by the students, who even issued a periodical mouthpiece called *Harte Zeiten* (Hard times), Janssen came under the scrutiny of the Swiss Secret Service, which at the time was keenly recording all supposed communist activity.[53] Bernhard Hoesli, dean of the architecture department at ETH, dismissed Janssen in spring 1971. Janssen's replacement was the Italian architect Aldo Rossi. The impact of his decidedly different approach, theoretically focused on the continuity of historic forms while remaining informed by Marxist thought, and its contrast with Janssen's tactics have been broadly discussed elsewhere.[54] What, though, is the significance of *archithese* giving his seminar a platform at a moment when it was being torn apart and denounced in the press by the Bund der Schweizerischer Architekten (Federation of Swiss Architects) as a potentially obnoxious aftershock of May '68?[55] The commitment to the contents of Janssen's seminar reflects the critical approach taken in other early *archithese* features, such as sociologist Eliane Perrin's analysis of "immigrant worker housing" barracks, which almost killed the periodical in its infancy. Perrin's article would later be followed by an entire thematic issue of *archithese* dedicated to the topic of *Hochschulpolitik* (higher education politics) and informed by a six-point questionnaire addressing educators as different as Alvin Boyarsky, Lucius Burckhardt, Kenneth Frampton, Roland Günter, and Charles Jencks.[56] *archithese* was a playground to negotiate and mediate the different positions. It hence proved its agency as a discursive architectural medium.

1   Ákos Moravánszky and Karl Kegler, eds., *Re-scaling the Environment: New Landscapes of Design, 1960–1980*, East West Central: Re-building Europe, 1950–1990, vol. 2 (Basel: Birkhäuser, 2016).

2   See Charles Jencks, *The Language of Post-modern Architecture* (New York: Rizzoli, 1977).

3   See Rolf Keller, *Bauen als Umweltzerstörung, Alarmbilder einer Unarchitektur der Gegenwart* (Zurich: Verlag für Architektur Artemis, 1973).

4   See Yuriko Furuhata, "Multimedia Environments and Security Operations: Expo '70 as a Laboratory of Governance," *Grey Room*, 54 (Winter 2004): 56–79.

5   See Irina Davidovici, "From Idealism to Disenchantment: Realism in and beyond archithese," 123–40 in this publication.

6   Ernst Neufert, *Architect's Data* (1936; London: Crosby Lockwood Staples, 1970); Le Corbusier, *The Modulor: A Harmonious Measure to the Human Scale, Universally Applicable to Architecture and Mechanics* (1950; Basel: Birkhäuser, 2004); Henry Dreyfuss with Alvin R. Tilley, *The Measure of Man: Human Factors in Design*, rev. and exp. 2nd ed. (New York: Whitney Library of Design, 1967); Alexander Kira, *The Bathroom: The Essence of Minimalism* (Ithaca, NY: Center for Housing and Environmental Studies, Cornell University, 1966). For an in-depth discussion of the different types and the development of standard graphic design "users," see Ellen Lupton, "Designing for People," in *Beautiful Users*, ed. Ellen Lupton, 20–31 (New York: Cooper Hewitt, Smithsonian Design Museum, 2014), 24–25.

7   See Anna-Maria Meister, "Formatting Modern Man on Paper: Ernst Neufert's 'Lehren,'" *History of Knowledge*, May 21, 2018, https://historyofknowledge.net/2018/05/21/formatting-modern-man-on-paper/.

8   Dreyfuss and Tilley, *The Measure of Man* (see note 6). See also Aimi Hamraie, *Building Access: Universal Design and the Politics of Disability* (Minneapolis: University of Minnesota Press, 2017), 19–40, here 37.

9   See Paul B. Preciado, "Architecture as a Practice of Biopolitical Disobedience," *Log* 25 (2012): 121–34.

10   Henri Lefèbvre, "Space and the State" (1978), in *Henri Lefebvre, State Space World: Selected Essays*, ed. Neil Brenner and Stuart Elden, 223–53 (Minneapolis: University of Minnesota Press, 2009), 235. See also Łukasz Stanek, *Henri Lefebvre on Space: Architecture, Urban Research and the Production of Theory* (Minneapolis: University of Minnesota Press, 2011), 71; Łukasz Stanek, "For and against the 'User,'" in *Use Matters: An Alternative History of Architecture*, ed. Kenny Cupers (London: Routledge, 2013), 139–52.

11   Kenny Cupers, "Introduction," in *Use Matters* (see note 10), 1–12, Where 1–2.

12   See Isabelle Doucet and Kenny Cupers, "Agency in Architecture: Reframing Criticality in Theory and Practice," in "Agency in Architecture: Reframing Criticality in Theory and Practice," ed. Isabelle Doucet and Kenny Cupers, special issue, *Footprint*, 4 (Spring 2009), 1–6.

13   See Kenny Cupers, "The Expertise of Participation: Mass Housing and Urban Planning in Post-war France," *Planning Perspectives* 26, 1 (January 2011): 29–53; Kenny Cupers, "The Infrastructure of Participation: Cultural Centers in Postwar Europe," in *Participation in Art and Architecture: Spaces of Interaction and Occupation*, ed. Martino Stierli and Mechtild Widrich, 13–39 (London: I.B. Tauris, 2015), 13.

14   Stierli and Widrich, *Participation in Art and Architecture* (see note 13), 3–4.

15   See Matrix, "Working with Women," in *Making Space: Women and the Man-Made Environment* (London: Pluto Press, 1984), 89–105; Matrix Open: Feminist Architecture Archive, http://www.matrixfeministarchitecturearchive.co.uk/.

16   Nancy Fraser, "Rethinking the Public Sphere: A Contribution to the Critique of Actually Existing Democracy," *Social Text* 25/26 (1990): 56–80.

17   Lauren Berlant and Michael Warner, "Sex in Public," in "Intimacy," special issue, *Critical Inquiry* 24, 2 (Winter 1998): 547–66.

18   See Bruno Latour, "On Actor-Network Theory: A Few Clarifications," *Soziale Welt* 47, 4 (1996), 369–82.

19   See Nishat Awan, Tatjana Schneider, and Jeremy Till, eds., *Spatial Agency: Other Ways of Doing Architecture* (London: Routledge, 2011).

20   See especially, Donna Haraway, "Situated Knowledges: The Science Question in Feminism and the Privilege of Partial Perspective," *Feminist Studies* 14, 3 (Autumn 1988): 575–99.

21   Shannon Mattern, "Maintenance and Care," *Places Journal*, November 2018, https://doi.org/10.22269/181120.

22   Colin Lorne, "Spatial Agency and Practicing Architecture beyond Buildings," *Social and Cultural Geography* 18, 2 (2017): 268–87.

23   See Jacques Blumer, "Atelier 5: 1955–1975: Experiments in Communal Living," 364–76 in this publication. First published in *archithese* 14 (1975): 37–42.

24   See Torsten Lange, "Between Crisis and Myth: The City at the End of Modernity," 213–31 in this publication.

25   See Franziska Bollerey, Kristiana Hartmann, "Collective Housing: Theories and Experiments of the Utopian Socialists Robert Owen (1771–1858) and Charles Fourier (1772–1837)," 252–71 in this publication.

26   See Jacques Blumer, "Atelier 5: 1955–1975: Experiments in Communal Living" (see note 23), 369.

27   David P. Handlin, "Group Portraits and Self-Portraits: Some Remarks on Recent Approaches to Town Planning," 350–62 in this publication. First published in *archithese* 9 (1974): 45–52.

28   Herbert Gans, *The Urban Villagers: Group and Class in the Life of Italian-Americans* (New York: Free Press of Glencoe, 1962).

29   Ibid.

30   Handlin, "Group Portraits and Self-Portraits," (see note 27), 356.

31   Ibid., 361.

32   In the same thematic issue that featured Handlin's contribution, *archithese* also published a more optimistic article on that very topic. See Praful C. Patel, Jeff Racki, and Reena Racki, "Squatters: The Seven Housing Systems of Nairobi*," 450–67 in this publication. First published in *archithese* 9 (1974): 27–38. See also Samia Henni, "The Colonial Order of Things," 389–403 in this publication.

33   For a different take, see Henni, "The Colonial Order of Things," 389–403 in this publication.

34   Handlin, "Group Portraits and Self-Portraits" (see note 27).

35   Denise Scott Brown, "Signs of Life: Symbols in the American City," 378–85 in this publication, here 385. First published in *archithese* 19 (1976): 29–33.

36   Marianna Charitonidou, "Denise Scott Brown's Active Socio-plastics and Urban Sociology: From Learning from West End to Learning from Levittown," *Urban, Planning and Transport Research* 10, 1 (2022): 131–58, here 133, 136; Denise Scott Brown, "Towards an Active Socio-plastics," in Denise Scott Brown, *Architecture Words 4: Having Words* (London: Architectural Association, 2009), 22–54.

37   Herbert J. Gans, *The Levittowners: Ways of Life and Politics in a New Suburban Community* (New York: Pantheon Books, 1967).

38   Charitonidou, "Denise Scott Brown's Active Socioplastics" (see note 36), 136–37.

39   Scott Brown, "Signs of Life" (see note 35), 378

40   Ibid.

41   Pierre Bourdieu, *Distinction: A Social Critique of the Judgement of Taste* (London: Keegan Paul, 1984). First published as *La distinction: Critique sociale du jugement* (Paris: Les Editions de Minuit, 1979).

42   Scott Brown, "Signs of Life" (see note 35), 378.

43   See Davidovici, "From Idealism to Disenchantment" (see note 5).

44   Scott Brown, "Signs of Life" (see note 35).

45   See Handlin, "Group Portraits and Self-Portraits" (see note 27).

46   See Roland Günter, Janne Günter, and Karl Wiemer, eds., *Die Arbeitersiedlung Eisenheim in Oberhausen*, Rheinische Kunststätten 541 (Cologne: Rheinischer Verein für Denkmalpflege und Landschaftsschutz, 2013).

47   See Leopold Banchini and Lukas Feireiss, eds., with text by Lloyd Kahn, *Shelter Cookbook* (Berlin: Spector Books, 2023).

48   See Marianne Günter and Roland Günter, "Citizens' Action Groups: How, Where, Why?," 338–49 in this publication. First published in *archithese* 1 (1972): 20–26.

49   Ibid., 346.

50   Even though the third-party parity council of the department of architecture had advised keeping them, the three German guest lecturers of the so-called experimental phase, Hans-Otto Schulte, Jörn Janssen and Hermann Zinn, were dismissed by the ETH board. Only the sociologist Lucius Burckhardt was allowed to keep his visiting lectureship for another year. In 1973 he left to become a professor at the newly established reform university Gesamthochschule (GhK) in Kassel.

See Peter Sutter, "Lucius Burckhardt-Wackernagel," in Ueli Mäder, Peter Sutter, Markus Bossert et al., eds., *Raum und Macht: Die Stadt zwischen Vision und Wirklichkeit; Leben und Wirken von Lucius und Annemarie Burckhardt* (Zurich: Rotpunktverlag, 2014), 21–70, here 46–47. See Bruno Reichlin and Jörn Janssen in conversation with Anne Kockelkorn and Axel Sowa, "Zurich, 1971: A Conversation on the Housing Question, Academic Intrigue, and an Italian Maestro," *Candide: Journal for Architectural Knowledge* 7 (October 2013): 113–40. See Hartmut Frank in conversation with Andreas Müller, Beat Schweingruber, Jan Verwijnen, and Adolf Max Vogt, "Zeitzeugen über die 68er-Ereignisse an der ETH Zürich. Das Phänomen 'Göhnerswil,'" *Werk, Bauen + Wohnen* 87, 7/8 (2000): 32–35.

51   See Jörn Janssen, "Die Architekten im Arbeitsprozess der Bauproduktion: Scheinselbständig," in *Produktionsbedingungen der Architektur: Zwischen Autonomie und Heteronomie*, ed. Tilo Amhoff, Henrik Hilbig, and Gernot Weckherlin (Dresden: Thelem, 2017), 41–50; Bruno Reichlin et al., "Zurich, 1971" (see note 50), 118–19.

52   Reichlin et al., "Zurich, 1971" (see note 51), 118–19.

53   Ibid., 130–31.

54   See Aldo Rossi, Judith Hopfengärtner, and Ákos Moravánszky, *Aldo Rossi und die Schweiz: Architektonische Wechselwirkungen* (Zurich: gta Verlag, 2011).

55   Reichlin et al., "Zurich, 1971" (see note 51), 132–33.

56   There were many more. Eliane Perrin, "Immigrant Worker Housing in Switzerland," 404–19 in this publication. First published in *archithese* 1 (1971): 2–11. See also "Hochschulpolitik," special issue, *archithese* 4 (1972).

Projektstudium an der ETH: kritisch statt technokratisch

Dieser Text wurde von einem Redaktionskollektiv des Seminars Janssen an der ETH verfasst und erschien zuerst in der Seminarzeitschrift *Harte Zeiten* vom 5. Juli 1971. Wir geben hier eine leicht gekürzte Fassung.

Im vergangenen Sommer beschloss das ETH-Präsidium die Lehraufträge dreier Gastdozenten der Architekturabteilung nicht mehr zu verlängern, mit der Begründung, man hätte in ihren Seminarien linke Agitation betrieben. Es handelt sich um die Soziologen Hermann Zinn, Hans-Otto Schulte und Jörn Janssen; mit ihnen verloren auch zehn Assistenten die Stelle.

Das Ereignis hat Wellen geworfen. Fronten haben sich gebildet, und verhärtet. Das hat sein Gutes: es bringt einige der wichtigsten offenen Fragen der heutigen Architektursituation aufs Tapet. Es hat aber auch sein Schlechtes: gerne wird nun Information durch doktrinäre Simplifikate ersetzt – zu beiden Seiten.

Wir haben uns entschlossen, einige Texte aus den umstrittenen Seminarien abzudrucken; zunächst, um einen Versuch zu machen, den allgemeinen Informationsmangel abzubauen. Aber auch, weil wir überzeugt sind, dass sich Architektur nicht nur im technischen organisatorischen oder visuellen, sondern auch im sozialen und politischen Raum abspielt. Sofern man von einer Hochschule wissenschaftliche Analysen gegebener Zustände erwartet, so gehören, scheint uns, derartige Untersuchungen in ihr Studienprogramm; sofern man von einer Architekturschule den Bezug zur Praxis fordert, so gehört (wenn auch nicht ausschliesslich!) die soziale und politische Praxis dazu.

Das sind Lappalien, die heute weiterum selbstverständlich sind. Vielleicht werden nur wenige Jahre vergehen, bis auch die obersten ETH-Instanzen stolz daran erinnern werden, dass im Jahre 1970-71 die ersten «kritischen Projektseminarien» durchgeführt wurden. Der erste Versuch ist gescheitert – nicht zufällig zum gleichen Zeitpunkt, wo in Paris die Schliessung des «Institut de l'Environnement» verfügt wurde. Aber die Arbeit geht weiter. S.v.M.

Das didaktische Modell des sogenannten Projektstudiums wird seit längerer Zeit in vielen Hochschulen diskutiert. Diese Diskussion beschränkt sich nicht nur auf Architekturschulen. Ein Projektstudium kann auch in anderen Fachbereichen, z. B. der Soziologie, der Medizin und der Rechtswissenschaften durchgeführt werden.

Im Falle der Architektur geht die Diskussion über das Projektstudium vom traditionellen Berufsbild des Architekten und Planers aus. Die heutige Ausbildung des Architekten richtet sich noch weitgehend nach diesem veralteten Berufsbild. Es handelt sich dabei um den freischaffenden, selbständigen Künstlerarchitekten. Er erhebt den Anspruch, einzelne Fachbereiche zu koordinieren. Seine Forderung nach Selbstverwirklichung seiner Persönlichkeit findet ihre Grenze erst in den Schranken der finanziellen Möglichkeiten des Auftraggebers.

Die Entwicklung in der Bauwirtschaft fordert nun eine neue Berufsausbildung der Architekten. Die Bauwirtschaft verbindet sich nämlich zunehmend mit der Struktur anderer Industrie- und Wirtschaftszweige. Dies hat zur Folge, dass in jüngster Zeit Unternehmen der chemischen, metallverarbeitenden und der Elektro-Industrie, wie auch reine Finanzierungsunternehmen, im Bereich des klassischen Bauhauptgewerbes tätig geworden sind. Mit der fortschreitenden Wirtschafts- und Kapitalkonzentration vergrössert sich die Abhängigkeit der Architekten und Planer. Sie sind nur kleingewerblich-ständisch organisiert und können somit keinen Einfluss auf diese Entwicklung nehmen. Damit zeigt sich, dass das traditionelle Berufsbild nicht mehr der Realität entspricht, und somit die alten Ausbildungskonzepte neu gestaltet werden müssen.

Die Notwendigkeit einer Neugestaltung der Ausbildung wird in weiten Kreisen gesehen. Einmal ist die Bauwirtschaft selbst nicht mehr zufrieden mit der wenig wirkungsvollen Ausbildung der Architekten und Planer. Die Ausbildungskosten scheinen ihr zu hoch im Verhältnis zum vermittelten Stoff. Andererseits sind gesellschaftliche Widersprüche vor allem in der Stadtplanung vermehrt deutlich geworden. Die bisherige Ausbildung der Architekten hat jedoch diese Widersprüche bewusst ausgeklammert.

Es gibt zwei mögliche Reaktionen auf diese Entwicklung:

1. Die technokratische Hochschulreform, die von der Industrie und Verwaltung gefordert wird. Ihr Ziel liegt in einer Ausbildung, die den wach-

Project-Based Learning at the ETH: Critical Rather Than Technocratic

Author:
Seminar Jansen
[AA.VV]

Source:
archithese, 3+4 (1971): 62–66

Translated by:
Steven Lindberg

This text was written by the editorial collective of the Janssen Seminar at the ETH [Swiss Federal Institute of Technology in Zurich] and first published in the seminar's journal *Harte Zeiten* on July 5, 1971. We offer a slightly abridged version here.

Last summer, the ETH board voted not to extend the teaching contracts of three visiting lecturers in the architecture department, with the justification that they had engaged in leftist agitation in their seminars. The lecturers in question were the sociologists Hermann Zinn, Hans-Otto Schulte, and Jörn Janssen; along with them, ten assistants also lost their positions.

The event made waves. Fronts formed and became entrenched. That has its good side: it brings up for discussion several of the most important open questions of the current situation in architecture. It also has its bad side, however: now, information is often replaced by doctrinaire simplifications — on both sides.

We have decided to reprint several texts from the controversial seminars; first, in an effort to remedy the general lack of information, but also because we are convinced that architecture plays out not only in technical, organizational, or visual space but also in social and political space. To the extent one expects scientific analyses of given circumstances from a university, such studies, it seems to us, belong in their programs; to the extent an architecture school is expected to have a connection to practice, social and political practice is part of that (albeit not exclusively!).

These are trifles that again seem self-evident today. Perhaps only a few years will pass before the supreme authorities at the ETH, too, proudly recall that the first "critical project seminars" were held in the years 1970–71. The first attempt failed — not coincidentally, at the same time as the closing of the Institut de l'Environnement in Paris was decreed. But the work goes on.

S.v.M.

The didactic model of the so-called project-based learning has been discussed for some time at many universities. This discussion is not limited to architecture schools. Project-based learning can also be carried out in other disciplines; for example, sociology, medicine, or law.

In the case of architecture, the discussion of the project-based learning derives from the traditional profile of the profession of the architect and planner. Today's education of architects is still largely based on this outdated profile of the profession; namely, the freelance, independent artist-architect. He claims to coordinate several specialist fields. His demand for the self-fulfillment of his personality finds its limits only in the restrictions of his client's financial means.

The evolution of the construction business now demands a new professional education of architects. For the construction business increasingly joins with the structure of other branches of industry and business. As a consequence, companies from the chemical, metalworking, and electronics industries, as well as purely financial enterprises, have recently become active in the traditional mainstream construction sector. As the concentration of business and capital progresses, the dependence of architects and planners increases. They are organized only as small businesses and professions and therefore cannot influence this evolution. This makes it clear that the traditional profile of the profession no longer corresponds to reality, and hence the old concepts of education have to be redesigned.

The need to redesign education is widely recognized. First, the construction business itself is no longer satisfied with the impractical education of architects and planners. The education's costs seem to them too high relative to the material conveyed. On the other side, social contradictions have become increasingly evident, especially in urban planning. Until now, however, the education of architects has consciously ignored these contradictions.

There are two possible reactions to this development:

1. The technocratic university reform demanded by the industry and the administration. The goal of this reform is an education that satisfies the increasing planning needs of the industry and the administration.

2. The critical university reform demanded by those affected by building planning. The goal of this reform is the education of architects and planners who are conscious of their growing political role. Only then they can act entirely responsibly toward society.

Both approaches call for a stronger connection to practice, which project-based learning might enable. They are referring, however, to two different forms of project study that hardly overlap—apart from the call for a connection to practice, specialization, and group work. These overlaps cannot conceal the different goals of the two forms of project study.

Technocratically oriented project-based learning serves only to consolidate the existing social conditions. Social contradictions are not addressed, much less eliminated. The technocratically educated architects serve above all the interests of those who invest their capital in the construction business.

Critically oriented project-based learning ought to consider the interests of the majority of the population. This necessarily happens against the interests of business and bureaucracy.

Critically educated architects are supposed to reveal existing injustices and study their social contexts. They ought to develop solutions that may also lie outside the realm of architecture. If the problem cannot be solved by means of architecture, political measures can also be proposed—for example, the *Recht auf Wohnung* [Right to Housing] initiative—as opposed to trying to lower rents by reducing the floor area.

Here, then, is an example to illustrate the contrast between the technocratic and critical project-based learning:

Example of Technocratic Project-Based Learning

As part of a reform of the construction guidelines for the area around Tessinerplatz, the municipal council of Zurich voted in 1947 to eliminate Venedigstrasse. Because this area is part of the core area, this resolution meant that the adjoining properties could be used more intensely than before. In recent times, these properties have all been held by one owner, so nothing stands in the way of an extensive redevelopment following modern principles.

1. A search for alternative proposals for the use of the area described (i.e., an ideas competition; work required: ca. two weeks).

2. Compilation of a catalog of criteria for selecting the optimal proposal (to be performed as work in groups).

3. Selection of an alternative to be refined collectively, after establishing a binding space allocation plan.

4. Individual students work out their plans by the end of the semester.

5. Work in small groups to find the best designs based on organizational/functional, constructional, or formal/design criteria.

6. Final presentation of the groups' work in the presence of several interested representatives (i.e., of the city planning office, the *Rentenanstalt* [Pension Company], and the Hatt-Haller company).

The "Critical" Alternative

In a critical project seminar, by contrast, such an assignment would have to look fundamentally different. A chair could not formulate it in advance or provide such

senden Planungserfordernissen der Industrie und Verwaltung genügen sollen.

2. Die kritische Hochschulreform, die von den Betroffenen der Bauplanung gefordert wird. Ihr Ziel liegt in der Ausbildung von Architekten und Planern, die sich ihrer wachsenden politischen Funktion bewusst sind. Nur so können sie gesellschaftlich voll verantwortlich handeln.

Beide Richtungen fordern einen grösseren Praxisbezug, der sich im Projektstudium realisieren liesse. Es handelt sich jedoch um zwei verschiedene Formen von Projektstudium, die sich kaum überschneiden — abgesehen etwa von der Forderung des Praxisbezugs, der Spezialisierung und der Gruppenarbeit. Diese Überschneidungen können nicht über die unterschiedlichen Ziele der beiden Formen des Projektstudiums hinwegtäuschen.

Das technokratisch ausgerichtete Projektstudium dient allein der Festigung der bestehenden gesellschaftlichen Verhältnisse. Gesellschaftliche Widersprüche werden dabei nicht berührt oder gar beseitigt. Die technokratisch ausgebildeten Architekten dienen vor allem den Interessen jener, die ihr Kapital in der Bauwirtschaft anlegen.

Das kritisch ausgerichtete Projektstudium soll die Interessen der Mehrheit der Bevölkerung berücksichtigen. Dies muss notfalls gegen die Interessen der Wirtschaft und der Verwaltung geschehen. Kritisch ausgebildete Architekten sollen vorhandene Missstände aufzeigen und ihre gesellschaftlichen Zusammenhänge untersuchen. Sie sollen Lösungen suchen, die möglicherweise auch ausserhalb des architektonischen Bereiches liegen können. Lässt sich das Problem nicht mit architektonischen Mitteln lösen, so können auch politische Massnahmen vorgeschlagen werden — wie zum Beispiel die Initiative « Recht auf Wohnung », statt des Versuches, die Wohnungsmiete durch eine Verkleinerung des Grundrisses zu senken.

Ein Beispiel soll den Gegensatz von technokratischem und kritischem Projektstudium aufzeigen:

Beispiel eines technokratischen Projektstudiums

Der Zürcher Gemeinderat beschloss im Jahre 1947 — im Rahmen einer Neuordnung der Baulinien für das Gebiet um den Tessinerplatz — die Aufhebung der Venedigstrasse. Da dieses Gebiet zum Kerngebiet gehört, ist durch diesen Beschluss für die anliegenden Grundstücke eine intensivere Nutzung als bisher möglich. Seit kurzem befinden sich diese Grundstücke in einer Hand, womit einer

Etudes critiques ou études technocratiques à l'ETH ?

Actuellement, la formation de l'architecte se réfère encore largement à une conception surannée de la profession : à l'idéal de l'architecte-artiste, indépendant et libéral. Or cette conception est de plus en plus contestée aujourd'hui. Le développement de l'industrie du bâtiment exige à cet égard, une réforme de la formation professionnelle de l'architecte, correspondant aux impératifs de l'industrialisation. L'architecte doit devenir en quelque sorte un expert technique qui concrétise le plus fidèlement possible les desiderata de l'industrie du bâtiment.

Tout ceci est d'autant plus problématique que la concentration du capital dans le commerce et l'industrie a eu des conséquences socialement irresponsables, en particulier quant au développement des villes.

Alors que la Direction de l'ETH présente un programme officiel de réformes qui entend avant tout tenir compte des exigences de l'industrie du bâtiment, nos auteurs proposent l'étude critique de projets architecturaux et urbanistiques. Cette étude offrirait à l'architecte un aperçu des mécanismes de décision qui déterminent actuellement la construction et lui permet de s'assumer dans ce contexte une responsabilité active. Alors que la réforme technocratique tient essentiellement compte des intérêts de l'industrie du bâtiment, les propositions de nos auteurs s'efforcent de tenir compte des besoins réels de la population.

Les auteurs illustrent cette alternative en citant un exemple zurichois récent: en 1947, la Municipalité de Zurich décida de transformer l'ancien quartier d'habitation de la Venedigstrasse en zone de développement urbain. Dans le cadre d'une étude technocratique, on se limiterait à mettre sur pied, par un travail de groupe, un projet de construction de haute qualité architecturale pour remplacer l'ancienne zone d'habitation.

Une étude critique devrait, au contraire, soupeser d'abord les avantages et les désavantages que pourrait entraîner cet « assainissement » pour la population et envisager ensuite la solution la plus acceptable pour les gens du quartier, en tenant compte en particulier des croissantes difficultés des classes les plus défavorisées de se reloger.

De tels critères ont été appliqués à l'occasion d'un séminaire de Jörn Janssen, dans l'analyse de la construction d'un ensemble d'habitation dans la banlieue zurichoise. Il s'agit de l'ensemble réalisé par le consortium Göhner dans la commune de Volketswil.

Les résultats préliminaires de cette analyse montrent avec évidence que cet ensemble — en dépit de la crise du logement surtout des travailleurs étrangers — est destiné exclusivement à la couche supérieure de la classe moyenne ; que l'on avait systématiquement éludé les procédés démocratiques de décision ; que la commune de Volketswil connaît maintenant de sérieuses difficultés, les moyens nécessaires aux installations subséquentes manquant. De plus, l'ensemble Göhner est en opposition flagrante avec les lignes directives de la planification régionale.

Malheureusement, les spécialistes suisses jusqu'ici n'ont jamais examiné vraiment de tels procédés. De même la Direction de l'ETH semble-t-elle chercher également à éviter de discuter ces problèmes. Il faut d'ailleurs comprendre dans ce sens la décision des autorités de l'Ecole de renoncer à l'enseignement des deux sociologues J. Janssen et H. Zinn.

grosszügigen Überbauung nach neuzeitlichen Gesichtspunkten nichts mehr im Wege steht.
1. Gesucht sind alternative Nutzungsvorschläge für das beschriebene Gebiet (d.h. ein Ideenwettbewerb; Arbeitsaufwand: ca. 2 Wochen)
2. Aufstellen eines Kriterienkataloges zur Auswahl des optimalen Vorschlages (dies soll in Gruppenarbeit geschehen).
3. Auswahl einer Alternative zur gemeinsamen Weiterbearbeitung, nach Erstellen eines verbindlichen Raumprogrammes.
4. Individuelle Entwurfsbearbeitung bis zum Ende des Semesters.
5. Ausarbeitung der besten Entwürfe in kleinen Gruppen nach organisatorisch-funktionellen, baukonstruktiven oder formal-gestalterischen Kriterien.
6. Abschliessende Präsentation der Gruppenarbeit in Anwesenheit einiger interessierter Herren aus der Praxis (Vertreter des Stadtplanungsamtes, der Rentenanstalt und der Firma Hatt-Haller).

Die «kritische» Alternative

In einem kritischen Projektseminar dagegen müsste eine solche Aufgabenstellung grundsätzlich anders aussehen. Eine Vorformulierung durch einen Lehrstuhl und die Aufstellung eines so exakten Zeitplans wären nicht möglich. Die Arbeit müsste sich an einem Rahmenthema orientieren, das ein bestimmtes Problemfeld beschreibt. Dieses Rahmenthema müsste für mehrere Projektseminare verbindlich sein, d.h. etwa vom Abteilungsrat für mehrere Semester als Forschungsaufgabe gestellt werden.

Es könnte in unserem Beispielfall verkürzt folgendermassen lauten: Im Kerngebiet der Stadt Zürich sind deutliche Entmischungstendenzen zu erkennen. Die wachsende wirtschaftliche Bedeutung der Stadt und die damit verbundene Konzentration von Verwaltungsbauten in der City hat eine Verschärfung des Wohnungsmarktes zur Folge. Die Abteilung I beabsichtigt deshalb, in den nächsten Semestern die mit dieser Tendenz zusammenhängenden Phänomene sowohl auf ihre Ursachen hin als auch in ihren Auswirkungen zu untersuchen. Im Anschluss daran sollen Strategien entwickelt werden, die geeignet erscheinen, die gegenwärtig zu beobachtenden Widersprüche zu beseitigen. Alle Projektseminare sollen an diesem Problemkreis orientiert werden und selbstgewählte damit zusammenhängende Fragestellungen bearbeiten. Die für den Fortgang dieser Arbeit erforderlichen Grundkurse — z.B. über Bauwirtschaft und Konjunktursteuerung, Betriebsorganisation und Kalkulation in Baubetrieben, Statistik, Sozialpsychologie, Soziologie u.ä. — werden von der Abteilung eingerichtet, sobald inhaltliche Vorschläge seitens der Projektseminare vorliegen.

Folgende spezielle Fragestellungen können beispielsweise Projektinhalte darstellen:
1. Welchen Einfluss haben die Hypothekenbanken und Versicherungen auf die Zürcher Stadtplanung?
2. Welcher Zusammenhang besteht zwischen den Bodenmarktverhältnissen in Zürich und der Verkehrsplanung, insbesondere der U-Bahnplanung?
3. War die Bildung des Bewohnervereins Venedigstrasse ein Schritt zur Demokratisierung der Planung?
4. Müssen die aus der Innenstadt verdrängten Wohnungsmieter Nachteile in Kauf nehmen, z.B. hinsichtlich Grundriss, Grösse, Ausstattung und Preis ihrer Wohnung?
5. Ist die Bauproduktion der Region in der Lage, eine genügende Anzahl billiger Wohnungen in der erforderlichen Zeit zu produzieren?
6. Welche Sozialisationsschäden ergeben sich aus der Wohnungsnot für die niedrigen Einkommensgruppen? Schaffen Notwohnungsamt und Mietgerichte genügend Abhilfe? u.a.m.

Seit einem Jahr wird an der Architekturabteilung der ETH Zürich in den jetzt liquidierten Seminarien systematisch an der Verwirklichung eines solchen kritischen Projektstudiums gearbeitet. Allerdings unter sehr erschwerten Umständen. Diese Seminare standen sehr isoliert da und mussten sich alle Grundkenntnisse intern selbst erarbeiten.

Als Beispiel: Das Seminar «Ökonomische Kriterien für Planungsentscheidungen»

Dieser Abschnitt wurde ebenfalls vom Redaktionskollektiv der Seminarzeitschrift *Harte Zeiten* verfasst und erschien zuerst in Nr. 6 vom 24. Juni 1971. Wir geben eine leicht gekürzte Fassung.

Als Projekt wurde die Zürcher Vorortsgemeinde Volketswil gewählt. Diese Gemeinde hat sich in den letzten Jahren vor allem «dank» der Bautätigkeit der Generalunternehmung Ernst Göhner AG von einem Dorf zu einer städtischen Vorortsgemeinde entwickelt. Zusammen mit Greifensee, Schwerzenbach und Fällanden weist sie, laut Volkszählung, zwischen 1960 und 1970 den grössten Bevölkerungszuwachs von allen Gemeinden des Kantons Zürich auf. Der Wohnungsbau in dieser Gemeinde geschieht in einem

an exact timeline. The work would have to be oriented around a framing theme that describes a specific set of problems. This framing theme would have to be binding for several project seminars; that is, set by the department committee as a research task for several semesters.

In short, in our example it might read as follows: The core area of the city of Zurich shows discernable tendencies toward a reduction of mixed use. The growing economic importance of the city and the associated concentration of government buildings in the city center has further aggravated the housing market. In the coming semesters, Department I therefore intends to study both the causes and the effects of the phenomena associated with this trend. Thereafter, strategies will be developed that seem suited to eliminate the conflicts that can be observed today. All the project seminars shall be oriented around this set of problems and work on related issues the students select themselves. The required introductory courses to pursue this work—for example, on the construction business and business cycle stabilization, company organization and calculation in the construction business, statistics, social psychology, sociology, etc.—will be established in the department as soon as proposals for the content of the project seminars are available.

The following special issues may, for example, be the subject matter of projects:

1. What influence do mortgage banks and insurance companies have on urban planning in Zurich?

2. What connection exists between the conditions of the land market in Zurich and transportation planning, especially subway planning?

3. Was the formation of the Bewohnerverein Venedigstrasse [Venedigstrasse Residents' Association] a step toward the democratization of planning?

4. Must the displaced tenants of urban housing accept disadvantages in, for example, floor plan, size, fixtures, and the cost of their homes?

5. Is construction in the region prepared to produce a sufficient number of cheap apartments in the required time?

6. What damages to socialization result from the housing shortage for lower-income groups? Are the office of emergency housing and the housing courts providing adequate remedies? And much more.

For a year, the now dissolved seminars have worked systematically toward implementing this sort of critical project-based learning at the architecture department of the ETH Zurich. Albeit under much more difficult conditions. These seminars are isolated and have to acquire internally, on their own, all the basic knowledge required.

An Example: The "Economic Criteria for Planning Decisions" Seminar

This section was also written by the editorial collective of the seminar journal *Harte Zeiten* and first published in issue no. 6 of June 24, 1971. We offer a slightly abridged version.

The Volketswil municipality of suburban Zurich was chosen as a project. This municipality has in recent years—above all, "thanks" to the construction activities of the Ernst Göhner AG general contracting company—developed from a village into an urban-suburban community. According to the census, it had the largest population increase of all the municipalities of the Canton of Zurich from 1960 to 1970, alongside Greifensee, Schwerzenbach, and Fällanden. Housing construction in the Volketswil municipality employed prefabricated elements, and a factory was built in the municipality itself for their production. The factory was built by the construction companies Losinger and Göhner (51 percent) under the name IGECO Volketswil. Of its production volume during the first five years (3,400 apartments), around 30 percent (1,200 apartments) were built in Volketswil.

The fifth semester, the winter semester of 1970–71, served almost exclusively for the gathering of empirical data on the developments of the Volketswil municipality, the Canton of Zurich, IGECO-Produktion, and the Göhner group.

The wealth of material that was within reach and soon obtained alone demonstrated the impossibility of conducting a so-called objective analysis. There were two main reasons for this:

1. For reasons of methodology and time, it was necessary to establish priorities for

collecting and organizing the material. Some of the available material, as well as potential further information, had to be disregarded.

2. Other available material could not be processed because it was not accessible. The owners of the information could easily block access to it (and did so).

That means: An "objective" analysis is already impossible because the owners of the information have no interest in an objective study from the opposite perspective.

The above-mentioned monopoly that certain information owners had on specific important materials occasionally forced our seminar to perform a kind of secret-service activity that is difficult to reconcile with the idea of independent scholarly research. It did not so much produce new information as reassess existing, unfortunately inadequate information (e.g., Ernst Göhner AG's cost estimate).

During the ongoing sixth semester, students began to analyze and problematize the material.

The overarching theme was now made more precise: "The influence of the construction industry on building planning." This influence will be described provisionally in the following areas:

The building production group is concerned with the technical process of housing production at Göhner. It is studying, for example, the question of where specific savings and improvements exist in the production of concrete-slab elements using the IGECO process; whether it is not perhaps the case that, under the pretext of an imperative for industrialization, quite different objectives are being pursued. What do these transformed conditions of production mean, precisely, for the true producers of the apartments; namely, the Italian and Spanish foreign workers? What influence does the demand for a return on capital investment (increasing competition, concentration, monopolization) have on the extent and structure of housing provision and the necessary upgrade of infrastructure?

The site selection study group observed that all the larger housing developments in the Zurich region were always built precisely where they did not belong, according to the official development plan of the regional planning authorities. On studying this phenomenon more closely, the group discovered the crucial role that land acquisition and the land market play in the housing production of a large company like Göhner. It therefore studied the origin and function of land prices and is currently working on various economic theories of ground rent.

We want to describe here in greater detail the work of the municipality autonomy group, because it played out in a way that seems typical of the development of project-oriented work in groups.

Initial studies and an interview with a representative from the municipal authorities made clear that satisfying needs had not been the primary planning motive, but had been integrated only so that the planning result—the built housing project—would be economically feasible (no exchange value without use value).

Consequently, the group described its theme as follows: It was decided to employ an empirical study in order to identify changes in the population's income and employment structure as a result of the development of the municipality from a village to a suburb of the city. The municipality's tax roll served as evidence to that end. Three years that exemplify the development of Volketswil were selected, and the relationships between income groups and professional groups as well as their shifts over the last seven years were studied.

Those and other preceding studies led to the following general conclusions:

1. Above all, the percentage of the upper middle class increased greatly in Volketswil; that is, the planning is for "high-income" classes.

2. Structures of democratic decision-making were completely steamrolled by the development, resulting in enormous difficulties for the municipality, which, both in terms of its powers and funds, struggles to cope with the accrued consequences of planning by private companies.

These results raised a question: What role does democratic decision-making play in the planning process? That is: the group now needs to look at the historical development of planning

Elementbauverfahren, für dessen Produktion in der Gemeinde selbst ein Werk errichtet worden ist. Das Werk wurde von den Baufirmen Losinger und Göhner (51 %) unter dem Namen «IGECO Volketswil» errichtet. Vom Produktionsvolumen der ersten fünf Jahre (3400 Wohnungen) wurden ca. 30 % (1200 Wohnungen) in Volketswil gebaut.

Das 5. Semester, Wintersemester 1970-71, diente fast ausschliesslich der Erhebung empirischen Materials über die Entwicklung der Gemeinde Volketswil, des Kantons Zürich, der IGECO-Produktion und des Göhner-Konzerns.

Schon die Fülle des erreichbaren und bald vorhandenen Materials zeigte, dass es unmöglich ist, eine sogenannt objektive Analyse durchzuführen. Dies vor allem aus zwei Gründen:

1. Aus arbeitstechnischen und zeitlichen Gründen war man gezwungen, bei der Beschaffung und Ordnung des Materials Prioritäten zu setzen. Vorhandenes und möglicherweise erreichbares Material musste also teilweise unberücksichtigt bleiben.

2. Anderes vorhandenes Material konnte nicht verarbeitet werden, weil es nicht zugänglich war. Informationsbesitzer konnten den Zugang zum Material leicht sperren (was auch geschah).

Das heisst: Eine «objektive» Analyse wird schon dadurch unmöglich, weil die Informationsbesitzer gar kein Interesse an einer objektiven Untersuchung von anderer Seite haben können.

Das oben erwähnte Monopol gewisser Informationsbesitzer über bestimmtes wichtiges Material drängte unser Seminar zum Teil in eine Art Geheimdiensttätigkeit, die sich nur schlecht mit der Vorstellung unabhängiger wissenschaftlicher Forschungsarbeit verbinden lässt. Es wurden weniger neue Erkenntnisse produziert als vielmehr vorhandene, nur leider unzugängliche, neu erarbeitet (z.B. die Kostenkalkulation der Ernst Göhner AG).

Während des laufenden 6. Semesters wurde die Analyse und Problematisierung des Stoffes begonnen.

Das Oberthema wurde jetzt präziser gefasst: «Der Einfluss der Bauwirtschaft auf die Bauplanung». Dieser Einfluss soll vorläufig in folgenden Bereichen beschrieben werden:

Die Gruppe Bauproduktion befasst sich mit dem technischen Verfahren der Wohnungsproduktion bei Göhner. Sie untersucht z.B. die Frage, worin bei der Herstellung von Schwerplatten-Betonelementen nach dem IGECO-Verfahren die konkreten Einsparungen und Verbesserungen denn nun bestehen; ob nicht vielleicht unter dem Vorwand einer notwendigen Industrialisierung objektiv ganz andere Ziele verfolgt worden sind. Was bedeuten diese veränderten Produktionsbedingungen nun gerade für die eigentlichen Produzenten der Wohnungen, nämlich die italienischen und spanischen Fremdarbeiter? Welchen Einfluss haben die Notwendigkeiten der Kapitalverwertung (Verschärfung der Konkurrenz, Konzentration, Monopolisierung) auf den Umfang und die Struktur des Wohnungsangebotes und der notwendigen Ergänzung der Infrastruktur?

Die Gruppe Standortwahl machte die Beobachtung, dass alle grösseren Siedlungen in der Region Zürich immer gerade dort entstanden sind, wo sie gemäss offiziellem Konzept der Regionalplanung gar nicht hingehört hätten. Bei den näheren Untersuchung dieses Phänomens erkannte die Gruppe die entscheidende Rolle, welche die Landbeschaffung und der Bodenmarkt für die Wohnungsproduktion eines Grossunternehmers wie Göhner spielen. Sie beschäftigte sich deshalb mit der Entstehung und Funktion der Bodenpreise und arbeitet im Augenblick über die verschiedenen ökonomischen Theorien der Grundrente.

Die Arbeit der Gruppe Gemeindeautonomie wollen wir im folgenden etwas genauer darstellen, weil uns ihr Ablauf typisch erscheint für die Entwicklung einer projektorientierten Gruppenarbeit.

Anhand erster Untersuchungen und eines Interviews mit einem Vertreter der Gemeindebehörde stellte sich deutlich heraus, dass eine Bedürfnisbefriedigung nicht der Anlass der ganzen Planung gewesen war, sondern nur deshalb einbezogen werden musste, damit das Planungsresultat — die gebaute Siedlung — wirtschaftlich verwertbar würde (kein Tauschwert ohne Gebrauchswert).

Daher umschrieb die Gruppe ihr Thema folgendermassen: Es wurde beschlossen, mittels einer empirischen Untersuchung die Veränderung der Einkommens- und Berufsstruktur der Bevölkerung zu ermitteln, als Folge der Entwicklung der Gemeinde von einem Dorf zur städtischen Vorortsgemeinde. Das Steuerregister der Gemeinde diente als Unterlage dazu. Es wurden drei für die Entwicklung von Volketswil exemplarische Jahre herausgenommen und die Relationen zwischen Einkommens- und Berufsgruppen und deren Verschiebungen in den letzten sieben Jahren untersucht.

Diese und die vorausgegangenen Untersuchungen führten zu den folgenden generellen Schlüssen:

1. Vor allem der gehobene Mittelstand hat in Volketswil prozentual sehr stark zugenommen, d. h. es wird für «kaufkräftige» Schichten geplant.

2. Demokratische Entscheidungsstrukturen werden von der Entwicklung völlig überrollt und daraus resultieren für die Gemeinde enorme Schwierigkeiten, die ihr überlassenen Folgen privatwirtschaftlicher Planung mit ihrer Kompetenz und finanziell nur einigermassen zu bewältigen.

Diese Resultate drängten die Frage auf: Welche Rolle spielen demokratische Entscheidungsabläufe im Planungsprozess? Das heisst: die Gruppe hat sich nun mit der historischen Entwicklung der Planung in dieser zürcherischen Vorortsregion zu beschäftigen, genauer, mit der Frage wo, wodurch bedingt, welche Entscheidungen gefällt wurden, die «Planungsresultate» wie Volketswil zustande gebracht haben; welches die rechtliche und politische Stellung der Gemeinde in diesen Entscheidungsstrukturen sei, und, ganz generell, welche politischen Konsequenzen der Einfluss der Bauwirtschaft auf die Bauplanung und welche Rolle dabei der Staat als «Krisendämpfer» zu spielen habe.

Solche Fragen und Probleme wurden — wie wir in den bisherigen Untersuchungen festgestellt haben — von den zuständigen Fachleuten überhaupt nicht bearbeitet, meist nicht einmal erkannt. Und sie sollen offenbar nach dem Willen der Schulleitung von den in Ausbildung begriffenen Planern und Architekten auch in Zukunft nicht erkannt oder gar gelöst werden.

Perspektiven zum 7. und 8. Semester

In Entsprechung zu den bereits formulierten Zielen des Projektstudiums käme es in den folgenden Semestern darauf an, eine reale Planungsaufgabe im Zusammenhang mit der Fallstudie zu wählen, die geeignet wäre, die in der Analyse erkannten Widersprüche und Konflikte auszutragen und zu lösen.

Denn: Die Hochschulen haben keine Aufgaben an sich, sondern nur in Bezug auf die Gesellschaft. Ihre Entwicklung in Richtung «Massenstudium» wird mit Sicherheit zu Konflikten führen, die über den Rahmen der Hochschule hinausgreifen und nur gesamtgesellschaftlich betrachtet und gelöst werden können. Das heisst: in unserer Situation der allgemeinen Verschleierung gesellschaftlicher Zusammenhänge hat die Hochschule die Aufgabe, kritisches Bewusstsein zu wecken und aktiv mitzuarbeiten bei der Lösung gesellschaftlicher Probleme.

in this suburban region of Zurich, specifically the questions of which decisions were made where and under what conditions that have led to "planning results" like those of Volketswil; what was the legal and political role of the municipality in these decision-making structures; and, more generally, what political consequences did the influence of the construction industry have on building planning and the role the state plays as a "crisis manager"?

Such questions and problems—we have determined in our studies thus far—were not addressed at all by the responsible experts and usually not even recognized. And apparently the administration also does not want them to be recognized, much less solved, in the future by the planners and architects now being educated.

Perspectives for the Seventh and Eighth Semesters

In accordance with the goals of the project-based learning already formulated, in the semesters to follow students will select a real planning task in the context of the case study that is suited to addressing and resolving the contradictions and conflicts recognized in the analysis.

Because: Universities do not have mandates per se, other than in relation to society. Their evolution in the direction of "mass studies" will certainly lead to conflicts that extend beyond the framework of the university and can be observed and resolved only by society as a whole. That means: In our present situation when social relations are systematically concealed, the task of the university is to awaken critical consciousness and to actively contribute to solving social problems.

Marianne Günter und Roland Günter

Bürgerinitiativen - wie

In der westdeutschen Hauptstadt Bonn existieren zur Zeit acht Bürgerinitiativen: die Aktionsgemeinschaft Tieflage Bundesbahn und Fernstrassenumgehung, das Stadtentwicklungsforum, die Arbeitsgemeinschaft Bonner Aerzte zum Umweltschutz (die erste Aerzte-Bürgerinitiative in Deutschland), die Bürgerinitiative Südstadt, die Aktion Nahverkehr, das Rote-Punkt-Komitee, die Planungsgruppe Kultur und die Bürgerinitiative Kommunales Kino.

Für eine Stadt von nicht ganz 300 000 Einwohnern, die bis vor nicht allzu langer Zeit zudem sehr konservativ und wenig lebendig war, sind Zahl und Bilanz erstaunlich. 1969 gelang es der Bürgerinitiative Stadtentwicklungsforum durch eine bundesweite Aktion, das Bundeskabinett zu veranlassen, die Fehlplanung für ein Regierungsviertel zu stoppen. Die Bürger erzwangen ein erheblich verbessertes Planungsverfahren (Expertenkolloquium Bundesbauten Bonn 1970, öffentliche Hearings, Diskussionen mit den Planern) und die Ausschreibung des bislang grössten bundesdeutschen Wettbewerbes. Bonner Bürgerinitiativen erreichten weiterhin nach zweijähriger erbitterter Kampagne, dass der Stadtrat seinen Beschluss aufhob, die Bundesbahn und eine Stadtautobahn mit einer 110 m breiten Schneise ebenerdig durch die Innenstädte von Bonn und Bad Godesberg zu führen. Sie sollen zumindestens in einen Tunnel kommen.

Zur Zeit kämpfen die Bürgerinitiativen gemeinsam darum, dass keine Autobahn durch die Zentren geschlagen wird: eine Umweltvergiftung und Stadtzerstörung katastrophalen Ausmasses soll verhindert werden. Zehntausende von Menschen würden das Opfer abstruser «Stadterneuerungsbestrebungen» werden: im Rahmen der Hausabrisse und städtebaulichen Umstrukturierungen (Wohnquartiere zu Bürovierteln) droht ihnen die Deportation an den Stadtrand. Bonner Bürgerinitiativen setzten die Errichtung eines Abendgymnasiums durch, verhinderten eine Müllverbrennungsanlage, die ein Versicherungskonzern für seine riesigen Büros in der Innenstadt anlegen wollte, setzten eine Anzahl Modifizierungen von Stadtratsbeschlüssen durch, verjagten Spekulanten und wirkten vor allem als Ideenfabrik für die Stadtplanung: sie können in der Regel Schwarz auf Weiss nachweisen, dass nahezu alle wichtigen Verbesserungen in der Bonner Stadtplanung der letzten zwei Jahre auf ihre Anregung, ihren politischen Druck oder geschickte Einflüsterungen zurückgehen.

Bonn ist nur ein Beispiel für eine Stadt, in der Bürgerinitiativen zunehmend eine wichtige Rolle spielen — einerseits zur Erhaltung städtischer Substanz angesichts drohender Stadtzerstörung, andererseits zur Verbesserung der Lebensumwelt unter gesamtgesellschaftlichen Aspekten. Einer Leverkusener Bürgerinitiative gelang es im Jahre 1971 (u. a. mit Bonner «Nachbarschaftshilfe»), die Planung einer Grosswohnanlage für 16 000 Menschen im Abgasbereich der Bayer-Werke zu verhindern. Das Projekt war nach Aussage eines Gutachters «wie ein Bauantrag mittlerer Grösse geplant» gewesen. Es ist nur eines von vielen Beispielen dafür, mit welchem Mass an stadtplanerischem Dilettantismus unsere zukünftige Lebensumwelt angelegt wird. Eine Wiesbadener Bürgerinitiative, vorwiegend von Jungsozialisten getragen, sorgte dafür, dass die vorgesehene Umwandlung eines ausgedehnten Wohngebietes zum Kerngebiet nicht zustande kam. Teilerfolge in dieser Richtung hatten auch die Bürgerinitiati-

Citizens' Action Groups: How, Where, Why?

Authors:
Marianne Günter
Roland Günter

Source:
archithese, 1 (1972): 20–26

Translated by:
Steven Lindberg

In the West German capital, Bonn, there are currently eight citizens' actions groups: the Aktionsgemeinschaft Tieflage Bundesbahn und Fernstrassenumgehung [Railway Tunnel and Highway Bypass Action Association]; the Stadtentwicklungsforum [Urban Development Forum]; the Arbeitsgemeinschaft Bonner Aerzte zum Umweltschutz [Bonn Physicians for Environmental Protection Working Association], the first citizens' action group of physicians in Germany; the Bürgerinitiative Südstadt [Südstadt Citizens' Action Group]; the Aktion Nahverkehr [Local Transportation Action Group]; the Rote-Punkt-Komitee [Red Dot Committee]; the Planungsgruppe Kultur [Culture Planning Group]; and the Bürgerinitiative Kommunales Kino [Communal Cinema Citizens' Action Group].

For a city with not quite 300,000 residents, which until not too long ago was also very conservative and not very lively, this number and balance are astonishing. In 1969, the Stadtentwicklungsforum citizens' action group organized a federal action that managed to prompt the Federal Cabinet to stop the misguided planning of a government quarter. The citizens compelled a considerably improved planning procedure (the Bundesbauten Bonn expert colloquium in 1970, public hearings, discussions with planners) and the largest architectural competition ever in West Germany. Citizens' action groups in Bonn managed, after a bitter, two-year campaign, to get the town council to repeal its decision allowing the federal railroad and a highway to pass via a 111-meter-wide ground-level strip through the center of the cities of Bonn and Bad Godesberg. It should at least pass through a tunnel.

At the moment, the citizens' action groups are fighting together to prevent the highway passing through the town centers: this is to prevent environmental pollution and destruction of cities on a catastrophic scale. Tens of thousands of people were victims of abstruse "urban renewal efforts": as part of the demolition of buildings and urban restructuring (residential neighborhoods into office districts), they were threatened with deportation to the outskirts of the city. Citizens' action groups in Bonn managed to get an evening secondary school built, prevented a refuse-incineration facility that an insurance group wanted to build for its enormous offices in the center of the city, got the town council to modify several resolutions, chased away speculators, and above all functioned as an idea factory for urban planning: as a rule, they can demonstrate in black-and-white that nearly all the important improvements in Bonn's town planning of the past two years can be traced back to their motivation, political pressure, or effective whispering.

Bonn is just one example of a city in which citizens' action groups are increasingly playing an important role—on the one hand, preserving the fabric of the city in the face of the threat of its destruction; on the other hand, improving the living environment for society as a whole. A citizens' action group in Leverkusen managed in 1971 (in part with "help from neighbors" in Bonn) to prevent the planning of a large housing development for 16,000 residents in an area exposed to fumes from Bayer's factories. According to an expert report, the project had been "planned like a medium-size building permit application." This is just one of many examples of the extent to which our future environment is being determined by amateurish town planning. A citizens' action group in Wiesbaden, largely supported by young socialists, saw to it that a planned transformation of an extended residential neighborhood into an inner-city zone was not carried out. Such partial successes were also enjoyed by citizens' action groups in the Westend district of Frankfurt and the Lehel district of Munich.

Citizens' action groups are sprouting from the ground not just in West Germany—they are in fact much older and more widespread in the Netherlands. For the most part, they are even more successful there: they have thus far succeeded in preventing the establishment of a chemical giant here, and in Amsterdam for twenty years they have prevented the threatened demolition of the large district of Jordaan (20,000 residents).

Citizens' action groups were initially viewed by the political parties with distrust, usually even as competition. In the meanwhile, however, it has become clear that they are by no means an "uprising of the apolitical community gardeners" but rather political enterprises: often they see the socioeconomic conflicts of interest far more clearly than the professional politicians; they distrust the pros because they have experienced on many occasions how, for them, money often counts more than the voice and will of the voters. Citizens' action groups are essentially an effort by those affected to act politically on their own initiative and thus to take democracy seriously. In the Federal Republic of Germany, this "grassroots work" has already begun to have an effect on the parties: many young members of the SPD [Sozialdemokratische Partei Deutschlands, or Social Democratic Party of Germany] and the FDP [Freie Demokratische Partei, or Free Democratic Party] are actively involved in citizens' action groups because they see them as an opportunity to outmaneuver the party hierarchy, which is often no longer interested in "grassroots problems." The pinnacle of recognition: Recently, the FDP and its leading politicians organized a forum of West German citizens' action groups in Baden-Baden.

Town planning today pursues the same goals nearly everywhere. The trend is to make profits in housing construction just as in industry. Conflicts of interest are growing along with it. Slogans such as "economic construction" often conceal an economy whose profits grow to the same extent as the living conditions of those affected are reduced. Housing construction follows the motto, "As long as people are surviving, it can't be that bad." Or, "Length times width times money." Citizens' action groups have the task of pointing out the resulting psychological and social damage of such planning and buildings. They should challenge projects that include, for example, housing types that reproduce the low emancipation of women.

So-called urban renewal, in particular, often turns out to be social warfare. In many cities, such mellifluous language is a guise: it is intended to cover up the ongoing brutal conquest of land in attractive locations in city centers where the socially disadvantaged have been living for centuries. This social conflict is disguised by such philanthropic terms as *responsibility* and *welfare*: keywords such as *cleanliness*, *better toilet*, and *white facade* are used to carry out a downright deportation of thousands of people to city outskirts with inadequately planned infrastructure. Social connections, friendships and neighborhoods, memory, and identification are all sacrificed to it. Those affected also pay for this isolation,

fig. 1 Bonn, Südstadt district. Urban destruction in a historical residential neighborhood near the center of the city. An office district is being built here. The citizens' action groups are defending themselves against it.
(Photo: Waldemar Haberey, Bonn)

wo - wozu?

ven im Frankfurter Westend und im Münchner Lehel.

Aber nicht nur in Westdeutschland spriessen die Bürgerinitiativen aus dem Boden — viel älter und verbreiteter sind sie in den Niederlanden. Dort waren sie grossenteils noch weitaus erfolgreicher: es gelang ihnen, die Ansiedlung eines Chemiegiganten und in Amsterdam den seit 20 Jahren drohenden Abriss des ausgedehnten Stadtteils Jordaan (20 000 Einwohner) bis heute zu verhindern.

Bürgerinitiativen wurden von den Parteien zunächst argwöhnisch, meist sogar als Konkurrenz betrachtet. Inzwischen ist sichtbar geworden, dass sie keineswegs der «Aufstand der unpolitischen Gartenlaube» sind, sondern politische Unternehmungen: häufig sehen sie die sozioökonomischen Interessenkonflikte wesentlich schärfer als die professionellen Politiker; sie misstrauen den Profis, weil sie vielerorts erfahren haben, dass für jene das Geld häufig mehr zählt als Stimme und Wille der Wähler. So sind Bürgerinitiativen im wesentlichen der Versuch von Betroffenen, eigeninitiativ politisch zu handeln und damit Demokratie ernst zu nehmen. Diese «Basisarbeit» beginnt in der Bundesrepublik bereits in Parteien zu wirken: viele junge Mitglieder der SPD und FDP beteiligen sich aktiv an Bürgerinitiativen, weil sie darin eine Chance sehen, die Allmacht der Parteihierarchie, die sich für die «Basisprobleme» oft

←fig. 2
Bonn, Südstadt district. Simrock-Strasse before its demolition. A bank headquarters swallows one hundred apartments.
(Photo: Waldemar Haberey, Bonn)

↑ fig. 3 Bonn-Bad Godesberg. The FDP faction of the town council and the Bürgerinitiative Stadtentwicklungsforum demonstrate to residents the planned effect of the inner-city highway along a fifty-meter-long firewall: its 120-meter-wide strip would destroy the spa town of Bad Godesberg with noise and exhaust fumes. (Photo: Roland Günter)

nicht mehr interessiert, auszumanövrieren. Höhepunkt der «Anerkennung»: Unlängst veranstaltete die FDP mit ihren Spitzenpolitikern in Baden-Baden ein «Forum der bundesdeutschen Bürgerinitiativen».

Die Stadtplanung folgt heute fast überall denselben Zielen. Der Trend wird immer stärker, im Wohnungsbau in ähnlicher Weise wie in der Industrie Profite zu machen. Damit wächst der Widerspruch der Interessen. Hinter einem Schlagwort wie «ökonomischer Bauweise» versteckt sich oft eine Oekonomie, deren Gewinnspanne in dem Masse wächst, wie die Lebensumwelt für die Betroffenen reduziert wird. Wohnungsbau nach dem Motto: Solange die Leute überleben, kann es nicht so schlimm sein. Oder: Länge mal Breite mal Geld. Bürgerinitiativen haben die Aufgabe, darauf hinzuweisen, welche psychischen und sozialen Schäden durch solche Planungen und Bauten entstehen. Sie sollen Planungen hinterfragen, z. B. wie in einer Wohnsiedlung die mangelhafte Emanzipation der Frau durch die Wohnform verewigt wird.

Vor allem das sogenannte Sanierung entpuppt sich oft als sozialer Krieg. In vielen Städten ist sie ein sprachlich gut klingender Deckmantel: er soll verschleiern, dass in den Cities eine brutale Eroberung des standortgünstigen Bodens stattfindet, auf dem seit Jahrhunderten die sozial Schwächeren wohnen. Diese gesellschaftliche Auseinandersetzung wird mit philanthropischen Begriffen wie «Verantwortung» und «Fürsorge» getarnt: unter den Stichworten «Sauberkeit», «besseres WC» und «weisse Fassade» wird eine regelrechte Deportation von Tausenden von Menschen an den infrastrukturell unzulänglich geplanten Stadtrand angeordnet. Ihr fallen die sozialen Bindungen, Freund- und Nachbarschaften, Erinnerung und Identifikation zum Opfer. Für diese Isolierung, ferner für die längeren Anfahrtswege zur Arbeit und damit für den Freizeitverlust bezahlen die Betroffenen zudem noch das Zwei- und Dreifache ihrer früheren Mieten.

In Amsterdam versuchen eine Anzahl von Bürgerinitiativen in vielfältiger Weise, sogar mit einem eigenen Sender («Radio Sirene»), das Bewusstsein dieser Situation zu fördern. Schreckbild aller Abrissbedrohten ist hier die neue Satellitenstadt Bijlmermeer für 120 000 Menschen, zuweilen als «Märkisches Viertel» von Amsterdam bezeichnet. Nicht die Betroffenen werden hier saniert, sondern Kapitalanleger und Baufirmen. Der Blick in deutsche Samstagzeitungen zeigt, dass reiche Leute in Berlin ihre Steuern in ausgedehntes Wohneigentum plus hohe Verzinsung verwandeln können — dafür zahlen die Zwangssanierten des Stadtteils Kreuzberg das Mehrfache ihrer früheren Miete.

Neben missratenen Neubauplanungen und Sanierungen sind Verkehrsprobleme ein weiteres wichtiges Arbeitsfeld von Bürgerinitiativen. Die Folgen einer falschen Verkehrspolitik, die das Auto zuungunsten der öffentlichen Transportmittel begünstigte (Hand in Hand mit flächenextensiver Siedlungsplanung, die eine günstige Erschliessung mit Bahn und Bus nicht zuliess), Lärm, zunehmende Vergiftung durch Abgase und nicht zuletzt eine nur noch durch den Krieg übertroffene Stadtzerstörung durch breite Schneisen in historischen Altstätten und älteren Wohnvorstädten — dies alles hat an vielen Orten den Aufstand der Bevölkerung veranlasst.

In München protestiert sie gegen einen Altstadtring. Seine gebauten Teilstücke zeigen, dass jede Verkehrsmassnahme weitreichende Folgen für die Umstrukturierung ausgedehnter Stadtbereiche hat: Kampf um neue prestigeverheissende Standorte und Verdrängung der Wohnbevölkerung. Ganz besonders grotesk ist diese Fehlplanung deshalb, weil sie verkehrlich überhaupt nicht funktioniert: die seitlichen Strassensysteme halten die Verkehrsüberflutung nicht aus, häufig bricht der Verkehrsfluss zusammen.

Viele Bürgerinitiativen bleiben deshalb erfolglos, weil ihre Teilnehmer nicht wissen, wie man sie organisiert, wie und wo sie handlungsfähig werden — kurz: wie man Bürgerinitiative «macht». Bürgerinitiative wird anfangs oft mit Erwartungen überladen — werden sie nicht schnell genug erfüllt, fallen ihre Teilnehmer in Resignation zurück. Oder: sie wissen nicht, wie man sich Informationen besorgt, sie analysiert und verwertet. Viele moralisieren bloss mit barockem Pathosblick zum Himmel oder verlegen sich nach jahrhundertealter Sitte aufs Bitten.

Bürgerinitiativen wie z. B. in Amsterdam, Bonn, Frankfurt, München und Wiesbaden hatten Erfolg, weil sie, abgesehen von sachlich hervorragender Arbeit, die *politischen* Strukturen durchschauten und nüchtern benutzten, sowie sich in der Sozialpsychologie der Politik ausserordentlich geschickt bewegten. Dazu im Folgenden einige Hinweise.

Bürgerinitiativen brauchen Personen, über

↓ fig. 4 Amsterdam. The satellite city Bijlmermeer for 120,000 residents is the bugaboo of the residents of Amsterdam who are threatened with being forced out of the center of the city. (Photo: Roland Günter)

die die Bevölkerung sich mit der Aktion identifizieren kann. Das war z. B. im Münchner Lehel ein Lehrer mittleren Alters: «der Herr Lichtl». Die Aktionsgruppe im Amsterdamer Jordaan gewinnt vor allem über Kinder Sympathie. «Kinder sind sehr wichtig, um die Familien zu interessieren.» Die Gruppe baute eigene Spielplätze — einen unter dem Namen «Freiheitsgarten». Sie besitzt ein eigenes Café. Es dient als Kommunikationszentrum, in dem die Bevölkerung sich informieren kann, andererseits aber auch die emotionalen Faktoren findet, die für die Sympathie, den Zusammenhalt und die Energie einer Bürgerinitiative sehr wichtig sind. Auch weitere holländische Gruppen haben Informationszentren.

Juristische Fixierungen in bestimmten Organisationsformen (Verein u. a.) sind erfahrungsgemäss nur hinderlich. Wozu Menschen nicht wirklich motiviert sind, das erfüllen sie auch nicht, wenn sie es unterschrieben haben. Warum sollen Kräfte in monatelangen Satzungsdebatten und Satzungsänderungen verbraucht werden — an meist platonischen Problemen? Wenn Mitgliederverzeichnisse existieren, ist zudem die Gefahr «schwarzer Listen» der Verwaltung gross: man darf nicht vergessen, dass in jeder Stadt vielfältige wirtschaftliche Verflechtungen herrschen. Wer hohe Risiken läuft, kann sich auch anders als mit «öffentlichem Bekennermut» nützlich machen: mit Informationen, Spenden u. a.

Viele Bürgerinitiativen scheitern einfach daran, dass sie ohne Rücksicht auf die sozioökonomischen Verhältnisse Rollenanforderungen an ihre Mitglieder stellen, die sie nur um den Preis des sozialen Selbstmordes leisten könnten. Die Bonner Bürgerinitiativen hatten nicht zuletzt deshalb so grosse Erfolge, weil sie sehr geschickt die Rollen differenzierten: Information — Expertenwissen — forensischer Auftritt — weitere Arbeit. Sympathisierende Verwaltungsbeamte, das sogenannte Frustrationspotential des Mittelbaues, können deshalb mitmachen, weil sie absolut vor Risiken geschützt werden: der jeweilige Informant darf nur einer einzigen Person bekannt sein. Experten, die oft in mannigfaltigen Auftragsverflechtungen stehen,

← fig. 5 Amsterdam, Jordaan. The citizens' action group built this playground with parents and children: the Vrijheidstuin (Freedom Garden). (Photo: Roland Günter)

↑ fig. 6 Amsterdam, Jordaan. Information center of the citizens' action group that has thus far successfully prevented the demolition of the district. (Photo: Roland Günter)

↓ fig. 7   Munich. Renters' radial march.
(Photo: Dieter Hinrichs, Munich)

brauchen sich nicht zu exponieren, sondern liefern in Kleingruppensitzungen Wissen: die Fülle der sogenannten Gefälligkeitsgutachten wird analysiert.

Exponenten der Bürgerinitiativen sind nur die, die es sich leisten können, weil sie unantastbar sind. Politik kann nicht auf der Basis von individuellem Heldentum gemacht werden.

Da angesichts des wenig entwickelten Standes der Demokratie die Möglichkeiten formeller, d. h. institutioneller Machtausübung, für Bürgerinitiativen entfallen, müssen die informellen umso intensiver genutzt werden. Eine einzige Aktion hat nirgendwo Wirkung — nur eine Bündelung vielfältiger Massnahmen. Diese müssen oft über ein bis zwei Jahre kontinuierlich verfolgt werden. Die Analyse gelungener Aktionen, so der Baustopp verfehlter Regierungsviertelplanungen in Bonn, zeigt eine Art Mosaiktechnik: Ueber Teilerfolge an verschiedenen Stellen wurde die Entwicklung langsam in die Richtung verändert, in der der Gesamterfolg erst möglich wurde. Politik ist eben «ein starkes, langsames Bohren von harten Brettern» (Max Weber).

Der Katalog von Aktionsmöglichkeiten ist umfangreich. Erfahrungsgemäss ist es für einen Kommunalpolitiker, der auch in seiner eigenen Partei mannigfache Konkurrenzen hat, ausserordentlich unangenehm, wenn seine Bürgerversammlung umfunktioniert wird. Wenn dies mit schöner Regelmässigkeit geschieht, muss er um seine Kandidatur in der Partei und Wahl fürchten. Dabei sind nicht nur die tatsächlichen Risiken wichtig, sondern oft noch mehr die vorgestellten: in der politischen Psychologie spielen Fiktionen — z. B. die Möglichkeit eines viel weitergehenden Aufbegehrens der Bevölkerung — eine grosse Rolle. Bürgerinitiativen können häufig nur über solche Nervenkriege Erfolg haben. Mit gezielten Kampagnen sollte die Wiederwahl einzelner Abgeordneter verhindert werden — schon die Androhung einer solchen Aktion kann wirksam sein.

Die Aktionsgruppe im Amsterdamer Jordaan bestreitet mit dem Erlös eines Cafés den schmalen Lebensunterhalt für fast ein Dutzend junger Leute: sie sind eine Art städtische Entwicklungshelfer für das Quartier. Einmal in der Woche fahren sie mit den Kindern aufs Land, organisieren Ferien auf einem Bauernhof in Friesland, vermitteln Tausch — vom Teller bis zum Kaninchen und Möbeln, wenn sich eine Fa-

↑ fig. 8   Bonn. Protest against air pollution from a planned highway through Bonn's small city center. Beethoven is given a breathing mask.

as well as for longer commutes to work and hence a loss of free time, with rents that are two to three times their previous ones.

In Amsterdam, several citizens' action groups are trying in various ways—even with their own radio station (Radio Sirene)—to increase awareness of this situation. The local bugaboo threatening demolition is the new 120,000-person satellite city of Bijlmermeer, which is sometimes called Amsterdam's "Märkisches Viertel." The renewal here is not benefiting those affected but the investors and construction companies. A look at weekend newspapers in Germany shows that the rich in Berlin can transform their taxes into extensive property holdings and high interest rates—yet the residents of the Kreuzberg district who were subjected to forced urban renewal pay many times their previous rent.

Alongside misguided plans for new buildings and urban renewal, traffic problems are another important area for the work of citizens' action groups. The consequences of bad transportation policies that benefit cars to the disadvantage of public transportation (hand in hand with the planning of extensive housing developments that do not allow for affordable train and bus lines), are noise, increased pollution from exhaust fumes, and, not least, a destruction of the city, exceeded only by the war, by broad strips cutting through historical old towns and older residential suburbs—all of this has caused an uprising of the residents in many places.

In Munich, they are protesting a ring road around the old town. The parts of it that have been built demonstrate that every transportation measure has far-reaching consequences for the restructuring of extended areas of the city: a battle over new, prestigious locations and residents' displacement. This misguided planning is particularly grotesque because it does not work for transportation at all: the system of side streets cannot handle the inundation of vehicles, and the flow of traffic often breaks down.

Many citizens' action groups remain unsuccessful because their members do not know how to organize or how and where they can be effective—in short, how citizens' action groups are "made." The expectations of citizens' action groups are often too high in the beginning—if they are not met quickly enough, their members become resigned. Or they do not know how to get information and analyze and evaluate it. Many simply moralize while raising their eyes toward heaven with baroque pathos or resort to petitions following a centuries-old custom.

Citizens' action groups such as those in Amsterdam, Bonn, Frankfurt, Munich, and Wiesbaden succeeded because, setting aside their objectively outstanding work, they saw through the *political* structures and soberly exploited them or maneuvered with extraordinary skill within the sociopsychology of politics. A few tips on that follow.

Citizens' action groups need people through whom residents can identify with the action. In the Lehel district of Munich, for example, that was a middle-aged teacher: Mr. Lichtl. The citizens' action groups in the Jordaan district of Amsterdam gained sympathy above all with children. "Children are very important as a way of gaining the interest of families." The group built its own playground and called it the Vrijheidstuin (Freedom Garden). The group owns its own café. It serves as a communication center where residents can get information but also finds the emotional factors that are very important for the sympathy, cohesion, and energy of a citizens' action group. Other Dutch groups also have information centers.

Experience has shown that legal entities in certain forms of organization (associations and so on) are merely a hindrance. When people are not truly motivated, they do not do something even if they have signed the form. Why waste energy on month-long debates over statutes and changes to bylaws—usually Platonic problems? When membership lists exist, moreover, there is also a big risk of administrative "black lists": One must not forget that every city has intertwined business networks. Anyone at high risk can also be useful in ways other than the "courage of one's convictions": with information, donations, and so on.

Many citizens' action groups fail simply because they do not consider socioeconomic circumstances and expect their members to play roles they could fill only at the cost of social suicide. The citizens' action groups in

Bonn had great success not least because they very cleverly distinguished among roles: information—expert knowledge—forensic evidence—other work. Sympathetic civil servants, the so-called frustration potential of the middle management, could participate because they were absolutely protected against risks: the information in question could be known only to a few people. Experts, who often have a complicated set of contractual agreements, need not expose themselves but can instead provide information to small groups in meetings: the wealth of "favorably slanted reports" is then analyzed.

The proponents of citizens' action groups are not just those who can afford to do so because they are untouchable. Politics cannot be pursued on the basis of individual heroism.

Because in the face of the underdeveloped state of democracy, citizens' action groups lack the opportunities to exercise their power formally—that is, through institutions—and thus informal paths must be used all the more intensely. Only a bundling of diverse measures will have an effect—isolated action will have no effect anywhere. They often have to be pursued continuously for one to two years. Analysis of successful actions, such as stopping the misguided plans to build a government district in Bonn, reveals a kind of mosaic technique: by means of partial successes in various areas, developments slowly changed in the direction that made overall success possible in the first place. Politics is precisely "a slow, powerful drilling through hard boards" (Max Weber).

The catalog of possible actions is extensive. Experience has taught that it is extraordinarily uncomfortable for a municipal politician, who also has many competitors within his own party, when his town meeting is taken over. When that happens with regularity, he necessarily fears for his candidacy in the party and in the election. What is often even more important than the actual risks are the imagined ones: in political psychology, fictions—for example, the possibility of a much-broader uprising of the people—play an important role. Citizens' action groups can often succeed only through such wars of nerves. Through focused campaigns, the reelection of specific members can be prevented—even the threat of such action can be effective.

The citizens' action group in the Jordaan district of Amsterdam uses the profits from a café to provide a modest living for nearly a dozen young people who function in a sense as urban development aid workers for the neighborhood. Once a week, they travel to the countryside with children, organize vacations on a farm in Friesland, facilitate swaps—everything from plates to rabbits and furniture when a family grows. They organize transportation and help restore buildings. In addition, around forty people are active part-time. Workers in the trades form consulting teams to explain to people how to maintain the houses and apartments with little money but lots of self-help and help from neighbors, while their rent remains the same or increases only insignificantly. The restored buildings are symbols of neighborhood spirit and a successful battle against the resignation on which the interests of capital speculate in many places.

Many citizens' action groups mediate expert consultation, press contacts, and "political channels." Several of them also advise parties—almost always the opposition in the municipal parliament. One of the most important tasks of citizens' action groups is providing clear information to the population: above all, memorable reminders of the consequences of planning. Together with the FDP faction on Bonn's town council, the members of an action group painted the traffic system to scale on an enormous firewall, whose sixteen lanes of noise and exhaust fumes would mean the end of the spa town of Bad Godesberg. To protest the danger to the public represented by this 110-meter-wide, city-destroying highway, a breathing mask was placed over the mouth of the Beethoven monument at Münsterplatz in Bonn. Women and children from a citizens' action group in Bonn wore breathing masks when protesting in front of the town hall. A magazine made the protests famous across the country. Photomontages of a highway spider with the cathedral of Münster as a rest stop and the Beethoven at its center illustrated the specter of the German capital as a transportation facility. Newspaper campaigns with articles, interviews, open letters, and letters to the editor, as well

milie vergrössert. Sie machen Transporte und helfen beim Häuser-Restaurieren. Ausserdem arbeiten rund 40 Leute einen Teil ihrer Zeit aktiv mit. Handwerker bilden Beraterteams, die der Bevölkerung erklären, wie sie mit wenig Geld und mit viel Selbst- und Nachbarschaftshilfe ihre Häuser und ihre Wohnungen erhalten: zur alten oder nur unerheblich gestiegenen Miete. Die restaurierten Bauten bilden Symbole des Quartiergeistes und der erfolgreichen Abwehr der Resignation, auf die die Kapitalinteressen vielerorts spekulieren.

Viele Bürgerinitiativen vermitteln Sachberatung, Pressekontakte und «politische Kanäle». Einige beraten auch Parteien — so gut wie immer die Opposition im Stadtparlament. Eine der wichtigsten Aufgaben der Bürgerinitiativen ist die verdeutlichende Information der Bevölkerung: vor allem der einprägsame Hinweis auf Planungsfolgen. Zusammen mit der Bonner FDP-Stadtratsfraktion malten Aktionsgruppenmitglieder auf eine riesige Brandmauer in Originalgrösse die Verkehrsanlage, die mit 16 Spuren Breite, Lärm und Abgasen das Ende des Badeortes Bad Godesberg bedeuten würde. Aus Protest gegen die Abgasgefährdung der Bevölkerung durch diese 110 m breite, stadtzerstörende Autobahn wurde dem Beethovendenkmal auf dem Bonner Münsterplatz ein Mundschutz umgehängt. Frauen und Kinder den Bonner Aktionsgruppen demonstrierten mit Atemschutz vor dem Rathaus. Eine Illustrierte machte die Proteste bundesweit bekannt. Fotomontagen einer Autobahnspinne, in deren Mitte die Münsterbasilika als Autobahn-Raststätte und das Beethovendenkmal stehen, führten das Gespenst der deutschen Bundeshauptstadt als Verkehrsanlage («programmierter Selbstmord») vor Augen. Zeitungskampagnen mit Artikeln, Interviews, offenen Briefen, Leserbriefen, ferner Broschüren, Plakate — auch in vielen Wartezimmern von Aerzten — sowie Sonderdrucke von Zeitungen und Zeitschriften und sogar Postkarten informierten die Bevölkerung. Hinzu kamen kleine Ausstellungen an Bauzäunen und bei Veranstaltungen.

Die Aktion Maxvorstadt in München organisierte einen Mietersternmarsch. Dabei führte sie einen Bagger mit, dessen Greifer ein historisches Haus, im Modell dargestellt, hochzog. Planspiele zeigen Problemalternativen und Folgen. Sie sollten nicht zu kompliziert sein, damit jeder damit umgehen kann. Kleinplakate im

← fig. 9
Amsterdam. Sign prohibiting demolition.
(Photo: Roland Günter)

← fig. 10
Amsterdam. The Nieuwmarkt citizens action group had its own radio station for a time: Radio Sirene.
(Photo: Roland Günter)

DIN-A-4 Format finden auf jedem Laternenpfahl Platz. Die holländischen Bürgerinitiativen haben häufig Quartierzeitungen: um den Aufwand möglichst gering zu halten und um jedem das Gefühl zu geben, dass sie nicht von Fachleuten, sondern von Laien gemacht werden, verzichten sie auf jeglichen Anspruch auf Perfektion.

Zur Aktionsgruppe im Jordaan-Viertel in Amsterdam gehören auch Filmemacher. Ihre Streifen werden in ganz Holland gezeigt. Im Märkischen Viertel in Berlin wurden Filme zur Problemdarstellung und Solidarisierung der Bevölkerung mit bedrängten Mietern ausserordentlich erfolgreich eingesetzt. Ueber die Bürgerinitiativen im Münchner Lehel gibt es einen Fernsehfilm: «Herr Lichtl sucht die Wahrheit» — im Münchner Rathaus und hinter den Kulissen. Bürgerinitiativen erfinden oft sehr einprägsame Slogans. In Bonn tauften sie in einer Aktion das «Amt für Stadterneuerung» in «Amt für Stadtzerstörung» um — eine Bezeichnung, die sich seither beharrlich hält.

Die in vielen deutschen Bürgeraktionen lange Zeit praktizierte Verunsicherungspsychologie mit Bierernst und bedrohender Aggressivität hat sich als Fehlschlag erwiesen: sie bestärkte lediglich die vorhandenen Aengste der Bevölkerung und trieb sie weiter zur Resignation. Die holländischen Bürgerinitiativen stärkten mit emotionalen Mitteln, vor allem mit Humor, das Selbstbewusstsein und schufen damit bessere psychologische Voraussetzungen für die Handlungsfähigkeit der Bevölkerung. Eine wichtige Rolle für die Solidarisierung spielten dort z. B. Stadtteilfeste.

Bürgerinitiativen bestreiten das Monopol der politischen Parteien, für Betroffene zu sprechen. Sie bestehen darauf, dass jeder der beste Experte für sich selbst ist. Bürgerinitiativen sollten auch klarstellen, dass Stadtplanung eine politische Auseinandersetzung verschiedener Interessen ist — meist zwischen denen, die eine möglichst günstige Lebensumwelt für ihre Entfaltung wünschen, und den Interessen der Kapitalverwertung, deren Vorteil in dem Masse steigt, wie sie an dieser Lebensumwelt durch Reduzierung der Bauleistungen (oft «Rationalisierung» genannt) Einsparungen vornehmen können und damit Gewinne machen. Den Betroffenen wird oft Sand in die Augen gestreut: Technische Argumente werden vorgeschoben, um Ziele und Interessenkonflikte zu verdecken.

Die Aufgabe der Bürgerinitiativen ist es, Grundlagen und Methoden von Planungen und Gutachten auf unausgesprochene oder tabuisierte Annahmen hin zu untersuchen, ferner die Rolle der Experten aufzudecken, die sich mit Gefälligkeitsgutachten in Priesterpose zur Absegnung missbrauchen lassen.

Angriffspunkte sind: schlechte Datenbasis, methodische Unzulänglichkeiten, isolierte Problemsicht, Mangel an Komplexität, spekulative Thesen, lineare Hochrechnungen, Scheinalternativen, logische Fehler, Beschreibungen von historischen, d. h. veränderbaren Tatbeständen als unveränderbare Norm, fehlende dialektische Analyse, vorgeschobene Risiken, die geringen Wahrscheinlichkeitsgrad haben, und selbstgesetzte Sachzwänge.

Bürgerinitiativen können in vielfältiger Weise Erfolge haben: sie leisten einen Beitrag zur Bewusstseinsbildung angesichts folgenreicher gesellschaftlicher Widersprüche; sie helfen, die Resignation abzubauen und das Selbstbewusstsein der Bevölkerung zu stärken; sie lassen sichtbar werden, dass der einzelne nicht bloss sein eigenes Interesse verfolgt (wie man ihn oft glauben machte), sondern ein gemeinsames, das sich nur in Gruppen durchsetzen lässt; sie zeigen, dass Planung kein unentrinnbares Schicksal, sondern teilweise gestaltbar ist; sie machen deutlich, dass Konflikte meist nicht durch den bösen Willen, die Unkenntnis oder die Dummheit anderer Leute entstehen, sondern durch unterschiedliche ökonomische und soziale Interessenlagen, in denen der Stärkere aus der schlechten Position des Schwächeren Vorteile zieht.

as brochures and posters—many of them in physicians' waiting rooms—and offprints from newspapers and magazines and even postcards, informed the public. Small exhibitions also appeared on fences at construction sites and at events.

The Aktion Maxvorstadt in Munich organized a radial march for renters. They brought along an excavator, which lifted a model of a historical house in its bucket. Planning simulations highlight collateral problems and consequences. They should not be too complicated for people to follow. Small posters in A4 format find room on every lamppost. The Dutch citizens' action groups often have neighborhood newspapers. To reduce the workload and give everyone the feeling that it is being done not just by experts but by laypersons, they do not even try to be perfect.

The citizens' action group in the Jordaan district includes filmmakers. Their films have been shown throughout Holland. In Berlin's Märkisches Viertel, films were used with extraordinary success to depict the problem and to foster among the wider public a sense of solidarity with the evicted renters. A television film depicts the citizens' actions groups in the Lehel district of Munich: *Herr Lichtl sucht die Wahrheit* [Mr. Lichtl seeks the truth]—specifically, at Munich's city hall and behind the scenes. Citizens' action groups often come up with very catchy slogans. In Bonn, for one action they renamed the Amt für Stadterneuerung [Office of Urban Renewal] the "Amt für Stadtzerstörung" [Office of Urban Destruction]—a name that has stuck ever since.

The psychology of creating uncertainty that has long been practiced by many German citizens' action groups with deadly seriousness and menacing aggressiveness has proven to be a misstep: it merely reinforces the existing fears of the people and drives them even further into resignation. The Dutch citizens' action groups build self-confidence using emotional means, above all humor, and thereby create better psychological conditions for the people to take action. For example, neighborhood festivals played an important role in creating solidarity there.

Citizens' action groups challenge the monopoly that the political parties have on speaking for the affected. They insist that everyone is the best expert when it comes to oneself. Citizens' action groups should also make clear that urban planning is a political debate among different interests—usually between those who want living conditions that are as favorable as possible to their development and the interest of capital investment, whose benefits increase to the extent they can save money on the living environment by reducing construction costs (often called "rationalization"), thus increasing their profits. Sand is often thrown in the eyes of those affected: technical arguments are advanced to cover up the real objectives and conflicts of interest.

The task of citizens' action groups is to study the principles and methods of planning and reports for unspoken or taboo assumptions and to uncover the role of experts who allow themselves to be misused by posing as priests while blessing favorably slanted reports.

The points of attack are: poor underlying data, methodological inadequacies, isolated perspectives on the problems, lack of complexity, speculative theses, linear projections, pseudo-alternatives, logical errors, descriptions of historical and hence changeable states of affairs as inalterable norms, lack of dialectical analysis, assumed risks with a low degree of probability, and self-imposed situational constraints.

Citizens' action groups can succeed in many ways: they contribute to building awareness of consequential conflicts in society; they help to overcome resignation and increase the self-confidence of the public; they make clear that individuals are not simply pursuing their own interests (as they are often led to believe) but a common interest that is best achieved by working in groups; they show that planning is not an inescapable fate but can in part be shaped; they make clear that conflicts usually result not from the ill will, ignorance, or stupidity of other people but from different economic and social interests in which the stronger take advantage of the bad position of those who are weaker.

Group Portraits and Self Portraits

Some Remarks on Recent Approaches to Town-Planning

Author:
David P. Handlin

Source:
archithese, 9 (1974): 45–52

Until about ten years ago most architects and planners believed that it was both possible and desirable to formulate a single concept of urban development that could be applied everywhere and for everyone. They chose general names like *La Ville Radieuse* or *Broadacre City* to indicate the universality of their concepts, and they did not hesitate, if given the opportunity, to build projects in countries that had unfamiliar cultures.

A new generation has reacted against this notion. They rely on cultural anthropologists and sociologists to tell them something about the life patterns of the people for whom they are building. This concern is present not just when designing for a distant culture; architects and planners often feel estranged from sections of their own country, or even their own city.

As an antidote to this condition, the idea that populations are made up of enclaves or groups that have their own cultures and, therefore, particular requirements in their built environments has seemed especially attractive.[1] Some architects and planners have found it sensible not to devise an ideal and uniform pattern at, for instance, an urban scale, but instead to think of the city as a set of separate "urban villages," each with its own sub-culture and architecture. This view has had a particular relevance in the United States, which has been described as "a nation of nations." Because Americans come from so many different backgrounds, it would seem appropriate, at least at first glance, to adopt a pluralistic approach to physical design and planning.

I have used the term "urban village" deliberately, because one way to understand whether there is any substance in these ideas is to examine an important work of sociology which has this phrase in its title.[2] In the late 1950s, when Herbert Gans did his research for *The Urban Villagers*, the West End—an area of 7000 inhabitants near downtown Boston—was scheduled to be torn down for urban renewal. To most superficial observers the West End seemed a slum, but Gans did not think so. If he could show that the West Enders had a culture that was different from that of most other Americans, but in its own way healthy and stable, it would be possible not only to correct the impression that the area was a slum, but also to indicate a set of criteria that could be used in future planning for the area.

David P. Handlin

Group portraits and self portraits

Some remarks on recent approaches to town-planning

Until about ten years ago most architects and planners believed that it was both possible and desirable to formulate a single concept of urban development that could be applied everywhere and for everyone. They chose general names like *La Ville Radieuse* or *Broadacre City* to indicate the universality of their concepts, and they did not hesitate, if given the opportunity, to build projects in countries that had unfamiliar cultures.

A new generation has reacted against this notion. They rely on cultural anthropologists and sociologists to tell them something about the life patterns of the people for whom they are building. This concern is present not just when designing for a distant culture; architects and planners often feel estranged from sections of their own country, or even their own city.

As an antidote to this condition, the idea that populations are made up of enclaves or groups that have their own cultures and, therefore, particular requirements in their built environments has seemed especially attractive.[1] Some architects and planners have found it

Gruppenportraits oder Selbstportraits?

Eine frühere Generation von Stadtplanern ging davon aus, dass die modernen Planungsprinzipien überall anwendbar seien; neuerdings wird aber mit Recht gefordert, dass jede Region und jede Bevölkerungsgruppe einer spezifischen Planungsmethode bedarf. Auf die universalen Konzepte wie *Ville Radieuse* oder *Broadacre City* folgte das Interesse für das soziale Geflecht städtischer Gemeinschaften. Jedoch bereitet die Analyse dieser städtischen Bevölkerungsgruppen grosse Schwierigkeiten, selbst für die erfahrensten Soziologen. Die berühmte Arbeit von Herbert Gans, *The Urban Villagers* (New York, 1962) entbehrt nicht der Widersprüche und Ungenauigkeiten, sind doch die unterprivilegierten Bevölkerungsgruppen weder stabil noch homogen. Infolgedessen sind auch ihre Bedürfnisse nur schwer definierbar. Auf welche anthropologischen Fakten soll sich in solchen Fällen eine Planung stützen?

Diese Frage wird von radikalen Planungstheoretikern häufig umgangen. Da die soziologischen «Gruppenbilder» keine adäquaten Planungsgrundlagen liefern, greift man auf die Idee des «Selbstporträts» zu-

sensible not to devise an ideal and uniform pattern at, for instance, an urban scale, but instead to think of the city as a set of separate "urban villages", each with its own sub-culture and architecture. This view has had a particular relevance in the United States, which has been described as "a nation of nations". Because Americans come from so many different backgrounds, it would seem appropriate, at least at first glance, to adopt a pluralistic approach to physical design and planning.

I have used the term "urban village" deliberately, because one way to understand whether there is any substance in these ideas is to examine an important work of sociology which has this phrase in its title.[2] In the late 1950's, when Herbert Gans did his research for *The Urban Villagers*, the West End — an area of 7000 inhabitants near downtown Boston — was scheduled to be torn down for urban renewal. To most superficial observers the West End seemed a slum, but Gans did not think so. If he could show that the West Enders had a culture that was different from that of most other Americans, but in its own way healthy and stable, it would be possible not only to correct the impression that the area was a slum, but also to indicate a set of criteria that could be used in future planning for the area.

The bulk of *The Urban Villagers* focussed on what Gans called the West End's peer group society, a close-knit set of people who seemed to reject the values of "middle-class" America. In fact, Gans found that West Enders treated the representatives of this "outside world", whether doctors, social workers, politicians, librarians, or teachers, with suspicion and hostility. Even consumer goods and the mass media were only partially accepted in this recreation of a village society in an urban area.[3] Gans, therefore, treated the West End as if it were uniform and unchanging. The only danger to the stability of the pattern of life there came from the incursions of outsiders. Of all possible perils, urban renewal, of course, was the most formidable.

Gans presented a wealth of information in *The Urban Villagers*, but it is still debatable whether his description was an adequate group portrait of the inhabitants of the West End. In composing such a portrait it was important to establish who, in fact, "the West Enders" were. Gans is a conscientious sociologist, so at the beginning of *The Urban Villagers* he had to come to terms with the fact that the West End was not at all homogeneous. Italian-Americans made up the largest group, about forty per cent, but the area also had sizable contingents of Jewish-, Polish-, Albanian-, Ukranian- and Greek-Americans. To complicate matters even further, the West End contained other categories of inhabitants, which Gans listed as: pathological households, middle-class professionals and students, artists and bohemians, and staff from a nearby hospital.[4]

Faced with such a bewildering heterogeneity, Gans chose to write about the Italian-Americans in the West End, but his task became still more complicated because there were important distinctions even among these people. Gans acknowledged that Sicilian-Americans differed from Italian-Americans and also that, if "class" was defined by income and education, there was a broad spectrum within the group that he had decided to analyze. Nevertheless, Gans ignored these differences, partly because, in the case of Sicilian- and Italian-American traits, they were "not visible to the non-Italian observer", but mainly because he thought that "the major criteria for ranking, differentiating,

---

rück: d. h. man sieht die Lösung des Problems in der totalen Selbstbestimmung des Wohnraums durch die Individuen oder die Familien, die die Städte bewohnen.

Aber auch diese Lösung des Problems erweist sich bei näherer Betrachtung als eine romantische Fiktion. In den Vereinigten Staaten ist das Eigenheim ein volkstümliches Ideal. Jedoch: in den meisten Fällen gleichen sich diese Eigenheime wie ein Ei dem anderen, und es ist alles andere als eine erwiesene Tatsache, dass ihre Bewohner sich dafür interessieren, die Architektur dieser Eigenheime zu «personalisieren». Sie interessieren sich kaum für veränderbare Räume: «Flexibilität» ist in ihren Augen bloss ein provisorischer Ersatz für Eigentum. Daher ist es auch fraglich, ob die architektonische «Spontaneität» der südamerikanischen «Squatters» und ihrer Bidonvilles als Vorbild für amerikanische Stadterneuerung dienen kann, wie das etwa Robert Goodman (*After the Planners*, New York, 1972) vorschwebt. Wer sich ein Eigenheim baut, der tut es, um den Status eines Hauseigentümers zu erreichen, und keineswegs, um sich der «bürgerlichen Repression» zu entziehen. Aehnlich utopisch und irrational ist die Verherrlichung des «mobile home» als einer neuen städtischen Wohnform: in Wirklichkeit tun die Verkäufer wie auch die Eigentümer von «mobile homes» alles, um diese moderne Form der städtischen Behausung der traditionellen Form des Eigenheims anzugleichen.

46

programs of the 1950s were the culmination of these early studies. photograph ca. 1860.

and establishing compatibility are ingroup loyalty and conformity to established standards of personal behavior".[5]

Using these criteria Gans outlined four categories of Italian-Americans: "routine-seekers" who wanted a stable way of life, "action-seekers" who tended to live more for the moment, the "maladapted" who were entirely unable to control their behavior because of alcoholism or other problems, and the "middle-class mobiles" who were striving to better themselves. Of these four groups Gans concentrated most of his analysis on the routine-seekers, because they were the people who seemed to reject the "middle-class values" that urban renewal was supposed to promote.[6]

Gans disposed of these ticklish questions about the composition of the West End in the introduction to The Urban Villagers. Once he had dealt with this definitional problem, he rarely mentioned the West End's heterogeneous composition again. In fact, a reader who skips the introduction might easily think that Gans was discussing the entire community. A telling transformation in terminology helped establish this impression. After the introductory chapter Gans only infrequently used the cumbersome, but accurate, term "routine-seeking Italian American". Instead he refered to the people he was describing as "the West Enders".

The continuing use of this term not only contradicted what had been discussed in the introduction and, therefore, was misleading about the composition of the group portrait, but it also reflected upon the accuracy of Gans' description of the routine-seeking Italian Americans. If the West End had been homogeneous, then it would have been proper to discuss only the contacts that the area's inhabitants had with outsiders. Since it was not, however, Gans should have told how the routine-seeking Italian Americans interacted with other West Enders. Surely such contacts — whether at school, at work, in play, or casually in stores and on the streets — must have existed in such a small area.[7]

How they occurred would perhaps have revealed something significant about the routine-seeking Italian American's self-definition and, therefore, his attitude toward social mobility and residence in the West End. By ignoring these matters Gans presented an incomplete portrait of his subjects, so one should be skeptical about his conclusions. It is significant, for instance, that although he frequently mentioned the routine-seeking Italian-American's fear of suburbia, he never confronted the fact that the population of the area had declined from 18,500 in 1920 to 7,000 in 1957. A few demographic statistics about length of residence and change of occupation would have clarified many questions about mobility, but Gans never took the trouble to find them.

There are two lessons to be bearned from

47

these contradictions and inconsistencies in *The Urban Villagers*. First of all, if a competent sociologist like Herbert Gans has so much difficulty in composing an adequate group portrait of the inhabitants of an area like the West End, then it is doubtful that architects and planners will be more successful in trying to establish a cultural or sociological basis for their designs.[8] More importantly, the inability to come to terms with the composition of the West End illustrates the inevitable pitfalls of the notion that a community is uniform and unchanging.

There is a compelling temptation to claim that "the community" speaks with a single voice. It makes good rhetoric, especially if that rhetoric emphasizes the differences between "insiders" and oppressive "outsiders". Besides, the uniform and unchanging community is methodologically neat. It would certainly be more complicated, if not impossible, to formulate a renewal plan, or even a lay-out for a block of apartments, if several cultural patterns or interests had to be accommodated in a physical design.

Unfortunately, in the United States there are very few homogeneous communities in which, no matter what the issue, there is a clear-cut distinction between insider and outsider. Those who have tried to organize communities, for whatever purpose, have generally been unsuccessful, if they have not recognized this fact and learned how to deal with it.[9] To continue to believe the myth of the uniform and unchanging community has most often led to disillusionment and frustration. In the late 1960's this was a common syndrome in the United States.

The current interest in the personalization of housing can partly be explained as an attempt to fill the vacuum of social concern that was left by the gradual realization that community feeling, especially in the depressed areas of American cities, could not be crystallized and used as an input for design. In other words, if it is not possible to design buildings or reconstruct neighborhoods from the information provided by group portraits, then perhaps, as an alternative, individuals or families can compose self portraits by making an imprint on the place in which they live.

There are many complicated issues in this proposition, but, if the personalization of housing is truly an issue, it must first be discussed in terms of home ownership. "The joy of home possession", a sentimental, but nevertheless telling, nineteenth century phrase, is still the dream of most American households and the means by which they can best feel an attachment to their everyday environments. This is the context in which the issue of personalization has generally been discussed. But this connection is now only infrequently made, because the embarrassing fact is that till recently most of those who disparaged home ownership also favored an architecture that denigrated any manifestation of "personality".

The classic critique of home ownership was made by F. Engels in his pamphlet *The Housing Question*. Engels thought that a desire for possession, whether for land or for housing, was an atavism. He encouraged workers to flock to large cities, where, unencumbered by their age-old bonds to the land, they would form a revolutionary group and produce a new social order. Housing reformers were among the enemies of this idea. Engels attacked them because the inexpensive homes they favored tied workers down with heavy mortgages, reduced their mobility, and, therefore, made it risky for them to strike against their employer. This was the case in America where — Engels learned from Eleanor Marx-Aveling, Karl Marx's daughter — "miserable wooden huts" with heavy mortgages were being erected for workers on the outskirts of large cities.[10]

Engels did not discuss what housing would be like after the dramatic transformation he anticipated.[11] But some American critics in the 1930's had specific ideas about this matter.[12] It would be too lengthy to characterize all the points of view that were involved in the debate that resulted in the formulation of a national housing policy in the United States in the late 1920's and 1930's. But at that time many architects, planners, and social commentators analyzed the housing question in terms that were similar to those that Engels had used. As an alternative to the system then operating in America, they envisioned a "collectivist" society that would combine socialist ideals and the spirit of an American agrarian tradition.[13]

This transformation would be accompanied by the evolution of a new individual who would not be interested in selfish matters.[14] Land and buildings in this society would, therefore, be held in common, and houses would not have

The bulk of *The Urban Villagers* focused on what Gans called the West End's peer group society, a close-knit set of people who seemed to reject the values of "middle-class" America. In fact, Gans found that West Enders treated the representatives of this "outside world," whether doctors, social workers, politicians, librarians, or teachers, with suspicion and hostility. Even consumer goods and the mass media were only partially accepted in this recreation of a village society in an urban area.[3] Gans, therefore, treated the West End as if it were uniform and unchanging. The only danger to the stability of the pattern of life there came from the incursions of outsiders. Of all possible perils, urban renewal, of course, was the most formidable.

Gans presented a wealth of information in *The Urban Villagers*, but it is still debatable whether his description was an adequate group portrait of the inhabitants of the West End. In composing such a portrait it was important to establish who, in fact, "the West Enders" were. Gans is a conscientious sociologist, so at the beginning of *The Urban Villagers* he had to come to terms with the fact that the West End was not at all homogeneous. Italian-Americans made up the largest group, about forty per cent, but the area also had sizable contingents of Jewish-, Polish-, Albanian-, Ukrainian- and Greek-Americans. To complicate matters even further, the West End contained other categories of inhabitants, which Gans listed as: pathological households, middle-class professionals and students, artists and bohemians, and staff from a nearby hospital.[4]

Faced with such a bewildering heterogeneity, Gans chose to write about the Italian-Americans in the West End, but his task became still more complicated because there were important distinctions even among these people. Gans acknowledged that Sicilian-Americans differed from Italian-Americans and also that, if "class" was defined by income and education, there was a broad spectrum within the group that he had decided to analyze. Nevertheless, Gans ignored these differences, partly because, in the case of Sicilian- and Italian-American traits, they were "not visible to the non-Italian observer," but mainly because he thought that "the major criteria for ranking, differentiating, and establishing compatibility are ingroup loyalty and conformity to established standards of personal behavior."[5]

Using these criteria Gans outlined four categories of Italian-Americans: "routine-seekers" who wanted a stable way of life, "action seekers" who tended to live more for the moment, the "maladapted" who were entirely unable to control their behavior because of alcoholism or other problems, and the "middleclass mobiles" who were striving to better themselves. Of these four groups Gans concentrated most of his analysis on the routine-seekers, because they were the people who seemed to reject the "middle-class values" that urban renewal was supposed to promote.[6]

Gans disposed of these ticklish questions about the composition of the West End in the introduction to *The Urban Villagers*. Once he had dealt with this definitional problem, he rarely mentioned the West End's heterogenous composition again. In fact, a reader who skips the introduction might easily think that Gans was discussing the entire community. A telling transformation in terminology helped establish this impression. After the introductory chapter, Gans only infrequently used the cumbersome, but accurate, term "routine-seeking Italian-American." Instead he referred to the people he was describing as "the West Enders."

The continuing use of this term not only contradicted what had been discussed in the introduction and, therefore, was misleading about the composition of the group portrait, but it also reflected upon the accuracy of Gans' description of the routine-seeking Italian-Americans. If the West End had been homogeneous, then it would have been proper to discuss only the contacts that the area's inhabitants had with outsiders. Since it was not, however, Gans should have told how the routine-seeking Italian-Americans interacted with other West Enders. Surely such contacts —whether at school, at work, in play, or casually in stores and on the streets—must have existed in such a small area.[7]

How they occurred would perhaps have revealed something significant about the routine-seeking Italian-American's self-definition and, therefore, his attitude toward social mobility and residence in the West End. By ignoring these matters Gans presented an incomplete portrait of his subjects, so one should be skeptical about his conclusions. It is significant, for instance, that although he frequently mentioned the routine-seeking Italian-American's fear of suburbia, he never confronted the fact that the population of the area had declined from 18,500 in 1920 to 7,000 in 1957. A few demographic statistics about length of residence and change of occupation would have clarified many questions about mobility, but Gans never took the trouble to find them.

There are two lessons to be learned from these contradictions and inconsistencies in *The Urban Villagers*. First of all, if a competent sociologist like Herbert Gans has so much difficulty in composing an adequate group portrait of the inhabitants of an area like the West End, then it is doubtful that architects and planners will be more successful in trying to establish a cultural or sociological basis for their designs.[8] More importantly, the inability to come to terms with the composition of the West End illustrates the inevitable pitfalls of the notion that a community is uniform and unchanging.

There is a compelling temptation to claim that "the community" speaks with a single voice. It makes good rhetoric, especially if that rhetoric emphasizes the differences between "insiders" and oppressive "outsiders." Besides, the uniform and unchanging community is methodologically neat. It would certainly be more complicated, if not impossible, to formulate a renewal plan or even a lay-out for a block of apartments, if several cultural patterns or interests had to be accommodated in a physical design.

Unfortunately, in the United States there are very few homogeneous communities in which, no matter what the issue, there is a clear-cut distinction between insider and outsider. Those who have tried to organize communities, for whatever purpose, have generally been unsuccessful, if they have not recognized this fact and learned how to deal with it.[9] To continue to believe the myth of the uniform and unchanging community has most often led to disillusionment and frustration. In the late 1960's this was a common syndrome in the United States.

The current interest in the personalization of housing can partly be explained as an attempt to fill the vacuum of social concern that was left by the gradual realization that community feeling, especially in the depressed areas of American cities, could not be crystallized and used as an input for design. In other words, if it is not possible to design buildings or reconstruct neighborhoods from the information provided by group portraits, then perhaps, as an alternative, individuals or families can compose self-portraits by making an imprint on the place in which they live.

There are many complicated issues in this proposition, but, if the personalization of housing is truly an issue, it must first be discussed in terms of home ownership. "The joy of home possession," a sentimental, but nevertheless telling, nineteenth century phrase, is still the dream of most American households and the means by which they can best feel an attachment to their everyday environments. This is the context in which the issue of personalization has generally been discussed. But this connection is now only infrequently made, because the embarrassing fact is that till recently most of those who disparaged home ownership also favored an architecture that denigrated any manifestation of "personality."

The classic critique of home ownership was made by F. Engels in his pamphlet *The Housing Question*. Engels thought that a desire for possession, whether for land or for housing was an atavism. He encouraged workers to flock to large cities, where, unencumbered by their age-old bonds to the land, they would form a revolutionary group and produce a new social order. Housing reformers were among the enemies of this idea. Engels attacked them because the inexpensive homes they favored tied workers down with heavy mortgages, reduced their mobility, and, therefore, made it risky for them to strike against their employer. This was the case in America where—Engels learned from Eleanor Marx-Aveling, Karl Marx's daughter—"miserable wooden huts" with heavy mortgages were being erected for workers on the outskirts of large cities.[10]

Engels did not discuss what housing would be like after the dramatic transformation he anticipated.[11] But some American critics in the 1930's had specific ideas about this matter.[12] It would be too lengthy to characterize all the

any of the quirks of "personality" that characterized the homes then common in America.[15] In arrangement they would be "mass", not detached, and in appearance they would be "objective".[16] The first projects of the Public Housing Administration, the same kind of buildings that are now called bleak and dehumanizing, were admired as examples of this "objective" architecture.[17]

In its own way this was a coherent vision, but few people liked it. In *Modern Times,* the quintessential statement of the 1930's, Charlie Chaplin's domestic ideal was a simple suburban house, and so it has been ever since. Whether this is wise from a financial point of view is still not clear. Not much is known about mortgage foreclosures in the United States, although the little evidence that has been uncovered does show that the loss of a home by foreclosure has not been a frequent occurrence.[18] Similarly, there has been a continuous, and unresolved, debate about whether home ownership is advantageous as an investment.[19] Nevertheless, there can be little question that home ownership is immensely popular in the United States. A better arrangement may be possible in some undisclosed future, but most people have wanted a home of their own in the here and now.

Despite its overwhelming popularity, many American architects still will not acknowledge the validity of home ownership and the suburban house. Instead they have devised a number of methods of accommodating the self-portrait in the collectivist ideal. Some believe that it is possible, for instance, to personalize what used to be considered "mass" and "objective" housing. It is not clear, however, that "people", whoever they are, truly desire such personalization. One should be skeptical of the universal applicability of such an idea when it is put forth mainly by architects, especially architectural students, who generally are known to enjoy such activities as taking out wall partitions and building furniture. It can also be argued that spatial flexibility, which is often considered a requisite for personalization, is bought at a great price. Movable partitions transmit sound easily and, because they cannot carry pipes and conduits, create house planning difficulties that may negate the advantages that such devices are intended of offer. Architects are becoming more familiar with these matters.[20] If such devices make living in anonymous buildings more palat-

↓ fig. 3 Cartoon from an "Own Your Own Home" campaign, 1920s.

able, then they should be encouraged. Nevertheless, I think most families would still prefer a home of their own and will always consider such attempts at personalization as substitutes for the ultimate state of home ownership.

This is the context in which the fascination with the compelling image of the self-built South American shanty town must be seen. At the end of *After the planners*, a broad critique of city planning and architecture in the United States, Robert Goodman points to such squatter settlements as hinting at "a more spontaneous, less

← fig. 4
The ideal American home, as viewed around 1930.

fig. 5 Squatter settlements in Lima, Peru.

bourgeoise, 'aesthetic' environment".[21] These images, especially when photographed, may have a kind of visual complexity that appeals to an architect who is repelled by other kinds of "mass" housing, but I think few people in the United States would choose to live in such places, if given the possibility of owning their own home. Most self-built houses in the United States have been erected not so that their inhabitants can escape bourgeois repression, but instead, so that they can achieve the status of home owner.[22] The uniform texture of a squatter settlement may suggest a "people's" architecture, but in the United States the image of the suburban house still fulfills this purpose.

A similar point can be made about mobile homes. Many architects have seen these houses as part of a new world of anti-materialistic impermanency. The portability of these houses conjures up visions of a disposable architecture which would be part of a cultural or even a spiritual awakening.[23] But anyone who has read the literature put out by the mobile home industry or has visited a park of these houses knowns that such a concept of flexibility or impermanency is exactly the opposite of what the purchaser of a mobile home wants.[24] Most Americans choose this kind of house because it is now the easiest way to live in that circumstance which approximates what they consider ideal. Consequently, mobile homes are styled, both by

the manufacturer and later the purchaser, to look as much like the personal, detached house as possible.

Undoubtedly many former residents of the West End have now achieved a kind of self portrait in a detached house, whether it is conventionally built or a mobile home.[25] By moving to the suburbs they have not shed all social pathologies, as many architects and planners in earlier decades predicted they would. But, by the same token, just because they live in individual houses does not mean that they have lost all

fig. 6 Self-built house, Beverley, Massachusetts.

↓ fig. 7   Archigram's image of mobility and flexibility.

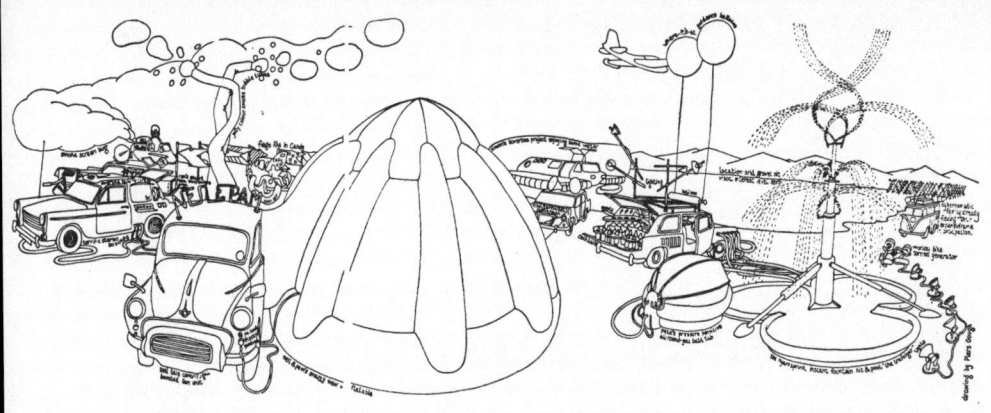

group affiliation. Americans have a long tradition of participation in a broad array of voluntary organizations, and there is no sign that this activity is abating. One might even be able to find evidence of specific group affiliations in the way that particular Americans choose their individual homes.

[1] The popularity of E. T. Hall's books is evidence of this interest.
[2] Herbert Gans, *The Urban Villagers* (New York, 1962).
[3] *The Urban Villagers*, pp. 45—228.
[4] *The Urban Villagers*, pp. 6—11.

There's a little bedroom up under those eaves. (Burkin Homes)

[5] *The Urban Villagers*, p. 27.
[6] *The Urban Villagers*, pp. 27—32. Of course, such a system of classification is by no means beyond dispute. I am sure many sociologists would disagree with the appropriateness of Gans' categories.
[7] For instance, on p. 8 Gans mentions in a footnote: "Most of the West End stores were owned by Jews, as were the medical, dental, and legal offices." Yet, there is no mention of the implications of this intermixing in the rest of the book.
[8] I will not discuss whether it is possible from good sociological data to extract a proper physical design. This is another questionable issue altogether.
[9] This, in fact, is what the most skilled politicians have learned to do. See, for instance: Edward C. Banfield and James Q. Wilson, *City Politics* (New York, 1963), pp. 115—137.
[10] Frederick Engels, *The Housing Question* (London, 1935), p. 35.
[11] The implications of this fact are discussed in: Leonardo Benevolo, *The Origins of Modern Town Planning* (London, 1963).
[12] I am referring primarily to Lewis Mumford because he was the most articulate of a group of critics concerned with housing in the 1930's.
[13] Lewis Mumford, *Technics and Civilization* (New York, 1962), pp. 400—435.
[14] *Technics and Civilization*, pp. 321—363.
[15] The essence of "personality" was expressed in: Emily Post, *The Personality of the House* (New York, 1930).
[16] *Technics and Civilization*, pp. 357—363. Lewis Mumford, *The Culture of Cities* (New York, 1966), p. (26).
[17] *The Culture of Cities*, p. (26).
[18] Stephan Thernstrom, *Poverity and Progress* (New York, 1969), pp. 116—122, 199—201.
[19] John P. Dean, *Home Ownership: Is It Sound?* (New York, 1945).
[20] See, for instance, the recent survey of this subject in the November, 1973 edition of *Architectural Design*.

↑ fig. 8   Mobile home's image of stability and permanence.

[21] Robert Goodman, *After the Planners* (New York, 1972), p. 242.
[22] See, for instance: John F. C. Turner and Robert Fichter, *Freedom to Build* (New York, 1972), ill. 24.
[23] This seems to be the message at the end of: Martin Pawley, *Architecture Versus Housing* (New York, 1971).
[24] Al Griffin, *So You Want to Buy a Mobile Home* (New York, 1970).
[25] Indeed, the weakness of Herbert Gans' *The Levittowners* is that he does not explain why the inhabitants of the area he studied left their previous neighborhoods. Could they too have at one time been "routine-seekers"?

Sources of illustrations:

New York Sanitary Association, *Report of the Citizen's Committee on the Sanitary Conditions of New York*, New York, 1863 (1; 2). Blanche Halbert, ed., *The Better Houses Manual*, Chicago, 1932 (3; 4). Robert Goodman, *After the Planners*, New York, 1972 (5). John F. C. Turner and Robert Fichter, *Freedom to Build*, New York, 1972 (6). Martin Pawley, *Architecture versus Housing*, London, 1971 (7). Al Griffin, *So You Want to Buy a Mobile Home*, New York, 1970 (8).

archithese   Bibliographie neuer Architekturbücher

Auch im Lehmhaus lässt sich's leben. Von René Gardi. Bern 1973. 249 Seiten mit 213 schwarzweissen und 30 farbigen, meist ganzseitigen Abbildungen. 30,5 x 24,5 cm. Ueber traditionelles Bauen und Wohnen in Westafrika. Der bekannte Afrikakenner führt uns mit diesem Buch in die Bau- und Wohnkunst der Tuareg, der Musgum und anderer Stämme ein. Verlag René Gardi. Fr. 85.—.

Funktionsmischung. Von J. Wiegand. Zur Planung gemischter Gebiete als Beitrag zur Zuordnung von Wohn- und Arbeitsstätten. Niederteufen 1973. 314 Seiten mit Tabellen, Skizzen und Fotografien. 22,5 x 15 cm. Nach einem Ueberblick über die Vor- und Nachteile der verschiedenen Formen von Funktionsmischung folgen detaillierte Ausführungen über in Frage kommende Gewerbezweige, die heute und in absehbarer Zukunft für die Funktionsmischung möglich sind. Anmerkungen über städtebauliche, rechtliche und wirtschaftliche Voraussetzungen. Niggli-Verlag, brosch. Fr. 48.50.

Der Architekt und der Computer. Von Boyd Auger. Stuttgart 1973. 96 Seiten mit 62 schwarzweissen Abbildungen. 20,5 x 23,5 cm. Das vorliegende Buch erläutert, wie der Computer in der Bauplanung eingesetzt werden kann und erörtert neben der allgemeinen Situation der Architektur Aufbau und Wirkungsweise des Computers. Niggli-Verlag. Fr. 41.—.

Die Architektur von Ludwig Wittgenstein. Eine Dokumentation. Hrsg. Bernd Leitner. Halifax 1973. 127 Seiten mit 65 Abbildungen und zahlreichen Briefdokumentationen. 27,5 x 19 cm. Dieser ab-norme Bau, der 1928 vollendet und 1971 beinahe wieder abgebrochen wurde, wird in diesem Band vom Nova Scotia College, das sich für die Erhaltung des Wittgenstein-Hauses eingesetzt hat, hervorragend dokumentiert. Das Aeussere des Baues erinnert in seinen kubischen Formen an die Architektur von Adolf Loos. Das Innere ist beispiellos in der Geschichte des Bauens im 20. Jahrhundert. Alles wird neu durchdacht. Nichts in dieser Architektur ist direkt übernommen; weder von einer Bautradition, noch von einer fachlichen Avantgarde. Text in deutscher und englischer Sprache. König-Verlag, brosch. Fr. 32.10.

Projects. Architectural Association 1946—1971. Hrsg. James Gowan. London 1973. 127 Seiten mit zahlreichen Skizzen, Grundrissen und Fotografien. 28 x 23 cm. Diese Publikation wurde anlässlich des 125jährigen Bestehens der AA herausgegeben, beschränkt sich jedoch auf die Tätigkeit der letzten 25 Jahre. Architectural Ass. London, broschiert Fr. 15.—.

The Anti-Rationalists. Von Nikolaus Pevsner und J. M. Richards. London 1973. 210 Seiten mit 280 schwarzweissen Abbildungen. 30,5 x 24 cm. In diesem Buch werden bisher unbekannte Vertreter der Art Nouveau vorgestellt, deren Werk von Spanien über Tschechoslowakei und Ungarn, von Glasgow nach Wien und Berlin, von Pubs bis zu Kapellen reicht. Architectural Press. Fr. 58.90.

Italian Architecture 1965—1970. Second Itinerant Triennial Exhibition of Contemporary Italian Architecture. Rom 1973. 392 Seiten mit zahlreichen schwarzweissen Abbildungen. Inhaltsverzeichnis. 20,5 x 20,5 cm. Vorwort von Giuseppe Tucci. Beiträge von G. Ferrara, G. Mariotti, C. Cresti u. a. Projekte von V. Gregotti, P. Portoghesi, A. Rossi u. a. Das Buch ist eingeteilt in folgende Kapitel: Suche nach neuen Städtemodellen. Neue Wohnformen. Restaurierung alter Städte. Architektonische Phantasien. Architekten und Gruppen. Englischer Text. IsMeo, brosch. Fr. 18.90.

Die bemalte Stadt. Initiativen zur Veränderung der Strassen in USA. Beispiele in Europa. Von H. Schmidt-Brümmer / F. Lee. Köln 1973. 198 Seiten mit 10 farbigen und 176 schwarzweissen Abbildungen. 20,5 x 15 cm. In diesem Band werden Beispiele aus Amerika und Europa gezeigt, wie Veränderungsmöglichkeiten gesucht werden, die verödete Landschaft betonkahler Häuserblocks etwas menschlicher zu gestalten in Form von popigen Wandmalereien oder satirischen Karikaturen usw. DuMont Verlag, brosch. Fr. 26.60.

Begegnung mit Pionieren. GTA Bd. 8. Von Alfred Roth. Basel 1973. 254 Seiten mit zahlreichen zum Teil mehrfarbigen Abbildungen. Namenregister. Abbildungsverzeichnis. 25 x 16,5 cm. Begegnung mit Le Corbusier, Piet Mondrian, Adolf Loos, Josef Hoffmann, Auguste Perret, Henry van de Velde. Sozusagen als Abschluss seiner zwölfjährigen Lehrtätigkeit an der ETH Zürich hat Roth dieses Buch herausgegeben und beschreibt darin seine frühen Begegnungen mit hervorragenden Persönlichkeiten der Architektur und Malerei. Birkhäuser Verlag. Fr. 44.—.

points of view that were involved in the debate that resulted in the formulation of a national housing policy in the United States in the late 1920's and 1930's. But at that time many architects, planners, and social commentators analyzed the housing question in terms that were similar to those that Engels had used. As an alternative to the system then operating in America, they envisioned a "collectivist" society that would combine socialist ideals and the spirit of an American agrarian tradition.[13]

This transformation would be accompanied by the evolution of a new individual who would not be interested in selfish matters.[14] Land and buildings in this society would, therefore, be held in common, and houses would not have any of the quirks of "personality" that characterized the homes then common in America.[15] In arrangement they would be "mass," not detached, and in appearance they would be "objective."[16] The first projects of the Public Housing Administration, the same kind of buildings that are now called bleak and dehumanizing, were admired as examples of this "Objective" architecture.[17]

In its own way this was a coherent vision, but few people liked it. In *Modern Times*, the quintessential statement of the 1930's, Charlie Chaplin's domestic ideal was a simple suburban house, and so it has been ever since. Whether this is wise from a financial point of view is still not clear. Not much is known about mortgage foreclosures in the United States, although the little evidence that has been uncovered does show that the loss of a home by foreclosure has not been a frequent occurrence.[18] Similarly, there has been a continuous, and unresolved debate about whether home ownership is advantageous as an investment.[19] Nevertheless, there can be little question that home ownership is immensely popular in the United States. A better arrangement may be possible in some undisclosed future, but most people have wanted a home of their own in the here and now.

Despite its overwhelming popularity, many American architects still will not acknowledge the validity of home ownership and the suburban house. Instead they have devised a number of methods of accommodating the self-portrait in the collectivist ideal. Some believe that it is possible, for instance, to personalize what used to be considered "mass" and "objective" housing. It is not clear, however, that "people," whoever they are, truly desire such personalization. One should be skeptical of the universal applicability of such an idea when it is put forth mainly by architects, especially architectural students, who generally are known to enjoy such activities as taking out wall partitions and building furniture. It can also be argued that spatial flexibility, which is often considered a requisite for personalization, is bought at a great price. Movable partitions transmit sound easily and, because they cannot carry pipes and conduits, create house planning difficulties that may negate the advantages that such devices are intended to offer. Architects are becoming more familiar with these matters.[20] If such devices make living in anonymous buildings more palatable, then they should be encouraged. Nevertheless, I think most families would still prefer a home of their own and will always consider such attempts at personalization as substitutes for the ultimate state of home ownership.

This is the context in which the fascination with the compelling image of the self-built South American shanty town must be seen. At the end of *After the Planners*, a broad critique of city planning and architecture in the United States, Robert Goodman points to such squatter settlements as hinting at "a more spontaneous, less bourgeoise, 'aesthetic' environment."[21] These images, especially when photographed, may have a kind of visual complexity that appeals to an architect who is repelled by other kinds of "mass" housing, but I think few people in the United States would choose to live in such places, if given the possibility of owning their own home. Most self-built houses in the United States have been erected not so that their inhabitants can escape bourgeois repression, but instead, so that they can achieve the status of home owner.[22] The uniform texture of a squatter settlement may suggest a "people's" architecture, but in the United States the image of the suburban house still fulfills this purpose.

A similar point can be made about mobile homes. Many architects have seen these houses as part of a new world of anti-materialistic impermanency. The portability of these houses conjures up visions of a disposable architecture which would be part of a cultural or even a spiritual awakening.[23] But anyone who has read the literature put out by the mobile home industry or has visited a park of these houses knows that such a concept of flexibility or impermanency is exactly the opposite of what the purchaser of a mobile home wants.[24] Most Americans choose this kind of house because it is now the easiest way to live in that circumstance which approximates what they consider ideal. Consequently, mobile homes are styled, both by the manufacturer and later the purchaser, to look as much like the personal, detached house as possible.

Undoubtedly many former residents of the West End have now achieved a kind of self-portrait in a detached house, whether it is conventionally built or a mobile home.[25] By moving to the suburbs they have not shed all social pathologies, as many architects and planners in earlier decades predicted they would. But, by the same token, just because they live in individual houses does not mean that they have lost all group affiliation. Americans have a long tradition of participation in a broad array of voluntary organizations, and there is no sign that this activity is abating. One might even be able to find evidence of specific group affiliations in the way that particular Americans choose their individual homes.

ENDNOTES

1   The popularity of E.T. Hall's books is evidence of this interest.

2   Herbert Gans, *The Urban Villagers* (New York, 1962).

3   Ibid., 45–228.

4   Ibid., 6–11.

5   Ibid., 27.

6   Ibid., 27–32. Of course, such a system of classification is by no means beyond dispute. I am sure many sociologists would disagree with the appropriateness of Gans' categories.

7   For instance, on p. 8 Gans mentions in a footnote: "Most of the West End stores were owned by Jews, as were the medical, dental, and legal offices." Yet, there is no mention of the implications of this intermixing in the rest of the book.

8   I will not discuss whether it is possible from good sociological data to extract a proper physical design. This is another questionable issue altogether.

9   This, in fact, is what the most skilled politicians have learned to do. See, for instance: Edward C. Banfield and James Q. Wilson, *City Politics* (New York, 1963), 115–37,

10   Frederick Engels, *The Housing Question* (London, 1935), 35.

11   The implications of this fact are discussed in: Leonardo Benevolo, *The Origins of Modem Town Planning* (London, 1963).

12   I am referring primarily to Lewis Mumford because he was the most articulate of a group of critics concerned with housing in the 1930s.

13   Lewis Mumford, *Technics and Civilization* (New York, 1962), 400–35.

14   Ibid., 321–63.

15   The essence of "personality" was expressed in: Emily Post, *The Personality of the House* (New York, 1930).

16   Mumford, *Technics and Civilization*, 357–63; and Lewis Mumford, *The Culture of Cities* (New York, 1966), (26).

17   Mumford, *The Culture of Cities*, (26).

18   Stephan Thernstrom, *Poverty and Progress* (New York, 1969), 116–22, 199–201.

19   John P. Dean, *Home Ownership: Is It Sound?* (New York, 1945).

20   See, for instance, the recent survey of this subject in the November 1973 edition of *Architectural Design*.

21   Robert Goodman, *After the Planners* (New York, 1972), 242.

22   See, for instance: John F.C. Turner and Robert Fichter, *Freedom to Build* (New York, 1972), ill. 24.

23   This seems to be the message at the end of: Martin Pawley, *Architecture versus Housing* (New York, 1971).

24   Al Griffin, *So You Want to Buy a Mobile Home* (New York, 1970).

25   Indeed, the weakness of Herbert Gans' *The Levittowners* is that he does not explain why the inhabitants of the area he studied left their previous neighborhoods. Could they too have at one time been "routine-seekers"?

Atelier 5: 1955–1975

Experiments in Communal Living

Author:
Jakob K. Blumer

Source:
archithese, 14 (1975): 37–44

Translated by:
Steven Lindberg

That form reflects contents seems self-evident to us. And that contents should result in special forms is a postulate well-known and almost venerable in architecture. It is much the same with the statement that the form of a settlement reflects a certain form of society or class of society. The proof of that is easy to offer and can also be extensively illustrated. One need think only of the villa neighborhoods and working-class housing developments of the nineteenth century or of medieval forms of buildings and cities and the associated feudal society of estates. A congruence between the nature of a settlement and its social content can thus be noted.

On closer inspection, however, deviations are revealed in specific cases. The social content of cities surely influenced their form, but the forms of the past have also continued to be used for new social contents. We must even recognize that explicit alternative proposals for a social order have adopted a traditional form of expression for their habitat. The congruence between the form and the social content is thus not always absolute. Such reflections are important today in the practical debates over housing development. They helped clarify the efforts of Atelier 5 in this area.

One of the tasks given to the architect, and in which he can develop and expand his ability as an architect, is the design of housing developments. To conceive an inhabitable structure that allows one to live well. The task he sets himself is to answer the question of "well-being." He can do so only if he sets out from hypotheses that he must often formulate as assertions, since they are not always supported by the existing social reality. If we consider, for instance, the professional situation of the medieval carpenter or master builder and his relationship to the form of his own work, the parallel phenomenon for us today is not the so-called good architect but, say, the "National Association of Home Builders" in the United States, *Haus und Herd* [Home and Hearth] in Switzerland, and similar phenomena. That is, somebody who is in tune with their work, with widely accepted social behavior and the associated ideas of taste, form, and organization. The "medieval carpenter" today would help shape an image of the housing development centered on the individual as a mobile, interchangeable, transforming, but also isolated element. Single-family housing developments, disjointed apartment blocks, shopping

Jakob K. Blumer

Atelier 5:
1955—1975

Versuche im gemeinsamen Wohnen

↑ fig. 1   Atelier 5: Thalmatt housing development in Stuckishaus, Bern. Opening celebration in August 1974, with "newcomers" from the adjacent Halen housing development.

Dass Formen Inhalte reflektieren scheint uns selbstverständlich. Und dass Inhalte in speziellen Formen resultieren sollten ist in der Architektur ein recht bekanntes und schon beinahe ehrwürdiges Postulat. Aehnlich ist es mit der Aussage, dass eine Siedlungsform die Reflexion einer bestimmten Gesellschaftsform, resp. Gesellschaftsschicht, darstelle. Der Beweis dafür ist leicht anzutreten und auch umfänglich illustrierbar. Man denke etwa an Villenquartiere und Arbeitersiedlungen im 19. Jahrhundert, oder an die Haus- und Stadtformen des Mittelalters und die dazugehörige feudale Ständegesellschaft. Es wäre also eine Kongruenz zwischen der Art einer Siedlung und ihrem sozialen Inhalt festzustellen.

Bei genauerer Betrachtung zeigen sich aber im Einzelfall Abweichungen. Wohl hat der soziale Inhalt der Städte ihre Form geprägt, vergangene Formen wurden aber auch durch neue soziale Inhalte weiterverwendet. Es ist sogar zu beachten, dass ausgesprochene Alternativvorschläge zu einer gesellschaftlichen Ordnung für ihren Lebensraum auf eine überlieferte Ausdrucksweise griffen. Die Kongruenz zwischen der Form und dem sozialen Inhalt ist also nicht immer absolut. Solche Ueberlegungen sind heute bei den praktischen Auseinandersetzungen mit dem Siedlungsbau wichtig. Für die Anstrengungen des Atelier 5 in dieser Richtung waren sie klärend.

Eine der Aufgaben, die dem Architekten gestellt wird, und in der er seine Fähigkeit als Architekt entwickeln und ausbauen kann, ist der Siedlungsbau. Ein bewohnbares Gebilde sich auszudenken, in dem sich's wohl sein lässt. Die Aufgabe, die er sich selber stellt, ist: die Frage nach dem «Wohlsein» zu beantworten.

Dies kann er nur, wenn er von Thesen ausgeht, die er oft als Behauptungen aufstellen muss, da sie von der gegebenen gesellschaftlichen Realität nicht immer getragen werden. Betrachten wir nämlich die Situation des mittelalterlichen Zimmermannes oder Baumeisters in seinem Beruf und sein Verhältnis zur Form der eigenen Arbeit, so ist für uns heute die Parallelerscheinung nicht der sogenannte «gute Architekt», sondern die «national home builders association» in den USA etwa, oder Haus und Herd in der Schweiz und ähnliche Erscheinungen. Das heisst, jemand, der mit seiner Arbeit im Einklang steht, mit einem weitgehend gültigen Gesellschaftsverhalten und den damit zusammenhängenden Geschmacks-, Form- und Organisationsvorstellungen. Der «mittelalterliche Zimmermann» hätte heute also ein Siedlungsbild mitzuformen, das auf den Einzelnen als mobiles, austauschbares, sich veränderndes, aber auch vereinzeltes Element ausgerichtet ist. Die Einfamilienhaussiedlungen, die unzusammenhängenden Mietsblöcke, die Shoppingcenters, alles schön addiert und einander nicht störend (sie taten ihm nichts, also auch nichts Gutes, heisst es in «Andorra» von M. Frisch), das ist heute ein ebenso natürlicher Ausdruck wie die Handwerkergassen mit ihren heute als pittoresk bezeichneten Häusern einer anderen Epoche. Na nu, warum daraus nicht die Konsequenzen ziehen, warum diesen Weg nicht weitergehen? Resultate sind heute bekannt: Venturi & Rauch und ihr eher grotesker und oft alptraumhafter «kapitalistischer Realismus» oder die Quadratkilometervereinzelung der Levittowns mit ihren organisierten Gemeinschaften.

Es ist hier offensichtlich ein Missbehagen

Résumé Blumer

L'architecte chargé de préparer les plans d'un ensemble d'habitations se trouve en face d'un problème difficile. Il essaye de donner une réponse à la question: que faut-il pour que l'on se trouve bien? Pour arriver à cette réponse, il pourrait évidemment adopter les idéaux du bien-être tels qu'ils sont diffusés par la société de consommation. Il pourrait s'adonner au nouveau «réalisme capitaliste» genre Levittown.

Mais il y a là un malaise. L'auteur croit que de créer un cadre de vie véritablement humain signifie formuler des thèses, des propositions qui ne sont souvent pas conformes à la réalité sociale donnée.

Ces thèses, dont l'Atelier 5 à Berne se fait le porte-parole, sont, entre autres:

— L'ensemble n'est pas uniquement la somme de ses éléments; il est une «unité» comportant des espaces privés et publics — comme c'est le cas dans les cellules individuelles.
— Les cellules sont indépendantes et permettent des transformations;
— Entre cellules privées et espaces publics il y a une multitude d'espaces qui permettent une transition graduelle entre sphère privée et domaine public;
— A côté de la fonction d'habitation il y a possibilité d'accomodation d'autres fonctions.
— Establissement d'un nouveau type de propriété coopérative comme cadre juridique de cette nouvelle forme d'habitat communautaire.

festzustellen. Und es könnte also etwa die Behauptung aufgestellt werden, die sich heute manifestierenden üblichen Siedlungsformen entsprächen zwar der gesellschaftlichen Situation, befriedigten aber nicht die echten Bedürfnisse der Bewohner. Oder, was das gleiche ist, die manifeste Umgebungsform zeige das Ungenügen der gesellschaftlichen Form und damit die Notwendigkeit von neuen Versuchen und neuen Umgebungen. Hier stehen verschiedene Wege offen. Man könnte neue Formen des Zusammenlebens suchen (die Regeln und die Leute) und neue Orte dafür schaffen. Das wurde und wird getan (Fourier, Owens, Kommunehäuser etc.). Man könnte aber auch neue Umgebungen schaffen nicht in Erwartung, dass dadurch zwangsläufig ein gesellschaftliches Verhalten geändert wird, aber doch in der Hoffnung, dass die Möglichkeiten zu einem anderen Verhalten teilweise genutzt würden. Hier liegt die Arbeit des Atelier 5. Also Modellansätze und praktische Erfahrung.

Oft wird nun das Argument ins Feld geführt, dass die Komplexität einer Umgebung von den Mitteln abhängt, die zu ihrer Realisierung zur Verfügung stehen. Das heisst, dass ein Zusammenhang besteht zwischen den effektiven Bauten und der sozialen Klasse, die sie überhaupt benützen kann. Das ist sicher richtig. Man könnte daraus folgern, dass es müssig sei, das Bedürfnis des Wohnens mit differenzierten Formen zu lösen, die sich allenfalls eine ausgewählte Klasse erlauben kann. Es ist jedoch leicht zu zeigen, dass der ökonomische Rahmen eine Funktion des grösseren gesellschaftlichen Verhaltens ist, und dass selbst innerhalb der marktwirtschaftlich-kapitalistisch organisierten Gesellschaften die Schwankungen sehr gross sind, so dass ökonomische Parameter für die Demonstration des «Gebildes, in dem man sich wohl fühlt» nicht absolut ausschlagebend sein können. Man denke nur etwa an sozialen Wohnungsbau in Grossbritannien, im Vergleich zu den Vertikalghettos in den USA oder auch den Vorstädten von Paris oder Mailand. Auch hier liegt ein Ansatz der Arbeiten des Atelier 5. Also Demonstrationsobjekte, deren Klassenbezug zwar bestehen kann, deren Wirkungsmöglichkeiten aber darüberhinausgehen sollten.

. . . Ein Gebilde auszudenken, in dem sich's wohl sein lässt . . . Das war die Ausgangslage.

Die Frage nach dem Wohlsein ist nur zu beantworten, wenn Ausgangsthesen aufgestellt werden. Diese können nicht im «allgemeinen Volksempfinden» gefunden werden. Aber man kann auch nicht (zumindest in unserer heutigen Situation) ein neues gesellschaftliches Verhalten voraussetzen. Ausgangsthesen müssen so formuliert werden, dass Widersprüche und Gegensätze unter den Bewohnern (bezüglich Gemeinschaftsverhalten, Geschmack, persönlicher Ausdruck etc.) weiterbestehen können, aber im Rahmen einer Umgebung, in der diese Widersprüche gegebenenfalls auch aufgehoben werden können. Das heisst, dass die Hauptaufgabe, die man sich stellt, nicht die ist, eine Umgebung zu schaffen, durch die eine bessere Gemeinschaft entstehen muss, oder eine Umgebung für eine bessere Gesellschaftsform vorzuschlagen, sondern Möglichkeiten zur Befriedigung von Grundbedürfnissen zu schaffen. Dadurch versucht man, einen höheren Grad von Gemeinsamkeit zu provozieren, ohne dass dies als Voraussetzung bei den Bewohnern schon vorhanden wäre. Es sind also in diesem Sinne subjektiv gesetzte Wegweiser und Versuche für Veränderungsmöglichkeiten.

Grundlage für die Arbeit ist also eine Reihe von Thesen, begründet durch Beobachtungen und Erfahrungen. Wir gehen davon aus:
— dass eine Siedlung mehr ist als die Summe der Einzelteile, aus denen sie zusammengestellt wird, das heisst, dass die einzelnen Elemente ein neues gemeinsames, auch räumlich erfahrbares Element bilden; wir postulieren also einen gestalteten öffentlichen Aussenraum, der ebenso intensiv und einfach gebraucht werden kann wie die einzelnen Wohneinheiten selber;
— dass die individuelle Abschirmung der einzelnen Wohneinheiten gewährleistet wird, und dass diese auch selbständig organisier- und transformierbar sein können;
— dass zwischen Wohnelementen und dem öffentlichen Aussenraum Uebergänge halböffentlichen Charakters geschaffen werden, die das Teilnehmen an der Oeffentlichkeit graduell erlauben;
— dass verschiedene Wohnmöglichkeiten für verschiedene Bedürfnisse innerhalb der gleichen Siedlung und der gleichen Baustruktur auftreten sollen, ein maximal mögliches Angebot an gemeinsamen Funktionen realisiert wird und neben der Wohn-

↓ figs. 2-3 Thalmatt housing development: overviews.

nutzung andere Nutzungen ermöglicht werden;
— dass für die öffentlichen Räume und gemeinsamen Elemente eine gemeinsame Verantwortung besteht (z. B. Miteigentum);
— dass es möglich gemacht werden sollte, innerhalb der gleichen Baustruktur verschiedene ökonomische Ansprüche und Möglichkeiten zu befriedigen.

Es ist selbstverständlich, dass nicht in allen Fällen alle hier angedeuteten und daraus resultierenden Ansprüche erfüllt und mit gleicher Intensität angestrebt werden. An zwei Beispielen soll die Weiterführung der in der Halensiedlung realisierten Grundkonzeption gezeigt werden:
— Siedlung Thalmatt
  wo die Ausgestaltung des individuellen Elementes im Gesamtkontext der Baustruktur konsequent durchgehalten wurde.
— Siedlung Werther
  sozialer Wohnungsbau in der BRD in Westfalen, wo der Widerspruch zwischen den Aspirationen der Bewohner und der zur Verfügung gestellten Umgebung zu einer Transformation derselben führte.

Siedlung Thalmatt

Die Siedlung Thalmatt begann als Experiment nach der Vollendung der Halensiedlung. Wir stellten uns damals, nachdem man Halen als eine Siedlung von grundsätzlich zwei Normtypen ausgeführt hatte, die Frage, ob es möglich sei, einerseits einen klar formulierten

↑ fig. 4 Detail of a single home in the Thalmatt housing development.

centers, all accurately combined and not interfering with one another (they did nothing to him, so nothing good either, it says in *Andorra* by M. Frisch)—that is just as natural an expression today as the craftsmen's alleys, with their houses from a bygone era, that we would now describe as picturesque. Well, why not draw the consequences from that, why not continue on that road? The results are known today: Venturi & Rauch and their rather grotesque and often nightmarish "capitalist realism" or the quarter-acre isolation of the Levittowns with their organized communities.

A sense of discontent is clearly evident here. And some might claim that the common forms of settlement that become manifest today correspond to the social situation but do not satisfy their residents' real needs. Or, amounting to the same thing: the manifest form of the environment reflects the inadequacy of the social form and hence the necessity of new efforts and new environments. This opens up different paths. One could seek new forms of living together (the rules and the people) and create new places for them. That was and is being done (Fourier, Owen, communal houses, etc.). But one could also create new environments not in anticipation that doing so will necessarily result in changes in social behavior, but in the hope that the possibilities for different behavior may be seized at least in part. That is the work of Atelier 5: model approaches and practical experience.

It is now often argued that the complexity of an environment depends on the funds available to realize it. That means a connection exists between effective buildings and the social class able to use them. That is surely correct. One might conclude from this that it would be futile to solve the needs of housing with differentiated forms that only a select class is able to afford. It is, however, easy to show that the economic framework is a function of the broader social behavior, and that even within market-based, capitalist societies the variations are very large, so that economic parameters cannot be absolutely decisive for the demonstration of the "structure in which one feels comfortable." One need think only of the council housing in Great Britain in comparison to the vertical ghettos in the United States or even the suburbs of Paris or Milan. Here, too, lies the approach of the work of Atelier 5; that is, demonstration objects that can have a relationship to class but whose possible effects are intended to go beyond that.

… Coming up with a structure in which to live well … That was the starting point. The question of well-being can be answered only when the initial hypotheses are established. They cannot be found in "universal popular opinion." But neither can one (at least not in our present situation) assume a new social behavior. The initial hypotheses must be formulated such that conflicts and oppositions among the residents (concerning community behavior, taste, personal expression, etc.) can continue to exist but within the framework of an environment in which these conflicts can, if necessary, also be resolved. This means that the main task to set yourself is not to create an environment from which a better community ecessarily results, or to propose an environment for a better form of society, but rather to create the means for satisfying basic needs. By doing so, one tries to stimulate a higher degree of commonality without this existing among the residents in advance. In that sense, they are subjectively developed guides and efforts to promote change.

The basis for this work is a series of hypotheses justified by observations and experiences. We assume:

— that a housing development is more than the sum of the parts from which it is assembled; that means, that the individual elements form a new, common unit that can be spatially experienced; we postulate a designed, public exterior space that can be used as intensively and simply as the individual housing units themselves;
— that the individual housing units are successfully screened off for privacy and that they can also be individually organized and transformed;
— that semipublic threshold spaces are created between the housing elements and the public outdoor spaces, permitting gradual participation in the public sphere;
— that various housing possibilities for various needs within the same development and the same building structure should be available,

a maximum possible number of communal functions offered, and uses other than housing be possible;
— that there be shared responsibility for public spaces and common elements (e.g., shared ownership);
— that different economic ambitions and opportunities may be satisfied within the same building structure.

It goes without saying that of the standards outlined here, as well as those deriving from the points above, not all can be achieved or aimed at with the same intensity in all cases. Two examples will demonstrate how the basic concept realized at the Halen housing development has been furthered:
— Thalmatt housing development, where the design of the individual elements was rigorously sustained in the overall context of the building structure.
— Werther housing development, social housing construction in Westphalia, Federal Republic of Germany, where the discrepancy between residents' aspirations and the produced environment led to a transformation of the latter.

Thalmatt Housing Development

The Thalmatt housing development began as an experiment after completing the Halen development. At the time, having just built Halen as a development of basically two standard types, we asked ourselves whether it would be possible to create, on the one hand, a clearly articulated and cohesive public outdoor space and, on the other hand, differentiated housing units adapted to the various needs of individual clients. Or, expressed romantically: Can one create a new environment as coherent and organic as those we know from Mediterranean cities? (The Mediterranean city is a matter of taste here; one could also take another coherent form of settlement as the initial basis.) The answer would at first surely be: No.

The coherent settlements of the past are the result of many individual acts of building over an extended period and a consequence of repeated changes. Moreover, they were the expression of a clearly ordered social structure that was expressed in a regulated use of forms and materials. Today, the architect determines the expression, and so a development is often more a picture of the architect's aesthetic taste than an expression of the fundamental needs of the residents.

Despite all these concerns, we continued to pursue the initial idea. The main argument for doing so was rooted in the observation that the most differentiated housing forms, which address somewhat more directly the needs of the client, are built as freestanding, single-family homes. They have no context and can therefore lack common public outdoor space, which in our view is an essential element for any living situation. The artificiality of a highly differentiated environment produced all at once seemed to us the lesser evil.

So as not to get lost from the outset in arbitrary and pretentious planning, we formulated a few principles:
a) The coherence of the housing development should not be achieved by any refined composition of building volumes but rather by establishing a basic architectural and organizational structure. For that reason, we consistently chose a terraced housing scheme that could be adapted to the various needs of the clients (distance between supports, finished floors, interior organization, etc.).
b) To handle the technical, organizational, and construction problems of the building process (all of the houses were built at the same time, after all), we dispensed with any overlapping of units. Every unit stands on its own land.
c) The scale of the outdoor spaces of a housing development cannot be reconciled with the scale of motor vehicles. The housing development was planned as a pure pedestrian zone.

The development consists of two rows of houses with a public space between them. All of the houses are accessed from this public area. The houses are arranged such that the upper row can see over the lower one. That means the lower row had to be limited to two stories. The size of the house, its fittings, its interior organization, and so on, were determined by the residents' needs.

Such a procedure was possible only because fifteen of eighteen clients were known in advance.

fig. 5 Atelier 5 with Niklaus Morgenthaler, Architekten: Wertherberg development, near Münster, Westphalia; 1966–68. View of the inner courtyard.

und zusammenhängenden öffentlichen Aussenraum und andererseits differenzierte, den verschiedenen Bedürfnissen einzelner Bauherren angepasste Wohneinheiten zu schaffen. Oder romantisch ausgedrückt: Kann man eine Umgebung so kohärent und gewachsen, wie wir sie aus Mittelmeerstädten kennen, neu schaffen? (Die Mittelmeerstadt ist hier Geschmackssache, man könnte jede andere kohärente Siedlungsform als Ausgangsbasis nehmen.) Die Antwort darauf wäre zuerst einmal sicher: nein.

Die kohärenten Siedlungen der Vergangenheit sind das Resultat von vielen baulichen Einzelhandlungen über längere Zeit hinweg und eine Folge von immer wieder erfolgten Aenderungen. Zudem waren sie der Ausdruck eines klar geordneten gesellschaftlichen Aufbaus, der sich in einem geregelten Gebrauch von Formen und Material ausdrückte. Heute bestimmt der Architekt den Ausdruck, und so ist denn eine Siedlung öfters ein Abbild der ästhetischen Geschmacksrichtung des Architekten, als der Ausdruck grundsätzlicher Bedürfnisse der Bewohner.

Trotz all diesen Bedenken haben wir die Ausgangsidee weiterverfolgt. Das Hauptargument dafür lag in der Beobachtung, dass die meisten differenzierten Wohnformen, die etwas direkter auf die Bedürfnisse des Bauherrn eingehen, als freistehende Einfamilienhäuser erstellt werden. Sie weisen keinen Zusammenhang auf und lassen somit den gemeinsamen öffentlichen Aussenraum, ein unserer Meinung nach wesentliches Element für jede Wohnsituation, vermissen. Demgegenüber schien uns die Künstlichkeit einer in einem Zug erstellten differenzierten Umgebung das kleinere Uebel.

Um sich aber nicht von Anfang an in ein zufälliges und geschmäcklerisches Projektieren zu verlieren, formulierten wir ein paar Grundsätze:

a) Der Zusammenhang der Siedlung sollte nicht durch irgendeine raffinierte Komposition der Baumassen erreicht werden, sondern dadurch, dass eine bauliche und organisatorische Grundstruktur aufgestellt wurde. Wir wählten daher durchgehend ein

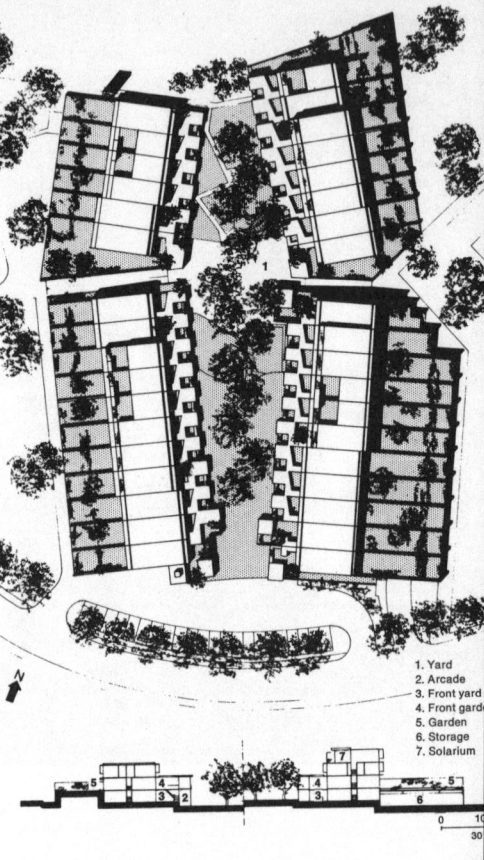

↓ fig. 6   Wertherberg housing development: site plan and section.

1. Yard
2. Arcade
3. Front yard
4. Front garden
5. Garden
6. Storage
7. Solarium

Reihenhausschema, das den verschiedenen Bedürfnissen der Bauherren angepasst werden konnte (Achsmass, ausgebaute Stockwerke, innere Organisation etc.).
b) Um die technischen, organisatorischen und konstruktiven Probleme des Bauvorganges bewältigen zu können (alle Häuser wurden ja zur gleichen Zeit gebaut), verzichteten wir auf eine Ueberlappung der Einheiten. Jede Einheit steht für sich auf eigenem Boden.
c) Die Masstäblichkeit der Aussenräume einer Siedlung lassen sich mit dem Masstab der Motorfahrzeuge nicht vereinbaren. Die Siedlung wird als reiner Fussgängerbereich geplant.

Die Siedlung besteht aus einer Doppelreihe von Häusern mit dem dazwischenliegenden öffentlichen Bereich. Alle Häuser werden aus diesem öffentlichen Bereich heraus betreten. Die Häuser werden so angeordnet, dass die obere Reihe über die untere hinwegsehen kann. Das bedeutet eine Beschränkung auf zwei Geschosse in der unteren Reihe. Die Grösse des Hauses, sein Ausbau, seine innere Organisation etc., wurden nach Bedarf der Bewohner bestimmt.

Ein solches Vorgehen wurde nur dadurch möglich, dass 15 von 18 Bauherren schon zum voraus bekannt waren. Die Eigentumsorganisation ist analog Halen gelöst. Das heisst privates Grundstück und Miteigentum. Die gemeinsamen Einrichtungen sind hier sehr bescheiden. Das Schwergewicht liegt auf der einzelnen Einheit. Die Siedlung ist eben erst bezogen worden.

Wertherberg — einige Jahre später

Schwierigkeiten bei der Mitbestimmung im Bauen

Der Stein der Weisen, der in regelmässigem Rhythmus alle paar Jahre wieder in neuer Form gefunden wird, liegt auf dem Gebiet der Architektur schon seit einiger Zeit da, wo von Mobilität, Austauschbarkeit und Mitformulierung der Umgebung durch den Bewohner gesprochen wird. Zweifelsohne an einer schönen Stelle. Vor allem von unserem alltäglichen Standort aus gesehen, der bestimmt wird durch eine meist langweilige, uniform ausgerichtete, gebaute Umwelt. Wenn es hochkommt, findet sich etwas Architektur, aber dann oft als Manifestation persönlicher Gefallsucht des Architekten. Also sollen die Leute doch lieber ihre Umgebung selber gestalten. Daran könnte man sich sicher begeistern. Was dieses Gestalten aber sei, darüber herrscht dort, wo davon gesprochen wird, nicht unbedingt Klarheit. Besteht die Gestaltung darin, innerhalb einer Wohnfläche beliebig Trennwände zu verschieben, oder aus einem gegebenen Baukastensystem sich die individuelle Kombination zusammenzustellen, oder mit individuellen Mitteln, mit dem, was man «auf dem Markt» findet, so weit wie möglich seine Wohnung innen und aussen zu gestalten? Diese Frage ist sicher schwer zu beantworten; und ebenso schwer ist es, in der neueren Architektur Beispiele zu finden, wo eine «Mitformulierung» gewollt oder gegen die Absicht der Architekten stattgefunden hat. Ein Beispiel ist Wertherberg, die Siedlung, die das Atelier 5 dort geplant und realisiert hat.

Vier Jahre später sieht Wertherberg anders aus. Es wurde von den heutigen Bewohnern in seinem Gesamtcharakter wesentlich modifiziert. Geändert oder von Anfang an individuell gestaltet wurden Räume und Elemente innerhalb des Hauses, geändert und modifiziert wurden die hofseitigen Vorplätze, die Eingänge und die Aussenhaut der Vorbauten. Nicht geändert wurde die kubische und funktionelle Organisation der Siedlung. Zufrieden sind die Leute generell mit der Organisation der Häuser und der Siedlung. Nicht zufrieden sind sie mit dem Gesicht der Häuser: äusseres Aussehen, Materialien, Eingänge, etc.

«Es geht auch anders, aber so geht es auch.» Mit «Wertherberg heute» hatte man nicht gerechnet, die Möglichkeit der Veränderung aber war eingeplant. So hatte man es den Bewohnern von Anfang an freigestellt, ihre Küchen einzubauen wie sie wollten. Die inneren Trennwände der Wohnungen sind aus Holz konstruiert

fig. 7   Wertherberg housing development: yard with greenery.

und können auf einfache Weise verschoben werden. Die äusseren Bauelemente wurden als Ständerkonstruktion mit Füllungen aus Betonbrettern konzipiert und machten so ein Ersetzen der Ausfachungen sehr leicht (Trennmauern, Eingänge etc.). Und schliesslich wollten die Architekten keinerlei Vorschriften für Aenderungen an der äusseren Form der Bauten erlassen.

Die Siedlung wurde fertig. Ein sehr differenziertes, in seiner räumlichen Gestaltung sehr reiches Gebilde. In ihrer Organisation eine Anlage, wo die Privatsphäre des einzelnen Wohnelementes äusserst geschützt wird, und die gleichzeitig von einem räumlich klar formulierten gemeinsamen Aussenraum bestimmt wird. Eigenheime, die zusammen ein grösseres Ganzes bilden. Eigenheime, denen jedoch die geläufigen Kennzeichen von Eigenheim fehlten. Die heutigen Bewohner waren zwar während der Planung der Siedlung dabei und konnten auf die Vorschläge der Architekten reagieren. Es musste aber gespart werden. Es musste vereinfacht werden. Die Architekten verfolgten konsequent und dadurch provokativ diese Richtung. Doch dann, als die Siedlung fertig war, da fehlte die Identifikation bei dem Bewohner, und es fehlte der Wille, das Ungewohnte kennen und gebrauchen zu lernen. Der Beton wurde als hässlich empfunden, die Gartenwände als schäbig und die Hauseingänge nicht auf der Höhe eines Eigenheimes. Der Eingangsgarten, die Visitenkarte, der Ort des gepflegten Rasens, die Tummelfläche der Gartenzwerge fehlte.

Modifiziert wurden die Vorbauten gegen den Platz hin. Gedeckte Sitzplätze wurden eingeglast, offene Partien überdeckt, die Terrassen möbliert und behängt. Immer liebevoll, manchmal ansprechend, öfters banal und geschmacklos.

Geändert wurden die Eingangspartien. Die Betonbretter wurden herausgenommen und durch durchbrochene Gitter ersetzt, oder durch Klinker oder hochpolierte Holzverkleidungen mit Eingangstüren und Frontbeleuchtungen, wie es sich für ein Eigenheim gehört. Materialien sind Klinker, Holzverkleidung, farbige und klare Glasbausteine, Wellplastik etc., alles was man normalerweise so im «Katalog» findet, und was nach üblichen Begriffen in den Eigenheimstatus hineinpasst.

Verändert wurde der Beton. Vordächer wurden gestrichen, und an einem beträchtlichen Teil der Siedlung wurde die Betonstruktur der Terrassen über dem Platz mit einer grauen Pappe beklebt, gemauerte Konstruktion vortäuschend.

Die Siedlung Wertherberg sieht anders aus. Man könnte sagen: Individualisierung und Differenzierung durch die Eigentümer. Oder man könnte sagen: Orgie in Kitsch und Geschmacklosigkeit. Beide Aussagen treffen jedoch nur die Oberfläche. Wertherberg als strukturierte Wohnsituation, als komplexe Organisation von Gemeinschaft und Privatheit wird heute noch ebenso erlebt wie gerade nach der Fertigstellung. Das Konzept dieser Wohnform hat nach wie vor seine gleichen Vor- und Nachteile. Geändert hat sich das Gesicht der einzelnen «Teilnehmer» an diesem Unterfangen. Oder man könnte auch sagen, erst jetzt habe sich dieses Gesicht herausgebildet. Und dieses Gesicht will nicht unbedingt gefallen.

Die Bewohner fangen an, ihre Umgebung zu gestalten. Darüber zu meckern, steht niemandem zu. Erschreckend ist nur die Art der Veränderung. Diese geht ja nicht dahin, den Gebrauchswert der Anlage zu steigern, etwa den öffentlichen Raum durch neue Funktionselemente zu bereichern oder die eigene Wohnsituation zu erweitern (hier gibt es allerdings Ansätze), sondern sie bemüht sich um das «make up», um eine neue Gesichtscrème und Perücke. Und der Spiegel, in dem sich der Einzelne schminkt, reflektiert die Aspirationen auf einen höheren sozialen Status und zeigt die Elemente an, die man mit diesem Status verbindet. Das, wodurch man die Behausung des «besser Gestellten» zu erkennen glaubt, wird in verkleinerter (und billigerer) Form an das eigene Haus geklebt. Beton ist hässlich, Sichtbackstein ist entsprechender. Eine neue, ungewohnte Wohnsituation anzunehmen, sie zu gebrauchen, ihre Vorteile auszunützen und sie zu ergänzen, diese Arbeit konnte in Wertherberg nicht geleistet werden. Es

← fig. 8
Typical "arcade" with entrances to the units.

43

wurde für die Eigentümer wichtig, wieder diejenigen Werte in ihre Siedlung herein- und zurückzubringen, mit denen sie sich identifizieren konnten, Werte, die vom Fernsehen bis zur Illustrierten, von *Schöner Wohnen* bis zum Versandhauskatalog angeboten werden. Bei diesem Angebot bleibt wenig Raum, um über eigene, wirkliche Bedürfnisse zu reflektieren.

Der Architekt steht diesen gesellschaftlichen Phänomenen etwas hilflos gegenüber. Er kann sich damit zufrieden geben, die Veränderung seines Baues miteingeplant zu haben. Die weitere Entwicklung kann er entweder als Zuschauer verfolgen oder versuchen, sie unter Kontrolle zu halten. Aus höherer Warte eine Umgebung zu erklären, d. h. die Einwohner darauf zu fixieren, ist aber — abgesehen von der Arroganz einer solchen Haltung — wenig intelligent. Es wird wiederum ein Beispiel hingestellt mit dem Anspruch, sich darauf auszurichten, d. h. es unreflektiert zu erstreben. Dadurch wird ein ähnlicher Mechanismus gefördert wie er heute die Leute zwingt, unreflektiert einem als Beispiel hingestellten Status mit seinen entsprechenden Insignien nachzueifern.

Darüber hinauszukommen und echter Bedürfnisse bewusst zu werden ist jedoch ein Emanzipationsprozess, der nur im grösseren gesellschaftlichen Rahmen geleistet werden kann. Das Heil von der Architektur zu erwarten, wäre naiv.

Die Aufgabe des Architekten, die Umgebung zu gestalten und neue, heutige Wohnformen zu planen und zu bauen, bleibt bestehen. In der Auseinandersetzung zwischen einer neuen Wohnsituation und den Aspirationen der Bewohner verändert sich unsere Umwelt. In diesem Prozess wird die Architektur oft strapaziert, eine sorgfältig durchgeformte Umgebung verkleidet. Der Gebrauch einer neuen, richtig konzipierten Wohnform dürfte aber das Bild dessen verändern, was man als erstrebenswerte Umgebung empfindet. Es wird ein neues Modell hingestellt, auf welches später als bekanntes, und somit «besser annehmbares» Beispiel zurückgegriffen werden kann. Aus dieser Perspektive sind die äusseren Veränderungen in Wertherberg eine «normale» Erscheinung. Die Leute haben sich mit ihrer Umgebung auseinandergesetzt. Das ist erfreulich, und kein Grund, sich die Haare auszuraufen. Oder dann nur als «Architekt», der sich in seiner Tätigkeit darum bemühte, eine Umgebung zu formen, die intelligent organisiert ist, reich im Gebrauch und deren Formen und Materialien, kohärent mit dem Ganzen zusammenspielen. Da ist es einem in Wertherberg ob so vieler unnützer Kosmetik schon eher ums Heulen.

↑ figs. 9–10   Wertherberg housing development: after "conversions" by the residents.

The organization of owners was dealt with in a way similar to Halen. That is, private lots and shared ownership. The common facilities are very modest. The focus is on the individual unit. The housing development is only now beginning to be occupied.

Wertherberg—Several Years Later Difficulties with Resident Participation in Construction

In the field of architecture, the philosopher's stone that is discovered anew at regular intervals every few years, for some time now lies where there is talk of mobility, interchangeability, and resident participation in the design of the environment. A good place without a doubt. Especially when seen from our everyday position, which is defined by a mostly boring, uniformly arranged built environment. We find some architecture, at best, but often it is merely a manifestation of the architect's own vanity. Let people design their surroundings themselves, then. There surely would be much enthusiasm for it. Yet what design might mean in those instances where it is being discussed is not necessarily clear. Does design entail randomly moving partitions within residential space, or assembling an individual combination from a predefined modular construction kit, or designing one's own apartment inside and out as much as possible using individual means, with whatever one finds "on the market"? This question is certainly difficult to answer, and it is just as difficult to find examples in recent architecture where "participation" was desired or happened against the intention of the architects. One example is Wertherberg, the housing development that Atelier 5 planned and realized there.

Four years later, Wertherberg looks different. Its overall character was fundamentally modified by the current residents. The rooms and elements within each house were changed or designed individually from the outset; the front yards facing the courtyard were changed and modified, as were the entrances and the outer skin of the front buildings. What was not changed was the cubic and functional organization of the housing development. In general, people are satisfied with the organization of the buildings and overall scheme. They are not satisfied with the face of the buildings: outward appearance, materials, entrances, and so on.

"It would also work another way, but it works like this too." We had not reckoned with "Wertherberg today," but the possibility of change had been planned into it. From the outset, residents were free to install their kitchens as they wished. The internal partition walls of the apartments are constructed of wood and can be easily moved. The external components were conceived as a frame construction with cement-board infills, allowing a simple replacement of the infill panels (partition walls, entrances, etc.). Finally, the architects did not want to issue any rules concerning changes to the outer form of the buildings.

The project was completed. A highly differentiated form of very lavish spatial design. In its overall disposition, it is a scheme in which the privacy of the individual housing unit is highly protected while at the same time being defined by a spatially clearly defined common outdoor space. Single-family homes that together form a larger whole. But they are single-family homes that lack some of the common characteristics of single-family homes. The present residents were involved in the planning of the development and could react to the architects' proposals. But costs had to be cut. It had to be simplified. The architects pursued that line rigorously and quite provocatively. But as the development was finished, the residents failed to identify with it, and they were unwilling to get to know and learn to use the unfamiliar. The concrete was perceived as ugly, the garden walls as shabby, and the entrances to the houses as not on the level of the single-family home. A front garden—the calling card, the place of the manicured lawn, the playground of garden gnomes—was lacking.

The front buildings facing the square were modified. Glass walls were installed in the covered seating areas, open sections were covered, furniture and hangings placed in the terraces. Always lovingly, sometimes attractively, often tritely and tastelessly.

The entrances were changed. The cement boards were removed and replaced by openwork grilles, brickwork, or highly polished wood panels with front doors and facade lighting, as suits a single-family home. The materials are clinker, wood paneling, tinted and clear glass bricks, corrugated plastic, and so on—everything one usually finds in the "catalog" and that suits the ordinary image of the single-family home.

The concrete was changed. Canopies were painted, and in a considerable section of the development the concrete structure of the terraces above the square was pasted over with gray cardboard to simulate masonry construction.

The Wertherberg housing development looks different. One could say: individualization and differentiation by the owners. Or one could say: an orgy of kitsch and tastelessness. Both statements, however, apply only to the surface. Wertherberg as a structured residential environment, as a complex organization of community and privacy, is experienced just as much today as it was just after its completion. The concept of this form of housing had and has the same advantages and disadvantages. What has changed is the look of the individual "participants" in this enterprise. Or one could also say: only now has this look taken shape. And this look does not necessarily wish to please.

The residents are beginning to design their surroundings. No one is entitled to complain about it. Only the nature of the change is alarming. It is not about increasing the use value of the grounds, improving the public space by adding new functional elements, or extending one's own living situation (though there are attempts to do that); rather, it is concerned with "makeup," with a new facial cream and wig. And the mirror in which the individual applies that makeup reflects aspirations to a higher social status and indicates the elements that are associated with that status. That which is thought to identify the housing of the "better off" is pasted onto one's own house in miniaturized (and cheaper) form. Concrete is ugly. Exposed brick is more appealing. Accepting a new, unusual housing situation, using it, making use of its advantages, and supplementing it—that work could not be done in Wertherberg. It became important to the owners that they bring in and bring into their development those values with which they could identify—values that are offered from the television to the magazine, from *Schöner Wohnen* [Beautiful living] to the mail-order catalog. Such offerings leave little room to reflect one's own, real needs.

The architect is rather helpless in the face of these social phenomena. He can be satisfied that he planned the possibility of change into his building. He can either watch the further development as a bystander or try to control it. Formulating surroundings from a lofty vantage point and declaring their form sacrosanct—that is, set in stone for the residents—is, however, not very intelligent, to say nothing of the arrogance of such an attitude. It holds out another example with the ambition of orienting oneself around it; that is, to strive for it without thinking. That encourages a mechanism similar to the one that now compels people to emulate unthinkingly a status that is held out as an example and all its corresponding insignia.

Getting beyond that and becoming aware of real needs is, however, a process of emancipation that can be achieved only within the larger social framework. To expect salvation from architecture would be naive.

The architect's task of designing the surroundings and planning and building new, current housing forms remains. In the interaction between a new housing situation and the aspirations of the resident, our environment changes. In this process, architecture often strains to put cladding on carefully formed surroundings. The use of a new, properly conceived housing form, however, may be able to change the picture of what is perceived as surroundings worth striving for. A new model is held out on which one can later fall back as a familiar and hence "more acceptable" example. From this perspective, the outward changes in Wertherberg are a "normal" phenomenon. The people engaged with their surroundings. That is heartening and no reason to pull one's hair out. Or, if so, only as an "architect" whose work was an effort to form surroundings that are intelligently organized, offer a wealth of uses, and whose forms and materials interact coherently with the whole. That is what really makes one want to weep about the many useless cosmetics in Wertherberg.

Signs of Life

Symbols in the American City

Author:
Denise Scott Brown

Source:
archithese, 19 (1976): 29–34

Translated by:
Steven Lindberg

Letter to the Editors

Asked to contribute to the realism issue of "archithese," I am sending photographs of panels we created for our current exhibition, "Signs of Life: Symbols in the American City," for the Smithsonian Institution. The exhibition is a critical documentation of American taste.

As this makes clear, we are studying the urban environment as we find it; we are trying to understand its symbols in order to establish a point of departure for our own work. You might say that our concept of "reality" is an empirical one, founded more on sociological and architectural perception than on philosophical trains of thought. We are, in a sense, simple sociologists who gain insights from observing behavior and taste and combine them with observation of the environment we as architects make. Peter Smithson once called this attitude "active socioplastics."

We share an interest in the concept of "realism," but we approach it from our own, pragmatic standpoint. That means that we try to form our ideas about architectural reality by induction: by deriving theories from specific examples and not the other way around. We do not believe our path is the only one or the only right one to approach the problem; rather, it supplements the theoretical approaches that many of our European colleagues have chosen. D.S.B.

**Signs of Life
Symbols in the American City**

I
What makes a house look like a house, a school look like a school, or a bank like a bank? What makes a petrol station look like a good neighbor? The elements of architecture have symbolic meaning and give messages about the environment that make it comprehensible and therefore usable by people in their daily lives.

The flashing electric sign on Route 66 tells us specifically, EAT HERE, and its design may suggest the kind of dining available—family, soft-lights sophisticated, country inn, etc. Off the main highway, however, the curving roads, well-tended lawns, colonial doorways,

Denise Scott Brown

ZEICHEN DES LEBENS

Symbole in der amerikanischen Stadt

Brief an die Herausgeber

Aufgefordert, zum Realismus-Heft von archithese beizutragen, schicke ich Fotografien von Tafeln, die wir für unsere gegenwärtige Ausstellung «Signs of Life: Symbols in the American City» im Auftrag der Smithsonian Institution ausgearbeitet haben. Die Ausstellung ist eine kritische Dokumentation des amerikanischen Geschmacks.

Wie daraus ersichtlich ist, studieren wir die städtische Umwelt (environment), so wie wir sie vorfinden; wir versuchen, ihre Symbole zu verstehen, um einen Ausgangspunkt für unsere eigene Arbeit zu gewinnen. Man kann sagen, dass unser Begriff von «Wirklichkeit» ein empirischer ist, mehr auf soziologische und architektonische Wahrnehmung gegründet als auf philosophische Gedankengänge. Wir sind, in einem gewissen Sinn, einfache Soziologen, die aus der Beobachtung des Verhaltens und des Geschmacks der Leute Einsichten gewinnen und diese verbinden mit der Beobachtung der Umwelt, die wir als Architekten machen. Peter Smithson nannte diese Haltung einmal «active socioplastics».

Wir teilen das Interesse für den «Realismus»-Begriff; wir nähern uns diesem allerdings von unserem eigenen, pragmatischen Standpunkt aus. Das heisst, wir versuchen, unsere Vorstellungen über die architektonische Wirklichkeit durch Induktion zu bilden: indem wir von den konkreten Beispielen aus zu Theorien gelangen, und nicht umgekehrt. Wir sind nicht der Meinung, unser Weg sei der einzige oder einzig richtige, um sich dem Problem zu nähern: er ergänzt vielmehr die theoretischeren Annäherungen, die viele unserer europäischen Kollegen gewählt haben.

D. S. B.

**Zeichen des Lebens
Symbole in der amerikanischen Stadt**

I

Was bewirkt, dass ein Haus wie ein Haus aussieht, eine Schule wie eine Schule oder eine Bank wie eine Bank? Was bewirkt, dass eine Tankstelle aussieht wie ein guter Nachbar? Diese Ausstellung soll zeigen, dass die Architektur-Formen symbolische Bedeutung haben und Mitteilungen machen über die Umwelt (environment), die diese für die Leute in ihrem täglichen Leben verständlich und brauchbar werden lassen.

So sagt uns das aufleuchtende Schriftzeichen an der *Route 66* ausdrücklich EAT HERE und seine Gestaltung kann uns zu verstehen geben, von welcher Art das Essen ist: gutbürgerlich, vornehm oder ländlich. Aber abseits der grossen Autobahnen, in Suburbia, erzählen uns die gewundenen Strassen, die gepflegten Rasen, die Häuser mit Giebeldächern, die Eingänge im Kolonialstil und die mit Läden versehenen Fenster, ohne Schriftzeichen zu benötigen, dass es hier Sinn für Tradition, Besitzerstolz und Landleben gibt.

Die Ausstellung ist auch ein Versuch, die pluralistische Aesthetik der amerikanischen Stadt und ihrer Vororte zu untersuchen und zu verstehen, was die Stadtlandschaft für die Leute bedeutet. Dies mittels einer Analyse ihrer Symbole und deren Herkunft. Wir haben unsere Aufmerksamkeit besonders auf die Ladenstrasse des 20. Jahrhunderts (strip) und auf die wuchernden Vororte (sprawl) gerichtet, weil in dieser Umwelt der Gebrauch von Symbolen seit dem 19. Jahrhundert andauert, während in anderen Gebieten diese Tradition durcheinandergebracht oder gebrochen wurde durch den Versuch der modernen Architekten, historische und symbolische Anspielungen aus der Architektur zu tilgen.

Unsere Dokumentation von Vorort, «Strip» und Stadt, im Zusammenhang mit einander und mit der Stadt des 19. Jahrhunderts, ist Teil einer breiter angelegten Bemühung, den unterschiedlichen architektonischen Geschmack in Amerika zu verstehen und die Rolle des Architekten in Beziehung zu ihm zu bestimmen. Wir behaupten:

— dass die Durchwirkung mit Symbolen und Zeichen, wie sie in der historischen Stadt bestand, in der heutigen Stadt weiterlebt, wenn auch in anderer Form;
— dass Symbole und Zeichen in der Umwelt der Stadt allgegenwärtig sind, was aber nicht anerkannt wird;
— dass die «gewöhnlichen» Symbole und Zeichen der Umwelt der Geschäfts- und Wohnviertel bedeutsam sind für das tägliche Leben;
— dass wir uns und unsere Umwelt besser verstehen, wenn wir die Symbole und Zeichen zu verstehen lernen;
— dass ein notwendiges Vorspiel zur Verbesserung unserer Umwelt darin besteht, dass wir ihre raison d'être verstehen.

Ein weiteres Ziel dieser Ausstellung ist es, den Architekten und Planern vorzuschlagen, die heutige Stadtlandschaft mit offenen Augen zu studieren und besonders die symbolischen Bedeutungen, mit denen die Leute sie belegen. Wenn sie das tun, werden sie mehr lernen über die Bedürfnisse, die Vorlieben und den Geschmack der Leute, deren Leben sie beeinflussen. Das gilt vor allem für den Geschmack von Gruppen, deren Werte sich von ihren eigenen unterscheiden.

II

Der Teil der Ausstellung, der «Das Heim» zum Gegenstand hat, untersucht vorstädtische und städtische Wohnviertel und Wohnhäuser. Seine Aufmerksamkeit gilt im besonderen dem Zierat, den die Leute ihren Häusern und Gärten hinzufügen, wenn sie sie einmal bewohnen. Die Untersuchung schliesst auch die Stile der von den Unternehmern erstellten Häuser ein und der Häuser, die in den Werbesendungen der Television, den Wohnjournalen, den Anzeigen der Automobilindustrie, den Karikaturen im *New Yorker* oder in den Versandhaus-Katalogen erscheinen. Der Grund dafür ist, dass diese Massenmedien ihren Markt zu erreichen suchen, indem sie die Symbole aus dem Bereich des Wohnens verwenden, die die gängigen gesellschaftlichen und persönlichen Wünsche spiegeln.

Die Elemente von Suburbia — die Strassen, Häuser, Dächer, Rasen und Haustüren — dienen praktischen Zwecken, sie bieten beispielsweise Zugang und Schutz, aber sie dienen den vorstädtischen Bewohnern auch als Mittel der Selbstdarstellung.

Sich windende Strassen, romantische Dachlinien, Haustüren im Kolonialstil und Laternen von Kutschen; sie alle sind zierende Elemente mit symbolischen Obertönen, die die Bewohner verwenden, um sich anderen mitzuteilen. Die Mitteilung betrifft hauptsächlich gesellschaftlichen Status, soziales Streben, individuelle Freiheit und Nostalgie für eine andere Zeit oder einen anderen Ort. Die symbolischen Inhalte dieser Elemente stammen aus Geschichte und Patriotismus, Leben auf dem Land und den Landsitzen der Reichen.

Eine Warnung: der Symbolismus im Bereich des vorstädtischen Wohnens gibt keine Auskunft darüber, *warum* die Leute in Suburbia leben, er verrät auch nicht viel über die Probleme, denen die Leute dort begegnen; er zeigt bloss einige der Wünsche an, die sie haben, während sie dort wohnen. Das gleiche gilt für das Wohnen in der Stadt. Und noch etwas: obschon die Massenmedien interessante Aufschlüsse geben über die Haltung bestimmter Gruppen gegenüber dem Wohnen, dürfen diese Quellen nicht als der Weisheit letzten Schluss

↓ fig. 1   The visual language of Levittown. Panel from the *Signs of Life* exhibition (1976).

fig. 2   The visual language of the row house (*Signs of Life*, 1976).

figs. 3–4   A popular row house; outside (3) and inside (4) (*Signs of Life*, 1976).

bezüglich der persönlichen und gesellschaftlichen Werte dieser Gruppen verstanden werden. Dennoch gibt die Selbstdarstellung der Amerikaner in ihrem Heim und darum herum einen wichtigen Hinweis auf ihre Haltungen, umso mehr, als diese Form der Selbstdarstellung von fast allen sozialen Gruppen praktiziert wird, von Jungen und Alten, Reichen und Armen, Mietern und Eigentümern, Städtern und Vorstädtern.

(Diese beiden Texte gehören zur Ausstellung *Signs of Life: Symbols in the American City*, die diesen Sommer im Auftrag der Smithsonian Institution in der Renwick Gallery in Washington eingerichtet wurde von Venturi und Rauch, Architekten und Planer. Verantwortlich für Forschung und Texte: Denise Scott Brown; für Gestaltung und Einrichtung: Steven Izenour.)
(Uebersetzung: Martin Steinmann)

figs. 5–6   An elegant home of the elite; outside (5) and inside (6) (*Signs of Life*, 1976).

Signes de vie, symboles dans la ville américaine

I

Qu'est-ce qui fait qu'une maison a l'air d'une maison, qu'une école a l'air d'une école, qu'une banque a l'air d'une banque? Qu'est-ce qui fait qu'une station d'essence a l'air d'une chose familière? Cette exposition doit montrer que les formes de l'architecture ont des significations symboliques et donnent des messages qui rendent l'environnement compréhensible et par conséquent utilisable par les gens dans leur vie quotidienne.

Par exemple, l'enseigne lumineuse clignotante de la *Route 66* nous dit de manière précise, MANGE ICI, et son type de design nous suggère le genre de repas qu'on peut y faire, peut-être familial, ou sophistiqué à lumières tamisées, ou encore auberge de campagne traditionnelle. Mais, loin de l'autoroute, les routes sinueuses d'une agglomération suburbaine, les étendues de gazon, les maisons avec leur toit en pente, leur entrée coloniale et leurs fenêtres à volets nous disent, sans avoir besoin d'aucun signe, qu'ici il y a une communauté qui chérit les traditions, la fierté de la propriété et la vie rurale.

Cette exposition essaie également d'étudier l'esthétique pluraliste de la ville américaine et de ses banlieues, et de comprendre ce que le paysage urbain signifie pour les gens, ceci à travers l'analyse de leurs symboles, de leurs sources et de leurs antécédents. Nous nous sommes particulièrement concentrés sur les enseignes commerciales et les nouvelles agglomérations suburbaines du vingtième siècle, parce que dans ces environnements la tradition — qui existait dans la ville du dix-neuvième siècle — d'utiliser des symboles en architecture s'est perpétuée, alors que dans les régions où l'architecte exerce un contrôle plus direct la tradition est devenue moins nette ou a même été rompue par les efforts des architectes «modernes» pour éliminer de l'architecture toute association historique et symbolique et toute décoration.

Notre documentation de l'agglomération suburbaine, des enseignes commerciales et de la ville fait partie d'un effort plus large de comprendre les différents goûts qui existent en Amérique en matière d'architecture, et de définir le rôle de l'architecte en relation avec ces goûts. Nous soutenons que:
— le foisonnement des symboles et des signes qui existait dans la ville historique continue dans la ville d'aujourd'hui, quoique sous une forme différente;
— il existe partout des signes et des symboles dans notre environnement urbain mais ils ne sont pas reconnus;
— les symboles et les signes «ordinaires» de l'environnement commercial et de l'environnement résidentiel sont importants dans notre vie quotidienne;
— en apprenant à comprendre nos symboles et nos signes nous en arrivons à nous comprendre mieux nous-mêmes et à mieux comprendre notre paysage;
— comprendre la *raison d'être* de notre environnement physique est le prélude nécessaire pour l'améliorer.

Cette exposition vise également à suggérer aux designers, aux architectes et aux planificateurs d'étudier sans préjugé le paysage urbain actuel et spécialement les significations qu'ont les gens y mettent. Ce faisant, ces urbanistes apprendront plus qu'ils n'en savent maintenant au sujet des besoins, des goûts et des préférences des gens dont ils influencent la vie, et particulièrement au sujet des groupes dont les valeurs sont différentes des leurs.

II

La partie de l'exposition qui a comme sujet le «home» étudie les quartiers résidentiels urbains et suburbains et les maisons individuelles. L'attention est centrée tout particulièrement sur les décorations que les gens ajoutent à leur maison et à leur jardin une fois qu'ils y viennent s'installer. Mais on y étudie aussi les styles des maisons construites par des entrepreneurs, ainsi que le contenu relatif au logement dans la publicité de la télévision, les «Home Journals», la publicité des automobiles, les dessins de la revue *The New Yorker*, la publicité des entrepreneurs de construction et les catalogues de vente par correspondance, parce que toutes ces sources de mass media essaient d'atteindre leur clientèle en utilisant des symboles du logement qui reflètent les aspirations sociales et personnelles.

Les éléments physiques des zones suburbaines — les routes, les maisons, les toits, le gazon et les portes d'entrée — correspondent à des nécessités pratiques telles que voies d'accès et protection, mais elles servent aussi comme moyens pour les résidents suburbains d'exprimer leur propre personne.

Les chemins qui serpentent, les toits aux silhouettes romantiques, les ornements dans le jardin, les portes d'entrée coloniales et les lanternes de calèche sont des éléments décoratifs avec des implications symboliques que les résidents utilisent pour communiquer aux autres quelque chose sur eux-mêmes. La communication tourne principalement autour du statut social, des aspirations sociales, de l'identité personnelle, de la liberté individuelle et de la nostalgie pour d'autres temps et d'autres lieux. Les sujets symboliques de la décoration du logement viennent de l'histoire, de la vie rurale, du patriotisme et des résidences des riches.

Un avertissement: le symbolisme du logement suburbain ne nous dit pas pourquoi les gens vivent dans les suburbs et ne nous révèle pas non plus beaucoup sur les problèmes que les gens ont dans les suburbs; il ne fait qu'indiquer quelques-unes de leurs aspirations quand ils y sont. Il en va de même avec le logement urbain. Quant à la source des mass media, quoique fournissant une information intéressante sur l'attitude d'un groupe vis-à-vis du logement, elle ne devrait pas être prise comme le dernier mot sur les valeurs personnelles et sociales aux Etats-Unis. Cependant, l'expression personnelle des Américains à l'intérieur et autour de leur «home» est un indice important de leurs attitudes, ceci d'autant plus que cette forme d'expression est pratiquée par presque tous les groupes sociaux, par les jeunes et les vieux, les riches et les pauvres, les locataires et les propriétaires, les habitants des villes et ceux des suburbs.

(Ces deux textes font partie de l'exposition *Signs of Life: Symbols in the American City*, qui a été préparée par Venturi et Rauch, architectes et planificateurs, pour la Smithsonian Institution à Washington (Renwick Gallery, été 1976). Responsable pour la recherche et les textes: Denise Scott Brown. Présentation: Steven Izenour.)

(Trad. Irène von Moos)

and shuttered windows of suburbia tell us, without need of signs, that here is a community that values tradition, pride of ownership, and the rural life.

The exhibition is also an attempt to survey the pluralist aesthetic of the American city and its suburbs and to understand what the urban environment means to people, through an analysis of its symbols, their sources, and their antecedents. We have focused particularly on the twentieth century commercial strip and suburban sprawl, because it is in these environments that the new symbolism has emerged since the nineteenth century. In areas more directly controlled by architects, the tradition of using symbolism in architecture has been confused or broken by their attempts to wipe the slate clean of all historical and symbolic associations.

This effort to document sprawl, strip, and city in the context of one another and of the nineteenth-century city is part of a broader effort to understand American architectural tastes and the role of the architect in relation to them. We argue that:
— the influence of the historic city's symbols and signs are still felt in today's city, but in a different form.
— symbols and signs are omnipresent in the city's environment, but this is not acknowledged.
— "ordinary" symbols and signs of the commercial and residential environments are significant in our daily lives.
— to better understand ourselves and our environment, we must learn to understand its symbols and signs.
— to improve our environment, we must first understand how and why it came to be.

A further aim is to suggest to urban designers, architects and planners, and the decision-makers they influence, that they shall study these environments, especially the symbolic meanings people ascribe to or invest in them. In so doing, they will learn more than urbanists now know about the needs, tastes, and preferences of the people whose lives they influence, particularly about the tastes of groups whose values and culture patterns are different from those of the professionals.

II

The section of the exhibition titled "The Home" surveys suburban neighborhoods and individual houses, particularly the decorations people add to their houses and yards once they occupy them. But it surveys, too, the housing content of television commercials, home magazines, automobile advertisements, *New Yorker* cartoons, and mail-order catalogs, because these mass media sources attempt to reach their markets by using residential symbols that reflect current social and personal aspirations.

The physical elements of suburbia—the roads, houses, roofs, lawns, and front doors—serve practical purposes such as giving access and shelter, but they also serve as means of self-expression for suburban residents.

Winding roads, romantic roof lines, garden ornaments, and colonial front doors—all are decorative elements with symbolic overtones that residents use to communicate with others about themselves. The communication is mainly about social status and social aspirations, personal identity and individual freedom, and nostalgia for another time or place. The symbolic subject matter of residential decoration comes from history, rural life, patriotism, and the states of the rich.

A warning: Suburban housing symbolism, however, does not tell us why people live in suburbia or much about the problems they experience in suburbia; it merely tells us some of their aspirations while they are there. The same holds true for dwelling in the city. Moreover, although the mass media are an interesting source of information on group attitudes to housing, they should not be taken as the last word on personal and social values in the United States. Nevertheless, the use of symbolic decoration by Americans in and around their houses is an important clue to American attitudes because it is practiced by almost all social groups, by young and old, rich and poor, renters and owners, urbanites and suburbanites.

(These two texts are taken from the exhibition *Signs of Life: Symbols in the American City*, which was curated by Venturi and Rauch, Architects and Planners, for the Smithsonian Institution at the Renwick Gallery in Washington. Responsibility for the research and texts: Denise Scott Brown; for design and installation: Steven Izenour.)

V Territory and Shelter

389
The Colonial Order
of Things
    by Samia Henni

405
Immigrant Worker
Housing in Switzerland:
Experiments in
Communal Living
    by Eliane Perrin

420
Military Theories and
Collective Housing
    by Teresa Zarebska

431
Remarks on an Ill-Defined
Problem: The Architecture
of Nonarchitects
    by André Corboz

450
Squatters: The Seven
Housing Systems of Nairobi
    by Praful C. Patel,
    Jeff Racki, and Reena Racki

468
An Architecture of Resistance:
Slums in Asia
    by Jin-Bak Pyun

The Colonial Order of Things

Samia Henni

The essays authored by Eliane Perrin, Teresa Zarebska, André Corboz, Praful C. Patel, Jeff Racki, Reena Racki, and Jin-Bak Pyun and published in *archithese* from 1971 to 1974 recall the claim that "there is no modernity without coloniality."[1] That is, coloniality constitutes modernity. It cannot be divided from it. It is not it. It is in it. The times in which and the spaces from which these essays were written echo this constitution. Some of the authors reproduced it. Others critiqued it and revealed the dynamics of Eurocentric—embodied in U.S.-centric—socio-economic and political apparatuses used to make space and impose power. This is not the same as claiming the essays offer no examples of resistance to these forms of modernity/coloniality.

In the selected essays, echoes of coloniality's constitution of modernity appear in various forms of spatial practice and architectural discourse, including debates about modern housing, "indigenous" housing, housing for the working class, self-built housing (or "informal" settlements), climate and hygiene questions; the housing policies and knowledge produced by national or international professional organizations, public institutions, and the United Nations Habitat programs; detailed surveys of slums built by the so-called other; and histories and theories of the military architecture of the Renaissance, which cannot be dissociated from European colonization.

By either embracing or opposing this constitution—consciously or unconsciously—the authors of the selected essays confront their readers with the power dynamics of architecture and the built environment. They offer connections among architectural history, theory, practice, and the colonial world order (or disorder). Aníbal Quijano, a Peruvian sociologist, argues that one of the fundamental principles of the coloniality of power "is the social classification of the world's population around the idea of race, a mental construction that expresses the basic experience of colonial domination and pervades the more important dimensions of global power, including its specific rationality: Eurocentrism."[2] One might regard these contributions as a way of exposing this coloniality of power—which is still in vogue today—and of searching for postmodernity.

Ethnography and Colonial Constructs
In his 1974 article "Remarks on an Ill-Defined Problem: The Architecture of Nonarchitects," Swiss architectural historian Corboz questions the hierarchical designation of the built environment and analyzes the ramifications, which persist to this day, of bourgeois cultural imperialism in architecture. He argues that the terms "spontaneous, popular, vernacular, minor, indigenous, primitive, anonymous, and without architects" are problematic and discriminatory because of their existence in relation or opposition to their dominant privileged antonyms.[3] This classification was constructed through a gaze that assessed the built environment based on what was familiar, accredited, and, ultimately, normalized. This was an approach that patronized and essentialized "the other," often reproducing imperial and colonial attitudes rooted in what Frantz Fanon, psychiatrist and political philosopher from the French colony of Martinique, denounced in his 1952 *Peau noire, masques blancs* (*Black Skin, White Masks*), and which Palestinian American cultural theorist Edward Said later theorized as "orientalism."[4] This phenomenon often characterizes West European and North American art and architectural history, as well as literature and cultural studies.[5]

The effort to classify and label the unfamiliar built environment culminated in the exhibition *Architecture without Architects* (Museum of Modern Art, New York, 1964) and the accompanying publication, *Architecture without Architects: A Short Introduction to Non-pedigreed Architecture*, curated and written by Austrian American architect Bernard Rudofsky. In his acknowledgments, Rudofsky uses the terms *non-formal architecture* and *non-classified architecture* to refer to the photographed buildings and spaces from around the world that he exhibited in New York. He credits, among other people and institutions, the Musée de l'Homme (Museum of Man) in Paris, the Hispanic Society in New York, the Frobenius Institute in Frankfurt, and the Islamic Archives in Washington, DC.[6] The majority of the collections and archives of these institutions came from European and North American colonies, colonial expeditions, ethnographic missions, and trading companies. For instance, the Parisian Musée de l'Homme—established in 1937 on the occasion of the Exposition Internationale des Arts et Techniques dans la Vie Moderne (International Exposition of Art and Technology in Modern Life) as an ethnography research center and ethnography museum to replace the Musée d'Ethnographie du Trocadéro (founded in 1882)—studied and collected artifacts, documents, customs, rituals, photographs, and reports about the people of Africa, Asia, and Oceania, portions of which were then part of the French Empire.[7]

Presenting and representing these populations and their built environments was an activity that developed across Central Europe, the United States, and Japan in the nineteenth and twentieth centuries. With the organization of large world's fairs and colonial exhibitions from 1879 to 1948, colonizing authorities—including Belgium, France, Germany, Great Britain, Italy, Portugal, Spain—celebrated the accomplishments of colonialization; portrayed a colonial world order; and displayed events, people, and places from the colonies. For example, in Switzerland, African people—children, women, and men locked up in confined spaces—were exhibited in the so-called *village nègre* in Geneva in 1896, in *Negerdörfli* in Altstetten in Zurich in 1925, and in the *Negerdorf aus Senegal* at the Basel Zoo in 1926.[8] These human zoos, also called "ethnological expositions," turned human lives and their habitats into consumable spectacles and lucrative attractions, while propagating racist prejudices and discriminatory constructs.[9] While colonial exhibitions varied in design, size, and duration, they typically shared common biased misinterpretations and misrepresentations of the displayed races, customs, religions, genders, and architectures.

This attitude is often reflected in urbanism and architectural discourses and publications in Europe and its vast empires. In 1931, a year after the French colonial regime organized monumental celebrations in Algiers and other parts of Algeria on the one hundredth anniversary of its French colonization, known as "Le Centenaire de l'Algérie Française" (The Centenary of French Algeria), the Bois de Vincennes in Paris hosted the International Colonial Exhibition, which displayed people, artifacts, resources, and goods from the French colonial empire.[10] Presided over by Marshal Hubert Lyautey, French army officer and colonial administrator, the exhibition organizers maintained both their "civilizing mission" toward people from the colonies and the seduction strategies they used to incite Europeans to move to and settle in the colonies. As the director of the exhibition congress argued,

> It was desirable that the number of Europeans in the colonial countries should always increase. It is, in fact, only this growth that will make it possible to stand up to the nationalist tendencies of the indigenous populations, which Bolshevik or other propaganda is trying to overexcite and develop. All the efforts of town planners must therefore tend to *encourage European immigration* to the colonies and to *obtain*, for this purpose, the maximum advantage for the urban population of the white race in the cities they organize.[11]

To respond to the colonization and migration of people from various parts of Europe to the colonies and to establish a colonial order, the exhibition hosted an International Congress of Urbanism in the Colonies and in Tropical Countries. In the extensive two-volume publication that resulted from the congress (1932), French architect and urbanist Jean Royer and Henri Prost, a French urbanist who worked in Turkey and the French Protectorate of Morocco, gathered lectures and essays written on European urbanism in the colonies by military officers and civil servants active there. The first volume of the manuscript is divided into six geographic areas: North Africa, Tropical Africa, the Orient, the Far East, the Americas, and Ancient Cities. According to Prost, the goal of the congress was to define the best provisions for cities where races of different customs coexisted; design housing that respected local climate and traditions; study ventilation, hygiene, sanitation, and new construction processes; and incite collaboration between modern builders and local artisans, preserve ancient cities, and protect historic monuments for tourism purposes.[12] Contrary to these integrationist premises, European architects and urbanists in Algiers took another trajectory, encouraging assimilation to French norms and forms.

Urbanism and Hygiene Narrative
The influential Association of Urbanism of the Amis d'Alger, the Algiers Group of the Société des architectes modernes (Society of Modern Architects), and the Trade Union Association of Architects Graduated and Admitted by the French Government organized the first Exposition d'Urbanisme et d'Architecture Moderne (Exhibition of Town Planning and Modern Architecture) in 1933. The French architect Marcel Lathuillière served as deputy president of the exhibition's organization committee; Albert Seiller, an Algiers-born-and-based architect, was the general curator; and Pierre-André Emery, Swiss-born and the future leader of the Algiers section of the Congrès Internationaux d'Architecture Moderne (International Congresses of Modern Architecture, CIAM), was the general secretary. In a special issue of the architectural magazine *Chantiers* dedicated to the exhibition, the articles and projects presented are divided into two parts: first, urbanism and the large-scale planning and development of cities; second, architecture and modern construction. One of the articles included in this publication is "Tous urbanistes!" (All town planners!) by Rudolphe Rey—the president of both the exhibition committee and the Amis d'Alger association —who invited Le Corbusier to Algiers. He asserts that "planners and architects in Algeria, closely united in the continuation of their generous effort, will not cease to guide public authorities in their great task of remodeling and developing our African cities."[13]

Lathuillière published an article titled "L'architecture moderne et l'aménagement de l'habitation" (Modern architecture and the configuration of housing), while Seiller reported his ideas in "L'hygiène dans l'habitation" (Housing hygiene). Both contributions ignore the question of housing designed for Algerians, a question that only one of the articles in the special issue deals with directly: "L'habitation indigène et les quartiers musulmans" (Indigenous housing and muslim neighborhoods), written by François Bienvenu, an architect who was born and based in Algiers and who worked for the French general government. Bienvenu describes the ongoing public debates on the types of housing in which Algerians—or, as they were called, the *indigènes* (indigenous or native people) —were expected to live. He describes two opposing schools of thought, neither of which had been able to forge an acceptable compromise. The debates centered on a rhetorical question: Is it necessary to conceive and build dwellings that would satisfy the traditional lifestyle of the "indigenous" population, or would it instead be better to envisage the adaptation of "indigenous" modes of living to the French modern lifestyle through European-type housing?

This "traditional/modern" dichotomy—or, to use Rudofsky's terms, "non-pedigreed/pedigreed"—dominated the debates about architecture in European empires. On the occasion of the second edition of the Exposition de la Cité Moderne: Urbanisme, architecture, habitation (Exhibition of the Modern City: Urbanism, Architecture, Housing) in Algiers in 1936, the French architecture magazine *L'architecture d'aujourd'hui*, directed by André Bloc, an Algiers-born French editor, dedicated a special issue to Algeria, Morocco, Syria, Lebanon, and Guadeloupe. The issue was titled "France d'outremer" (Overseas France) and was edited by Pierre Vago, a Budapest-born French architect. In his essay "L'habitation indigène dans les colonies françaises" (Indigenous housing in French colonies), Moscow-born French architect Alexandre Persitz describes and discusses the houses and housing built by people from North Africa, West and Equatorial Africa, Madagascar, Indochina, and Oceania. He argues, however, that "the real colonial urbanism requires a perfect understanding between the medical-hygienists, the architects, the ethnographers, the administration and … the native."[14]

The combination of sanitation, hygiene, and colonial ethnography in the colonies, which intersected with surveillance and confinement during fascist regimes in the years leading up to and during the Second World War, obsessed European architects, planners, civil servants, and military officers.

In the aftermath of the disasters and losses of the Second World War, European authorities and institutions became more concerned with the dynamics of the nascent Cold War, the escalating activities of civil rights and independence movements, and the launching of state-led reconstruction and modernization plans. This had a significant impact on architects and architectural discourses; it was evident in the postwar anxieties of some of the members of CIAM.[15] This reaction was combined with an interest in the living strategies and building patterns that colonized people had invented and implemented. For example, in 1953, at the ninth meeting of the CIAM in Aix-en-Provence, two grid presentations marked a methodological and epistemological turn. The first presentation was of the GAMMA Grid by the Groupe d'Architectes Modernes Marocains (Modern Moroccan Architects Group, GAMMA).[16] The second presentation was the Grid Mahieddine, given by the members of the CIAM-Algiers group.[17] Through a series of plans, sections, elevations, drawings, diagrams, photographs, and interviews with residents, each group documented the built environments and dwelling practices of an existing *bidonville* (shantytown or slum) in Casablanca and Algiers. To a group of international professionals, they presented a typical architecture designed and realized under colonial conditions by its residents—"architecture without architects." In doing so, they also illustrated the harsh conditions that people from Morocco and Algeria (the so-called indigenous) had to endure. A few years later, the *bidonville* would become an object of study in major European cities hosting migrant workers, often from the colonies. One of the most notable examples was the *bidonville de Nanterre*, in the suburb of Paris, populated by Algerian migrant workers, which was mapped and studied by the Parisian Institut de l'environnement (Environmental Institute) in the early 1970s.[18]

Housing and "Other" Climates

In parallel with these international gatherings and postwar frictions, European architecture journals and publishers began featuring the work of European architects in the overseas colonies or in recently independent countries such as India. In 1953, *Architectural Review* published a collection of surveys and projects, titled "The African Experiment," that British architects Jane Drew and Maxwell Fry had completed in the British colonized territories of West Africa. The two architects published a series of illustrated volumes and technical manuals, including *Village Housing in the Tropics: With Special Reference to West Africa* (1947), *Tropical Architecture in the Humid Zone* (1956), and *Tropical Architecture in the Dry and Humid Zones* (1964). The five chapters of the last of these manuals are titled "Climate," "The Dwelling," "Housing and Town Planning," "Civic, Commercial and Industrial," and "Health, Hygiene and Hospitalization." In the manual's introduction, they write, "It is necessary to recognize that we, the authors, are not inhabitants of the tropic zone but have to come to it from the temperate zone. We have experienced its climate, lived with its people and dealt with its problems as they have affected our work." They believed that architects and planners working in these regions had to respond to local conditions and that on the (Western) professionals "falls the major burden of creating an environment in which the tropical peoples may flourish."[19]

Drew and Fry's architectural experiences in independent India and British West Africa served as the foundation for the Department of Tropical Studies at the Architectural Association (AA) in London following the 1953 Conference on Tropical Architecture held at University College London.[20] The department was directed by Otto H. Koenigsberger, a German architect who had worked in Egypt and India before joining the AA. Drew, Fry, Koenigsberger, and others contributed to the institutionalization of architectural research, training, and education in Britain that addressed the tropics of the British Empire and where the question of climate and hygiene became essential. The AA was a link between Britain and its formerly colonized territories. It offered training for architects from Europe and the tropics and helped to prolong colonial activities overseas by producing, consuming, and exporting knowledge. It also shaped the forms and norms of future international urban development principles and protocols, especially through Koenigsberger's popular 1974 textbook the *Manual of Tropical Housing and Building*, which was translated into several languages.[21]

In addition to directing the AA's Department of Tropical Studies, Koenigsberger served as a consultant to the United Nations (UN) Technical Assistance Administration and the Housing Committee of the UN Economic and Social Council. He served on housing and urban planning committees in several countries, including India and Nigeria. His teaching materials and pedagogical design projects often served UN goals. And, in 1969 the department was renamed the Department of Development and Tropical Studies. Koenigsberger was also involved in conceiving *Habitat International*, a journal for the study of human settlements and their design, planning, production, and management that was established at the first UN conference on human settlements and sustainable urban development, known as Habitat I, held from May 31 to June 11, 1976, in Vancouver, Canada.[22] One of the outcomes of this conference was the establishment of the UN Human Settlements Program (UN-Habitat) in 1978, with headquarters in Nairobi, Kenya. UN-Habitat focuses on urban legislation, planning, research, capacity building, housing, and slum upgrading on five continents. This focus led to the consolidation of "modernization" and "development" theories and practices in Western academic settings and among international bodies like the UN, which were based on Eurocentric principles of economic growth, surplus value, technological advancement, and industrialized production processes.

Construction and the Immigrant Labor Force
Before the advent of this worldwide, institutionalized endeavor and the financial recession of the 1970s, European territorial empires were being gradually dismantled. Over the turbulent 1950s and 1960s, revolutions, conflicts, protests, and wars broke

out across Asia, Africa, the Middle East, Europe, and other parts of the world. Civil rights and independence movements called and fought for the end of dispossession, exploitation, and colonialism. This pivotal moment resulted in the establishment of independent nation-states and new markets, migration and the displacement of people and goods, proliferation of self-built settlements, refinement of police and military tactics and strategies, consolidation of solidarity alliances, the Non-Aligned Movement, and a fierce race for a new world order.[23] Architects and architecture schools attempted to understand how newly independent societies—often called "underdeveloped," "less developed," or "developing" countries—contributed to the formation of built environments. Patel, Racki, and Racki's "Squatters: The Seven Housing Systems of Nairobi" and Pyun's "An Architecture of Resistance: Slums in Asia," both published in *archithese* in 1974, are part of this enterprise. Patel, Racki, and Racki, who then were graduate students at the Massachusetts Institute of Technology (MIT), analyze the housing typologies, programs, and policies being implemented in Nairobi.[24] Pyun disapproves of the prejudices being imposed on the population living in the slums and calls for a more accurate understanding of the self-built settlements, which he deems sociospatial environments capable of generating culture.

The UN debates and policies on slum clearance and housing typologies and markets were equally important to European cities during the era of reconstruction and modernization plans that followed the Second World War. Supported by the U.S. Marshall Plan for European recovery, several countries adopted state-led planning and control of an entrepreneurial economy and witnessed rapid economic growth, high productivity and consumption, and attendant social benefits. One of the fastest-developing industries was mass housing construction, which required impressive labor force numbers, leading to the immediate importation of "young, healthy, and strong" male workers from the Mediterranean basin to major European cities and industrial regions. Italian, Spanish, and Portuguese permanent and seasonal immigrant workers were swiftly joined by men from colonized territories, especially from North Africa.[25]

Many cities across Europe struggled to provide proper housing and adequate shelter for the vital immigrant construction labor force brought in to reconstruct the devastated cities and infrastructure. In addition to the propagation of self-built settlements on the outskirts of major European cities, squatted lands and rapidly constructed shelters proliferated around agricultural and industrial areas. In her 1971 article "Immigrant Worker Housing in Switzerland," which was released in the first issue of *archithese*, the Swiss sociologist Perrin denounces the conditions of housing available to the labor class in Switzerland.[26] Perrin analyzes the division of labor, the hierarchization of the foreign labor force—which amounted to 16 percent of the total population in 1969—the juridical status and rights of immigrant workers, and the expenses, contracts, and conditions of lodging that border workers, as well as seasonal and annual employees, faced in Switzerland.

Perrin contends that the quantitative disaster—what, she argues, "the bourgeoisie call the 'housing crisis'"—is bound up with a qualitative one, as well as with the bourgeoisie's need to turn working-class districts (often located in the decaying historic center of cities and characterized by low rents due to inadequate building conditions) into offices, banks, hotels, and supermarkets, thus pushing workers out of city centers to the outskirts of cities or into suburbs, banlieues, and dormitory cities.[27] Perrin associates the "housing crisis" with the capitalist production and consumption of properties, condemning the precarization of labor and ghettoization of urban areas and criticizing the unhygienic conditions of such ghettos. The phenomenon witnessed in Switzerland's cities was hardly unique; it proliferated in the majority of cities in Europe and elsewhere in the aftermath of the Second World War.

Some questioned Perrin's analysis and critique of working-class conditions and the Swiss bourgeoisie, thereby also questioning *archithese's* editorial decision to publish her article, since it might have outraged some of the journal's subscribers. In *archithese's* 1971 second issue, Hans Reinhard, the central president of the Fédération Suisse des architectes indépendants / Verband freierwerbender Schweizer Architekten (Swiss

Federation of Independent Architects, fsai), which published *archithese*, issued a note distancing the fsai from *archithese's* positions: "The FSAI is the publisher of 'archithese.' However, it does not identify with the opinions of different collaborators. On the other hand, it shares the editors' wish for lively responses and an active participation in the discussions."[28] As in other parts of Western Europe, Switzerland's early 1970s were characterized by the demands of the '68 movements and the fears of workers, students, and leftwing claims. However, Switzerland had been uniquely lagging among the Western nations in terms of its emancipatory drive. Women did not gain the right to vote in federal elections until 1971.[29]

Territories and the Military Domain
In parallel with the search for new construction markets domestically and internationally and the competing "zoning" of the East/West/nonaligned territories and industries was a widespread fear of a nuclear strike. Military and civil research and studies that explored the relationship between armed conflicts and the built environment began to emerge and resulted in a series of protocols and publications addressing the historical connections between policies — decreed by military authorities and institutions — and the protection and distribution of people and buildings in a given territory. For example, the Swiss federal authorities had been committed since the 1960s to keeping its people safe from atomic attack by providing a civil shelter for all and requiring the systematic construction of bunkers (fallout shelters) in all newly built residential buildings — a policy that is still mandatory today.[30] In the Soviet Union and the United States, secret cities were being built at record speed to intensify scientific research and create nuclear weapons for mass destruction. French cultural theorist Paul Virilio conducted an inquiry into the hundreds of bunkers and defensive fortifications that Nazi Germany had built along the western and northern coasts of France and Scandinavia, called the Atlantic Wall. These studies culminated in a well-illustrated publication, *Bunker Archéologie: Étude sur l'espace militaire européen de la Seconde Guerre Mondiale* (*Bunker Archeology:*

Studies on the European Military Space of the Second World War).[31]

The dynamics of the Cold War clearly influenced the methodologies and thematic interest of art and architectural historians in the 1970s as they scrutinized how armed conflicts shaped spaces, places, and people. In 1974, Stanislaus von Moos, the Swiss art historian who cofounded and was the first editor of *archithese*, released *Turm und Bollwerk: Beiträge zu einer politischen Ikonographie der italienischen Renaissancearchitektur* (Tower and bulwark: Contributions to a political iconography of Italian Renaissance architecture), in which he analyzes the development of defensive techniques and architecture in Renaissance theory from Leon Battista Alberti to Niccolò Machiavelli, investigating the psychological impact of such military architecture.[32] A preview of this study is provided in von Moos's article "Zur Ingenieurkunst der Renaissance" (On Renaissance Engineering), published in *archithese* 5. In her article "Military Theories and Collective Housing," Polish architectural historian Zarebska cites von Moos's article. Zarebska elaborates on the guiding principles of military urbanism, architecture, engineering, and theories during the Italian Renaissance and investigates the Dutch royal planning of military dwellings and camps for army officers, including mobile, defensive, and offensive settlements.[33] She focuses on the typologies of those settlements rather than on their military functions and aims, which included the colonization of overseas territories and the foundation of what is today called "globalization," a phenomenon that, in many ways, is merely the prolongation of the colonial order.[34]

Zarebska begins her article by warning readers that "It may seem curious for a magazine devoted to the architectural issues of our own time to turn to military matters. And yet, the waging of war has long been an integral part of the arts, crafts, and sciences of past eras. It has motivated research and influenced methodology across the disciplines."[35] Also uncommon about this architectural journal was that it reminded architects that architecture cannot be divided from its social, economic, political, and psychological constituents. Giving voice to students, architects, art and architectural historians, sociologists, and other professionals to lay down the "cartographies of power" and to depict the transitions and distresses that many populations around the world were experiencing at that time was to say that architecture is not, and cannot be, neutral. To search for postmodernity was to understand and expose the impacts of language, dispossession, migration, exploitation, climate, and wars on the built and living environment. Therefore, if one agrees that "there is no modernity without coloniality," then one should accept that there is no postmodernity without postcoloniality.[36]

1   Walter Mignolo and Catherine E. Walsh, *On Decoloniality: Concepts, Analytics, Praxis* (Durham, NC: Duke University Press, 2018), 4.

2   Anibal Quijano, "Coloniality of Power, Eurocentrism, and Latin America," *Nepantla: Views from South* 1, 3 (September 2000): 533–80.

3   André Corboz, "Remarks on an Ill-Defined Problem: The Architecture of Nonarchitects," 430–49 in this publication. First published in *archithese* 9 (1974): 2–14.

4   Frantz Fanon, *Black Skin, White Masks*, trans. Markmann Charles Lam (1952; London: Pluto Press, 2008); Edward W. Said, *Orientalism* (London: Routledge and Kegan Paul, 1978). On Fanon's seminal work, see Frantz Fanon, *Pour la révolution africaine; Écrits politiques* (Paris: F. Maspero, 1964); Frantz Fanon, *The Wretched of the Earth*, trans. R. Philcox (New York: Grove Press, 2004); Frantz Fanon, *A Dying Colonialism* (New York: Grove Press, 1967).

5   Samia Henni, "Colonial Ramifications," e-Flux Architecture, History/Theory, gta Institute, ETH Zurich, October 31, 2018, https://www.e-flux.com/architecture/history-theory/225180/colonial-ramifications/.

6   Bernard Rudofsky, *Architecture without Architects: A Short Introduction to Non-pedigreed Architecture* (New York: Museum of Modern Art, 1964), acknowledgments.

7   See, for example, Patricia Morton, *Hybrid Modernities: Architecture and Representation at the 1931 Colonial Exposition*, Paris (Cambridge, MA: MIT Press, 2000).

8   Swiss actors, such as merchants, missionaries, and scientists, were involved in both the transatlantic slave trade and colonial endeavors. See, for example, Patricia Purtschert and Harald Fischer-Tiné, eds., *Colonial Switzerland: Rethinking Colonialism from the Margins* (London: Palgrave Macmillan, 2015).

9   Pascal Blanchard and Musée du quai Branly, *Human Zoos: The Invention of the Savage* (Arles: Actes Sud, 2011); Rikke Andreassen, *Human Exhibitions: Race, Gender and Sexuality in Ethnic Displays, Studies in Migration and Diaspora* (Farnham, UK: Ashgate, 2015).

10   Edmond Chappuis et al., *1830–1930: Le centenaire de l'Algérie française* (Strasbourg: Compagnie alsacienne des arts photomécaniques A. et F. Kahn, 1930); Gustave Mercier et al., *Le centenaire de l'Algérie: Exposé d'ensemble* (Alger: P. et G. Soubiron, 1931).

11   "Il était souhaitable que le nombre des Européens dans les pays coloniaux allat toujours croissant. C'est, en effet, cet accroissement qui, seul, permettra de tenir tête aux tendances nationalistes des populations indigènes qu'une propagande bolcheviste ou autre s'efforce de surexciter et de développer. Tout l'effort des urbanistes doit donc tendre à *favoriser l'immigration européenne dans les colonies et à procurer*, à cet effet, le *maximum d'avantages aux citadins de race blanche* dans les cités qu'ils organisent."

Jean Royer et al., eds., *L'urbanisme aux colonies et dans les pays tropicaux. communications et rapports du Congrès international de l'urbanisme aux colonies et dans les pays de latitude intertropicale, [Paris-Vincennes, du 10 au 15 octobre 1931]* (La Charité-sur-Loire, France: Delayance, 1932), 12; emphasis in original.

12   Ibid., 12.

13   Rudolphe Rey, "Tous urbanistes!," *Chantiers*, 3 (March 1933): 237.

14   "[L]e veritable urbanism colonial demande une entente parfaite entre les medecins-hygienistes, les architectes, les ethnographes, l'administration et... l'indigène." Marcel Persitz, "L'habitation indigène dans les colonies françaises," *L'architecture d'aujourd'hui*, 3 (March 1936): 13–19, here 13.

15   Eric Paul Mumford, *The Discourse of CIAM Urbanism, 1928–1959* (Ann Arbor, MI: UMI Dissertation Services, 1996); Eric Paul Mumford, *Defining Urban Design: CIAM Architects and the Formation of a Discipline, 1937–69* (New Haven: Yale University Press, 2009).

16   The CIAM group in Morocco included Georges Candilis, Shadrach Woods, and Alison Smithson and Peter Smithson. See, for example, Tom Avermaete, *Another Modern: The Post-war Architecture and Urbanism of Candilis-Josic-Woods*; Serhat Karakayali, "Colonialism and the Critique of Modernity," in *Colonial Modern: Aesthetics of the Past, Rebellions for the Future*, ed. Tom Avermaete, Serhat

Karakayali, and Marion von Osten (London: Black Dog Publishing, 2010), 16–32.

17 The group was led by Emery and included Louis Miquel, Jean de Maisonseul, Pierre Bourlier, and Roland Simounet. See, for example, Jean-Lucien Bonillo, "Le CIAM-Alger, Albert Camus et Le Corbusier: Modernité et identité," in *Le Corbusier, visions d'Alger* (Paris: Éditions de la Villette, 2012), 218–37; Zeynep Çelik, "Bidonvilles, CIAM et grands ensembles," in *Alger: Paysages urbain et architectures, 1800–2000* (Paris: Les Éditions de l'Imprimeur, 2003), 186–227; Zeynep Çelik, "Learning from the Bidonville: CIAM Looks at Algiers," *Harvard Design Magazine*, 8 (2003): 70–74; Sheila Crane, "The Shantytown of Algiers and the Colonization of Everyday Life," in *Use Matters: An Alternative History of Architecture*, ed. Kenny Cupers (New York: Routledge, 2013), 111–27.

18 See, for example, Victor Collet, *Nanterre, du bidonville à la cité* (Marseille 2019); Isabelle Herpin and Serge Santelli, *Cahiers d'architecture 1: Bidonville à Nanterre: Étude architecturale*, Unité Pédagogique d'Architecture 8 (Paris: Institut de l'environnement, 1971); Isabelle Herpin and Serge Santelli, *Bidonville à Nanterre: Étude architecturale...* (Paris: Ministère des Affaires culturelles, Institut de l'environnement, 1973). On the relationships between the slums in France's colonies and the metropole, see, for example, Samia Henni, *Architecture of Counterrevolution: The French Army in Northern Algeria* (Zurich: gta Verlag, 2017), 149–78. On the Institut de l'environnement, see, for example, Tony Côme, *L'Institut de l'environnement: Une école décolonisée* (Paris: Éditions B42, 2017).

19 Maxwell Fry and Jane Drew, *Tropical Architecture in the Dry and Humid Zones* (Malabar, FL: R.E. Krieger, 1982).

20 See, for example, Jiat-Hwee Chang, *A Genealogy of Tropical Architecture: Colonial Networks, Nature and Technoscience* (London: Routledge, 2016).

21 Otto H. Koenigsberger, *Manual of Tropical Housing and Building* (London: Longman, 1974).

22 See, for example, Tom Avermaete, Maristella Casciato, and Mirko Zardini, *Casablanca Chandigarh: A Report on Modernization* (Zurich: Park Books,

2014); United Nations et al., *Climate and House Design* (New York: United Nations, 1971); Duanfang Lu ed., *Third World Modernism: Architecture, Development and Identity* (London: Routledge, 2011).

23 See, for example, Ákos Moravánszky and Judith Hopfengärtner, eds., *Re-humanizing Architecture: New Forms of Community, 1950–1970* (Basel: Birkhäuser, 2017); Ákos Moravánszky and Karl R. Kegler, eds., *Re-scaling the Environment: New Landscapes of Design, 1960–1980* (Basel: Birkhäuser, 2017); Ákos Moravánszky and Torsten Lange, eds., *Re-framing Identities: Architecture's Turn to History, 1970–1990* (Basel: Birkhäuser, 2017).

24 Praful C. Patel, Jeff Racki, and Reena Racki, "Squatters: The Seven Housing Systems of Nairobi," 450–67 in this publication. Published in *archithese* 9 (1974): 27–38. Their article was based on research undertaken in 1971–1972 at MIT and included two visits to Nairobi. For a longer version of the article, see Jeffrey Racki et al., "Housing Systems Analysis: An Aid to Policy Development," *Ekistics* 38, 227 (1974): 281–86, available at https://www.jstor.org/stable/43618420; Jin-Bak Pyun, "An Architecture of Resistance: Slums in Asia," 468–78 in this publication. First published in *archithese* 9 (1974): 39–44.

25 See, for example, Charles Oman and Ganeshan Wignaraja, *The Postwar Evolution of Development Thinking* (New York: St. Martin's Press, 1991); Peter M.R. Stirk and David Willis, *Shaping Postwar Europe: European Unity and Disunity, 1945–1957* (New York: St. Martin's Press, 1991); Theodore H.M. Prudon, Hélène Lipstadt, and Sites and Neighbourhoods of the Modern Movement International Working Party for Documentation and Conservation of Buildings, *Import-Export: Postwar Modernism in an Expanding World, 1945–1975: Proceedings VIIIth International Conference*, September 26–October 2, 2004, Columbia University, New York City (New York: DOCOMOMO International, 2008).

26 Eliane Perrin, "Immigrant Worker Housing in Switzerland," 404–19 in this publication. First published in *archithese* 1 (1971): 2–11.

27 Ibid., 2, 6: "Ce que la bourgeoisie appelle 'la crise du logement.'"

28 Hans Reinhard, "Editorial," *archithese* 2 (1971): n.p.; Oral panel discussion on occasion of the exhibition Sammelstelle archithese, Nidwaldner Museum Stans (2017–2018), with Hans Reinhard, Stanislaus von Moos, Ákos Moravánszky, Katalin Deér, and Nina Paim, moderated by Gabrielle Schaad, January 31, 2018, Stans.

29 Appenzell Innerrhoden, Switzerland's smallest canton, granted women the vote on local issues only in 1990, becoming the last canton to adopt women's suffrage.

30 Switzerland became one of the most prominent exporters of bunker-building technology and knowledge. See, for example, Silvia Berger Ziauddin, "Calculating the Apocalypse: The Unexpected Career of the Swiss Nuclear Bunker," in *War Zones: gta papers* 2, ed. Samia Henni (Zurich: gta Verlag, 2018), 38–48.

31 Paul Virilio, *Bunker Archaeology* (1967; New York: Princeton Architectural Press, 1994).

32 On contemporaneous publications, see, for example, Quentin Hughes, *Fortress, Architecture and Military History in Malta: Quentin Hughes, ... with Photographs by David Wrightson* (London: L. Humphries, 1969); Alexander H. Thompson, *Military Architecture in Medieval England* (Totowa, NJ: Rowman and Littlefield, 1975).

33 Teresa Zarebska, "Military Theories and Collective Housing," 420–29 in this publication. First published in *archithese* 8 (1973): 9–14.

34 See, for example, Samia Henni, "Anticolonial Remedies: From Colonization to Globalization," in "Onus," ed. Caroline Acheatel et al., special issue, *Perspecta* 53 (2020): 193–203.

35 Zarebska, "Military Theories and Collective Housing," (see note 33), 420–29 in this publication.

36 Mignolo and Walsh, *On Decoloniality* (see note 1), 4.

Eliane Perrin

Le logement des travailleurs étrangers en Suisse

Deutscher Text: Seite 11

La question du logement des travailleurs immigrés en Suisse est particulièrement intéressante pour deux raisons. Elle ne peut être abordée pour elle-même car elle nous renvoie immédiatement à la dimension politique de l'immigration pour la bourgeoisie nationale et internationale, la division de la classe ouvrière. D'autre part, elle nous renvoie au problème du logement pour toute la classe ouvrière, aux conditions de logement de tous les travailleurs, à ce que la bourgeoisie appelle « la crise du logement ».

Il est donc nécessaire de restituer ce problème dans le contexte économique, politique et social de la Suisse actuelle.

La situation politique actuelle en Suisse: division de la classe ouvrière et la « paix du travail »
Comme dans tous les pays capitalistes développés (ou impérialistes), la bourgeoisie et le patronat mènent une politique de division de la classe ouvrière à travers la hiérarchie des postes de travail, des salaires, etc. et par une politique d'importation d'une marchandise particulièrement rentable et mobile: *la main-d'œuvre étrangère*.

Ainsi, en 1969, la Suisse a-t-elle compté 991 000 travailleurs étrangers (ou plus exactement 972 000 si l'on exclut de ce chiffre les fonctionnaires internationaux) sur une population totale de 6 184 000 habitants, c'est-à-dire 16 %.

Mais la bourgeoisie ne s'arrête pas là dans sa politique de division: les travailleurs immigrés ne comptent pas moins de trois types de statut: frontalier, annuel, saisonnier.

Les frontaliers (de nationalité française, allemande et italienne pour la plupart) ont un permis de travail uniquement, ce qui signifie l'obligation de passer la frontière chaque matin et chaque soir, donc de faire de longs trajets quotidiens.

Les annuels ont un permis de travail renouvelable chaque année, résiliable à chaque instant, et le droit, s'ils trouvent un appartement

Immigrant Worker Housing in Switzerland

Experiments in Communal Living

Author:
Eliane Perrin

Source:
archithese, 1 (1971): 2–11

Translated by:
Brett Petzer

The issue of housing for immigrant workers in Switzerland is of particular interest for two reasons. On the one hand, it defies analysis in isolation, because it is so closely connected to the political dimension of immigration for the national and international bourgeoisie, as well as the division of the working class. On the other hand, this subject leads us directly to the problem of housing for the working class as a whole, to the housing conditions of all workers, to what the bourgeoisie refer to as "the housing crisis."

It is therefore necessary to place this problem in the economic, political, and social context of Switzerland today.

The Current Political Situation in Switzerland: Division of the Working Class and the "Labor Peace"

As in all developed capitalist (or imperialist) countries, the bourgeoisie and the bosses have pursued a policy of dividing the working class through a hierarchy of jobs, wages, and so on, and through a policy of importing one particularly profitable and mobile commodity: foreign labor.

In Switzerland in 1969, for example, there were 991,000 foreign workers (or, more precisely, 972,000 if international civil servants are excluded) out of a total population of 6,184,000, or 16 percent.

But the bourgeoisie did not stop there in its policy of division. Immigrant workers are classified according to no less than three types of status: cross-border, annual, and seasonal.

Cross-border workers (mostly French, German, and Italian nationals) hold a work permit only, which means that they must cross the border every morning and evening, necessitating long daily journeys.

Annual workers have a work permit that is renewable every year and can be canceled at any time. They may also, if they find an apartment or if their boss provides them with one, bring their wife and children to join them. In 1969, there were 316,595 annual workers.

Seasonal workers hold a permit for a maximum legal duration of nine months (or eleven months if the boss requires it) per year. The other three months must be spent in their country of origin. They are not allowed to rent an unfurnished apartment or room. They are also not allowed to bring their wives to join them (unless she is working, which allows employers in some related sectors, such as cleaning, or ice cream sales in the summer, to hire them for almost nothing). Under no circumstances may their children join them (it goes without saying that a large number of women and children are currently in Switzerland clandestinely). In 1969, there were 655,200 seasonal workers.

This portrait of the divisions within the working class becomes more complete when we add that, in 1969, for example, there were 531,501 workers of Italian nationality, 115,606 of German nationality, 97,862 of Spanish nationality, 49,538 of French nationality, 43,052 of Austrian nationality, 20,809 of Yugoslav nationality, 10,064 of Turkish nationality, 8,590 of Greek nationality, and 94,773 of other nationalities.

The situation of immigrant workers in Switzerland's production system only reinforces these divides. They hold the majority of all manual jobs and are lowest in the wage hierarchy. Indeed, in the construction sector, one of the most backward in terms of rationalization and standardization, immigrant workers are practically alone in performing productive labor; the few remaining Swiss work as supervisors, foremen, site foremen, and so on. They also occupy a very large proportion of the lowest positions in sectors such as metals, textiles, food, tobacco, restaurants and hotels, hospital services, watchmaking, and so on. As a result, they constitute the most heavily exploited part of the working class in Switzerland.

The hierarchical division of the working class as a whole (for Swiss workers, this divide is between foremen, office workers, technicians, etc.) is reproduced within the immigrant worker community through nationality. In French-speaking Switzerland, for example, the first large wave of immigrants, the Italians, had moved up a few steps in the hierarchy of qualifications and wages (their qualifications had been recognized, whereas previously bosses had not recognized qualifications on the pretext that they were foreign or on grounds of seniority) by the time the second wave arrived. These were the Spaniards, who now find themselves in a better position than the Turks, Greeks, Yugoslavs, and so on.

The objective division of the working class in Switzerland by employers (through the hierarchy of jobs and wages) and by the bourgeoisie (through differences in status) would not be so consequential if it were not also subjective; that is, if workers could unite around struggles based on common interests.

In fact, the Swiss component of the working class happens to constitute the vast majority of union members. It has, by means of the unions making up the only major central body (the Swiss Union of Trade Unions), renounced that fundamental working-class method of attack and defense: the right to strike (it is worth noting that the Swiss Union of Trade Unions is social-democratic in orientation and fully aligned with the Swiss Socialist Party; no union has ever aligned with the very marginal Swiss Communist Party).

This renunciation takes the form of agreements made every three or four years by branch associations and, at the national level, between the trade union and bosses. These agreements give rise to "summit" negotiations between respective leaders on wage increases, vacations, and so on, premised on the understanding that unionized workers are not to go on strike during the coming three- or four-year period. If a strike is then called and the employer in question can prove that even one striker was unionized, the union must pay a fine to compensate the employer! Bosses, for their part, undertake to refrain from lockouts (although to circumvent this, they need only dismiss their workers one by one).

The trade unions are thus closely connected to the bourgeoisie and the bosses, their role being to keep the peace.

Moreover, where the immigration of foreign workers is concerned, they have already (both before, and in response to, the Schwarzenbach initiative "against foreign overpopulation") resolutely abandoned any stance that defends the interests of all workers. Instead, they limit themselves to advocating only for Swiss workers and "the interests of the national economy." They have thus endorsed a reduction in the number of immigrant workers but oppose the Schwarzenbach initiative as "too brutal and inhumane."

Consequently, immigrant workers, the most exploited section of the working class, not only lack all political rights but find themselves without union rights. It is easy to understand,

fig. 1 Abandoned villa inhabited by seasonal and annual workers in the Grottes district, Geneva.

ou si leur patron leur en procure un, d'amener leur femme et leurs enfants. En 1969, on comptait 316 595 annuels.

Les saisonniers ont un permis d'une durée légale maximum de 9 mois (qui dure 11 mois si le patron en a besoin) par an. Les trois autres mois doivent être passés au pays d'origine. Ils n'ont pas le droit de louer un appartement ou une chambre non meublés. Ils n'ont pas le droit de faire venir leur femme (à moins qu'elle ne travaille, ce qui permet au patronat dans certaines branches annexes — nettoyages, vente des glaces en été — de les engager pour quasi rien) et en aucun cas leurs enfants. (Inutile de dire qu'il y a actuellement un grand nombre de femmes et d'enfants clandestins en Suisse.) En 1969, il y avait 655 200 saisonniers.

Le tableau de la division de la classe ouvrière n'est complet que lorsque l'on sait qu'en 1969, par exemple, il y avait 531 501 travailleurs de nationalité italienne, 115 606 de nationalité allemande, 97 862 de nationalité espagnole, 49 538 de nationalité française, 43 052 de nationalité autrichienne, 20 809 de nationalité yougoslave, 10 064 de nationalité turque, 8 590 de nationalité grecque et 94 773 d'autres nationalités...!

La situation des travailleurs immigrés dans le système de production en Suisse ne fait que renforcer encore ces divisions: ils occupent en majorité et prioritairement tous les postes manuels et les plus bas dans la hiérarchie des salaires. En effet, dans le secteur du bâtiment, l'un des plus en retard du point de vue de la rationalisation et de la standardisation, les travailleurs immigrés sont pratiquement seuls aux postes de travail productif, les quelques Suisses restant sont chefs d'équipe, contremaîtres, chefs de chantier, etc. Ils occupent également une très grande proportion des postes de travail les plus bas dans la métallurgie, l'industrie textile, l'alimentation, l'industrie des tabacs, la restauration et l'hôtellerie, des services hospitaliers, de l'horlogerie, etc. Ils constituent par conséquent la partie la plus durement exploitée de la classe ouvrière en Suisse.

La division hiérarchique de toute la classe ouvrière (pour la partie suisse, entre contremaîtres, employés de bureau, techniciens,

↑ fig. 2 Barracks at the Pont de l'Ecu in Vernier.

etc.) se reproduit à l'intérieur des travailleurs immigrés en se recoupant avec leur division par nationalité: en Suisse romande par exemple, la première grande vague d'immigrés, les Italiens, ont grimpé quelques échelons dans la hiérarchie des qualifications et des salaires (on a reconnu leurs qualifications que le patronat ne reconnaissait pas auparavant sous prétexte que les certificats étaient étrangers, ou par simple ancienneté) lorsqu'est arrivée la deuxième vague, les Espagnols, qui eux-mêmes se trouvent actuellement mieux placés que les Turcs, les Grecs, les Yougoslaves, etc.

La division objective par le patronat (hiérarchie des postes de travail et des salaires) et la bourgeoisie (différences de statut) de la classe ouvrière en Suisse ne serait pas si grave si elle n'était pas en même temps subjective, s'il y avait des luttes pour des intérêts communs à travers lesquelles les travailleurs retrouvent leur unité.

En effet, la partie suisse de la classe ouvrière, qui se trouve constituer la très grande majorité des syndiqués, a, par l'intermédiaire des syndicats groupés dans l'unique grande centrale (l'Union Syndicale Suisse) d'obédience social-démocrate (liée totalement au Parti Socialiste Suisse — il n'y a jamais eu de syndicat lié au Parti Communiste très minoritaire —) renoncé au moyen de défense et d'attaque fondamental de la classe ouvrière, le droit de grève.

Cette renonciation intervient lors d'accords passés tous les trois ou quatre ans par branches de métier et au niveau national entre le syndicat et le patronat. Ces accords donnent lieu à des négociations « au sommet » entre les directions respectives sur les augmentations de salaires, les vacances, etc., avec à la clé, pour les syndicats ouvriers, l'engagement à ne pas déclencher de grève pendant la nouvelle période de trois ou quatre ans (si se déclenchent des grèves et que le patron visé peut prouver qu'il y avait ne serait-ce qu'un seul syndiqué gréviste, le syndicat s'engage à payer une amende dédommageant le patron!!!), et pour le patronat, l'engagement à ne pas avoir recours au lock-out (il lui suffit de congédier les ouvriers l'un après l'autre...)

Les syndicats sont ainsi totalement liés à la bourgeoisie et au patronat; ils jouent le rôle de facteur d'ordre.

De plus, sur la question de l'immigration des travailleurs étrangers, ils ont, avant déjà, et à l'occasion de l'initiative Schwarzenbach « contre la surpopulation étrangère » abandonné résolument toute position de défense des intérêts de tous les travailleurs, défendant les seuls travailleurs nationaux et « l'intérêt de l'économie nationale » se prononçant pour la diminution du nombre de travailleurs immigrés, mais contre l'initiative Schwarzenbach « trop brutale et inhumaine ».

Ainsi, les travailleurs immigrés, partie la plus exploitée de la classe ouvrière, non seulement n'ont aucuns droits politiques, mais se trouvent sans droits syndicaux. On comprend ainsi aisément que les immigrés provenant de pays où il y a des luttes ouvrières, Italiens et Espagnols en particulier, non seulement ne se syndiquent pas (les autres non plus d'ailleurs, mais de manière moins consciente), et se trouvent politiquement profondément divisés des travailleurs suisses, véritable aristocratie ouvrière, mais se sont lancés depuis une année dans une série de luttes, dans une série de grèves sauvages capitales pour la recomposition de l'unité des travailleurs sur une base de classe.

↑ fig. 3 This insalubrious building is inhabited by seasonal and annual

En Suisse, ce que la bourgeoisie appelle la «crise du logement» pour perpétuer l'idée que le problème du logement n'est que passager et en voie de résolution «naturelle» grâce à quelques mesures le plus souvent étatiques (encouragement à la construction de logements à loyers modérés ou bas, baisse du taux d'intérêt des banques sur les prêts destinés à la construction de logements, facilité de prêt bancaire encourageant la petite bourgeoisie à investir dans la construction de pavillons, etc.), quelquefois privées (construction de logements des entreprises pour leurs travailleurs par exemple). Ces mesures sont régulièrement présentées comme provisoires, destinées à disparaître au profit du marché libre.

La «crise du logement», se caractérisant par la rareté et le prix élevé des appartements dans les régions fortement concentrées industriellement et démographiquement, touche en premier lieu la classe ouvrière et s'étend régulièrement, dans les périodes de pénurie grave, à toutes les classes moyennes, petite bourgeoisie, etc.

Elle est structurellement liée au mode de production capitaliste puisqu'elle tient essentiellement au prix du capital (taux hypothécaire), de la construction, au développement économique et au degré de concentration industrielle des régions (spéculation foncière, zones déclassées), donc à la production du logement dans la production du domaine bâti en général, et à l'organisation du marché locatif (régies, logements construits et loués par les entreprises, etc.). Cette «crise» est, pensons-nous, étroitement liée à une phase précise du développement capitaliste de restructuration monopoliste, liée à l'accentuation de la concurrence au niveau européen et entre l'Europe et les Etats-Unis d'Amérique et déterminant pour les bourgeoisies nationales et les différents capitalistes une priorité aux investissements dans la production visant la modernisation et la rationalisation de la production aux dépens notamment du logement, en particulier du logement ouvrier, moins rentable parmi les moins rentables!

De plus, cette «crise du logement», crise quantitative, est accompagnée d'une crise «qualitative», liée à la nécessité pour la bourgeoisie de réorganiser la ville en détruisant tous les logements situés au centre de la cité (logements pour la plupart anciens, donc abandonnés par la bourgeoisie et devenus les quartiers ouvriers, ou constituant les quartiers ouvriers traditionnels) pour y reconstruire des bureaux, des banques, des super-marchés, des hôtels, etc., donc de rejeter la classe ouvrière dans des logements situés à l'extérieur de la ville, cité-dortoirs, baraques, etc.

Le logement des travailleurs immigrés
Dans cette situation économique et politique générale — division de la classe ouvrière et pénurie de logements — quelles sont les conditions de logement des travailleurs immigrés? Comme on pouvait s'y attendre, elles renforcent la division de la classe ouvrière déjà instaurée par le patronat au niveau du travail (logements ségrégés), et sont qualitativement pires que celles des H.L.M. bien que participant au même type de «solution».

Rappelons avant d'analyser de plus près les habitations des travailleurs étrangers qu'il existe du point de vue de la location

then, that immigrants from countries with a tradition of working-class struggle (such as Italians and Spaniards, in particular) do not unionize (of course, other workers do not unionize either, but this is less deliberate). What is more, these workers find themselves deeply divided from Swiss workers, who form a veritable workers' aristocracy. And yet, for the past year, immigrant workers have been engaged in a series of struggles and wildcat strikes that may prove essential for the rebuilding of worker unity on the basis of class.

In Switzerland, the bourgeoisie use the term *housing crisis* to perpetuate the idea that the housing problem is merely temporary and will resolve itself "naturally" thanks to a number of measures. Most of these are state-led, including promoting the construction of moderate- or low-rent housing, lowering bank interest rates on house-building loans, or bank loan facilities promoting investment in new detached housing by the petit bourgeoisie. Some measures involve the private sector, like building company housing. However, they are all routinely framed as temporary; their destiny is to vanish so that the free market can resume its work.

The "housing crisis," characterized by the scarcity and high cost of flats in regions where industry and population are concentrated, affects the working class first and foremost. In periods of severe scarcity, it regularly extends to all the middle classes, petty bourgeoisie, and so on.

It is also structurally linked to the capitalist mode of production. The "crisis" essentially arises from the price of capital (mortgage rate), construction, economic development, and the degree of industrial concentration of the regions (including land speculation and decommissioned areas). It is therefore an outcome of the production of housing within the production of the built environment in general. It is also an outcome of how the rental market is organized (housing associations, company-built and -rented housing, etc.). This "crisis" is, in our view, closely connected to a specific phase of the development within capitalism of monopolistic restructuring, which is in turn linked to intensifying competition at the European level, as well as between Europe and the United States of America. This phase also demands that national bourgeoisies and various capitalists prioritize investments in the modernization and rationalization of production. This comes at the expense of housing in general and worker housing in particular—the least profitable of the least profitable investments!

Moreover, this "housing crisis" is a quantitative crisis accompanied by a qualitative one, owing to the bourgeoisie's need to reorganize the city by destroying all the housing in the center to build offices, banks, supermarkets, and hotels instead. As these are mostly older residences, they have been abandoned by the bourgeoisie and become working-class neighborhoods or have always been traditional working-class neighborhoods. The result is that the working class is driven to peripheral housing, bedroom suburbs, and barracks.

Housing for Immigrant Workers

What, then, are the housing conditions of immigrant workers within this economic and political context of working-class division and housing scarcity? As might be expected, they reinforce the division of the working class that bosses have already established in the workplace (segregated housing) and are qualitatively worse than conditions in the HLM [*Habitation à loyer modéré*, rent-controlled housing], although the latter form part of the same kind of "solution."

Before analyzing the housing of foreign workers more closely, it should be noted that rentals can be of two kinds, according to whether immigrant workers hold seasonal or annual permits. These permits are linked to measures taken by the Swiss Federal Council to limit the number of foreign workers by company, sector, or canton. This means that a given employer may take on only a specified number of seasonal and annual workers.

Seasonal workers are not allowed to rent an apartment (something they could not do in any event, given the housing shortage, rent prices, and their wages) or an unfurnished room. Moreover, an employer can dismiss them from one day to the next, with or without issuing a *carte libre* or "free card" that allows the worker fourteen days to find a new employer. This lack of security means that no rental agency will rent to a seasonal worker directly. Rooms or flats are rented to bosses, who deduct their cost from wages and pay the agency.

Annual workers, who are allowed to bring their families to Switzerland, may rent a flat. However, in most cases, they cannot find one unless their employer provides it or surety that they will pay or, as with seasonal workers, withholds the rent from their wages. In practice, rental agencies give preference to Swiss workers, who are considered to be a "safer bet."

The vast majority of immigrant workers live in what we might call wooden or stone barracks.

Wooden Barracks

Wooden barracks are temporary structures, or were until October 1970, when an official regulation was issued regulating and legalizing their construction. They lack foundations, but the best of them sit on a concrete slab. Their external walls are of wood, and internal walls are of wood or Pavatex (wood-fiber insulating board), enclosing twenty to forty beds per barrack. Most often, they lack warm water, and have two washbasins inside, with a few metal sinks outside for laundry; these are also used for bathing (as two washbasins for twenty to forty persons is hardly adequate for morning ablutions). Showers are on the outside (in Geneva, the worst case encountered offered four showers for 270 construction workers; in another case, the ratio was 18 to 400). The toilets are squat toilets, serving an average of twelve to thirteen persons each. Most barracks have electricity, which the managers turn on from 6 to 9 a.m., from 12 to 3 p.m., and from 6 to 10 p.m. only. There is generally a heating system in the center of the barrack, usually oil-fired, so that those nearby are warm while it is on, while the rest shiver from cold; this lasts from October to April. Drafts are a constant, as air passes under doors and through windows that do not fully shut. The internal layout varies (but only in detail), from the "two-bed room" in the best cases to twelve-bed, military-style dormitories. What management and the state deem a "room" varies from a space enclosed on all sides by wooden partitions with a door, to one with partitions on three sides with only a curtain separating it from the central corridor. The beds are simple bases with hard, deformed horizontal supports. Each bed has its own stool or chair and wardrobe and sometimes a table for two or four beds. There is no individual lighting (in general, four people are lit by one bulb). None of these "rooms" are truly sound-insulated. There is almost never a kitchen, so there are canteens. In some barracks, workers who do not eat in the canteen are quickly dismissed under some pretext or other, the canteen being a source of profit for management. Portions here are generous (as these are construction workers) but of the lowest possible quality. In Geneva, barracks can be found alone or in groups, the largest of which houses 400 workers across twenty barracks. The distance between two barracks is often as little as two meters, with an earthen perimeter (rather than tarmac).

The average price of a bed was sixty-five Swiss francs in 1970 (actual prices range from sixty to one hundred francs). Electricity and gas costs are often added to this by management. Managers also frequently try to charge seasonal workers for the three months they are obliged to spend in their home country, on pain of losing their bed in the spring. Since rent is most often deducted from seasonal workers' wages by the boss, and workers are paid fortnightly, this amounts to charging thirteen months' rent! As the state will increase rents by 30 percent from 1971, barrack rents will be increasing too.

Barracks are always built with the complicity of the state. Indeed, they are most often located on land where construction is banned, such as railway verges, riverbanks, wet or unstable soil, motorway verges, airport land, and so on. They are also generally beyond the city limits, necessitating long daily commutes to building sites.

Barracks are sometimes built and owned by the state itself, which contracts charities to manage them (these can be Catholic, such as Caritas, or Protestant, such as the Salvation Army or Centre Social Protestant); they can also be built by companies to house their own workforce. The job of barracks manager is usually entrusted to a particularly docile and submissive immigrant worker, who is then granted the right to bring his family to join him. He is tasked with maintaining order in the barrack and, in the event of unrest, with submitting the names and car registration numbers of "outsiders" to his superiors. Barracks managers are also responsible for calling the police when there are internal conflicts or external agitators

deux situations différentes selon que les immigrés se voient délivrer un permis de saisonnier ou un permis d'annuel. Ces permis sont liés à des mesures du Conseil fédéral, ayant comme objectif le contingentement par entreprise ou par branche d'industrie et par canton de la main-d'œuvre étrangère. Tel patron n'a donc le droit d'engager que tant de saisonniers et tant d'annuels.

Les saisonniers n'ont pas le droit de louer un appartement (ce qu'ils n'arriveraient de toute manière pas à faire, vu la pénurie, le prix des loyers et le montant de leur salaire) ou une chambre non meublés. De plus, leur « insécurité » de l'emploi, c'est-à-dire le fait que leur patron peut les renvoyer d'un jour à l'autre en leur donnant ou non « carte libre », c'est-à-dire un délai de quinze jours pour trouver un nouvel employeur, a pour conséquence qu'aucune régie n'accepte de louer directement à un saisonnier: elle loue la chambre ou l'appartement au patron qui retient le prix sur le salaire de ses ouvriers et le verse ensuite à la régie.

Les annuels, qui ont le droit de faire venir leur famille, ont le droit de louer un appartement. Cependant, ils n'en trouvent le plus souvent aucun à moins que leur patron leur en fournisse un, se portant garant du fait qu'ils paieront, ou retenant comme pour les saisonniers leur loyer sur leur salaire. En effet, les régies louent en priorité aux travailleurs suisses, jugés « plus sûrs »...

Les travailleurs immigrés habitent dans leur grande majorité ce que nous appelons les baraques en bois et les baraques en pierre.

Les baraques en bois

Les baraques en bois sont des constructions provisoires (ou du moins l'ont été jusqu'à la parution d'un règlement officiel des baraques qui en fait depuis le mois d'octobre 1970 un type de construction admis, légal...), sans fondations, avec, dans le meilleur des cas une dalle en béton, des murs extérieurs en bois et des cloisons internes en bois ou en pavatex contenant entre 20 et 40 lits par baraque. Elles n'ont le plus souvent pas d'eau chaude, deux

↑ figs. 4–5   Salvation Army barracks in Prébois, Meyrin.

figs. 6–7 →
frigério barracks in Gourgas, Geneva.

lavabos internes, et quelques éviers en zinc pour faire la lessive à l'extérieur, mais qui sont aussi utilisés pour se laver (2 robinets internes pour 20 à 40 personnes ne sauraient suffire le matin). Elles ont des douches à l'extérieur (à Genève, dans le pire des cas 4 pour 270 travailleurs du bâtiment, dans un autre cas 18 pour 400 travailleurs). Les WC sont turcs, en moyenne un pour 12 à 13 personnes. Elles ont pour la plupart l'électricité, que le gérant branche en général de 6 à 9 h, de 12 à 15 h, et de 18 à 22 h uniquement. Il y a en général un chauffage au centre de la baraque, le plus souvent au mazout, ce qui fait que ceux qui se trouvent à proximité ont chaud pendant qu'il est allumé, alors que les autres grelottent au fond de la baraque, et ceci du mois d'octobre au mois d'avril. Les courants d'air sont la règle générale: l'air passe par les fenêtres qui ferment mal et sous les portes. L'organisation interne varie (ce ne sont que des variations de détails!) de la « chambre à deux lits » dans le meilleur des cas au dortoir à 12 lits de type militaire. Ce que les gérants et l'Etat appellent « chambre » varie entre la chambre à quatre parois en bois, avec porte en passant par trois parois avec rideaux jusqu'au trois parois sans fermeture (donc ouvertes sur le couloir central). Les lits sont de simples sommiers à ressorts horizontaux durs et déformés. A chaque lit correspond un tabouret ou une chaise, une armoire, et quelquefois une table pour deux ou quatre. La lumière est collective (une ampoule pour quatre personnes en général). Aucune « chambre » n'est réellement insonorisée. Il n'y a presque jamais de cuisine, aussi y a-t-il des cantines. Dans certaines baraques, les travailleurs qui ne mangent pas à la cantine sont rapidement renvoyés sous un prétexte quelconque, la cantine étant un des moyens de faire des bénéfices pour les gérants. Les plats sont quantitativement copieux (il s'agit de travailleurs du bâtiment) mais qualitativement de dernier choix. A Genève, la plus grande concentration de baraques est de 20 (logeant 400 travailleurs) et va jusqu'à la baraque unique. La distance entre deux baraques n'est souvent que de deux mètres, les alentours sont en terre battue (pas de goudron).

Le prix moyen du lit était de 65 fr. en 1970, ce qui recouvre des variations entre 60 fr. et 100 fr. Souvent, les gérants ajoutent les frais d'électricité, de gaz, etc. Souvent aussi ils essaient de faire payer les travailleurs saisonniers pendant les trois mois qu'ils sont obligés de passer dans leur pays sous peine de ne plus retrouver leur lit au printemps. Comme le plus souvent le loyer est retenu sur le salaire des saisonniers par le patron, et qu'ils sont payés tous les quinze jours, cela revient en fait à leur faire payer 13 mois de loyer! Sur l'initiative de l'Etat augmentant le prix du loyer de 30 % dès 1971, toutes les baraques vont augmenter également leurs prix.

Les baraques sont toujours construites avec la complicité de l'Etat. En effet, elles sont le plus souvent situées sur des terrains interdits à la construction: au bord des lignes de chemin de fer, au bord des rivières, sur des terrains trop humides, pas solides, au bord des autoroutes, de l'aéroport, etc.; et le plus souvent à l'extérieur de la ville, d'où la nécessité de faire de très longs trajets de la baraque au chantier chaque jour.

Elles sont quelquefois directement construites par l'Etat qui en est donc propriétaire, et qui confie la gérance à des organisations de bienfaisance catholiques (Caritas par exemple) ou protestantes (l'Armée du Salut, le Centre Social Protestant par exemple), ou construites directement par les entreprises qui y logent leurs travailleurs. La gérance en est le plus souvent confiée à un travailleur immigré particulièrement docile et soumis, auquel on accorde alors le droit de faire venir sa famille. Il est chargé de faire régner l'ordre à l'intérieur, et en période d'agitation de communiquer les noms, les numéros de plaques de voitures, etc. de ceux qui viennent de « l'extérieur » dans les baraques. Ils sont également chargés d'appeler la police lorsqu'il y a des conflits internes ou des agitateurs externes dans les périodes de grèves ou de graves tensions. En effet, les baraques sont propriété privée, ce qui permet aux gérants d'exiger que tout ce qui est distribué aux travailleurs immigrés habitant les baraques passe par sa censure (qui s'exerce naturellement contre tous les tracts politiques et non contre la propagande religieuse ou ne concernant pas la situation des travailleurs immigrés en Suisse), et de faire appel à la police qui encercle les baraques avec des chiens policiers pour empêcher tout contact des travailleurs avec l'extérieur, notamment les travailleurs de la même entreprise habitant dans d'autres baraques ou dans des baraques en dur, comme cela s'est produit lors de la grève de la Murer à Genève. Les personnes voulant pénétrer dans les baraques pendant les périodes de grèves sont toutes interpellées et arrêtées par la police.

Les baraques constituent donc une sorte de ghetto éparpillé à l'intérieur et aux alentours des grandes villes ou en rase campagne.

A Genève, à la suite de plusieurs conflits et d'une grève sauvage qui contenaient tous un ou deux points portant sur les baraques et qui ont ébranlé la « paix du travail », la bourgeoisie a décidé en octobre 1970 d'un règlement des baraques, ceci à travers l'Etat. Aussi a-t-elle décidé d'institutionnaliser ce qu'elle avait toujours présenté comme provisoire.

Ce règlement définit des conditions d'hygiène « élémentaire », précisant que « le volume d'air de la pièce à destination de logement doit être d'au moins 15 mètres cubes pour la première personne logée et 10 mètres cubes pour chaque personne suivante. Les dégagements sont compris dans ces volumes » (Art. 3 et 8), que « chaque travailleur doit disposer d'un lit personnel constitué par un sommier métallique et un matelas en bon état garni de draps, des couvertures en suffisance et d'un oreiller muni d'une taie, ainsi que d'une armoire personnelle pouvant être fermée à clé (...). Chaque chambre comprend une table suffisamment grande, ainsi qu'un siège et une table de nuit ou étagère par personne logée. » (Art. 2 et 7), etc.

Il n'est pas difficile d'imaginer dans quel état sont les baraques (aucune n'est conforme à ce règlement à Genève aujourd'hui...) pour que la bourgeoisie soit obligée de préciser dans un texte de loi que chaque travailleur doit avoir un lit personnel! Et qu'il doit disposer de couvertures en suffisance ainsi que d'une table suffisamment grande, de douches et de WC en nombre suffisant... Qu'est-ce que suffisant? Ce ne sont certainement pas les baraques en tant que telles.

← figs. 8–9
Substandard building inhabited by seasonal and annual workers in the Grottes district, Geneva.

Les baraques en pierre
Ce que nous appelons les baraques en pierre sont les vieilles maisons, situées le plus souvent au centre de la ville, quelquefois

à l'extérieur (vieilles villas, etc.) qui se trouvent dans des zones qui, selon le plan de réorganisation de la ville par la bourgeoisie sont destinées à plus ou moins long terme à être détruites et qui, par conséquent, n'ont plus fait l'objet de réparations depuis plusieurs années, et ont, à un moment donné, été déclarées insalubres. La plupart des Suisses en ont été expulsés ou sont en voie de l'être.

Ces maisons sont louées quelquefois entièrement, quelquefois uniquement par appartement par les entrepreneurs aux régies; celles-ci les «meublent» (de lits, de chaises et de rares tables) et y placent leurs saisonniers et leurs annuels. Ceci a de nouveau lieu avec la complicité de l'Etat (puisqu'il les a déclarées insalubres auparavant).

Il existe donc trois types de conditions de location: 1. le travailleur signe un contrat de bail avec une régie ou l'office de la ville pour l'usage d'un logement. Il paie son loyer à la régie. Ceci est le cas pour les Suisses et pour quelques annuels; 2. le travailleur a accès à un appartement pour lui et sa famille que lui procure son patron. Il paie son loyer au patron quand celui-ci ne le lui retient pas sur son salaire; 3. le travailleur a accès à un lit. Il est logé avec d'autres travailleurs dans une chambre. Le patron retient le loyer sur le salaire. C'est le cas de tous les saisonniers.

Ces différences font que dans un même immeuble, pour deux appartements semblables, les travailleurs paieront des loyers différents, n'auront pas le même bailleur et surtout pas les mêmes droits sur le logement.

Ainsi les saisonniers ne pourront pas décider de l'utilisation de leur logement (nombre de personnes habitant ensemble) et ne pourront changer de travail sans perdre du même coup leur logement.

Mais pour le patronat et l'Etat, ces différences permettent de reprendre le plus possible sur le logement de ce qu'ils ont donné d'un autre côté en salaire, et cela dans l'arbitraire le plus complet. Par exemple, un taudis du quartier des Pâquis à Genève, lorsqu'il était habité par des Suisses, rapportait 700 fr. par mois (10 appartements de 70 fr.); maintenant, en y logeant 4 saisonniers par chambre, il rapporte 10 fois plus (70 fr. par lit) c'est-à-dire 7000 fr. par mois! Il est évident que les installations sanitaires ne sont pas multipliées...

Malgré ces différences de loyers, de droits, de statuts, les travailleurs habitant ces taudis et ces zones réservées à la démolition sont logés dans les mêmes conditions que les habitants des baraques: les immeubles sont extrêmement dégradés, n'ont pas de chauffage central, pas d'eau chaude, pas d'installations sanitaires (un WC à l'étage) et sont toujours humides. On n'y fait plus de réparations, ce qui fait que, pour y habiter, les travailleurs sont obligés de faire des réparations à leurs frais, ce qui objectivement doit être ajouté au prix du loyer et le double très facilement (chauffage, peinture, installation d'eau chaude, etc.).

Aussi pouvons-nous dire en conclusion que les travailleurs logés en ville, même s'ils ont l'illusion d'être mieux logés que ceux des baraques en bois (surtout à cause de la possibilité de se faire de la cuisine, du bruit, et l'impression d'être moins surveillés) sont en réalité le plus souvent dans des conditions similaires si ce n'est pires.

En plus de notre expérience personnelle, nous nous sommes basés pour rédiger cet article sur les livres et documents suivants:

F. Engels: *La question du logement*, Ed. Sociales, Paris, 1969.

F. Alberoni: «Tipologia delle migrazioni esteriore», in *Studi di sociologia*, n° 3, 1963.

S. Zanolli: *L'assimilation des travailleurs étrangers*, Juris-Verlag, Zürich, 1964.

B. Schmutz: *La signification des facteurs de mouvements de la main-d'œuvre dans les transformations de la structure professionnelle*, Ed. La Baconnière, Neuchâtel, 1965.

R. Descloîtres: «Adaptation des travailleurs ruraux et étrangers à l'industrie», in *Rapports de l'OCDE*, Paris, 1965.

during a strike or periods of tension. Indeed, the barracks are private property, which allows managers to insist that anything distributed to immigrant workers in the barracks be censored (this censorship is naturally limited to political tracts and anything connected to the situation of immigrant workers in Switzerland; religious or other propaganda is exempt). It also allows managers to summon the police, who then surround the barracks with police dogs to prevent any contact with the outside. This applies especially to workers employed by the same company who live in other barracks, or in permanent structures, as occurred in the strike of [the building contractor] Murer in Geneva. Anyone who tries to enter the barracks during a strike is questioned and arrested.

The barracks thus constitute a kind of ghetto that is scattered within or on the edges of the major cities and around the countryside.

In Geneva, following several conflicts and a wildcat strike (all of which made barrack-related demands) that broke the "labor peace," the bourgeoisie decided in October 1970 to regularize the barracks through state channels. This amounted to institutionalizing something that had always been framed as provisional.

This regulation defined "basic" hygiene conditions, specifying that "the volume of air in the room used for accommodation shall be at least 15 cubic meters for the first person housed, plus 10 cubic meters for each subsequent person. Headroom is included in these volumes" (Articles 3 and 8). It was further stated that "each worker shall have access to a bed for personal use, consisting of a metal base and mattress in good condition, and furnished with sheets, sufficient blankets and a pillow with pillowcase, as well as a lockable personal wardrobe… . Each room shall include a table of sufficient size, as well as one seat and bedside cabinet per person accommodated" (Articles 2 and 7), and so on.

Given that the bourgeoisie felt the need to specify that each worker should have their own bed (when none of these barracks currently comply with the Geneva regulation), one can only imagine their condition! And as for specifying "sufficient" bedding and a table of "sufficient" size—what defines *sufficient*? Certainly not the barracks as they are.

Stone Barracks

Stone barracks refers to old houses, most often in the city center but sometimes in the suburbs (e.g., old villas), which are situated in zones earmarked for eventual demolition in the redevelopment plans of the bourgeoisie. As a result, they have not been maintained in years, and sooner or later they are declared unfit for habitation. By then, most Swiss citizens have been or are in the process of being evicted.

Sometimes these houses are rented out in their entirety; sometimes, entrepreneurs rent individual flats to rental agencies. The entrepreneurs will then "furnish" these flats (with beds, chairs, and very occasionally tables) for their seasonal and annual workers. Once again, this process depends on the complicity of the state, because the buildings have already been declared unfit for habitation.

Consequently, there are three types of rental conditions. In the first, the worker signs a rental contract with a rental agency or municipality for the use of a dwelling. He then pays his rent to the agency. This is the case for Swiss citizens and some annual workers. In the second situation, the worker has access to an apartment for himself and his family, provided by his employer. He pays his rent to the employer, unless the latter deducts it from his wages. In the third situation, the worker has access to a bed. He is housed in a room with other workers. The boss deducts the rent from his wages. This is the case for all seasonal workers.

These differences mean that in the same building, in two similar apartments, the workers may pay different rents, may not have the same landlord, and, above all, will not have the same housing rights.

This means that seasonal workers will not be able to determine how their accommodation is used (such as the number of persons living together) and cannot change jobs without simultaneously losing their accommodation.

But for bosses and the state, these differences allow them to make back as much as possible of what they have paid out in wages, in the most arbitrary way. For example, when it housed Swiss citizens, a slum in Geneva's Pâquis district brought in seven hundred Swiss francs per month (for ten flats at seventy francs each). Now that it houses four seasonal workers per room, at seventy francs per bed, it brings in ten times as much—or seven thousand francs per month! It goes without saying that the sanitary facilities have not been likewise multiplied.

Despite these differences in rents, rights, and status, the workers living in these slums and areas reserved for demolition are housed in the same conditions as the inhabitants of the barracks. The buildings are extremely dilapidated, have no central heating, no hot water, no sanitary facilities (there is one toilet per floor), and have permanent damp. As repairs are no longer being made, workers must make repairs at their own expense in order to live there; these expenses (heating, painting, hot water installation) are in reality part of the rent and can easily exceed it.

We can conclude by noting that workers housed in the city, even if they believe themselves better housed than workers in barracks (because they can cook and make noise and are not as closely monitored), are in reality often living in conditions that are similar if not worse.

In addition to our personal experience, we have based this article on the following books and documents:

F. Engels, *La question du logement* (Paris: Ed. Sociales, 1969).

F. Alberoni, "Tipologia delle migrationzioni esteriore," *Studi di sociologia* 3 (1963).

S. Zanolli, *L'assimilation des travailleurs étrangers* (Zurich: Juris-Verlag, 1964).

B. Schmutz, *La signification des facteurs de mouvements de la main-d'œuvre dans les transformations de la structure professionnelle* (Neuchâtel: Ed. La Baconnière, 1965).

R. Descloîtres, "Adaptation des travailleurs ruraux et étrangers à l'industrie," *Rapports de l'OCDE* (Paris), 1965.

H. M. Hagmann, *Les travailleurs étrangers, chance et tournant de la Suisse* (Lausanne: Ed. Payot, 1966).

H. M. Hagmann, *Pour une politique active d'assimilation des travailleurs étrangers en Suisse* (Lausanne: Ed. Payot, 1967).

R. Descloîtres, "Le travailleur étranger," *Rapports de l'OCDE* (Paris), 1967.

D. Maillat, *Structure des salaires et immigration* (Neuchâtel: Ed. La Baconnière, 1968).

H. M. Hagmann, "Migration des hommes ou migrations des capitaux?," *Revue migrations* (Geneva), 11 (1968).

E. Cinnani, *Emigrazione e imperialismo* (Rome: Ed. Riuniti, 1968).

S. Passigli, *Emigrazione e comportamento politico* (Bologna: Ed. Il Mulino, 1969).

A. Macheret, "L'immigration étrangère à l'heure de l'intégration européenne," in *Etudes suisses de droit européen* (Geneva: Ed. Georg, 1969).

F. Alberoni and G. Baglioni, *L'integrazione dell'immigrato nella società industriale* (Bologna: Ed. Il Mulino, 1969).

G. Blumer, *L'emigrazione italiana in Europa* (Milan: Ed. Feltrinelli, 1970).

B. Granotier, *Les travailleurs immigrés en France* (Paris: Ed. Maspéro, 1970).

S. Soldini, M. Rossi, E. Poglia, G. Pellicciari, L. Persico, and F. Cavalli, *L'immigrazione in Svizzera* (Milan: Ed. Sapere, 1970).

P. Baran and P. Sweezy, *Le capitalisme monopoliste* (Paris: Ed. Maspéro, 1970).

Groupe Action Travailleurs Immigrés, *Baraques et saisonniers* (Geneva, 1970).

Résultats de l'enquête au quartier des Grottes, in *Bulletin du "Comité logement-luttes ouvrières"* (Geneva), 1 (November 1970).

"Règlement relatif au logement des travailleurs saisonniers," in *Feuille d'Avis Officielle de la République et Canton de Genève*, October 2, 1970.

Die Wohnbedingungen der Fremdarbeiter in der Schweiz

Die Frage der Unterkunft der Fremdarbeiter in der Schweiz ist nur von der wirtschaftlichen, politischen und sozialen Gesamtsituation her zu verstehen: d.h. im Zusammenhang mit der Aufspaltung der Arbeiterklasse innerhalb der kapitalistischen Wirtschaftsordnung einerseits und durch die allgemeine « Wohnbaukrise » andererseits. Die in der Schweiz beschäftigten Fremdarbeiter (991 000; 16 % der Gesamtbevölkerung) stehen auf der tiefsten Stufe einer bereits hierarchisch (in verschiedene Salärklassen, etc.) aufgespaltenen Arbeiterschaft; überdies besitzen sie weder politische noch gewerkschaftliche Rechte und insbesondere kein Streikrecht.

Was die « Wohnbaukrise » betrifft (Mangel an preiswerten Wohnungen), so ist sie nur durch die Struktur der kapitalistischen Produktionsweise zu verstehen (da der Wohnbau ein wenig rentabler Sektor der Produktion ist) — die verschiedenen staatlichen Förderungsmassnahmen können — keine Lösung des Problems bringen.

Die Arbeiterklasse ist durch diese « Krise » am unmittelbarsten betroffen — und innerhalb der Arbeiterklasse haben die Fremdarbeiter ihre Folgen am härtesten zu spüren. Auf der Ebene der Unterkunft wiederholt und verstärkt sich die Aufspaltung der Arbeiterklasse, die das Bürgertum bereits auf der Ebene der Arbeit verwirklicht hat. Unter Mitwissen des Staates und unter direkter Kontrolle durch die Arbeitgeber ist die grosse Mehrzahl der Fremdarbeiter in « Baracken » untergebracht: entweder in « provisorischen » Holzschuppen oder in Altbauten, die bereits für den Abbruch bestimmt sind. Diese Wohngelegenheiten bilden ein über Stadt und Land verstreutes Ghetto.

Die Verfasserin stützt sich auf Beispiele aus Genf (Mietpreise, Zahlungsmodalitäten, Wohnbedingungen, sanitäre Einrichtungen, usw.), wo die jüngsten Konflikte den Staatsrat genötigt haben, eine Reihe sehr vielsagender « elementarer Sanitätsvorschriften » für die Baracken zu erlassen. — Trotz einiger Vorteile (relative Unabhängigkeit, keine direkte Kontrolle durch den Arbeitgeber) ist die Situation in den « Steinbaracken » aber keineswegs besser als diejenige in den Holzschuppen.

H. M. Hagmann: *Les travailleurs étrangers, chance et tournant de la Suisse*, Ed. Payot, Lausanne, 1966.

H.-M. Hagmann: *Pour une politique active d'assimilation des travailleurs étrangers en Suisse*, Ed. Payot, Lausanne, 1967.

R. Descloîtres: « Le travailleur étranger », in *Rapports de l'OCDE*, Paris, 1967.

D. Maillat: *Structure des salaires et immigration*, Ed. La Baconnière, Neuchâtel, 1968.

H. M. Hagmann: « Migration des hommes ou migrations des capitaux? » in *Revue Migrations*, n° 11, Genève, 1968.

E. Cinnani: *Emigrazione e imperialismo*, Ed. Riuniti, Roma, 1968.

S. Passigli: *Emigrazione e comportamento politico*, Ed. Il Mulino, Bologna, 1969.

A. Macheret: « L'immigration étrangère à l'heure de l'intégration européenne », in *Etudes suisses de droit européen*, Ed. Georg, Genève, 1969.

F. Alberoni e G. Baglioni: *L'integrazione dell'immigrato nella società industriale*, Ed. Il Mulino, Bologna, 1969.

G. Blumer: *L'emigrazione italiana in Europa*, Ed. Feltrinelli, Milan, 1970.

B. Granotier: *Les travailleurs immigrés en France*, Ed. Maspéro, Paris, 1970.

S. Soldini, M. Rossi, E. Poglia, G. Pellicciari, L. Persico e F. Cavalli: *L'immigrazione in Svizzera*, Ed. Sapere, Milano, 1970.

Baran et Sweezy: *Le capitalisme monopoliste*, Ed. Maspéro, Paris, 1970.

Groupe Action Travailleurs Immigrés: *Baraques et Saisonniers*, Genève, 1970.

Résultats de l'enquête au quartier des Grottes, in *Bulletin du « Comité logement-luttes ouvrières »*, n° 1, Genève, nov. 1970.

« Règlement relatif au logement des travailleurs saisonniers », in *Feuille d'Avis Officielle de la République et Canton de Genève*, 2 octobre 1970.

Military Theories and Collective Housing

Author:
Teresa Zarebska

Source:
archithese, 8 (1973): 9–14

Translated by:
Brett Petzer

It may seem curious for a magazine devoted to the architectural issues of our own time to turn to military matters. And yet, the waging of war has long been an integral part of the arts, crafts, and sciences of past eras. It has motivated research and influenced methodology across the disciplines. This is also a subject that *archithese* has dealt with before, in an excellent article by Stanislaus von Moos.[1]

Von Moos pointed out that the significance of technique, and especially military technique, had been underestimated in both architectural theory and practice by historiographers of the Italian Renaissance.[2] This argument can be further extended by taking stock of an even more serious lacuna in the subsequent phase of development of military architecture, one dominated by the Dutch and their neighbors. Indeed, monographs on Francesco di Giorgio Martini, Leonardo da Vinci, Peruzzi, the Sangallo family, Michelangelo, and Scamozzi do address their military activities. However, such celebrated names are largely absent from the late-sixteenth and early seventeenth centuries. Not only are there no monographs, but the various histories of the architecture of this period fail even to mention serious authors such as Daniel Speckle,

Jacques Perret, Jean Errard de Bar-le-Duc, Samuel Marolois, Pietro Sardi, Simon Stevin, Adam Freytag, Nicolaus Goldmann, Georg Andreas Böckler, Antoine de Ville, Wilhelm Dilich, or Matthias Doegen. These names pioneered the military architecture of their time and often appeared alongside classical greats such as Vegetius, Aelianus, Frontinus, and Vitruvius.

Although military and urban planning had already begun to emerge as distinct disciplines by the mid-sixteenth century,[3] a kind of all-purpose "civil and military" architect still existed at this time. These architects were prepared to undertake various tasks. They marked out the city limits, defensive perimeter, and often a fortress. Inside these, they designed the street plan and built palaces, churches, municipal offices, and quite often they even designed model houses.[4] Later, military engineers would gradually replace architects in these roles. By the end of the sixteenth century, engineers were already being warned not to usurp the role of architects in tasks such as the planning of squares, streets, and buildings. City walls and fortresses were then also considered to fall under the architect's purview, leaving military

Teresa Zarebska

Théories militaires
et habitations collectives

Il peut sembler insolite qu'une revue consacrée aux problèmes architecturaux proches de notre temps fasse place au domaine militaire. Pourtant c'est un domaine qui fut intégré dans l'ensemble des sciences, techniques et arts des époques passées et qui a inspiré les recherches et influencé les méthodes des différentes disciplines. Ce problème a d'ailleurs déjà été abordé dans *archithese*, dans l'excellent article de Stanislaus von Moos[1]. L'auteur mettait alors en relief le fait que l'importance de la technique surtout de la technique militaire) dans la théorie aussi bien que dans la pratique architecturale avait été sous-évaluée par les historiographes de la Renaissance italienne.[2] On peut compléter cette thèse en relevant qu'une même lacune, encore plus grave, existe pour la phase suivante du développement de l'architecture militaire, phase dominée par les auteurs hollandais et leurs voisins. En effet, les monographies sur Francesco di Giorgio Martini, Leonardo da Vinci, Peruzzi, les Sangallo, Michelangelo et Scamozzi traitent aussi de leur activité militaire. En revanche, à la fin du XVIième et dans la première partie du XVIIième siècle, on ne trouve pas de noms si brillants. Et souvent, non seulement il n'existe pas de monographies mais les diverses histoires de l'architecture ne mentionnent même pas des auteurs valables tels que Daniel Speckle, Jacques Perret, Jean Errard-de-Bar-le-Duc, Samuel Marolois, Pietro Sardi, Simon Stevin, Adam Freytag, Nicolaus Goldmann, Georg Andreas Boekler, Antoine de Ville, Wilhelm Dillich ou Matthias Doegen, qui ont tracé le chemin à l'architecture militaire de leur temps, et dont les noms figuraient alors souvent à côté des classiques (Vegetius, Aelianus, Frontinus, Vitruvius).

Bien que vers le milieu du XVIième siècle les problématiques militaire et urbanistique commencent déjà à s'individuer comme disciplines particulières[3], il existe encore à cette époque un type d'architecte universel, «civil et militaire». Celui-ci est encore préparé à des tâches variées: il projette la ville, son enceinte

Militärische Theorien als Grundlage der Planung von Kollektivwohnungen

Die militärischen Planer und Festungsarchitekten des 16. und 17. Jahrhunderts leisteten einen wesentlichen Beitrag zur Vorgeschichte des sozialen Siedlungsbaus. Der strategische Zwang, neue Festungs- und Stadtanlagen rasch, aber technisch genau zu bauen, erforderte eine weitgehende Rationalisierung der Planung und Arbeitsorganisation.

Im späten 16. und in den ersten Hälfte des 17. Jahrhunderts fehlen glanzvolle Namen unter den Festungsplanern und Baumeistern, aber die Publikationen und Entwürfe von Speckle, Perret, Errand-de-Bar-le-Duc, Marolois, Sardi, Freytag, Dögen u. a. hinterliessen ihre Spuren in der Geschichte kollektiver Unterkünfte. Militärische Anlagen jeder Art besitzen zwangsläufig kollektiven Charakter, wurden auf «öffentlichem Boden» errichtet und verfügten öfters über Behausungen und Hospitäler für ausgediente Soldaten. Zugang, Unterkunft für Menschen, Tiere und Geräte, Warenlager, die Zuordnung verschiedenster Funktionen, und die gesamte Raumnutzung wurden koordiniert, in der Absicht, universale Planungskonzepte zu entwikkeln.

Schon im 14. Jahrhundert errichtete Venedig Sozialsiedlungen für Seeleute, und im 17. Jahrhundert entstand z. B. in Kopenhagen die Siedlung «Nyboder» in der Neustadt. Im allgemeinen handelt es sich dabei um langgestreckte Häuserzeilen in der Tradition militärischer Lager, die kleine Gärten und Höfe zwischen sich einschliessen.

9

de fortifications es aussi souvent une forteresse; à l'intérieur de l'enceinte il trace le réseau des rues, construit des palais, des églises, le palais communal, et il lui arrive même souvent de projeter des maisons modèles[4]. Plus tard, l'architecte sera peu à peu remplacé dans ces tâches par l'ingénieur militaire. Déjà à la fin du XVIième siècle on entend des mises en garde contre l'usurpation par l'ingénieur de tâches telles que la planification des places, des rues et des édifices, et l'on dit alors que l'enceinte de la ville de même que la forteresse sont du ressort de l'architecte et que la fonction de l'ingénieur militaire doit se limiter à la construction d'éléments purement militaires, tels que bastions, casemates, caponnières, etc. Une fois de plus, l'architecte se propose comme «uomo universale»: c'est à lui qu'il convient de coordonner et de surveiller les travaux et de réaliser l'ensemble spatial.

De toutes façons, à l'époque de Bacon et de Descartes, de Galilée et de Kepler, le modèle de l'«homme universel», qui avait inspiré l'architecte encore récemment, est dépassé. La collaboration des divers spécialistes, qui pourront compléter réciproquement leur science et échanger leurs expériences et méthodes, s'impose. La fondation d'une ville et la construction d'une nouvelle forteresse est un exemple de tâche complexe, qui requiert une collaboration interdisciplinaire. A cette fin Francesco de Marchi propose la formation d'une commission d'experts, laquelle devrait travailler sous la direction de l'architecte «qui sait faire les dessins et diriger les chantiers». A cette commission devraient participer: «un soldat expérimenté et connaisseur de la milice, qui connaisse le site où construire la forteresse, qu'elle puisse être défendue des ennemis. Il faut aussi un médecin très savant, pour connaître l'air, l'eau, les fruits. Ensuite il faut un homme expert en agriculture, qui connaisse la fertilité du sol et qui sache s'il y aura de l'eau, des prés, du bois, des terrains pour semer toutes sortes de grains et planter des vignes; et il faut un homme capable et averti dans les arts minéraux, qui puisse reconnaître s'il y a des mines, desquelles le Prince puisse se prévaloir. Il faut encore un astrologue très savant...»[5] Cette dernière figure d'expert symbolise les époques passées et nous rappelle que nous sommes précisément au seuil d'une nouvelle conception et organisation du travail. Dans le dernier quart du XVIième et la première moitié du XVIIième siècle on assiste en effet à un développement extraordinaire des méthodes de planification et de réalisation des grandes constructions.

Un des meilleurs auteurs hollandais de manuels de mathématique, perspective et fortification, Marolois, nous en donne un exemple[6], en faisant le récit d'un concours urbanistico-militaire dont le thème était la modernisation de l'enceinte défensive de la ville de Herdewyck. Mais le niveau élevé d'organisation de tout processus de construction d'une ville nouvelle est illustré de manière encore plus frappante par les recherches de Enrico Sisi sur la ville de La Valette[7]. De ce travail il résulte clairement que déjà vers 1560 il était possible non seulement de projeter un ensemble urbain basé sur des analyses préliminaires et des prémices théoriques, mais aussi d'effectuer une réalisation vraiment moderne. L'auteur du projet, l'ingénieur Laparelli, compte tous les groupes de parcelles et d'espaces publics, et établit des relations mathématiques entre les différentes zones du territoire fortifié[8]. Le plan de travail est établi avec une précision telle qu'on peut mettre à l'ouvrage simultanément un grand nombre d'ouvriers (3500 à 5000). Avec l'aide des règlements adéquats sur les servitudes liées aux parcelles, Laparelli dirige de manière conséquente la construction de toute la ville.

La construction d'une forteresse se faisait presque toujours à vitesse accélérée. De la rapidité des travaux dépendait le succès de l'entreprise, car seulement l'enceinte une fois complète, la citadelle pouvait se prétendre inexpugnable. Cette nécessité de construire à la fois avec rapidité et précision a favorisé le perfectionnement des méthodes. On pensa à créer non seulement des points fortifiés, mais des lignes de défense formées par tout un réseau de forteresses; le meilleur exemple en est la fortification contre les Turcs en Europe méridionale, et surtout en Hongrie[9]. D'autre part, les guerres entre l'Espagne et la Hollande furent également très stimulantes pour la modernisation des systèmes de défense[10].

L'efficacité de la défense ne dépendait pas seulement des constructions militaires: les habitants de la forteresse, civils et militaires, devaient être préparés à un long siège, c'est-à-dire qu'ils devaient être logés assez confortablement. Le problème des casernes et des maisons familiales modestes devint un des éléments des

↓ fig. 1 Jozef Naronowicz-Naroński, design for the Polish-Lithuanian army camp.

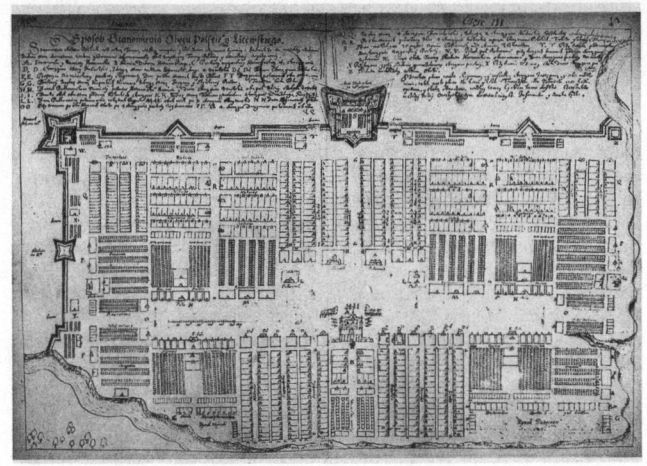

← fig. 2
Samuel Marolois, military camp (from *Fortification ou architecture militaire*, [The Hague, 1615], pl. 27).

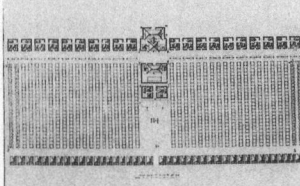

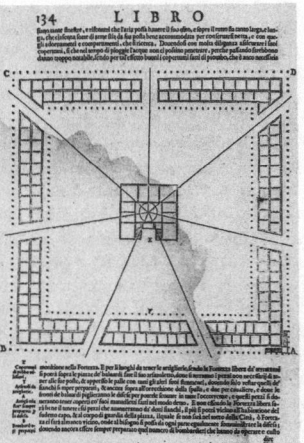

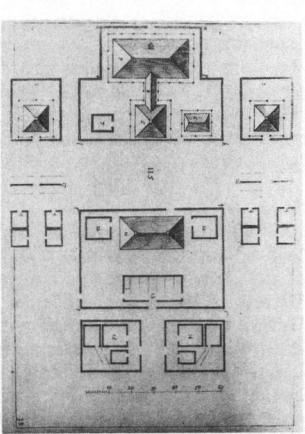

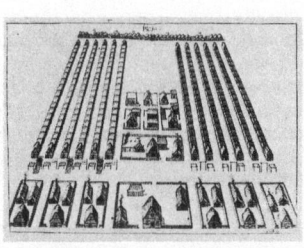

↑ fig. 3 Buonaiuto Lorini, the square in the center of the heptagonal fortress (*Delle fortificationi* [Venice, 1597], p. 146).

↑ fig. 4 Samuel Marolois, detail of the military camp (*Fortification ou architecture militaire* [The Hague, 1615], pl. 28).

↑ fig. 5 Adam Freytag, section of the camp of an infantry regiment (*Architectura*, plate after p. 136).

études théoriques de l'architecture militaire. Dans les traités militaires de la période «italienne» on trouve des fragments de textes sur la répartition des blocs dans les forteresses, sur la nécessité d'assurer aux défenseurs des habitations fonctionnelles, situées rationellement du point de vue militaire, bien accessibles, sûres et suffisamment spacieuses. Malheureusement des dessins de ces maisons-casernes sont très rares et schématiques. Un dessin de Buonaiuto Lorini montrant les casernes entourant la place d'armes au centre de la forteresse peut nous en donner une idée (Fig. 3) [11].

Le thème des «habitations collectives» pour les soldats est devenu très important dans la période «hollandaise» de la théorie militaire. A cette époque les théoriciens développèrent de façon complexe la technique de planification du campement militaire. Il s'agissait d'un type d'installation temporaire, parfois pour quelques jours seulement, d'autres fois pour plusieurs mois lorsque le siège devait durer longtemps. «Camp volant», «camp de défense», «camp d'attaque»[12], sont les termes qui expriment une hiérarchie des types de campements selon leurs dimensions et leur durée. Le point de départ était sans doute le *castrum romanum*, connu par le schéma publié par Machiavel[13] et par des descriptions[14]. Vers la fin du XVIème siècle, le schéma romain était rejoint conjointement au schéma moderne, carré, de composition centrale, souvent avec deux axes de symétrie[15]. Les projets sont basés sur des données mathématiques: la surface occupée par un soldat de telle ou telle arme et le terrain nécessaire pour un régiment quelconque sont multipliées pour trouver la superficie totale du campement. La connaissance des mesures générales était importante pour pouvoir simultanément tracer la rue intérieure du camp et construire les fortifications externes.

Il semble que ce soit Marolois qui ait inauguré cette méthode, dans une publication de 1615 (Fig. 2—4). L'auteur dessine les longues rangées de baraques, les magasins de victuailles, à part les habitations des officiers, et au centre la place d'armes. Les détails de la place d'armes sont indiqués dans un dessin plus grande échelle; on y voit les maisons, les écuries, les dépôts, etc. Après ce schéma traditionnel Marolois en élabore un autre, comportant un carré au centre, de 300 pieds de côté, complété par des rectangles de même longueur.

Il est possible que ce module de 300 pieds vienne de la pratique militaire. On le retrouve chez plusieurs auteurs, en particulier chez Simon Stevin[16] et Adam Freytag[17], de qui l'on possède une image en perspective des «quartiers» de la cavalerie et de l'infanterie comme éléments du camp (Fig. 5).

Un autre théoricien de cette lignée est Jozef Naronowicz-Naronski, auteur d'excellents manuels de mathématiques, géométrie, cartographie, perspective et architecture militaire[18]. Il fit le projet pour l'ensemble du grand campement de l'armée polacco-lituanienne. Il détermina d'abord les unités: les parcelles individuelles, destinées aux officiers et à leurs aides et serviteurs (Fig. 7), et aussi celles des simples chevaliers et de leurs hommes. On y voit les tentes ou baraques d'habitations, l'emplacement de la cuisine, les écuries, les dépôts, les emplacements pour les chars, les latrines, etc. De ces unités Naronski passe à des fragments plus grands, et finit par un grandiose plan génial du camp (Fig. 1). Cet ensemble spatial situé au bord du fleuve est conçu — comme dit l'auteur — en accord avec la tradition polonaise, mais on y remarque à la fois l'influence de la tradition antique comme celle de la coutume moderne. Le schéma est à un axe, avec une place allongée au centre, sur laquelle se trouve la résidence du commandant; tous les régiments ont leurs «quartiers» projetés avec grand soin, selon divers modèles, et dans la périphérie, près du fleuve, sont prévues deux places de marché.

Les constructions d'habitations militaires de tous genres, dans les citadelles et dans les camps comme dans les villes fortifiées, avaient généralement un caractère collectif. Elles étaient réalisées sur un terrain appartenant au souverain ou à l'état ou à des fonds publics. Parfois elles avaient aussi un caractère social. Par exemple pour les soldats méritants on construisait divers types de logements et d'hôpitaux. A Venise, pour les familles des marins on avait construit un quartier déjà au Moyen-Age[19]. A Copenhague, un quartier très fameux pour les marins et autres dépendants de la marine, le «Nyboder», avait été tracé en 1631 (Fig. 6). La distribution des rues et des maisons — originairement à un étage — est frappante: les maisons juxtaposées forment des bandes, entre lesquelles se trouvent, en alternance, soit des rues assez larges soit des files de petits jardins.

engineers to limit themselves to purely military elements, such as bastions, casemates, and caponiers. Once again, the architect presents himself here as an *uomo universale*: it falls to him to coordinate and supervise the work and to deliver the spatial ensemble.

In any event, by the time of Bacon and Descartes, Galileo and Kepler, the model of the "universal man" that had inspired architects until recently was out of date. Collaboration between various specialists, who could complement each other's expertise and exchange findings and methods, was becoming indispensable. Founding a city and constructing a new fortress were complex undertakings requiring interdisciplinary collaboration. To this end, Francesco de Marchi proposed an expert commission, which was to work under the direction of the architect, "who knows how to draft the drawings and manage the building sites." This commission was to include "an experienced soldier with a good knowledge of the militia, who knows the site on which the fortress is to be built, so that it can be defended from enemies. Also needed is a very knowledgeable doctor, to survey the air, water sources, and fruits. Next, an expert in agriculture, who can judge the fertility of the soil, and who can say where and whether there will be water, meadows, wood, and land on which to sow all kinds of seeds and plant vines. Also required is a man capable and knowledgeable about minerals, who can determine whether there are mines that the Prince might take advantage of. There must also be a very learned astrologer …"[5] This final expert symbolizes bygone eras and serves as a reminder that this period was on the cusp of a new conception and organization of work. Indeed, the last quarter of the sixteenth century and the first half of the seventeenth century bore witness to an extraordinary period of development in the planning and construction methods used for major works.

One example of this can be found in Marolois, one of the greatest Dutch writers of treatises on mathematics, perspective, and fortification.[6] He writes of a military and urban planning competition for the modernization of the defensive perimeter of the town of Harderwijk. But the higher level of organization inherent in the construction of a new town is even more strikingly illustrated by Enrico Sisi's research on the city of Valletta.[7] His work shows that as early as 1560 it was already possible not only to plan an urban ensemble based on preliminary analyses and theoretical premises but to execute the project in a truly modern way. The engineer Laparelli, the author of the project, made an inventory of all the groups of plots and public spaces and established mathematical relationships between the different sections of the fortified area.[8] The plan of work was drawn up with such precision that a large number of laborers (3,500–5,000) could be put to work simultaneously. By virtue of regulations for the easements serving the plots, Laparelli was able to manage the construction of the entire settlement.

The construction of a fortress was almost always carried out at high speed. The success of the undertaking depended on the speed of the work, because only once the enclosure was complete could the citadel call itself impregnable. The need to build both rapidly and accurately spurred further refinement in methods. The creation of fortified sites gave rise to the concept of defensive lines formed by entire networks of fortresses; the best examples hereof can be found in the defenses built against the Turks in southern Europe, especially Hungary.[9] On the other hand, the wars between Spain and the Netherlands were also a great stimulus for the modernization of defense systems.[10]

An efficient defense depended on more than military structures. The inhabitants of a fortress, both civilian and military, had to be prepared for a long siege, meaning that their lodgings had to be relatively comfortable. The study of barracks and housing for laborers' families became part of the theory of military architecture. Military treatises from the "Italian" period include fragments of texts on the distribution of functional blocks inside fortresses and on the necessity of providing defenders with housing that is functional, easily accessible, safe, sufficiently spacious, and rationally located (in military terms). Unfortunately, drawings of these barrack-houses are schematic and very rare; a drawing by Buonaiuto Lorini of the barracks surrounding the parade ground in the center of the fortress gives us some idea (Fig. 3).[11]

The concept of "collective housing" for soldiers became very important in the "Dutch" era of military theory. Theorists of the time developed more complex techniques for the planning of military camps. These were a kind of temporary facility that sometimes lasted only a few days and sometimes for several months, in the case of lengthy sieges. The terms *flying camp*, *defensive camp*, and *offensive camp*[12] describe a hierarchy of types of camps according to scale and duration. The point of departure for these was doubtless the *castrum romanum*, known to us from the schema published by Machiavelli[13] and from various descriptions.[14] Toward the end of the sixteenth century, the Roman plan was used in conjunction with the modern, square, centrally composed plan, often with two axes of symmetry.[15] Designs were based on mathematical data: the area occupied by a soldier and his weapons, plus the land needed for a given regiment, were multiplied to find the total area of the camp. Knowing these general measures made it possible to mark out the internal streets of the camp while constructing the external fortifications at the same time.

Marolois seems to be the one who introduced this method in a publication of 1615 (Fig. 2–4). His drawing depicts long rows of barracks, the victuals stores apart from the officers' quarters, and, in the middle, the parade ground. Details of the parade ground are shown at a larger scale in another drawing, which also includes the houses, stables, storehouses, and so on. Another sketch follows this traditional Marolois drawing; it shows a square in the center, three hundred feet wide, with rectangles of the same length on all sides. This three-hundred-foot module may have been derived from military practice. It can be found in the works of several authors, particularly Simon Stevin[16] and Adam Freytag,[17] from whom we have a perspective image of the cavalry and infantry "quarters" as elements of the camp (Fig. 5).

Another theorist in this tradition is Józef Naronowicz-Naroński, the author of excellent treatises on mathematics, geometry, cartography, perspective, and military architecture.[18] He drew up the plans for the grand encampment of the Polish-Lithuanian army. He first determined the units, meaning the individual plots intended for the officers and their assistants and servants (Fig. 7), as well as those for the common knights and their men. Also shown are the tents or barracks, the location of the kitchen, the stables, depots, wagons, latrines, and so on. From these units, Naroński progresses to larger portions, culminating in an expansive and ingenious plan of the camp (Fig. 1). This spatial ensemble situated on a riverbank is designed, as the author states, in accordance with Polish tradition. However, the influence of both ancient and modern customs is also apparent. The schema has a single axis, with an elongated square in the center, where the commander's quarters are found. Each regiment has its quarters, laid out with great care according to various models, and on the periphery near the river, two marketplaces have been planned.

The construction of military housing of all kinds, in citadels and camps as well as in fortified towns, was generally of a collective nature. Housing was built on land belonging to the sovereign or the state or to public funds. Sometimes this housing had a social character. For example, various types of housing and hospitals were built for deserving soldiers. In Venice, a district for sailors' families had already been constructed in the Middle Ages.[19] In Copenhagen, the "Nyboder," a very well-known district for sailors and other dependents of the navy, had been laid out in 1631 (Fig. 6). The layout of the streets and houses, originally single-story, is striking: the terrace houses form rows facing onto wide streets and backing onto small gardens. These rows are cut diagonally by converging streets. The latter are a remnant of Copenhagen's central plan of 1629, which was abandoned in the middle of that century.[20] As for the parallel streets that form the elongated blocks (nicknamed "sandwiches" or "sticks"[21]), should they be interpreted as an allusion to the rows of barracks in military camps? The proximity of the fortress, which was built contemporaneously, and the site's location near the fortified line are further points in favor of attributing a semi-military character to Nyboder. The church in the center of the district has been destroyed.

According to theorists, every fortress had to be equipped with a church or chapel, as well

fig. 6 Copenhagen city plan (1649) with superimposed drawing of the Swedish attack (1658). In the center, the Nyboder district (engraving by Erik Dahlberg).

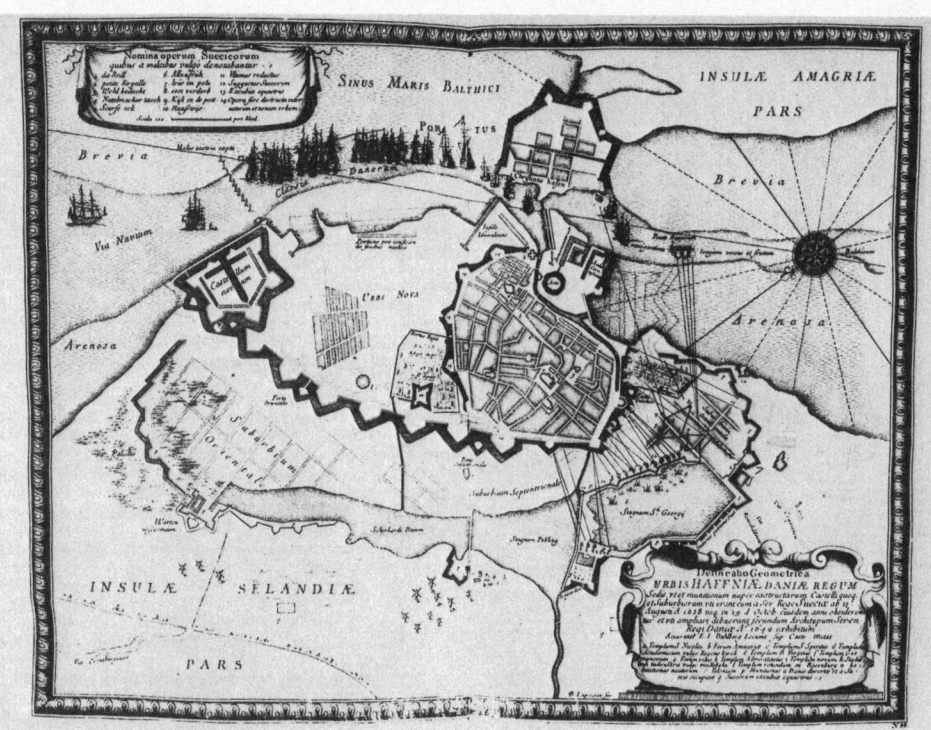

Les bandes parallèles sont coupées en diagonale par des rues convergentes. Celles-ci peuvent être expliquées facilement comme des vestiges du plan central de Copenhagen de 1629, abandonné au milieu du siècle [20]. En revanche les rues parallèles, formant les blocs allongés («en sandwich»; «les baguettes» [21]) sont-elles à interpréter comme des réminiscences des rangées de baraques dans les camps militaires? Le voisinnage de la forteresse, construite à la même époque, la localisation du quartier près de la ligne des fortifications, renforcent la possibilité d'attribuer au Nyboder un caractère semi-militaire. L'église au centre du quartier à été détruite.

Toute forteresse devait être, selon les théoriciens, munie d'une église ou d'une chapelle et du tribunal — pour maintenir le niveau moral des habitants. De même la résidence du commandant avait à la fois un but représentatif et disciplinaire. Pour la santé des habitants, beaucoup d'auteurs exigeaient un hôpital avec un personnel suffisant. Pour assurer des réserves de vivres et d'armements, les édifices adéquats étaient prévus.

Bien que les quartiers pour soldats représentent un type spécifique d'habitat collectif, on peut supposer que leur popularité dépassait le milieu militaire. Les succès militaires intéressaient le larges couches de la société. Beaucoup de dessins et de gravures montrent non seulement les batailles fameuses, mais décrivent aussi les villes, les forteresses et les camps mi-fig. 7 J. Naronowicz-Naroński, the plots of the military camp for officers. Measures vary according to rank (Budownictwo wojenne, 1659, in Warsaw University Library, Ms. no. 106, p. 105).

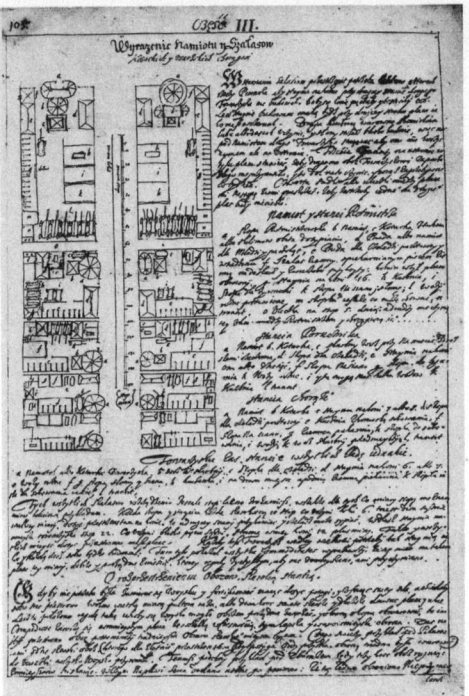

litaires, thèmes qui étaient souvent illustrés dans les tableaux des palais princiers.

On peut supposer que la planification des habitations militaires dans la première moitié du XVIIième siècle, épisode dans le développement des méthodes de planification, constitue une étape non négligeable entre le «schéma idéal» du quartier d'habitation de la Renaissance et le projet détaillé de l'Illuminisme.

[1] S. von Moos, «Zur Ingenieurkunst der Renaissance», archithese, 5, 1973, p. 39 seg.
[2] Cf. T. Zarebska, «Technical Aspects of the Italian Townplanning Theory in the XVth and XVIth Century», Actes du XIième Congrès International d'Histoire des Sciences, Varsovie-Cracovie, 1965, Wroclaw 1968, vol. VI, p. 130 seg.

[3] Le processus d'émancipation de l'architecture militaire est présenté de manière convaincante par Horst De la Croix, «Military Architecture and the Radial City Plan in Sixteenth Century Italy», Art Bulletin, XLII, 1960, p. 263 seg. Cf. également P. Cataneo, I quattro primi libri di architettura, Vinegia, 1554. Dans l'introduction de son livre, Cataneo déclare: «La più bella parte dell'Architettura certamente sarà quella che tratta della città ...»
[4] J. Kowalczyk, «Biblioteka Jana Szymona Wolffa, inzyniera ks. Janusza Wisniowieckiego na Zbarazu» («Bibliothèque de J. S. Wolff, ingénieur du prince J. Wisniowiecki di Zbaraz»), Biuletyn Historii Sztuki, XXIII, 1, Varsovie, 1961, p. 77 seg.
[5] Francesco de Marchi, Della architettura militare, libri tre, Brescia, 1599, f. 5 v., cap. XIX.
[6] Samuel Marolois, Fortification ou architecture militaire tant offensive que defensive, Hagae Comitis, 1615, tab. 22, pl. 102.
[7] E. Sisi, «Nascita di una città: La Valetta», Urbanistica, 22, 1957, p. 121 seg.
[8] La même fonction de Laparelli pour La Valette a été exercée par exemple par l'architecte Morando pour Zamosc (1579) et par Lemercier pour Richelieu (mais cette dernière ville n'a presque pas de fortifications).
[9] L. Gerö, «Wloskie fortyfikacje bastionowe na Wegrzech» («Les bastions fortifiés italiens en Hongrie»), Kwartalnik Architektury i Urbanistyki, IV, 1—2, Varsovie, 1959, p. 23 seg.
[10] C'est pendant ces guerres que fut élaboré le système de fortification «hollandais», ancien et nouveau.
[11] Buonaiuto Lorini, Delle Fortificationi, Venise, 1597, p. 146.
[12] Classification de Matthias Dögen dans L'Architecture militaire moderne ou Fortification, Amsterdam, 1648, p. 470.
[13] N. Macchiavelli, Libro dell'arte della guerra, Firenze, 1524, v. 112 r (dans l'édition de 1529, f. 111), publié in: T. Zarebska, Teoria urbanistyki wloskie j XV i XVI wieku, Varsovie, 1971, p. 163.
[14] On en trouve dans les bibliothèques princières et royales, même dans des pays éloignés de l'Italie, par exemple dans la bibliothèque du roi de Pologne, datant du milieu de XVIième siècle.
[15] P. Cataneo compare les deux schémas dans la seconde version de son Trattato, de 1567: libro I, p. 46 et 48. Reproduction: T. Zarebska, Teoria . . . , op. cit., p. 115.
[16] Simon Stevin est l'auteur de plusieurs traités, publiés au tournant du siècle. Il discute des logements collectifs dans une œuvre consacrée spécialement aux campements militaires: Castrametatio, das ist Legermeting, Rotterdam, 1617, p. 35—37.
[17] Adam Freytag, Architectura militaris nova et aucta, Leyden, 1631, S. Herbst, A. Freytag, «Polski Slownik Biograficzny», VII/2, n. 32, p. 135, édité par A. Gruszecki, Bastionowe zamki w Malopolsce (Les châteaux à bastions en Pologne mineure), Varsovie, 1962, p. 30.
[18] Jozef Naronowicz-Naronski, Budownictwo wojenne (Constructions militaires), édité par J. Nowakowa, Varsovie, 1957.
[19] E. Trincanato, «Residenze collettive a Venezia», Urbanistica, 42—43, 1965, p. 7 seg.
[20] O. Thomassen, «Quartieri residenziali storici di Copenhagen», Urbanistica, 42—43, 1965, p. 36 seg.
[21] P. Lavedan, Histoire de l'Urbanisme, Renaissance et temps modernes, Paris, 1959, p. 402 seg.

as a court, for the moral upkeep of the inhabitants. Likewise, the commander's residence had both a representative and a disciplinary purpose. Many authors demanded a hospital with sufficient personnel, for the health of the inhabitants. Adequate buildings were planned to ensure reserves of food and armaments.

Although soldiers' quarters represent a specific type of collective housing, it can be assumed that their popularity extended beyond the military milieu. Military successes were of interest to the broader society. Many drawings and engravings not only depict famous battles but describe cities, fortresses, and military camps; these themes often appeared in paintings in the princely palaces.

It can be assumed that the planning of military dwellings in the first half of the seventeenth century, as a phase in the development of planning methods, constitutes a significant step between the "ideal schema" of the Renaissance residential district and the detailed project of the Enlightenment.

ENDNOTES

1   S. von Moos, "Zur Ingenieurkunst der Renaissance," *archithese* 5 (1973): 39 seq.

2   See T. Zarebska, "Technical Aspects of the Italian Town Planning Theory in the 15th and 16th Century," *Actes du XIe Congres International d'Histoire des Sciences, Varsovie-Cracovie*, 1965 (Wrocław, 1968), 6:130 seq.

3   The process of emancipation of military architecture is convincingly presented by Horst De la Croix, "Military Architecture and the Radial City Plan in Sixteenth Century Italy," *Art Bulletin* 42 (1960): 263 seq. See also P. Cataneo, *I quattro primi libri di architettura* (Venice, 1554). In the introduction to his book, Cataneo states, "La più bella parte dell'Architettura certamente sarà quella che tratta della città …"

4   J. Kowalczyk, "Biblioteka Jana Szymona Wola, inżyniera ks. Janusza Wiśniowieckiego na Zbarażu" [Library of J. S. Wolff, engineer of the prince J. Wiśniowiecki di Zbaraz], *Biuletyn historii sztuki [Bulletin of art history]* 23, 1 (1961): 77 seq.

5   Francesco de Marchi, *Della architettura militare*, libri tre (Brescia, 1599), f. 5 v., cap. XIX.

6   Samuel Marolois, *Fortification ou architecture militaire tant offensive que défensive* (Hagae Comitis, 1615), tab. 22, pi. 102.

7   E. Sisi, "Nascita di una citta: La Valletta," *Urbanistica* 22 (1957): 121 seq.

8   What Laparelli did for Valletta, the architect Morando did for Zamość (1579) and Lemercier for Richelieu (although the latter city has almost no fortifications).

9   L. Gerö, *Włoskie fortyfikacje bastionowe na Węgrzech* [Italian fortified strongholds in Hungary], *Kwartalnik architektury i urbanistyki* 4, 1–2 (1959): 23 seq.

10   During these wars, the old and new "Dutch" fortification systems were developed.

11   Buonaiuto Lorini, *Delle fortificationi* (Venice, 1597), 146.

12   Classification of Matthias Dögen in *L'architecture militaire moderne ou fortification* (Amsterdam, 1648), 470.

13   N. Machiavelli, *Libro dell'arte della guerra* (Florence, 1524), v. 112 r (in the edition of 1529, f. 111), published in T. Zarebska, *Teoria urbanistyki włoskie j XV i XVI wieku* (Warsaw, 1971), 163.

14   These can be found in princely and royal libraries, even in countries far from Italy; for example, in the library of the king of Poland, dating from the middle of the seventeenth century.

15   P. Cataneo compares the two diagrams in the second version of his *Trattato* of 1567: libro 1, 46, 48. Reproduction: T. Zarebska, *Teoria urbanistyki*, 115.

16   Simon Stevin is the author of several drafts published at the turn of the century. He discusses collective housing in a work devoted especially to military camps: *Castramentatio, das ist Legermeting* (Rotterdam, 1617), 35–37.

17   Adam Freytag, *Architectura militaris nova et aucta* (Leiden, 1631); and S. Herbst and A. Freytag, *Polski słownik biograficzny*, VII/2, 32, 135, published in A. Gruszecki, *Bastionowe zamki w Małopolsce* [Bastion castles in Lesser Poland] (Warsaw, 1962), 30.

18   Józef Naronowicz-Naroński, *Budownictwo wojenne* [Military structures], published in J. Nowakowa (Warsaw, 1957).

19   E. Trincanato, "Residenze collettive a Venezia," *Urbanistica* 42–43 (1965): 7 seq.

20   O. Thomassen, "Quartieri residenziali storici di Copenhagen," *Urbanistica* 42–43 (1965): 36 se.

21   P. Lavedan, *Histoire de l'urbanisme, Renaissance et temps modernes* (Paris, 1959), 402 seq.

André Corboz

Remarques sur un problème mal défini:

1. Terminologie

Spontanée, populaire, vernaculaire, mineure, indigène, primitive, anonyme, sans architectes: la multiplicité des qualificatifs indique déjà combien cette architecture — ces architectures, plutôt, échappent à nos catégories, dérangent. Chaque adjectif suppose une vue différente (affective, scientifique, polémique) avec toutes les nuances qui s'échelonnent du lyrisme au mépris. Spontanée, c'est-à-dire élevée sans effort comme par une grâce de nature; populaire: non contaminée par la culture des classes dominantes; vernaculaire: issue d'une tradition circonscrite, quoique touchante; mineure: marginale et en sourdine; indigène: relevant de l'enquête ethnographique; primitive: venue du fond des âges, mais fossilisée; anonyme: faisant partie de séries non différenciées; sans architectes: digne d'avoir été conçue par des professionnels.

Cette dernière expression, la plus répandue depuis le succès d'un livre fameux[1], consacre en somme la distinction fondamentale qui s'est introduite dans la pratique du bâtiment, depuis la Renaissance, entre l'architecture (pensée par un artiste doté d'une biographie) et le reste des constructions (dues à des tâcherons sans importance occupés à des problèmes de quantité). Même si cette discrimination caricaturale ne recoupe nullement la réalité historique, la notion même d'une architecture «spontanée» ou «populaire» ou «mineure» implique un second terme qui serait, grosso modo, une architecture «majeure». Laquelle se trouve avoir aujourd'hui mauvaise presse jusque chez ceux qui en sont, par formation, les représentants.

2. Approches

Les instruments d'analyse dont nous disposons nous obligent à appréhender comme de biais l'ensemble des édifices qui n'entrent pas ordinairement dans les ouvrages d'histoire de l'architecture. Les notions d'art et d'œuvre, comme celle d'objectivité, se sont précisées au XIXe siècle en tant que moyens de l'impérialisme culturel de la bourgeoisie dans sa phase d'apothéose; l'histoire de l'art, d'où celle de l'architecture est sortie, fut d'abord encline à valoriser les symboles de la richesse et du pouvoir des classes dominantes. Impossible, avec ces lunettes-là, d'apercevoir ce qui était exclu d'emblée du champ visuel. Telle est du moins l'explication couramment admise, encore qu'elle ne dise pas pourquoi — Marx lui-même l'a relevé — ces produits architecturaux sont néanmoins irréductibles aux conditions qui les ont suscités, qui pourquoi ce sont eux qui explicitent le plus complètement la totalité de leurs contenus.

Avant la révolution industrielle, la démarcation passait plutôt entre la ferme et la demeure urbaine qu'entre les bâtisses des architectes à brevet et les autres. Et lorsque la distinction intervient, c'est aussitôt pour des motifs sociaux, et non architectoniques: William Morris déclare sa préférence démocratique pour la maison du paysan, voire pour la baraque de son garçon d'écurie: ici, le contenu qualifie le contenant.

Dans la seconde partie du XIXe siècle commencent les admirables campagnes de relevés, comme celle de Jakob Hunziker pour la Suisse[2], dont les critères sont soit sociologiques, soit

Remarks on an Ill-Defined Problem: The Architecture of Nonarchitects

Author:
André Corboz

Source:
archithese, 9 (1974): 2–14

Translated by:
Brett Petzer

1. Terminology

Spontaneous, popular, vernacular, minor, indigenous, primitive, anonymous, without architects: the multiplicity of qualifiers indicates how much this architecture—these architectures, rather—challenge and trouble our existing categories. Each of these adjectives implies a different perspective (affective, scientific, polemical) and every nuance from lyricism to contempt. *Spontaneous*: arising effortlessly, as if by the grace of nature. *Popular*: uncontaminated by the culture of the dominant classes. *Vernacular*: derived from a limited, albeit affecting, tradition. *Minor*: marginal and muted. *Indigenous*: subject to ethnographic investigation. *Primitive*: emerging from the depths of time but fossilized. *Anonymous*: part of an undifferentiated series. *Without architects*: worthy of having been professionally designed.

This last expression is now the most widespread owing to the success of a well-known book.[1] It also sums up the fundamental distinction introduced into building practice since the Renaissance: that between architecture (as conceived by an artist with a biography) and all other construction (as produced by nameless factotums responding to quantitative challenges). This caricature of the distinction may well overstate the historical reality, but the very notion of "spontaneous" or "popular" or "minor" architecture implies a second term that, roughly speaking, would be "major" architecture. Currently, this word is given a bad press even by those who are, by training, its representatives.

2. Approaches

The instruments of analysis available to us compel us to consider all buildings that are not usually included in architectural histories as mere noise. The notions of *art* and *artwork*, like that of objectivity, were refined in the course of the nineteenth century as instruments of the cultural imperialism of the bourgeoisie in its climactic phase. The history of art, from which the history of architecture emerged, was initially inclined to value symbols of the wealth and power of the dominant classes. This lens precludes any accounting for the objects excluded from the visual field at the outset. This, at least, is the commonly accepted explanation. However, it does not explain why—as Marx himself pointed out—these architectural products are nonetheless irreducible to the conditions that gave rise to them, or why they themselves provide the most complete explication of their total contents.

Before the Industrial Revolution, the major divide was that between farmhouses and urban dwellings and not between buildings by licensed architects and all others. When the latter distinction did emerge, it was for social rather than architectural reasons, such as when William Morris declared his democratic preference for the houses of peasants; indeed, for his stable boy's hut. Here, the content qualifies the container.

The second half of the nineteenth century saw the beginning of the remarkable survey campaigns, such as Jakob Hunziker's for Switzerland,[2] which were based on both sociological and technical criteria. Some were concerned with architecture as an expression of a way of life; others marveled at the common sense and ingenuity manifest in the buildings. Yet both approaches presuppose the need for solutions. At a time when Viollet-le-Duc believed he could exhaustively explain the Gothic through close analysis of the balance of thrusts, the very same engineering mentality was deconstructing the Alpine chalet into primary factors: orientation, protection against the elements, wood technology, crop conservation, and so on. In these projects, the distribution of buildings was deemed to be entirely determined by the patriarchal family, the modes of operation, and the structure of trade in a given area. These two approaches resulted in cartographic classifications that were as faithful as possible to Linnaeus's illustrious model, conceptualized as typologies.

The "functionalist tradition" dear to the heralds of utilitarianism was reflected in irreplaceable descriptions, in the face of which the almost purely morphological sampling of someone like Rudofsky is a regression to the picturesque. Paradoxically, the aesthetic apprehension of "uncultivated" architecture seems the more recent. The Arts and Crafts movement, Muthesius, or Le Corbusier were evidently sensitive to traditional constructions, and Japan seduced men as far opposed as Mies and Wright, for very different reasons, in which the indigenous idea of Japanese architecture played no part. As an impetus for invention, the conspicuous qualities of anonymous architecture differ according to one's perspective, and, like their precursors, they are usually recorded only after the fact. However, only from 1945 onward, possibly in reaction to the inadequate definition of architecture outlined by the CIAM, do modern architects begin a new phase, one of large-scale exploitation of the formal repertoire of the Greek islands or the cottages of northern Italy. The old condescension suddenly gives way to a fervor in which methodological preconceptions are abolished. At this point, it ceased to matter whether the well-apportioned volumes we admire in Tuscan or Dalmatian farmhouses were intended as such, for they are the outcome of a program, a practice, and a custom.

3. The Nature of the Phenomenon

In addition to the research of the folklorists, ethnographers also brought an unprecedented variety of architectonic solutions to the marketplace of forms. Statistically, their number far exceeded that of the architecture in the textbooks. It had to be conceded, even if only de facto, that various "minor," "indigenous," and "primitive" architectures existed. This entailed the realization that "the birth of music does not date from that of the symphony orchestra" (Rudofsky)—even if, as Boudon[3] said, each of them can only strictly be called *architecture* from the moment they were seen and perceived by an architect and presented as such.

The fact remains that each of the approaches adopted (sociological, technical, typological, aesthetic) overestimated one component. By necessity, these approaches flattened all phenomena through reduction, each according to its own preliminary frameworks and codes.[4] Yet the chief characteristic of all "spontaneous" architecture, from the Trobriand Islands to the Dogons and from the Pueblos to Galicia, is, on the contrary, what could be called a global (i.e., cultural) function. This is prior to its role in creating protection from the sun or from wild animals, such that people and livestock can rest; prior to projecting a social structure onto the landscape; and prior to producing technical solutions. Before all of that, the architecture of traditional cultures is a semantic act: it affirms an order, restores it, and reinforces it through repetition.

l'architecture des non-architectes

techniques: les unes s'attachent à l'architecture comme expression d'un mode de vie, les autres s'émerveillent devant le bon sens et l'ingéniosité dont les bâtisses témoignent. Dans les deux cas, la démarche postule la *nécessité* des solutions. Au moment où Viollet-le-Duc croit pouvoir épuiser le gothique par une analyse fine de l'équilibre des poussées, la même mentalité d'ingénieur décompose le chalet alpin en facteurs premiers qui se nomment orientation, protection contre les éléments, technologie du bois, conservation des récoltes et j'en passe. Quant à la distribution, la voici dans ces ouvrages entièrement déterminée par la famille patriarcale, le mode d'exploitation et la structure des échanges dans un terroir donné. Ces deux démarches aboutissent à des classifications cartographiées, aussi fidèles que possible à l'illustre modèle de Linné, et conceptualisées sous forme de typologies.

La «tradition fonctionnaliste» chère aux hérauts de l'utilitarisme s'est reflétée dans des descriptions irremplaçables, au regard desquelles l'échantillonage presque uniquement morphologique d'un Rudofsky fait figure de régression au pittoresque. Paradoxalement, il semble que l'appréhension esthétique de l'architecture non «cultivée» soit la plus récente. Les «Arts and Crafts», Muthesius ou Le Corbusier étaient certes tout qu'insensibles aux constructions traditionnelles et le Japon a séduit des hommes aussi opposés que Mies et Wright, pour des motifs très différents, dans lesquels l'idée autochtone de l'architecture nippone n'avait aucune part. En tant que stimulant de l'invention, les qualités éminentes d'une architecture non si-

gnée varient avec le regard qui se porte sur elles et, comme les précurseurs, elles sont généralement désignées après coup. Mais c'est surtout à partir de 1945, en réaction peut-être contre l'insuffisance de la définition de l'architecture esquissée par les CIAM, que commence sur une large échelle, de la part des architectes dits modernes, la phase d'exploitation du répertoire formel des îles grecques ou des chalets de l'Italie septentrionale. A l'ancienne condescendance fait brusquement place une passion où s'abolissent tous les préliminaires méthodologiques. Peu importe, à ce point, si le volume bien divisé que nous admirons dans la ferme toscane ou dalmate ne soit pas voulu comme tel, mais résulte d'un programme, d'une pratique et d'une coutume.

3. Nature du phénomène

Aux recherches des folkloristes s'ajoutaient celles des ethnographes, qui déversaient elles aussi sur le marché des formes une variété inouïe de solutions architectoniques; statistiquement, leur importance dépassait de beaucoup celle de l'architecture des manuels. Il fallut bien reconnaître au moins *de facto* l'existence des diverses architectures «mineures», «indigènes» et «primitives» et se rendre compte que «la naissance de la musique ne date pas de celle de l'orchestre symphonique» (Rudofsky) — même si, pour le dire avec Boudon[3], chacune d'elles n'est devenue précisément architecture qu'à partir du moment où elle était regardée par un architecte, perçue et présentée comme telle.

Il n'en restait pas moins que chacune des

1. Terminologie

Die Vielfalt der Adjektive, mit denen man die «Architektur ohne Architekten» zu kennzeichnen versucht, beweist, wie schwierig es ist, das Problem begrifflich zu fassen. Jede Kennzeichnung verweist implizit auf eine andere Architektur, die «wirkliche», die hinter der sogenannt «spontanen» liegt. Dadurch wird die zwar seit Jahrhunderten überlieferte, aber theoretisch fragwürdige Unterscheidung von »Architektur« und «Bauen» immer wieder von Neuem bestätigt.

2. Methoden

Unsere Instrumente architekturkritischer Analyse leiten sich von einem veralteten Architekturbegriff her: daher die Schwierigkeit, die «volkstümliche» Architektur überhaupt adäquat zu erfassen. Die frühesten Beschreibungen und Inventare beruhen auf einer deterministischen Optik und beschränken sich fast ausschliesslich auf technische oder soziologische Aspekte (d. h. man lobte v. a. die Scharfsinnigkeit und die Oekonomie der Konstruktion im Hinblick auf die gegebene Lebensform). Die rein ästhetische Degustation der «spontanen» oder «anonymen» Architektur ist neueren Datums. (Beispiel: Bernard Rudofsky, *Architecture Without Architects*, New York, 1965).

3. Natur des Phänomens

Die Untersuchungen der Volkskundler legen folgenden Schluss nahe: die Vielfalt des erarbeiteten Materials kann nicht in den traditionellen, westlichen Begriffen von Architektur erfasst werden. Die frühen enzyklopädischen Beschreibungen «volkstümlicher» Architektur (z. B. Jakob Hunziker, *Das Schweizerhaus nach seinen landschaftlichen Formen und seiner geschichtlichen Entwicklung dargestellt*, 8 Bde., 1900 bis 1914) sind heute noch unentbehrlich; aber sie beruhen im Allgemeinen auf einer einseitigen Optik (d. h. man berschränkte sich auf technische, soziale, typologische, morphologische Aspekte) und wer-

approches adoptées (sociologique, technique, typologique, esthétique) procédait par surévaluation d'une composante: nécessaires, elles aplatissaient pourtant tous les phénomènes par une opération réductrice. A chacune sa grille de lecture, son code [4]. Mais la caractéristique principale de toute architecture «spontanée», des îles Trobriand aux Dogons et des Pueblo à la Galice, c'est au contraire ce qu'on pourrait appeler une fonctionnalité globale, c'est-à-dire culturelle. Avant d'offrir une protection contre le soleil ou les fauves et de permettre le repos des hommes et du bétail, avant d'inscrire au sol une organisation sociale, avant de définir des solutions techniques, l'architecture des cultures traditionnelles est un acte sémantique: elle affirme un ordre, le réinstaure et le confirme par la répétition.

L'idéologie positiviste empêchait une description exhaustive: en analysant les paramètres climatique, technique, social, etc., comme autant de sous-ensembles, elle croyait avoir exposé la totalité des phénomènes constitutifs, mais le problème de l'origine restait entier [5]. Sur ce point, tout se passait comme si les hypothèses du XVIIIe siècle sur la hutte primitive étaient vérifiées: on concluait implicitement à la naturalitée des établissements humains. Or, aussi loin que les traces nous permettent de remonter, on peut affirmer que ces établissements sont, d'abord, un acte culturel, auquel les paramètres viennent s'ajuster. Et lorsqu'il y a conflit entre le modèle culturel (c'est-à-dire, en dernier ressort, mythique) et la fonction telle que nous la définissons aujourd'hui, c'est toujours le modèle qui a le dessus. Dans les maisons paysannes de Magyarpolány, la seule pièce d'habitation ouvre ses deux fenêtres sur la rue, mais on ne l'utilise que pour exposer les morts: comment expliquer ce «gaspillage» en termes de nécessité pratique? Même chez Vitruve, les problèmes de salubrité sont ramenés à des clauses magiques et astrologiques.

Notre méthode d'aménagement consiste à élaborer des sous-modèles (économique, social, politique, etc.), dont nous cherchons ensuite la combinaison la plus favorable par un processus d'optimisation; le modèle global résulte donc d'une série d'opérations analytiques partielles. Les sociétés traditionnelles ont choisi la voie inverse: elles projettent sur le terrain leur modèle culturel comme une grande forme à la fois primordiale et résolutoire, dans laquelle les sous-modèles s'inscrivent: le modèle global précède; en d'autres termes, la société, le pouvoir, les échanges, les techniques et leurs interactions ne sont et ne peuvent être, chez elles, que des facettes de la «culture»; et ceci vaut pour l'habilitation comme pour le territoire.

4. Spontanéité?

Dans ces conditions, parler d'architecture «spontanée», c'est croire au primitif libre-et-vertueux et vanter la «sérénité» de ses constructions consiste à faire la révérence au Bon Sauvage. Malheureusement, aucun âge d'or n'a jamais trouvé son lieu sur cette planète: loin de justifier nos nostalgies, l'architecture «spontanée» parle plutôt des difficultés de la survie, de divinités susceptibles, de rapports de force à l'intérieur de sociétés implacablement hiérar-

fig. 2 [Democratic Republic of] Congo: village on the shores of Lake Kivu.

den daher der Komplexität ihres Gegenstandes nicht gerecht. In Wirklichkeit unterliegt jede sogenannt «spontane» Architektur zuallererst einer umfassenden, kulturellen Funktionalität. Mit anderen Worten: diese Architektur ist in erster Linie ein semantischer Akt, Bestätigung einer kulturellen Ordnung, und erst in zweiter Linie eine Schutzvorkehrung, ein Ausdrucksmittel oder ein Stück Baukonstruktion. Wo Widersprüche zwischen dem kulturellen Modell (dem «Mythos») einer Gesellschaft und der praktischen «Funktion» auftauchen, da ist es im allgemeinen das kulturelle Modell, welches die Lösung determiniert. Zumindest in traditionellen Gesellschaften; die Lösungen, die für die industrielle Gesellschaft typisch sind, beruhen zumeist auf einer Absolutsetzung eines architektonischen (oder anderen) Aspektes der gegebenen Aufgabe.

4. Spontaneität?

Es gibt keine spontane Architektur! Jene Architektur, die wir als «spontan» empfinden, ist in Wirklichkeit Ausdruck einer Gesellschaft, die streng hierarchisch gegliedert ist. Das physische Ueberleben ist ihr Hauptproblem. Innovation wird abgelehnt: sie könnte das Gleichgewicht der Gruppe stören. Wo wir «Freiheit» vermuten, ist in Wirklichkeit strenge Zensur am Werk. Wir

fig. 1
Northern China: a fortified village

chisées, de civilisations où le moi est faible. On pourrait aussi bien la décrire comme une architecture de censure, dans laquelle toute innovation est proscrite, parce que dangereuse pour l'équilibre du groupe. Cette nature-là ressemble étrangement à un produit de la culture . . .

La connaissance toujours plus précise des circonstances a fini par faire justice des aménagements d'apparence anarchique en montrant que les chercheurs leur avaient d'abord appliqué des critères inadéquats: animés par une idée de l'ordre urbain empruntée au néo-classi-

cisme, les premiers historiens de la ville n'ont rien compris aux tracés urbains irréguliers, «chemins des ânes». Après la réhabilitation esthétisante de Sitte[6], il fallut attendre Piccinato[7] pour saisir qu'irrégularité ne signifiait pas manque de plan, Guidoni[8] pour retrouver les tracés complexes et symboliques et Pierotti[9] pour revendiquer l'actualité méthodologique des anciens processus de design urbain.

Quant à l'architecture anonyme ou sans architectes des campagnes européennes ou des îles du Pacifique, cela signifie simplement qu'elle n'est pas érigée par quelqu'un du métier (encore que l'on confonde volontiers architecte inconnu avec absence d'architecte). Mais non par quelqu'un d'ignare. Ni même par quelqu'un. Après les destructions des Français au XVIIe siècle, les habitants de la Franche-Comté reconstruisent leurs villages: qui veut bâtir ou rebâtir va couper son bois et le laisse d'abord sécher une trentaine d'années; puis toute la population discute les plans (et ainsi se transforment les types, par légères retouches) tandis que charpentiers, maçons et serruriers, formés sur place par tradition orale et pratique, et faisant partie intégrante ou groupe, construisent tous les édifices: critique constante et chantiers tournants; la coordination est spontanée, le reste se décidant collectivement. On a décrit le contrôle communautaire exercé pendant trois siècles sur son habitat par la population d'un village italien[10]. Et l'on rencontre parfois de vieux contremaîtres villageois «encore capables de construire selon une série de considérations très compliquées sur l'orientation, le climat, les matériaux souvent même codifiés dans les statuts communaux (...) afin que ce soit l'habitant, avec ses besoins et ses faiblesses, qui donne forme à la demeure, et non le contraire»[11].

Même si tel bourg de la haute vallée du Tibre, couronne brune enracinée dans une terre dont elle paraît le produit, évoque un temps où l'homme ne se concevait pas différent de l'animal, ni même de la plante, l'illusion de la spontanéité doit faire place à la certitude que ce bourg est issu d'une longue négociation inscrite dans les limites des connaissances et des habitudes d'esprit de ses habitants. Que les décisions obéissent à une espèce de guidage inconscient dû à l'évidence des règles de comportement fournie par la société ne signifie pas non plus que nous ayons affaire à une mentalité prélogique: l'important, c'est qu'il y ait raisonnement, intégrant l'ensemble des données disponibles: nous n'agissons pas autrement.

5. Difficultés

Si j'apprécie tel détail de construction, telle combinaison volumétrique, tel escalier, c'est ordinairement en fonction de leur position dans une série historique. Une voûte nervurée surprend en 1060, mais non en 1450, ou l'ébauche de la Scala dei Forbici (Palais royal de Turin, 1720) à la villa Contarini (Piazzola sul Brenta, XVIe), mais non plus sa réplique abâtardie dans un hôtel de la Riviera. Cette donnée essentielle qu'est le degré d'innovation fait généralement défaut dans la critique de l'architecture «populaire». Celle-ci n'appartient à l'histoire que par grands pans indivisibles, car ses éléments semblent suspendus dans le temps, comme s'ils étaient simultanés. L'histoire s'intéresse aux

Here, positivist ideology stood in the way of an exhaustive description: it was believed that, by analyzing climatic, technical, social, and other parameters in terms of subsets, the constituent phenomena would be brought to light in their entirety. Yet the problem of origins remained intact.[5] On this point, it was as if eighteenth-century hypotheses on the primitive hut had been verified, the implicit conclusion being that human settlements were naturalized. In fact, for as far back as the evidence takes us, these settlements can be characterized as cultural acts to which the parameters were then adjusted. Where conflicts arose between the cultural (i.e., ultimately mythical) model, and the function as we define it today, it was always the model that prevailed. In the peasant houses of Magyarpolàny, the single dwelling room has two windows opening onto the street but is used only to display the dead. How can this "waste" be explained in terms of practical necessity? Even Vitruvius reduces questions of public health to magical and astrological terms.

Our method of planning consists of developing submodels (economic, social, political, etc.) and determining the most favorable combination of these through a process of optimization. The overall model is thus derived from a series of partial analytical operations. Traditional societies have chosen the opposite approach. They project their cultural model onto their territory as a framework that is both primordial and resolution-oriented, within which submodels are incorporated. In other words, the overall model is prior to society, power, exchange, and technology, and these societies' interactions are, and can only be, aspects of the "culture." This applies to authorization as well as to the land itself.

4. Spontaneity

Under these conditions, to speak of "spontaneous" architecture is to believe in the free and virtuous primitive, and extolling the "serenity" of these buildings amounts to adulation of the "Noble Savage." Regretfully, our planet has never seen a golden age. Far from a justification for our nostalgia, "spontaneous" architecture is rather a testament to the difficulties of survival, of easily offended gods, of power relations within implacably hierarchical societies, and of civilizations where the self is weak. It could just as well be described as an architecture of censorship, in which any innovation is prohibited because it endangers the equilibrium within the group. This characteristic bears a curious resemblance to something produced by culture.

Our increasingly precise grasp of these conditions eventually showed that the apparent anarchy of arrangements resulted from the inadequate criteria initially applied by researchers. Operating within an idea of urban order derived from neoclassicism, the first urban historians failed to understand irregular plots or "the pack mules' routes" through the city. Following Sitte's[6] aestheticizing rehabilitation, further progress was attendant on Piccinato,[7] who realized that irregularity did not mean the absence of a plan; for Guidoni,[8] who revealed the complexity and symbolism of these patterns; and for Pierotti,[9] who posited that ancient urban design processes were subject to methodological evolution.

As for the anonymous or nonarchitect architecture of the European countryside or the Pacific islands, this simply means that it has not been produced by a member of the profession (bearing in mind that the designations "unknown architect" and "no architect" are often confused). It does not mean that the makers are unschooled or even unknown. After the destruction wrought by French forces in the seventeenth century, the inhabitants of Franche-Comté rebuilt their villages. Whoever wanted to build or rebuild would cut wood and set it to dry for about thirty years. Then, the whole community would discuss the plans (so that, by small adjustments, types are gradually transformed). Meanwhile carpenters, masons, and locksmiths, trained on the job by oral and practical tradition, and forming an integral part of the group, would erect all the buildings. This is achieved through continual critique and rotating work sites, spontaneously coordinated; the rest is decided collectively. One study has described the community control exerted on its environment by an Italian village over three centuries.[10] Sometimes one encounters old village foremen who are "still able to build according to a series of very complicated considerations regarding orientation, climate, and materials. Often, these are even codified in communal statutes ... so that it is the inhabitant, with their needs and weaknesses, who gives shape to the dwelling, and not the other way round."[11]

This Upper Tiber Valley village, a brown corona seemingly rooted in the land from which it has emerged, may well bring to mind a time when man did not see himself as different from animals or even plants. Even so, the illusion of spontaneity must yield to the certain knowledge that this village is the result of a long negotiation bounded by the limits of its inhabitants' understandings and habits of mind. Nor does the contention that decision-making here is subject to a kind of unconscious guidance, based on the rules of behavior provided by society, mean that we are dealing with a prelogical mentality. What matters is that reasoning does take place, integrating all the available data; we do not do things any other way.

5. Difficulties

When I admire a construction detail here, or a volumetric combination or staircase there, it is usually because of their position in a historical series. A ribbed vault is surprising for 1060, but not for 1450. Likewise for the sketch of the Scala dei Forbici (Royal Palace of Turin, 1720) at the Villa Contarini (Piazzola sul Brenta, sixteenth century) but not its bastard replica in a hotel on the Riviera. This essential fact of the degree of innovation is generally unacknowledged in the criticism of "people's" architecture. The latter exists in history only in large indivisible sections, because its components seem suspended in time, as if they were contemporaneous. History is interested in phenomena in the making, and this kind of architecture has little of it — has the *mazot* [a kind of Alpine hut] evolved since the Neolithic era?

Circumstances such as these favor the synchronic collection of data. This has, in fact, been attempted in recent research taking a structuralist perspective. This literature has argued that the concept of space is multifaceted, which is perhaps its most interesting contribution. Rather than one space that exists a priori, there is a space for every society, even for every social group. Consequently, one can no longer speak of "popular" or "primitive" architecture (a residual category for everything not considered "real" architecture), for there are as many architectures as there are units capable of producing spatial systems. Accordingly, the dwelling sometimes takes the form of a cell, because it is part of a larger social whole, and sometimes presents itself as a complete unit, serving as a total framework for the life associated with it.[12]

In an initial phase, the document, if it escaped history, could not escape classification (Leroi-Gourhan); now, classification can be made explicit through systems of meaningful relationships. The fragmentation of the field into a series of objects of study should mean an end to the practice of hastily applying rather rough-hewn notions to the available facts. It should then be possible to move forward by ever-finer distinctions until each object is fairly treated and correctly identified.

To these general considerations, others must be added regarding the very possibility of isolating observable reality. In Europe, in particular, cases of "pure" phenomena are extremely rare. The *mazot* and its relatives in the Alps are probably the last examples of an architectural concept that dates directly back to prehistory without alteration across the millennia, although this hypothesis has yet to be proved. In almost all other cases, "vernacular" architecture has maintained a confusingly complex relationship with its opposite, in particular with courtly architecture.

6. Exchanges

In periodizing, we use certain signs that often relate to treatments rather than to the architectural unit itself. We date these in reference to an expressive vocabulary that provides a terminus a quo. An ogee window in the Canton of Grisons or a volute corbel in Apulia obviously refers to the stylistic fields of "Gothic" and "baroque." Sometimes the building technique, which at first glance appears native to the site, stems from practices within "major" architecture. Roberto Pane established a correlation between the vaults of Capri and those of the twelve imperial villas built on the island by Rome.[13] The tiny churches of the Aegean would not exist without those of Byzantium. The phenomenon thus includes an element of recuperation and bricolage.

fig. 5 Iran: caravanserai at Qum (near Tehran).

phénomènes en devenir et ceux-ci n'en ont guère: le mazot s'est-il modifié depuis le néolithique?

De telles circonstances favorisent la saisie synchronique des données: c'est précisément ce que la recherche récente a tenté dans une perspective structuraliste. Elle a conclu à la multiplicité du concept d'espace, ce qui forme peut-être son apport le plus intéressant: non pas un espace à priori, mais un espace par société, ou même par groupe social. Et par conséquent, non plus une architecture «populaire» ou «primitive» (ensemble résiduel de tout ce que ne contient pas l'architecture «proprement dite»), mais autant d'architectures que d'unités productives de systèmes spatiaux. Ainsi, l'habitation tantôt prend la forme d'une cellule, parce qu'elle fait partie d'un ensemble social plus grand, et tantôt se présente comme une unité complète, cadre total de la vie associée [12].

Dans une première phase, le document, s'il échappait à l'histoire, ne pouvait échapper à la classification (Leroi-Gourhan); maintenant, la classification peut s'expliciter en systèmes de relations signifiantes. La fragmentation du champ en une série d'objets d'étude devrait permettre d'abandonner les notions mal dégrossies à plaquer tant bien que mal sur les faits disponibles et de procéder par découpages de plus en plus fins, qui restitueront finalement l'identité de chaque objet et lui rendront justice.

A ces considérations générales, il faut en ajouter d'autres, qui touchent la possibilité même d'isoler la réalité observable. Dans l'aire européenne en particulier, les cas de phénomènes «purs» sont rarissimes: le mazot et ses cousins des Alpes offrent sans doute les derniers spécimens d'une conception architecturale qui remonte directement à la préhistoire sans avoir subi d'altération au cours des millénaires — encore s'agit-il d'une hypothèse. Dans presque tous les autres cas, l'architecture «vernaculaire» a entretenu avec l'autre, et en particulier avec l'architecture aulique, des rapports d'une complexité déroutante.

6. Echanges

Lorsque nous périodisons, nous le faisons en fonction de certains signes qui souvent n'intéressent pas l'organisme architectural, mais son traitement: nous datons en fonction d'un vocabulaire expressif de référence qui fournit un *terminus a quo*. Une fenêtre à accolade dans les Grisons ou une console à volute en Apulie renvoie évidemment aux domaines stylistiques du «gothique» et du «baroque». Parfois, c'est la technique de construction, à première vue aborigène, qui découle d'une pratique de l'architecture «majeure»: Roberto Pane a établi une corrélation entre les voûtes de Capri et celles des douze villas impériales que Rome avait bâties dans l'île [13]. Les minuscules églises égéennes n'existeraient pas sans celles de Byzance. Le phénomène contient donc une composante de récupération et de bricolage.

Dans ces cas comme dans bien d'autres, l'architecture «mineure» ne s'oppose donc pas à celle de l'élite: elle en est comme l'ombre portée. L'architecture «populaire» vise à assurer la conservation d'une société, mais il serait erroné de la décrire uniquement en termes de ré-

↓ fig. 6 Attic in Bruson (Valais, Switzerland).

↓ fig. 7 Tunisia: houses and attic in Metameur.

sistance à la culture dominante. En Occident, le devenir appartient partout à l'architecture «cultivée», qui souvent fournit des thèmes à l'autre. A cet égard, la pénétration et la persistance des pratiques «gothiques», puis «baroques», jusque dans des zones fort éloignées des centres de production du nouveau langage indiquent bien une continuité verticale entre la «grande» architecture et ses transcriptions locales. Suivant les provinces, on peut même parler d'homogénéité. La preuve que cette diffusion capillaire de modèles étrangers n'est pas subie, mais assumée, un village comme Bissone et plus encore Au, dans le Vorarlberg, l'administrent surabondamment: le premier exporte ses architectes dans la moitié de l'Europe, l'autre couvre une immense région de ses *Wandpfeilerbasilika*.

A cela s'ajoute que l'on qualifie souvent de «populaires» des constructions qui le sont devenues par le changement de leur fonction primitive (c'est le cas de quasi tous les édifices agricoles anciens de la Campagne romaine, non pas ruraux, mais ruralisés)[14] ou qui dérivent en droite ligne de bâtiments érigés hors les murs par l'aristocratie urbaine: «la configuration des fermes arétines (...) dans une zone où la présence et les conseils de Vasari ne furent pas étrangers, témoignent de l'incidence de ces images sur la réalité historique, dans un échange tacite entre tradition spontanée et élaboration intellectuelle»[15].

L'intervention d'un architecte, formé comme tel, sur un organisme traditionnel complète le tableau de ces passages du populaire au cultivé. Cette fois, la coutume ne se borne plus à absorber une pratique extérieure, elle s'offre elle-même, dans sa substance, comme thème principal. Biagio Rossetti, au début du XVIe siècle, rationalise la demeure ferraraise et après lui Sebastiano Serlio, Pierre Le Muet (XVIIe siècle), Charles-Etienne Briseux (XVIIIe siècle) et beaucoup d'autres proposent des habitations urbaines fondées sur les habitudes locales. La villa palladienne elle-même procède largement à partir de distributions spatiales déjà consolidées: elle leur «impose la proportion» bien avant que Ledoux n'énonce une telle formule. Il arrive même que cette circularité des modèles s'avère difficile à analyser au point que l'on ne peut démêler qui s'inspire de quoi.

7. Coupure

La révolution industrielle tarit la tradition dans tous les territoires où elle s'étend. Au même moment, l'architecture de l'élite connaît sa crise la plus grave. Les structures agraires et celles du prolétariat urbain sont entraînées dans la mutation, sans parvenir à y trouver une nouvelle assiette. Partout, la coutume architecturale se disloque sous l'effet de leur aliénation. La créativité populaire a perdu ses modèles et adopte le kitsch sous la pression des valeurs culturelles bourgeoises. Un décalage s'installe alors entre ses aspirations désormais régressives et ce que l'on commence à nommer l'avant-garde[16]. Françoise Choay parle du «scandale des niveaux politologiques», désignant ainsi la coexistence en un même temps de conceptions diverses de la ville et de son espace, les unes projetées dans l'avenir, d'autres accrochées au

wissen heute, dass die unregelmässigen Stadtanlagen des Mittelalters Resultat sorgfältiger Planung sind. Was die Vorstellung einer «anonymen» Architektur betrifft, so bleibt zunächst einmal von Fall zu Fall abzuklären, ob diese «Anonymität» etwa bloss darauf zurückzuführen ist, dass man den Namen des Architekten nicht kennt. Im übrigen bedeutet «Anonymität» nichts anderes, als dass die Bauten nicht von einem einzelnen Fachmann entworfen wurden. Aber die Gemeinschaft, die für das Bauen verantwortlich ist, arbeitet keineswegs «spontan», sondern aufgrund von bewährten Regeln hinsichtlich Orientierung, Klima, Materialien. Die Schreiner, Maurer und Schlosser entstammen demselben Milieu wie diejenigen, für die sie bauen, d. h. sie arbeiten entsprechend den Kenntnissen und Gewohnheiten ihrer Klienten. Das einzige, was wirklich spontan ist, ist die Koordination der Arbeit.

5. *Schwierigkeiten*

Wir sind uns gewohnt, Architektur danach zu beurteilen, ob und inwiefern sie eine neue Lösung für ein vertrautes Problem offeriert. Mit anderen Worten: wir interessieren uns zuallererst für die Stellung eines Bauwerks innerhalb eines zeitlichen Ablaufs. Im Hinblick auf «volkstümliche» oder «anonyme» Architektur ist dieses Vorgehen höchst fragwürdig: solche Architktur ist häufig gar nicht datierbar; man kann sie bestenfalls einer Epoche oder einem Jahrhundert zuordnen. Sie scheint sich eher einer synchronen als einer diachronen Betrachtungsweise zu erschliessen.

Insofern sind volkstümliche Siedlungsbilder scheinbar immobil. Daraus leitet sich die bekannte Schlussfolgerung des Strukturalismus ab: es gebe nicht Raum an sich, sondern soviele Räume, wie es Gesellschaften oder gesellschaftliche Gruppen gibt. Dagegen ist allerdings zu sagen, dass es zumindest in Europa nur ganz wenige architektonische Phänomene gibt, die einem derart

↑ fig. 8 Andalusia: Mijas.

↓ fig. 9   Caucasus: fortified village in the Svanetia Valley.

«immobilen» Urzustand entsprechen (wie etwa die Walliser Sennhütte); die meisten scheinbar «spontanen» Bauformen Mitteleuropas sind in irgendeiner Form von Architektur (d. h. von bestimmten Werken bestimmter Architekten) beeinflusst.

6. Wechselwirkungen

Das «anonyme» oder «volkstümliche» Bauen steht in jedem Falle in einem komplexen Verhältnis zur Architektur der «Elite». Die Uebernahme eines Stilelements (z. B. einer gotischen Fensterform) in einem «anonymen» Bauwerk erlaubt Rückschlüsse auf sein Entstehungsdatum, zumindest die Festlegung eines

↑ fig. 10   Greece: churches in Siphnos.

↓ fig. 11　Andalusia: Mijas.

↓ fig. 12　Italy: Procida.

présent, la plupart remontant à divers moments du passé. C'est en somme la notion de contemporain chez René Grousset, pour qui les hommes d'une même époque vivent dans des temps historiques différents, ou encore celle du déphasage des constellations psychiques à une époque donnée, selon Jung[17].

Cette situation nouvelle, due à l'irruption de la conscience historique, interdit tout accès direct à une tradition désormais close. Pendant la phase fonctionnaliste-rationaliste du mouvement moderne, toute relation avec l'histoire cesse dogmatiquement: le rapport de l'architecture avec la pratique indigène est coupé du même coup. La méthode nouvelle, fondée sur l'analyse des programmes et l'économie de la construction, postule un langage architectural ne devant rien à aucune tradition. Pourtant, les grands de l'entre deux-guerres vouent à l'architecture «mineure» un intérêt (d'origine romantique) à la fois complexe et respectueux. La génération suivante, qui tente de poser les problèmes dans une optique plus large que ses prédécesseurs, revalorise notamment les composantes formelles du phénomène architectonique; pour certains insatisfaits de la jeune tradition moderne, celle de l'âge d'or paraît alors à portée de main. Quelques exemples périlleux fournis par les maîtres en personne (comme la morphologie algérienne des chapelles à Ronchamp) les y incitent; ils y sont ensuite encouragés par des imprudents bien intentionnés, tel Rudofsky, selon qui les constructions vernaculaires constituent «la plus grande source inviolée d'inspiration architecturale pour l'homme industrialisé»[18].

8. Architecture octroyée contre bidonville consolidé

Les grands de l'architecture contemporaine étaient non seulement des puritains (en vertu de leur commune origine protestante), mais aussi des pré-freudiens. Leur pratique visait à remplacer tous les chaos urbains de l'Occident par de vertigineuses épures en trois dimensions, échelle grandeur, sur la foi d'un petit nombre de normes techniques et sanitaires où se concrétisait leur vision éthique et politique des rapports sociaux. Le plan Voisin a traumatisé plusieurs générations. Appliquées mécaniquement par les municipalités, applaudies par la spéculation immobilière, ces conceptions servirent surtout à remembrer les slums et à balayer les campements des squatters. L'habitation minimum, née dans un souci tout socialiste de la dignité humaine, devint un instrument de profit et une arme politique.

Les nouveaux logements, même inaugurés avec des discours émus, répondaient malheureusement mal au mode de vie de leurs destinataires, qu'ils ramenaient au niveau de l'utilité minimum; dans cet habitat «prêt à porter», beaucoup ne lisaient que le symbole de leur mise en condition. Architecture faite pour le peuple, mais surtout architecture de charité, bâtie pour une société de personnes mineures; architecture inflexible; architecture paternaliste comme les premières constitutions de XIXe siècle, architecture octroyée[19].

Monde industrialisé ou tiers monde, ces expériences furent des échecs à des titres divers. Certes, les problèmes eux-mêmes ne sont pas identiques dans les deux zones: dans la pre-

↓ fig. 13 Italy: farm near Florence.

terminus a quo, ohne dass das Bauwerk als Ganzes diesem Stil zuzuordnen wäre. Oft erweist es sich, dass eine konstruktive Form, die man früher als autochton gedeutet hat, in Wirklichkeit von einer Bauform der «hohen» Architektur abgeleitet ist (z. B. die Gewölbeformen von Wohnhäusern auf Capri). Es gibt demnach, streng genommen, keinen Gegensatz zwischen der Architektur des Volkes und Architektur der Elite: häufig erscheint die eine als der Schatten der anderen. Beispiel: die Stilformen der Gotik wie auch diejenigen des Barock haben die volkstümliche Architektur bis hinauf in die hintersten Bergtäler entscheidend beeinflusst. Im übrigen werden häu-

↑ fig. 14 Italy: Castellina in Chianti (near Siena), "Il Cennino."

In these cases, as in many others, the "minor" architecture is not opposed to that of the elite: it is like a shadow cast by the elite. The aim of the "people's" architecture is to ensure the preservation of a society, but to describe it only in terms of resistance to the dominant culture would be wrong. In the West, the future belongs everywhere to the "cultivated" architecture, which is often a source of themes for the other. In this respect, the penetration and persistence of "Gothic" and then "baroque" practices, even in areas far removed from the centers of production of the new language, indicate a vertical continuity between "major" architecture and its local transcriptions. Depending on the province, one can even speak of a certain homogeneity. A village like Bissone (Canton of Ticino) or Au in Austria's Vorarlberg provides ample proof that this capillary diffusion of foreign models was actively exploited rather than passively endured. Bissone exported architects to half of Europe, while Au built its *Wandpfeiler* basilicas over an immense region.

To this group may be added buildings that are now considered "popular" because of a change in function. This category includes, for example, almost all the old agricultural buildings of the countryside around Rome, which are ruralized rather than rural.[14] Another example is the buildings derived directly from those put up by the urban aristocracy outside city walls: "the layout of the farmsteads of Arezzo … in an area where Vasari's presence and counsel were not unknown, bears witness to the impact of these images on historical reality, in a tacit exchange between spontaneous tradition and intellectual development."[15]

The intervention that an architect—someone with architectural training—makes on a traditional entity completes our tableau of the steps that lead from the popular to the cultivated. This time, architectural custom no longer contents itself with absorbing outside practices; instead it offers itself, in substance, as the primary theme. At the start of the sixteenth century Biagio Rossetti rationalized residential building in Ferrara. Subsequently, urban housing based on local custom was proposed by Sebastiano Serlio, Peter the Mute in the seventeenth century, Charles-Étienne Briseux in the eighteenth century, and many others. The Palladian villa is itself largely based on spatial distributions that had already been consolidated. It "imposed proportion" on them long before Ledoux formulated his formula. At times this circular quality in the models can even be an impediment to analysis, due to the difficulty of determining who was inspired by what.

7. Breach

The Industrial Revolution trampled tradition wherever it spread. At the same time, the architecture of the elite was undergoing its most serious crisis. Agrarian structures and those of the urban proletariat became embroiled in the transformation without managing to acquire a new base. Everywhere, architectural custom started to disintegrate as a result of their alienation. Deprived of its models, popular creativity turned to kitsch under pressure from bourgeois cultural values. A discrepancy then appears between its aspirations, which have become regressive, and what is beginning to be called the avant-garde.[16] Françoise Choay speaks of the "scandal of political levels," referring to the coexistence at one and the same time of diverse conceptions of the city and its space. Some of these were projections into the future, others clung to the present, and the majority drew on various moments in history. This is, in short, René Grousset's notion of the contemporary, in which people of the same era inhabit different historical times, or perhaps Jung's[17] notion of the dephasing of psychic constellations in a given era.

This new situation, due to the irruption of historical consciousness, precludes any direct access to a tradition that is now closed. During the functionalist and rationalist phase of the modern movement, any relationship with history was terminated as a question of dogma. In the same instance, the relationship between architecture and indigenous practice was severed. The new method, based on analysis of construction programs and building economics, postulated an architectural language that owed nothing to any tradition. Yet the greats of the interwar period took an interest in "minor" architecture that, although it originated in romanticism, was both complex and respectful.

The next generation, which attempted to frame these problems more broadly than its predecessors, reasserted the value of the formal components of the architectural phenomenon. For anyone dissatisfied with the young modernist tradition, that of the golden age thus seemed within reach. Some perilous examples provided by the masters themselves (such as the Algerian morphology of the chapels at Ronchamp) encouraged them to do so. They were subsequently encouraged by well-meaning, reckless people, such as Rudofsky, who called vernacular buildings "the greatest unspoiled source of architectural inspiration for industrialized man."[18]

8. Concessionary Architecture versus the Consolidated Slum

The greats of contemporary architecture were not only Puritans (by virtue of their shared Protestant origin), but also pre-Freudians. Their practices sought to replace all of the urban chaos of the West with high-rise, three-dimensional, large-scale sketches based on a handful of technical and sanitary standards that gave expression to their ethical and political vision of social relations. The Plan Voisin traumatized several generations. Cheered on by property speculators, cities applied these designs by rote, mainly for the purpose of consolidating slum districts and sweeping away squatter settlements. The minimum dwelling, born out of a socialist commitment to human dignity, was transformed into a source of profit and a political weapon.

However moving the speeches at every ribbon-cutting ceremony, this new kind of housing unfortunately failed to respond to its inhabitants' way of life, which it reduced to calculations of minimum utility. In this "ready-to-wear" housing, many saw nothing more than a symbol of the social condition that had been attributed to them: an architecture made for the people, yes, but also an architecture of charity, built for a society of lesser citizens; an inflexible architecture, as paternalistic as the first constitutions of the eighteenth century, a concessionary architecture.[19]

Whether in the industrialized world or the Third World, these experiments failed in various ways. Admittedly, the problems themselves differ across the two contexts. In the industrialized world, planning is essential because the sprawl of single-family dwellings based on a petty-bourgeois model is self-limiting. In the Third World, other avenues must be explored as an alternative to the hubris of the *grands ensembles*. Hence the work of people like Bugnicourt in Africa and Turner in America.[20] If popular architecture is understood to mean the built consequences of settling a population on a site, then people at the margins of industrial civilization must be included in a broader definition of "popular" architecture. The truly "spontaneous" architecture of today is that of *barriadas*, favelas, and slums.

These marginalized people include, in varying proportions, peasants in the process of being urbanized and city dwellers rejected by the capitalist city. Their cultural backgrounds are therefore very diverse: some are wholly cut off from tradition; others have brought with them models of behavior now severed from their socioeconomic roots; all are poor and live in solidarity with one another. The problem is further complicated by the fact that some of these disadvantaged people want to leave what we might call the city's waiting room as soon as possible, while others have found a greater sense of security within it (since the psychosocial qualities of the environment make up for its physical defects).

The approach taken by J. Bugnicourt consists in recovering from indigenous architecture whatever proves useful in solving the challenges of urbanization and population growth (such as building systems and natural ventilation techniques). Here, the existing cultural foundations have not disappeared, and creativity has not been delegated to the elite, so that the continuity of a people's culture becomes a realistic, rather than utopian, expectation. And yet the powers that be, in their preoccupation with the prestige of achieving a Western condition, seem oblivious to the riches they have at their disposal.

Stabilizing this seemingly inchoate habitat and furnishing the means to consolidate it for good are points of action that should enable a rekindling of the creativity that has been lost, suspended, or suppressed. As might be expected,

fig Bauten als «volkstümlich» bezeichnet, die ganz einfach ihre ursprüngliche Funktion verloren haben und landwirtschaftlichen Zwecken zugeführt wurden. Was das landwirtschaftliche Bauen betrifft, so richtet es sich häufig nach den Vorbildern von Landsitzen, wie sie die städtische Oberschicht zum Vergnügen und zur Ueberwachung des landwirtschaftlichen Gutsbetriebs gebaut hat. Umgekehrt haben Architekten immer wieder städtische Wohnbauten nach dem Vorbild lokaler Bautraditionen gestaltet. In diesen Fällen ist das «volkstümliche» Bauen nicht Resultat, sondern Ausgangspunkt der Wechselwirkung von «oben» nach «unten».

7. *Einschnitte*
Die industrielle Revolution unterbricht diese Wechselwirkungen. Die «volkstümliche» Architektur verliert ihre Basis; sie überlebt bestenfalls; die Architektur der Elite geht durch eine Reihe von Krisen. Die moderne Bewegung bricht mit der Geschichte und der Tradition. Nach 1945 gerät allerdings die Formensprache des «anonymen» Bauens neuerdings in den Gesichtskreis der Architektur. Es kommt zu häufig zu rein formalen Uebernahmen, unter Verzicht auf die um 1920 postulierten Prinzipien.

8. *«Verordnete» Architektur oder Bidonville?*
Unter dem Zwang, die Probleme der rapiden Verstädterung unter Kontrolle zu bringen, haben sowohl Stadtverwaltungen als auch die Bauspekulation jene Planungsprinzipien übernommen, welche die Protagonisten der modernen Architektur um 1920 erarbeitet hatten. Die «grands ensembles», ursprünglich aus der Sorge um Gerechtigkeit und Menschenwürde ersonnen, erwiesen sich nun manchenorts als Fehlschläge. In der Dritten Welt werden gegenwärtig andere, neuere Planungsmethoden ausprobiert: aufgrund traditioneller Baumethoden und aufgrund eines vertieften Verständnisses der

mière, il est impossible de survivre sans planifier, car la prolifération des maisons individuelles sur la base d'un modèle petit-bourgeois mène à une impasse. Dans la seconde, d'autres voies devraient s'ouvrir comme une réponse à l'impertinence des grands ensembles. D'où les travaux d'un Bugnicourt en Afrique et d'un Turner en Amérique [20]. Si l'on entend par architecture populaire les conséquences bâties de l'installation d'une population sur un site, alors il faut inclure les marginaux de la civilisation industrielle dans une définition élargie de l'architecture «populaire». La véritable architecture «spontanée» actuelle est celle des barriadas, des favellas et des bidonvilles.

Ces marginaux comprennent, selon des dosages variables, des paysans en voie d'urbanisation et des citadins rejetés par la cité capitaliste. Leurs origines culturelles s'avèrent donc très diverses: les uns sont coupés de toute tradition quelconque, les autres ont apporté avec eux des modèles de comportement désormais dépourvus de racines socio-économiques; tous sont pauvres et vivent de solidarité. Le problème se complique encore par le fait qu'une partie de ces défavorisés aspirent à sortir au plus vite de cette espèce d'antichambre urbaine que forme le bidonville tandis que d'autres y ont au contraire trouvé une sécurité plus grande (les qualités psycho-sociales du milieu compensant ses défauts physiques).

La voie choisie par J. Bugnicourt consiste à récupérer dans l'architecture indigène ce qui sera utile pour résoudre l'urbanisation et la poussée démographique (systèmes de construction, techniques de ventilation naturelle, etc.).

Ici, les assises culturelles n'ont pas disparu et la créativité n'a pas été déléguée à l'élite, si bien que la continuité populaire n'apparaît pas comme une utopie. Sauf que les pouvoirs, soucieux d'une occidentalisation de prestige, ne semblent guère se rendre compte de la chance dont ils disposent.

Stabiliser cet habitat à première vue informe, fournir les moyens de le consolider «en dur», telle est l'hypothèse qui devrait permettre de réamorcer une créativité disparue, en veilleuse ou brimée: l'école américaine, comme on pouvait s'y attendre, évite de poser directement le problème en termes politiques. On peut se demander si cette planification «par le bas» permettra de faire du bidonville le lieu d'une autogestion suffisante: ne devrait-elle pas, pour réussir vraiment, constituer l'un des aspects d'une opération plus générale, dont l'autre consisterait à acquérir des moyens de production, qui seuls assurent la couverture de la vie quotidienne? Et dans une optique plus radicale, ne pourrait-on pas penser que le bidonville consolidé consolide du même coup le système qui le produit? La gauche est prise dans un dilemme: ou la politique du pire, qui hâtera l'avènement de ce qu'elle souhaite, ou la modification immédiate des conditions de vie de ceux qu'elle veut sauver. Mais comment choisir entre l'amélioration des conditions du prolétariat, qui profite immédiatement au capital, et la volonté de gripper les mécanismes de production, qui pour un temps au moins fera empirer le sort des exploités? Sur le plan urbain, les actions réformistes ne peuvent pas relever d'autre chose que de la «morale croix-rouge».

↓ fig. 15 Spain: granary in Galicia.

«Bidonvilles» und ihres sozialen Gefüges. Diese «Bidonvilles» sind die eigentliche «spontane» Architektur der Gegenwart. Freilich: die soziale Struktur der «Bidonvilles» ist nicht homogen und ihre Konsolidierung gleicht einer paternalistischen «Rotkreuz»-Lösung. So oder so: jede ernsthafte Diskussion «spontaner» Architektur führt uns zwangsläufig abseits jener Sphäre der Poesie, die frühere Generationen mit der Idee «anonymen» Bauens verbanden.

Uebersetzung: S. v. M.

Discours désabusé, qui nous a menés terriblement loin de la poésie immédiate et des formes heureuses auxquelles les amateurs de folklore nous avaient rendus sensibles...

[1] B. Rudofsky, *Architecture Without Architects. — A Short Introduction to Non-Pedigreed Architecture*, New York 1965.
[2] J. Hunziker, *Das Schweizerhaus nach seinen landschaftlichen Formen und seiner geschichtlichen Entwicklung dargestellt*, 8 vol., Aarau 1900—1914. cf. aussi A. De Foville, *Enquête sur les conditions de l'habitation en France — Les maisons-types*, Paris 1894.
[3] Ph. Boudon, *Sur l'espace architectural — Essai d'épistémologie de l'architecture*, Paris 1971, p. 48.
[4] cf. J. M. Fitch. *American Building — The Environmental Forces that Shaped it*, New York 1966; "New Uses for the Artistic Patrimony", in *Journal of the Society of Architectural Historians*, vol. XXX, 1871, pp. 3—16.
[5] Cf. J. Rykwert. *On Adam's House in Paradise — The Idea of the Primitive Hut in Architectural History*, New York 1972.
[6] C. Sitte, *Der Städte-Bau nach seinen künstlerischen Grundsätzen*, Vienne 1889.
[7] L. Piccinato, «Urbanistica medioevale», in *L'urbanistica dall'antichità ad oggi*, Florence 1943.
[8] E. Guidoni, *Arte e urbanistica in Toscana 1000 al 1315*, Rome 1970.
[9] P. Pierotti, *Urbanistica: storia e prassi*, Pise 1973.
[10] L. Benevolo, «Pescocostanzo», in *Quaderni dell'Istituto di storia dell'architettura*, Rome, juin 1955.
[11] E. Battisti, *L'Antirinascimento*, Milan 1962, p. 316.
[12] Cf. R. Cresswell, «Les concepts de la maison: les peuples non industriels», in *Zodiaque*, no 7, pp. 183 à 197.
[13] R. Pane, *Capri*, Venise 1954.
[14] Cf. R. Freddi, *Edifici rurali nella pianura romana*, Rome 1970.
[15] V. Stefanelli, Introduction à: G. Vasari il Giovane, *La Città ideale*, Rome 1970, p. 49. Voir aussi L. Gori-Montanelli, *L'architettura rurale in Toscana*, Florence 1964, et G. Ferrara, G. Biffoli, *La casa colonica in Toscana*, Florence 1966.
[16] Cf. A. Corboz, «Encore Pessac», in *archithèse* no 1, 1972.
[17] C. G. Jung, *Essais de psychologie analytique*, Paris 1931, p. 28.
[18] Cf. aussi S. Moholy-Nagy, *Native Genius in Anonymous Architecture*, New York 1957, et M. Golfinger, *Villages in the Sun — Mediterranean Community Architecture*, New York 1969.
[19] Cf. l'article de Jin-Bak Pyun dans ce numéro d'*archithèse*, p. 39.
[20] Cf. l'article de J. et R. Racki dans ce numéro d'*archithèse*, p. 27.

the American school avoids posing the problem in openly political terms. One wonders whether this "bottom-up" planning will turn slums into self-sufficient, self-governing places. Does true success not require that it be part of a more widespread effort, including acquisition of the means of production, which are the sole means of providing the necessities of everyday life? And, to take a more radical point of view, is it not also possible that the consolidation of slums would, in the same moment, consolidate the system that produces them? The Left is caught in a dilemma. On the one hand, doomsday politics that will hasten the onset of its objectives; namely, an immediate transformation of the living conditions of those it wants to save. This, however, means choosing between improving the conditions of the proletariat, who benefit from capital in an immediate sense, and the prospect of seizing the means of production, which will—temporarily at least—worsen the lives of the worst off. In urban terms, reformist efforts can never be anything other than a "Red Cross morality."

This rather disenchanted line of thought has brought us quite a distance from the immediate poetry and happy forms that folklorists have taught us to perceive.

ENDNOTES

1   B. Rudofsky, *Architecture without Architects: A Short Introduction to Non-pedigreed Architecture* (New York, 1965).

2   J. Hunziker, *Das Schweizerhaus nach seinen landschaftlichen Formen und seiner geschichtlichen Entwicklung dargestellt*, 8 vols. (Aarau, 1900–1914). See also A. De Foville, *Enquête sur les conditions de l'habitation en France—Les maisons-types* (Paris, 1894).

3   Ph. Boudon, *Sur l'espace architectural: Essai d'épistémologie de l'architecture* (Paris 1971), 48.

4   See J. M. Fitch, *American Building: The Environmental Forces That Shaped It* (New York, 1966); and "New Uses for the Artistic Patrimony," *Journal of the Society of Architectural Historians* 30 (1871): 3–16.

5   See J. Rykwert, *On Adam's House in Paradise: The Idea of the Primitive Hut in Architectural History* (New York, 1972).

6   C. Sitte, *Der Städte-Bau nach seinen künstlerischen Grundsätzen* (Vienna, 1889).

7   L. Piccinato, "Urbanistica medioevale," in *L'urbanistica dall'antichità ad oggi* (Florence, 1943).

8   E. Guidoni, *Arte e urbanistica in Toscana 1000 al 1315* (Rome, 1970).

9   P. Pierotti, *Urbanistica: Storia e prassi* (Pisa, 1973).

10   L. Benevolo, "Pescocostanzo," *Quaderni dell'Istituto di storia dell'architettura* (Rome), June 1955.

11   E. Battisti, *L'Antirinascimento* (Milan, 1962), 316.

12   See R. Cresswell, "Les concepts de la maison: Les peuples non industriels," *Zodiaque* 7 (1960): 183–97.

13   R. Pane, *Capri* (Venice, 1954).

14   See R. Freddi, *Edifici rurali nella pianura romana* (Rome, 1970).

15   V. Stefanelli, introduction to G. Vasari il Giovane, *La città ideale* (Rome, 1970), 49. See also L. Gori-Montanelli, *L'architettura rurale in Toscana* (Florence, 1964); and G. Ferrara and G. Biffoli, *La casa colonica in Toscana* (Florence, 1966).

16   See A. Corboz, "Encore Ressac," *archithese* 1 (1972).

17   C.G. Jung, *Essais de psychologie analytique* (Paris, 1931), 28.

18   See also S. Moholy-Nagy, *Native Genius in Anonymous Architecture* (New York, 1957); and M. Gol[d]finger, *Villages in the Sun: Mediterranean Community Architecture* (New York, 1969).

19   See Jin-Bak Pyun's article in this issue of *archithese*, 39, 468–78 in this publication.

20   See J. and R. Racki's article in this issue of *archithese*, 27, 450–67 in this publication.

Squatters: The Seven Housing Systems of Nairobi*

Authors:
Praful C. Patel
Jeff Racki
Reena Racki

Sources:
archithese, 9 (1974): 27–38
Ekistics 277 (October 1974): 286
(EN, partial reprint)

Translated by:
Steven Lindberg

Planning practices in developing countries are necessarily derived from strategies common in the industrialized world. The choice of technologies, the nature of the interventions of public authorities, the establishment of relatively high housing standards, and the widespread view that housing construction is nothing other than providing a complete package of accommodations reflect this practice. In other words, housing construction is generally understood to be a product not a process. This view is dubious even in industrialized countries; it is completely inappropriate under the conditions of the Third World.

The dominant theories of development assume that a higher standard of living for the broad population is conceivable only on the basis of economic growth and industrialization that is as comprehensive as possible. From such a perspective, investments in housing construction seem unproductive, so obtaining the capital necessary for housing construction is very difficult.

That accounts for the necessity of state interventions. Nevertheless, in the Third World, institutions capable of successfully implementing public services and housing construction programs exist only in the rarest cases. To the extent that state loans are made available at all, they are accessible only to a wealthy small minority. The difficulty of obtaining favorable loans reflects, in some cases, rising inflation, and that in turn causes low interest on savings. In such a situation, land speculation and constantly increasing land costs appear to be an antidote to inflation. But where effective tax and other state controls are lacking, land and building speculation operate outside the legal framework.

For the majority of the population in developing countries, income is low and uncertain, to say nothing of widespread underemployment and unemployment. Population growth far exceeds job growth, and this trend is only exacerbated by growing inequality between the countryside and the cities, which are growing explosively thanks to their services, infrastructure, and potential labor market.

The consequences of this situation are not difficult to foresee. The public authorities are not in a position to create sufficient housing, and what is actually built corresponds to international notions of "modern" housing standards. For all the state funding, the cost

Praful C. Patel,
Jeff Racki und Reena Racki

SQUATTERS:

Die sieben Wohnbausysteme von Nairobi *

Planungspraktiken in Entwicklungsländern leiten sich zwangsläufig von den Strategien her, die in der industrialisierten Welt üblich sind. Die Wahl der Technologien, die Art der Eingriffe von Seiten der öffentlichen Hand, die Festlegung relativ hoher Wohnungsstandards und die weitverbreitete Auffassung, wonach Wohnbau nichts anderes sei als die Bereitstellung eines kompletten Paketes von Unterkünften, spiegeln diese Praxis. Mit anderen Worten: Wohnbau wird im allgemeinen als Produkt, nicht als Prozess verstanden. Diese Auffassung ist fragwürdig in den industrialisierten Ländern; sie ist vollkommen unangemessen unter den Bedingungen der Dritten Welt.

Die vorherrschenden Entwicklungstheorien gehen davon aus, dass ein höherer Lebensstandard für die breite Bevölkerung nur auf der Grundlage wirtschaftlichen Wachstums und möglichst umfassender Industrialisierung denkbar sei. In einer solchen Perspektive erscheinen Investitionen in den Wohnbau als unproduktiv, und so hat denn auch der Wohnbau grosse Schwierigkeiten, das notwendige Kapital zu beschaffen.

Daher die Notwendigkeit staatlicher Eingriffe. Jedoch, in der Dritten Welt bestehen nur in den seltensten Fällen arbeitsfähige Institutionen, die imstande sind, öffentliche Dienstleistungen und Wohnbauprogramme erfolgreich durchzuführen. Sofern überhaupt öffentliche Kredite gewährt werden, sind sie nur einer kleinen Minorität von Wohlhabenden zugänglich. Die Schwierigkeit, günstige Kredite zu erlangen, spiegelt z. T. die steigende Inflation und diese wiederum wirkt sich in geringen Ersparniszinsen aus. In einer solchen Situation erscheinen die Bodenspekulation und die ständig steigenden Bodenpreise als ein Gegengift gegen die Inflation. Wo aber wirksame Steuer- und andere staatliche Kontrollen fehlen, spielt sich Boden- und Bauspekulation ausserhalb des gesetzlichen Rahmens ab.

Für die Mehrheit der Bevölkerung in Entwicklungsländern ist das Einkommen gering und unsicher, ganz abgesehen von der weitverbreiteten Unterbeschäftigung und Arbeitslosigkeit. Der Bevölkerungszuwachs übertrifft bei weitem den Zuwachs an Arbeitsplätzen, und dieser Trend wird noch verschärft durch das wachsende Gefälle zwischen der Landschaft und den Städten, die dank ihrer Dienstleistungen, Infrastrukturen und dank ihrem potentiellen Arbeitsmarkt explosiv anwachsen.

Die Folgen dieser Situation sind unschwer abzuschätzen. Die öffentlichen Instanzen sind ausserstande, genügend Wohnraum zu beschaffen; und was tatsächlich gebaut wird, das entspricht den internationalen Vorstellungen «moderner» Wohnbaunormen. Bei aller staatlichen Förderung führen der Geldpreis, die relativ hohen Wohnbaunormen und die herrschenden Bodenpreise zu Wohnungen, die nur für Angehörige der Mittelklasse und für eine massiv unterstützte Minderheit der unteren Einkommensschichten erschwinglich sind.

Die Mehrheit der Bevölkerung ist daher zur Selbsthilfe gezwungen. Das Resultat ist eine «Selbsthilfe-Architektur», die im allgemeinen von den Instanzen, die den Wohnbau kontrollieren, negativ beurteilt wird. Charles Abrams ist einer der ersten, die versuchten, die positiven Eigentümlichkeiten dieser Siedlungen zu erfassen, welche ausserhalb und unterhalb der staatlichen Normen entstanden. Ihm folgte John Turner, der für die spontanen Besiedelungsformen der «Squatters» als Resultate von Prozessen würdigte, welche den wechselnden Anforderungen und Bedürfnissen ihrer Benützer weit unmittelbarer entsprechen als die von oben verordneten Wohnformen (s. Bibliographie).

Was sich dabei abzeichnete war die Erkenntnis, dass Menschen, die selbst für ihren Wohnraum aufkommen müssen, im allgemeinen weit besser imstande sind, ihre Bedürfnisse abzuschätzen als jene Spezialisten und Fachleute, welche von der Obrigkeit mit dem Bau und der Kontrolle von Wohnraum beauftragt werden.

Allerdings: fehlender Zugang zu den fundamentalen Ressourcen des Bauens (Boden, Kredit, Materialien, Information, Berufswissen, Dienstleistungen) erschweren oder verunmöglichen gar die Versuche baulicher Selbsthilfe. Darin liegt eine echte Herausforderung an die

Les sept systèmes de logement de Nairobi

Les programmes de logement dans les pays en voie de développement sont invariablement dérivés de stratégies utilisées dans les pays industrialisés. Le logement est conçu principalement comme un produit, non comme un processus. Cette approche, déjà douteuse dans les pays développés, l'est encore plus dans le contexte du tiers-monde.

Les auteurs ont identifié sept systèmes de logement dans le secteur pauvre de Nairobi, qui représente 75 % de la population. 1. Les «Squatters»; 2. «Company Houses» (logements construits par des sociétés privés); 3. «Public Packages» (logements construits par l'état); 4. Mise à disposition de terrains équipés par l'état; 5. Anciens immeubles locatifs; 6. Pavillons individuels privés; 7. Logements mis à disposition par les employeurs.

Ces différents systèmes, qui se développent à des vitesses variées, se distinguent non seulement au niveau de l'environnement physique (arrangement des maisons, systèmes de circulation) mais aussi — et de manière encore plus frappante — au niveau du rapport des habitants avec leur environnement, en termes de promotion, propriété et contrôle.

Etant donné le peu de mobilité économique à Nairobi et, par ailleurs, le taux de croissance urbaine très élevé — surtout dans le secteur pauvre — tous les systèmes de logement doivent être prises en considération. Si l'on arrive à évaluer leurs potentiels et leurs insuffisances, ou pourra établir de manière réaliste les besoins en logement et les stratégies possible pour y faire face, à Nairobi comme dans d'autres villes du tiers-monde.

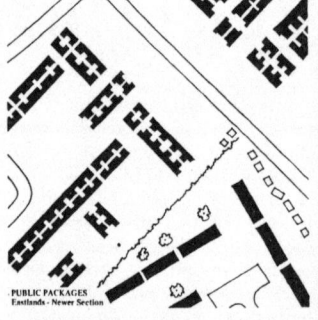

PUBLIC PACKAGES
Eastlands - Newer Section

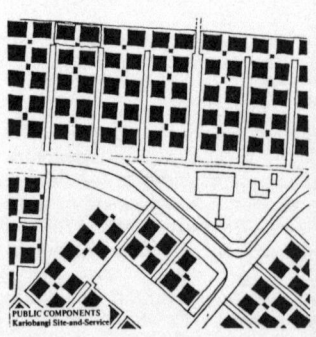

PUBLIC COMPONENTS
Kariobangi Site-and-Service

Fachleute: ihre Aufgabe sollte zuallererst darin bestehen, der Bevölkerung zu helfen, von technischen Einrichtungen und ökonomischen Ressourcen Gebrauch zu machen. Das ist nur möglich auf der Grundlage des Wissens um die ungleiche Verteilung von Reichtum und Entwicklungschancen innerhalb der Gesellschaft.

Dazu gehört auch ein Verständnis dessen, was im Wohnungsbau tatsächlich vorgeht. Im Grunde handelt es sich um eine Reihe von Systemen, und diese Systeme operieren auf Grund eines komplexen Zusammenwirkens von bereitliegenden Möglichkeiten und von Leuten, die diese ins Werk setzen. Es ist entscheidend wichtig, diese Systeme korrekt zu identifizieren und ihre Chancen abzuschätzen. Wir stehen heute erst am Beginn der Entwicklung von Methoden, die imstande sind, abzuklären, welche Schritte in einer gegebenen Situation notwendig sind, um mit einem Minimum an finanziellem und zeitlichem Aufwand ein Maximum an praktischem Nutzen zu erzielen.

Das Beispiel von Nairobi

Nairobi wurde vor knapp 75 Jahren gegründet; heute wächst seine Bevölkerung von 580 000 Einwohnern jährlich um 7½ %. Davon ist bloss 2½ % das Resultat von Neugeburten; 59 % der jährlichen Zunahme wird durch die Zuwanderer bestritten. Kenyas Bevölkerung lebt zu 90 % von der Landwirtschaft; bloss 10 % seiner Bevölkerung ist in Städten von mehr als 20 000 Einwohnern ansässig. Die Gegensätze zwischen der Hauptstadt Nairobi und den kleineren Städten, ganz zu schweigen von der umgebenden Landschaft, sind dramatisch. Der industrielle Reichtum Kenyas ist weitgehend in Nairobi konzentriert, und dort befinden sich auch 40 % aller Industrien des Landes.

Dies erklärt die Anziehungskraft Nairobis. Die Stadt ist für einen andauernden Strom von Zuwanderern der Inbegriff wirtschaftlicher Chancen. Diese Zuwanderer hoffen, dort bessere materielle Existenzbedingungen zu finden;

fig. 1 Comparison of the various settlement patterns of Nairobi.

aber nicht alle beabsichtigen, sich ganz in der Stadt anzusiedeln. Viele von ihnen haben vielmehr vor, nach einigen Jahren wieder in ihr Heimatdorf zurückzukehren und unterhalten daher sehr enge Verbindungen mit ihren Angehörigen «draussen» auf dem Land. Tom Weisner und andere haben jenes typische «Stadt-Land-Kontinuum» beschrieben, mit seinem Netz von engen familiären Beziehungen, häufigen Besuchen in beiderlei Richtung, und mit seinem dauernden Austausch von Geld und Gütern. Unsere Untersuchung der Armenquartiere von Nairobi hat ihre Erfahrungen bestätigt. Diese engen Beziehungen, welche typisch sind für die Angehörigen der unteren Einkommensschichten, zeigt sich etwa darin, dass sie es in den meisten Fällen vorziehen, ihre Ersparnisse nach Hause zu schicken, statt sie in ihre städtische Unterkunft zu investieren. Welches die Aspirationen der in den letzten zehn Jahren (seit dem Begin der nationalen Unabhängigkeit) geborenen Kinder dieser Zuwanderer sein werden, das kann man allerdings noch nicht abschätzen.

Nairobi ist eine gespaltene Stadt, sowohl im Hinblick auf ihre physische Gestalt als auch im Hinblick auf ihre sozio-ökonomische Struktur. Entsprechend der drastisch unterschiedlichen Einkommenskategorien unterscheiden sich auch die Wohnquartiere der verschiedenen Klassen und Einkommensgruppen. Die Reichen wohnen vornehmlich im Westen; die Armen im Osten — und diese Spaltung hat ihren Ursprung in der sozialen und wirtschaftlichen Geschichte der Stadt. In der Zeit vor der nationalen Unabhängigkeit fiel diese Grenze zwischen arm und reich mit derjenigen zwischen schwarz und weiss zusammen, wobei die asiatische Bevölkerung zwischen beiden rassischen «Ghettos», allerdings näher bei den Schwarzen, angesiedelt war. Das hat sich selbstverständlich in den letzten Jahren geändert.

Die sieben Wohnbausysteme

Wir haben im östlichen Teil von Nairobi, d. h. in jenem Sektor, in dem die unteren Einkommensschichten wohnen, sieben verschiedene Wohnbausysteme identifiziert, von denen einige wichtiger sind und schneller wachsen als andere. Im Rahmen dieser Arbeit haben wir jene Bewohner der «unteren Einkommensschicht» zugewiesen, welche nicht imstande sind, die Kosten für eine moderne Minimalwohnung, wie sie von der Administration geliefert werden, selbst zu tragen. In Nairobi fallen ungefähr 75 % der Bewohner in die so definierte Kategorie der «unteren Einkommensschicht». In der Tat sind bloss ca. 25 % der Einwohner Nairobis in der Lage, eine nicht subventionierte Unterkunft oder eine Minimalwohnung zu mieten oder zu kaufen. — Andererseits lebt die überwältigende Mehrheit der der unteren Einkommensschicht zugehörigen Familien in einer Dichte, die weit über den von der Regierung festgelegten Normen liegt; der Durchschnitt ist ein Raum pro Familie.

Wir haben für diese verschiedenen Wohnbausysteme die populären Bezeichnungen übernommen, und dort, wo es keine solchen gab, neue geschaffen. Nämlich:

1. «Squatters» — d. h. unrechtmässige Ansiedler (dorfartige Siedlungen von hoher Dichte).
2. «Company Houses» (genossenschaftlicher Wohnbau).
3. Alte Wohnblöcke (asiatische Hofbauten).
4. «Public Packages» (öffentlicher Wohnbau).
5. «Public Components» (Bereitstellung erschlossener Grundstücke durch die Verwaltung).
6. Eigentumswohnhäuser (Dagoretti).
7. Wohnungen, die vom Arbeitgeber zur Verfügung gestellt werden.

Die baulichen Unterschiede zwischen diesen Wohnbausystemen sind radikal, vor allem was die Wohnungsgrundrisse und die Verkehrssysteme anbelangt. Es ist aber wichtig, festzuhalten, dass diese Wohnbausysteme mehr sind als bloss materielle Unterkünfte. Wichtiger als die physische Endform ist das Netz der Beziehungen zwischen den Bewohnern und ihrer Umwelt, d. h. die Art und Weise, wie diese Bauten errichtet, verwaltet und kontrolliert werden. In jedem dieser Wohnbausysteme ist ein spezifisches Netz von Beziehungen am Werk; Beziehungen einerseits zwischen den verschiedenen am Bauprozess Beteiligten untereinander, aber auch Beziehungen dieser Entscheidungsträger zur gebauten Endform selbst.

Im Rahmen unserer Untersuchung hat es sich als nützlich erwiesen, die an diesen Bauprozessen Beteiligten in drei Gruppen zu unterteilen: der öffentliche, der private und der volkstümliche Sektor. Der öffentliche Sektor hat ungefähr 30 % des Wohnbauvolumens in Nairobi produziert, der private Sektor rund 25 % und der volkstümliche Sektor 47 %. Noch aufschlussreicher ist aber die Wachstumsrate des von diesen drei Sektoren produzierten Wohnbauvolumens. Die Produktion des öffentlichen und privaten Sektors wächst jährlich um je ca. 1 bis 2 %, während die Produktion des volkstümlichen Sektors rapide zunimmt, mindestens um jährlich 10 %. Obwohl vollkommen illegal, ist der volkstümliche Sektor offenbar als einziger imstande, mit dem Bevölkerungszuwachs Schritt zu halten.

Um besser feststellen zu können, wie weit die Zuwanderer in der Lage sind, ihre Unterkunft zu finanzieren, und vor allem, um besser abklären zu können, welches das Verhältnis des Aufwandes für die Wohnung verglichen mit demjenigen für andere Güter ist, mussten wir die «untere Einkommensschicht» noch weiter aufgliedern nach sehr niederem, niederem und bescheidenem Einkommen. Das heisst:

1. Sehr niederes Einkommen: genügt für das lebenswichtige Minimum an Nahrung und Brennstoff für die Familie, aber nicht für Ausgaben für Unterkunft und Verkehr.
2. Niederes Einkommen: genügt für das Existenzminimum plus bescheidene Ausgaben für die Unterkunft.
3. Bescheidenes Einkommen (zwei- bis fünfmal Existenzminimum): genügt bestenfalls für die Finanzierung einer unsubventionierten Minimalwohnung, oder für die Finanzierung eines kleinen Eigenheims.

Arbeitsstatistiken erlauben den Schluss, dass ca. 15 % der Bevölkerung von Nairobi ein sehr niederes Einkommen beziehen; 25 % ein niederes und weitere 25 % ein mittleres bis hohes. Da die Arbeitslosigkeit ständig zunimmt, ist zu erwarten, dass einerseits der Anteil der «niederen Einkommensschicht» innerhalb der Bevölkerung von Nairobi prozentual zunehmen wird, und dass auch der Anteil der Bewohner, die ein sehr niederes Einkommen beziehen, innerhalb der «niederen Einkommensschicht» sowohl zahlenmässig als auch prozentual zunehmen wird.

Wir geben im folgenden eine knappe Beschreibung der wesentlichen Eigentümlichkeiten der sieben weiter oben erwähnten Wohnbausysteme.

1. «Squatters» (d. h. unrechtmässige Ansiedler)

Dieses System ist ganz vom volkstümlichen Sektor getragen, sowohl was Entstehung, Entwurf, Bau und Unterhalt betrifft. Landbesitz, Grundrissgestaltung und Bauweise liegen vollkommen ausserhalb der rechtlichen Normen des Wohnbaus. Die Verwaltung verhält sich im allgemeinen dieser Bauform gegenüber negativ oder paternalistisch; d. h. sie schwankt zwischen direkter Zerstörung und passiver Duldung — sie ist jedenfalls nicht willens, die lebensnotwendigen und positiven Aspekte dieses Wohnbausystems anzuerkennen. In Wirklichkeit stellt es die Voraussetzung des Ueberlebens für seine Bewohner dar, in Ermangelung von brauchbaren Alternativen (d. h. Unterkünften, die für sie erschwinglich sind und die in angemessener Distanz zu Arbeitsplätzen und öffentlichen Dienstleistungen liegen). Die zentrale Lage zahlreicher Squatter-Siedlungen und ihr minimaler Kostenaufwand erlaubt selbst den Bezügern von sehr niederen Einkommen in einer unsicheren Umgebung zu überleben. Es kann vorkommen, dass sich die Verwaltung dazu bereitfindet, in bereits existierenden Siedlungen Erschliessungen einzurichten, auch kann gelegentlich durch politische Druckmittel die drohende Zerstörung von Squatter-Siedlungen aufgehalten werden — aber die Verwaltung verfügt über keine positive Politik des Verständnisses der Squatters und ihrer wirtschaftlichen Probleme.

70 % der Squatters verdienen weniger als das Lebensnotwendige. Etwa die Hälfte von ihnen ist seit mehr als fünf Jahren in Nairobi ansässig; d. h. ihre wirtschaftliche Mobilität ist relativ gering. Die Squatters machen etwa 18 % der Bevölkerung von Nairobi aus, oder ¼ der «niederen Einkommensschicht». Zahlreiche Squatters senden monatlich 10—25 % ihres Einkommens nach Hause. Die Hälfte der Squatter-Familien bezahlen keine Miete und haben keine Ausgaben für ihre Unterkunft zu entrichten.

Es gibt zwei Sorten von Squatter-Siedlungen in Nairobi: eigentliche Squatter-Dörfer oder kleine, in bestehende Baulücken eingefügte Siedlungssplitter. Die Dörfer verfügen über Gemeinschaftseinrichtungen und sind normalerweise an Flussufern angeordnet, z. B. am Ufer des Mathare River. Jedes Dorf ist von einem Streifen kultivierten Landes umgeben, selbst wenn es sich im Zentrum der Stadt befindet. Die «infill squatters» sind demgegenüber kleine

↓ fig. 2   Nairobi. Detail: Squatter settlement on the bank of the Mathare River.

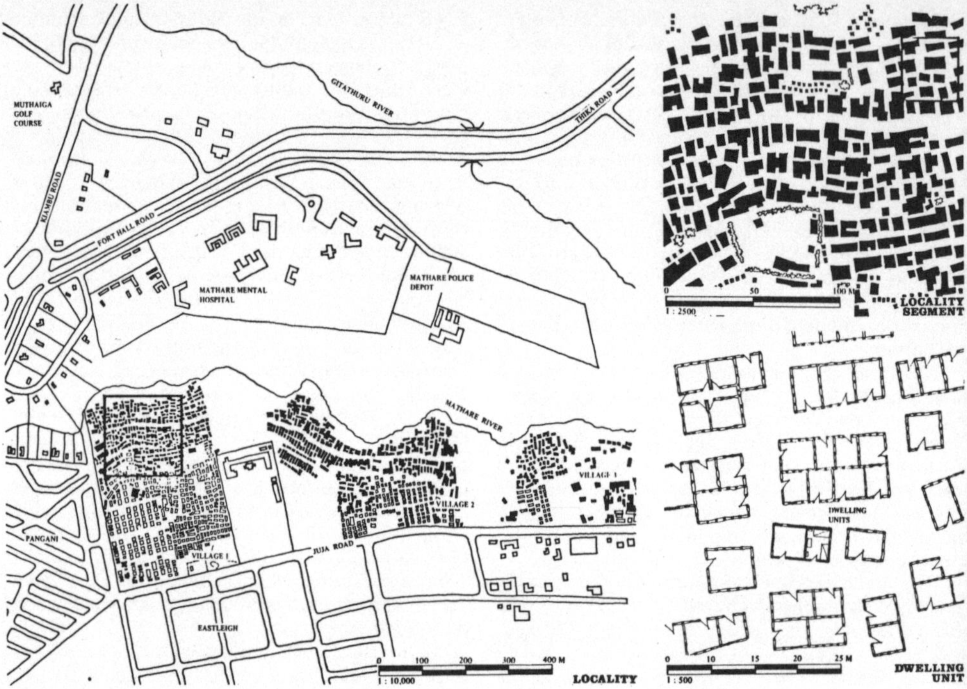

Gruppen von Familien, die sich auf verstreuten unbenützten Stücken öffentlichen oder privaten Grundes im Stadtzentrum etabliert haben. In einigen Fällen wurden Squatter-Dörfer von der Verwaltung mit elementaren Dienstleistungen versehen, aber die meisten Squatters stehen unter dem beständigen Druck drohender Zerstörung.

Die «autonomen» Körperschaften der Squatters repräsentieren nicht nur reale Bedürfnisse, sondern auch eine wichtige Voraussetzung für die Schaffung neuen Wohnraums. Aber sie befinden sich in ständiger Gefahr: die Schwierigkeit, Arbeit zu finden, die Unmöglichkeit, gut gelegenes und erschlossenes Land zu erwerben, restriktive Bauvorschriften und die Zerstörungspraktiken der Verwaltung erschweren jeden Versuch, ihr Los zu verbessern. Der Versuch der Bewohner des Squatter-Dorfes am Mathare River, das Land, auf dem sie sich eingerichtet haben, käuflich zu erwerben, scheiterte an den ständig steigenden Bodenpreisen.

↑ fig. 3   Squatter settlement in the Mathare River Valley, Nairobi. The huts are built of clay, wattle, and discarded materials.

of money, the relatively high standards for housing, and the dominant land costs lead to apartments that are affordable only for members of the middle class and a massively subsidized minority of the lower income strata.

A majority of the population is thus forced to rely on self-help. The result is a "self-help architecture" that is generally judged negatively by the authorities that control housing construction. Charles Abrams was one of the first to attempt to appreciate the positive features of these settlements created outside of and below state standards. He was followed by John Turner, who assessed the spontaneous settlement forms of "squatters" as the result of processes that correspond much more directly to the changing requirements and needs of their users than do the housing forms decreed from above (see Bibliography).

The insight that emerged was that people who have to come up with their housing themselves are in general far better able to assess their needs than the specialists and experts who are commissioned by the authorities to build and regulate housing.

However, lack of access to the fundamental resources of building (land, loans, materials, information, professional knowledge, services) makes attempts at self-help building more difficult or impossible. Therein lies a true challenge to the experts: their task should first and foremost be helping the population to make use of technical facilities and economic resources. That is possible only on the basis of knowledge of the society's unequal distribution of wealth and opportunities for advancement.

That includes an understanding of what actually happens in housing construction. In essence, it amounts to a series of systems, and these systems operate on the basis of a complex interaction of existing possibilities and of people who implement them. That these systems be correctly identified and their possibilities be evaluated is crucially important. Today, we stand at the beginning of the development of methods that are capable of clarifying what steps are necessary in a given situation to maximize practical use with a minimum investment of finances and time.

The Example of Nairobi

Nairobi was founded just over seventy-five years ago; today, its population of 580,000 residents is growing 7.5 percent per annum. Of that, just 2.5 percent is the result of births; 59 percent of the annual increase consists of migrants. Ninety percent of Kenya's population makes a living from agriculture; just 10 percent of the population is located in cities with more than 20,000 residents. The contrasts between the capital, Nairobi, and the smaller cities— to say nothing of the surrounding countryside —are dramatic. Kenya's industrial wealth is largely concentrated in Nairobi, which also has 40 percent of the country's industrial base.

That explains Nairobi's attractiveness. The city is the epitome of economic opportunity for a constant stream of migrants. These migrants hope they will find better material conditions for life there, but not all of them intend to settle permanently in the city. Rather, many of them intend to return to their native village after several years and therefore retain very close ties to their family and friends "outside" in the countryside. Tom Weisner and others have described this typical "urban-rural continuum," with its network of close family relationships, its frequent visits in both directions, and its constant exchange of money and goods. Our study of the poor neighborhoods of Nairobi confirmed their experiences. These close relationships, which are typical of the members of lower-income levels, are revealed, for example, in the fact that most prefer to send their savings home rather than invest them in their urban home. It is, however, too early to assess what aspirations the children born to these migrants over the past ten years (since the beginning of national independence) will have.

Nairobi is a divided city, in terms of both its physical form and its socioeconomic structure. The residential neighborhoods of the different classes and income groups differ in accordance with the drastically different income categories. The rich live primarily in the west and the poor in the east—and this division has its origin in the city's social and economic history. In the period prior to national independence, this line between poor and rich coincided with that of black and white, with the Asian population located between the two race "ghettos," though closer to the blacks. That has, of course, changed in recent years.

The Seven Housing Systems

In the eastern part of Nairobi—that is, in the sector in which the lower-income classes live—we identified seven systems for housing construction, some of which are more important and growing more quickly than others. In the course of this work, we assigned to the "lower-income class" those residents who are not in a position to bear the costs themselves for a modern minimal dwelling of the sort provided by the administration. In Nairobi, around 75 percent of the residents belong to the category of the "lower-income class" as defined in this way. Only around 25 percent of the residents in Nairobi are in a position to rent or purchase nonsubsidized housing or a minimal dwelling. On the other hand, an overwhelming majority of families belonging to the lower-income class live in a density far above the standards established by the government; the average is one room per family.

We have used the popular names for these housing systems and created new ones where there were none. Namely:
1. Squatters—that is, Illegal Settlers (Village-like Settlements of High Density).
2. Company Houses (Cooperative Housing).
3. Old Tenements (Asian Courtyard Buildings).
4. Public Packages (Public Housing).
5. Public Components (Provision by the Government of Properties with Access to Public Supply Network).
6. Popular Ownership (Dagoretti).
7. Employer-Provided Housing.

The architectural differences between these housing systems are radical, especially insofar as apartment floor plans and transportation systems are concerned. It is important to clarify, however, that these housing systems are more than just material accommodations. More important than their final physical form is the network of relationships between the residents and their environment; that is, the way these buildings are constructed, managed, and controlled. In each of these housing systems, a specific network of relationships is at work; relationships, on the one hand, among the different participants in the construction process but also the relationships of these decision makers to the final built form itself.

In the course of our study, it proved to be useful to divide the participants in these construction processes into three groups: the public, the private, and the popular sector. The public sector has produced around 30 percent of the volume of housing in Nairobi, the private sector around 25 percent, and the popular sector 47 percent. Even more revealing, however, is the rate of growth of the volume of housing produced by these three sectors. The production of the public and private sectors is growing per annum by circa 1 to 2 percent each, whereas the production of the popular sector is increasing rapidly, at least 10 percent per annum. Although completely illegal, the popular sector is apparently the only one capable of keeping up with the population increase.

To understand better the extent to which migrants are in a position to finance their accommodations and, above all, to clarify the ratio of the cost of housing to that of other goods, we had to subdivide the "low-income sector" even further according to very low, low, and modest income. That means:
1. Very Low Income: Sufficient for the minimum of food and fuel necessary for a family to live but not for expenses for housing and transportation.
2. Low Income: Sufficient for the subsistence minimum plus modest expense for accommodations.
3. Modest Income (two to three times the subsistence minimum): Sufficient at best to finance an unsubsidized minimal dwelling or to finance a small home of one's own.

Labor statistics permit the conclusion that circa 15 percent of the population of Nairobi has a very low income, 25 percent a low one, and another 25 percent a moderate to high one. Because unemployment is constantly increasing, the "low-income sector," on the one hand, is expected to increase as a proportion of the population of Nairobi and, on the other hand, residents of the "low-income sector" with a very low income will increase both in terms of numbers and as a percentage.

fig. 4 Squatter settlement in Nairobi: The clothing and household items are in keeping with the rural origins of the residents.

2. «Company Houses» (genossenschaftlicher Wohnbau)

Die «Company Houses» wurden von Baugenossenschaften errichtet, die, als Aktiengesellschaften organisiert, Landkäufe tätigen und Wohneinheiten bauen, teils mit beachtlichen Gewinnmargen. Die Leistung dieser Baugenossenschaften ist phänomenal, obwohl sie erst seit 1969 am Werk sind. Während z. B. der öffentliche Sektor in einem Jahr bloss 1000 Wohneinheiten errichtete, schufen die Baugenossenschaften deren 7000. Aber auch dieses genossenschaftliche Bauen ist illegal, da es den offiziellen Baunormen nicht entspricht.

Der Grund dieses Erfolges liegt in den enormen Gewinnen, die das genossenschaftliche Bauen gegenwärtig abwirft, oft bis zu jährlich 50 % — freilich verbunden mit extremen Risiken. Die Genossenschaftswohnbauten versorgen Zuwanderer, die der mittleren und unteren Einkommensschicht angehören, und deren Bedürfnisse gegenwärtig von keinem anderen Wohnbausystem befriedigt werden. Freilich, sie sind immer noch viel zu teuer für die Bezüger sehr niederer Einkommen, für die das Squatting die einzige realistische Unterkunftsmöglichkeit darstellt. Die Bewohner dieser Wohnblöcke geben denn auch einen hohen Prozentsatz ihres Einkommens für die Miete aus, oft bis zu 50 %. Ueberdies haben die emporschnellenden Bodenpreise zur Folge, dass auch die Mieten dieser Einraum-Wohnungen ständig ansteigen. Wären die Risiken dieses Wohnbausystems geringer und gäbe es eine wirksame Bodenpreiskontrolle, so wäre diese Art der Wohnraumbeschaffung sozial durchaus verantwortbar. Die Gewinnmargen könnten dann in demselben Ausmass reduziert werden wie die Risiken, und die geringeren Kosten würden sich auch günstig auf die Mietpreise auswirken.

3. Alte Wohnblöcke (asiatische Hofbauten)

Diese Wohnblöcke im Stadtzentrum wurden von Asiaten für ihre grossen Familien sowie einige Mieter gebaut, und sie verfügen häufig über einen Laden auf dem Strassenniveau, der von der Familie selbst betrieben wird. Im Anschluss an die Unabhängigkeit Kenyas sind zahlreiche asiatische Familien ausgewandert, wodurch diese Wohnblöcke frei wurden und sich jenem Teil der schwarzen Bevölkerung anboten, der über ein bescheidenes Einkommen verfügt. Heute werden keine solchen Wohn-

figs. 5–6 "Company houses, that is, cooperative housing, Nairobi.

↓ fig. 7 "Company houses" above the Mathare River Valley, Nairobi.

↓ fig. 8 Old housing blocks in the center of Nairobi (Asian courtyard buildings).

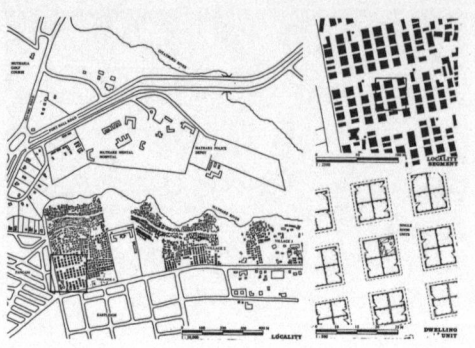
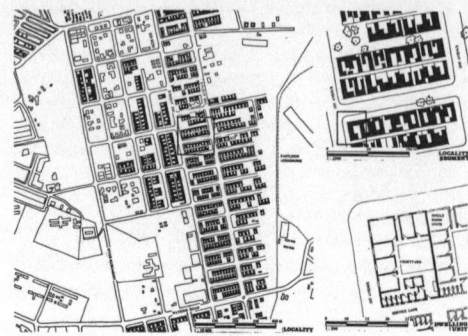

blöcke mehr gebaut, und die Mieten sind denn auch im allgemeinen weit höher als diejenigen der genossenschaftlichen Wohnbauten, da, unter anderem, die Qualität der Bauten, ihrer Erschliessungen und der verfügbaren Dienstleistungen viel besser sind. Da diese Wohnblöcke auf für 90 Jahre gepachtetem Land stehen, das in weniger als 30 Jahren wieder an die öffentliche Hand zurückfallen wird, findet sich niemand, der daran interessiert ist, anstelle dieser Wohnblöcke gewinnträchtigere Neubauten zu errichten. Die Wohnblöcke weisen eine hohe Dichte auf: ungefähr 200 Personen per acre und 4,5 Personen per Wohnraum. Die Gemeinschaftseinrichtungen befinden sich in den Innenhöfen. Da die Mieten ständig ansteigen, treten Mieter der mittleren Einkommensschicht anstelle von solchen der niederen Einkommensschicht, obwohl diese durchaus imstande wären, die Mieten moderner Minimalwohnungen zu zahlen, sofern es deren in genügender Zahl gäbe. Unter den Angehörigen der mittleren Einkommensschicht, die diese Wohnblöcke bewohnen, sind denn auch viele auf den Wartelisten für den öffentlichen Wohnbau eingetragen.

4. «Public Packages» (öffentlicher Wohnbau)

Hier handelt es sich um Wohnbauprojekte, die direkt vom Gemeinderat von Nairobi finanziert, gebaut und verwaltet werden. Es handelt sich um ein komplettes Paket von Einrichtungen, an deren Entstehung und Verwaltung der volkstümliche Sektor vollkommen unbeteiligt ist. Obwohl der Bau dieser Wohneinheiten subventioniert und die Mieten einer strengen Kontrolle unterworfen sind, haben die hohen Baunormen zur Folge, dass diese Wohnungen für die überwältigende Mehrheit der Angehörigen der niederen und sehr niederen Einkommensklasse unerschwinglich sind. So sind es vor allem zahlreiche Angehörige der mittleren und oberen Einkommensklassen, die von den staat-

↑ figs. 9–11 One- or two-story courtyard buildings, often with stores along the street facade.

In what follows we briefly describe the essential properties of the seven housing systems mentioned above.

1. Squatters (i.e., Illegal Settlers)

This system is initiated, designed, built, and controlled by the popular sector. The form of land tenure, building subdivision pattern, and construction standards fall outside the legally acceptable development framework or the planning process, as it presently operates. Public action is usually destructive or paternalistic toward this system; that is, it oscillates between direct destruction and passive tolerance—it is, in any case, unwilling to recognize the vital and positive aspects of this housing system. In reality, it represents the precondition for the survival of its residents, for lack of useful alternatives (i.e., accommodations they can afford that are located at a reasonable distance from jobs and public services). The central locations of many of these settlements and their minimum cost commitment enable very low-income people to survive in an insecure environment. The existing public policy might allow the installation of utility systems and prevent demolition. There is no really positive policy which reflects an understanding of the users' economic problems and need.

Seventy percent of the squatters earn less than the subsistence minimum. About half of them have been in Nairobi for more than five years, indicating a fairly low level of economic mobility for a sizable proportion of them. The total squatter population is about 18 percent of Nairobi's population and about a quarter of the low-income population. Many squatters send 10 to 25 percent of their income to their families in villages. Half of the squatter families pay no rent and have no expenditures at all on housing.

There are two sorts of squatter settlements in Nairobi: squatter villages proper and small splinter settlements introduced into existing vacant sites. Squatter villages have community organizations and distinct physical and social units, such as those of the Mathare River Valley. Each village is bounded by an area of cultivation, including those that are located in the inner ring of the city. The "infill squatters," by contrast, are small groups of families who have established themselves on scattered unused pieces of public or private land in the center of the city. Post facto government action has initiated the installation of basic services and utilities into some of the villages as a result of political pressure exerted by the villagers and their tribesmen, but many of the squatters live insecurely under the constant threat of demolition.

The "autonomous" squatter village community organizations and initiatives represent an assertion of real need and a major housing resource. Lack of access to employment opportunities, suitably located and basically serviced land, restrictive building standards and codes, and demolition practices constantly hamper the squatters' attempts to improve their lot. Attempts of the Mathare Valley village residents to buy the land legally on which they are located were thwarted by steeply rising land values which priced them out of the market.

2. Company Houses (Cooperative Housing Construction)

The "Company Houses" were built by building cooperatives that, organized as joint-stock companies, purchase land and build housing units, sometimes at considerable profit margins. Although they have only been in existence since 1969, their output has been very high. For example, they built 7,000 single-room dwelling units in one year as compared with the 1,000 units per year output of the public sector. The company development is, however, illegal, since it does not conform to official modern standards of building and subdivision.

The high output is a result of the enormous profit-making capacity. The returns of as much as 50 percent per annum are accompanied by extremely high risks. Company housing caters to an obviously unmet demand of the moderate- and low-income migrants. Admittedly, they are always still much too expensive for those with very low incomes, for whom squatting represents the only realistic possibility to get housing. The low-income households living in the tenements must spend up to 50 percent of their earnings on rent. The current spiraling land costs are increasing the rents of the company rooms. If their risks were reduced and the land costs controlled, rents could be reduced and this building resource would become an asset to the city.

3. Old Tenements (Asian Courtyard Buildings)

These housing blocks in the center of the city were built by Asians for their large families as well as some tenants, and they often have a street-level store run by the family itself. Following Kenya's independence, numerous Asian families emigrated, freeing up these housing blocks, which were then offered to the sector of the black population that has a modest income. Today, such housing blocks are no longer being built, and the rents are in general also much higher than those of the cooperative apartment buildings, since, among other reasons, the quality of the buildings, access to infrastructure, and available services are much better. Because these housing blocks often stand on land leased for ninety years, which in less than thirty years will return to state ownership, no one can be found who is interested in building more profitable new apartments to replace these housing blocks. The housing blocks have high density: approximately 200 people per acre and 4.5 people per housing unit. The common facilities are located in the interior courtyards. Because rents are constantly increasing, renters from the moderate-income sector apply, rather than from the lower-income sector, even though the latter would certainly be in a position to pay the rents for modern minimal dwellings if there were a sufficient number of them. Many of the members of the moderate-income sector who occupy these housing blocks are also on the waiting lists for public housing.

4. Public Packages (Public Housing)

These are housing construction projects financed, built, and managed directly by the Nairobi City Council. They consist of a complete package of furnishings, and the popular sector takes no part in their production and management. Although the building of these housing units is subsidized and the rents subject to strict control, the high construction standards mean that these apartments are unaffordable for the overwhelming majority of the members of the low- and very low-income sectors who profit from state subsidies—renters who in general scarcely pay more than 5–10 percent of their income for housing. That represents a considerable loss for the city as a whole. The high costs of construction and management in public housing do not benefit those who are truly dependent on state aid. If it even belongs to the tasks of the public sector to provide housing for the moderate-income sector, it should be done on the basis of current market prices and the resulting profits used to support the lower-income sectors. In any case, the current achievements of public housing construction are so modest and their administrative provisions so complicated that the development of new, alternative housing construction methods seems inevitable—to say nothing of the fact that current practices run counter to the interests of the lower-income sectors.

5. Public Components (Properties Developed by the Municipal Administration)

The Nairobi City Council has also arranged for the public sector to make available to migrants developed land on which they can build homes. The experiments carried out in Nairobi excluded the very low-income sector, however. That was primarily because many squatters who were dislocated to the land provided by the city were not willing or able to construct buildings that met specific minimum standards, even when those standards were far below those of modern minimal dwellings. Moreover, the peripheral location of these developed urban lands represents a crucial disadvantage for many squatters, who prefer to earn some money from the sale of their property and use it to return to one of the squatter villages in the center of the city. Communal self-help is lacking almost entirely in these settlements, and one consequence, among others, of the bureaucratic process of selecting residents is that developed plots stand vacant for long periods, while the waiting lists for potential residents continually grow. Because the settlement of these developed lands is not accompanied by the economic improvement of the residents, it is decidedly only a partial solution, one that continues to place the main burden on the shoulders of the poor themselves, with no attempt being made to understand their real needs and priorities. Nevertheless, this housing system represents a solution that is potentially more useful, if it is put into practice on a broader foundation, than the experiences in Nairobi might suggest.

↓ figs. 12–13   "Public packages" (public housing) in the eastern part of Nairobi.

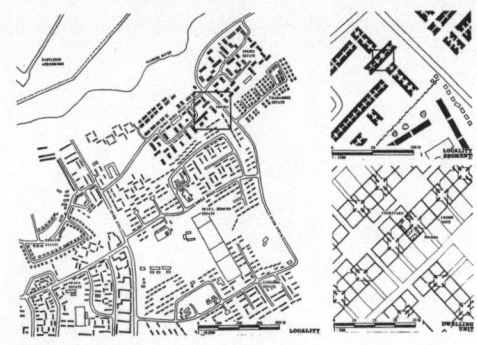

lichen Subventionen profitieren, Mieter, die im Allgemeinen kaum mehr als 5 oder 10 % ihres Einkommens für ihre Unterkunft ausgeben. Für die Stadt als Ganzes bedeutet das einen beachtlichen Verlust. Die hohen Bau- und Verwaltungskosten im öffentlichen Wohnbau kommen nicht jenen zugute, die wirklich auf staatliche Hilfe angewiesen sind. Wenn es überhaupt zu den Aufgaben des öffentlichen Sektors gehört, die mittlere Einkommensschicht mit Unterkünften zu versorgen, so sollte er dies auf der Basis der gängigen Marktpreise tun und die Gewinne, die dabei erzielt werden, dazu verwenden, die unteren Einkommensschichten zu unterstützen. Jedenfalls sind die Leistungen des öffentlichen Wohnbaus gegenwärtig so bescheiden und die administrativen Umstände derart komplex, dass die Entwicklung neuer, alternativer Wohnbaumethoden unausweichlich scheint, ganz abgesehen von der Tatsache, dass die heutigen Praktiken den Interessen der unteren Einkommensschichten zuwiderlaufen.

5. «Public Components» (durch die Verwaltung erschlossene Grundstücke)

Im Uebrigen hat der Gemeinderat von Nairobi veranlasst, dass der öffentliche Sektor den Zuwanderern erschlossenes Land zur Verfügung stellt, auf dem sie ihre Unterkünfte bauen können. Die Experimente, die in Nairobi durchgeführt wurden, fanden aber unter Ausschluss der sehr niederen Einkommensschichten statt. Dies liegt hauptsächlich daran, dass viele Squatters, die auf das von der Stadt bereitgestellte Land disloziert wurden, nicht willens oder nicht imstande waren, Bauten auf der Grundlage von spezifischen Minimalnormen zu errichten, selbst wenn diese Normen weit unter denjenigen moderner Minimalwohnungen liegen. Ueberdies stellte die periphere Lage dieser erschlossenen städtischen Terrains für viele Squatters einen entscheidenden Nachteil dar; sie zogen es vor, durch den Verkauf ihres Grundstückes etwas Geld zu verdienen und damit in eines der Squatter-Dörfer im Stadtzentrum zurückzukehren. Gemeinschaftliche Selbsthilfe fehlt fast vollkommen in diesen Siedlungen, und der bürokratische Prozess der Auswahl von Ansiedlern hat unter anderem zur Folge, dass erschlossene Terrains für lange Perioden leerstehen, während andererseits die Wartelisten potentieller Ansiedler ständig anwachsen. Da die Besiedlung dieser erschlossenen Terrains nicht durch einen wirtschaftlichen Aufstieg der Bewohner unterstützt wird, handelt es sich um eine ausgesprochene Teillösung; die Hauptlast liegt nach wie vor auf den Schultern der Armen selbst, ohne dass ein Versuch unternommen würde, ihre wirklichen Bedürfnisse und Prioritäten zu verstehen. Trotzdem stellt dieses Wohnbausystem, sofern es auf einer breiteren Grundlage ins Werk gesetzt wird, eine brauchbarere Lösung dar als es aufgrund der bisherigen Erfahrungen in Nairobi scheinen mag.

↓ figs. 14–15 "Public components" (properties developed by the municipal authorities).
Most of these housing units now belong to owners who live in other parts of the city.

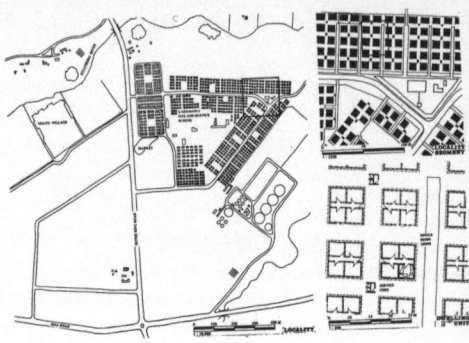

6. Volkstümliche Eigentumswohnhäuser (Dagoretti)

Unmittelbar im Anschluss an die Unabhängigkeit Kenyas erhielten alle Dorfbewohner von Dagoretti, einer Vorortszone von Nairobi, den Status von Eigentümern des von ihnen besiedelten Bodens. Ueberdies wurde das Gebiet als ausserhalb der städtischen Gesetzgebung liegend deklariert — eine politische Entschädigung für eine Bevölkerungsgruppe, die am meisten unter der Not unmittelbar vor der Unabhängigkeitserklärung gelitten hatte. Die kleinen Parzellen innerhalb dieser Dörfer sind zu klein, um den meist arbeitslosen Bewohnern eine für den Lebensunterhalt ausreichende Bewirtschaftung des Bodens zu ermöglichen. Daher haben viele von ihnen Wohnräume angebaut, deren Vermietung ihnen ein bescheidenes Einkommen sichert, oder sie haben ihre Grundstücke an nicht-ansässige Wohnbauspekulanten verkauft, die, wie wir gesehen haben, äusserst rasch und erfolgreich operieren. 40 % der Bewohner sind Bezüger sehr niederer Einkommen, einige leben sogar vollkommen ausserhalb jeder Geldwirtschaft. Dagoretti gilt als «hypertrophiertes» Dorf, als ländliches Gebiet, obwohl es innerhalb der Stadtgrenzen von Nairobi liegt, und obwohl es von zahlreichen seiner Bewohner als eine vorübergehende Unterkunft betrachtet wird, die ihnen erlaubt, in der Stadt zu arbeiten, und dabei genügend Geld für die spätere Rückkehr nach Hause beiseitezulegen. Zahlreiche Bewohner überleben bloss dank der landwirtschaftlichen Bewirtschaftung des umliegenden Geländes, die ihnen die lebensnotwendige Nahrung sichert; Gelegenheitsarbeiten ermöglichen es ihnen, Schulgebühren und Steuern zu bezahlen.

Aber die Bodenspekulation in den rasch anwachsenden Wohnblock-Dörfern in der unmittelbaren Umgebung des Zentrums von Nairobi trägt viel dazu bei, dass die Zimmermieten rasch ansteigen. In einigen Fällen haben die Bodenpreise innerhalb von fünf Jahren um 500 % zugenommen. Gegenwärtig leben 10 % der Bevölkerung von Nairobi in Dagoretti.

7. Wohnungen, die vom Arbeitgeber zur Verfügung gestellt werden

In den Häusern der Oberschicht war es üblich, dem «Dienstpersonal» Wohnraum auf dem eigene Grundstück zur Verfügung zu stellen, und diese Gewohnheit haben auch einige private Firmen übernommen. Ungefähr 10 % der Bevölkerung der unteren Einkommensschicht ist in Wohnungen untergebracht, die von den Arbeitgebern zur Verfügung gestellt werden; aber diese Kategorie von Bewohnern ist ziemlich stabil. Viele Bedienstete sind alteingesessene Bewohner von Nairobi. Und da immer weniger Stadtbewohner es sich leisten können, Dienstpersonal zu halten, ist es höchst unwahrscheinlich, dass diese Art der Beschäftigung und der Behausung zunehmen wird.

*

Heute ist die wirtschaftliche Mobilität in Nairobi minim, andererseits unterliegt die Stadt einem rapiden Wachstum, besonders auf der Ebene der sehr niederen Einkommensschichten.

↓ fig. 16   Popular owner-occupied apartments on small lots.

↓ fig. 17   A complex of owner-occupied apartments with a *shamba*; that is, land that can be used for cultivation.

← fig. 18
Popular owner-occupied apartments in Dagoretti (in the village of Kawangwar

↓ fig. 19 Apartments provided by the employer. Detail: middle-class house with neighboring housing for servants. Upper Nairobi.

Unter diesen Umständen gilt es, sämtliche heute bestehenden Ressourcen des Wohnbaus auszunützen. Vor allem aber stellen die verschiedenen Wohnbausysteme mit ihrem komplexen Netz von verantwortlichen Entscheidungsträgern eine wichtige Voraussetzung dar, um vor allem den verschiedenen Sektoren der unteren Einkommensklasse Wohnraum zu erschliessen.

Nur wenn es gelingt, jedes dieser Wohnbausysteme im Hinblick auf seine positiven Aspekte, seine Möglichkeiten und Mängel abzuschätzen, ist es möglich, die Wohnbedürfnisse der Bewohner realistisch zu erfassen und mögliche Strategien zu entwerfen — in Nairobi und auch anderswo.

Uebersetzung: S. v. M.

* Der vorliegende Aufsatz ist die gekürzte Fassung einer Arbeit, die 1971—1972 in der School of Architecture and Planning des Massachusetts Institute of Technology (MIT) zusammengestellt wurde. Es liegen ihr zwei Studienaufenthalte in Nairobi zugrunde. Aufgrund der vorliegenden Analyse wurde die Arbeitsgruppe vom Gemeinderat von Nairobi eingeladen, ein Wohnbauprojekt für diese Stadt auszuarbeiten.

Eine umfassendere Dokumentation der Analyse und des Projekts wird in einer demnächst erscheinenden Nummer von Ekistics (Athen) erscheinen.

Bibliographie
Charles Abrams, *Housing in the Modern World*, Faber and Faber, London, 1964.
David Etherton, u. a., *Mathare Valley — Report*, Nairobi Housing Research and Development Unit, Nairobi, 1971.
Ford Foundation Urbanization Study, New York, 1973.
William Grindley und Robert Merril, «Survey of Sites and Services», International Bank for Reconstruction and Development (Weltbank), Section Working Paper (vervielfältigtes Ms.), Washington, D. C., 1972.
Kenya Government, *Statistical Abstracts and Population Census*, Nairobi, 1962, 1968, 1969 und 1972.
Philip M. Hauser und Leo F. Schnore, *The Study of Urbanization*, John Wiley, New York, 1967.
John Harris, «Some Thoughts on Housing Policy for Nairobi», MIT-Research-Paper (vervielfältigtes Ms.), Cambridge, Mass., 1970.
Nairobi Urban Study Group, *Working Papers on Nairobi*, Nairobi City Council, 1971—1972.
S. H. Ominde, *Land and Population Movements in Kenya*, Heinemann-Books, 1968.

John F. C. Turner und Robert Fichter, *Freedom to Build*, McMillan, New York, 1972.
E. A. K. Senkubuge, *Dagoretti-Study*, University of Nairobi, Nairobi (Diss.), 1971.
Thomas Weisner, «One Family, Two Households. A Rural-Urban Network» (vervielfältigtes Ms.), Nairobi, 1969.

↑ fig. 20 Typical middle-class residence in Nairobi. The housing for service personnel is located at the back of the lot.

6. Popular Ownership (Dagoretti)

Immediately following Kenya's independence, all the village dwellers of Dagoretti, a suburban zone of Nairobi, were granted ownership of the land they had settled. In addition, the region was declared to be outside of the city's jurisdiction—a political redress for a population group that had suffered most in the period immediately before the declaration of independence. The lots in these villages are too small to provide the residents, most of whom are unemployed, with agriculture adequate to earn a livelihood. For that reason, many have built additions to their houses, the rent from which provides them with a modest income, or they have sold their properties to nonresident housing speculators, who, as we have seen, operate extremely quickly and successfully. Forty percent of the residents receive very low income; some even live entirely outside the money economy. Dagoretti is considered a "hypertrophied" village, a rural region even though it lies within the city limits of Nairobi and even though many of its residents regard it as temporary housing that enables them to work in the city while setting aside enough money to return home later. Numerous residents survive only thanks to agricultural use of the surrounding land, which ensures them the food necessary for life; occasional work enables them to pay school fees and taxes. But the land speculation in the rapidly growing villages of housing blocks in the immediate surroundings of the center of Nairobi contributes greatly to the rapid increase in room rents. In several cases, the land prices have increased by 500 percent within five years. Currently, 10 percent of the population of Nairobi lives in in Dagoretti.

7. Employer-Provided Housing

In the homes of the upper classes, it was common to make living space on the property available to "service personnel," and some private companies have also adopted this habit. Approximately 10 percent of the population of the lower-income sector is housed in apartments provided by employers, but this category of residents is rather stable. Many servants are long-established residents of Nairobi. And because fewer and fewer city dwellers can afford to keep servants, it is highly improbable that this kind of employment and housing will increase.

Today, economic mobility in Nairobi is minimal; on the other hand, the city is undergoing rapid growth, especially in the lower-income sectors. Under such conditions, it is necessary to exploit all existing resources for housing construction. Above all, however, the various housing systems, with their complex network of responsible decision-makers, represent an important precondition for providing living space, especially for the various sectors of the lower-income class.

Only if each of these housing systems can be judged with an eye to its positive aspects, its possibilities, and its shortcomings can the housing needs of the residents be assessed realistically and possible design strategies proposed—in Nairobi and also elsewhere.

* The present essay is an abridged version of work compiled in 1971–72 at the School of Architecture and Planning of the Massachusetts Institute of Technology (MIT). It is based on two study trips to Nairobi. On the basis of the present analysis, the study group of the Nairobi City Council was invited to work out a housing construction project for that city. A more detailed documentation of this analysis and project will be published in an upcoming issue of *Ekistics* (Athens).

BIBLIOGRAPHY

Charles Abrams. *Housing in the Modern World*. London: Faber and Faber, 1964.

David Etherton et al. *Mathare Valley*. Report, Nairobi Housing Research and Development Unit. Nairobi, 1971.

Ford Foundation Urbanization Study. New York, 1973.

William Grindley and Robert Merrill. "Survey of Sites and Services." International Bank for Reconstruction and Development, Section Working Paper, Washington, DC, 1972.

Kenya Government. *Statistical Abstracts and Population Census*. Nairobi, 1962, 1968, 1969, and 1972.

Philip M. Hauser and Leo F. Schnore. *The Study of Urbanization*. New York: John Wiley, 1967.

John Harris. "Some Thoughts on Housing Policy for Nairobi" (mimeographed MS). Research paper, MIT, Cambridge, MA, 1970.

Nairobi Urban Study Group. *Working Papers on Nairobi*. Nairobi City Council, 1971–72.

S.H. Ominde. *Land and Population Movements in Kenya*. London: Heinemann Books, 1968.

John F.C. Turner and Robert Fichter. *Freedom to Build*. New York: Macmillan, 1972.

A.K. Senkubuge. "Dagoretti Study." Thesis. University of Nairobi. Nairobi, 1971.

Thomas Weisner. "One Family, Two Households: A Rural-Urban Network" (mimeographed MS). Nairobi, 1969.

An Architecture of Resistance: Slums in Asia

Author:
Jin-Bak Pyun

Source:
archithese, 9 (1974): 39–44

Translated by:
Brett Petzer

Architecture can become a means of controlling the social environment, but it can also be an effective tool for the liberation of man and community. To fulfill its liberating mission, it must strongly support and make manifest the values of humanity. As a cultural support system, it is not and should not be passive and negative but become active and dynamic. The architecture of slums represents the real significance of architecture in a society where people are increasingly oppressed.

This brief account of the issue of slums in the urban centers of South Asia and the Far East is based on a literature review and on the author's experience in Seoul, the capital of South Korea. Despite the lack of direct observation of the other territories concerned, the problem in the various countries is sufficiently homogeneous to allow for a degree of generalization. This article argues that the slum gives rise to and shapes a dynamic culture, and it analyzes the attitude of the authorities toward this mass phenomenon.

As we shall see, the real problem of the slum is not its alleged state of social disorganization or juvenile delinquency but the antipathy of "high culture" to this "popular culture."[1]

Among authorities, the policy of clearing slums and displacing their residents and then imposing a new environment on these people is commonplace, even though it produces an absurd result in the form of empty architecture. In reality, architecture must be the outcome of a popular process of adaptation to the sociophysical environment. If we allow that urban planning and state oversight of housing are among the necessary evils of our society, official intervention should be limited to efforts to understand the sociospatial environment and the provision of an effective environment to inhabitants.[2] This is the only possible alternative to initiatives that are as misguided as they are unsympathetic.

Slum Culture

The slum is a unique sociospatial environment that constitutes a culture. Living in a slum requires that one adapt to this milieu.

Slum culture is both a way of life for disadvantaged city dwellers and a mechanism for adaptation to the urban condition. Because the inhabitants of this environment are rural and poor immigrants who are unskilled or semiskilled, the productivity of squatters is very low in the slum's initial phase. They are

Jin-Bak Pyun

Une architecture de résistance: Les bidonvilles asiatiques

L'architecture peut devenir un moyen de contrôler le milieu social, mais elle peut être aussi un outil efficace de la libération de l'homme et de la collectivité. Pour remplir sa mission libératrice, elle doit soutenir et manifester vivement les valeurs d'humanité. Comme système de soutien culturel, elle n'est pas et ne doit pas être passive ni négative, mais devenir active et dynamique. L'architecture des bidonvilles représente cette juste valeur d'architecture dans la société où l'homme est de plus en plus oppressé.

Ce bref exposé du problème des bidonvilles dans les centres urbains de l'Asie méridionale et de l'Extrême-Orient se fonde sur une étude bibliographique et sur l'expérience de l'auteur dans le cas de Séoul, capital de la Corée du Sud. Malgré le manque d'observation directe des autres territoires concernés, la problématique dans les divers pays est assez homogène pour qu'une certaine généralisation soit possible. L'article présente le bidonville comme formant une culture dynamique et se propose d'analyser l'attitude des autorités vis à vis de ce phénomène de masse.

Comme nous le verrons, le vrai problème du bidonville n'est pas son état prétendu de désorganisation sociale ni la délinquence juvé-

Die asiatischen Bidonvilles: eine Architektur des Widerstandes

Architektur kann ein Mittel der Kontrolle des sozialen Milieus durch die Bürokratie sein, sie kann aber auch als wirksames Mittel der Befreiung des Menschen und der Gemeinschaft dienen. Aber sie kann ihre befreiende Funktion nur ausüben, wenn sie humane Werte unterstützt und zum Ausdruck bringt, und wenn sie sich diesen Werten gegenüber nicht passiv und negativ, sondern aktiv und dynamisch verhält. Die Architektur der Bidonvilles entspricht diesem Anspruch mehr als jede andere moderne Siedlungsform.

Der vorliegende Aufsatz zum Problem der Bidonvilles in den städtischen Ballungszentren Asiens und des Fernen Ostens stützt sich hauptsächlich auf die Erfahrungen des Verfassers in Söul, der Hauptstadt Südkoreas. Der Aufsatz schildert die Bidonvilles als dynamisches soziales Milieu und versucht, das Verhalten der staatlichen Instanzen gegenüber diesem Massenphänomen zu analysieren. Dabei zeigt es sich, dass das wirkliche Problem der Bidonvilles nicht in seinem vermeintlichen Mangel an sozialer Ordnung oder gar in der Jugendkriminalität liegt, sondern in der Skepsis und Antipathie der Elite gegenüber dieser «volkstümlichen» Kultur und Lebensform. Im allgemeinen beschränken sich die staatlichen Planungsinstanzen darauf, diese Elendsquartiere einzureissen, die Bevölkerung zu dislozieren und ihr eine neue, fremde Umwelt aufzuzwingen. In Wirklichkeit aber sollte die Architektur nicht Resultat einer bürokratischen Massnahme sein, sondern vielmehr Resultat eines von den Bewohnern selbst vollzogenen Prozesses der Adaptation an das veränderte sozioökonomische Milieu. Ueberall dort, wo Stadtplanung und Wohnbauförderung unumgänglich sind, sollten sich die behördlichen Eingriffe darauf beschränken, den Bewohnern eine Umwelt bereitzustellen, die ihren gesellschaftlichen und räumlichen Gewohnheiten entspricht.

nile, mais plutôt l'antipathie de la «haute culture» face à cette «culture populaire»[1]. La politique de destruction des taudis et de déplacement de la population ainsi que l'imposition d'un environnement étranger, attitudes courantes des autorités, ne produit qu'un non-sens: il en découle une architecture vide. En réalité, l'architecture doit résulter d'un processus populaire d'adaptation au milieu socio-physique. Si la planification urbaine et le contrôle de l'habitation sont l'un des maux nécessaires de notre société, l'intervention officielle devrait se limiter à comprendre le milieu socio-spatial et à fournir à l'habitant un environnement effectif[2]. Telle est la seule alternative possible à l'égard d'initiatives aussi erronées qu'antipathiques.

Culture de bidonville

Le bidonville est un milieu socio-spatial propre qui constitue une culture. Habiter le bidonville signifie donc s'adapter à ce milieu.

La culture de bidonville constitue à la fois un mode de vie pour les citadins défavorisés et un mécanisme d'adaptation à la condition urbaine. Etant donné que ce milieu est habité par des immigrants ruraux et pauvres, non spécialisés ou semi-spécialisés, la productivité des squatters est très faible dans la phase initiale du bidonville; ils sont le plus souvent en chômage ou sous-employés. Comme milieu adapté à la condition marginale, un mode de vie et des normes originales peuvent s'y développer par la suite. Dans ces conditions, le bidonville peut former une culture de pauvreté dans le sens d'Oscar Lewis[3], mais ce n'est pas sa caractéristique véritable, car la culture de bidonville se distingue par la mobilité sociale «vers le haut» et le sens de la communauté, que la culture de pauvreté ne connaît pas.

On observe en général trois types d'établissement urbain des pauvres: slum, taudis bâti par le gouvernement, bidonville ou colonie de squatters[4]. Le slum s'implante dans un quartier dévalorisé du centre-ville et appartient généralement à la culture de pauvreté où la mobilité «vers le haut» s'avère très limitée. Le taudis bâti par le gouvernement comprend les projets d'habitation, statiques et vite dépréciés, qui ont une haute probabilité de devenir bientôt des taudis de désespoir. Le bidonville ou la colonie de squatters, sous-produit du «phénomène de capitale», s'installe soit près du centre-ville soit à la périphérie où se trouvent diverses sources d'emplois non spécialisés ou semi-spécialisés.

La mobilité socio-économique «vers le haut» constitue l'une des caractéristiques fondamentales de la culture de bidonville. Dans ce milieu, le besoin d'équipements communautaires est généralement ressenti plus fortement que celui du logement fini, au point d'être prioritaire. Cela implique non seulement l'aspiration à la sécurité dans la possession du terrain dont les squatters se sont emparés illégalement, mais aussi l'intention de participer à la vie politique et de «monter» vers la classe moyenne ou plus haut encore. L'investissement à la fois psychologique et matériel considérable que les pauvres de Séoul ont effectué en est le meilleur exemple. Dans une économie très restreinte où les fonds publics sont fort limités, l'accès à une institution d'éducation supérieure coûte trop cher pour que la famille pauvre puisse en supporter la charge. (Pour cette raison, les businessmen considèrent que les établissements d'instructions privés sont l'une des entreprises les plus rentables.) La volonté de s'élever dans la hiérarchie sociale incite ceux qui ne peuvent y parvenir eux-mêmes à s'endetter leur vie durant pour permettre à leurs enfants d'étudier et de réussir à leur place.

L'interaction dynamique sociale est une autre caractéristique fondamentale du milieu des squatters. La cause réside surtout dans la nécessité de l'auto-défense collective vis à vis de l'antipathie des autorités. Le niveau de l'organisation sociale des squatters est beaucoup plus élevé que celui des classes sociales plus hautes. Les diverses activités de l'habitation, comme l'auto-construction et l'entraide mutuelle, engendrent l'interaction sociale la plus intense.

Enfin, le bidonville forme une société autonome, mais d'une façon différente de ce qu'on croit généralement en pensant à sa pauvreté. C'est plutôt dans les taudis du gouvernement que l'indépendance diminue. Au départ déjà, le bidonville comme expression du droit d'habiter n'attend rien d'une société incapable de la protéger. Comme la sécurité socio-économique des squatters n'est pas garantie, même après l'occupation illégale du terrain et la construction de la première boîte en bidon et en carton, ils doivent se débrouiller: chercher un emploi (plutôt que d'attendre longtemps les soins méprisants des autorités) et agrandir leur logement petit à petit. L'auto-construction se développe écologiquement et les squatters organisent souvent eux-mêmes les services publics essentiels. La culture de bidonville, fondée sur cet esprit d'autonomie, est en effet le bien le plus précieux dans une économie de subsistance. En réalité, il ne faut pas non plus sous-estimer la capacité d'épargne des squatters. Si l'on tient compte du nombre des squatters et de leur ténacité, cette épargne constitue un potentiel financier considérable dans une économie restreinte. Le bidonville n'est donc pas un taudis stagnant et désespéré, mais un taudis montant, une société d'espoir.

Etant donné le nombre considérable des squatters et le dynamisme de la culture de bidonville, il est fort probable que cette classe sociale pourra devenir plus tard la classe moyenne majoritaire. Il n'est même pas exagéré de dire que l'Asie urbaine est formée par la masse des familles habitant de telles colonies. Dans l'Inde de 1970, on considérait qu'environ 25 % de la population urbaine des villes comme Calcutta, Bombay et Dehli vivaient dans un bidonville; à Formose, en 1966, environ 25 %; à Karachi, en 1968, 27 %; à Manille, la même année, 1,100,000 habitants, soit 35 %; à Séoul, en 1970, une population de 1,370,000 âmes, soit 30 % [5]. Cette population urbaine constitue donc bel et bien une potentialité énorme comme nouvelle classe sociale et nouvelle force politique; elle remplira probablement le vide qui existe entre l'actuelle classe dirigeante, formée d'élites urbaines, et la masse des paysans. Il est à noter que beaucoup de jeunes fonctionnaires en Corée ont des parents qui étaient squatters dans la période initiale du bidonville.

Haute culture contre culture populaire

> "There were distinctions, profound distinctions, between high culture (accessible to the elite) and popular culture (accessible to all)."
> Norman Birnbaum, in *The crisis of industrial society*.

L'autorité publique, avec son élite technocratique et son idéologie de la planification moderne, intervient dans les espaces collectifs des squatters au nom du bien-être public, de la rentabilité du sol ou encore du développement économique. C'est là que s'établit la problématique de la haute culture face à la culture populaire. Premièrement, le fossé culturel ne permet pas facilement la communication entre les deux conceptions. L'idéologie imposée d'en haut n'étant pas accessible à la plus grande partie de la population, aucune espérance de participation n'est possible. Ensuite, les normes, les goûts, les standards exprimés par les technocrates de l'élite ne reflètent que le milieu social d'où ils proviennent. Enfin, la culture parachutée dans le milieu architectural des squatters s'inspire très souvent de l'image des villes occidentales, ce qui constitue un écart de plus entre la culture traditionnelle et la culture imposée.

Lorsque j'ai quitté Séoul en 1968, je n'avais pas encore une vue claire de la vie en appar-

↑ fig. 1   Seoul 1971: Architecture that has been parachuted into a working-class neighborhood.

tement. C'était pour moi une espèce de mode étrangère: il n'y avait d'ailleurs qu'un petit nombre de ces appartements en Corée. Lorsque je suis retourné à Séoul en 1971, la capitale avait été complètement transformée. Les bidonvilles qui couvraient les collines de Séoul étaient remplacés par de hauts immeubles d'appartements. Cette grande production de logements est assez surprenante au premier coup d'œil. Mais cette opération de symbiose entre les pouvoirs publics et le secteur privé n'a pas résolu véritablement le problème des logements, si l'on tient compte de la capacité économique des squatters à l'égard de ce nouvel habitat de standard minimum et de la mauvaise qualité de l'environnement. En effet, plusieurs colonies de bidonvilles, cette fois-ci conçues par le gouvernement, ont été installées en banlieue de Séoul pour des milliers de familles relogées. Une barrière physique, nommée «green belt», a été plantée entre le centre-ville et ces bidonvilles «officiels». Les familles relogées en banlieue souffrent de devoir s'adapter une fois encore à une marginalité pire que la précédente, parce que l'accès à l'emploi et les équipements communautaires sont éloignés et qu'il est impossible de rétablir le dynamisme social dans le nouvel habitat. C'est la version coréenne de la «cité-jardin» de Howard et de la rénovation urbaine de type nord-américain, que Charles Abrams a critiqué il y a longtemps déjà.

Parmi les divers problèmes, celui de la densité revêt une importance particulière, car non seulement elle est un outil de planification publique, mais elle détermine largement le dynamisme socio-économique. Ce problème n'est pas encore résolu au point de constituer un outil effectif de planification. C'est un concept absurde, parce que non objectif, comme René Dubos l'a montré [6]. La densité est étroitement associée au mode de vie d'un milieu culturel. Lorsqu'on impose une limite de densité, on doit supporter le changement brusque qu'elle entraîne dans le milieu. Le cas de Puerto Rico montre que la population peut évoluer de 600 ans en 20 ans; en Nouvelle-Guinée, elle a même sauté plus de 2000 ans [7]. C'est à la communauté seule de régler elle-même sa propre densité et de procéder à sa propre animation.

L'écart fondamental entre les aspirations et ce qui est fourni découle du fait que le problème du logement est traduit uniquement en termes de manque de logements. Mais ce manque n'est qu'un aspect surestimé d'un ensemble plus vaste, qui est le fait d'*habiter*, lié de façon cohérente au milieu socio-économique. La définition de l'ONU (habitation comme «milieu habité») le qualifie exactement: cela signifie que le logement est un élement d'appui du dévoloppement socio-économique de chaque famille et de chaque communauté. John Turner distingue le *produit* (nom) et le *processus* (verbe) d'habitation [8]: pour lui, le logement s'associe à diverses activités qui relèvent de l'habiter plutôt que du produit final; il s'agit donc d'un processus. En effet, même le logement produit dans le milieu pauvre n'est jamais perçu d'abord comme un lieu de confort, mais comme un lieu permettant l'adaptation de la famille à ses divers besoins socio-économiques.

En réalité, lorsque j'ai visité cette nouvelle forme d'habitat collectif, une transformation était en train de s'effectuer. Des épiciers, des cordonniers, des tailleurs, etc., avaient déjà commencé à s'installer dans un couloir obscur des étages supérieurs et devant l'entrée, tandis que de petits manufacturiers occupaient des appartements; les balcons étaient devenus des extensions de la cuisine et servaient de buanderie; les blocs de charbon s'empilaient dans les corridors. Le milieu architectural issu de ces conditions extrêmes n'avait plus rien à faire avec l'image imposée par le designer. J'étais en présence de deux conceptions architecturales antagonistes: une architecture de résistance, et même de révolte, s'opposait à une architecture de contrôle.

Il est bien clair qu'une intervention hors contexte et paternaliste ne pourra jamais intégrer les squatters à la vie urbaine globale. Tout au plus entraînera-t-elle la ségrégation sociale, qui produit des conflits violents. L'élimination de certaines possibilités socio-économiques, tels que l'engagement communautaire et la prospérité commerciale, est elle aussi très grave. Lorsque les petits commerces sont relogés, il est évident qu'ils commencent par perdre leur clientèle et qu'il leur est difficile de redémarrer. Le relogement implique une discrimination politique, parce qu'elle détruit la vie associée des personnes déplacées. C'est bien l'architecture et la planification qui sont devenues les outils les plus efficaces pour contrôler le milieu des squatters. La question de la morale de l'architecture et de l'architecte se pose donc sérieusement.

most often unemployed or underemployed. In this environment oriented to a marginal position in society, new norms and ways of living may then start to develop. Under these conditions, the slum may form what Oscar Lewis[3] refers to as a "culture of poverty," but this is not a defining quality: slum culture is distinguished by upward social mobility and a sense of community, which are absent from cultures of poverty.

There are generally three types of urban settlements that house the poor: ghettos, government-built tenement neighborhoods, and shantytowns or squatter settlements.[4] Ghettos form in run-down inner-city neighborhoods and generally belong to the culture of poverty, where upward mobility is very limited. Government-built tenement neighborhoods include housing projects that rapidly deteriorate after handover because they are "static" and thus likely to become slums of desperation. The shantytown or squatter settlement, a by-product of the "phenomenon of capital," arises either close to the city center or on the urban periphery, where various sources of unskilled or semiskilled employment can be found.

Upward socioeconomic mobility is one of the fundamental characteristics of slum culture. In this environment, residents' need for community facilities outweighs their need for finished housing, sometimes so much so that the former becomes top priority. This not only suggests that residents aspire to security of tenure over the land they have illegally appropriated but that they intend to participate in political life and raise themselves to middle-class status or higher.

The best example of this is the extent to which Seoul's poor invest in this aim, both psychologically and materially. In a very restricted economy where public funds are severely limited, access to institutions of higher education is beyond the financial reach of low-income families (this is why businesspeople consider private education to be among the most profitable of commercial ventures). A desire to move up in the social hierarchy encourages those who will never do so themselves to take on lifelong debt so that their children can study and succeed in their stead.

Dynamic social interaction is another fundamental characteristic of the squatter environment. This is mainly due to the need for collective self-defense against official animosity. Squatters have a much greater level of social organization than higher social classes. The many and varied activities in the settlement, such as self-building and mutual aid, produce the most intense social interaction.

Ultimately the slum forms an autonomous society, but in a way that differs from the general view on poverty. A reduction in independence is more often found in government tenements. The slum, as an expression of the right to shelter, is premised from the outset on the expectation that no help or protection will be forthcoming from the rest of society. Since the socioeconomic security of the squatters is not secure, even after illegal occupation of the land and the construction of the first cardboard-and-container shanty, the squatters must make do. They seek jobs (instead of a lengthy wait for grudging assistance from the authorities) and gradually add to their dwellings. Self-construction develops organically, and squatters often organize essential public services themselves. Slum culture, based on this spirit of self-reliance, is the most valuable asset in a subsistence economy. In reality, squatters' capacity to save money should not be underestimated either. Considering their numbers and their self-discipline, these savings represent a considerable financial resource in a small economy. Accordingly, the slum is not a stagnant and desperate shantytown but a rising one—a society built on hope.

Given the considerable number of squatters and the dynamism of slum culture, it is very likely that this social class may later come to constitute the majority of the middle class. It is no exaggeration to say that urban Asia consists of families living in such settlements. In India in 1970, about 25 percent of the urban population of cities such as Calcutta, Bombay, and Delhi were considered to live in a slum; in Formosa [Taiwan] in 1966, about 25 percent; in Karachi in 1968, 27 percent; in Manila in the same year, 1.1 million inhabitants, or 35 percent; in Seoul in 1970, a population of 1,370,000, or 30 percent.[5] This urban population therefore has enormous potential as a new social class and a new political force; it will probably fill the gap between the present ruling class of urban elites and the mass of peasants. In this regard it is worth noting that many young civil servants in Korea have parents who were squatters in the early slum period.

High Culture versus Popular Culture

> "There were distinctions, profound distinctions, between high culture (accessible to the elite) and popular culture (accessible to all)."
> Norman Birnbaum, in *The Crisis of Industrial Society*

Public authorities, with their technocratic elitism and ideology of modern planning, make interventions in squatters' collective spaces in the name of public welfare, land values, or economic development. This is where the problem of high culture versus popular culture emerges. First, the cultural gap prevents easy communication between the two perspectives. Since a majority of the population has no access to the ideology imposed from above, meaningful participation is impossible. Second, the norms, tastes, and standards expressed by elite technocrats solely reflect their own social background. Finally, the culture that is air-dropped into the squatters' architectural environment is very often in the image of Western cities, which constitutes another gap between traditional and imposed culture.

When I left Seoul in 1968, I still did not have a clear understanding of apartment living. To me, it was a kind of foreign trend, and there were only a few of these apartments in Korea. When I returned to Seoul in 1971, the capital had been completely transformed. The slums that covered the hills of Seoul had been replaced by high-rise apartment buildings. This large-scale production of housing is quite surprising at first glance. But the symbiosis between the public authorities and the private sector did not really solve the housing problem, if one considers the squatters' financial means to pay for these minimum-standard dwellings and the poor quality of these neighborhoods. Indeed, several slum settlements, this time designed by the government, have been created on the outskirts of Seoul for thousands of rehoused families. A physical barrier, called a "green belt," has been planted between the city center and these "official" slums. Families relocated to the suburbs face a second adaptation, this time to a condition even more marginal than before, because restoring social dynamism in the new habitat is impossible and because of the longer distances they must travel to access jobs and community facilities. This is the Korean version of Howard's "garden cities" and North American-style urban renewal, which Charles Abrams criticized so long ago.

Among these diverse problems, density is particularly important, since it is not only a tool for public planning but a determinant of socioeconomic dynamism. This problem has not yet been sufficiently resolved to serve as an effective planning tool. As a concept, it is absurd in its lack of objectivity, as René Dubos has shown.[6] Density is closely linked to the way of life found within a cultural environment. When a limit on density is imposed, inhabitants must contend with the abrupt change it produces in the environment. The case of Puerto Rico shows that six hundred years of population shifts can repeat themselves in twenty years; in New Guinea, the same period has produced change equivalent to the past two thousand.[7] It is up to the community alone to regulate its own density and begin with its own facilitation process.

The fundamental discrepancy between community aspirations and what is eventually provided stems from the fact that the housing problem is articulated in terms of a lack of housing alone. However, this need is but one overemphasized aspect of a much larger whole; namely, the fact of *inhabiting* the city in a way that coheres with the socioeconomic environment. The UN definition (which refers to housing as the "inhabited environment") captures this precisely: housing is one supporting element in the socioeconomic development of each family and community. John Turner distinguishes between the *product* (noun) and *process* (verb) of housing.[8] For him, housing is associated with various activities that make up the act of inhabiting rather than the final product; it is, therefore, a process. Indeed, even the housing produced in low-income environments is never perceived primarily as a place of comfort but as a place that allows the family to adapt to its various socioeconomic needs.

In fact, when I visited this new form of collective housing, a transformation was taking

↓ fig. 2   In this country, urbanization often means entry into an aggregate of rural folklore rather than a truly urban way of life.

↓ fig. 4   Official architecture is the only horizon now open to those who are still intrepid enough to build their house.

↓ fig. 5   The third generation. Nature, already invaded by squatters, will soon disappear under slum settlements.

←fig. 3   The *jangdok* (marinade jars) have pride of place in every Korean family home. But where should they be kept? Official architecture failed to anticipate this need, but users have found a solution.

Dans les bidonvilles, la qualité de l'environnement s'affirme à tous points de vue supérieure à celle des logements à mode de vie imposé. La surface habitable est généralement assez vaste pour accueillir une parenté étendue et souvent même pour permettre de louer une pièce. Elle permet également une adaptation spatiale aisée à diverses économiques, comme le petit commerce ou la manufacture. En outre, les espaces publics expriment la structure sociale et religieuse. Dans un groupe rigidement soumis à un système socio-religieux, cette expression spatiale est particulièrement claire, comme l'étude de Rory Fonseca l'a démontré[9]. Une telle compatibilité socio-spatiale concrète peut former la clef du nouvel aménagement. Ap-

↑ fig. 6   Here, squatting makes its assault on official architectural standards.

↑ fig. 7   Finding a foothold for one's business in the street is a question of survival.

proche significative, car elle ne bloque pas la continuité historique et culturelle et donc n'implique aucun péril d'adaptation dans la période transitoire. Fonseca, décrivant le cas du Vieux-Delhi, observe que «not only is its structure meaningful but provides valuable clues to the resolution of planning, housing, and related community development problems arising from the continuing rapid rate of urbanization».[10]

L'écart est trop large entre les designers et les usagers, entre les besoins représentés par l'architecture officielle et ceux des occupants, entre ceux qui dirigent et ceux qui sont dirigés, en d'autres termes entre la haute culture et la culture populaire. Dans ce contexte, la démocratisation de la planification urbaine et de l'architecture est possible. D'où la nécessité d'un rapprochement entre la haute culture et la culture populaire.

Vers la démocratie de la culture urbaine

> «Ce qui est le plus nécessaire, c'est la manifestation publique de cette évidence afin de provoquer une réaction en chaîne d'amélioration de ces peuplements à travers le monde. Il est temps d'en finir avec les attitudes et les approches négatives et improductives vis à vis du problème des taudis et des zones de peuplement non règlementées.»
> O.N.U.

Les colonies de bidonvilles doivent être intégrées à la ville toute entière avec l'ensemble de leurs réseaux socio-spatiaux. L'objectif fondamental d'une collectivité démocratique suppose la distribution démocratique des biens matériels et la communication réciproque entre les divers groupes sociaux, qui n'est ni la négociation inégale ni l'ordre imposé. C'est uniquement dans ces conditions que le milieu architectural comme représentation d'une culture globale équilibrée devient lui-même démocratique et qu'une morale architecturale s'établit.

L'intégration des squatters à la collectivité urbaine est le fondement de leur participation à la vie politique et aux divers processus d'aménagement, de planification, de design et de production. Cette participation constitue un outil important non seulement dans le processus de prise de décision, mais aussi en tant que processus d'information et d'apprentissage. Pour une meilleure participation, le gouvernement doit disposer de toutes les informations concernant l'avenir des squatters: ceci est un premier pas dans la participation. En même temps, il faut démystifier les langages de haute culture, surtout le langage technocratique. Il faut aussi assurer légalement le processus de participation: il y a d'innombrables normes touchant le produit architectural, fondées sur le standard minimum, mais la notion de standard minimum n'a pas été étendue aux processus d'information et de décision. Cette remise en cause politique de l'acte architectural serait un pas remarquable vers une démocratie de la culture urbaine.

Par manque de formation, donc par défaut d'une certaine capacité d'élaborer des projets de développement, les squatters font appel à une aide extérieure. Le type de relation des travailleurs sociaux avec les squatters doit être également adopté par les architectes. Au-delà du paternalisme, l'architecte peut jouer un rôle décisif pour le développement socio-économique des squatters. C'est de tels architectes que les pays en voie de développement ont besoin. Cela implique évidemment une orientation nouvelle dans l'éducation des jeunes architectes, comme leur confrère égyptien Hassan Fathy l'espère intensément[11].

La culture urbaine des pays de l'Asie du Sud ne s'affirmera que lorsqu'elle aura intégré celle des bidonvilles.

---

[1] A propos de la distinction entre la haute culture et la culture populaire, voir p. ex. Norman Birnbaum, *The crisis of industrial society*, Oxford 1969.
[2] Le cadre du concept, environnement effectif, se réfère à Herbert J. Gans, *People and plans: essays on urban problems and solutions*, New York 1968.
[3] Cf. Oscar Lewis, *La vida: a Puerto Rican family in the culture of poverty*, New York 1966.
[4] A propos de la typologie des slums urbains, voir aussi Alejandro Portes, «The urban slum in Chile: types and correlates», in *Land Economics*, Vol. XLVII, No. 4, novembre 1971, pp. 235—248.
[5] Source des statistiques: ONU, *Amélioration des taudis et des zones de peuplement non réglementées*, New York 1971.
[6] René Dubos, «The perils of adaptation», in *Arts of the environment*, New York 1972, pp. 32—39.
[7] Cf. *Ekistics*, Vol. 32, No 191, octobre 1971, p. 274.
[8] Cf. John F. C. Turner, «Housing as a verbe», in *Freedom to build*, New York 1972.
[9] Voir Rory Fonseca, «The walled city of Old Delhi», in *Shelter and society*, New York 1969.
[10] Rory Fonseca, *op. cit.*, p. 106.
[11] Cf. Hassan Fathy, *Architecture for the poor*, Chicago 1973.

place. Grocers, shoemakers, tailors, and others had already begun setting up shop in a dark hallway on the upper floors and in front of the entrance. Meanwhile, small-scale manufacturers were operating out of apartments. Kitchens extended onto balconies to make space for laundering. Coal was heaped up in the corridors. The architectural environment produced by these extreme conditions had completely parted ways with the image imposed by the designer. I was in the presence of two antagonistic conceptions of architecture: an architecture of resistance, even revolt, was opposed to one of control.

Clearly, any intervention grounded in paternalism and oblivious to context could not possibly integrate squatters into global urban life. At most, such efforts will lead to social segregation, which will, in turn, produce violent conflict. The elimination of certain socioeconomic opportunities, such as community engagement and commercial prosperity, also has a severe impact. When small businesses are relocated, they necessarily lose their customer base and find it difficult to resume trading. Relocation also involves political discrimination, because it destroys displaced persons' networks and community life. Architecture and planning have thus become the most effective of the tools used to control the world of the squatter settlement. For this reason, the question of architecture's morality, and of architects' morality, is a weighty one.

In the slums, the quality of the environment is, in every respect, better than in housing in which a particular way of living has been imposed. The habitable area is generally large enough to accommodate the extended family; sometimes, it even allows for the rental of a room. It further supports straightforward adaptation to the spatial needs of various economic activities, such as small-scale trading or manufacturing. In addition, the public spaces express the slum's social and religious structure. Among groups subject to a rigid socioreligious system, this spatial expression is particularly clear, as Rory Fonseca's study[9] has shown. This concrete compatibility between the social and the spatial could offer the key to the new spatial planning. Significantly, this approach does not obstruct historical and cultural continuity and so avoids all the risks of adaptation in the transitional period. As Fonseca observes in a description of Old Delhi, "not only is its structure meaningful, but [it] provides valuable clues to the resolution of planning, housing, and related community development problems arising from the continuing rapid rate of urbanization."[10]

There is too wide a gap between designers and users, between the needs that official architecture represents and the needs of the occupants, between those who direct and those who are directed—that is, between high culture and popular culture. In this context, the democratization of urban planning and architecture is possible. Hence the need for a rapprochement between high culture and popular culture.

Toward a Democracy of Urban Culture

> "What is most needed is for this evidence to be publicly displayed to provoke a chain reaction of improvements in these settlements all around the world. It is time to put an end to negative and unproductive attitudes and approaches to the problem of slums and unregulated settlements."
> UN

Slum settlements must be integrated, with all of their sociospatial networks, into the city as a whole. The fundamental objective of a democratic community is premised on the democratic distribution of material goods and on mutual communication between various social groups. This is neither lopsided negotiation nor imposed order. Only under these conditions can the architectural environment, as the representation of a balanced global culture, become democratic in itself and a moral architecture be established.

The integration of squatters into the urban community is the basis for their participation in political life and in the various processes of planning, design, and production. As a tool, this participation is important not only in the process of decision-making but in the processes of information gathering and learning. To improve the quality of participation, the state must possess all the information relevant to the squatters' future; this is a first step in participation. At the same time, the languages of high culture, especially technocratic language, must be demystified. The process of participation must also be legally guaranteed:

there are countless standards for architectural output, based on minimum standards, but the notion of a minimum standard has not been extended to public information and decision-making processes. Such a political reassessment of how architecture is actually practiced would constitute a remarkable advance toward a democracy of urban culture.

Due to a lack of training and a corresponding lack of capacity to formulate development projects, squatters must call on help from the outside. The kind of relationship that exists between social workers and squatters should be adopted by architects as well. Beyond paternalism, the architect can play a decisive role in the squatters' socioeconomic development. This is the kind of architect that developing countries need. This obviously implies a new orientation in how young architects are educated, as per the ardent hopes of their Egyptian colleague, Hassan Fathy.[11]

The urban culture of the countries of South Asia will succeed in asserting itself only once it has integrated the urban culture of the slums.

ENDNOTES

1   On the distinction between high and popular culture, see, for example, Norman Birnbaum, *The Crisis of Industrial Society* (Oxford, 1969).

2   The framework of the concept of effective environment is found in Herbert J. Gans, *People and Plans: Essays on Urban Problems and Solutions* (New York, 1968).

3   See Oscar Lewis, *La Vida: A Puerto Rican Family in the Culture of Poverty* (New York, 1966).

4   On the typology of urban slums, see also Alejandro Portes, "The Urban Slum in Chile: Types and Correlates," *Land Economics* 47, 4 (November 1971): 235–48.

5   Statistics sourced from the United Nations, *Amélioration des taudis et des zones de peuplement non réglementées* (New York, 1971) [English edition, New York, 1971].

6   René Dubos, "The Perils of Adaptation," in *Arts of the Environment* (New York, 1972), 32–39.

7   See *Ekistics* 32, 191 (October 1971): 274.

8   See John F.C. Turner, "Housing as a Verb," in *Freedom to Build* (New York, 1972).

9   See Rory Fonseca, "The Walled City of Old Delhi," in *Shelter and Society* (New York, 1969).

10   Ibid., 106.

11   See Hassan Fathy, *Architecture for the Poor* (Chicago, 1973).

A Conversation with Stanislaus von Moos

Self-Organized Magazine?

Gabrielle Schaad: Among the things that stick out about *archithese* is the fact that it appears as relatively "self-organized." Compared to other publications founded around 1970 it didn't have an institutional base. For instance, *ARCH+* in Germany or *Oppositions* in the United States emerged from an established discussion culture: the former at the Institut für Grundlagen moderner Architektur und Entwerfen (Institute for Principles of Modern Architecture, IGmA) established 1967 in Stuttgart, and the latter at the Institute for Architecture and Urban Studies (IAUS; 1967–1985) in New York. For *archithese*, the situation was different. As a federation of practice-oriented architects, the Association of Independent Swiss Architects (FSAI) may have occasionally provided a framework for roundtables and conferences that could result in a publication. Yet, unlike the IGmA or the IAUS—not to mention the recently founded Institute for the History and Theory of Architecture (gta; 1967) at the Swiss Federal Institute of Technology (ETH Zurich)—FSAI was not a significant institutional space for intellectual exchange.

Stanislaus von Moos: In fact, it resulted from a strange kind of convergence of interests. I had played around with doing "little magazines" ever since my student years. So, I suspect the subject was in the air when I first sat together with Hans Reinhard, who was then at the helm of FSAI (Fig. 1). On the other hand, it is fair to assume that he thought the upgrade of the FSAI's quarterly bulletin (to which I had occasionally contributed as an author) to a small magazine might add some cultural and intellectual luster to the federation's then still somewhat uncertain status within the profession (Fig. 2). Reinhard assumed the publication would allow for voices to be raised against the de facto monopoly in matters of architectural culture then largely claimed by the Bund Schweizerischer Architekten / Federation of Swiss Architects (BSA / FAS) and its organ, the journal *Werk*. Be that as it may, five years later, in 1976, when BSA and FSAI came together to decide on the

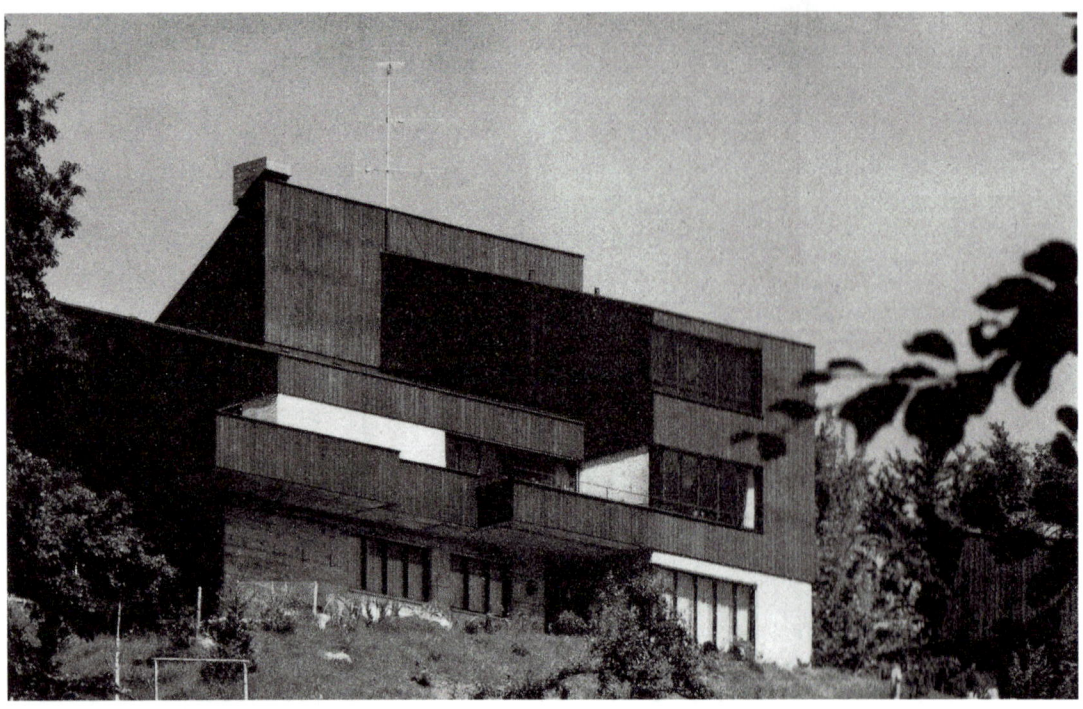

Fig. 1—Hans Reinhard, "Wohnhaus in Hergiswil, 1969 [Reinhard's private mansion, 1969]," *fsai. Verband freierwerbender Schweizer Architekten* 2 (1969): 8–9.

fsai

Verband freierwerbender Schweizer Architekten
Fédération suisse des architectes indépendants
Federazione svizzera degli architetti indipendenti

2/69

Redaktion: Hans Reinhard, 6052 Hergiswil NW

Inserate: Roger Düby, 4460 Gelterkinden

Herausgeber: Zentralvorstand FSAI, 1002 Lausanne

Druck: Buchdruckerei Maihof, Luzern

Juni 1969

S. von Moos:
Anmerkungen zum Bauen in der Schweiz (2)

Zum Stand der Dinge

Heute versucht die Planung, das Baugeschehen unseres Landes von A bis Z in den Griff zu bekommen. Das ist ebenso notwendig wie schwierig in einem Land, das (im Verhältnis zu seinem bewohnbaren und kultivierbaren Boden) die grösste Einwohnerdichte Europas besitzt. Aber nicht davon soll hier die Rede sein – auch nicht von den Reibungen und Komplikationen, die auf allen Ebenen den Gang der Dinge erschweren, weil hierzulande Besitz und administrative Kompetenz aufgesplittert sind wie kaum anderswo. Es geht um das Bauen selbst.

Ob es sich in planerisch geordneten oder ungeordneten Bahnen bewegt ist zwar eine wichtige Frage, aber das Bemühen, verschiedene Kräfte miteinander in ein gewisses Gleichgewicht zu bringen, sagt noch nichts über die tatsächlichen visuellen Erscheinungsformen dieser Kräfte aus. Darum geht es hier.
Das Bauen in der Schweiz bewegt sich in zwei Hauptströmen. Da ist auf der einen Seite das weite Feld der Trivialarchitektur, der Genossenschaftssiedlungen und der Verwaltungsbauten in unseren Städten. Nur ein Teil davon wurde von Architekten entworfen, denn überregionale Generalunternehmerfirmen rechnen ihren Bauherren mit immer grösserem Erfolg vor, dass heute ein einzelner Architekt diesen Ansturm von Problemen des Planens und Bauens, des Ent-

Otto Glaus und Ruedi Lienhard, Architekten ETH/SIA: Wohnsiedlung Jakobsgut I und II in Zürich-Höngg, 1967.

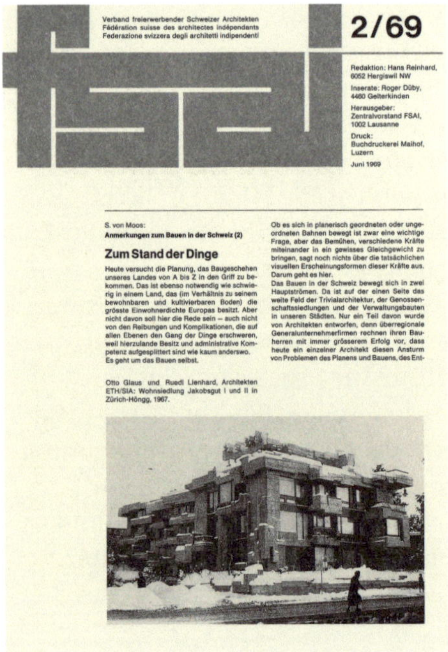

Fig. 2—*fsai. Verband freierwerbender Schweizer Architekten* 2 (1969), 29.7 × 21 cm.

upcoming merger of the two journals *Werk* and *archithese*, that mission at least could be said to have been "accomplished"![1]

I can only say that, for Reinhard, working with us as editors probably turned out to be more of a challenge than it was for us to work with the FSAI. A report on the housing conditions of immigrant workers in Switzerland published in the very first issue almost brought about the end of the adventure—it had caused an uproar within the association. But the FSAI president's unwillingness to compromise on the principle of our editorial independence saved the operation.[2]

Torsten Lange: Since you mentioned it, I would like to briefly focus on *archithese*'s "first cycle"; that is, the first four numbers published in Lausanne (1971). What strikes us most today is the variety of authors and themes featured in those issues. Journalistic criticism of then-recent architecture alternates with scholarly discussions that speak to the then-emerging interest in preservation. The politics of housing and the role of architects in society are also addressed—often from a distinctly Marxist perspective.[3] Then, there is an interview with the philosopher Henri Lefèbvre and an article by Yona Friedman that extends over two issues. Grappling with so many challenges and crises at once somehow looks like a welcome escape from an art historian's solitary work in the Biblioteca Hertziana in Rome.

Fig. 3—Stanislaus von Moos, *Turm und Bollwerk: Beiträge zu einer politischen Ikonographie der italienischen Renaissancearchitektur* (Zurich: Atlantis-Verlag, 1974).

SvM: The architectural journalist Jean-Claude Widmer was my first-year coeditor of the magazine together with the architect Albert Büsch, who represented the FSAI. The interview with Lefèbvre—a highlight of the entire series—and the contacts with Yona Friedman and Ionel Schein go entirely on Widmer's account.[4] Charles Jencks, Jacques Gubler, André Corboz, and others were my "acquisitions." Anyway, you are right, I was in Rome at that time, and it might have been better to remain focused on my dissertation during my tenure at the Swiss Institute there.[5] But then, in the way I tried to understand them, the issues at stake in the fifteenth and sixteenth centuries are often not that different from those of today (Fig. 3).

Fig. 4—Colin Rowe and Robert Slutzky, *Transparenz, Kommentar von Bernhard Hoesli* (Le Corbusier-Studien 1), "gta" 4 (Basel: Birkhäuser Verlag, 1968).

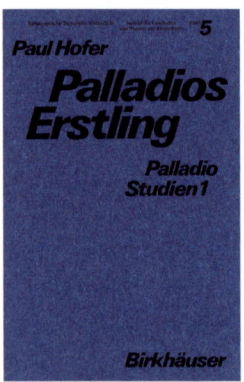

Fig. 5—Paul Hofer, *Palladios Erstling – Die Villa Godi-Valmarana* (Palladio-Studien 1), "gta" 5 (Basel: Birkhäuser Verlag, 1969).

TL: Well, but—from a Zurich point of view—what made *archithese*'s eclectic approach so different, so appealing in comparison to the recently published first issues of the gta publication? You had lampooned the latter for its antiquated methods and for the inconsistency between the scholarly posture of its work in comparison to the neo-avant-garde allure of Hans-Rudolf Lutz's graphics for gta.[6] You also criticized the series' underlying editorial strategy as a mixed-bag approach that included Étienne-Louis Boullée, Rowe and Slutzky's "Transparency" essay, and a collection of writings rescued from the drawers of one of the gta chairs—including one about a hitherto neglected Palladio villa (Figs. 4–5).[7]

SvM: Looking back, the gta publication roster's variety is one of its virtues. It is granted that my somewhat insolent book review didn't earn me many friends at the ETH [laughs]. As to *archithese*'s even more strident eclecticism of subjects and approaches, it may well have been one reason for its short-term collapse—after only one year of operation. However, when we founded the magazine, the gta Institute was undoubtedly the least among our worries. We had neither cash nor an academic base to work from, nor were we confronted with the challenge of a weathered institutional aura that needed to be defended and illustrated.

But since you are pointing to a particular strategic "indecision" that both operations seem to have shared in their early moments, let me point at two differences. First, as you suggested, *archithese*, perhaps just following the zeitgeist, ventured into an area of sociopolitical analysis and critical theory that was somewhat off-limits for the gta at the time—due to chronic territorial claims within the school and the generation gap.[8] Second, there is also a "structural" difference. While the gta book series was conceived as a venue for the faculty who ran the institute, you will find but a few articles by Jean-Claude Widmer and myself in *archithese*. We both liked to see our names printed but were realistic enough not to think of the magazine as being primarily a stage for our ambitions as authors. In the long run, *archithese* (if not indirectly the FSAI) may even have played a role in fostering academic careers. After all, a few of our most productive collaborators later joined the ranks of the gta Institute—even its board of directors (André Corboz, Werner Oechslin, and Kurt W. Forster, in particular)!

GS: Was it ever the magazine's ambition to reach out to non-academic audiences? Looking back: Did you target the academic, the professional, or the broader public audience with *archithese*?

SvM: We never really thought about it—but then again, in the early ("luxury") version of *archithese*, we decided to have pieces that were "scholarly" or in any way "theoretical" printed on gray paper, with more journalistic and less formal essays on white. We thought that would help readers to choose between the "lighter" and the "heavier" offerings. ... Something like the "Schweiz" [Switzerland] and the "Literatur und Kunst" [Literature and art] sections in the Swiss newspaper *Neue Zürcher Zeitung*, although the initial model was the *Architectural Review*, with its light-blue or yellow pages for the "intellectually highbrow" articles. Academic audiences were on our radar. Then came what you call "the broader public": people interested in the political and economic contexts of architectural production. No doubt we somewhat neglected the strictly "professional" audience—and, understandably, we were criticized for it.

GS: But wasn't it precisely this fluid and dynamic character that made the journal more "postmodern" in its pluralistic approach to topics and methodology?

SvM: Our "pluralism" was structural: the lack of an institutional structure or of a compact group of colleagues behind me that could have secured a unity of interest, orientation, let alone doctrine. "Postmodern?"—I don't know. In my own work, I avoid the term, knowing well that we are all part of the phenomenon.

TL: Referring to what you just said about *archithese*'s role in paving the way toward "careers:" What about yourself as a teacher? Have you benefitted from your past as *archithese*'s editor?

SvM: Probably, yes—although outside of Switzerland more than inside. At least for the architects among my colleagues at the Technical University in Delft, the two *werk.archithese* issues about "Monotony" may have carried more weight than my so-called academic credentials.[9] But that is a mere suspicion!

Looks and Politics

GS: Published in Switzerland, *archithese* in its early period was very much produced "on the move." It is tempting to think that its "clip, stamp, fold" approach was partly born from your own nomadic lifestyle and from the aesthetic, political, and even academic sympathies and affiliations that came along with time.[10] Digital communication channels did not yet exist when the magazine began. The FSAI granted for the production just enough to cover the printing, distribution, and some modest author fees. In that sense, yours was probably not a job to make a living at. Does *archithese*'s international outlook therefore need to be seen as a reflection both of the limited means at your disposal and of your own itinerant career—kicked off, I assume, more by your work on Le Corbusier than by your Renaissance studies?[11] After your stay in Rome and the first issues appeared in print, Cambridge, Massachusetts, became your primary address. Still, when referring to the beginnings of *archithese*, Kurt W. Forster, a one-time director of the Swiss Institute in Rome, pointed to the variety of small architectural magazines then circulating in Italy and their role as instigators of architectural discussions in that country and beyond.[12]

SvM: I was hopelessly fascinated by these magazines, as Forster probably was too. In my case, by their looks perhaps even more than by their contents. I spent more time browsing through them in the libraries than researching and studying their contents. Of course, there was Paolo Portoghesi's rather

Fig. 7—*op. cit.* 129 (May 2007), 14.5 × 22.7 cm.

Fig. 6—*sele arte* 8, 49 (January–February, 1961); (*sele arte: architettura, scultura, pittura, grafica, arti decorative e industriali, arti della visione*, Florence: 1952–1966), 21.5 × 15.5 cm.

Fig. 8—*Contropiano* 2 (1970), 20 × 13 cm.

omnivorous *Controspazio*. I heard of *Contropiano*, its more radical Marxist and theory-oriented counterpart, much later. But for me, the motivation to do a magazine was not primarily political in a partisan sense. Furthermore, my interest went toward the art criticism–oriented *sele arte*, edited by Carlo L. Ragghianti, and *op. cit.*, edited by Renato De Fusco. I found them informative, intellectually elegant, and extremely handsome. Italy provided the most immediate plausible models indeed (Figs. 6–9).

GS: It is intriguing that you were so impressed by *op.cit*. The magazine was founded in 1964 by the art historian Renato De Fusco in Naples. Inspired primarily by Max Bill, the Swiss concrete art protagonist, De Fusco had joined the Italian Movimento per l'arte concreta in the early 1950s. The magazine *arte concreta*, running fifteen issues, was the loose movement's mouthpiece from 1951 to 1953. In your student years you did an entirely lowercase magazine for literature and criticism called *ventil*. While its title sounds vaguely technoid, the graphics are distinctly inspired by the typographical aesthetics of "konkrete kunst." Here, perhaps, we have one of the sources for *archithese*'s "look" (Fig. 10)?

Fig. 9—Renato De Fusco, *Architettura come mass medium: Note per una semiologia architettonica* (Bari: Dedalo, 1967).

SvM: I'm thrilled to learn about De Fusco's early involvement with *arte concreta*—I had no idea about it. Through *op.cit*. I knew of his notoriety in semiology and his interest in mass culture—only later did I discover his important book *Architettura come mass medium* (1967) (Fig. 9).[13] My infatuation with "straight," sans-serif typography and lower case—or, more broadly, with Max Bill and what I thought he stood for in terms of form-giving, art, design, and architecture—was rather naive.[14] When Marcel Wyss, who ran the splendid and opulently printed neoconstructivist magazine *spirale*, agreed to exchange ads with our mini-journal *ventil*, it was for me like a knightly accolade! Then, somewhat later, I was blinded by the graphics of Gerstner, Gredinger and Kutter (GGK), the notorious Basel advertising agency as reflected in a series of "youth supplements" I ran with my friend Felix Bucher for the *Luzerner*

Fig. 10 — *archithese* (dummy) (1970);
Cover design and layout by Stanislaus von Moos,
17.5 × 22 cm.

Fig. 11—*Forum* [supplement to *Luzerner Neuste Nachrichten LNN*], May, 6, 1961; guest editors Felix Bucher and Stanislaus von Moos.

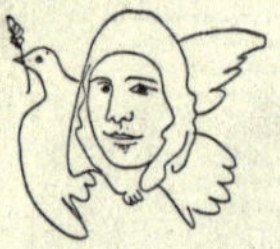

Fig. 12—Markus Kutter, *Schiff nach Europa* (Teufen: Arthur Niggli, 1957); Cover (above) and layout page 155 (below). Design and typography by Karl Gerstner.

Fig. 13—*konkrete poesie* 1 (1960), 21 × 15 cm.

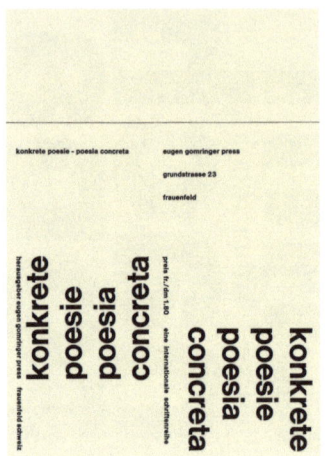

Fig. 14—Ordering coupon for *konkrete poesie*, ca. 1962; left and above: design and typography by Eugen Gomringer.

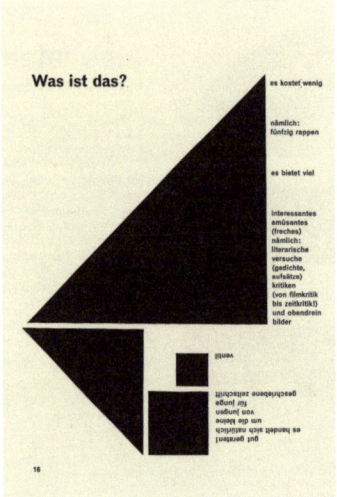

Fig. 15—Advertisement leaflet for *ventil*, ca. 1960, 21 × 14.3 cm.

Fig. 16—*ventil* 6 (November, 1960), 14.5 × 14.5 cm.

Fig. 17—Advertisements leporello for *ventil*; Design and typography by Melchior Küttel, 45.1 × 15.4 cm.

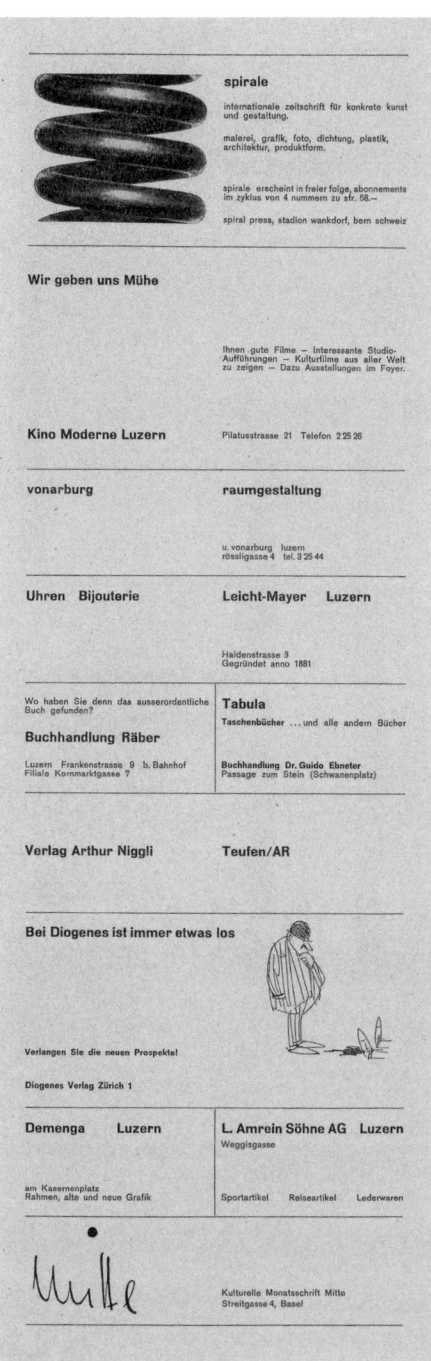

Fig. 18—Advertisements leporello for *ventil*, verso with sponsoring ads by, e.g., *spirale*, Diogenes Verlag, etc., 45.1 × 15.4 cm.

Fig. 19—*spirale: Internationale Zeitschrift für Konkrete Kunst und Gestaltung* 6/7 (1958); Cover design by Marcel Wyss, 35 × 35 cm.

Neueste Nachrichten (Lucerne latest news, LNN] around 1961 (Figs. 11–19).[15] But all this certainly stood behind my fascination with those Italian magazines.

GS: But then, your friends from the FSAI didn't like your first design proposals for *archithese*.

SvM: No, no, they decided to hire a professional designer, Paul Diethelm, who translated my minimalist and deliberately "ascetic" proposals into something that had the allure of a design brochure or a product catalog. I was not too happy with the compromise, but then, while the typeface for "archi / these" (on two lines) looked too bombastic for me, at least it was consistent with the lowercase dogma (Fig. 20).

GS: After just one year, however, *archithese* was taken over by Arthur Niggli, an internationally known publisher of architecture and art books working from Teufen, near Appenzell in remote rural Switzerland. He dropped both the graphic formula and the French-speaking coeditor (Fig. 21).

SvM: Alas, the first year had resulted in an economic fiasco. It had become clear that the formula we had agreed upon—every issue covering a somewhat arbitrary range of approaches and subjects—failed to trigger both the advertisements and the subscriptions needed to keep the magazine above water. Also, working with a print shop that was not itself involved in marketing the magazine (in our case the Imprimeries Réunies in Lausanne) and with a professional graphic designer proved too heavy a burden on the budget. What ultimately saved the project was the generosity of the members of the FSAI who agreed to cover the accumulated debts and to try a fresh model.

GS: But how did the collaboration with Arthur Niggli come about? I understand you had known him before.

SvM: I had never met him personally, but he knew of my earlier stabs in the field of publishing and magazine making.

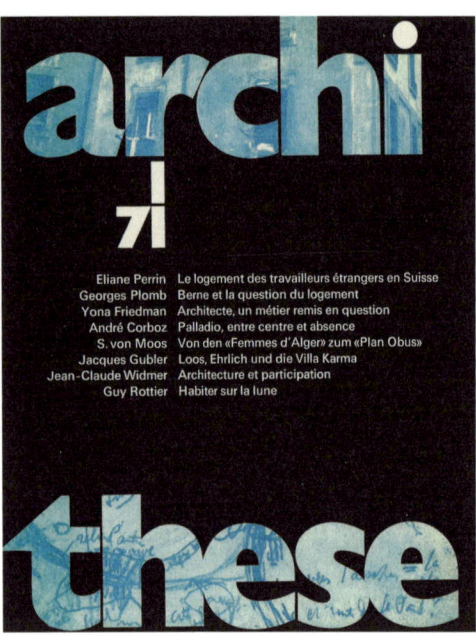

Fig. 20—*archithese* 1–4 (1971);
Cover design and typography by Paul Diethelm.

Fig. 21—Double spread from Jean-Claude Widmer,
"Architecture et participation," *archithese* 1 (1971): 22–24.

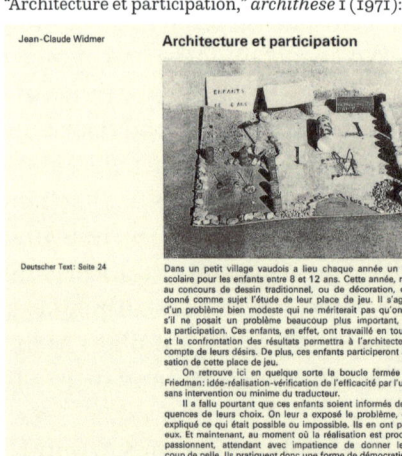
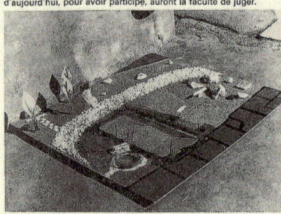

In fact, I had contacted him around 1961, hoping he would post an ad in the student paper *ventil*—which he in fact did (as did Diogenes Verlag in Zurich, among others). So, when I approached Niggli ten years later, he was quite open to the idea of a collaboration. But above all, he must have liked the first four 1971 *archithese* issues, for he decided to stick to the given format of a "little magazine," albeit under the condition that it would become a "journal in the format of a series of thematic publications [*Zeitschrift als Schriftenreihe*]."[16] In this way, he hoped to sell subscriptions as well as individual issues in the bookshops. On the other hand, he didn't like the idea of there being two editors instead of just one (good for me that, among the two options, he preferred the one who spoke German). To compensate for the loss of the French-speaking coeditor, Irène von Moos, my wife, provided in-house German-French-German translations to keep the readership from the French-speaking part of Switzerland happy. Finally, and perhaps most important, Niggli was determined to provide graphic design in-house. So, he kept the small format, kept Diethelm's typeface for the title, but dismissed the graphic designer, thus granting himself as well as his editor a considerable margin of creative improvisation regarding cover design, layout, and typography.

GS: For the Niggli series, you adopted a simple grid system to distribute texts and images on the spreads, but then you undermined the canonic "Swiss style" with interspersed historical, sometimes almost "mannerist" typefaces! You seem to have enjoyed this unorthodox playfulness—perhaps you saw it as highlighting the magazine's interest in history, everyday life, and popular culture?—a playfulness that seems to have allowed the journal to forge different and new arguments to reflect architecture's changing role and impact through the centuries critically. In a way, your informal DIY graphic design looks like the perfect vehicle for the "search for postmodernity" that we claim as a motivation for the present book.

SvM: I love your way of reasoning by looking! However, the "mannerism" was not exclusively mine. It is in fact Niggli who needs to be credited for the covers of the first five or six numbers of the new series that started in 1972 ("Zürich & Co.," I find the most beautiful among them).[17] Later, Niggli lost interest in hand-crafting the covers, and nos. 8–20 certainly go on my account (my wife, Irène, helping!).

Remember that Niggli had done many books about typography. The three volumes entitled *Lettera* are reference works in the field—a treasure trove of normal as well as utterly fanciful historical and historicist typefaces (Figs. 22–23).[18] With these three books, Niggli contributed to a substantial modification of "Swiss style" in graphics, and *archithese* thus became one among his playing fields, and mine.[19] The result, in terms of "corporate identity" of the magazine, was indeed a mess of rather haphazardly executed graphic ideas—all betraying a process of rapid deprofessionalization of most aspects of design a magazine is confronted with. All in all a curious anticipation of what was later to become the paradigm for a growing part of suburban building and living in Switzerland ... On the other hand, and as a short-term side effect, the new freedom allowed us to differentiate ourselves from the "official" Swiss professional magazine *Werk*. Meanwhile, Peter Eisenman and his friends from the Institute of Architecture and Urban Studies in New York (IAUS) began publishing *Oppositions*, thus demonstrating that orthodox "Swiss style" in graphic design was far from dead (Fig. 24)!

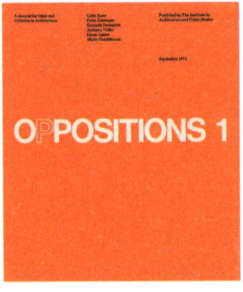

Fig. 24—*Oppositions 1* (1973); Cover design and typography by Massimo Vignelli.

Transcultural, Trans-Atlantic

TL: One step in the 1972 relaunch was the deliberate deprofessionalization in design; the other was the move from thematically open issues to the format of a thematic serial publication. Also, the journal now featured an impressive and extensive list of permanent staff (Max Bill, Lucius Burckhardt, Walter M. Foerderer, to name only a few), an editorial board of sorts that consisted predominantly of historians and thinkers. Did they contribute to a shift in the journal's focus?

Fig. 22—"Zürich & Co.,"special issue, *archithese* 3 (1972); Cover design by Arthur Niggli.

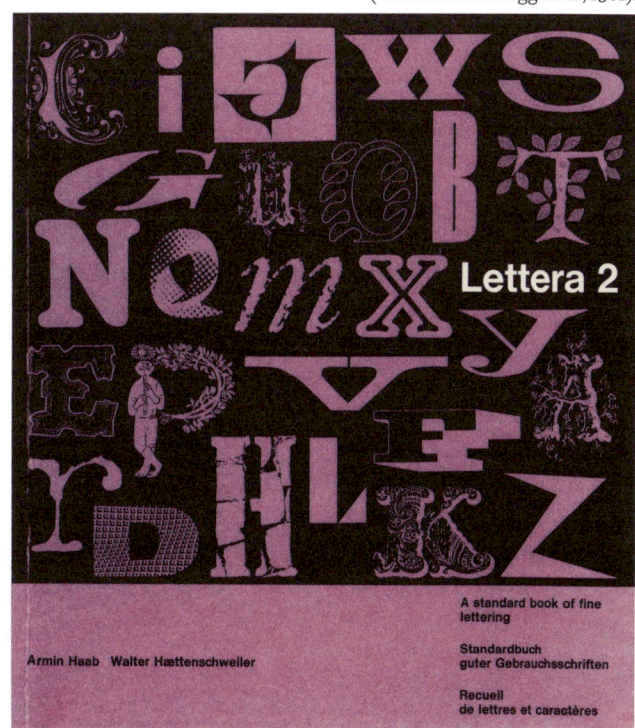

Fig. 23—Armin Haab and Walter Haettenschweiler, *Lettera 2* (Teufen: Arthur Niggli Ltd., 1961).

SvM: "Permanent staff?" I don't think that is precisely the right term … The list came together rather empirically and was a way to compensate for the lack of an institutional base for the magazine. It consisted of people we had already been in contact with through the early issues or whom we hoped to recruit as authors for upcoming topics. In fact, the "editorial board" never actually met and never intervened (except for Max Bill, who occasionally voiced his discontent with our choices).[20] In the end, some of our most interesting issues ended up being prepared or edited by our "board members": Kurt W. Forster, Martin Steinmann, Werner Oechslin, Erwin Mühlestein, Claude Schnaidt, Lisbeth Sachs.

TL: Besides, there are some "elder statesmen" on the list (Max Bill, Julius Posener, Hans Curjel). Why did you not include Reyner Banham? In terms of approach and subject matter, your own work seems closer to Banham's writing than to the majority of the "board members."

Fig. 25—Jul Bachmann, Stanislaus von Moos, *New Directions in Swiss Architecture* (New York: George Braziller, 1969).

SvM: A surprising observation, but you may be right. It so happens that I am a "Banham fan," although I only met him in person twice. His solid, unadorned, and often witty (perhaps "pop") pragmatism in history writing strikes me as more inspiring than the gnawing profundity of many among his Mediterranean colleagues. Though he knew about my work, it did not even occur to me to ask for his participation (Fig. 25).[21] That's perhaps because my primary London contact in those days was Charles Jencks, Banham's doctoral student. In hindsight, I am even more worried by Alan Colquhoun's absence from the "board."

GS: Though it may not be apparent from your "board," the United States (or "America") was a major preoccupation throughout the history of *archithese*. On the other hand, we see hardly a trace of the French architectural debate— except for the first year, when Jean-Claude Widmer was coeditor. The transcontinental cross-examination began early on, with *archithese* 4, "Hochschulpolitik" [Higher education politics; de facto: "Politics of Architectural Education"], with Kenneth Frampton and Michael Mostoller (at Columbia and Harvard respectively) as respondents to *archithese*'s questionnaire on how to outline architectural pedagogies in the aftermath of 1968. Later, from 1973 to 1976, the cross-examination developed around three major thematic clusters: social housing, realism, and "Metropolis." Then, "USA/Switzerland" literally brought the subject home.[22] Was the Swiss fascination with the "Big Brother" what led to framing those topics? Or was it the "expatriate's" frustration with the perceived gridlock and retardation of the situation at home?

SvM: Probably a bit of both. In view of "USA/Switzerland" we had invited Peter W. Gygax, Niklaus Morgenthaler, and Dolf Schnebli to speak about their experience as architects in the United States. At a symposium we organized at Bürgenstock, a mountain resort overlooking Lake Lucerne, they presented their respective musings. Morgenthaler offered a sharp characterization of the U.S. and the political torments that shaped the American everyday at that time (Fig. 26). Schnebli, in turn, presented a detailed scrutiny of the beautiful law school extension he (or rather the team Schnebli, Anselevicius, Montgomery) had built on the campus of Washington University in St. Louis. Later, these talks, supplemented by a long, illustrated list of projects built in the USA by Swiss architects, appeared in *archithese*. By the way, this was the one instance where Niggli was thoroughly "not amused" by the typeface I chose for the cover!

Visiting St. Louis a few years ago, I tried to find Schnebli's 1960s law school, but it had since been replaced by a piece of neo-neo-Victorian campus architecture. As to France: Please don't forget that the late Jean-Louis Cohen's first magazine essay was published in *archithese*![23]

GS: Morgenthaler is primarily known as one of the designers of the Halen settlement near Bern (1955–1962, together with Atelier 5), so his humorous recollections were a particular

Fig. 27—Double spread from Niklaus Morgenthaler, "Amerika–Schweiz: Mutwillige Vergleiche," in "u.s.a. – switzerland," special issue, *archithese* 16 (1975), 10–11.

Fig. 28—Peter Blake, *God's Own Junkyard: The Planned Deterioration of America's Landscape*, (New York: Holt, Rinehart & Winston, 1964).

Fig. 29—Rolf Keller, *Bauen als Umweltzerstörung: Alarmbilder einer Un-Architektur der Gegenwart* (Zurich: Verlag für Architektur Artemis, 1973).

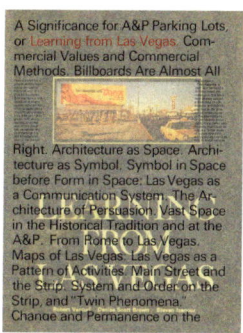

Fig. 26—Robert Venturi, Denise Scott Brown, and Steven Izenour, *Learning from Las Vegas* (Cambridge, MA: MIT Press, 1972).

surprise (Fig. 27). As to your essay "Phase Shifts," it, too, is based on the talk you gave on this occasion.[24] Blatantly inspired by Robert Venturi and Denise Scott Brown's *Learning from Las Vegas* (1972), you were trying to analyze the Bürgenstock resort as well as similar locations in terms of architecture as a "language of signs."[25] You also took advantage of the occasion by reflecting critically architect Rolf Keller's book *Bauen als Umweltzerstörung* [Building as environmental sack] (1973) and his very striking and figurative accusations of the "monotony" and "chaos" in 1960s urban development (Figs. 28–29).[26]

SvM: The essay in fact reflects my perhaps rather naive curiosity for an ethnographic or socio-anthropological reading of architectural form—or rather, for everyday "architectural semiotics" (though I never used the term). I am still struck by how this approach has hardly been implemented in the European context.

TL: How do you explain this paradox? You once mentioned that, while attempting to implement Venturi/Scott Brown's tools, you found that their method's usefulness turns out to be rather limited in a European situation, particularly so in Switzerland.

SvM: I think it is because the local culture does not yield the same extremes as the U.S. The settings here seem to be both more complex and more nuanced than along the American "Strip," where Venturi's and Scott Brown's "pop-theorizing" originated and to which it is so easily applicable.

GS: And yet, as reflected in "Phase Shifts," I think your stance does reveal an interest in semiology—albeit semiology understood as a way of recovering the "meanings" architecture can embody, be they intended by the designer, attributed by the public, or arbitrarily aggregated by circumstance—including metaphor, ambiguity, rhetorical nuance, and metonymy, as they inevitably occur in the production of space, in design,

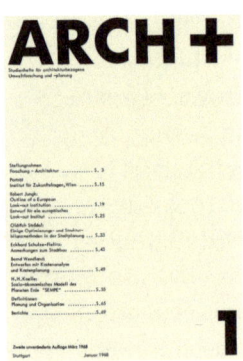

Fig. 30—*ARCH+* 1 (1968).

and in architectural writing. At the opposite end of this discourse, we could locate the semiotically inspired structuralist, systems-theory-linked approach taken, for example, by the magazine *ARCH+* in its founding years (Fig. 30). There, cybernetic thinking was enlisted to help analyze, theorize, and improve the (built) environment. However, cybernetics and information theory were hardly ever invoked on the pages of *archithese*—except perhaps in a rather flippant side remark in your editorial for the issue dedicated to HfG Ulm (Fig. 31).[27]

TL: There are other overlooked areas in the history of *archithese*. Browsing through the "little magazines" that were so instrumental in shaping architectural discourse around 1968, one keeps stumbling over playful openings and flashes of critical thinking by way of paper architecture, imaginatively visualized radical utopias, or even dystopias. In turn, *archithese*, inspired by the work and writing of Venturi and Scott Brown, was content to prompt the idea of "realism" in architecture and graphic discourse. This turn to "realism," not least by way of critically revisiting the failed historical utopias of the twentieth century— including Karl Moser's redevelopment plan for Zurich's old town (1933), or the dreams of "socialist architecture" in the USSR, or even the most recent utopias from the 1960s—seems indicative of a magazine "in search of postmodernity."

GS: Despite its distinctive graphic design, *archithese* never adopted the visual language of, for example, science fiction, as found in radical paper architecture and many of the "little magazines"—though you seem to have been interested, to a certain extent, in Archizoom's ambiguous synthesis of the real and mass media.

SvM: After all, the very first issue of the relaunched *archithese* in 1972 opened with Superstudio's "Cautionary Tales"—a classic in the field of reasoning by way of radical utopias![28] That the Superstudio "cartoon" remained a maverick in *archithese* has little to do with a theoretical stance against this sort of work (Fig. 32). I wish we would have had more contributions of that

Fig. 31 — "hfg ulm. ein rückblick une rétrospective,"
special issue, *archithese* 15 (1975).

Twelve Cautionary Tales for Christmas

PREMONITIONS OF THE MYSTICAL REBIRTH OF URBANISM

SUPERSTUDIO evoke twelve visions of ideal cities, the supreme achievement of twenty thousand years of civilization, blood, sweat and tears; the final haven of Man in possession of Truth, free from contradiction, equivocation and indecision; totally and for ever replete with his own PERFECTION.

First city
2,000-ton city

Even and perfect, the city lies amid green lawns, sunny hills and wooded mountains; slim, tall sheets of continuous buildings intersect in a rigorous, square mesh, one league apart. The buildings, or rather the single, uninterrupted building consists of cubic cells 5 cubits each way; these cells are placed one on top of another in a single vertical stack, reaching a height of a third of a league above sea-level, so that the relative height of the building varies in relation to the level of the ground on which it rises. Each cell has two external walls. Cell walls are of opaque material, porous to air, rigid, but light. The wall facing north (or if this is an external wall, the wall facing west) is capable of emitting 3D images, sounds and smells. Against the opposite wall is a seat capable of moulding perfectly to the human body, even of enclosing it completely. Incorporated in this seat is an apparatus for satisfying all physiological needs. When not in use, this membrane and all apparatus withdraw and the wall reforms. The floor is a simulator, and can evoke all sensations of living things. The ceiling is a brain-impulse-receiver.

In each cell is an individual whose brain impulses are continually transmitted to an electronic analyser set at the top of the building, beneath a continuous semi-cylindrical vault. The analyser selects, compares and interprets the desires of each individual, programming the life of the entire city moment by moment. All citizens are in a state of perfect equality.

Death no longer exists. Sometimes someone indulges in absurd thoughts of rebellion against the perfect and eternal life granted to him. At first the analyser ignores the crime; but if it is repeated, the man who has shown himself unworthy is rejected. The ceiling panel descends with a force of two thousand tons until it reaches the floor.

At this point, in this marvellous economy, another life is initiated.

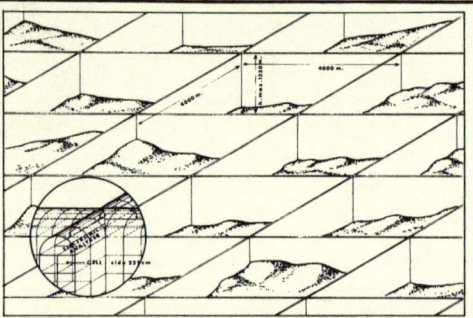

The panel returns to its original height, and all the individuals living in cells within a distance of a quarter of a league from the empty cell donate an ovum or a group of spermatozoa, which are transported in channels created for this purpose in a mad race to the now-empty seat. Here, an ovum is fertilized and the seat is transformed into a uterus, protecting the new son of the city for nine months, until his happy dawn.

Second city
Temporal cochlea-city

The city is an endless screw, 4.5 Km. in diameter, completing one revolution a year.

Its lower extremity, facing the centre of the earth, consists of an excavating apparatus (a kind of turbine, with blades) that, in revolving, crushes rock, forcing all matter towards the centre of the cylinder and through a duct up to the ground. Above the turbine is the propulsion apparatus, an atomic power centre set to last 10,000 years and the automatic plant and electronic computers that control the city.

The upper extremity grows gradually, remaining constantly at the level of the ground outside. Growth is realized through the continuous construction of new sections of city by means of an automatic building-site placed like a bridge between the centre and the perimeter. On this site, rock detritus from the excavations at the bottom is used as building material.

The city is composed of living-cells arranged in a double row of concentric circles. Between the two contiguous circles of cells runs a roadway. Each cell has a single opening, a door giving on to the circular roadway; the other three walls backing onto other cells are totally opaque and soundproof.

The floor of the cells is soft, all apparatus required for the satisfaction of individual living needs are hidden in the ceiling and are tele-controlled. The entire city is climatized at a constant 25°C. with 60% humidity. Each cell is constantly lit to an intensity of 150 lux; the roads are illuminated to an intensity of 500 lux; this light contains all the wavelengths of the visible spectrum; that of the roads also contains small quantities of ultra-violet light.

The cells have no system for closing or screening.

Inhabitants live one to a cell, and possess no clothes or other objects because the city provides for their every need. They are absolutely free to act and organize their lives, both as individuals and as a community; to be alone; to gather in groups; to create laws or regulations; the only restriction is that they cannot go outside the city because the upper ends of the circular roads are closed by the automatic building-site.

Each cell contains an "automatic obstetrician" which, applied to the abdomen of the future mother, extracts the foetus painlessly. The baby is transported by pipeline to a cell in the newly-built section, where it is fed and looked after automatically. Only in this phase is the door of the cell sealed by a steel panel. For four years the child remains in his cell, during which time he learns the ethics and working of

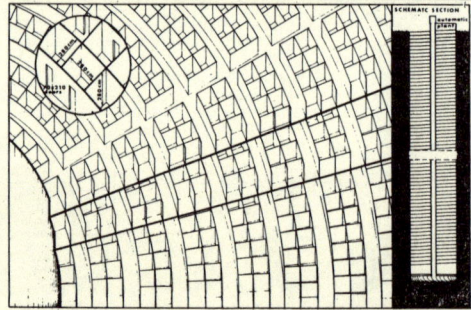

his city. Thereafter the metal door slides away and disappears forever into the wall.

Materials used for building the city remain unaltered for a century, without maintenance; then they begin to degenerate; this is also true of the equipment and machinery. Naturally, load-bearing structures and the general equipment of the city are an exception.

The inhabitants spend a lot of time in the roads near their cells; often, in groups or alone, they climb the spiral roads until they reach the children's zone and beyond, into the last four deserted and silent spirals where the newborn babies live. Often, placing their hands and ears against the warm, vibrating metal walls of the building-site, they try to penetrate the mystery of the outside world. But it is rare for someone to go down the road beyond the zone of extreme old age, into the spirals of decay and putrefaction of things and men, and yet further into the uncertain light and the heat, into the spirals scattered with detritus, dust, bones, until they reach the dark, suffocating and vibrant zones spiralling towards indefinite depths.

737

Fig. 32—Superstudio, "Twelve Cautionary Tales for Christmas: Premonitions of the Mystical Rebirth of Urbanism,"
Architectural Design (December 1971): 737–742.

type. But I must admit, after 1971, when I was teaching in the U.S. at Harvard's Visual Arts Center, I was quite disconnected from the avant-garde paper architecture scene, except for occasional visits to the Architectural Association School of Architecture in London. Whereas, due to my day-to-day job, I was naturally drawn to the kind of subjects that became titles in the *archithese* series. As to the term *realism*, it was nothing like the series' chosen motto. I believe it was not even explicitly referred to in *archithese* before 1975.

GS: And yet, in art-historical discourse, "realism" or the idea of engaging with "reality" could be called excessive throughout the 1960s and early 1970s—think only of the then emerging performance art. The epoch-making documenta 5 (1972) in Kassel that promised an "inquiry into image worlds" was touted by its director, Harald Szeemann, as "questioning of reality." You once mentioned that, for you, realism meant "the reality of experiencing the built environment" and that the Zeitgeist centered around "realism" had no effect on your interest in Renaissance architecture.[29]

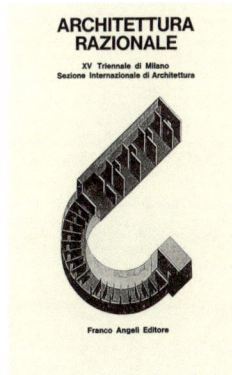

Fig. 33—Ezio Bonfanti, Ricco Bonicalzi, Aldo Rossi et al., *Architettura Razionale: XV Triennale di Milano. Sezione Internazionale di Architettura* (Milan: Franco Angeli Editore, 1973).

SvM: What I remember is that the term *realism* wasn't really part of my critical vocabulary before 1975—even though surely it ought to have been. After all, I rationalized my interest in the pragmatics and the semiotics of Renaissance military architecture as being clearly antithetical to the (in my view esoteric) idealism of Rudolf Wittkower's *Architectural Principles in the Age of Humanism* (1949).[30] Thus "realism," in fact, was just around the corner, as was "brutalism," for that matter. In retrospect, these preoccupations probably had more to do with the "Return of the Real" as later theorized by Hal Foster than I could have realized then.[31]

GS: What about the theorizations of an "inner-architectonic reality" of buildings in the aftermath of Aldo Rossi's *Architettura razionale* exhibition at the Triennale di Milano (1973) and his earlier teaching at ETH Zurich (1972); for example, in *archithese* 19 ("Realismus/réalisme") (Figs. 33–34)? Your guest editors,

Fig. 34—"Realismus – réalisme," special issue, *archithese* 19 (1975).

Bruno Reichlin and Martin Steinmann, celebrated Rossi's "realism" to the point of (over)identification, but you didn't participate in the discussion.

SvM: Not directly, except for having introduced the term *realism* in an earlier issue and except for having designed the cover. I did return to the subject in another context, however.[32] As to "inner-architectonic reality," I still find this notion somewhat mysterious. Architecture inevitably serves a multitude of practical and symbolic functions, including imperatives that have little or nothing to do with the art of building as such. To locate the demands of "reality" inside the art of building seems either tautological or oxymoronic, depending on one's definition of architecture. In preparing the issue, Reichlin and Steinmann, my two guest editors, had asked Aldo Rossi to submit a text. Did the master sense the risk of being trapped by the straitjacket of a theory he would have to reject, even though it was concocted by close Zurich friends and former collaborators? Be that as it may, he ended up submitting a poetic text that spoke about literature and cinema and thus reframed architecture in the wider field of art ("Une éducation réaliste" / "A realist education").[33] Rossi's failure to play the role his friends had assigned him as the mastermind of "realism" appears to have been a major disappointment to my guest editors. Reichlin's uncharacteristically self-ironic recollections of the episode still carry a scent of bitterness.[34]

Theory / History Today

TL: From today's perspective, the combination of rigor and apparent ease with which the authors covered their wide-ranging topics is remarkable, even irritating at times. The journal *archithese* carved out its specific niche, bridging between academic and professional worlds, history and theory, activism and criticism. What has changed since then regarding criticism and given the widespread institutionalization of architectural history and theory at architecture schools?

SvM: I think I know what you mean by "irritating" [laughs]! — To return to your question, I wonder myself. In any case, at the time we began with *archithese*, "theory" still played but an unclear role in architectural education. Ten years earlier, when I began studying at the ETH, the school had just reorganized its program following the model of a Bauhaus-inspired "Grundkurs" [foundational course]. Here, theory meant coming to terms with the dialectics of figure and ground, positive and negative space, with using line drawing for exploring three-dimensionality, experiencing rectangle and sphere as a means of form giving, et cetera. Then, in the "structure" classes, design at least was grounded in facts, albeit still taught as a craft or at best as an "approach" — in no way as an intellectual pursuit. Only in the architectural history classes or when teachers occasionally talked about their experience with buildings that they considered important did one begin to suspect that there must be more to design than just structure and form. If I left ETH after just one year in architecture, it was because I found more answers to my queries outside architecture school than within (and besides, mathematics was not my thing to begin with).

Ten years later, with the freshly founded gta Institute within the school, the situation was certainly no longer the same. But room nevertheless appears to have been left among students or even faculty for critical perspective. In hindsight, that appetite for, if you will, the philosophical dimension of design may have been our chance as a magazine.

TL: In the subsequent years, theory and history offerings exploded in most schools of architecture — especially so in the U.S., to the point of moving the very culture of architectural design (the "craft" or the "art" part of architecture) out of focus.

SvM: I couldn't agree more. The good thing however is that more and more architects learned to write. Many have made brilliant careers as historians, theoreticians, and critics — especially those inspired by art. Meanwhile, outside of academia, the fascination with theory has slowly but conspicuously given way to other discursive elixirs. Or do you know of a contemporary "starchitect" who would defend his position in terms of theory? When I look back, it bugs me to realize that from 1971 to 1976 in *archithese* there was almost no reflection of what was going on in art at the time—or in the sociology of art.

TL: Architectural theorist Joan Ockman recently summarized the shift toward more research-oriented forms of academic architectural practice as "privileging hunting and gathering over more sedentary tasks like reflecting and questioning." She argues that—and I'd like to cite her here—"instead of history/theory today, what we now have is 'research': Research as the holy grail of contemporary architecture education. The 'laboratories' in which it is carried out—by white-coated architectural technicians, figuratively speaking—are its shrines. As for criticism: arguably, we now have something like 'curation.' History/theory has turned into research/curation."[35]

SvM: Joan Ockman is probably right. As a former editor of *archithese* I should deplore this trend. But then, as a historian, I am inevitably of those who are first engaged in "hunting and gathering," granted that, in history writing, that works only in conjunction with "reflecting and questioning." ... In my case it never worked the other way around, but that is because I am neither philosopher nor theoretician. Does "History/Theory" versus "Research/Curation" make sense at all as an alternative?

Fig. 35—Manfredo Tafuri, *Progetto e Utopia: Architettura e Sviluppo Capitalistico* (Bari: Laterza & Figli, 1973).

GS: In Italy a similar "impasse" was brought into focus when Manfredo Tafuri set out to criticize *storia operativa* (operational historiography) as practiced by architect/historian Bruno Zevi, among others, and pleaded—demonstratively so in Zevi's book *Michelangiolo architetto* (1964)—for a "critical" history of architecture in a Marxist sense.[36] In an essay published in 1982, you, too, looking back upon your experience with *archithese*, seemed to disassociate yourself from *storia operativa* in favor of a position that is, after all, close to Tafuri's. What brought you in contact with Tafuri? It is intriguing that, in his seminal study *Progetto e Utopia* (1973), he should discuss the very same "case" you had chosen for your first article ever published in *archithese*:

511

Fig. 36 — "Monotonie," special issue, *werk.archithese* 1 (1977).

Fig. 37 — "'Stadtgestalt' oder Architektur," special issue, *werk.archithese* 33–34 (1978).

Le Corbusier's Plan Obus for Algiers (Fig. 35). Needless to say, he followed a different agenda.[37] Whereas you never relied on bolstering your reading with authoritative sources like Althusser, Benjamin, et cetera, Tafuri heavily drew on Marxism and critical theory.

SvM: I always had a tremendous respect for Tafuri's work, even though I read and understood only parts of it. Tafuri for me was synonymous both with my fear of theoretical or heavily philosophical or psychoanalytical writing in art and architecture and my secret "homesickness" for it. You are right, I certainly shared his critique of *storia operativa*—the article you quoted may serve as an example. Although, probably, much of what I myself was writing about Venturi and other architects at that time was itself a form of *storia operativa* and hence part of the problem. I first met Tafuri during a visit in Rome while preparing *archithese* 7 ("Socialist Architecture? USSR 1917–1932," 1973).[38] He knew of me because of Le Corbusier and probably saw "my" magazine (and, later, *werk.archithese*) as a potential echo chamber, or at least as a vehicle for having his work brought to a German-speaking audience. His contributions, especially the later one for *werk.archithese*, became notorious among my Zurich friends, particularly the ones among them who were summoned to help with the predictably herculean task of translation (Figs. 36–37).[39] More than one of these essays later appeared as chapters in Tafuri's *La sfera e il labirinto* (1980).[40]

TL: I would like to briefly talk about the last numbers of the Niggli series—17, 18, and 20—all entitled "Metropolis" and centered on New York (interrupted only by no. 19, "Realism") (Fig. 38). The subject appears to have arisen from Werner Oechslin's research interest in American architectural history. He also supervised them editorially, focusing on history—thus, somewhat contrasting with your interests in method transfer in contemporary criticism and theory. I guess Rem Koolhaas's essay about the "Rockettes"—a preview of what would later become a chapter in his *Delirious New York* (1978)—fell rather in line with your interests?[41]

Fig. 38—"Metropolis," special issue, *archithese* 17 (1976).

Fig. 39—Double spread from Andreas Adam, "Skyline," in "Metropolis," special issue, *archithese* 17 (1976): 4–14, here 4–5.

SvM: Werner's role was crucial with these three issues, yet recruiting the many authors and editing their essays was definitely a collective effort. William Curtis I knew from my time in Cambridge, Massachusetts; Rem Koolhaas I had first met around 1975, when he began working on *Delirious New York* (I remember we had breakfast at Kenneth Frampton's house in New York); Rosemarie Haag Bletter, Cervin Robinson, and other contributors to these three issues were also contacted then.

TL: To see the FSAI, a Swiss federation of practicing architects, sponsor three "volumes" of academic deliberations about the American metropolis is rather unexpected! And at a time when the resulting lessons were even less likely to be applied in Europe than the critical tools of Venturi/Scott Brown.

SvM: Of course, we never planned to produce three numbers. But Manfredo Tafuri's and Mario Maniera-Elia's responses to Werner Oechslin's "call for papers" were so extensive that it became clear we needed more than one issue to host their texts. Obviously, some leftovers hadn't made their way into the great volume on the history of the American city that had just been published in Italian (1973).[42] (The book, by the way, never appeared in German.) All this and a shared gusto for accuracy and footnotes among Italian and Italophile scholars created a momentum of its own. Hence, within weeks, we had an overflow of valuable material, including Andreas Adam's incredible collection of postcards from New York (second only to Madelon Vriesendorp's) (Fig. 39).[43] For a "poor" journal, it would have been crazy to forego the chance to publish it all. Sometime later, Academy Editions in London played with the idea of producing the material in one volume as a book (with Banham as proposed author of the introduction)—a pity this collaboration never materialized.

TL: This planned anthology truly sounds like it would have hit a nerve. Indeed, the topic of the early twentieth century American metropolis very much appears to have been "in the air" at the time—perhaps unsurprisingly, given New York's drastic transformation on its way to becoming a global city, as Saskia Sassen later analyzed. Rosemarie Haag Bletter's *Skyscraper Style* (1975) shortly preceded your "Metropolis" series. Only a couple of years after it, in 1978, Koolhaas released his retroactive manifesto *Delirious New York*. And Tafuri's *La sfera e il labirinto*, with one of its chapters dedicated to the New York skyscraper, was published in 1980. Moreover, these last two projects first saw the light in *archithese*, where they were presented in their early stages.

GS: So, maybe the publisher, Academy Editions, felt that everything had been said? Andreas Adam's postcard collection, on the other hand, got turned into a richly illustrated book recently. I guess this proves not only the series editors' foresight but also the lasting fascination of the American city.

1   Over the years, *archithese* has had several publishers and name changes. It was first published by Imprimeries Réunies, Lausanne (issues 1–3/4, 1971); then by Niggli Verlag, Niederteufen (issues 1–20, 1972–1976); then, as *werk. archithese*, also published by Niggli Verlag (1976–1978); and finally in 1980, again as *archithese*.

2   Eliane Perrin, "Immigrant Worker Housing in Switzerland," 404–19 in this publication. First published in *archithese* 1 (1971): 2–11.

3   See, for example, ibid.

4   See J.-C. Widmer, "Questions for Henri Lefebvre," 232–40 in this publication. First published in *archithese* 2 (1971): 11–15.

5   A member of the Swiss Institute in Rome from 1968–1971, von Moos was then working on the book version of his PhD thesis, published later as see Stanislaus von Moos, *Turm und Bollwerk: Beiträge zu einer politischen Ikonografie der italienischen Renaissancearchitektur* (Zurich: Atlantis-Verlag, 1976).

6   See Sylvia Claus, "Phantom Theory: The gta Institute in Postmodernist Architectural Discourse," *gta papers* 3 (2019): 121–35, here 124; Stanislaus von Moos, "Schriftenreihe des Instituts für Geschichte und Theorie der Architektur an der ETH Zürich," *Zeitschrift für Schweizerische Archäologie und Kunstgeschichte* 27, 4 (1970): 236–43, here 236.

7   Adolf Max Vogt, *Boullées Newton-Denkmal Sakralbau und Kugelidee*, "gta" 3 (Basel: Birkhäuser, 1969); Colin Rowe and Robert Slutzky, *Transparenz*, Kommentar von Bernhard Hoesli (Le Corbusier-Studien 1), "gta" 4 (Basel: Birkhäuser-Verlag, 1968); Paul Hofer, *Palladios Erstling—Die Villa Godi-Valmarana* (Palladio-Studien 1), "gta" 5 (Basel: Birkhäuser-Verlag, 1969).

8   See AA.VV, "Project-Based Learning at the ETH: Critical Rather Than Technocratic," 328–37 in this publication. First published in *archithese* 3/4 (1971): 62–66.

9   See *werk.archithese 1* (1977); *werk.archithese* 17–18 (1978).

10   Beatriz Colomina and Marie Theres Stauffer, "Interview with Stanislaus von Moos," in *CLIP/STAMP/FOLD: The Radical Architecture of Little Magazines, 196X to 197X*, ed. Beatriz Colomina and Craig Buckley (New York: Actar; Princeton, NJ: Media and Modernity Program, Princeton University, 2010), 483–88.

11   Stanislaus von Moos, *Le Corbusier: Elements of a Synthesis* (Cambridge, MA: MIT Press, 1979). Originally published as *Le Corbusier: Elemente einer Synthese* (Zurich: Huber, 1968), with French, Spanish, Japanese, and Korean editions following.

12   Colomina and Stauffer, *CLIP/STAMP/FOLD* (see note 10), 483–88.

13   Renato De Fusco, *Architettura come mass medium: Note per una semiologia architettonica* (Bari: Dedalo, 1967).

14   Von Moos's assessment of the term *concrete* in art theory triggered an angry letter from Bill. See "diesen sommer ... oder: was heisst 'konkret,'" *ventil* 6 (Summer 1960): 30–31.

15   Upon reading a high school student paper von Moos had written about *Schiff nach Europa* (Teufen, Switzerland: Arthur Niggli, 1957), Markus Kutter offered him a job at GGK (founded by Karl Gerstner, Paul Gredinger and Markus Kutter). Von Moos turned down the offer, though, and chose to enroll as an architecture student at the ETH Zurich instead.

16   See Editorial, *archithese* 2 (1972): n.p.: "archithese ist eine Zeitschrift in Form einer Schriftenreihe. Jedes Heft enthält ein in sich abgeschlossenes Thema. Die Hefte werden fortlaufend numeriert [*sic*]. Dies ist Heft 2/1972."

17   *archithese* 3 (1972).

18   Armin Haab and Alex Stocker, *Lettera: A Standard Book of Fine Lettering / Standardbuch guter Gebrauchsschriften / Nouveau répertoire d'alphabets originaux* (Teufen: Arthur Niggli, 1954). Followed by Armin Haab and Walter Haettenschweiler, *Lettera 2* (Teufen: Arthur Niggli, 1961); Armin Haab and Walter Haettenschweiler, *Lettera 3: A Standard Book of Fine Lettering / Standardbuch Guter Gebrauchsschriften / Nouveau répertoire d'alphabets originaux* (Teufen: Arthur Niggli, 1968).

19   Christof Bignens, *Swiss Style: Die grosse Zeit der Gebrauchsgrafik in der Schweiz 1914–1964* (Zurich: Chronos, 2000).

20   Max Bill was at odds with von Moos's commissioning of Claude Schnaidt as guest editor for a retrospective on the Hochschule für Gestaltung in Ulm (Ulm School of Design) published as *archithese* 15 (1975).

21   See Jul Bachmann, Stanislaus von Moos, *New Directions in Swiss Architecture* (New York: George Braziller, 1969); Reyner Banham, "Jul Bachmann and Stanislaus von Moos, Swiss Architecture; Robert Stern, American Architecture; Udo Kultermann, African Architecture; Francisco Bullrigh, Latin American Architecture, Braziller (New Directions Series)," *Art Bulletin* 54, 4 (1972): 565.

22   See *archithese* 16 (1975). The essays included in this issue had been presented in talks given at a symposium organized by the FSAI at Bürgenstock near Lucerne in 1975.

23   Jean-Louis Cohen, "Villejuif, une architecture dans les lutes," *archithese* 7 (1973): 42–48.

24   Stanislaus von Moos, "Phase Shifts," 92–107 in this publication. First published in *archithese* 16 (1975): 26–36.

25   Robert Venturi, Denise Scott Brown, and Steven Izenour, *Learning from Las Vegas* (Cambridge, MA: MIT Press, 1972).

26   Rolf Keller, *Bauen als Umweltzerstörung: Alarmbilder einer Un-Architektur der Gegenwart* (Zurich: Verlag für Architektur Artemis, 1973). See also Peter Blake, *God's Own Junkyard: The Planned Deterioration of America's Landscape* (New York: Holt, Rinehart and Winston, 1964).

27   See Editorial, *archithese* 15 (1975) 2–4, here 4.

28   Superstudio, "Three Warnings against a Mystical Rebirth of Urbanism," 242–51 in this publication. First published in *archithese* 1 (1972): 3–6, 36.

29   Colomina and Stauffer, "Interview with Stanislaus von Moos" (see note 10), 485.

30   Stanislaus von Moos, "Kunstgeschichte der Technik? Zum Problem der 'Zeitbedingten Optik' in der Architekturgeschichte," *Orbis Scientiarum* 2, 1 (1972): 73–90; Stanislaus von Moos, "Poscritto sul tema: Fortificazioni e architettura moderna," in *L'architettura militare Veneta del Cinquecento*, ed. André Chastel and Antonio Corrazin (Venice: Centro Internazionale di Studi di Architettura Andrea Palladio di Vicenza; Milan: Electa, 1988), 170–78.

31   Hal Foster, *The Return of the Real* (Cambridge, MA: MIT Press, 1996).

32   Stanislaus von Moos, "Zweierlei Realismus," *werk.archithese* 7–8 (1977): 58–62.

33   Aldo Rossi, "A Realist Education," 188–93 in this publication. First published in *archithese* 19 (1976): 25–26.

34   Bruno Reichlin, "'Amarcord' Erinnerung an Aldo Rossi," in *Aldo Rossi und die Schweiz*, ed. Ákos Moravánszky and Judith Hopfengärtner (Zurich: gta Verlag, 2011), 29–44.

35   Joan Ockman, "Slashed," *e-flux Architecture: History/Theory*, October 27, 2017, https://www.e-flux.com/architecture/history-theory/159236/slashed/.

36   Paolo Portoghesi and Bruno Zevi, *Michelangiolo architetto* (Rome: Einaudi, 1964).

37   See Manfredo Tafuri, *Progetto e utopia: Architettura e sviluppo capitalistico* (Bari: Laterza e Figli, 1973); Stanislaus von Moos, "Von den 'Femmes d'Alger' zum 'Plan Obus': Hinweis auf die Kunsttheorie Le Corbusiers," *archithese* 1 (1971): 25–37.

38   See Manfredo Tafuri, "Les premières hypothèses de planification urbaine dans la Russie soviétique 1918–1925," *archithese* 7 (1973): 34–41.

39   Manfredo Tafuri, "Borromini und Piranesi: Die Stadt als 'zersprengte Ordnung,'" *werk.archithese* 33/34 (1979): 6–12.

40   Manfredo Tafuri, *La sfera e il labirinto: Avanguardie e architettura da Piranesi agli anni '70* (Rome: Einaudi, 1980).

41   Rem Koolhaas, "Roxy, Noah, and the Radio City Music Hall," 296–307 in this publication. First published in *archithese*, 18 (1976), 37–43.

42   Giorgio Ciucci, Francesco Dal Co, Mario Manieri-Elia, and Manfredo Tafuri, *La città americana dalla Guerra Civile al New Deal* (Bari: Laterza, 1973).

43   Andreas Adam, "Skyline," *archithese* 17 (1976): 4–14.

Image Credits:

Page 512 (top): © 1977 werk·archithese, No. 1, © Verlag Werk AG
Page 512 (bottom): © 1978 werk·archithese, No. 33–34, © Verlag Werk AG

APPENDIX

521
Name index

524
Contributors

526
Acknowledgments
Imprint

527
Register of *archithese*
1971–1976

Name index

A
Aalto, Alvar 28, 146
AA.VV (editorial collective of the Janssen Seminar) 3, 310, 311, 329–37
Abrams, Charles 457, 474
Abramovitz, Max 50
Adam, Andreas 24, 515, 516, 517
Adams, Thomas 280
Adamson, Glenn 6
Adorno, Theodor W. 205, 206
Aelianus, Claudius 420
Alberti, Leon Battista 401
Albini, Franco 156
Van Alen, William 112
Alexander, Christopher 12
Allemann, Richard 220
Althusser, Louis 200, 513
Angreß, Gina 214
Anselevicius, George 501
Argan, Giulio 35
Aristarco, Guido 188
Associated Architects 117, 296, 299, 301
Aureli, Pier Vittorio 137

B
Bader, John 146
Bacon, Francis 260, 425
Balibar, Étienne 200
De Balzac, Honoré 206
Banham, Reyner 43, 500, 516
Bar-le-Duc, Jean Errard de 420
Barthes, Roland 206
Bauman, Zygmunt 8
Bell, Daniel 44
Benjamin, Walter 274, 513
Benda, Julien 43
Bense, Max 12
Berkeley, Bubsy 289, 291
Berlant, Lauren 315
Bernini, Gian Lorenzo 101
Bienvenu, François 394
Bill, Max 219, 488, 489, 500, 525
Birnbaum, Norman 474
Bishop, Claire 315
Blake, Peter 94, 95, 101, 502
Bletter, Rosemarie Haag 2, 10, 22, 26, 27, 28, 110–19, 224, 227, 291, 516, 517
Bloc, André 394
Bloch, Ernst 135, 183, 184
Blumer, Jacques (Jakob K.) 3, 310, 311, 364–76
Böckler, Georg Andreas 420
Bofill, Ricardo 238
Bollerey, Franziska 2, 10, 13, 212, 216, 222, 223, 227, 252–71
Borromini, Francesco 177
Bosshard, André E. 220
Boudon, Philippe 175
Boullée, Étienne-Louis 263, 484

Bourdieu, Pierre 320
Bourriaud, Nicolas 315
Boyarsky, Alvin 324
Bragdon, Claude 273
Brecht, Bertolt 135, 200
Briseux, Charles-Étienne 445
Buonarroti, Michelangelo 187
Bucher, Felix 488
Buckley, Craig 13
Bugnicourt, Jacques 446
Bunshaft, Gordon 50
Buonarroti, Michelangelo 18, 144, 187, 420
Burckhardt, Lucius 10, 219, 324, 498
Burkhalter, Marianne (Burkhalter Sumi) 28, 146
Burle Marx, Roberto 102

C
Cacciari, Massimo 11
Calamai, Clara 188, 193
Caminada, Gion 134
Campi, Mario 27
Candilis, Georges
Canova, Antonio 84
De Carlo, Giancarlo 314
Chakrabarty, Dipesh 15
Chaplin, Charles 361
Cheney, Sheldon 111
De Chirico, Giorgio 90, 91
Choay, Françoise 445
Chomsky, Noam 44
Christiaanse, Kees 135,
Churchill & Lippmann 117
Clemens, Paul 66
Clinton & Russell 112
Dal Co, Francesco 12
Cohen, Jean-Louis 501
Colomina, Beatriz 138
Colquhoun, Alan 2, 122, 124, 127, 128, 129, 131, 145, 166–75, 194, 500
Considerant, Victor 223, 265, 267, 268
Consolascio, Eraldo 126
Corbett, Harvey Wiley 273, 274, 275, 280, 291
Corboz, André 3, 10, 11, 388, 389, 390, 431–49
Croly, Herbert David 286
Cupers, Kenny 314
Curran, Henry 291
Curtis, William 516

D
Dahinden, Justus 103
Davidovici, Irina 2, 15, 18, 123–40, 524
Dehio, Georg 66
Delano, Frederick A. 279
Derrida, Jacques 205
Descartes, René 425

Diethelm, Paul 9, 10, 495, 496, 497
Dilich, Wilhelm 420
Doegen, Matthias 420
Doucet, Isabelle 314
Doxiadis, Constantinos A. 52
Drew, Jane 396
Dreyfuss, Henry 313
Dubos, René 474

E
Eisenman, Peter 11, 498
Eisenstein, Sergei 188
Emery, Pierre-André 393
Emery, Fred E. 33
Emerson, Ralph Waldo 285
Engels, Friedrich 263, 356, 361

F
Fanon, Frantz 390
Fathy, Hassan 478
Faulkner, William 188
Fellini, Federico 188
Ferriss, Hugh 117, 225, 273, 275
Filarete (Antonio di Pietro Averlino) 178, 187
Fischer, Theodor 66
Fischer von Erlach, Johann Bernhard 83
Fitzgerald, F. Scott 286
Fitzgerald, Zelda 286
Flagg, Ernest 279
Focillon, Henri 200
Foerderer, Walter M. 104, 498
Fonseca, Rory 477
Forster, Kurt W. 11, 222, 485, 486, 500
Foster, Hal 6, 136, 507
Fourier, Charles 13, 222, 223, 252, 253, 259, 264, 265, 266, 267, 268, 269, 270, 271, 316, 369
Frampton, Kenneth 324, 501, 516
Franzen, Ulrich 146
Fraser, Nancy 315
Frassinelli, (Gian) Piero 10, 221
Freud, Sigmund 33, 38, 206, 446
Freytag, Adam 420, 423, 426
Friedman, Yona 238, 483
Frisch, Max 369
Fritz, Erwin 316
Fröhlich, Martin 13, 219
Frontinus, Sextus Julius 420
Fry, Maxwell 396
Fuller, Richard Buckminster 43, 44, 163
De Fusco, Renato 488

G
Galbraith, John Kenneth 38, 59
Galileo (Galilei) 425
Gans, Herbert J. 3, 310, 318, 320, 350, 355, 356
Gerber, Samuel 316
Gerstner, Karl 488, 401
Giedion, Sigfried 102, 145, 163
Ginzburg, Moisei 200
Gisel, Ernst 100
Godin, Jean-Baptiste André 268
Goebbels, Joseph 51

Goldmann, Nicolaus 420
Goodman, Robert 361
Göhner, Ernst 323, 324, 333, 334
Grassi, Giorgio 2, 122, 124, 127, 128, 129, 130, 131, 135, 176–87
Gredinger, Paul 488
Gregotti, Vittorio 35
Gropius, Walter 29, 44, 156, 194
Grousset, René 445
Gubler, Jacques 123
Guidoni, Enrico 437
Günter, Marianne (Janne) 3, 310, 311, 321, 322, 324, 338–49
Günter, Roland 3, 310, 311, 321, 322, 324, 338–49
Guyer, Esther 100
Guyer, Rolf 100
Gygax, Peter W. 501

H
Habermas, Jürgen 315
Hadid, Zaha 135
Handlin, David P. 3, 310, 317, 318, 319, 320, 321, 350–62
Haraway, Donna (Jeanne) 315
Harrison, Wallace Kirkman 50, 283, 299
Hartmann, Kristiana 2, 13, 212, 216, 222, 223, 227, 252–71
Hassan, Ihab 8
Hastings, Thomas 280, 291
Hays, K. Michael 137, 138
Helmle & Corbett 273, 274, 275, 285
Helmle, Corbett & Harrison 283
Hemingway, Ernest 188
Henderson, Rose 285
Henni, Samia 3, 17, 18, 388, 389–403, 525
Hesterberg, Rolf 326
Hertzberger, Herman 172, 173
Herzog, Jacques 133, 134, 135
Hilberseimer, Ludwig 83
Hitler, Adolf 51
Hoesli, Bernhard 198, 200, 324, 484
Holton & George 112
Holz, Hans Heinz 36, 77, 127
Hood, Raymond 117, 280, 285, 291
Hostettler, Hans 316
Howard, Ebenezer 274, 474
Huber, Benedikt 220
Huet, Bernard 134, 135
Hunziker, Jakob 432

I
Izenour, Steven 146, 153, 159, 386, 503

J
Jacobs, Jane 214, 215
Jakobson, Roman Osipovich 199
Jameson, Fredric 8, 9, 137
Janssen, Jörn 3, 13, 310, 323, 324, 329–37
Jefferson, Thomas 94
Jencks, Charles 2, 10, 16, 22, 30, 31, 32, 33, 34, 38–61, 124, 312, 324, 483, 500

Joedicke, Jürgen 12
Johns, Jasper 146
Johnson, Philip 50, 51
De Jouvenel, Bertrand 43
Joyce, James 145, 206
Jung, Carl Gustav 445

K
Kagel, Mauricio 73
Kahn, Ely Jacques
    (Buchman & Kahn)
    274, 276, 280, 285, 286, 292
Kahn, Louis I. 146
Kallmann, McKinell & Knowles
    99, 102
Keller, Rolf 94, 96, 97, 99,
    101, 312, 503
Kepler, Johannes 425
Kira, Alexander 313
Klee, Paul 200
Koenigsberger, Otto H. 396, 397
Koestler, Arthur 33
Kollhoff, Hans 135
Koolhaas, Rem 2, 10, 14, 135,
    212, 216, 226, 227, 228,
    296–307, 513, 516, 517
Kuhn, Thomas 168
Kutter, Markus 488, 491

L
Lang, Fritz 117, 273
Lange, Torsten 2, 5–19, 212,
    213–31, 479–518
Laparelli, Francesco 425
Lathuillière, Marcel 393
Leach, Edmund 52
Le Corbusier 29, 31, 43, 51, 99,
    105, 111, 142, 145, 146, 170, 171,
    173, 175, 178, 187, 199, 200,
    202, 232, 268, 291, 313, 315,
    318, 393, 432, 484, 486, 513
Ledoux, Claude-Nicolas 445
Lefaivre, Liane 135, 136
Lefèbvre, Henri 2, 212, 217, 218,
    219, 220, 221, 232–40
Leonidoff, Leon 305
Leroi-Gourhan, André 438
Lévi-Strauss, Claude 33
Lewis, Oscar 473
Lichtenstein, Claude 224
Lichtenstein, Roy 146
Linnaeus, Carl 432
Llorens, Tomás 136
Lobsinger, Mary Lou 137
Loos, Adolf 183, 184
Lorca, Federico García 188
Luckhardt, Wassili 44
Lukács, Georg [György] 129,
    178, 199
Lyautey, Hubert 392
Lynch, Kevin 215
Lyotard, Jean François 8, 15

M
Mácel, Otakar 127
Machiavelli, Niccolò 401, 426
Mann, Thomas 66
Mahaffey, Noel 146
Maniera-Elia, Mario 516

De Marchi, Francesco 425
Marcuse, Herbert 222
Marinetti, Filippo Tommaso 51
Marolois, Samuel 420, 423,
    425, 426
Martin, Reinhold 7, 137
Martini, Francesco di Giorgio 420
Marx, Karl 38, 52, 102, 356, 431
Marx-Aveling, Eleanor 356
May, Ernst 90, 91
McKenzie, Voorhees &
    Gmelin 279
McLuhan, Marshall 38
Meili, Marcel 133, 134, 135
Meister, Anna-Maria 313
Mendelsohn, Erich 110, 111
De Meuron, Pierre 133, 134
DeMille, Cecil B. 117
Meyer, Hannes 184
Meyer, Peter 105
Mignolo, Walter D. 15
Mitscherlich, Alexander 215
Moholy-Nagy, Sibyl 51
Montgomery, Robert 501
Moravánszky, Ákos 18, 131
More, Thomas 260
Morgenthaler, Niklaus 11, 37,
    371, 501
Morris, William 432
Moser, Karl 13, 502
Mostoller, Michael 501
Mühlestein, Erwin 500
Mujica, Francisco 280, 284,
    286, 287, 288, 291, 292
Müller, Michael 155
Müller, Werner 220
Mumford, Lewis 280
Murchison, Kenneth M. 286
Mussolini, Benito 51
the Mute, Peter 445
Muthesius, Hermann 432

N
Naef, Joachim 108
Naronowicz-Naroński, Józef 426
Negri, Antonio (Toni) 11
Nervi, Pier Luigi 51
Neuenschwander, Eduard 220
Neufert, Ernst 313
Neurath, Otto 194
Niemeyer, Oscar 49, 237, 238
Nieuwenhuys, Constant Anton 238
Niggemeyer, Elisabeth 215
Niggli, Arthur 9, 10, 14,
    491, 495, 497, 498, 501, 513
Nixon, Richard 146
Nouvel, Jean 135

O
Ockman, Joan 224, 225, 511
Oechslin, Werner 224, 225,
    485, 500, 513, 516
Oldenburg, Claes 146, 163
Ortner, Laurids 135
Otto, Frei 163
Owen, Robert 2, 212, 222, 223,
    252, 255, 257, 259, 260,
    263, 264, 268, 316, 369
Owen, William 260

P
Pagano, Giuseppe 51
Pane, Robert 438
Park, Edwin Avery 111
Patel, Praful C. 3, 388, 398,
    450–67
Paul, Jürgen 2, 22, 28, 29, 62–75
Pavese, Cesare 188
Pavitt, Jane 6
Perret, Jacques 420
Perrin, Eliane 3, 10, 324, 388,
    389, 399, 405–19
Persitz, Alexandre 394
Peruzzi, Baldassare 420
Pessina, Franco 27
Peter, Markus 134
Peverelli, Diego 10
Pevsner, Nikolaus 43
Piazzoli, Niki 27
Piccinato, Luigi 437
Piermarini, Giuseppe 178, 187
Pierotti, Piero 437
Pini, Alfredo 316
Plato 260
Poirier, Richard 145, 155
Ponti, Gio 51, 101
Pope, Alexander 84
Popper, Karl 168, 205
Posener, Julius 500
Post, George B. 279
Prost, Henri 392
Pudovkin, Vsevolod 188
Pyun, Jin-Bak 3, 388,
    398, 468–78

Q
Quijano, Aníbal 390

R
Racki, Jeff 3, 389, 398, 450–67
Racki, Reena 3, 389, 398, 450–67
Ragghianti, Carlo L. 488
Rancière, Jacques 315
Rausser, Edwin 103
Rey, Rudolphe 393
Reichlin, Bruno 2, 10, 22, 28, 34, 35,
    76–91, 122, 123, 124, 126, 127,
    130, 131, 191, 194–209, 509
Reinhard, Andrew 299
Reinhard, Hans 9, 24, 399, 482, 483
Reinhart, Fabio 2, 22, 28, 34,
    35, 76–91, 126, 130, 134, 191
Rittel, Horst W. J. 12, 214
Robertson, Paul 279, 291
Robinson, Cervin 516
Rockefeller, John D., Jr. 296
Root, John 285
Rosa, Alberto Asor 11
Rosenquist, James 146
Rossellini, Roberto 188
Rossetti, Biagio 445
Rossi, Aldo 2, 15, 35, 77, 78, 87,
    88, 122, 175, 188–93,
    200, 201, 203, 205, 207, 215,
    321, 324, 506, 509
Rothafel, Samuel Lionel (Roxy)
    227, 296, 299, 300, 305, 306
Rousseau, Jean Jacques 112
Rowe, Colin 198, 200, 484

Royer, Jean 392
Ruchat-Roncati, Flora 132
Rudofsky, Bernard 391, 394,
    432, 446
Ruscha, (Ed) Edward Joseph
    146, 151
Ruskin, John 112

S
Saarinen, Eliel 279
Saarinen, Eero 51, 285
Sachs, Lisbeth 500
Said, Edward 390
Sardi, Pietro
Scamozzi, Vincenzo 420
Schaad, Gabrielle 2, 3, 5–19,
    311–26, 479–518
Schein, Ionel 483
Schinkel, Karl Friedrich 31
Schlippe, Joseph 65, 66, 68
Schmidt, Georg 194
Schmidt, Hans 194
Schnaidt, Claude 500
Schnebli, Dolf 99, 102, 501
Schnitter, Beate 220
Schoen, Eugene 285
Schroeder-Keller, Sibylle 219
Schulte, Hans-Otto 329
Schultze-Naumburg, Paul 51, 66
Schwarz, Fritz 99
Scott Brown, Denise 2, 3, 10, 11,
    15, 17, 123, 124, 125, 126, 127,
    130, 133, 135, 138, 142–64,
    310, 311, 320, 321, 378–86,
    502, 504, 516
Seiller, Albert 393, 394
Seminar Janssen [AA.VV]
    3, 13, 310, 323, 324, 329–37
Semper, Gottfried 34, 81, 83, 84
Serlio, Sebastiano 445
Shaw, Wini 291
Sheller, Charles 112
Shklovsky, Viktor 136
Shreve, Lamb & Harmon 112
Siedler, Wolf Jobst 214
Šik, Miroslav 134
Sisi, Enrico 425
Siti, Walter 199
Sitte, Camillo 66
Sloan, John 291
Slutzky, Robert 198, 200, 484
Smith, Al 274
Smithson, Peter 320, 378
Solon, Leon 280
Speckle, Daniel 420
Stanek, Łukasz 218
Stauffer, Marie Theres 2, 15,
    18, 22, 23–37
Stein, Clarence 274
Steinmann, Martin 2, 122, 123,
    124, 126, 127, 130, 131, 135,
    194–209, 219, 500, 509
Stevin, Simon 420, 426
Stierli, Martino 315
Stirling, James 205
Strand, Paul 112
Studer, Ernst 108
Studer, Gottlieb 108
Sullivan, Louis 112, 279, 280, 286

Sumi, Christian (Burkhalter Sumi) 134
Superstudio 210, 212, 216, 212, 222, 227, 242–51, 504, 506
Szacka, Léa-Cathrine 10
Szeemann, Harald 507

T
Tafuri, Manfredo 2, 10, 11, 12, 14, 135, 212, 216, 218, 222, 224, 225, 226, 227, 273–94, 511, 513, 516, 517
Terragni, Giuseppe 51
Tessenow, Heinrich 183, 184
Tomashevsky, Boris 168
Tronti, Mario 222
Tschumi, Bernard 226
Turner, John F. C. 446, 457, 474

U
Ungers, Oswald Mathias 227

V
Vago, Pierre 394
Van der Rohe, Ludwig Mies 29, 31, 43, 44, 51, 178
Da Varallo, Tanzio 193
Vegetius Renatus, Flavius 420
Venturi, Robert 2, 11, 15, 17, 32, 94, 105, 122, 124, 125, 126, 127, 131, 133, 135, 142–64, 200, 202, 205, 206, 369, 385, 503, 504, 513, 516
Verdi, Giuseppe 188
De Ville, Antoine 420
Da Vinci, Leonardo 420
Viollet-le-Duc, Eugène 432
Virilio, Paul 400
Visconti, Luchino 188
Vitruvius (Pollio), Marcus 420, 437
Vogt, Adolf Max 126
Von Bertalanffy, Karl Ludwig 33
Von Moos, Irène 497
Von Moos, Stanislaus 2,5, 9, 10, 11, 13, 18, 22, 23, 24, 25, 26, 28, 92–108, 93, 122, 123, 124, 125, 126, 142–64, 213, 219, 420, 479–518
Vriesendorp, Madelon 516

W
Wandeler, Hugo 220
Walker & Gillette 112, 115
Walker, Ralph 277, 279, 280, 285
Warhol, Andy 146
Warner, Michael 315
Webber, Melvin M. 214
Weber, Max 346
Weeber, Carel 135
Whitman, Walt 112, 285
Whitwell, Thomas Stedman 257, 259, 260, 263
Widmer, Jean-Claude 2, 212, 217, 232–40, 483, 484, 496, 500
Widrich, Mechtild 315
Wright, Frank Lloyd 51, 291, 432
Wright, Henry 274, 280, 285, 286

Y
Yamasaki, Minoru 48, 101, 312

Z
Zarebska, Teresa 3, 380, 389, 401, 420–29
Zevi, Bruno 511
Zinn, Hermann 329
Zumthor, Peter 134

Contributors

Editors

Torsten Lange is Lecturer in Cultural and Architectural History at Lucerne University of Applied Sciences and Arts, Switzerland. He studied architecture as well as the history and theory of architecture at Bauhaus-Universität Weimar and The Bartlett School of Architecture in London, where he received his PhD in 2015. His work focuses on the conditions underpinning the production of the built environment during late socialism and on writing histories of queer spatial practices. He is co-editor of *Re-Framing Identities: Architecture's Turn to History* (Basel, Berlin: Birkhäuser, 2017), the special issue "Architectural Historiography and Fourth Wave Feminism" of *Architectural Histories* (8/2020), and of *Care: gta papers* 7 (Zurich: gta Verlag, 2022), and published several essays and articles.

Gabrielle Schaad is an art historian and postdoc at the Chair of Theory and History of Architecture, Art, and Design, TU Munich. She coordinates the study program *Exhibiting and Making Public* at the Zurich University of the Arts ZHdK, where she is a Lecturer and Curator in the Bachelor Fine Arts. Her doctoral thesis received from the Institute for the History and Theory of Architecture (gta), ETH Zurich, focused on techniques aimed at emancipation in art and architecture and their pitfalls, transforming space-time in Cold War Japan ("Performing Environmental Textures – Intersected Bodies of Gutai and Metabolism (Japan, 1955–1972)"). She has been awarded research scholarships by the SNSF, the MEXT Japan (2013–2015), and Schloss Solitude, Stuttgart. In addition to her monograph Shizuko Yoshikawa (Zurich: Lars Müller Publishers, 2018) and academic contributions, she recently co-edited *Care: gta papers* 7 (Zurich: gta Verlag, 2022).

Authors

Irina Davidovici is an architect, historian, and the director of the gta Archives at ETH Zurich. Her doctoral thesis on German-Swiss architecture in the 1980s and 1990s received the RIBA President's Research Award for Outstanding Doctoral Thesis in 2009. Her ETH Habilitation thesis *Collective Grounds: Housing Estates in the European City, 1865–1934* is a comparative study of early housing estates in London, Paris, Amsterdam and Vienna focusing on their urban aspects. She is, among many other publications, the author of Forms of Practice. *German-Swiss Architecture 1980–2000* (Zurich: gta Verlag, 2012, 2nd expanded edition 2018) and editor of *Colquhounery. Alan Colquhoun from Bricolage to Myth* (London: AA publications, 2015). After *The Autonomy of Theory: Ticino Architecture and Its Critical Reception* (Zurich: gta Verlag, 2023) she is currently working on *Common Grounds: A Comparative History of Early Housing Estates in Europe* (Zurich: Triest Verlag, 2024).

Samia Henni is a historian of the built, destroyed and imagined environments. She is the author of the multi-award-winning *Architecture of Counterrevolution: The French Army in Northern Algeria* (Zurich: gta Verlag 2017), and *Colonial Toxicity: Rehearsing French Radioactive Architecture and Landscape in the Sahara* (Amsterdam, Zurich: If I Can't Dance, edition fink, 2023), and the editor of *Deserts Are Not Empty* (Columbia Books on Architecture and the City, 2022) and *War Zones* (Zurich: gta Verlag, 2018). She is also the maker of exhibitions, such as *Performing Colonial Toxicity* (Amsterdam, 2023–04), *Discreet Violence: Architecture and the French War in Algeria* (various exhibition venues, including Zurich, Rotterdam, Berlin, Paris and Johannesburg, 2017–22), *Archives: Secret-Défense?* (ifa Gallery, SAVVY Contemporary, Berlin, 2021), and *Housing Pharmacology* (Manifesta 13, Marseille, 2020). Currently, she is an invited visiting professor at the Institute for the History and Theory of Architecture (gta) at ETH Zurich.

Marie Theres Stauffer is professor for the history of architecture and urbanism at the University of Geneva. She has published on topics of the 20th century, such as *Figurationen des Utopischen. Theoretische Projekte von Superstudio und Archizoom* (Berlin: Deutscher Kunstverlag, 2008), or *Ensembles urbaines Genève 21 Alfred-Bertrand. Champel* (with Raphaël Nussbaumer; Gollion: Infolio 2023). A second focus is on the architecture of the 17th/18th century, including her habilitation thesis *Spiegelung und Raum. Semantische Perspektiven* (University of Bern, 2008), as well as *Machines à percevoir/Maschinen der Wahrnehmung/Perceptual Maschines* (with Stefan Kristensen: Köln: Böhlau 2016). She has taught at the Universities of Konstanz, Bern, Zurich and at the ETH Zurich. Her research has been awarded the Prix Jubilé of the Swiss Academy of Humanities and Social Sciences (SAGW) (2004) and the Swiss Art Award of the Federal Office of Culture (2006), among others, and she has also received fellowships from the Max Planck Society and the Alexander von Humboldt Foundation.

Stanislaus von Moos is an art historian and professor emeritus of Modern Art at the University of Zurich (1982–2005) and the founding editor of archithese (1971–1976). Apart from his doctoral thesis (*Turm und Bollwerk. Beiträge zu einer politischen Ikonographie der italienischen Renaissancearchitektur* (Zürich, Freiburg: Atlantis Verlag 1976)), his monographs on Le Corbusier (*Le Corbusier. Elements of a Synthesis*, first ed. in German 1968, with revised and extended editions in several languages from 1972 to 2014), he has published on *Venturi, Scott Brown & Associates* (vol.1, 1987; vol.2, 1999) as well as on artists and architects like Karl Moser, Max Bill, Thomas Hirschhorn, Peter Fischli / David Weiss, among others. He has curated major exhibitions and held lecture- and professorships in Europe and overseas. His most recent books include *Eyes That Saw. Architecture After Las Vegas* (ed., together with Martino Stierli, Zurich: Scheidegger & Spiess, 2020), *Erste Hilfe. Architekturdiskurs nach 1940. Eine Schweizer Spurensuche* (Zurich: gta Verlag, 2021) as well as *Twentyfive x Herzog & de Meuron* (together with Arthur Rüegg; Göttingen: Steidl, 2024). In 2023 the Swiss Federal Office of Culture awarded him the Grand Prix Meret Oppenheim.

Acknowledgments

The publisher and editors thank Verein pro archithese, in particular Christoph Schuepp, for the generous permission to print the facsimile pages and the covers of the issues of *archithese* between 1971–1976.

The editors and the publisher would like to express their sincere thanks to all institutions and foundations for their support, without which the realization of this publication would not have been possible.

Swiss National Science Foundation (SNSF)

Department of Architecture, ETH Zurich

Institute for the History and Theory of Architecture (gta), ETH Zurich

Lucerne School of Engineering and Architecture, HSLU Lucerne

HSLU Foundation

Pro Helvetia

Dr. Adolf Streuli-Stiftung

Kulturstiftung Kanton Luzern

Kulturstiftung Kanton Nidwalden

Imprint

Editors
  Gabrielle Schaad, Torsten Lange

Authors (essays)
  Irina Davidovici, Samia Henni, Torsten Lange, Gabrielle Schaad, Marie Theres Stauffer

Translation
  German → English, Steven Lindberg
  French → English, Brett Petzer
  Italian → English, Shanti Evans

Editing
  Gabrielle Schaad, Torsten Lange

Copy-editing and proofreading
  Chris Davey

Design concept, layout, and typesetting
  Eliot Gisel and common-interest
  (Nina Paim, Mariachiara De Leo)

Lithography
  Carsten Humme, Frank Berger

Printing and binding
  DZA Druckerei zu Altenburg

Paper
  Munken Print White

Fonts
  CoFo Robert, Univers Next

© 2024 Triest Verlag für Architektur, Design und Typografie, Zürich and the authors.
triest-verlag.ch

For all articles and covers from *archithese* printed in this publication: © archithese, Verein pro archithese.

The prepress of this publication was funded by the Swiss National Science Foundation.

Triest Verlag receives a grant for the years 2021 to 2024 from the Federal Office of Culture as part of the Swiss publishers' subsidies.

ISBN 978-3-03863-059-3

Register of archithese 1971–1976

1971

1
Eliane Perrin, "Le Logement des travailleurs étrangers en Suisse"
Eliane Perrin, "Die Wohnbedingungen der Fremdarbeiter in der Schweiz"
Georges Plomb, "Berne et la question du logement"
Georges Plomb, "Bern und die Wohnbaufrage"
Yona Friedman, "Architecte: Un métier remis en question"
Jean Claude Widmer, "Architecture et participation"
Stanislaus von Moos, "Von den 'Femmes d'Alger' zum 'Plan Obus'"
Stanislaus von Moos, "Des 'Femmes d'Alger' au 'Plan Obus'"
André Corboz, "Palladio: Entre Centre et absence"
André Corboz, "Palladio: Gedanken zum Jahreskurs des Centro Internazionale di Studi di Architettura"
Jacques Gubler, "Loos, Ehrlich und die Villa Karma"
Guy Rottier, "Habiter sur la Lune"
Guy Rottier, "Wohnen auf dem Mond"

2
Stanislaus von Moos, "Industrialisierte Folklore"
Jean Claude Widmer, "Questions à Henri Lefèbvre"
Rudolphe Luscher, "Vers un urbanisme cohérent"
Yona Friedmann, "Architecte: un métier remis en question II"
Charles Jencks, "Heutige Architektur und 'Zeitgeist'"
André Corboz, "Un pont de Robert Maillart à Leningrad?"

3+4
Hans Curjel, "Wendepunkt des Theaterbaus – in Zürich?"
Max Bill, "Theaterprojekte in Zürich: Der grosse und der kleine Moloch"
Blaise Junod, "Extension du centre urbain de Neuchâtel et route national 5"
Werner Oechslin, "Städtebau und Denkmalpflege in Italien"
Ionel Schein, "A l'attention des jeunes architectes"
Claude Schnaidt, "L'etat et l'environnement"
Seminar Janssen, "Projektstudium an der ETH: kritisch statt technokratisch"

1972

1 Urbanismus? / Urbanisme?
Superstudio, "Drei Warnungen vor einer mystischen Wiedergeburt des Urbanismus"
Nikolaas J. Habraken, "Das Ende des Wohnbauprojektes"
Jean-Pierre Junker, "Zur Erhaltung und Wiedergewinnung innerstädtischen Wohnraumes"
Roland Günter, Marianne Günter, "Bürgerinitiative – wie, wo, wozu?"
André Corboz, "Encore Pessac"
Martin Steinmann, "Neuer Blick auf die Charte d'Athènes"

2 Vorgestern. Historismus und 20. Jahrhundert / Historisme et 20ième siècle
Stanislaus von Moos, "Schwierigkeiten mit dem Historismus"
André Corboz, "Un passé sans avenir"
Joachim Petsch, "Restaurative Tendenzen in der Nachkriegsarchitektur der Bundesrepublik"
Charles Jencks, "Rhetorik und Architektur"
Martin Fröhlich, "Hinter der Fassade"
Georg Germann, "Das organische Ganze"
Gregor Germann, "Frühe Nationaldenkmäler"

3 Zürich & Co.
Stanislaus von Moos, "Keinerlei Proportion"
Lucius Burckhardt, "Pro Memoria Zürich"
Max Bill, "Das verordnete Chaos"
Sibylle Schroeder-Keller und Luciana Greco (Interviews), "Aufruf zur Gründung eines Bauverhinderungsbüros"
Jürg P. Hartmann, "Der PTT Bunker: Ein Bauprojekt als Konflikt öffentlicher Interessen"
Ulrich Pfammatter, "Die Zürcher U-Bahn"
Martin Fröhlich and Martin Steinmann, "Zürich, das nicht gebaut wurde: Mythos und Realität planerischer Grosszügigkeit; Das Niederdorf als 'Village Radieux'"
Toni Stooss, "Das Alfred-Escher-Denkmal – ein Monument der Gründerjahre"
Hanspeter Rebsamen, "Bausteine zu einem Inventar"

4 Hochschulpolitik – eine Umfrage / Politique universitaire – un questionnaire
Stanislaus von Moos, "Vorbemerkungen der Redaktion"
"Die 6 Fragen / Les 6 questions"
Alberto Abriani
Alvin Boyarsky
Klaus Brake
Lucius Bruckhardt
Harald Deilmann
Kenneth Frampton
Roland Günter
Bernard Huet
Charles Jencks
Jürgen Joedicke
Cryrus Mechkat
Michael Mostoller
Julius Posener
Claude Schnaidt
Dolf Schnebli
Hans-Otto Schulte
Carlo Severati

1973

5 Zweck – From / Fonction – Forme
Rudolf Arnheim, "Funktion und Ausdruck"
Claude Schnaidt, "Convenance et altérations de la forme"
André Corboz, "A propos de la 'sincérité' dans l'architecture médiévale"
Stanislaus von Moos, "Zur Ingenieurkunst der Renaissance in Italien"

6 Tragende Häute / Peaux portantes
Frei Otto, "Die neue Zeit"
Lisbeth Sachs, "Biologie und Bauen"
Felix Candela, "Schalenbau – gestern und morgen"
Frei Otto, "Das Zeltdach – subjektive Anmerkungen zum Olympiadach"
Walter Bird, "Pneumatische Tragwerke – aus wirtschaftlicher Sicht, 'Schweizerische Beispiele'"

7 Sozialistische Architektur? / Architecture socialiste? UdSSR / URSS 1917–1932
Stanislaus von Moos, "UdSSR 1917–1932: Stichworte; Kleines Glossarium zur russischen Architektur der 1920er-Jahre / Petit glossaire: À propos de l'architecture russe des années vingt"
Konrad Farner, "Einige Thesen zum Problem 'Architektur der sozialistischen Gesellschaft' –Quelques thèse sur le problème de 'l'architecture dans la société socialiste'"

Adolf Max Vogt, "Das Motiv
  der Arbeit in der russischen
  Revolutionsarchitektur"
Francesco Dal Co, "La poétique
  'a-historique' de l'art
  de l'avant-garde en URSS"
Joachim Petsch, "Melnikows Pariser
  Ausstellungspavillon"
Manfredo Tafuri, "Les premières
  hypothèses de planification
  urbaine dans la Russie soviétique:
  1918–1925"
Jean-Louis Cohen, "Un exemple
  français: Villejuif, une
  architecture dans les luttes"

8 Anfänge des sozialen Wohnbaus / Origines de l'habitat social

Kurt W. Forster, "Sozialer Wohnbau:
  Geschichte und Gegenwart"
Teresa Zarebska, "Théories militaires
  et habitations collectives"
Franziska Bollerey und Kristina
  Hartmann, "Kollektives Wohnen
  – Theorien und Experimente
  der utopischen Sozialisten Robert
  Owen (1771–1858) und Charles
  Fourier (1772–1837)"
Jürgen Zänker, "Non Amor, sed
  'Labor Omnia Vincit' – Crespi
  d'Adda, eine Industriesiedlung des
  19. Jahrhunderts in Oberitalien"
David Handlin, "Les leçons de
  la 'Boston Cooperative
  Building Society'"
Roland Günter und Michael Weisser,
  "Eisenheim in Oberhausen
  – die Untersuchung der
  ältesten Arbeitersiedlung
  Westdeutschlands (1844–1901)"

1974

9 "Spontane" Architektur / Architecture "spontanée"

André Corboz, "Remarques sur
  un problème mal défini:
  l'architecture des non architectes"
Dennis J. DeWitt, "Neo-Vernacular
  – eine moderne Tradition"
Friedrich Achleitner, "Siphnos –
  Bemerkungen zu einer Baukultur"
Praful C. Patel, Jeff Racki und
  Reena Racki, "Squatters:
  Die sieben Wohnbausysteme
  von Nairobi"
Jin-Bak Pyun, "Une architecture
  de résistance: Les bidonvilles
  asiatiques"
David P. Handlin, "Group Portraits
  and Self Portraits – Some Remarks
  on Recent Approaches to
  Town Planning"

10 Architekturkritik / Critique de l'architecture

1. Theorie
  Antonio Hernandez,
    "Zur Geschichte der
    Architekturkritik"
  Klaus Brake, "'Architekturkritik'
    und die Realität der Bau-
    und Stadtplanung"
  Bruno Zevi, "Moses und Aaron"
2. Dokumentation
  Ulrich Conrads, "Rekapitulation"
    (1972)
  Peter Meyer, "Keine
    Architekturkritik" (1961)
  Peter M. Bode, "Architektur,
    Presse, Strategien
    und Modelle" (1970)
  Bruno Zevi, "Il Mummers Theatre
    di John Johansen" (1971)
  Ada Louise Huxtable, "The New
    Urban Image? Look Down,
    Not Up" (1974)
  Heinrich Klotz, "Der Wolkenkratzer
    des Aristoteles Onassis"
  Stanislaus von Moos, "Das Brasilia
    der Franzosen" (1971)
3. Neue Texte
  André Corboz, "'Place Boaventure',
    Kraak de l'Import-Export"
  Charles Jencks, "Stirling's Olivetti
    Training Center"

11 Denkmalpflege: Theorie / Théorie de la conservation

Stanislaus von Moos,
  "Die politische Herausforderung
  an die Denkmalpflege"
Alan Gowans, "Some General Remarks
  on Preservation"
Jürgen Paul, "Der Wiederaufbau
  des Kornhauses in Freiburg i. B.
  und einige Betrachtungen
  über Architektur und
  Geschichtsverständnis"
Bruno Reichlin and Fabio Reinhart,
  "Die Historie als Teil der
  Architekturtheorie"
Roland Günter und Eugen Bruno,
  "Von der Denkmalpflege zum
  Schutz der Stadt"
2. Fragen an die Denkmalpflege /
  Questions à propos de la
  conservation des monumentes
Beiträge von Ulrich Bellwald,
  Lucius Burckhardt, Pier Luigi
  Cervellati, Josef Grünenfelder,
  Hans Martin Gubler,
  Roland Günter, Italo Insolera,
  Gerhard Kapner, Albert
  Knoepfli, Fritz Lauber,
  Alfred A. Schmid

12 Das Kollektivwohnhaus / La maison collective (1900–1930)

Martin Steinmann,
  "Das Laubenganghaus"
Brian B. Taylor, "Sauvage and
  Hygienic Housing"
Jacques Gubler, "Le village des
  Faiseurs d'Or"
Tilmann Buddensieg, "Messel und
  Taut"
Stanislaus von Moos, "Wohnkollektiv,
  Hospiz und Dampfer"
William Curtis, "Berthold Lubetkin or:
  'Socialist' Architecture in the
  Diaspora"
Peter Haiko und Mara Reissberger,
  "Die Wohnhausbauten der
  Gemeinde Wien, 1919–1934"

1975

13 Las Vegas etc. – oder: Realismus in der Architektur / ou: réalisme en architecture

Stanislaus von Moos, "Las Vegas
  et cetera"
Interview Stanislaus von Moos
  mit Robert Venturi &
  Denise Scott Brown, "Lachen
  um nicht zu weinen"
Interview (Version française)
  "Rire pour ne pas pleurer"
Dominique Gilliard, "Le Quartier
  des Iris"
Othmar Birkner, "Das soziale
  Grün – Nutzgartenbewegung
  und Wohnreform"
Vera Ziroff, "Vom Weissenhof
  zum Kochenhof"

14 "Grosshaushalt" / "Macro-ménage" – Formen des kollektiven Wohnens / Formes d'habitat collectif, 1930–1975

Erwin Mühlestein, "Kollektives
  Wohnen, gestern und heute"
Erwin Mühlestein, "L'habitat collectif
  – hier et aujourd'hui"
William Curtis, "L'Université, la ville
  et l'habitat collectif"
Jakob K. Blumer, "Atelier 5: 1955–1975.
  Versuche im gemeinsamen
  Wohnen"